WHY I AM A HINDU

Shashi Tharoor served for twenty-nine years at
the UN, culminating as Under-Secretary-General.
He is a Congress MP in India, the author of fourteen
previous books, and has won numerous literary
awards, including a Commonwealth Writers' Prize.
Tharoor has a PhD from the Fletcher School, and
was named by the World Economic Forum in
Davos in 1998 as a Global Leader of Tomorrow.

SHASHI THAROOR

WHY
I AM A
HINDU

SCRIBE
Melbourne • London

Scribe Publications
18–20 Edward St, Brunswick, Victoria 3056, Australia
3754 Pleasant Ave, Suite 100, Minneapolis, Minnesota 55409 USA

Published in Australia, New Zealand, and North America by Scribe 2018

Printed and bound in Australia by Griffin Press

Printed and bound in the UK by CPI Group (UK) Ltd, Croydon CR0 4YY

Scribe Publications is committed to the sustainable use of natural resources
and the use of paper products maderesponsibly from those resources.

9781947534568 (US hardback edition)
9781947534551 (US paperback edition)
9781925713534 (ANZ edition)
9781925693355 (e-book)

A CiP record for this title is available from the National Library of Australia.

scribepublications.com
scribepublications.com.au

for my mother

Lily
Tharoor

whose devotion
is untainted
by her scepticism

What thing I am I do not know.
I wander secluded, burdened by my mind.
When the first-born of Truth has come to me
I receive a share in that self-same Word.

— *Rig Veda*, I.164.37

May we not anger you, O God, in our worship
By praise that is unworthy or by scanty tribute.

— *Rig Veda*, II.33.4

May He delight in these my words.

— *Rig Veda*, I.25.18

CONTENTS

Preface and Acknowledgements   xi

PART I
MY HINDUISM

1. My Hinduism   3
2. The Hindu Way   31
3. Questioning Hindu Customs   65
4. Great Souls of Hinduism   87

PART II
POLITICAL HINDUISM

5. Hinduism and the Politics of Hindutva   131
6. Beyond Holy Cows: The Uses and Abuses of Hindu Culture
   and History   183

PART III
TAKING BACK HINDUISM

7. Taking Back Hinduism   249

Notes   275
Bibliography   287
Index   291

PREFACE AND ACKNOWLEDGEMENTS

I wrote this book for two main reasons. The first was to try and understand for myself, and for whoever else was interested, the extraordinary wisdom and virtues of the faith I have lived for over six decades, a faith that I have tried to absorb through beliefs and practices handed down to me by my father and others, my own observations, as well as an extensive reading of the scriptures in translation and numerous scholarly treatises. The second reason I wrote this book was to show that the intolerant and often violent forms of Hindutva that began to impose themselves on the public consciousness of Indians in the 1980s went against the spirit of Hinduism, that most plural, inclusive, eclectic and expansive of faiths.

I am neither a Sanskritist nor a scholar of Hinduism and did not set out to write a scholarly exposition of the religion. Mine is a layman's view of Hinduism, and my exposition seeks to give the reader an overview of the faith as I understand it, as well as accessible summaries of its main features. As will be apparent, I have relied on some of its greatest teachers and adepts to explain its essence. My narrative weaves between personal witness and an attentive reading of the relevant scriptures and academic texts. I seek to bring together ideas of Hinduism from ancient texts, their development by many thinkers, and the practices and the challenges of Hindutva ideology. My approach is to present both the ancient texts of Hinduism and the modern beliefs of Hindutva descriptively and on their own terms, rather than through the theoretical approaches of historians, theologians and social scientists. In this way I seek to arrive at what I hope the reader will find is a lucid and reflective account of one of the world's oldest and greatest faiths and its contemporary existence.

But I do not pretend to offer a comprehensive view of Hinduism: that would go well beyond the space and scope of this book. Instead, I describe aspects of Hindu thought that matter to me, question practices I am less enthusiastic about, outline Hinduism's capacity to grow and reform and be revitalised for subsequent generations, summarise the history of Hinduism in India and provide a feeling for what being Hindu means in a multi-religious country. In the process I devote as much space to the ideological contestations and political challenges swirling around the faith today as I do to its timeless metaphysics.

The book is divided into three sections. The first section, 'My Hinduism', looks at every aspect of the religion—its principal schools, tenets, teachers, and teachings, as well as some of its more questionable social practices. The second section, 'Political Hinduism', explains the ways in which political leaders, strategists, thinkers and their religious allies have attempted to hijack the faith for their own ends. The third section, 'Taking Back Hinduism', talks about how we might free Hinduism from the excesses and perversions it has been subjected to, and restore it to its truest essence, which in many ways is that of an almost ideal faith for the twenty-first-century world.

To some readers, my title—'Why I am a Hindu'—begs the question of who really is this 'I' that I refer to. Is it the thoughtful Hindu layman, the product of a modern English-language education in contemporary India, who is interrogating himself about the faith to which he claims adherence? Or is it the politician steeped in the issues of the day, who is writing with a sense of urgency and despair conditioned by the experience of being called 'anti-Hindu' by those who understand far less of the faith but are inflamed by their own ideological certitudes? My claims about being Hindu are undoubtedly mediated by political contestations around the public expressions of Hinduism by those who see it as a badge of identity more than a system of transcendental beliefs. But where I disagree with them, I do so not as a secularist—or as they would allege, a 'pseudo-secularist'—standing outside the faith, but as a believing Hindu who seeks to challenge them from within the bounds of the religion to which we both claim allegiance.

In some ways I am guilty of the old Indian failing of trying to depict the elephant by describing its tail, tusk, girth and so on. As a result I can at best approximate a number of truths in my effort to describe the unknowable whole truth. Hinduism is uniquely difficult to encapsulate for reasons I describe in my opening chapter: no single founder or prophet, no organised church, no single holy book, and so on; the faith is almost Wikipedia-like in the authorial diversity of its scriptures and tenets. The metaphors used by scholars to describe Hinduism have ranged from the banyan tree and the jungle to a kaleidoscope and even a pan of lasagne. One scholar has pointed out that 'Hinduism' can stand for a civilisation as 'Hellenism' does, and also for a faith as 'Judaism' does; political ideologues in the mid twentieth century insisted it also stood for a 'race' of people embraced by its beliefs. But isn't it also true that our Indian understanding of what 'religion' means has been so drastically affected by colonisation, secularisation, modernity and interaction with global currents, that our own way of conceptualising our native conglomeration of tradition, belief and faith is irretrievably lost?

I cannot be sure, and yet I would argue it does not matter. Some might suggest that this book is an exercise in attempting to fit something unwieldy and unclassifiable into terms an English-speaking twenty-first century reader can understand.[1] Would what we call today 'Hinduism' be recognised by Yajnavalkya (mentioned in the Upanishads, as distinct from the putative author of the *Yajnavalkya-smriti*, mentioned later) or even Adi Shankara who reinterpreted the same faith nearly 2,000 years later? In essence, can today's Hinduism be divorced from the journeys that this aggregate of faiths took over three millennia of enquiry and exploration, resistance to assault and creative reform? Is it even possible, a thoughtful friend asks me, to think of Hinduism as 'pristine' and thus implicitly to say 'I am Hindu' without acknowledging that what one means is not some eternal category of belief but a set of self-descriptors that is contingent on history?

Some may well suggest that my portrayal of Hinduism means that I too have joined those who seek to 'tame' this most unruly of belief systems. Critics allege that the Indian secular liberals want to do just that to Hinduism because they cannot understand religious belief, while the Hindutvavadis want to do so because they cannot control too diverse a set of beliefs. Both sets of attempts result in an effort to 'homogenise' Hinduism for various ends. But the quotidian practices of Hindus involve intense prayer and meditation as well as fierce and bloody rituals, slavish devotion to gurus as well as philosophically abstruse speculations—a range of conduct that has little respect for a writer's need to describe religious phenomena in coherent terms.

As a Hindu, I write of my own faith, and confess that I am incapable of the detachment that one might find in conventional scholarly studies of Hinduism. Rather, mine is an engaged view of the religion, from within its confines—if something so capacious can be seen as confining at all. Though I have read a great deal of Western academic work on Hinduism, I do not partake of the hypercritical views of some twenti-eth-century Indologists, whose Orientalist gaze upon Hinduism, based perhaps understandably on modern notions of egalitarianism, rational-ism and social justice, has sparked hysterical accusations of Hinduphobia. While I do not go as far myself in rejecting their right to express such views, I fear that some Western writing on Hinduism has paradoxically provoked a backlash that has driven many Hindus into the arms of radicals. Despite the flaws in some of its practices, my admira-tion for and pride in Hinduism outweighs my critical concerns, and I make no apology for this.

This book could not have been written without the help of numer-ous people who have been kind enough to comment on various drafts of the text. My former aide and associate Manu S. Pillai, a gifted histo-rian himself, offered me useful guidance, as did my 'sister from another womb', Dr Nanditha Krishna of the Indian Council of Historical Research, who has authored several books herself on various aspects of Hinduism. (She has asked me to point out that she agrees with my depiction of Hinduism but not with my rejection of Hindutva.) My thanks to Nanditha for allowing me to use her translation of the Nasadiya Sukta (the Creation Hymn). Keerthik Sasidharan, an intel-lectual moonlighting as a banker, raised a number of the questions I have summarised in this Author's Note and offered other insights into the faith. Devdutt Pattanaik, undoubtedly India's most popular interpreter of Hinduism, came up with a number of pertinent suggestions on an earlier draft, which have helped influence my final text. Professor Sheeba Thattil's research was invaluable in assembling vast amounts of material on Hinduism, including several works now out of print. I would like to thank Dr Karan Singh for allowing me to use his translation of Mirabai's poem. As always, family played a vital part. My son Kanishk Tharoor and my niece Dr Ragini Tharoor Srinivasan read the manuscript attentively and offered invaluable suggestions and criticisms. Ragini's searching comments and criticisms were especially helpful in making me think through my own assumptions and arguments, and I am most grateful. My sisters Shobha and Smita offered thoughts on an early draft and have remained strongly supportive throughout.

While many minds have therefore contributed to the contents of this volume, the final responsibility for the arguments and interpretations in this book rests with me. If, after reading this book, Hindu and non-Hindu alike come away with a new appreciation of the faith I cherish, and the challenges it is currently dealing with in contemporary India, *Why I Am a Hindu* would have served its purpose.

Shashi Tharoor
January 2018
New Delhi

PART ONE

MY HINDUISM

1

MY HINDUISM

Why am I a Hindu?

The obvious answer to this question is, of course, that it's because I was born one. Most people have little choice about the faith they grow up with: it was selected for them at birth, by the accident of geography and their parents' cultural moorings. The overwhelming majority of Hindus in the world were born Hindu. A small handful, inspired by marriage, migration or philosophical conviction, have adopted the faith, usually by a process of 'conversion' unknown to most Hindus. Unlike that small minority, I was never anything else: I was born a Hindu, grew up as one, and have considered myself one all my life.

But what does being a Hindu mean? Many of us began having to interrogate ourselves in the late 1980s, when the world media first began to speak and write of 'Hindu fundamentalism'. This was odd, because we knew of Hinduism as a religion without fundamentals: no founder or prophet, no organised church, no compulsory beliefs or rites of worship, no uniform conception of the 'good life', no single sacred book.

My Hinduism was a lived faith; it was a Hinduism of experience and upbringing, a Hinduism of observation and conversation, not one anchored in deep religious study (though of course the two are not mutually exclusive). I knew few mantras, just a few snatches of a couple of hymns and practically no Sanskrit: my knowledge of Hindu sacred texts and philosophies came entirely from reading them in English translation. (When I went to a temple, I prayed in an odd combination of English, Sanskrit and my 'mother tongue' Malayalam, instinctively convinced that an omniscient God would naturally be multilingual.)

As a student of history I had always been curious about ancient Indian traditions and beliefs, and I had amassed a rather decent collection of books on the subject of Hindu thought, including multiple translations of the Bhagavad Gita. I had also been a passionate follower of the thoughts and speeches of Swami Vivekananda (as will be apparent in what follows). I had read widely in English about my faith, absorbing the wisdom of Dr Sarvepalli Radhakrishnan and Ananda Coomaraswamy, learning about the lives of such notable figures as Swami Vivekananda, Ramakrishna Paramahamsa and Paramahansa Yogananda, and delving into a variety of scholarly studies, from the old classics by A. L. Basham and R. C. Zaehner to the brilliantly interpretative translations and exegeses of Raimon Panikkar and Dr Karan Singh. From these, and others, notably my own father, I had acquired a set of personal convictions that made up 'my' Hinduism. But was that enough, and what did it amount to in the face of a violent new assertion of Hinduness in a form I could not recognise as bearing any relation to my own faith?

DEFINING HINDUISM

The first challenge, of course, was definitional. The name 'Hindu' itself denotes something less, and more, than a set of theological beliefs. In many languages, French and Persian amongst them, the word for 'Indian' is 'Hindu'. Originally, *Hindu* simply meant the people beyond the River Sindhu, or Indus. But the Indus is now in Islamic Pakistan; and to make matters worse, the word 'Hindu' did not exist in any Indian language till its use by foreigners gave Indians a term for self-definition. Hindus, in other words, call themselves by a label that they didn't invent themselves in any of their own languages, but adopted cheerfully when others began to refer to them by that word. (Of course, many prefer a different term altogether—Sanatana Dharma, or eternal faith, which we will discuss later.)

'Hinduism' is thus the name that foreigners first applied to what they saw as the indigenous religion of India. It embraces an eclectic range of doctrines and practices, from pantheism to agnosticism and from faith in reincarnation to belief in the caste system. But none of these constitutes an obligatory credo for a Hindu: there are none. We have no compulsory dogmas.

This is, of course, rather unusual. A Catholic is a Catholic because he believes Jesus was the Son of God who sacrificed himself for Man; a Catholic believes in the Immaculate Conception and the Virgin Birth, offers confession, genuflects in church and is guided by the Pope and a celibate priesthood. A Muslim must believe that there is no God but Allah and that Muhammad is His Prophet. A Jew cherishes his Torah or Pentateuch and his Talmud; a Parsi worships at a Fire Temple; a Sikh honours the teachings of the Guru Granth Sahib above all else. There is no Hindu equivalent to any of these beliefs. There are simply no binding requirements to being a Hindu. Not even a belief in God. I grew up in a Hindu household. Our home always had a prayer-room, where paintings and portraits of assorted divinities jostled for shelf- and wall-space with fading photographs of departed ancestors, all stained by ash scattered from the incense burned daily by my devout parents. I have written before of how my earliest experiences of piety came from watching my father at prayer. Every morning, after his bath, my father would stand in front of the prayer-room wrapped in his towel, his wet hair still uncombed, and chant his Sanskrit mantras. But he never obliged me to join him; he exemplified the Hindu idea that religion is an intensely personal matter, that prayer is between you and whatever image of your Maker you choose to worship. In the Hindu way, I was to find my own truth.

MY TRUTH

I think I have. I am a believer, despite a brief period of schoolboy athe-ism (of the kind that comes with the discovery of rationality and goes with an acknowledgement of its limitations). And I am happy to describe myself as a believing Hindu: not just because it is the faith into which I was born, but for a string of other reasons, though faith requires no reason.

One reason is cultural: as a Hindu I belong to a faith that expresses the ancient genius of my own people. I am proud of the history of my faith in my own land: of the travels of Adi Shankara, who journeyed from the southernmost tip of the country to Kashmir in the north, Gujarat in the west and Odisha in the east, debating spiritual scholars everywhere, preaching his beliefs, establishing his mutths (monasteries). I am reaffirmed in this atavistic allegiance by the Harvard scholar Diana Eck writing of the 'sacred geography' of India, 'knit together by countless tracks of pilgrimage'. The great philosopher–president of India, Dr Sarvepalli Radhakrishnan, wrote of Hindus as 'a distinct cultural unit, with a common history, a common literature, and a common civilisation'. In reiterating my allegiance to Hinduism, I am consciously laying claim to this geography and history, its literature and civilisation, identifying myself as an heir (one among a billion heirs) to a venerable tradition that stretches back into time immemorial. I fully accept that many of my friends, compatriots and fellow-Hindus feel no similar need, and that there are Hindus who are not (or are no longer) Indian, but I am comfortable with this 'cultural' and 'geographical' Hinduism that anchors me to my ancestral past.

But another 'reason' for my belief in Hinduism is, for lack of a better phrase, its intellectual 'fit': I am more comfortable with the tenets of Hinduism than I would be with those of the other faiths of which I know. I have long thought of myself as liberal, not merely in the political sense of the term, or even in relation to principles of economics, but as an attitude to life. To accept people as one finds them, to allow them to be and become what they choose, and to encourage them to do whatever they like (so long as it does not harm others) is my natural instinct. Rigid and censorious beliefs have never appealed to my temperament. In matters of religion, too, I found my liberal instincts reinforced by the faith in which I was brought up. Hinduism is, in many ways, predicated on the idea that the eternal wisdom of the ages and of divinity cannot be confined to a single sacred book; we have many, and we can delve into each to find our own truth (or truths). As a Hindu I can claim adherence to a religion without an established church or priestly papacy, a religion whose rituals and customs I am free to reject, a religion that does not oblige me to demonstrate my faith by any visible sign, by subsuming my identity in any collectivity, not even by a specific day or time or frequency of worship. (There is no Hindu Pope, no Hindu Vatican, no Hindu catechism, not even a Hindu Sunday.) As a Hindu I follow a faith that offers a veritable smorgasbord of options to the worshipper of divinities to adore and to pray to, of rituals to observe (or not), of customs and practices to honour (or not), of fasts to keep (or not). As a Hindu I subscribe to a creed that is free of the restrictive dogmas of holy writ, one that refuses to be shackled to the limitations of a single volume of holy revelation.

A Hindu can be *astika* (pious) or *nastika* (impious): the terms are said to relate more to orthopraxy (action) rather than orthodoxy (belief), but action proceeds from a set of convictions. As an *astika* he can accept the sacredness of the Vedas, the existence of *atman* (the soul) and belief in God, or he can reject one or more of these credos and still be Hindu, an adherent of the *nastika* variant of Hindu philosophy. As an *astika* Hindu he can subscribe to any of the six major schools of philosophy, the Shad Darshanas (which I describe later); as a *nastika* Hindu he can declare allegiance to one of five schools, including Buddhism and Jainism, which after arising as reform movements against the ritualistic Hinduism of their day, were practically re-absorbed into the parent faith (though their adherents may not see it that way). Or the *nastika* can attach himself to the materialist Charvaka School, whose followers denounced most religious practices and devoted themselves to wealth and profit. The palette of options available is as colourful as the most inventive artist's.

At the same time, as a Hindu, I appreciate the fact that Hinduism professes no false certitudes. Its capacity to express wonder at Creation and simultaneously scepticism about the omniscience of the Creator are unique to Hinduism. Both are captured beautifully in this verse from the 3,500-year-old *Rig Veda*, the Nasadiya Sukta or Creation Hymn:

Then there was neither non-existence nor existence,
Then there was neither space, nor the sky beyond.
What covered it? Where was it?
What sheltered it? Was there water, in depths unfathomed?

Then there was neither death nor immortality
Nor was there then the division between night and day.
That One breathed, breathlessly and self-sustaining.
There was that One then, and there was no other.

In the beginning there was only darkness, veiled in darkness,
In profound darkness, a water without light.
All that existed then was void and formless.
That One arose at last, born of the power of heat.

In the beginning arose desire,
That primal seed, born of the mind.
The sages who searched their hearts with wisdom,
Discovered the link of the existent to the non-existent.

And they stretched their cord of vision across the void,
What was above? What was below?
Then seeds were sown and mighty power arose,
Below was strength, Above was impulse.

Who really knows? And who can say?
Whence did it all come? And how did creation happen?
The gods themselves are later than creation,
So who knows truly whence this great creation sprang?

Who knows whence this creation had its origin?
He, whether He fashioned it or whether He did not,
He, who surveys it all from the highest heaven,
He knows—or maybe even He does not know.

— *Rig Veda*, X.129[1]

'Maybe even He does not know!' I love a faith that raises such a fundamental question about no less a Supreme Being than the Creator of the Universe Himself. Maybe He does not know, indeed. Who are we mere mortals to claim a knowledge of which even He cannot be certain?

Hindu thought also makes a virtue out of the unknowability of God. There is a marvellous story in the Upanishads about a sage who is asked to define the nature of God; the wise man, normally loquacious, falls silent. He is pressed by his disciples for an answer, and he replies that that *was* his answer, for the Absolute is silence; the mystery of the divine reality cannot be reduced to words or speech. Neither thought nor words can suffice: 'It is not understood by those who understand it,' says the Kena Upanishad, 'it is understood by those who do not under-stand it.' The final words of the Upanishads are '*neti, neti*'—'not this, not this'—signifying the indescribability of the Absolute. For many sages, their consciousness of the Divine is untranslatable to others, for those who have not attained the same realisation cannot grasp it through word or sign: it is 'that of which nothing can be said'.

And while I am, paradoxically, listing my 'reasons' for a faith beyond understanding, let me cite the fundamental point: above all, as a Hindu I belong to the only major religion in the world that does not claim to be the only true religion. I find it immensely congenial to be able to face my fellow human beings of other faiths without being burdened by the conviction that I am embarked upon a 'true path' that they have missed. This dogma lies at the core of the 'Semitic faiths', Christianity, Islam, and Judaism. The Bible contains the words 'I am the Way, the Truth and the Life; no man cometh unto the Father [God], but by me' (John 14:6); 'There is no God but Allah, and Muhammad is His Prophet', declares the Quran, denying unbelievers all possibility of redemption, let alone of salvation or paradise. Hinduism asserts that all ways of belief are equally valid, and Hindus readily venerate the saints, and the sacred objects, of other faiths. I am proud that I can honour the sanctity of other faiths without feeling I am betraying my own.

After all, as the philosopher Raimon Panikkar put it so brilliantly in his *The Vedic Experience*, 'It is precisely faith that makes thinking possible, for faith offers the unthought ground out of which thinking can emerge. It is faith that makes moral and other decisions possible, open-ing to us the horizon against which our actions become meaningful.' As a Hindu I seek meaning in my actions within the context of my reli-gious beliefs.

A FAITH WITHOUT DOGMA

And yet, Hinduism is a civilisation, not a dogma. There is no such thing as a Hindu heresy. Hinduism is a faith that allows each believer to stretch his or her imagination to a personal notion of the creative godhead of divinity. Hinduism is also a faith that uniquely does not have any notion of heresy in it: you cannot be a Hindu heretic because there is no standard set of dogmas from which you can deviate that make you a heretic. Indeed, not even what one might think of as the most basic tenet of any religion—a belief in the existence of God—is a pre-requisite in Hinduism. As I have noted, an important branch of Hindu philosophy, the Charvaka School, goes so far as to embrace atheism within the Hindu philosophical framework.

The Charvakas were an interesting example of the intellectual heterodoxy of ancient Hinduism. Not only were they unabashedly materialist, but they challenged the most cherished assumptions of the astikas. The sage Madhvacharya summarised the Charvaka School in his *Sarvadarsana Sangraha* as arguing that 'there is no heaven, no final liberation, no soul (which continues to exist) in another world, nor any ceremonies of castes or orders which are productive of future reward'. The Charvakas were in fact contemptuous of holy men and their practices: 'The Agnihotra sacrifice, the three Vedas, the mendicant's triple staff (*tridanda*), and the practice of smearing oneself with ashes, are only means of livelihood ordained by the creator for men who have neither understanding nor energy.' And they were also scathing about the theological claims of astika philosophers: 'If [it be true that] an animal slaughtered at the Jyotistoma sacrifice is [in consequence] exalted to heaven', they asked, 'why does the worshipper not immolate his own father?'[2]

Hinduism, in other words, incorporates almost all forms of belief and worship within it; there is no need to choose some or reject others. Mahatma Gandhi famously appreciated this quality of Hinduism: 'Its freedom from dogma makes a forcible appeal to me,' he wrote, 'inasmuch as it gives the votary the largest scope for self-expression.'[3] It is therefore a timeless faith, populated by ideas at once ancient and modern, hosting texts, philosophies, belief systems and schools of thought that do not necessarily all agree with each other. But none has ever been rejected by some supreme authority as beyond the pale; there is no such authority in Hinduism. There can be no Hindu Inquisition because there is neither an exacting theology that everyone must subscribe to as holy writ, nor an exalted authority empowered to appoint an Inquisitor. Hindu thought is like a vast library in which no book ever goes out of print; even if the religious ideas a specific volume contains have not been read, enunciated or followed in centuries, the book remains available to be dipped into, to be revised and reprinted with new annotations or a new commentary whenever a reader feels the need for it. In many cases the thoughts it contains may have been modified by or adapted to other ideas that may have arisen in response; in most, it's simply there, to be referred to, used or ignored as Hindus see fit.

Inevitably, though, the question 'who is a Hindu?' has been asked, and, equally inevitably, political figures have entered the definitional fray. The fighter for Indian independence, 'Lokmanya (accepted by the people)' Bal Gangadhar Tilak (1856–1920), suggested, in a meeting of the Sanatana Dharma Sabha (Association of Hindus), that 'a Hindu is he who believes that the Vedas contain self-evident and axiomatic truths',[4] thus seeking to create a religious identity, based on sacred texts, that would be eligible for special consideration from a British colonial regime that had already extended recognition to Muslims (as members of a defined religious community following the dictates of the Quran). Two decades later Mahatma Gandhi added to Tilak's basic view, writing that Hindus are people who believe in the Vedas, the Upanishads, the multiple Hindu scriptures, the various incarnations of God, rebirth or reincarnation, *varna* (caste) and *ashrama* (the four stages of life, which I describe later), and veneration and protection of the cow, and do not express disbelief in idol worship. This is a rather long and contentious list, since many Hindus (myself included) do not subscribe to some of these requirements and do not consider them-selves any less Hindu for not doing so. The foundational theorist of the political philosophy of Hindutva, V. D. Savarkar (whose ideas are discussed more fully below), asserted in the 1920s that one could be a Hindu even if one did not recognise the religious authority of the Vedas.[5] To him, the various religious disputes within Hindu religious thought—between monism and pantheism, between Dvaita and Advaita, between the Vedas and the Upanishads and even including agnosticism and atheism—were irrelevant to the issue of Hindu identity. Savarkar saw 'Hindu-ness' or 'Hindutva' as opposed to 'Hinduism' as a uniting cultural construct that underlay the identity of all those who belong to 'Bharatvarsha', the ancient land of India. Unsurprisingly, then, India's first prime minister, Jawaharlal Nehru, observed that 'Being a Hindu means all things to all men'.[6] British civil servant and historian Sir Alfred Lyall described Hinduism as a 'tangled jungle' full of paradoxes and contradictions, 'a religious chaos' spread all over India, difficult to comprehend and define. No wonder Dr Sarvepalli Radhakrishnan began his celebrated 1926 Upton Lectures on Hinduism by asking of his own faith: 'Is it a museum of beliefs, a medley of rites, or a mere map, a geographical expression?'.[7]

As I have argued, one corollary of this eclecticism is the willingness of Hindus to accept other faiths and modes of worship—indeed often embrace them for themselves. It is quite common for Hindus to show reverence to the religious places of other faiths, and to carry relics or sacred objects of other faiths. History is replete with accounts of Hindus thronging Sufi dargahs, Sikh gurudwaras and Christian shrines (notably the Basilica of Our Lady of Good Health in Velankanni town in Tamil Nadu, which has been described as the 'Lourdes of the East', or Mount Mary Church in Mumbai's Bandra) with the same reverence they might express in their own temples. My late father was a devout Hindu who prayed faithfully twice a day, after his baths. He regularly went on pilgrimages to all the major temples and religious sites in our land. When a fire engulfed the Guruvayur temple in the 1960s, he led a fund-raising drive in Bombay that saw much of his meagre savings diverted to the rebuilding of that shrine. Yet, when a Catholic friend— his life insurance agent, who had made a trip to the Vatican—presented him with an amulet of the Virgin Mary that had personally been blessed by the Pope, he accepted it with reverence and carried it around with him for years. That is the Hinduism most Hindus know: a faith that accords respect and even reverence to the sanctified beliefs of others.

This inclination to revere the Divine, whatever its source, is a notable Hindu trait, reflecting a traditional unwillingness to succumb to doctrinal absolutism. In his historic speech at Chicago's Parliament of the World's Religions on 11 September 1893, Swami Vivekananda spoke of Hinduism as teaching the world not just tolerance but acceptance. The Swami believed that Hinduism, with its openness, its respect for variety, its acceptance of all other faiths, was one religion that should be able to spread its influence without threatening others. At the Chicago Parliament, he articulated the liberal humanism that lies at the heart of his (and my) creed: 'I am proud to belong to a religion which has taught the world both tolerance and universal acceptance. We believe not only in universal toleration, but we accept all religions as true.'[8]

He went on to quote a hymn, the Shiva Mahimna Stotram, which he remembered from his formative years at school: 'As the different streams having their sources in different places all mingle their water in the sea, so, O Lord, the different paths which men take through different tendencies, various though they appear, crooked or straight, all lead to Thee...the wonderful doctrine preached in the [Bhagavad] Gita echoes the same idea, saying: "Whosoever comes to Me, through whatsoever form, I reach him; all men are struggling through paths which in the end lead to me".'[9]

This was a profoundly important idea, and central to the philosophy Vivekananda was preaching. Tolerance, after all, implies that you have the truth, but will generously indulge another who does not; you will, in an act of tolerance, allow him the right to be wrong. Acceptance, on the other hand, implies that you have a truth but the other person may also have a truth; that you accept his truth and respect it, while expecting him to respect (and accept) your truth in turn. This practice of acceptance of difference—the idea that other ways of being and believing are equally valid—is central to Hinduism and the basis for India's democratic culture.

'I challenge the world to find,' Vivekananda proudly declared in a different speech in Chicago, 'throughout the whole system of Sanskrit philosophy, any such expression as that the Hindu alone will be saved and not others. Says Vyasa, "We find perfect men even beyond the pale of our caste and creed".'[10]

One of Hinduism's great strengths—though there are some who see this as a weakness—is its lack of prescriptive tenets. The faith assumes that different people require different pathways to the Ultimate; even within Hinduism, there is no desire to require the same things of all people, it being accepted that people of different spiritual and intellectual attainments will employ different routes in seeking the Divine.

MULTIPLE DIVINITIES

As a result, Hindus allow themselves to worship the divine in multiple forms; the 333 million gods of legend (some versions say 33 million, 300 million and 330 million: even here we are flexible!) are in fact merely a reflection of the infinite aspects of divinity. While other faiths tend to personify the idea of God, seeing Him in anthropomorphic terms as a man-like Being, the Hindu idea of God is both simpler and more complicated. God, to the Hindu, is everywhere, a presence and an absence, within us and outside us. God transcends both time and space. God has no beginning and no end, but equally has no shape and no form. God can therefore be imagined in myriad ways, and in all conceivable shapes and forms, since there is nowhere that God is not, and nowhere that God cannot be. The highest form of God is the Brahman, the Absolute, the universal soul that suffuses all creation.

As a verse in the *Maitreya Upanishad* puts it:

> In the beginning everything was Brahman. He was one, and infinite; infinite in the East, infinite in the South, infinite in the West, infinite in the North, above and below and everywhere infinite. East and the other regions do not exist for him, nor across, nor below, nor above. The Highest Self is not to be fixed, he is unlimited, unborn, not to be reasoned about, not to be conceived. He is like the ether (everywhere), and at the destruction of the universe, he alone is awake. Then from that ether he wakes all this world, which consists of thought only, and by him alone is all this meditated on, and in him it

is dissolved. His is that luminous form which shines in the sun, and the manifold light in the smokeless fire, and the fire in the stomach which consumes the food. Thus it is said:

'He who is in the fire, and he who is in the heart, and he who is in the sun, they are one and the same.'[11]

One of the most famous dialogues in Hindu philosophy, from the *Chandogya Upanishad*, relates to a discussion between a *rishi* (sage) and his son about the existence of God. The young man, Svetaketu, asks his father, Uddalaka Aruni, how he can demonstrate that God exists when there is no visible proof of God's existence. In the typical Hindu manner of instruction, Uddalaka asks his son to fetch a fruit from the banyan tree and cut it open. Inside the fruit, the son finds a small seed. The father asks him to break it apart and see what there is in it, but the seed is all there is. Uddalaka tells his son that all he can see is a small seed; yet something exists in that seed that is so powerful that an immense banyan tree can grow out of it. Similarly, God is not visible, but exists, and the world has grown out of God.

The son is only partly persuaded, so the father asks him to mix salt and water in a bowl. Now, he tells Svetaketu, taste the water and the salt in different parts of the bowl, and once you have done so, separate the salt from the water. The son does as instructed, and points out that the water in every part of the bowl tastes equally salty, and that once dissolved, the salt cannot be separated from the water. Aha, says Uddalaka: you find the salt all-pervasive in the bowl; so too is the universal spirit, which is all-pervasive in creation. When, at the end of our lives, we human beings merge with Brahman, we cannot be separated from it any more than the salt can from the water in your bowl.

Since God is everywhere and in everything, this all-pervasive Universal Spirit is *nirguna*, without qualities, without shape and without gender; Hindus cannot refer to *nirguna* Brahman as 'He', since God can be and is also 'She' and 'It'. The Vedas use the interrogative pronoun '*ka*' (who?), or more precisely *kasmai* (to whom?) for the unknowable God. The impersonal pronoun often used in Sanskrit for God is '*tat*', 'that' in English; in other words, that which exists. Hindu meditation begins with the words '*Om tat sat*': *Om*, the primordial sound that encompasses past, present and future; *tat*, that which exists; *sat*, Truth. The *Chandogya Upanishad* tells the story of Svetaketu, who is taught metaphysics by his father in a series of lessons that each end with the statement '*Tat tvam asi*'—'That you are'—that you are the same as the Brahman that pervades the cosmos.

As the *Hiranyagarbha* hymn in the *Rig Veda* asks:

> O Father of the Earth, by fixed laws ruling
> O Father of the Heavens, pray protect us,
> O Father of the great and shining Waters!
> What God shall we adore with our oblation?

— *Rig Veda*, I.121.9[12]

But the sages realised that all this was rather abstruse, and would be difficult for the average human being to comprehend. The *nirguna* Brahman was a philosophical concept at the heart of Hinduism, but people needed to worship something they could imagine and visualise. Hence the idea of the *saguna* Brahman—the Absolute given form, qualities and attributes, also known as Ishvara or Bhagavan. Strictly speaking, Ishvara is the best translation of God in the Christian or Allah in the Muslim sense of these terms, since those faiths have no equivalent for God in the sense of Brahman. But the Hindu Ishvara takes multiple forms: there is the trinity of Brahma (the Creator), Vishnu (the Preserver) and Shiva or Mahesh (the Destroyer), all different manifestations of the God Principle, and their myriad manifestations, plus their *avatara*s, consorts and companions, who may all be worshipped depending on the preferences of the devotee. The *avatara* doctrine—under which these gods manifested themselves in different, recognisable human-like forms, such as Rama or Krishna—also had the distinct advantage of permitting the worshipper to venerate a personal god without this involving any rupture with the mainstream corpus of Hindu thought, which emphasised the impersonal formless aspect of divinity and insisted on '*neti, neti*'. The unknowable *nirguna* Brahman, after all, becomes all the more knowable when it takes human form as an *avatara*; the abstraction of Hindu philosophic thought becomes more accessible in the form of a recognisable figure. The idea of the *avatara* responded to the popular demand for devotion to personal gods, and to their recurrence in the life of the believer. As Krishna says in the Gita (4. 7–8): 'Whenever righteousness declines in the world and unrighteousness arises, I return to earth. For the deliverance of good, the destruction of evil and the re-establishment of dharma, I am reborn from time to time.'

At the same time it is remarkable how the ten avataras of Vishnu, the Dasavataras, seemingly chart the course of human evolution two millennia before Darwin, starting with Matsya (the fish), and proceeding successively through Kurma (the tortoise), Varaha (the boar), and Narasimha (the half man-half lion) to more recognisable human forms, Vamana (the dwarf) and Parasurama (who wields a great axe), then perfect men who are worshipped as divine (Sri Rama and Sri Krishna), then the Buddha (an interesting inclusion, of which more later) and finally Kalki, who is yet to be born, a brilliant youth on a white steed with a devastating sword, encircled by flames, who represents the destruction of the world as we know it.

Some speak simplistically of the holy trinity of Brahma, Vishnu and Shiva as three separate gods, but all three are in fact three sides of one complex being: aspects of the *uttama purusha*, the perfect personality. There is a God who created the gods (and the demons): Prajapati, Lord of all Creatures. There are multiple further manifestations of the divine in popular Hindu iconography: a myriad of gods and goddesses. This might well have resulted from the Vedic civilisation's absorption of the tribal and folk deities it found being worshipped in India before its advance through the country; each local manifestation of a god or a goddess was included in the all-embracing Hindu pantheon, so that as Hinduism spread, it accommodated earlier forms of worship rather than overthrowing them. Similarly, many tribes revered animals, but instead of disrespecting them, Hinduism absorbed the non-humans too, by making them the companions or vehicles (*vahanas*) of the gods. So Vedic gods found themselves riding a lion, mounting a peacock, reclining on a swan, or sitting on a bull. It was part of the agglomerative nature of Hinduism that it neither rejected nor dismissed the faiths it encountered, but sought to bring them into the fold in this way.

Hinduism, therefore, has given birth to a rich iconography, varying according to the specific divine form and further according to the role in which that divinity is depicted, whether at a peaceful moment or in an attack upon evil, for instance, or whether as 'Himself' or transformed for a specific purpose (Vishnu, for instance, became half-man half-lion, Narasimha, to kill a demon who could not be killed by a human). While the iconography of Shiva, Vishnu and the 'remover of obstacles', the elephant-headed Ganesha, is well known, every depiction of Ishvara (in whichever form) involves certain symbolic images and attributes, and the images of these gods were configured to embody profound conceptions of the universe, from the subduing of ignorance and the defeat of evil to the harmonies of destruction and regeneration.

Thus Brahma, the Creator, is always shown with four heads, facing all four directions, as befits the creator of the universe; he holds the Vedas in his hand, a prayer-vessel beside him, and sits on a lotus, the favoured flower in Hindu iconography since it remains pure and unsoiled by the mud and dirt from which it emerges. His consort is Saraswati, goddess of learning and wisdom, who is always depicted holding the musical instrument the *veena*, symbolising the music of the cosmos, the inner sound of Om from which the universe emerged. She has rosary beads in one hand to signify the importance of prayer and meditation, and palm leaf scrolls in another, to epitomise learning. She too sits on a lotus, but sometimes on a peacock, a symbol of the ego that should be suppressed in the pursuit of true knowledge, and her *vahana*, or vehicle, is the graceful swan.

Brahma is rarely worshipped—there are barely a handful of temples dedicated to him, the most remarkable at Pushkar in Rajasthan—but Saraswati is ubiquitous, widely honoured and portrayed, and there is a specific day devoted each year to her exaltation, Saraswati Puja, whereas there is none to Brahma. That she is merely a consort to one of the holy trinity is irrelevant to her importance. Hinduism cannot entirely be absolved of gender bias, but its reverence for the female principle in the godhead is exemplary.

No better example of this exists than the many manifestations of the goddess in the form of Shakti, which literally means strength—the power of the life-force that creates, nurtures, sustains and also destroys the world. The goddess is seen as a source of energy, without which the male aspect of the godhead would be ineffectual. This female energy takes many forms. As Saraswati, she embodies learning; as Lakshmi, wealth and prosperity. As Uma or Parvati, she is Shiva's gentle *ardhangani*, his half, as inseparable from the Lord as fire and heat, or *purusha* (the spirit) and *prakriti* (matter), are inseparable. As Kamakshi or Rajarajeshwari, she is the Great Mother. As Durga, she rides a tiger, bearing weapons to fight the eight evils of humankind—greed, hate, envy, contempt for others, passion, vanity, jealousy and illusion. In her most frightening form she is Kali, the personification of time (*kala*), dark, angry and armed, weapons flailing, her body dripping with blood, wearing the skulls of her victims, sometimes holding aloft the severed head of one or grinding her foot into the prone body of another.

If that sounds macabre, there are fifty-one Shakti-peethas (temples to the goddess) across India, each consecrated to a body part of Shiva's first wife, Sati, whose body was said to have been dismembered in fifty-one pieces by the flying Sudarshana Chakra weapon of Lord Vishnu. (Sati had killed herself during a fire sacrifice conducted by her father, and her disconsolate husband was carrying her body around in grief and mourning; Vishnu's act was intended to get Shiva to snap out of it. Sati was duly reincarnated as Parvati.) There are temples where the goddess retreats into seclusion for three days a month to menstruate, as in Chengannur in Kerala; others where Devi's footprint (on stone) alone is worshipped. My home state of Kerala overflows with temples to the goddess, often referred to simply as Devi or Bhagavathi (both of which simply mean the goddess), though the most popular form of Bhagavathi-worship is of the goddess as Bhadrakali, a form of Kali. One temple in Thiruvananthapuram, the Attukal Bhagavathi temple, is listed in the *Guinness Book of World Records* for the largest gathering of women in one place at one time: millions (2.5 million in 2009, a record that is broken every year, with 4.5 million reported in 2017) assemble each February for the Pongala, at which offerings are cooked and prepared for the goddess.

There is a marvellous Puranic story about the birth of Durga. It is said that a terrible buffalo-headed demon, Mahishasura, had succeeded in conquering all the gods (or *devas*) and established himself as the master of all creation. The gods, despairing in defeat, retreated to a conclave under Lord Indra to find a solution. They decided to pool their strengths, each contributing a particular weapon or personal attribute, and when they had made their contributions and due rituals had been conducted, a dazzling light engulfed the universe from which emerged a fierce female warrior, riding a snarling tiger, wielding a weapon in each of her eighteen arms. She engaged in furious and bloody battle with Mahishasura for nine days and nine nights, at the end of which she vanquished him. These nine days and nights are celebrated annually by Hindus as the nine-day Navaratri festival, which celebrates the defeat of terrible evil by the forces of good—though interestingly, some fringe groups have started to commemorate Mahishasura instead, claiming he is the symbol of the indigenous Adivasis (Tribal peoples) vanquished by the 'civilising' onslaught of the mainstream Hindus.

The various manifestations of Devi suggest that Hinduism took on board multiple goddess-worshipping cults; Kali seems to have been a pre-Vedic goddess converted by the Hindus into one more form of Shakti. Sometimes the same figures in Hindu texts have different genders: Vishnu famously adopted a female form for specific purposes. A female form of Ganesha, now little worshipped, was depicted as Vinayaki or Ganeshvari. In the *Mahabharata*, Arjuna becomes Arjuni (female) and Brihannala (of the third gender) without losing his masculine valour; indeed, the Madurai temple has sculptures of him in all three forms.

Similarly Hanuman, a monkey-god, was enlisted in the service of Lord Rama in the epic *Ramayana*; scholars see in his appearance the absorption of animist nature-worship into Vedic theism, and the accommodation of south Asia's indigenous peoples into the Hindu fold. Characters depicted in the epics as animals with anthropomorphic characteristics may in fact have been Adivasis: Hanuman was perhaps the leader of a monkey-totem Adivasi tribe, Jatayu that of a vulture-totem tribe and Jambuvan of a tribe using bear totems.[13]

Another interesting example is that of the god Jagannath in Odisha, famous for his *ratha* or chariot. It's a beautiful, elaborately carved wooden vehicle used for a sanctified purpose—to wheel an image of a deity worshipped by millions to a temple in full public view—but it has given its name to the English word, 'juggernaut'.

The word is a colonial mangling of Jagannath (Sanskrit for 'Lord of the World'), a manifestation of the god Krishna. Legend has it that in ancient times, King Indradyumna chanced upon the corpse of Lord Krishna, who had been slain by a hunter, and was informed by the god Vishnu that he should make a wooden statue of the Lord and inter his bones in it. The great sage Vishwakarma, the architect of the gods, undertook the task on condition that he not be disturbed while carving the statue. When, after fifteen days, the impatient king went to enquire about the progress of the sculpture, the irritated sage abandoned it unfinished, without hands or feet. King Indradyumna prayed to Brahma, the Creator, who breathed life into the statue by giving it eyes and a soul, though He could do nothing about the stumps where the deity's limbs should have been. This consecrated statue is worshipped at the Jagannath temple in Puri, in the eastern state of Odisha.

The legend almost certainly masks a different story. As I have noted, as Hinduism spread through the subcontinent, it absorbed local animist and tribal faiths it encountered, by accommodating their images of worship into the Hindu pantheon. Jagannatha was probably a Tribal god who was reimagined, through this legend, as a manifestation of Krishna (himself an incarnation of Vishnu), his somewhat rough and limbless appearance explained through an elaborate story that fits within Hindu lore. One of the ways of ensuring the new deity's acceptance by the people was by parading Him four times a year in elaborate *yatra*s (journeys) on land and water, of which the most famous is the *ratha* (chariot)-*yatra*, or chariot procession, in the month of Ashadha, according to the Hindu calendar (roughly mid-June to mid-July in the Gregorian). This is when the idol is wheeled to the temple in an enormous chariot as devotees line the streets in a frenzy, hailing the lord with chants and prayers and craning their necks for a glimpse of the deity seated in the chariot, followed by lesser chariots bearing statues of his brother Balarama and sister Subhadra.

How did the deity transported in this devotional procession become transmogrified into an English term for a relentless, remorseless, unstoppable force that destroys anything in its path? Orientalism began early, alas: four centuries before the British conquest of India, fantastical tales about India were propagated in the fourteenth-century travelogue of Sir John Mandeville, who described the festival in his *Travels* and depicted Hindus throwing themselves under the wheels of the enormous Jagannath chariots as a religious sacrifice and being crushed to death. Hinduism, in fact, has no concept of such human sacrifice; if Sir John really saw a Hindu killed under the wheels of a chariot, it can only be because a poor devotee stumbled and fell accidentally upon the path in the tumult and the enormous chariot could not easily stop or turn on the narrow road. Still, the tale, the false image of the faith it portrayed, and the unfortunate associations of the word persisted. By the eighteenth century 'juggernaut' was in common use as a synonym for an irresistible and destructive force that demands total devotion or unforgiving sacrifice—the sense in which it pops up in the novels of Charlotte Brontë and Charles Dickens, and even Robert Louis Stevenson, who applied it to Dr Jekyll's foil, Mr Hyde. It was only Mark Twain, in his *Autobiography*, who described Juggernaut as the kindest of gods; and a look at the lovely model of an eighteenth-century ratha in the British Museum's collection shows you why, for such an exquisite piece of art would only have been used to transport a figure of reverence, not of fear. But alas, by then the damage had been done.

But I digress. Hinduism did not stop with the absorption of earlier animist or tribal religions. It accepted the precepts of Mahavira, the founder of Jainism, treating his followers as a special sect of Hindus rather than as a separate faith. When Buddhism sought to reform Hinduism, Hinduism turned around and sought to absorb it too, by including the Buddha as a reincarnation of Vishnu and his agnostic teachings as merely a *nastika* form of the mother faith. As a result Buddhism has hardly any strength or presence in the land of its birth, having been absorbed and overtaken by the religion it sought to challenge. Hinduism could well have tried the same with Christianity and Islam, too, had it been allowed to do so; but these faiths were not interested in being embraced by Hinduism, since they saw themselves as the revealed Truth rather than as one among multiple versions of truth.

Hinduism is also unusual in seeing God, Man and the universe as co-related. As the philosopher Raimon Panikkar has explained, in Hindu thought, God without Man is nothing, literally 'no-thing'; Man without God is just a 'thing', without meaning or larger purpose; and the universe without Man or God is 'any-thing', sheer chaos, devoid of existence. In Panikkar's explanation, nothing separates Man from God: 'there is neither intermediary nor barrier between them'. So Hindu prayers mix the sacred with the profane: a Hindu can ask God for anything. Among the tens of thousands of sacred verses and hymns in the Hindu scriptures are a merchant's prayer for wealth, a bankrupt's plea to the divine to free him of debt, verses extolling the union of a man with a woman, and even the lament of a rueful (and luckless) gambler asking God to help him shake his addiction. Prayer and worship, for the Hindu, are thus not purely spiritual exercises: they enhance the quality of his life in the material world, in the here and now.

GANESH, MY ISHTA-DEVTA

Hindus are often asked, during certain ritual prayers, to imagine their *ishta-devta*, their personal God, or rather that way of imagining the abstraction of the Absolute in an anthropomorphic form that most appeals to them. I pick Ganesh—or Ganapathi, as we prefer to call him in the South—myself, not because I believe God looks like Him, but because of the myriad aspects of the godhead, the ones He represents appeal most to me.

> *Om maha Ganapathe namaha,*
> *sarva vignoba shantaye,*
> *Om Ganeshaya namaha...*

Every morning, for longer than I can remember, I have begun my day with that prayer. I learned it without being fully aware what all the Sanskrit words meant, knowing only that I was invoking, like millions of Hindus around the world, the name of the great elephant-headed god to bless all my endeavours to come.

Ganesh sits impassively on my bedroom shelf, in my office, in my living-room and my dining-room, as well as my prayer alcove, in multiple forms of statuary, stone, metal and papier-mache. There is nothing incongruous about this; he is used to worse, appearing as he does on innumerable calendars, posters, trademarks and wedding invitation cards. Paunchy, long-trunked (though with one broken tusk), attired in whatever costume the artist fancies (from ascetic to astronaut), Ganesh, riding his way across Indian hearts on a rat, is arguably Hinduism's most popular divine figure.

Few auspicious occasions are embarked upon without first seeking Ganesh's blessing. His principal attribute in Hindu mythology—a quality that flows from both his wisdom and his strength—is as a remover of obstacles to the fulfilment of desires. No wonder everyone wants Ganesh on their side before launching any important project, from starting a factory to acquiring a wife. My own student-day courtship violated time-honoured Indian rules about caste, language, region, age and parental approval; but when we got married, my then wife-to-be and I had an embossed red Ganesh adorning the front of our wedding invitations.

I have since developed an even more personal connection to Ganesh. The great 2,000-year-old epic, the *Mahabharata*, was supposedly dictated by the sage Veda Vyasa to Ganesh himself; since then, many a writer has found it helpful to invoke Ganesh in his epigraph. When I recast the characters and episodes of the *Mahabharata* into a political satire on twentieth-century Indian history, *The Great Indian Novel* (1989), I had it dictated by a retired nationalist, Ved Vyas, to a secretary named Ganapathi, with a big nose and shrewd, intelligent eyes, who enters with elephantine tread, dragging an enormous trunk behind him. Such are the secular uses of Hindu divinity.

For in my Hinduism the godhead is not some remote and forbidding entity in the distant heavens. God is immediately accessible all around us, and He takes many forms for those who need to imagine Him in a more personalised fashion. The Hindu pantheon includes thousands of such figures, great and small. Ganesh is the chief of the *gana*s, or what some scholars call the 'inferior deities'.[14] He is not part of the trinity of Brahma, Vishnu and Shiva, who are the principal Hindu gods, the three facets of the Ultimate First Cause. But he is the son of Shiva, or at least of Shiva's wife, Parvati (one theory is that she shaped him from the scurf of her own body, without paternal involvement).

As a writer I have always been interested in the kinds of stories a society tells about itself. So part of the appeal of Ganesh for me lies in the plethora of stories about how this most unflappable of deities lost his (original) head and acquired his unconventional appearance.

The most widely-held version is the one my grandmother told me when I was little, about the time that Parvati went to take a bath and asked her son to guard the door. Shiva arrived and wished to enter, but Ganesh would not let him in. Enraged by this effrontery, Shiva cut off the boy's head. Parvati, horrified, asked him to replace it, and Shiva obliged with the head of the first creature he could find, an elephant.

This was a salutary lesson in the perils of excessive obedience to your parents, though I don't think my grandmother intended me to take it that way. My mother, who always tried unsuccessfully to resist the temptation to boast about her children, had another version: a vain Parvati asked Shani (Saturn) to look at her perfect son, forgetting that Shani's gaze would reduce the boy's head to ashes. Once again, an elephant's was the head that came to hand.

Growing up in an India where loyalty seems all too often on sale to the highest bidder, I could not but be impressed by Ganesh's rare quality of stubborn devotion to duty. However he may have lost his head, it was Ganesh's obduracy as a guard that, in my grandmother's telling, cost him a tusk. 'The powerful avatar Parasurama,' she recounted, as we little ones gathered round her at dusk, 'possessor of many a boon from Shiva, came to call on the Great Destroyer at his abode of Mount Kailash. Once again, Ganesh was at the door, and he refused to let the visitor disturb the sleeping Shiva. Parasurama, furious, tried to force his way in, but found Ganesh a determined opponent.' (My eyes widened in excitement at this part.) 'Ganesh picked Parasurama up with his long trunk, swung him round and round till he was dizzy and helpless, and threw him to the ground. When his head cleared, Parasurama flung his axe at the obstinate Ganesh. Now Ganesh could have easily avoided the axe, but he recognised the weapon as one of Shiva's. He could not insult his father by resisting his weapon. So he took the axe humbly upon his tusk.' Ever since, Ganesh has been depicted with only one full tusk, the other half-amputated by the axe.

The thrill of that story did not diminish for me when I learned the more prosaic version which says that Ganesh wore down one tusk to a stub by using it to write down the epic verse of the *Mahabharata*. For this reason, the missing tusk signifies knowledge. As I grew older, I learned of more such symbols associated with Ganesh. Scholars of Hinduism tell us that Ganesh's fat body represents the hugeness of the cosmos, its combination of man and pachyderm signifying the unity of the microcosm (man) with the macrocosm (depicted as an elephant). Some suggest it has the less esoteric purpose of demonstrating that appearances mean little, and that an outwardly unattractive form can hide internal spiritual beauty. In any case, his looks do not prevent Ganesh, in most popular depictions, from being surrounded by beautiful women, including his twin wives, Siddhi and Buddhi. Siddhi represents spiritual power and Buddhi intellect; in some versions there is a third wife, Riddhi, embodying prosperity (though she usually replaces Buddhi—perhaps making the point that you can have either brains or wealth but not both!) Further, Ganesh's trunk can be curled into the symbol 'Om', the primal sound; and the snake found coiled around his waist represents the force of cosmic energy.

'But Ammamma,' I would ask my grandmother, 'why does Ganesh ride a rat?' For in most of the pictures in our prayer room, the deity is shown on this unusual mount. At the simplest level the sight of an elephantine god on a tiny mouse visually equates the importance of the greatest and smallest of God's creatures. And, as my grandmother explained, each animal is a symbol of Ganesh's capacities: 'like an elephant, he can crash through the jungle uprooting every impediment in his path, while like the rat he can burrow his way through the tightest of defences.' A god who thus combines the attributes of elephant, mouse and man can remove any obstacle confronting those who propitiate him. No wonder that many worship him as their principal deity, despite his formally more modest standing in the pantheon.

And what is the secret of his appeal to a twenty-first century urbanite like myself? As his unblinking gaze and broad brow suggest, Ganesh is an extremely intelligent god. When I was very young I heard the story of how Parvati asked her two sons, Ganesh and Kartikeya, to go around the world in a race. Kartikeya, the more vigorous and martial-minded of the two, set off at once, confident he would encircle the globe faster than his corpulent brother. Ganesh, after resting a while, took a few steps around his mother and sat down again. Parvati reminded him of her challenge. 'But you are my world,' Ganesh disarmingly replied, 'and I have gone around you.' Needless to say, he won the race—and my unqualified admiration.

So it is no surprise that Ganesh is worshipped in India with not just reverence but enthusiasm. Sometimes this can be carried to extremes, as when Ganesh devotees in Western India in the 1890s allowed the bubonic plague to take many lives rather than co-operate with a British campaign to exterminate the rats that carried it (for the rats were also, after all, Ganesh's mounts). Or when, in late September 1995, word spread around the world that statues of Ganesh had begun drinking milk. In some cases, statues of his divine parents, Shiva and Parvati, were also reported to be imbibing these liquid offerings, but Ganesh it was who took the elephant's share.

In India, the rationalists were quick to react. It was, they averred, a matter of simple physics. Molecules on the rough stone and marble surfaces of the statues had created a 'capillary action' which sucked in the droplets of milk. (*Om capillary actioneyeh namaha?*) These were not really absorbed into the statue but formed a thin layer of droplets on the surface which would be visible if the statue were dark. A team of government scientists proceeded to demonstrate this on television, placing green powder in the milk and showing a green stain spreading over the face of a white marble statue. Mass hysteria was alleged; Indian priests (who live off the offerings of devotees in the temples) were merely trying to whip up more custom, said some; it was all politics, said others, pointing to the need for the then-flagging Hindutva movement to attract the credulous to their credo. *The Pioneer* newspaper published a photograph of a spout emerging from the back of a temple from which milk poured into a bucket;[15] the implication was that it was chicanery, not divine ingestion, that accounted for the disappearing milk in the temples. Still, millions of devotees who flocked to temples worldwide saw in the phenomenon a simple message from the heavens that the gods remained interested in the affairs of ordinary mortals.

But Hindus have always believed that to be the case; the 'milk miracle' merely reinforced an unstated assumption about the nature of the godhead. Our gods crowd the streets, smile or frown on us from the skies, jostle us for space on the buses; they are part of our daily lives, as intimate and personal as the towels in which we wrap ourselves after a bath. As MP for Thiruvananthapuram (Trivandrum, in Kerala), I was struck by the fact that my constituency is the one place in the world where even the airport runway shuts down twice a year for a few hours so that Lord Padmanabhaswamy can be escorted on his usual traditional route across the airfield for His ritual seaside bath. And none in the city, of any faith, considers this remotely unusual.

So the intrusion of the gods into our lives through the milk-drinking episode is no great aberration. They are part of our lives anyway; we see ourselves in them, only idealised. My own affection is for Ganesh himself, a god who—overweight, long-nosed, broken-tusked and big-eared—cheerfully reflects our own physical imperfections. After all, a country with many seemingly insurmountable problems needs a god who can overcome obstacles.

When I was a child in Bombay, I was enraptured once a year by the city's great Ganesh Chaturthi festival, in which India's bustling commercial capital gives itself over to the celebration of this many-talented deity. Hundreds of statues of Ganesh are made, decorated and lovingly dressed; then they are taken out across the busy city streets in amid endless processions of followers, who collectively number over a million, before being floated out to sea in a triumphant gesture of release. As a little boy I stood on the beach watching the statues settle gradually into the water while the streams of worshippers dispersed. It was sad to see the giant elephant heads disappear beneath the waves, but I knew that Ganesh had not really left me. I would find him again, in my wall-calendars, on my mantelpiece, at the beginning of my books—and in the prayers with which I would resume my life the morning after the festival:

MY HINDUISM

Om maha Ganapathe namaha,
sarva vignoba shantaye,
Om Ganeshaya namaha...

Om, I invoke the name of Ganapathi;
Bringer of peace over all troubles,
Om, I invoke the name of Ganesh...

2

THE HINDU WAY

The sage Yajnavalkya was once asked to list the number of gods; it is said he began with the number 3,300 and ended by reducing them all to one—Brahman, the pervasive spirit of the cosmos that underlies all creation. The Rig Veda say '*ekam sat vipra bahudha vadanti*'. This was also Swami Vivekananda's favourite phrase about spirituality: 'That which exists is One; the sages call It by various names.'

Hindus therefore understand that all worship of God reflects an effort to reach out to that which cannot be touched or seen; since God is, in that sense, literally unknowable, one may imagine Him/Her/It in any form, since each form may be just as valid as another and none can be guaranteed to be more accurate than the next one. The various forms of God in Hinduism, reducing the abstract to the specific visual form, reflect the limitations of the human imagination rather than any shapes within which the divine must be confined. Indeed, Hindu legends have the gods manifesting themselves in so many shapes and forms that the notion of one agreed image of God would be preposterous. Thus one can imagine God as a potbellied man with an elephant head, and also as a ten-armed woman with a beatific smile; and since both forms are equally valid to the worshipper, why not also imagine God as a bleeding man on a cross? All are acceptable to the Hindu; the reverence accorded to each representation of the unknowable God by worshippers of other faiths is enough to prompt similar respect from the Hindu. Acceptance is always the name of the game.

As I have remarked at the outset, the key to understanding Hinduism is that it is one faith that claims no monopoly on the Truth. Hindus understand that theirs may not necessarily be the only path that leads to salvation; they are taught to respect all other paths that seek the Truth, knowing that these will vary depending on the circumstances of each individual's life, the culture in which they are born or live, their values and motivations. In the *Gita*, Lord Krishna says, 'Whosoever follows any faith and worships me under whatsoever denomination in whatsoever form with steadfastness, his faith I shall reinforce'.[1] The acknowledgement of multiple paths to the ultimate truth of creation is implicit in the philosophical disputes and arguments that have marked the faith for millennia.

One consequence of this acceptance of difference is that it flies in the face of the certitudes most other religions assert. The French traveller François Bernier, on his well-documented journey through India in the seventeenth century, tried to introduce some Brahmins in 1671 to Christianity, and was startled by their response: 'They pretended not [that] their law was universal; that God had only made it for them, and it was, therefore, they could not receive a stranger into their religion: that they thought not our religion was therefore false, but that it might be it was good for us, and that God might have appointed several different ways to go to heaven; but they will not hear that our religion should be the general religion for the whole earth; and theirs a fable and pure device.'[2]

We respect your truth, the Brahmins were saying; please respect ours.

Some scholars have described Hindus as henotheists, that is, people who worship their God but do not deny the existence of other gods. Every Hindu worships some god, but it may not be the same god worshipped by every other Hindu either. As Radhakrishnan puts it: 'God is more than the law that commands, the judge that condemns, the love that constrains, the father to whom we owe our being, or the mother with whom is bound up all that we can hope for or aspire to.'[3] God is all that, and infinitely more.

This henotheistic attitude means, however, undifferentiated respect for all the various possible ways of worshipping God, whether Hindu or not. A Hindu can accept the worship of the Abrahamic God as another practice of the same kind as he sees pursued by other Hindus. For him, someone worshipping Christ is essentially no different from himself worshipping Vishnu or Shiva. The acceptance of difference starts here for the Hindu. This was why it was possible for a large community of Jews, the Bene Israel, after arriving on the shores of western India around the time of Christ, to practise their faith for centuries in rural Maharashtra without being seen by their Hindu neighbours as practitioners of a different religion; Hindus used to seeing various Hindus pursue their own modes of devotion found nothing odd in a people with their own different practices, assuming them to be just another kind of Hindu, until a wandering rabbi from Jerusalem arrived in India centuries later and identified them as the Jews they were.

It didn't matter to the Hindus around them. The *Haristuti* has a prayer that says: 'May Vishnu, the ruler of the three worlds, worshipped by the Shaivites as Shiva, by the Vedantins as Brahman, by the Buddhists as the Buddha, by the Naiyayikas as the chief agent, by the Jainas as the liberated, by the ritualists as the principle of *dharma*, may he grant our prayers.'[4] This cheerful eclecticism was the attitude that enabled Swami Vivekananda, concluding the presentation of a paper at Chicago's Parliament of the World's Religions in 1893, to call upon the blessings of 'He who is the Brahman of the Hindus, the Ahura Mazda of the Zoroastrians, the Buddha of the Buddhists, the Jehovah of the Jews, and the Father in Heaven of the Christians.' To him they were one and the same: 'That which exists is One; the sages call It by various names.'

SEEING LIFE WHOLE

The British, who in their two centuries of imperial rule over India struggled to understand and come to terms with Hinduism, did a great deal to explore and debate its meanings as best they could. Some saw it, in E. M. Forster's notorious phrase, as 'a mystery and a muddle'; others tried to reduce it to terms they could relate to. Whether

Hinduism was polytheistic or monotheistic was a question that agitated many British minds. After the Census of 1911, one senior British official concluded that 'the great majority of Hindus have a firm belief in one supreme God—Parameshwara, Ishvara or Narayana.' The chief British census official in India, Sir Herbert Risley, observed that 'these ideas are not the monopoly of the learned: they are shared in great measure by the man on the street.' An 'intelligent Hindu peasant', he claimed, not only was familiar with Hindu concepts like the *paramatma* (supreme soul), *karma* (loosely translatable as 'fate'), *maya* (illusion), *mukti* (salvation) and so on, but had 'a rough working theory of their bearing upon his own future'.[5]

A few basic ideas were deeply ingrained into every Hindu, whether he lived up to them or not. Among these commonly-held beliefs were two four-fold divisions. The first was the organisation of life into four stages, or *ashramas*: these were *brahmacharya*, the bachelor existence, a time to be spent learning and acquiring mastery over the essential disciplines needed to lead a meaningful life; then *grihastha*, the life of a householder, when one married, procreated, and assumed the responsibilities of family life; then *vanaprastha*, when one retired and retreated to the forest to lead a life of contemplation in harmony with nature; and finally, sannyas, the stage of renunciation of all worldly ties, at which one seeks one's ultimate merger with Brahman, the spirit suffusing the cosmos.

The four stages of life also related to the four ends of life, the Purusharthas, that every Hindu had to pursue: *dharma*, the moral code (discussed more fully later), *artha*, prosperity or material well-being, *kama*, desire for pleasure and gratification, and ultimately *moksha*, or the salvation that comes from ultimate self-realisation, the fulfilment of which is the purpose of each individual life.

These stages and ends of life in Hinduism embraced an all-encompassing idea of human needs in a comprehensive vision. Every person needs to learn and to earn; to have sex, food and money; to love, to nurture, to assume responsibility; each individual also has a shared concern for the common good and an indefinable curiosity about the unseen, about that which can only be experienced and not understood through words. All of these urges coexist in all of us; they overlap and interact with each other; we pursue them systematically or randomly, or we stumble across them, but they are present in each of our lives in an interdependence of which we are barely conscious but which the Hindu *rishis* fully appreciated. The common expression '*mata, pita, guru, daivam*' encapsulates the human journey—one is first, from birth, totally dependent on the mother, then exposed to the outer world by the father, then taught and guided by the guru, until one finally finds God.

The Hindu appreciation of life saw it whole, recognised the supreme ends of life and the stages needed to progress towards their achievement. It did not seek to suppress or deny the normal lust for sex, wealth or possessions, but sublimated these in a larger purpose. (Kama even has its own *shastra*, Vatsyayana's Kama Sutra). Hinduism accommodated the acknowledgement of worldly desires within the quest for the eternal. As Radhakrishnan postulated, Hinduism 'binds together the kingdoms of earth and heaven'. Indeed, it is no coincidence that Hindu gods are all married; they are depicted with consorts, each of whom, like the gods and goddesses themselves, have multiple aspects and manifestations. It is a striking feature of Hinduism that our gods can be susceptible to desire; they are depicted falling for *apsaras* and seducing sages' wives. Lord Shiva even fell for Vishnu in the transformed appearance of the ethereally beautiful Mohini. Prudery appears to have been imported into Hindu social attitudes only in reaction to the Muslim invasions and Victorian colonial rule.

Hindus pursue their quest for the eternal—the search for 'the light beyond the darkness'—through three types of activity: *jnana* or the quest for knowledge, not merely theoretical learning but in the form of realised experience which leads to wisdom; *bhakti* or devotion, expressed principally through prayer, fasting, temple rituals and sacrifice, but also through meditation and self-interrogation; and karma or action and service in the fulfilment of *dharma*. (Karma is a concept that is variously translated as action, fate or destiny, and causality; it means all three, though the meaning depends on the context in which the phrase is used.)

Bhakti is of course the most popular path, and the easiest for most people to pursue, since a capacity for worship comes inborn in all of us. Purists categorise Hindu worship in a taxonomy that runs like this: the most simple Hindus worship spirits and animist forces; the next level of ordinary Hindus worship their own ancestors, popular deities and gurus or godmen; the level above that worships incarnations like Rama, Krishna, or Buddha; above this level are those who worship a personal god, or *ishta-devta;* and highest of all are those Hindus who worship the Absolute, in the form of Brahman. Those who worship the *ishta-devta* or personal *bhagavan* (in other words those trying to reach Brahman through a divine intermediary) must settle for a somewhat lower place in the hierarchy of spiritual yearning than those who seek Brahman for itself, in the quest for ultimate self-realisation. A verse from the *Kena Upanishad*[6] captures some of the exquisite literary talents of the ancients along with the profundity of their philosophical enquiry:

> Who sends the mind to wander afar? Who first drives life to start on its journey? Who impels us to utter these words? Who is the Spirit behind the eye and the ear?

> It is the ear of the ear, the eye of the eye, and the Word of words, the mind of mind, and the life of life. Those who follow wisdom pass beyond and, on leaving this world, become immortal.

> There the eye goes not, nor words, nor mind. We know not, we cannot understand, how he can be explained: He is above the known and he is above the unknown. Thus have we heard from the ancient sages who explained this truth to us.

> What cannot be spoken with words, but that whereby words are spoken: Know that alone to be Brahman, the Spirit; and not what people here adore.

> What cannot be thought with the mind, but that whereby the mind can think: Know that alone to be Brahman, the Spirit; and not what people here adore.

> What cannot be seen with the eye, but that whereby the eye can see: Know that alone to be Brahman, the Spirit; and not what people here adore.

What cannot be heard with the ear, but that whereby the ear can hear: Know that alone to be Brahman, the Spirit; and not what people here adore.

What cannot be indrawn with breath, but that whereby breath is indrawn: Know that alone to be Brahman, the Spirit; and not what people here adore.

Into all of this, great variations and choices enter. Some critics have described Hinduism as animism tempered by philosophy, or mysticism leavened by metaphysics. They are not wholly right, but they are not wrong either. Ultimately, all such worship is merely a means to an end. Some look for God in nature, in forests and rivers, some in images of wood or stone, and some in the heavens; but the Hindu sage looks for God within, and finds Him in his own deeper self.

THE BANYAN TREE OF HINDUISM

As a result of this openness and diversity, Hinduism is a typically Indian growth, a banyan tree. It spreads its branches far and wide, and these in turn sink back into the earth to take fresh root in the welcoming soil. In the shade of the vast canopy of this capacious banyan tree, sustained by multiple roots and several trunks, a great variety of flora and fauna, thought and action, flourishes.

The multiplicity of places of worship in India gives Hindus plenty of choice, and affords religious-minded temple-goers opportunities for extensive pilgrimages. Most Hindu families embark on these quite often; for some, the only holidays they undertake are to temple towns, to worship at the shrine of a powerful deity. While some pilgrimages, especially to well-established temple towns, take on the characteristics of a religious holiday, others can be quite arduous. The annual *yatra* to the ice-cave at Amarnath in Kashmir involves a major trek; that of Mount Kailash and Lake Mansarovar in Tibet, renowned as the abode of Shiva, has cost the lives of many of who have attempted it across the narrow and treacherous Himalayan passes. Pilgrimages to Kedarnath and Badrinath, and to the sources of the Ganga and the Yamuna at

Gangotri and Yamunotri respectively, are other Himalayan journeys that are not for the weak or faint-hearted. Other religious trips are to sites where large numbers of Hindus gather for a special occasion: from the Thrissur Pooram, an annual festival which involves the largest processional of caparisoned elephants in the world (usually up to a hundred pachyderms decked up to the hilt), to the *ratha-yatra* at the Jagannath temple in Puri, Odisha and the Kumbh Melas described below. *Utsava*s (religious festivals, from the Sanskrit '*ut*', to let go or remove, and '*sava*', worldly sorrows, hence an occasion to release one's burdens or cares) abound across the country. Regional festivals witness throngs of worshippers in different parts of the country on different occasions at fixed times of the year—Bengalis celebrating Durga Puja, Maharashtrians Ganesh Chaturthi, the Ram Leela across north India, Onam in Kerala, Pongal in Tamil Nadu. Holi, the festival of colours, is famously the most fun-filled of all *utsava*s, while an occasion like Makar Sankranti, marking the transit of the sun into the Makara rashi (Capricorn—sign of the zodiac) in Hindu astrology, is observed with due solemnity. The largest crowds gather during the Kumbha Melas that take place every twelve years in Haridwar, Allahabad (Prayag), Nasik, and Ujjain: the Allahabad Kumbh, at the confluence of the Ganga and the Yamuna, is an extraordinary sight, attracting some twenty million people each time.

Sometimes a pilgrimage may consist of a regular visit to one favourite temple: the Kerala political leader K. Karunakaran travelled to the fabled Krishna temple in Guruvayur on the first of every month (according to the Malayalam calendar) throughout his long life, and thousands do the same to the hilltop shrine to Ayyappa at Sabarimalai, or to Balaji at Tirumalai. Sometimes it is to a particular area where many temples abound: the temples to the nine planets at Kumbakonam, for instance. But quite often it can be an extensive circuit, such as the one my family undertook by car across southern India when I was fourteen, a three-week journey that enabled us to pray at Tirupati, Madurai (whose famed Meenakshi temple, dedicated to a warrior queen who became a consort of Shiva, boasts 33,000 sculptures), Thanjavur, Kanchipuram, Palani, Rameswaram and innumerable smaller towns in Tamil Nadu and Kerala, halting at each place just to worship at the principal temple, and moving on to the next one. My parents found this profoundly satisfying; for their children, it was all a bit of an adventure, though we learned a little about Hinduism at each stop.

The striking thing to a young boy during this journey was the remarkable variety of these places of worship, the differences in their architectural styles and physical appearances, the different manifestations of god being worshipped at different temples, the variety of rituals and the behaviour of the priests, the different materials presented as *prasadam* (offerings) to the gods, and the idiosyncratic practices associated with each shrine, most famously the shaving of the head at the Venkatachalapathi temple in Tirumalai, Tirupati (Andhra Pradesh), the richest temple in India,[7] where my fourteen-year-old locks were duly shorn as an offering to Lord Balaji.

The Hindu acceptance of variety goes much farther than this, however. Foreigners sometimes politely ask if Hinduism requires vegetarianism or abjures alcohol, and are puzzled when different Hindus give them different answers to the question. Versions of the faith come with their own prescriptions and proscriptions, but there is no universal requirement. There are Hindus, particularly Vaishnavas in the north, who recoil in horror at the very thought of consuming meat and others who will not touch even garlic or onion (considered *tamasik*[8] foods by purists), while there are Hindus who eat all of these and would consider it mildly uncivilised not to do so. Goats are routinely sacrificed at the Kalighat temple in Kolkata and other animals at Kali temples across the land, but most Hindu religious occasions are marked by ostentatious vegetarianism. My children's mother is half-Bengali, half-Kashmiri, descended from a long line of carnivorous Brahmins on both sides who were alternately horrified and mournful about my vegetarianism (some tried to excuse it on the grounds that I must be a 'Vaishnava', a worshipper of Vishnu, though I was too eclectic to be so typecast and had actually been named for Shiva, having been born on Maha Shivaratri. But then in Tamil, the word for vegetarian is 'shaiva'. Go figure!). We brought up our sons to 'eat everything', but their mixed genetic inheritance prevailed: one twin took to meat-eating with relish, while the other, at age seven, with no persuasion whatsoever from his father, turned staunchly vegetarian.

Alcohol offers its own contradictions. There is a strain of prohibition in some aspects of Hindu thought, but this coexists with the use of alcohol in some religious rituals (such as at the Kal Bhairava temples) and indeed with the routine habit, of some *sannyasis*, of consuming marijuana and other hallucinogens in the pursuit of spiritual experiences. In the Vedas, *soma* (or *som-ras*) was a favourite beverage of the Vedic deities, and much alcohol flowed during religious ceremonies and sacrifices; in the *Rig Veda*, Mandala IV, Hymn 18, the god Indra is said to have drunk three lakes of *soma* to fortify himself before slaying the dragon Vritra, who had imprisoned all the waters of the world.[9] The *Mahabharata* is replete with details of alcohol consumed by those who are worshipped as incarnations of Vishnu. In Puranic mythology, there is a Hindu goddess of wine, Varuni, who emerged from the primordial Churning of the Ocean, the Samudra Manthan, as one of fourteen 'ratnas' bestowed upon the world, including the moon. Sanskrit literature, including the poetry and plays of Kalidasa, India's greatest literary figure (even though only a fraction of his sublime work has survived), is replete with references to intoxicating drinks. Yet other texts also offer Dharmashastric objections to Brahmins consuming liquor, and Brahminical Hinduism has tended to disapprove of alcohol consumption.

There is doctrinal variety, as well. Those Hindus who are steeped in the *Upanishads* and the *Bhagavad Gita*, suffused with a sense of Brahman (the Ultimate Reality underlying all phenomena) pervading the cosmos and debating its unity with atman (the Universal Soul also present in each of us) would consider themselves monotheists; the 'common man', innocent of such texts, might think of the multiple deities he sees around him as different gods, and have no difficulty with being considered a polytheist. The truth is that it doesn't matter. These are all equally valid ways of being a Hindu.

This pervasive multiplicity of practices and beliefs makes it difficult to conceptualise Hinduism as one might other religions. As a term of description, indeed, 'Hindu' implies no monolithic identity; to speak of the 'Hindu community' as one might the 'Muslim ummah' is contestable, since Muslims are bound to each other by credos, convictions and rules of which Hindus are innocent. The absence of standard practices and belief systems, and the absence of ecclesiastical hierarchies and universal religious institutions, adds to the difficulty. When Christians disagree amongst each other, they disagree with reference to the interpretation of one single book, the Bible, whose teachings remain the fountainhead of their faith. The same is true of Muslims, though the room for interpretation is less, since the Quran is seen as the revealed word of God, though the Hadith offers more room for discussion. Hinduism has no such handy volume; when Hindus seek guidance, it is rarely to textual authority that they turn (though often to spiritual guides or gurus, whose knowledge, at least in theory, may be derived from their understanding of various scriptures).

In recent times, the *Bhagavad Gita* has become the equivalent of a 'sacred book' for the Hindus, due to its frequent use by twentieth-century gurus such as Swami Chinmayananda and political leaders like Mahatma Gandhi. The *Gita* subsumes the ideals of the Vedas and Upanishads in the words of the popular deity Krishna, and its exhortation to do one's duty irrespective of the consequences has been cited as an inspiration by various figures on the world stage, from Turkish Prime Minister Bulent Ecevit to justify his country's invasion of Cyprus, to my failed candidacy for the Secretary-Generalship of the United Nations.

But Hinduism cannot be reduced to the *Bhagavad Gita*, or any single holy book. Dr Radhakrishnan put it best: to him, Hinduism is 'not a definite dogmatic creed, but a vast, complex, but subtly unified mass of spiritual thought and realisation.' The spiritual leader Dada Vaswani calls Hinduism variously 'a fellowship of faiths', 'a federation of philosophies', and 'a league of religions'. Note the plural in that last word.

Indeed, the writer Rutvij Merchant adapted a phrase of mine to make the point. I had written in my book, *India: From Midnight to the Millennium*, that any truism about India can be immediately contradicted by another truism about India. He observed that 'Hinduism appears to be very much like India; an essential paradox, as any attempt at a truism about Hinduism can be immediately contradicted by another truism about Hinduism.' Remarking that there are as many Hinduisms as there are adherents, he goes on to add: 'Interestingly, Shashi Tharoor's statement about India "that the singular thing about the country is that you can only speak about it in the plural", applies to Hinduism perfectly; if religion is seen as a technology that can be leveraged to grow spiritually and eventually achieve union with the Supreme, there appears to be no uniformity or synchronisation to the Hindu way; indeed the term "the Hindu way" is in itself a fallacy as there is no one Hindu way.'[10]

Merchant interestingly defines a Hindu as one who is an ardent seeker of Truth: 'An individual who strives to actively discern the existence of the objective Reality otherwise termed as God and attain Him if convinced of His existence, using means that are inherently subjective and dependent on the individual's own proclivities, beliefs and values, is a Hindu.' This definition of Hinduism, if it can be called that—since it could apply to almost anyone of any culture or religious faith—emphasises the individualist nature of the quest for truth, the role of reasoning in the process, and the ultimate yearning for God (whether one uses that term or speaks of the soul's merger with Brahman, the idea is the same).

Some Hindus reject the term 'Hindu' altogether as a description of their faith, preferring to speak of 'Brahmanism', though this is used by some Dalits and others as a term of abuse against the Brahmins who have dominated the faith. But in its origins, the expression refers to the ideal of attaining the Brahman, the Universal Spirit that suffuses the cosmos. Many use the Sanskrit-Hindi phrase, 'Sanatana Dharma', or 'eternal faith' (though 'faith', as I explain shortly, is an inadequate translation of 'dharma'). Sanatana is eternal in the sense that it refers to a *dharma* that is old and new at the same time, ever-present and ever-evolving. In Hinduism, there is no difficulty in accepting that some aspects of *dharma* will be rendered irrelevant over the aeons and that other ideas, innovations and reforms will be infused into the faith and rejuvenate it. The essence of *dharma*, however, remains unchanged throughout eternity.

The Hindu concept of time is very different from Western ideas. In Hindu thought, the world has no beginning and no end, but only experiences endless repetitive cycles of time in four *yugas* (aeons or ages): Satya Yuga, the age of truth, Treta Yuga, Dvapara Yuga and Kali Yuga (the age of destruction and untruth, the one in which we are all living now). Each Kali Yuga ends with a great flood (*pralaya*) that destroys the world, only to start afresh with a new Satya Yuga. Some Hindus argue that Vaishnavites and Shaivites differ in their perception of time; after all, Vishnu is reincarnated in various *avatars*, while Shiva simply 'is'. Vaishnavites, in this reading, are constantly changing through time, while Shaivites are focused on the annihilation of the self. Though the distinction is interesting, both sets of Hindus relate to time very differently from followers of other faiths, whose temporal existence on this earth culminates, after death, in paradise or hellfire.

I mentioned earlier that *dharma* is often translated as faith, and that this is an inadequate translation. The concept of *dharma* is much broader, embracing an entire system of social ethics covering law-abiding conduct. Indeed, in an afterword to *The Great Indian Novel* in 1989, I listed a whole series of meanings that have been ascribed to the term '*dharma*', an untranslatable Sanskrit word that is, nonetheless, breezily defined as an unitalicised entry in many an English dictionary. (The *Chambers Twentieth-Century Dictionary*, for example, defines it as 'the righteousness that underlies the law'.) A passable effort, to be sure, but no one-word translation in English ('faith', 'religion', 'law'), can convey the full range of meaning implicit in the term. 'English has no equivalent for *dharma*,' writes P. Lal, defining *dharma* as 'code of good conduct, pattern of noble living, religious rules and observance'. Nanditha Krishna, author of several popular books on various aspects of Hinduism, translates *dharma* as 'law of righteousness'. In his book *The Speaking Tree*, Richard Lannoy actually defines *dharma* in nine different ways in different contexts. These include moral law, spiritual order, sacred law, righteousness, and even the sweeping 'totality of social, ethical and spiritual harmony.' Indeed, *dharma* in its classic sense embraces the total cosmic responsibility of both God and Man. My late friend Ansar Hussain Khan, author of the polemical *The Rediscovery of India*, suggested that *dharma* is most simply defined as 'that by which we live'.

The word *dharma* is formed from the Sanskrit root 'dhr', to hold. *Dharma* is therefore that which holds a person or object and maintains it in existence; it is the law that governs its being. To live according to *dharma* is to be in consonance with the truth of things. A moral life, for a Hindu, is a life lived in accordance with his *dharma*, which in turn must be in conformity with the absolute truth that encompasses the universe.

A POLYCENTRIC FAITH

Hinduism is a polycentric faith. Since it admits multiple centres of belief and practice, there is no single structure of theological authority or liturgical power. When there is no centre, there is no periphery either; Sanatana Dharma is inclusive, since there is no basis for excluding any belief. Radhakrishnan argues that Hindu tolerance is not indifference: Hindus understand that not all self-declared truths are of equal value. Still, they are all welcome in that gigantic buffet table of spiritual options the Hindu feels empowered to dip into. Of course, the flip side of the coin is that Hindus tend not to see non-Hindu religious traditions as 'other'; and in particular, they do not see them as challenging or putting into doubt Hindu beliefs and practices, which, after all, are timeless and eternal.

Unlike Hinduism, however, as we have seen, the Semitic (or Abrahamic) faiths believe themselves to be of divine origin. The True Faith was revealed by God to Abraham and was therefore beyond contestation, even if its three major variants, Judaism, Christianity and Islam (in order of appearance!) relied on different texts; and in Muslim belief, God revealed Himself further to Muhammad, who became the definitive Prophet of His Word. Since the word of God cannot be false, all three Semitic religions came to revolve around ideas of absolute truth; they were the only way to reach God, and those who chose other paths were doomed to hellfire or damnation. Many saw it as their duty to show the absolute truth they had found to those who were still in darkness but unaware of the error of their ways. If you resisted their truth, you were wrong and if you were unwilling to correct yourself, you must be either misguided, evil or blind—the only possible explanations for those unable or unwilling to see the truth laid before them by these 'revealed' religions. For this reason it was permissible, for some 'true believers', to convert you to the 'right' path by force or inducement.

Sanatana Dharma, however, saw its adherents engaged in a permanent quest for truth, which was not something revealed from on high by God or a prophet, but something that had to be searched for by prayer, meditation, good conduct and experience, and could well be attained only at the very end of one's life, if at all. Religion is, after all, experience; ideally, it is an experience of God. The *Svetashvatara Upanishad* says: 'God, the maker of All, the great spirit ever seated in the hearts of creatures, is fashioned by the heart, the understanding and the will. They who know that become immortal.' The heart, the understanding and the will each play their part; all are indispensable. This also means that religious experience is personal experience; self-realisation will vary from individual to individual. After all, the Divine, as Radhakrishnan argued, reveals itself to men within the framework of their intimate perceptions and prejudices. The Western faiths largely look outward to the heavens for their revealed truths; the Hindu looks within himself.

A Hindu could live his faith at one or more of several levels: the quotidian, with its temple rituals, religious observances, social customs and good deeds (the path of religious performance); the spiritual, with extensive prayer, meditation, worship of and service to a deity, penance and austerities (the path of devotion); and the intellectual, with a serious study of philosophy and theology (the path of knowledge). Most Hindus never get beyond the first stage; their Hinduism is a religion of temple visits, fasts to propitiate favourite gods, the observance of specific festivals according to the tradition in their geographic regions. But even for the others, who demand more from (and look for more in) their faith, their quest for the truth, their enquiry into the mysteries of Creation, would not end with a blinding flash of realisation from the pages of a sacred book. After all, unlike the Bible, the Dialogues of the Buddha, and the Quran, all the unchallengeable principal texts of their religions, even the *Vedas* are merely the first in a substantial corpus of scriptural works.

It is also true that in a religion as vast, capacious and evolving as Hinduism, there is much in the religious texts that contradict themselves, and each scholar can find scriptural justification for a point of view diametrically opposed to that of another scholar, also with his own scriptural justification. Take, for example, the place of women in Hindu society, which has undoubtedly undergone much transformation, for better and for worse. The epics, the *Manusmriti* and the dicta of Yajnavalkya, putative author of the *Yajnavalkya-smriti*, all contain much material that is bloodcurdlingly misogynist in relegating women to a place of inferiority in relation to men. Bhishma in the Anushasana Parva of the *Mahabharata* declares: 'Women have one eternal duty in this world: dependence upon and obedient service to their husbands.' And yet this is the faith that regarded wives as *ardhangini*, half of the whole, and *sahadharmini*, the partner of the man in the fulfilment of *dharma*. The sage Sayana, in his commentary on the *Rig Veda*, wrote: 'The wife and the husband, being the equal halves of one substance, are equal in every respect; both should join and take equal part in all work, religious and secular.' A warrior queen like Kaikeyi strode on to the battlefield alongside her husband. Swami Vivekananda pointed out with pride that some of the most exalted *rishi*s of the Hindu faith, the most learned and respected authorities on the scriptures, are women. (Twenty-one of the original *rishika*s to whom the *Vedas* were revealed were women: the names of Gargi and Maitreyi today adorn colleges in Delhi University; Vishavara, Ghosha and Apala were also prominent seers.) Adi Shankara, in a theological debate with his famous critic Madana Mishra, appointed as the judge between them the latter's learned wife Sarasavani. Even Manu declared, 'where women are honoured, there the gods rejoice, but where they are not honoured, there all rituals are useless.' Of the 210 Shiva-worshipping Lingayat saints, thirty-five are women. In other words, there is authority for different approaches in the ancient texts; the Hindu is invited to take his pick. If the Hindu chooses wrongly, or unwisely, among the opinions offered to him, it is not Hinduism's fault.

The Hindu understands that all scripture requires interpretation, and cannot be taken literally. In particular, there has long been an acknowledgement that what is laid down in ancient texts may not necessarily have been what was, or is, practised in the faith. The strong position held by the polyandrous, property-owning Nair women in Kerala's matrilineal society, the honoured position of Rajput women, who killed themselves en masse after their husbands fell on the battlefield, and the reverence accorded to women mystics like Mirabai and social reformers like Savitribai Phule, show Hinduism as accepting of women as figures of authority and respect. The fact that the *Manusmriti* is both misogynist and casteist does not preclude the possibility that throughout the ages, it was honoured in the breach.

Hinduism offers the believer much to choose from: what you choose to follow is your Hinduism, while others might find scriptural justification for a contrary view. Hindu philosophy testifies to the extent to which reasoned debate amongst the believers—in dialogue with but not restrictively bound by their scriptures—has allowed Hindu religious philosophers throughout history to reform themselves and their faith.

MANY SACRED BOOKS

As I have asserted, Hinduism has not one sacred book, but several, both complementary and contradictory to each other. The Hindu scriptures are commonly divided into Srutis, Smritis, Itihasas, Puranas, Agamas and Darshanas.

The Srutis are that which has been heard or revealed. The four *Vedas*—*Rig Veda, Sama Veda, Yajur Veda* and *Atharva Veda*—are Sruti, having been revealed to, or heard by, the *rishi*s, codified by Veda Vyasa and passed down through generations of disciples. But they are not revealed texts in the Christian or Muslim senses of the term; the *rishi* is a Mantra-Drashta, a seer of mantra or thought; the thought is not his own, but he 'hears' or 'sees' it. It is interesting that the Sanksrit word for philosophy is *darshana*, literally 'seeing': the perception of the seer is as important in Hinduism as his intellectual enquiry. In this, too, Hindu philosophy differs considerably from its Western counterparts.

In fact the *Rig Veda* is estimated to have taken perhaps half a millennium to attain its corpus of 10,552 mantras in verse, and in the course of these five centuries at least fifty poet-*rishis* had a hand in its composition. Their sacredness comes from their divine inspiration and sustained quality, not from having been handed down fully composed by God like the Quran. The story is no different with the later Vedas; the four Vedas are believed to have been created between 1500 BCE and 500 BCE, a period of one thousand years. In that period we see enormous evolution from the nomadic faith of the *Rig Veda*, in which animal sacrifices, including those of cattle, were offered to the gods[11] and the healthy scepticism in some of its verses, to the evidence in the later Vedas of adjustment to new social realities, such as the *Yajur Veda*'s references to new gods, clearly taken into Hinduism from prevailing local faiths—including Pashupati, Lord of the Beasts, and Aushadi, Lord of Medicinal Herbs.

Similarly the 108 *Upanishads*, which distil the essence of the Vedic philosophy, are also Sruti (revealed literature). They were also written over centuries: it is believed that the first eight go back to the period between the eighth century BCE to the fourth century BCE, congruent with the Age of the Buddha. The next three *Upanishads* are post-Buddhist and date from 300 BCE to 200 CE, whereas the remaining 97 *Upanishads* belong to the Puranic period—from the second century CE to the tenth century CE. The chronological gap between the earliest verses of the Rig Veda and the bulk of the *Upanishads* was greater than the time that separates us today from the life of Jesus Christ. An entire *Upanishad* (the *Mandukya Upanishad*) is devoted to the primal sound, Om. In the reckoning of many Hindus, the Upa-Vedas, or subsidiary vedas, include Ayurveda, the science of wellness, Dhanurveda, the science of weapons and the rules of warfare, Gandharva Veda, the science of the performing arts (including the classic text on music, dance and theatre, the *Natya Shastra*), and the Arthashastra, the treatise on statecraft that in many respects anticipated Machiavelli's *The Prince* by nearly two millennia. The Vedangas, the explanatory 'limbs' of the Vedas, deal with such matters as grammar, phonetics, etymology, the art of poetry, the science of rituals and (in the famous *JyotishaVedanga*) astronomy and astrology. All these again are the product of centuries of writing and reflection.

The Smritis are that which is remembered; they are composed by human beings without any specific divine inspiration and passed on to guide ordinary people in the conduct of their lives and the performance of their spiritual and worldly duties. The eighteen Smritis, written down largely over the five centuries between 300 BCE and 200 CE, are often referred to as the *Dharmashastras*, since they explicate how *dharma* must be observed, and these are seen as practices that must change with time and place. The Smritis describe the daily life of individuals, prescribing rituals and rules which vary according to each *varna* or social class and are collectively known as *varna-ashrama-dharma*. The Smritis also lay down the rules of governance, known as Raj Dharma, and adumbrate the earliest ideas of what may be considered a Hindu constitutional order, headed by a king. Among the most famous of the *smritis* is the Arthashastra, an ancient treatise on statecraft, economic policy and military strategy, composed between the 2nd century BCE and the 3rd century CE, and attributed by many to Chanakya or Kautilya, principal counsellor to the Emperor Chandragupta Maurya (though this is disputed). In its unsentimental explication of the duties and responsibilities of kings and states, and its ruthless advocacy of amoral policies including alliance-making, coercion and suborning of rivals, it anticipates by several centuries the prescriptions of Machiavelli.

Since the Smritis are purely man-made and mutable, Hinduism does not aver that laws laid down a millennium ago must be followed to the letter today. The foundational laws of Yajnavalkya and the Code of Manu, often cited as the source of 'Hindu law', are Smriti; no Hindu seriously argues that they must be observed to the letter today. (Indeed, it is debatable whether they were strictly followed even in the times it which they were propounded.) In fact, the Smritis were not all internally consistent:

> *A profusion of arguments! The Smritis differ among themselves.*
> *No one's opinion is final or conclusive.*

The essence of dharma is hidden and elusive.
The right path is the path followed by great men.

— *Yaksha Prashna*, Sloka 114[12]

The *Itihasas*, the epics, respond to the human need for instruction through story: the profound philosophical enquiries of the Srutis and the *Smritis* are more easily digested by the common people in the form of parables and epic narratives (which in turn easily lend themselves to theatrical form, dance and music, all the better to communicate their message to the masses). *Itihasa* literally means 'the way it was' and many take the epics literally, though they have been embroidered with mystical and fantastic elements, and it is quite probable that divinity was ascribed to their principal personages only in later retellings. Their principal purpose remains to impart the values of the *Dharmashastras* in story form. The *Ramayana* tells the story of a kingly figure, Rama, who upholds both his personal *dharma* and his raja *dharma*: in the earliest versions he was not portrayed as a god, but as an ideal man devoted to upholding truth. Indeed there is impressive evidence for the historicity of Rama in Valmiki's text, which is replete with astonishingly accurate geographical, botanical and zoological details about his journey from Ayodhya to Lanka and back.[13] He makes enormous sacrifices in his personal life, including giving up his beloved wife, in order to fulfil his *dharma*. The *Mahabharata* was told and retold, with countless interpolations and additions, till about 400 CE; it incorporates the classic poem, the Bhagavad Gita, the Song of the Lord, which distils the essence of the *Upanishads* and is to many Hindus the core religious text of their faith.

The two great Hindu epics, the *Ramayana* and the *Mahabharata*, tell stirring stories accompanied by digressive meditations on values, morals and principles. They are polycentric and fundamental texts about such key issues in society as what constitutes ethical conduct; how a just society is made and sustained; and the duties and obligations of kings, counsellors, warriors, women and sages. They deal with great moral dilemmas and issues of right conduct, justice and fidelity, violence and redemption; they give voice to a range of actors and concerns; they provide models for social and political action; and because they are told and retold as stories, they have embedded themselves in the popular consciousness of Hindus.

The *Ramayana*, the epic tale of an exiled prince's conquest of the demon kingdom where his wife is held hostage, is a stirring saga, intimately familiar to all Indians and most Southeast Asians. Lord Rama's ultimate triumph and his return to rule his own kingdom as a just and benevolent king is the archetypal story of the victory of good over evil; yet in many of its episodes, including what becomes of his queen, there are complex moral dilemmas unveiled that do not lend themselves to simplistic interpretations.

The *Mahabharata* deals much more with *adharma*: it is a tale of the real world, one whose heroes have feet of clay, whose stories have ambiguous ends, whose events range from great feats of honour and valour to dubious compromises, broken promises, dishonourable battles, expedient lies, dispensable morality. It asks profound questions about the nature of *dharma*: Yudhishthira says 'dharma is subtle' and each episode in the epic appears to be a case study of what this means—is *dharma* derived from the *shastras*, from precedents, from *nyay*, from *niti*? Is it determined by caste or gender? The *Mahabharata* offers much ground for reflection on weighty ethical and moral dilemmas. When the low-born Ekalavya becomes a master archer by eavesdropping on lessons offered by Dronacharya to his caste betters, the teacher asks for the boy's thumb in tribute, which would destroy his ability to practise what he has learned. When Draupadi, wife of the Pandavas, is 'lost' in a wager in a fixed game of dice, she questions the right of her husband to stake her and the propriety of the winners to seize her. By raising these questions, the epic obliges Hindus to interrogate themselves about their beliefs. The *Mahabharata* has come to stand for so much in the popular consciousness of Indians: the issues the epic raises, as well as the values it seeks to promote, are central to an understanding of what makes India India. Its characters and personages still march triumphantly in Indian minds, its myths and legends still inspire the Indian imagination, its events still speak to Indians with a contemporary resonance.

While the *Ramayana* (composed from around the 200 BCE to perhaps 200 CE) and the *Mahabharata* (said to be composed between about 400 BCE and 400 CE, after some eight centuries of retellings and interpolations)[14] are the two best-known epics whose core story (and many subsidiary tales) are widely known to practically every Indian, the Itihasas also include the *Yogavasishtha*, stories and fables imparted by the sage Vasishtha to Lord Rama, and the *Harivamsha*, which tells stories of creation and of the origins of Lord Krishna. When the *Ramayana* and the *Mahabharata* were retold in the vernacular languages, they acquired immense popularity and impact. The Kamban *Ramayana* in Tamil in the twelfth century CE, and Tulsidas's *Ramcharitmanas* in Awadhi in the sixteenth century, exalted Rama to his present place in the Hindu pantheon.

The *Mahabharata* incorporated the Bhagavad Gita, an extraordinary, inspirational and profoundly philosophical text which addresses in powerful and poetic language a basic conundrum of human existence: what human beings should do when they are pulled in contradictory directions by equally important but incompatible obligations. We are all faced in life with having to make hard choices; the Gita presents us with the searingly hard choice confronting the heroic warrior Arjuna, who finds himself on the battlefield, about to go to war, in the name of a just cause, whose triumph will involve the killing of several members of his own family. His duty and his moral commitment to one side of the battle stands against his love for his own kith and kin, whose blood he must shed, and that too in violation of the universal moral duty not to take life. But if, for this reason, he refuses to fight, his absence from the battlefield could allow the forces of unrighteousness to prevail; it would mean the victory of those who have committed wrongs, and it would violate his own duty and obligation as a warrior to deploy his martial skills in fulfilment of his duty and in defence of the right. Arjuna confesses his agonising dilemma to Lord Krishna, whose counsel makes up the bulk of the Gita. Perform your *dharma*, Krishna tells Arjuna: do your duty regardless of the outcome. The right action in conformity with your *dharma* is your only obligation; its consequences, even its success or failure, should have nothing to do with the moral motivation for your action. Your own feelings, or prospects of reward, are irrelevant to the need to act. Krishna's philosophical advice is essentially to do what is right regardless of the consequences. Implicit is an acknowledgement that doing the right thing is not always easy, that it can cause pain and grief to others, even others one loves or is bound to. But the path of *dharma*, leading a life of good conduct—what a Westerner might call a moral life—is a complicated and ambiguous task, not to be reduced to simple calculations of defeat or failure, life or death, reward or punishment. Armed with this advice, and with Krishna as his charioteer, Arjuna goes forth to sanguinary battle, and prevails, leaving the battlefield littered with the blood-soaked bodies of his own cousins.

The *Gita* is an amazing text, full of wisdom and philosophical reason, but also a call for action, an exhortation to fulfil one's duty with conviction and courage. It has probably inspired more commentaries per line of text than any other work in the vast canons of Hinduism. Swami Vivekananda and Mahatma Gandhi swore by it; each found different aspects of its poetic brilliance and profundity to live by.

The eighteen *Puranas* (composed roughly between 250 CE and 1000 CE) convey the truths of the Vedas and the Dharmashastras in short stories as well, and have formed the basis of religious education in rural India for millennia. They differ from the Itihasas since they do not comprise a grand epic narrative but several different stories featuring non-recurrent characters. The moral code conveyed through Puranic stories is still the basis for Hindu ethics, and the characters in many Puranic tales have come to epitomise the virtues of faith, chastity, obedience, loyalty, constancy, generosity and so on. Their names are often cited, whether in conversation or even political discourse, as emblematic of those virtues: Prahalada the faithful believer, Savitri the devoted wife, Dhruva the constant, Harishchandra the truthful, and so on. The *Puranas* also tell the stories of the ten incarnations of Vishnu; and the *Srimad Bhagavatam*, or *Bhagavata Purana*, focusing on the life and times of Lord Krishna, is still recited in temples and homes across India.

The *Puranas* mark a significant development in Hinduism, with a much greater emphasis on the worship of Gods in human form, unlike the earlier Vedic faith; where the latter had relied on rituals and sacrifices in which *homams* (prayer rituals around a fire), usually involving the fire god Agni, played a major role, the Puranic practice principally involved idol-worship and *pujas*. (It is suggested that while the Vedic era saw only the worship of a formless and imageless God, the conduct of rituals and the propitiation of the river and mountain and tree gods of local tribes—all of which were 'portable' and not confined to a fixed spot—it was the arrival of the Greeks under Alexander in the fourth century BCE that brought into India the idea of permanent temples enshrining stone images of heroes and gods.) Again, while the Hinduism of the Vedas emerged from mantras and rituals, including elaborate sacrifices, the *Puranas* promoted their values entirely on the basis of myths and stories. By developing the concept of the saguna Brahman to go with the exalted idea of the nirguna Brahman, the Puranic faith integrated the Vedic religion into the daily worship of ordinary people. Using the seductive power of *maya* (illusion), the *nirguna* Brahman of the Vedas took the form of *saguna* Brahman or Ishvara, the creator of *prakriti*, the natural world and the God or Bhagavan of all human beings. Vishnu and Shiva were recognised as Ishvaras; the followers of the former, the Vaishnavas, worshipped Him in several *avatars*, while the followers of Shiva, the Shaivites, confined their worship to Shiva alone, though in several aspects (the dancing Nataraja, the powerfully symbolic *lingam*), and his immediate family (his consort Parvati, his sons Ganesh or Vinayaka, and Skanda or Murugan). Puranic Hinduism witnessed the absorption (even 'Sanskritisation') of the existing local cultures and the adoption of their deities and heroes into Hindu mythology; it is in the Puranic age that both Vaishnavites and Shaivites accepted idol worship, which was earlier absent from the Vedic faith. The *Puranas* offered a bridge between the Vedic religion and local folkways, between highbrow philosophers and vernacular cultures, assimilating both in a narrative of inclusive ethics. It is in the *Puranas* that much of what we today understand by popular Hinduism is anchored.

Not quite fitting into any of these categories is another magnificent work of early Hinduism, authored in the South by Thiruvalluvar (born around 300 CE) whose *Thirukkural*, a collection of 1,330 couplets or *kurals* containing profound aphorisms and imparting moral lessons, has been called by some 'the Veda of the Tamils'.

By the sixth century CE India and Hinduism had a rich mythology, a corpus of elaborate rites and rituals, extraordinary heroic poetry, a well-developed system of popular ethics, an evolving religious architecture and a spiritual literature for the masses. It also had non-religious texts of universal significance, notably the fables of the *Panchatantra*, which imparted practical advice on worldly matters (and on the foibles of human character) in the form of entertaining tales featuring both humans and animals. There is cynicism, including about kings and political leaders; violence, often unfortunate; and humour, sometimes at the expense of the vainglorious. 'We are told quite frankly,' observes the historian Upinder Singh, 'that conventional virtues can lead to ruin. Truthfulness, kindness, and helpfulness to others lead to disaster. The idea of self-sacrifice (even feigned) is mocked. Cunning, quick thinking, and hard-headedness are valorised. The only social relationship that is celebrated is friendship, and even that does not emerge unscathed.'[15]

With idol worship came temple construction, a feature of Hinduism only since the fifth century CE, and reaching its apogee in the magnificent Chola temples of the eleventh to the thirteenth centuries, many of which are still in use today. The 108 Agamas lay down the disciplines and doctrines for the worship of specific deities, notably Shiva, Vishnu and Shakti, which in turn have given birth to cults focused on each of these manifestations of the divine. They also specify the rules for constructing temples in honour of each of these, and for observing related rituals and rites. They are meticulously detailed, ranging from the ablutions to be performed by the worshipper to the adornments on the idol, the timing and order of prayers and so on, and also replete with devotional songs and verses. However, most people worship daily in the privacy of their own homes: instead of idols consecrated in temples, they have portable idols installed in an alcove or puja-room. This practice is sanctified in the *Srimad Bhagavatham* or *Bhagavata Purana* (Part 11, Chapter 27, Sloka 12), which specifies that eight types of material engender permissible forms of idol worship: stone, wood, metal, clay, sand, crystal, a drawing or even just a mental image. Some of the prominent temples were located on the banks of sacred rivers—notably the Ganga, Yamuna, Narmada, Godavari, Krishna, and Kaveri—whose flowing waters were said to have cleansing properties that could purify those who immersed themselves in them.

The Darshanas are the texts of the six principal schools of Hindu philosophy, drawing from many, and are unabashedly intellectual and abstrusely academic in nature. The six (the Shad Darshanas) include three lesser-known schools of Hindu philosophy: the Nyaya School, which emphasises logic and debate; the Vaisheshika School, which sees the universe as made up of countless atoms, each with its own distinctive quality; and the Mimamsa School, which emphasises the role of sacrifice and ritual in seeking salvation (some scholars describe the Vedic religion as Mimamsa Hinduism to distinguish it from the Puranic Hinduism of later years). A fourth, the Yoga School, is better known around the world for its physical practices, but in fact principally focuses on the control of the mind, the breath and the body as the means to attaining the divine samadhi (a state of trance-like meditative consciousness). The central debate in Hindu philosophy is, however, between the two other schools, the oldest, the Sankhya School (so old that it is mentioned in the *Mahabharata*), based on reasoning, which argues the case for dualism or Dvaita (the idea that there is a clear distinction between spirit and matter, between the divine and the worldly) and the newest (founded just over a millennium ago), the Vedanta School, which rejects dualism (Advaita) and sees spirit and matter as essentially one. Vedanta, or 'the end of the Vedas', has, thanks to the initial efforts of Adi Shankara and the nineteenth-century preaching of Swami Vivekananda, become the principal school of Hindu philosophy today, as well as the most influential internationally, and is discussed more fully in the next chapter.

Hindus trust the Vedas, but most do not see them as immune to analysis or criticism; it has been axiomatic in Hinduism that what was valuable to its forefathers might be valuable to us today, but each generation is allowed to enquire into its own spiritual patrimony. The Vedas have a sanctified place in the Hindu consciousness, but the *Upanishads*, the *Puranas*, the epics, and other works of spiritual and philosophical enquiry are also counted among our most basic scriptures. The three prasthanas or divisions of the Vedanta—the *Upanishads*, the *Brahma Sutras* (555 aphoristic verses attributed to Badarayana and written down some time between 450 BCE and 200 CE, which summarise the spiritual and philosophical ideas in the *Upanishads*) and the Bhagavad Gita—correspond roughly, according to Hindu philosophers, with the three stages of faith, knowledge and discipline. Each has value and each can be understood and practised alone or in combination with the others.

That said, as we have seen, Hindus, unlike Muslims and Christians, do not see their religious texts as claiming to embody the ultimate truth. Indeed, it would be a problem if they did, because then different texts would offer contradictory truths and men might be obliged to fight each other to demonstrate the superiority of their truth. Instead, a work of scripture is, to a Hindu, a means of self-realisation; the words, and the insights they contain, are devices through which a diligent Hindu approaches self-transformation. A religious text is a breach in the fog of ignorance that enshrouds the human mind. Allow its insights, the magic of its words, the music of its mantras, to penetrate through the fog, and a transformation might follow. The transformation is not merely in understanding the words of the text as in an Abrahamic holy book, but in opening the mind to new possibilities—including the possibility that the literal claims of the text might be false. The purpose of the religious text is to enter the mind of the reader and help constitute the self.

As Swami Vivekananda put it: 'To the Westerners their religious books have been inspired, while with us our books have been expired; breath-like they came, the breath of God, out of the hearts of sages they sprang, the mantra-drashtas.'

Given this attitude to the Hindu holy texts, the Sanatana Dharma's attitude to the Bible, the Torah or the Quran is the same. Hindus do not look for the literal meanings of these holy books; and since they do not read them literally, they do not argue over them literally either. The Hindu has historically refused to pick a fight over the meaning of other people's religious texts; since they cannot literally be true, to the Hindu, they can either help in self-realisation or not, but they are not worth quarrelling about. You say your holy book is the word of God? Fine; if it helps you understand your true self, if it opens your mind's eyes to the ultimate truth of Creation and helps you merge your soul into the cosmos, it will have served its purpose. Ah, you say, that's not what your holy book is supposed to do? What use is it to you then? Come, let me read it; perhaps it will help open my eyes.

This approach to theological disputation left the honest Christian missionary in colonial times somewhat confused.

THE HINDU LIFE EXPERIENCE

As a result, Hinduism occupies a unique place among the world's faiths. In it, as Dr Radhakrishnan explained:

> 'Intellect is subordinated to intuition, dogma to experience, outer expression to inward realisation. Religion is not the acceptance of academic abstractions or the celebration of ceremonies, but a kind of life or experience. It is insight into the nature of reality (*darshana*) or experience of reality (*anubhava*).'

Hindus dislike people being drafted into truth-armies firing cannons of certitudes; their instinct is to remain sceptical, open, questioning. Reason and intuition must go together. Blind belief in dogma is absent in Hinduism; all spiritual teachings are subject to disputation, and perceptions must be tested through logical thought. The Hindu sacred texts 'are not so much dogmatic dicta as transcripts from life.'

This is all very well, one might say, but what of the vast majority of Hindus, who have not read most of these sacred texts, who are unaware of the glorious capaciousness of their faith, who are inured to theological heterodoxy and scriptural eclecticism? What of those who only know Hinduism as a cultural identity, who go to their temples to pray to their *ishta-devta* (their favourite gods) when they are in trouble or distress, who observe fasts for specific deities, celebrate joyously the major festivals in their area and are conscious of their difference from those who practise other faiths? Is the Hinduism I am describing their Hinduism too?

I would claim it is. Because ultimately the nature of any religious faith is not determined by its scholars, theologians and scriptural exegetes. It is precisely the ordinary believer, the worshipper who is indifferent to theories about his faith but believes in God and values his religion as his way of reaching his hands out to his Maker, who demonstrates the essence of his faith in his own practice of it. In Hinduism, there is an understandable tendency to see the faith through its remarkable Sanskrit scriptural and philosophical writings. But just as important to the practice of Hinduism are the non-Sanskritic, oral, vernacular and regional traditions of worship and ritual, which are indispensable to the way the faith is experienced in different parts of the country. And it is precisely because Hinduism has been practised in a certain way for millennia that is has survived as long as it has with its essential nature unchanged, even as it has faced the vicissitudes of reformist movements like Buddhism and Jainism, military assaults from Muslim invaders, conquest and Islamic rule, the conversion activity of Christian missionaries, reformist challenges like those of Ramananda, Chaitanya and Kabir (of whom later), syncretic movements like Sikhism and the Brahmo Samaj and attempts at conversion of its adherents to other faiths. Every Hindu may not be conscious of the finer points of his faith, but he has been raised in the tradition of its assumptions and doctrines, even when these have not been explained to him. His Hinduism may be a Hinduism of habit rather than a Hinduism of learning, but it is a lived Hinduism for all that.

These 'habits' vary enormously from place to place, caste to caste, and community to community. In South India it is entirely common to see celebrations and practices completely unfamiliar to a north Indian, and vice-versa. The Thaipusam festival, taking place in the Tamil month of Thai, in which devotees carry ceremonial offerings on wooden planks called kavadis and many pierce themselves through the body and march in excruciating processionals to demonstrate their devotion to Lord Murugan, is unknown in other parts of India. Pongal is a huge festival in Tamil Nadu and southern Kerala but a north Indian Hindu will have no clue what it signifies. While Diwali, the Festival of Lights, has over the years become, in popular perception, the standout Hindu festival, it is observed fairly modestly in the south; in Kerala, on the other hand, the festival of Onam is celebrated with enormous gaiety and piety unlike in the north, where it is not celebrated at all.

Onam, in fact, offers another striking example of Hindu diversity. It celebrates the annual return to earth of the *asura* King Mahabali, a wise and benevolent monarch under whose egalitarian rule the people of Kerala flourished in mythical times. The gods, jealous of his overweening power and popularity, sent Lord Vishnu to earth in the form of a Brahmin dwarf, Vamana, who asked the king for as much land as he could cover in three steps. The king, surprised by the modesty of his request, granted his wish; whereupon the dwarf grew to his celestial size as the Lord. With one step he covered the earth, with his second the heavens; and when he had nowhere left to place his third step, he turned to the king to fulfil his promise. King Mahabali humbly offered his own head; Lord Vishnu placed his foot on the monarch's head, driving the king through the ground into the netherworld. Onam commemorates Mahabali's annual return to earth to see how his people are getting on. Rather like Santa Claus, he is largely portrayed as a jolly rotund figure happy to see his subjects enjoying a good time, and Onam is an occasion for holiday cheer, gift-giving and enormous feasts. As I have noted, it is, however, not celebrated by north Indian Hindus, who instead observe, the day before Onam, a minor festival called Vamana Puja in which they worship Vishnu in the form of a dwarf. A Malayalam tweet by a north Indian politician, Bharatiya Janata Party (BJP) President Amit Shah, wishing Keralites well on the occasion of Vamana Puja, caused great offence to its intended audience, since it was portrayed as celebrating the ill-treatment of the popular local king vanquished by Vamana!

As a result of its huge diversity, and the multiple folk religious practices it has absorbed over the millennia, mainstream Hinduism abounds in festivals. There is no day in the calendar which is not associated with some auspicious occasion, or dedicated to a specific god, or assigned to a particular religious practice. The importance and significance of each day will again vary depending on which part of India one is in, and which community one belongs to. In Delhi it is entirely possible to see

Punjabis celebrating Lohri while Bengalis go about their business, Biharis enveloped in Chhath Puja while Maharashtrians remain ignorant of it and Malayalis in Onam holiday spirit while northerners are just gearing themselves up for Diwali.

Rituals are undoubtedly a precious part of religious practice for most Hindus. Some are conducted by priests in arcane Sanskrit while the devotee, having paid his fee, stands with hands folded and listens in incomprehension. (There is a distinction in many scriptural texts between the priest who performs the ritual and the *yajamana* or the person for whom it is performed, whose only role consists of offering a *dakshina* or gratuity to the priest.) Some—particularly the rituals associated with birth and naming, the first feeding of grain to a baby, the first instruction in the alphabet, and of course marriage, death and cremation—are full of inescapable meaning for every participant and bind the worshipper to his faith, family and community. Most often the rituals require a visit to a temple; sometimes they are performed at home. My sisters, who live abroad, do not go as often to temples as our mother, who lives in India, though they strive to keep up certain religious traditions and practices even in foreign lands. But they tell me that they are deeply comforted by the knowledge that on every special occasion in their family, our mother is going to an ancient temple to pray for them, to seek the Lord's blessings for their families, and to distribute alms to the poor in their name. In turn, whether in damp London or sunny California, they remember to light a lamp at dusk in their prayer-rooms, as Hindus have done for centuries.

Hindu rituals almost always require a priest, in most parts of India; however my own community, the Nairs of Kerala, dispenses with the services of a priest on the occasion of marriage, seeing it as a social contract to be performed under the guidance of family elders in the presence of large numbers of usually well-fed witnesses, which would be enough to seal a marriage in the eyes of the world. The eyes of a representative of God they consider much less important; whereas in the north, it would be unthinkable not to have a priest officiating— indeed the wedding might well be considered null and void if a priest didn't turn up to conduct it.

Given this dislike of priestly intermediaries in my gene pool, it is no wonder that as a young boy I asked my father why it was necessary to go to temples. If God is everywhere, I reasoned, isn't He (or She) at home, at school, at work? Why do we need to go to a temple to find Her? My father patiently explained that while God is everywhere, He was especially powerful in certain places, especially those where He had manifested himself through the spontaneous appearance of an idol (as in the Krishna idol in Guruvayur) or other miracles. Such places then became sanctified by the devotions of millions of worshippers over hundreds of years, and thus acquired even more religious significance. It was a self-perpetuating phenomenon: a temple became famous because of something associated with it, usually a legend involving the deity in question, then worshippers came and testified to its powers, saying their prayers at that place had been answered by the Goddess, for instance, and then more worshippers came and the more devotion the temple attracted, the more were the stories of miracles and blessings accruing from worship there, and the more people kept coming....

On that south Indian pilgrimage when I was fourteen, I also found myself asking my father about the behaviour of some of the priests at the more famous temples, who openly stuck out their hands for more money after performing the rituals my father had already paid for. He looked somewhat embarrassed at first, then replied softly but firmly that priests had to live too. They were performing a service to us devotees, but they had families they were responsible for, children they had to educate, and it was only fair they asked for help from the people on whose behalf they had interceded with God. After all, they had what today we would call 'domain knowledge'; they knew the scriptures, had mastered the mantras and could recite the appropriate ones with the required fluency. Why shouldn't they be rewarded for their expertise?

This left my teenage mind only partly mollified, and I have not been as enthusiastic a temple-goer as my parents, especially since I rationalised that praying in the privacy of my own home would be just as effective, as long as my heart was pure and my thoughts clear. I maintain an eclectic prayer-alcove in my home, where dozens of pictures, idols and relics of Hindu deities—including a print that reproduces one of my parents' religious pictures, that I saw my father pray before every day as I grew up—all compete for my reverential attention daily.

Still, the passion of other worshippers keeps drawing me back to temples, especially in my constituency, Thiruvananthapuram, which is blessed with more places of worship per square kilometre than any other metropolis in India, and where friends, colleagues and party workers insist on accompanying me, praying for me and promising assorted divinities that I will perform certain rituals in fulfilment of their undertakings. (I have, as a result, been weighed against bananas, coconuts and salt because *they* had sworn that I would be: this is a powerful incentive against weight-loss, since the heavier I was, the more the temples in question benefited from donations of those items). But I am not complaining. I find peace in the temples, and a strengthening of my ties to those who have accompanied me there, as if we have shared something indefinable in that common space where hope and need combine in supplication to the Divine.

* * *

Some have seen in Hinduism a selfish religion, a collection of individuals praying for themselves, with no equivalent of the Muslim Friday prayer or the Sunday Christian Mass with its service and sermon uniting a community in worship. Philosophically, after all, the most important claim the *Upanishads* make is that the essence of each individual is also the essence of all things; the human self, the *atman*, and the cosmic reality, Brahman, are essentially the same. This leads to the view that one only needs to look within to find divinity; one has no need of fellow worshippers or collective sermonising. Hindu religious practice is essentially contemplative, as the seeker turns his gaze inwards in quest of real awareness. The *Mundaka Upanishad* (II.2.3)[16] offers a marvellous metaphor: the Imperishable is the target for the seeker, the *Upanishads* are his bow, constant meditation is his arrow, and the string of the bow is drawn with his mind filled with Brahman. Because of this interiority, some Hindu critics see Hinduism as lacking the unity that strengthens other faiths and helps them to negotiate the modern world and social pressures better. Its focus on self-realisation rather than collective advancement, they say, might allow plenty of room for philosophical thought, but none for collective action. To such critics, this prevents Hindus from constituting a defined 'community' that can withstand external pressures. Such thinking partly animates the Hindutva project we shall discuss in Chapter Five.

The *Atharva Veda* points out that the quest for awareness, the search for answers, the journey towards self-realisation, never ceases:

> *How does the wind not cease to blow?*
> *How does the mind take no repose?*
> *Why do the waters, seeking to reach the truth,*
> *Never at any time cease to flow?*

— *Atharva Veda*, X.7.37[17]

And yet this process is not purely self-centred individualism, since the real self one discovers in this profound quest is the same self as everyone else's. Self-realisation leads ultimately to merging one's soul into the collective Brahman. So when one goes to a temple to worship, one is finding a common sanctified space to help one travel to the same destination as every other worshipper.

3

QUESTIONING HINDU CUSTOMS

Some of Thiruvananthapuram's old temples, especially the eleventh-century Sree Padmanabhaswamy Kshetram, recently revealed to be one of the richest temples in the world because of all the treasures deposited there by the triumphant Travancore maharajas of yore, are truly beautiful. This is where Vishnu is worshipped as Padmanabha, lying on the great serpent Ananta as he floats on the vast Ocean of Milk, the Kshir Sagar. It is in this posture that he is so revered that the kings of the Travancore kingdom called themselves 'Padmanabhadasa', servants of Padmanabha, and ruled in his name rather than in their own—a curious inversion of the concept of the divine right of kings, since here it was the kingly right of the divine.

If many temples are beautiful, though, not all old Hindu practices sanctified by these temples are. The ancient tradition of caste was one my nationalist parents tried to shield me from for years, and it was only at age eleven, when asked by a schoolmate in Mumbai what my caste was (in an incident I describe below), that I finally demanded an explanation. But caste as an instrument of discrimination was abhorrent to my liberal sensibilities from a very young age.

CASTE AND HINDUISM

It is difficult to pretend that Hinduism can be exempted from the problems of casteism, since the religion has been cited as legitimising this form of discrimination in some of its sacred texts. The *Rig Veda* does not mention caste in its original books and it first appears in the Purusha Sukta verse, a later interpolation that describes the sacrifice by the gods of Purusha, the cosmic man, to create all human life: according to this verse, from his mouth emerged the Brahmin, the priests and scholars; his arms were made into the Kshatriyas, the warriors and rulers; his two thighs were the general populace, the farmers, merchants and traders who made up the Vaishyas; and from his feet the Sudras, the workers, artisans and servants, were born.

The verse has been challenged, especially by the great constitutionalist and Dalit leader Dr Bhimrao Ambedkar, who considered it a fraudulent attempt to legitimise caste discrimination, but there is little doubt that many Hindus believed that the caste system had religious sanction. Ironically, as I have demonstrated in my 2017 book *Inglorious Empire: What the British Did to India*, India had castes, but not a caste system: the rigidities of caste as we understand it today were introduced by the British in their desire to understand, categorise, and classify the people they were ruling, in order to control them all the better. What the writer on Hinduism Devdutt Pattanaik describes as the attempt by the British to 'force-fit' some 3,000 *jatis* (castes, or some say sub-castes, grouped around hereditary professions) into the four varnas established in the Dharmashastras, has given us a complex 'caste system' whose uneven persistence in Hindu society has been the source of both iniquity and confusion.

The language of the Purusha Sukta verse would seem to rule out any but Brahmin priests in Hindu temples, and yet *shudra archakas* (low caste sacerdotes) perform rituals in many Hindu places of worship, and in October 2017 the Travancore Devaswom (temple board) officially appointed thirty-six non-Brahmin priests, including six Dalits (the former 'Untouchables' who were not even admitted to Kerala's temples till 1936 and who are still denied access to the sanctum sanctorum in many temples where that privilege is reserved only for those who wear the sacred thread, namely Brahmins). It is conventional wisdom that the caste system confined all learning to a narrow privileged caste of Brahmins, yet Veda Vyasa, the compiler of the Vedas, was born to a low-caste fisherwoman, and Valmiki, the author of the *Ramayana*, was a low-caste hunter; both are revered today, even by the Brahmins.

Caste may well have originated in Hinduism's desire to accommodate the different racial, sectarian, and occupational groups it encountered, in a social hierarchy: Dr Radhakrishnan called it 'the answer of Hinduism to the forces pressing on it from outside', an instrument to 'civilise' different tribes it absorbed. To this great scholar, caste 'stands for the ordered complexity, the harmonised multiplicity, the many in one which is the clue to the structure of the universe'.[1] That sounds almost admirable, till one understands that this complexity, in practice, ossified into impermeable social barriers that manifested themselves in degrading forms of social discrimination and economic oppression. It was not always the case: there was a famous 'fuzziness' to the operations of caste in the pre-colonial era, and many famous examples of caste mobility (beyond those of Veda Vyasa and Valmiki). Be that as it may, the workings of caste extended into religious worship as well. Many temples forbade entry of the 'lower' castes and the 'outcastes'; the latter became known as 'Untouchables' because of the innumerable social prohibitions and indignities to which they were subject.

There is no excusing such abhorrent practices, and many modern Hindus have grown up rejecting the discriminatory aspects of the caste system, while still observing caste preferences when it comes to arranging the marriages of their children. Their logic is simple: caste is a form of community organisation that has been in place for ever, and we are not about to jettison it. We are comfortable with the affinities it implies, and we would prefer to perpetuate our family by arranging marriages within our caste group. But that doesn't mean we will discriminate against people of other castes, or mistreat them: we are educated people, and we know that's wrong. This may strike many modern Indians as a dubious compromise, but the attitude I have summarised is far more common within the Hindu population than many imagine.

It should also be said that the most impressive of India's movements against caste discrimination, from those of Basava in the twelfth century to Sree Narayana Guru in the nineteenth, came from within Hinduism and retained a Hindu vocabulary and conceptual world, including reverence for Hindu deities. Sree Narayana Guru, forbidden as an Ezhava from worshipping at the Shiva temple, entered a river and unearthed a *lingam* (phallic statue) that he consecrated himself, thereby creating his own Shiva rather than rejecting the god who was denied to him. The fourteenth-century Bhakti saint Chokhamela was a Dalit whose fervour for God continued even though he was not allowed inside the temple. In one of his verses he addresses the deity as he might speak to a man of an upper caste: 'I am so hungry; I have come for your leavings, I am full of hope.' In another verse, he brings a 'bowl for your leftover food'; with no access to the shrine, he seeks to fulfil his devotion by serving the deity, submitting himself completely and eating the scraps left behind. This is alarmingly conformist, yet revealing of the extent to which Chokhamela's abject social condition had no bearing on his spiritual standing nor on the extent of his posthumous sanctification. Among the Lingayat saints, too, there were many of humble origins. While Basava, the founder of the sect, was born a Brahmin, many of his prominent disciples were of humbler origins: as Manu S. Pillai records, Allama Prabhu was a drummer, Siddharama a cowherd, Maccayya a washerman, and Kakkaya, a skinner of dead cows.[2]

Still, social mobility was relatively rare in Hinduism, and the lot of the outcastes was a terrible one. Was this because of the religion or the society that practised it? Arguably, Untouchability was a social practice for which it is impossible to find scriptural sanction. To suggest that to be a good Hindu you had to practise caste discrimination is therefore theologically unsound. As the philosopher Jonardon Ganeri has explained, 'Hinduism contains within itself the philosophical resources to sustain an internal critique of reprehensible and unjust social practices that have sometimes emerged in Hindu societies.' As those who are familiar with Adi Shankara's beliefs will testify, the Upanishadic insistence on the unity of being, a divinity available to everyone, the *atma* residing in everyone, and the idea that all human souls ultimately merge into the same Brahman, for instance, implies the equality of all souls and argues against caste discrimination. So does the Vedantic concept of the welfare of all human beings, irrespective of social or economic distinctions: '*bahujana sukhaya bahujana hitaya cha*'. Adi Shankara himself is said to have met an outcaste, Chandala, who was ordered by his disciples to move out of the path of the great sage. 'Who are you to ask me to move for you?' the outcaste asked the great *rishi*. 'Is the Self within me different from the Self within you?' Shankara was so struck by this enunciation of Advaita wisdom by the low-born Chandala that he prostrated himself before the Untouchable and proclaimed him to be his guru.

Manu S. Pillai recounts a legend from the same period: 'The sage Vararuchi, son of Sankaracharya's preceptor, married a pariah (low caste) woman, and fathered twelve children with her. One became a Brahmin, another a carpenter, and one was even a Muslim. Yet another sibling, when they all met for a feast, brought to the table food that he enjoyed: the udder of a cow, or beef if you will. Of course the story goes on to transform the meat into a plant that everyone then consumed, but the lesson is simply that though they were different in what they did and what they ate, they were all born of the same parents, and children of the same land.'[3]

Still, caste discrimination was widespread and iniquitous. Of course Hindus have long accepted the logic of 'reservations' (government legislated quotas in employment and education) in India as a means of making up for millennia of discrimination based on birth. This is why the Constitution inaugurated the world's oldest and farthest-reaching affirmative action programme, guaranteeing Dalits and Adivasis (Scheduled Castes and Tribes) not only equality of opportunity but guaranteed outcomes, with reserved places in educational institutions, government jobs and even seats in Parliament and the state assemblies. Given the appalling discrimination to which they had been subject for millennia—especially those subject to the unspeakable privations of Untouchability—this seems only fair to most, including many caste Hindus, who have not objected to these (SC/ST) reservations.

These reservations are granted to groups listed in Schedules of the Indian Constitution on the basis of their (presumably immutable) caste identities. The addition of the 'Other Backward Classes' (OBC) category in 1989 after the acceptance by the government of Prime Minister V.P. Singh of the recommendations of the Mandal Commission added more people to the numbers benefiting from such official reservations, but it didn't change the basis on which they benefited: despite the 'C' in 'OBC' referring to 'classes', the OBC lists contained castes and sub-castes just above the Dalits in the social pecking order. People like myself tend to disavow caste loyalties as unworthy relics of a more unequal pre-Independence past, but accept that granting benefits on the basis of caste is unavoidable. As for ourselves, as intellectual heirs of an anti-colonial freedom movement that explicitly rejected caste, and out-lawed caste discrimination, we aren't supposed to admit to caste feeling even if, in some cases, it lurks somewhere beneath the surface.

I am conscious of my own bias in the opposite direction; as the son of a newspaper executive from Kerala who dropped his caste name (Nair) at college in response to Mahatma Gandhi's exhortations to do so, moved to London and brought his children up in Westernised Bombay, I am a product of a nationalist generation that was consciously raised to be oblivious of caste.

I still remember my own discovery of caste. I was an eleven-year-old representing the seventh form in an inter-class theatrical event at which the eighth form sketch featured the scion of a famous Bollywood dynasty (who are Hindu). The boy would later become a successful screen heart-throb. I had acted, penned a humorous poem and organ-ised my class's efforts, and the young man was either intrigued or dis-concerted by what he had witnessed, for he sought me out the next morning at school.

'Tharoor,' he asked me at the head of the steps near the toilet, 'what caste are you?'

I blinked my nervousness at the Great Man. 'I—I don't know,' I stammered. My father, who never mentioned anyone's religion, let alone caste, had not bothered to enlighten me on such matters. 'You don't know?' the actor's son demanded in astonishment. 'What do you mean, you don't know? Everybody knows their own caste.'

I shamefacedly confessed I didn't.

'You mean you're not a Brahmin or something?'

I couldn't even avow I was a something. The Great Man never spoke to me again in school. But I went home that evening and extracted an explanation from my parents, whose eclectic liberality had left me in such ignorance. They told me, in simplified terms, about the Nairs; and so it is to that schoolboy, celluloid hero of the future, that I owe my first lesson about my genealogical past.

Despite this enforced awareness, I grew up thinking of caste as an irrelevance. The idea of caste as a badge of identity bothered me hardly at all, because I saw it as one of several such badges, to be donned or taken off according to my convenience. My caste identity was relevant to family holidays in my parents' ancestral villages, but irrelevant to my cosmopolitan schooling, and my parents never mentioned (or asked) the caste or religion of any schoolmate who came home to play with me or attend my birthday parties. I grew up ignorant of caste, married outside my caste, and brought up two children to be utterly indifferent to caste, indeed largely unconscious of it. Until my fifties, when I entered the caste-ridden world of Indian politics, it remained that way. Even then I deliberately abstained from finding out the caste of anyone I met or worked with; I hired a cook without asking his caste (the same with my remaining domestic staff) and have entertained all manner of people in my home without the thought of caste affinity even crossing my mind.

One of the key identities in India is, inescapably, caste. As has been noted, to some, it's an instrument of political mobilisation; as the political ascendancy in parts of north India has repeatedly demonstrated, when many Indians cast their vote, they vote their caste. English-speaking urban Indians may scorn such behaviour even while accepting it as part of political reality. After all, none of us would object if a Dalit leader advertised her pride in being a Dalit, or called for Dalit solidarity. Yet my obliviousness to caste is itself a confession of privilege; no Dalit, my Dalit friends tell me, can afford to be oblivious of caste. Much of the outrage at caste is, of course, when it's not a member of an oppressed community celebrating its achievements, but members of one of the so-called 'upper castes', someone at the top of the heap, celebrating their privileges, power and prominence.

Caste won't disappear from the landscape of Hinduism: too many political and administrative benefits (and disadvantages) derive from one's caste affiliation for that to happen, not to mention that for many Indians, it is still part of their lived reality, even though it doesn't pack the same punch it once used to. If it becomes more and more one of many interchangeable, mutable forms of identity—one fraternity of many that an Indian can lay claim to—it may cease to matter so much. The majority of Hindus aren't there yet, unfortunately. And politics may not let them get there either. In recent years we have witnessed the unedifying (and unwittingly hilarious) spectacle of castes fighting with each other to be declared backward: the competitive zeal of the Meenas and the Gujjars in Rajasthan to be deemed more backward than each other, and the agitations of privileged and powerful castes like the Marathas, the Patels and the Jats for reservations on the same basis, would be funny if all sides weren't so deadly serious. As an uncle of mine sagely observed, 'In our country now, you can't go forward unless you're a backward.' (That may seem a prejudiced remark, but such views are increasingly held by many whose castes are ineligible for reservations). Caste—ironically entrenched in India by British colonial rule, as I wrote in *Inglorious Empire*—has remained an inescapable feature of our lives.

The news that a recent survey has established that 27 per cent of Indians still practise caste Untouchability[4] is not, in many ways, news at all. Most Indians have grown up in an India where we have seen such behaviour, though the kind of people who read English-language books probably think of it as something that happens in rural, backward villages rather than bigger towns and cities.

But this survey also packs a few other surprises. It shows almost every third Hindu (30 per cent) admitted to the practice. That is, they refused to allow Dalits into their kitchen or to use their utensils. But data from the survey showed that Untouchability was also practised by Sikhs (23 per cent), Muslims (18 per cent) and Christians (5 per cent).[5] These are faiths that pride themselves on their enshrining of equality and the brotherhood of faith. Dr Amit Thorat, the survey's lead researcher, was quoted in the Indian media as saying, 'These findings indicate that conversion [to religions other than Hinduism] has not led to the total change of mindset that was hoped…caste identity is sticky baggage, difficult to dislodge in social settings.'[6]

My father's and my response—to be oblivious to caste and indifferent to the caste associations of friends, employees and associates—is no longer enough in today's caste-conscious India. For a long time I assumed this was the modern Indian ideal—the egalitarian spirit in which one judged people not by their caste but (to borrow from Martin Luther King Jr.) by the content of their character or the sum of their abilities. But living in India over the last decade, after thirty-four years based abroad, has taught me I was wrong. As an eighteen-year-old blogger, Tejaswini Tabhane, pointed out recently, 'A Brahmin's caste pride comes with humiliation for other castes'. Caste, she writes, 'is both the base and superstructure of Indian society and both the relations of power as well as the forces of production are mediated through it. Blindness to caste does not take away the social, political and economical privileges one gets because of one's "accident of birth" in a particular ("upper") caste.' In her words, anyone belonging to a hierarchically privileged caste 'is bound to get the advantages of his caste location, willingly or unwillingly, consciously or unconsciously. Caste governs the distribution of resources and opportunities in Indian society. Caste is very much present in your life even if it is not directly visible to you because your social and economic capital is a production of your caste only.'[7]

I have to concede she is right. And that makes her admonition strike home: 'To be born in a privileged caste is not anyone's fault but to refuse to even acknowledge "unearned benefits" accruing due to one's caste and thereby claiming that the very mechanism that enforces them is absent in one's life is not right.' On the other hand, 'For the people belonging to the marginalised lower strata of this system, caste is about humiliation, deprivation, oppression and imposed identity.'

Caste blindness, in other words, is itself an affectation available only to the privileged; the 'lower' castes cannot afford to be indifferent to

caste. Parallels are sought to be drawn to debates over race-blind policies in the West, but these are inexact: race, after all, is visible, whereas
caste is not, which makes it genuinely possible to be caste-blind in
one's social and personal relations in a way that is not feasible in multi-
race contexts (a white person cannot credibly say, 'I didn't realise he
was black', least of all when a white employer rejects a black applicant's job application, but an upper-caste Hindu can plausibly claim, 'I
didn't know she was a Dalit'). Still, the temper of the times demands
consciousness of caste and positive compensatory action for its disabilities, rather than blindness to it. Jawaharlal Nehru had hoped caste
would disappear from India's consciousness, as I had allowed it to from
mine. In today's India, that will no longer do.

The recent official findings confirming the persistence of the iniquitous practice of caste discrimination across India's religious communities
do not exonerate Hindu society. But caste, Swami Vivekananda told us,
has nothing to do with religion: it is a purely social practice, and many
Hindus can and should bring up their children to abhor the idea of caste.
In the *Puranas* there is the story of a debate between the *rishis* Vasistha and
Vishwamitra on whether the Vedic religion could be universalised or
whether it was intended for the Aryan people alone. The *Upanishads*
broadened the appeal of the ritualistic religion depicted in the Vedas, and
sages like Adi Shankara and Ramanuja democratised it further. Indeed,
Adi Shankara declared that any human being, merely by virtue of their
personhood, could attain the Supreme Consciousness through a study of
the scriptures, the *Puranas* and the epics, meditation (*japa*), fasting (*upav-
asa*) and worship (*puja*). Caste was never approved of by Adi Shankara.
The contemporary rejection of caste draws from a long reformist tradition in Hinduism that embraces all of them, as well as Kabir, Nanak,
Shirdi Sai Baba, Sree Narayana Guru and Mahatma Gandhi.

Hindu society may have maintained a distasteful practice, but no one
can credibly argue that it is intrinsic to the religion. There is a marvellous story of Utanga, a childhood friend of Lord Krishna, who had
received a boon from Krishna that the Lord would provide him water
whenever he needed it on his wanderings. On one occasion, overcome
by thirst in a remote place, Utanga called upon his boon. An outcaste

hunter soon appeared before him, clad in skins and dirty rags, offering him water from an animal-skin water bag. Utanga, a fastidious Brahmin, turned down his offer. The hunter continued his attempts to persuade him to drink the water but Utanga was haughtily unmoved, berating Lord Krishna in his mind for not having fulfilled his promise. The hunter, his generosity spurned even by a man in need, duly disappeared. Soon Krishna himself materialised before Utanga, informing him that he had sent Indra, the king of the Devas, in the guise of the hunter, to offer him not just water but *amrit*, the nectar of immortality. 'Since, instead of accepting his generosity, you chose to judge him by external factors like caste, you have forfeited the chance of immortality,' the Lord informed Utanga.

The Hindu who says that caste discrimination is incompatible with his *dharma* is a better Hindu than one who insists her religion does not permit her to engage a low caste cook in her house (as a senior government official recently did) or claims her faith will not allow her to serve a Dalit boss (which somehow no menial employee in India has yet done). Still, the battles over temple entry to Dalits occurred within living memory; and other instances of the pernicious effect of caste discrimination in the practice of religion are not hard to find. India's first artist to achieve mass popularity, Raja Ravi Varma, did so in the 1890s by printing lithographs of his paintings of Hindu gods, which enabled Dalits to worship in their homes images of the very deities they were not allowed to pray to in the temples, from which they were barred. As I've pointed out a few pages earlier, the great social reformer Sree Narayana Guru in Kerala installed a Shiva-lingam in a temple because Hindus of his Ezhava caste were forbidden from entering the area's established Shiva temples. So the Hindu religion has undoubtedly been complicit in caste discrimination, and the faith's identification with caste oppression has long been the principal negative held against it. Is a religion responsible for the worst behaviour of its followers? Perhaps not; but Hindus collectively need to continue doing all that they can to wash the stain of caste discrimination from the face of their faith.

WHY I AM A HINDU

GURUS AND THE 'GOD MARKET'

Another aspect of popular Hinduism that does not reflect well on it is superstition. Hindus are considered prone to believing in assorted signs and soothsayers; our fondness for astrology, for instance, is widely observed. It is true that a Hindu without a horoscope is like an American without a credit card, and is subject to many of the same disabilities. I even have two horoscopes: one cast for me soon after my birth in London by an expatriate Indian doctor there, another by the family astrologer at the village in Kerala. They didn't match, and to this day, it seems, I have been pursuing two mutually incompatible fates, in the worlds of public service and authorship.

Still, is it fair to saddle Hinduism with the burden of being responsible for its astrologers, many of whom are undoubtedly charlatans? Or should the belief of certain Hindus in astrology be seen as an emanation of Indian society rather than of the Hindu faith?

The latter case is undoubtedly strengthened by the Hindu affinity for gurus and godmen, whose claims to religious significance often do not extend much beyond their garb (and their gab). Hindus have flocked to ochre-robed dispensers of spiritual wisdom for centuries. There have been ascetic fakirs like Shirdi Sai Baba, performers of miracles like Sathya Sai Baba, teachers of meditation like Maharishi Mahesh Yogi and practitioners of sexual liberation like 'Bhagwan' Shri Rajneesh (who later transformed himself into the somewhat more austere Osho). The legendary Sathya Sai Baba has multiple millions of followers around the world; I have written elsewhere of the spotless town of Puttaparthi that serves as his spiritual headquarters, and continues to attract devotees years after his death. Among the 'living saints' of Hinduism, Mata Amritanandamayi, the 'hugging saint', is revered as the embodiment of unconditional love. Her ashram and spiritual retreat, Amritapuri in Vallikavu near Kollam, is a beehive of activity, thronged with followers from around the world; like Sathya Sai Baba, she channels the donations of her followers to major social welfare projects, running a university, medical college, hospital and a television studio.

Such revered figures follow in a long-established Hindu tradition. Advaita Vedantist Hindus have traditionally held gurus or teachers in high reverence, since many ancient texts suggest that one should seek a qualified and able guide in the pursuit of one's spiritual quest. Following a guru is thus seen by many Hindus as desirable though not mandatory, a path to an end rather than an end in itself; a guru is a guide towards the fulfilment of self-realisation, not a substitute for it. In the Advaita tradition, a competent teacher is vital to help a seeker attain correct knowledge and freedom from false knowledge; he (or occasionally she) serves as a revered instructor, counsellor, and shaper of their disciples' values. Since Hinduism emphasises *anubhava*, or the knowledge that comes from experience, as much as philosophical knowledge or *jnana*, which comes from study and reading, a guru can share his experience as a guide and model to the disciple. The best kind of guru is usually an inspirational teacher, a source of wisdom and instruction, a guide moulding the spiritual evolution of the disciple, an elder who imparts his values and a philosopher who reveals the meaning of life to the attentive seeker. Guru means 'dispeller of darkness'; the exalted place of the guru in Hindu thinking reflects the fact that while a mother merely gives us physical birth, a guru ensures our spiritual rebirth. Not all self-anointed gurus are, however, worthy of the appellation.

India is full of gurus; some are figures of great learning and erudition in the religious texts, some are capable of performing mystical and magical feats beyond rational explanation, and some merely impart a quiet wisdom that their followers find inspirational. Such gurus attract followings in the millions, and many have established ashrams to which their devotees flock, and in which many live either permanently or for regular periods, either conducting religious and spiritual practices, or performing social services in the name of their guru's order. But there are also, in the same domain yet of a different order, charlatans, poseurs and tricksters, in what has been dubbed 'the God Market', who woo the credulous with simplistic ideas of spirituality and amass huge fortunes at the expense of the gullible. These include a female guru who wears red mini-skirts and offers homilies on love, a baba who sits in a tree and dispenses benediction through a touch of his foot, and another who receives the world in his naked glory and whose ultimate blessing comes in the opportunity to grasp his exposed male member. Much of this has nothing to do with Hinduism, except that it is a manifestation of the Hindu's eternal search for spiritual truth, in whatever form it can be found.

Many of the devotees of these godmen are not Hindus. Equally, some of these godmen are not Hindu but count Hindus among their followers. It is important to note that the hold godmen have on their followers is not purely a function of religious devotion; rather it has a lot to do with a sense of drift in society, an aimlessness and hopelessness that requires a religious anchor. Clinching evidence for this proposition came in the person of a godman who is not strictly a Hindu, but a Sikh—the self-styled Baba Gurmeet Ram Rahim Singh Insan, whose name is a compound of Sikh, Hindu and Muslim names with 'Insan' meaning 'Human', and whose jailing in August 2017 precipitated a crisis across Punjab, Haryana and Delhi.

The flamboyant, jewellery-bedecked Gurmeet Singh had a reputation for sexually exploiting his female followers, but only two of them had the courage to sue. The case took fifteen years and 200 sittings of the court before he was convicted; during this time, numerous efforts were made by the Baba's devotees to pressure the investigators, the police, the judges and the complainants to withdraw the suit, but they did not give in.

Baba Gurmeet Ram Rahim Singh Insan was always a peculiar godman, eschewing spiritual asceticism for gaudy showmanship and ostentatious living. He liked his hair long, his motorcycles powerful, his cars expensive, his attire sequinned and his women clingy. He performed in popular music videos of his own composition—his biggest hit is called 'Love Charger'—and had a feature film made about himself called *Messenger of God*. This unlikely 'Rockstar Baba', however, amassed a mass following of fanatic worshippers estimated at over ten million.

He or his henchmen kept this flock together in ruthlessly effective ways. A crusading small-town journalist who reported the rape complaint against him was murdered in 2002. The Baba's movement, known as the Dera Sacha Sauda, amassed significant landholdings and property assets, and exerted influence over various aspects of life in the states of Punjab and Haryana; its reach extended to Delhi.

And yet the Dera Sacha Sauda fulfilled a genuine need in north Indian society, giving millions an identity and a standing they had not previously known. Sections of people who had long known only oppression found in the dera movement a measure of security, safety and dignity they and their families had not historically enjoyed, as well as (or so the cynics say) a simpler, more 'market-friendly' version of religious faith. The dera movement considerably predates Ram Rahim, and had established itself for valid and even admirable reasons well before he became its best-known exponent.

Dera members are overwhelmingly Sikhs, though there are many Hindus among them. Sikhism is a faith that enjoins equality among its faithful, a message that had in the past inspired conversions of people from the lower Hindu castes, particularly Dalits and the 'Other Backward Classes'. But so deep is the prejudice in Indian society that many converted Sikhs found themselves treated no better by their co-religionists of higher castes, who dominate the official Sikh religious bodies which run the major gurudwaras or Sikh shrines.

Faced with an entrenched status quo, many Sikhs of less privileged backgrounds became disillusioned. Their feelings of anger and helplessness, compounded by poor education and soaring unemployment, led them to alcohol and drugs. Punjab became known as the drug capital of India, a reputation underscored in the searing portrayal of mass drug addiction in the recent hit film *Udta Punjab*.

It is in this context that the Dera Sacha Sauda and its charismatic leader emerged as saviours. For all his bling, Baba Gurmeet Ram Rahim Singh Insan exemplified an alternative life. The dera offers free education to its members and their children, free food for the hungry, and meaningful employment in its enterprises; it keeps the faithful off drugs, and more than jobs, it gives them a sense of meaning and purpose to their lives. In the process, it gives them that most precious and intangible of human needs—dignity and a sense of belonging.

Politicians played along with the Baba and his dera, and indeed with several other such religious movements; Dera Sacha Sauda is one of the biggest, but far from the only, of several deras dotting Punjab and Haryana. The deras, after all, helped keep social peace, tamp down discontent, and channel frustrations towards constructive activity. Rather than disapprove of them as dangerous cults, successive governments rushed to embrace them. Their religious nature offered a far safer alternative to drugs and crime. The deras ended addiction, replaced anomie with community and redirected despair to divinity, even if it came attired in flashy silver jackets and drove a Range Rover.

The intense loyalty the deras in turn inspire cannot be underestimated. Their fulfilment of people's basic needs is suffused with the religious fervour that comes along with affiliation to a spiritual guru. And most of them are led by figures less ostentatious and controversial than Gurmeet Ram Rahim Singh Insan. But social and economic insecurity is at the heart of a dera's religious appeal and its fanatic following. Where government and civil society failed, a seeming charlatan with an insatiable lust succeeded, and his success mattered far more than his flaws. People who were willing to lend their wives and daughters to their guru could not understand why the same 'blessing' extended to two girls should land him in jail. As an anonymous posting on social media pointed out, 'a lost man doesn't care if a rapist gives him direction. A hungry man will take food from a murderer's hand'.

The mass upsurge by dera followers on their guru's conviction revealed their fears that without him and his organisation, they might once again slide back into the margins. This explains the intensity of their identification with him, whatever he does. They are literally willing to kill for him or, as they might see it, for themselves. Many Indians lamented that such blind religious devotion should thrive in their country in the second decade of the twenty-first century. But the violence that followed the jailing of this particular godman raises far more troubling questions than that.

The episode shows that India's much-vaunted economic growth and development has shallow roots indeed: that it has failed to deliver caste equality and social justice to the underclasses. It shows official institutions of governance all-too-readily subcontracting their responsibilities to religious orders, and enabling their leaders to live above the law. It shows the fragility of law and order systems, which failed so spectacularly in the face of mass fury. And it shows the hold of religious leaders on the loyalties, and the passions, of vast sections of people who find validation for their lives in such unthinking followership.

HINDU FATALISM

One unavoidable issue to be dealt with relating to popular notions of Hinduism is that of 'Hindu fatalism'. Does not our belief in destiny, in karma and predestination, make us inured to our lot in life and accepting of Fate, rather than seeking to change it?

There is an old story, from our ancient *Puranas*, the kind of story Hindus have often told to illustrate larger points about themselves.

A man—the quintessential Hindu, one might say—is pursued by a tiger. He runs fast, but his panting heart tells him he cannot run much longer or faster. He spots a tree. Relief! He accelerates and gets to it in one last despairing stride. He climbs the tree. The tiger snarls beneath him, but he feels he has at least escaped its snapping jaws. But no— what's this? The branch on which he is sitting is weak, and bends dangerously. That is not all; termites are gnawing away at it. Before long, they will eat through it and the branch will snap and fall.

The man realises this, sees the tiger below him waiting for him to tumble into its grasp. But as the branch bends, it sags over a well. Aha! Escape? Our hero looks hopefully into the well. Perhaps he can swim! But the well is dry. Worse, there are poisonous snakes writhing and hissing on its bed, waiting for prey.

What is our hero to do? As the branch bends lower, he perceives a solitary blade of grass growing on the wall of the well. On the tip of the blade of grass gleams a drop of honey.

What action does our Puranic man, the archetypal Indian, take in this situation?

He bends with the branch, and licks up the honey.

This story is at least 2,000 years old, but it could be told today. It speaks of what the Orientalists saw as Hindu fatalism, a tendency for us to be resigned to our lot and to accept the world as it is ordained to be. The story speaks of our self-absorption in the face of impossible circumstances, and our willingness to make the best we possibly can out of those impossible circumstances.

That is the Hindu answer to the insuperable difficulty. One does not struggle against that which one cannot overcome, but seeks instead to find the best path, for oneself, to live with it. In many ways, it explains what the West has regarded as Hindu fatalism, and to which V. S. Naipaul referred as a tendency for 'non-doing'.

And yet this is a very partial understanding of Hinduism. The *Bhagavad Gita* asks Hindus to raise themselves by the self; that is, to use whatever elements Fate has dealt them—the circumstances of their birth, their location, their access to wealth, the opportunities for education and so on—as best they can to move towards self-realisation. The fact that circumstances are what they are does not deny the Hindu the freedom of will to seek to change them. The position of the planets at the time of a Hindu's birth may have determined some of his or her possibilities, charting good phases and bad ones in their lives, but then it is up to them to make what they can of them. It is wrong to suggest that everything is willed by Fate for the quiescent Hindu, that his destiny is decreed. The Hindu works with God to fulfil his potential. God is not just above and beyond us; to the Hindu, He is also within us. He struggles with us, suffers with us, strives with us. To that degree, the Hindu knows he shapes his own fate, in partnership with God.

Early in my United Nations career, my first boss, a lay preacher in his native Denmark, asked me a pointed question: 'Why should a Hindu be good?' Not, I replied, in order to go to heaven or avoid hell; most Hindus do not believe in the existence of either. If heaven is a place where a soul should sprout white wings and sing the praises of God, it must be rather a boring place, hardly worth aspiring to, and God must be a rather insecure Being. And as for hell, the very notion of hell is incompatible with Hindu cosmology, since it suggests there is a place where God is not, and that, to the Hindu, is impossible to conceive, for God is everywhere or He would not be God.

If Hinduism is, indeed, a *manava dharma*, an ethical code applicable to the whole of humanity, then it is legitimate for a non-Hindu to ask: why indeed should a Hindu be good? First, because he is bound by the moral obligation to fulfil his *dharma*, the right action his religion enjoins upon him always to undertake.

The Hindu is taught that there are six principal obstacles to the performance of *dharma*: two are Purusharthas gone wrong, *kama* as lust
rather than desire, and *lobha* as greed and avarice for material possessions (beyond *artha* which is the legitimate acquisition of wealth and
worldly goods for a worthy life). Four other vices are personal failings
that are within an individual's capacity to prevent: *krodha* (hatred), *mada*
(vanity), *matsarya* (envy) and *moha* (delusion arising from ignorance or
infatuation). These six obstacles are prevented and overcome through
the practice of seven essential virtues laid down from the time of Adi
Shankara: *ahimsa* (non-violence), *satyam* (truth), *shivam* (piety), *sundaram*
(the cultivation of beauty), *vairagyam* (detachment), *pavitram* (purity)
and *swabhavam* (self-control). The rejection of these vices and the practice of these virtues are essential for a Hindu to lead a good life.

My boss wanted a more pragmatic reason for why a Hindu should
be good. If it was not the promise of a better life in the next world, or
a desire to avoid eternal damnation in Hell, what was a Hindu's incentive? I explained that whereas in Christianity the body has a soul, in
Hinduism the soul has a body. In other words, we are emanations of a
universal soul, the *atman*, which does not die; it discards its temporal
form, the body, from time to time. Since the purpose of the soul is
ultimately to reach moksha, to attain union with Brahman and stop the
endless cycle of birth and rebirth in various bodies, the incentive for a
Hindu to be good lay in the desire to progress towards this goal. An
amoral Hindu, one who lived in *adharma*, would be in disharmony with
the world and be set back in his soul's striving for *moksha*.

I am not sure he was satisfied with my answer, and I am not sure
you, the reader, will be. There was, however, a catch in what I was
propounding. If the soul is permanent and the body is not, it makes
sense that the soul sheds bodies and keeps returning to earth until it has
attained *moksha*; from this flows the doctrine of *punarjanmam* (reincarnation), the idea that one will be reborn until one has attained that
level of self-realisation.

The idea of reincarnation, emerging from the endless cycle of birth
and rebirth, is basic to Hinduism. If in other faiths the individual is a
body which has its own soul, in Hinduism the individual is a soul which

83

happens to be in temporary possession of a certain body; the immortal soul occupies a mortal corpus, which it discards at the end of its physical life, only to re-emerge in another form, until it accomplishes true self-realisation and *moksha*, and merges with Brahman. This cycle of birth, death and rebirth is known as Samsara, and it is a belief that addresses one of the central challenges facing every believer in God—if God is all-knowing, all-seeing, all-compassionate and merciful, why does He permit so much suffering, pain, inequality and inequity to bedevil his creations? The Hindu answer is that such suffering is the result of man's own actions in a previous life; our present circumstances are caused or enabled by our past deeds and misdeeds, action and inaction. The soul continues from life-cycle to life-cycle, hopping from body to body as a caterpillar climbs onto a blade of grass and jumps to a new one (the metaphor is Upanishadic, not my own.)

I always considered this deeply unfair: why should a human being, conscious only of himself in his present life, have to suffer for wrongs he does not recollect and misdeeds he has no memory of having committed in previous lives of which he is unaware? Still, I had to accept it was a more coherent explanation than the contradictory ones offered by other faiths, which struggled to reconcile the world's injustices with their theological belief in a merciful God. If you thought of God as, for instance, an old man in a white beard looking down benevolently at you from the heavens, listening to your prayers and interceding when He saw fit, then it was difficult to accept that His benevolence stopped short of your well-being despite your prayers, or that He was indifferent to the cruelty and suffering assailing His creatures. If you stopped thinking of God that way, however, but saw God in everyone and everything, in the bad and the good, in the unfair as well as the just, as an impersonal cosmic force that just *is*—then you can come to terms with the world's tragedies as well as its joys. The idea of reincarnation is related to that of *karma*, or action—the accumulated actions of your life. So the very circumstances of your birth—the home, the place, the nation and the opportunities into which you are born—are determined by your soul's actions in its previous incarnation.

The time and circumstances of your death, too, are beyond human agency; when you have finished enjoying the benefits earned from (and paying for the misdeeds committed in) your previous life, your time on earth ends and your soul discards your body, to enter another. This is known as *prarabdha karma*. Then there are your characteristics, tendencies and aptitudes, themselves emerging from the accumulated learnings of your previous lives; this is called *sanchita karma* and can be changed by your efforts, education and conduct in your present life. Finally there is *agami karma*, those of our actions which will pave the way for our future (reborn) life. Our evil words or deeds in the present life will mar our soul's prospects in the next, whereas good deeds, right actions and the fulfillment of our *dharma* without regard to reward, will ensure our rebirth at a higher stage of the progress towards *moksha*.

To some this suggests another, somewhat simplistic, answer to the question 'Why should a Hindu be good?' Be good so that you are reborn in a better situation in your next life than in the present one; if you are good, you may reappear as a king or a sage, whereas if you are bad, you might come back as an invalid or a mosquito. (Or as Amartya Sen, the Nobel laureate, put it: 'As a Hindu, if you are a good economist in this life, you come back in the next as a physicist. If you are a bad economist in this life, you come back in the next as a sociologist.') Jokes apart, your *prarabdha karma* is established by what your soul has experienced in its previous foray in a human body: your incentive to be good is to improve its chances of a better time in its next innings.

I was never comfortable with this idea, since it seemed to me to have been devised somewhat self-servingly by the upper castes to ensure social peace. Do not rebel if you are born poor or 'Untouchable', the doctrine seemed to imply, since it's merely your soul paying for the sins of your past life; and do not blame us for leading a much better life than you, since we are merely reaping the benefits of our past good deeds.

Behave, conform, accept your lot and serve your betters, the doctrine seemed to suggest, and you will enjoy the rewards next time around. As a philosophy to reconcile people with their lot, and that would help maintain social peace, such a belief-system was of inestimable value. (It also justified human suffering in terms that no other religion's theology could match.) But I found it ethically dubious—and so, no doubt unfairly, looked askance at the idea of reincarnation itself. I was wrong to do so, since the socio-political rationale was irrelevant to the Hindu sages who had advanced the theory of *punarjanmam*. They were less concerned about issues of socio-political conformism than I was; the *rishis'* interest lay in the soul's unsteady and imperfect progress towards self-realisation and merger with the cosmos. Their doctrine was about the divine soul, not the social circumstances of the body it happened to occupy.

4

GREAT SOULS OF HINDUISM

Much of what I believe as a Hindu comes from an early and intense reading of the writings and lectures of Swami Vivekananda (1863–1902), the magnetic-eyed saint with the majestic mien and marvellous oratorical skills, who did more than anyone else to place Hinduism on the world map in the late nineteenth century. Swami Vivekananda was an inspiration to me right from my formative years. One of the few accomplishments I remember from a hyperactive extra-curricular life at college relates to him. I was asked to deliver, at age eighteen in 1974, the annual Vivekananda Memorial Oration at Delhi University. The honour was given to me because of my fondness for his ideas and a willingness to recite them with something approaching the oratorical flourish for which he was famous; any fantasy of association with him, alas, ends there.

To understand Vivekananda's Hinduism one has to go much farther back in time. His ideas emerged from the Advaita Vedanta School of Hindu philosophy, anchored in the oldest *Upanishads* and established by Adi Shankara in the eighth century CE, which as we have seen is undoubtedly the most influential of the multiple schools of philosophy and theology that characterise Hinduism.

HINDUISM: THE EARLY DAYS

It is said that the roots of Hinduism can be traced to the Indus Valley civilisation that flourished around 3300 to 1500 BCE (although some sources claim that it is even older). Since the script of that civilisation has not yet been satisfactorily deciphered, it is difficult to aver this with any certainty, but the ruins of the Harappan cities reveal evidence that suggest a priestly hierarchy and a cult of worship, and Indus Valley seals show a cross-legged figure who seems to represent Shiva. At any rate, the worship of male and female gods clearly existed, as perhaps did a fertility cult, along with the worship of nature, animals and spirits. The doctrines of what we recognise today as Hindu *dharma* were first established (it is said, by the sage Yajnavalkya) in around 3000 BCE (many scholars dispute the historicity of this date, suggesting instead dates a millennia and a half later, 1500 BCE). They were reified in the four Vedas, composed roughly between 1700 and 500 BCE, laying down many of the mantras and benedictions, rituals and ceremonies of the faith, together with commentaries on these. The faith was then replenished by Veda Vyasa (the sage who is said to have codified the Vedas and is credited as the 'author' of the *Mahabharata*).

But despite the richness of the epics such as the *Mahabharata* and *Ramayana*, the religion of the later Vedas became excessively ritualistic and rigidly hierarchical. Other ideas and practices needed to be accommodated. Around 150 BCE, some centuries after Vyasa, Patanjali, a notable scholar of the Sankhya School of Hindu philosophy, compiled the *Yoga Sutras*, a classic text on yoga theory and practice, which laid the foundations of classical yoga. Patanjali's sutras lay down an eightfold path, *ashtanga* yoga, which involves a rigorous set of physical, psychological and moral pursuits, following the strictest discipline, which, if progressively followed under the guidance of a suitable teacher, would lead the practitioner to ultimate self-realisation and pure consciousness. Then the *Upanishads* emerged, throwing the light of sophisticated (and sometimes abstruse) philosophical enquiry on the faith. Building on the sacred Vedas, these were all foundational texts of Hinduism. The *Puranas* were composed, and their stories helped integrate the Vedic religion with the folk religions of India, absorbing them in a shared ethic.

Subsequently, Hinduism became paralysed by its own inflexible practices of orthodoxy, ritualism and formality, and the rise of mutually antagonistic sects locked in interminable conflict. Inevitably, reformers arose to challenge it, notably the ascetic Mahavira Jaina (c. 599 BCE–527 BCE) and the other-worldly Gautama Buddha (c. 563 BCE–483 BCE), whose followers branched out into new religions distinct from the Mimamsa Brahminism practised by mainstream Hindus. Both new faiths flourished for several centuries, as Hinduism descended into esoteric disputes over Sankhya dualism and Charvaka materialism. It was then, in the late eighth century CE, that a youthful South Indian sage rose to heal and rejuvenate a divided religion.

ADI SHANKARA

This was Adi Shankara, whose Advaita Vedanta was the philosophically robust response to that era of confusion, integrating diverse thoughts and Hindu practices into a philosophy based on the Vedic dictum of 'One Truth, Many Expositions'. Advaita Vedanta is only one—and arguably the last—of the six schools known as the 'six systems' (Shad Darshanas) of mainstream Hindu philosophy, but it has proved the most enduring. Shankara emphasised the importance of *pramanas* or methods of reasoning, tempered by *anubhava* or intuitive experience, which empower the seeker to gain the spiritual knowledge adumbrated by the sacred texts. He focused on selected texts—the Bhagavad Gita, the Brahma Sutras and ten of the 108 *Upanishads*—as the key reference works of Hindu *dharma*, illuminating them through his *bhashyas* (commentaries). Reasoning is essential to clarify the truth, according to the Advaita School, and Shankara was a famous debater of his time, challenging and being challenged by those of different philosophical persuasions but triumphing always through the power of his reasoning and the force of his arguments. His *bhashyas* are all written in prose, not verse, with lucidity and sharpness, and employ the Upanishadic question-and-answer format that the West calls 'Socratic'.

Adi Shankara also authored the *Vivekachudamani*, 581 verses spelling out the qualifications required in a student of Vedanta: to be able to discriminate between the real and the unreal; to be able to maintain a spirit of detachment from this world; to have the capacity to control sensory perceptions; and to feel an intense desire to attain self-realisation and *moksha*. The *Vivekachudamani* reviews the entire range of Hindu philosophical thought and argument, from the *Upanishads* to the Bhagavad Gita. More accessibly, and as part of his effort to popularise the faith, Adi Shankara also authored a hundred *stotrams*, verses that can be sung as *bhajans* by the worshipper (or *bhakt*)—many fairly brief but some quite long, like his most famous *bhajan*, the Bhaja Govindam. Most of the *stotrams* (hymns or verses) relate to the worship of the major Puranic gods, though some are devoted to spiritual themes and others are sung in praise of sacred rivers or the holy city of Kashi (Varanasi). To Adi Shankara, *bhakti yoga* (the practice of worship) was an important step towards *jnana yoga* (the cultivation of knowledge). The sage was very conscious of the need to revive the faith of which he was such a master. In Verse 7 of his Bhaja Govindam, he laments the fact that children are interested in play and young men in pretty girls, but the old worry since no one is interested in the Absolute.

Adi Shankara was not merely a philosophical thinker who reconciled the doctrines and traditions of the ancients with a robust interpretation for the future; he was also a practical reformer. He purified the worship of the Goddess, which had become somewhat questionable thanks to dubious practices introduced by the tantrics, and introduced the *samayachara* form of Devi worship, involving hymns of exquisite beauty like the Soundarya Lahari or the waves of beauty, composed by himself. His ready acceptance of many Buddhist principles and practices so narrowed the gap between the two faiths as to make the absorption of Buddhism by the parent faith inevitable in India.

Adi Shankara's extraordinary travels—which began when he was just eight years old and continued till his death at the age of thirty-two—took him to every corner of the Indian subcontinent, from Rameswaram in the extreme south to Srinagar in the Kashmir Valley in the extreme north, from Dwarka in Gujarat to Kamarupa in Assam in the north-east, and various points in between. He established temples almost everywhere he halted, all of which have remained in continuous use since, and left behind five major *mutths* headed by successor Shankaracharyas to this day: Jyotirmath near Badrinath (Uttarakhand), Govardhan Mutth in Puri (Odisha), Kalika Mutth in Dwarka (Gujarat), and two in the south, the Sarada Peetham in Sringeri (Karnataka) and the Kanchi Kamakoti Peetham in Kanchipuram (Tamil Nadu). (Most Hindus count only the first four as his major legacies, though the prominence in the twentieth century of the Shankaracharyas of Kanchi has elevated that *peetham* into a religious seat of equal if not greater significance.) In addition to these 'pontifical' seats, Adi Shankara is credited with the creation and organisation of the order of Dasanami Sannyasis, wandering monks who took the message of the faith across the country. Despite Shankara's skill in debate, Advaita nonetheless believes that pure logic cannot alone lead to philosophical truths; knowledge is all very well, but experience and meditative insights are essential too. Shankara's Advaita Vedanta was based on *shastra* ('scriptures'), *pramanas* or *yukti* ('reason') and *anubhava* ('experiential knowledge'), supplemented by *karmas* ('spiritual practices') and the purity and steadiness of mind achieved in yoga. None was sufficient in itself: the entire package, as it were, allowed the seeker to gain the knowledge and insights required to attain self-realisation.

Shankara also proposed the four '*mahavakyas*' or 'great sentences' of his doctrine—'Prajnanam Brahma' (knowledge is Brahman), 'Ayam Atma Brahma' (this atman is Brahman), 'Tat tvam asi' (that you are), and 'Aham Brahmasmi' (I am Brahman)—as the guiding principles of Hindu spiritual contemplation, all of which underscored his doctrine that the inner immortal soul, atman, and the great cosmic spirit, Brahman, are really one and the same. Atman and Brahman had been regarded by the 'dualist' Sankhya School of thought as separate entities, but Shankara argued that while they might seem different at the empirical level of reality, this is an illusion. Brahman, the spirit that suffuses the cosmos, is the sole reality; other than Brahman, everything else, including the universe, material objects and individuals, is ever changing, transient and illusory (*maya*). (As Radhakrishnan was later to explain, *maya* is not merely illusion, but 'a subjective misperception of the world as ultimately real.') Brahman is Paramarthika Satyam, Absolute Truth, and one's *atman* or self is identical to it. Realising this and accepting the true self, pure consciousness, as the only reality (*sat*), leads to *moksha* or salvation, defined by some as a state of bliss (*ananda*) and by others, more modestly, as the endless but not beginningless absence of pain, the pain all human beings suffer in the course of their ordinary lives. The supreme truth of Brahman is *sat-chit-ananda* (truth-consciousness-bliss), as Shankara wrote in his *Upadeshasahasri*:

> *I am other than name, form and action.*
> *My nature is ever free!*
> *I am Self, the supreme unconditioned Brahman.*
> *I am pure Awareness, always non-dual.*

— Adi Shankara, *Upadeshasahasri* 11.7[1]

As I have noted earlier, the *Manduka Upanishad* explains that Om is the bow, one's *atman* is the arrow, and Brahman the target. The term Advaita ('not-two') refers to the rejection of dualism: as Shankara's follower, the sage Anandagiri, put it, to say that Brahman and *atman* are separate would be like dividing a fowl in two and saying that one half can be cooked while the other half would lay eggs.

Shankara's Hinduism does not see God as external to the universe. God dwells in the universe, but God is not the universe; He is in it and beyond it. The world is in God, and the two are indivisible. Advaita Vedanta emphasises *jivanmukti*, the idea that *moksha* (salvation or liberation, the realisation of the ultimate purpose of each individual) is achievable in the course of our present life. Advaita's adherents seek their spiritual fulfilment in the acquisition of this profound spiritual knowledge and in immersing themselves in the indissoluble union of the true Self (*atman* or soul) with the highest metaphysical Reality (Brahman).

Shankara also asserted that the realisation of self-knowledge required the mind to be purified by an ethical life that observed essential precepts or Yamas such as *ahimsa* (non-injury, non-violence to others in body, mind and thoughts), *satya* (respect for truth, abstinence from falsehood), *asteya* (rejection of theft), *aparigraha* (abstaining from craving possessions) and a simple life of meditation and reflection. These ideas were to have a profound and lasting impact on Mahtama Gandhi twelve centuries later. (Of *ahimsa*, Gandhi wrote: 'Nonviolence is common to all religions, but it has found the highest expression and application in Hinduism.')

From the ancient texts, Advaita Vedanta accepted the idea of the Purusharthas, the four goals of human life. These, as we have seen earlier, are *dharma*, the right conduct of the individual in accordance with his duties and obligations; *artha*, the material possessions required to sustain the individual and those dependent upon him; *kama*, the pursuit of pleasure and comfort, including love and sexual pleasure; and *moksha*, the individual's ultimate salvation, his liberation from earthly bonds and his realisation of union with the divine spirit. This last involves a state of full awareness of the ultimate oneness of the soul, atman, and Brahman; the Hindu realises the Divine within himself, perceives the Divine in other beings, and accepts that Brahman is in everything, and everything is Brahman.

> *Without beginning and end is he; in the midst*
> *Of chaos is he, and brings forth all things. Creator*
> *Is he, and sole pervader, of manifold forms.*
> *When a man knows God he is freed from all fetters.*

> — *Svetashvatara Upanishad*, V.13.2[2]

Despite such ideas being seen by many as Brahminical and elitist, Advaita Vedanta, by conceiving of Oneness in this manner, lays the philosophical groundwork for the fundamental equality of all human beings. In the same section of his *Upadeshasahasri*, Adi Shankara posits precisely this ethical premise of equality; any *bheda* (discrimination) based on class or caste or parentage is, Shankara declared, a mistake, a sign of error and of lack of knowledge. Shankara's liberated individual understands and practises the ethics of non-discrimination, since the high-born and the low are all part of the same Oneness. This was all the more significant in a religion on which the pernicious practice of caste discrimination had begun to cast a blight. The Advaita Vedantist recognised all living beings as essentially one, and therefore as essentially equal.

The fully realised self is *sat-chit-ananda* incarnate, as Shankara himself sings:

'Atma Shatakam' (The Song of the Self):

> *I am not the mind, nor the intellect, nor the ego, nor the material*
> *of the mind;*
> *I am not the body, nor the changes of the body;*
> *I am not the senses of hearing, taste, smell, or sight,*
> *Nor am I the ether, the earth, the fire, the air;*
> *I am Existence Absolute, Knowledge Absolute, Bliss*
> *Absolute—I am Shiva, I am Shiva. (Shivoham, Shivoham).*
>
> *I am not the Prâna, nor the five vital airs;*
> *I am not the materials of the body, nor the five sheaths;*
> *Neither am I the organs of action, nor the object of the senses;*
> *I am Existence Absolute, Knowledge Absolute, Bliss Absolute—*
> *I am Shiva, I am Shiva. (Shivoham, Shivoham).*
>
> *I have neither aversion nor attachment, neither greed nor delusion;*
> *Neither egotism nor envy, neither Dharma nor Moksha;*
> *I am neither desire nor objects of desire;*
> *I am Existence Absolute, Knowledge Absolute, Bliss*
> *Absolute—I am Shiva, I am Shiva. (Shivoham, Shivoham).*
>
> *I am neither sin nor virtue, neither pleasure nor pain; Nor*
> *temple nor worship, nor pilgrimage nor scriptures, Neither*
> *the act of enjoying, the enjoyable nor the enjoyer;*
> *I am Existence Absolute, Knowledge Absolute, Bliss*
> *Absolute—I am Shiva, I am Shiva. (Shivoham, Shivoham).*
>
> *I have neither death nor fear of death, nor caste;*
> *Nor was I ever born, nor had I parents, friends, and relations;*
> *I have neither Guru, nor disciple;*
> *I am Existence Absolute, Knowledge Absolute, Bliss*
> *Absolute—I am Shiva, I am Shiva. (Shivoham, Shivoham).*
>
> *I am untouched by the senses, I am neither Mukti nor knowable;*
> *I am without form, without limit, beyond space, beyond time;*
> *I am in everything; I am the basis of the universe; everywhere am I.*

> *I am Existence Absolute, Knowledge Absolute, Bliss*
> *Absolute—I am Shiva, I am Shiva. (Shivoham, Shivoham).*

— Adi Shankara, *Nirvana Shatakam*[3]

All of this may seem somewhat abstruse to some, a sort of Hindu theological primer of no interest to most Hindus, let alone others. In fact there is far greater complexity to Advaita Vedanta than my simple summary can even begin to hint at. The *Kena Upanishad* makes that clear:

> *I do not think that I know it well. Nor do I know that I do not know it.*
> *Among us those who know, know it; even they do not know that they do not*
> *know.*

— *Kena Upanishad*, II.2[4]

However, there was the dawning realisation, among many of those who followed in his footsteps in the centuries following Adi Shankara's death in the mountain temple of Kedarnath at the young age of thirty-two, that there was a great need to make his breakthroughs intelligible to the common man. There were other even more compelling reasons for the faith to change and evolve.

REINVENTING HINDUISM

Though they were eclipsed and even reabsorbed into Hinduism, both Jainism and Buddhism had a lasting impact on the religion they had sought to transform. Buddhist monasticism led to the establishment of the concept of *sannyasis* (monks or ascetics) in Hinduism—who, inspired by the Buddhists, wear ochre robes, shave their heads and practise celibacy for life. (There was no pre-Buddhist equivalent of this: Hindu priests were *grihasthas*, married householders, and not *sannyasis*). Similarly the Buddhist monasteries prompted Sankaracharya to establish *mutths*, in which *sannyasis* and lay students could live together and learn in a sort of *gurukul* (or traditional school). As to Jainism, the acceptance of *ahimsa* as a basic principle in Hinduism was clearly a response to Mahavira Jaina's emphasis on this doctrine. The adoption of vegetarianism as a superior form of life by a large number of Hindus, especially Brahmins, is also a Jain contribution to Hinduism.

Hinduism reasserted itself in response to the rise of Buddhism and Jainism, largely supplanting or absorbing these faiths across the country, to the extent that the practice of Buddhism largely ended (so much so that that until the 1950s, the Buddha in Sarnath sported a Vaishnava namam, or holy mark on his forehead), and the Jains began to be regarded by a section of Hindus as a sort of Hindu sect (though many Jains disputed this) rather than as a rival faith. By the tenth century, Hinduism had reasserted its dominance, swallowed up its reformers, reformulated its popular doctrines, equipped itself with a higher philosophy which found acceptance among the intellectuals, accommodated popular forms of idol worship, created major spiritual centres and furnished itself with *sannyasis* to spread the word. Its supremacy in India seemed incontestable.

But around 1000 CE a new challenge arose from the northwest to the dominance of Hinduism in the subcontinent. The raids into India by Mohammed bin Qasim, who invaded Sind in 712 CE, Mahmud of Ghazni (who attacked India seventeen times between 1000 CE and 1027 CE) and Muhammad Ghori (who launched several bloody raids between the 1180s and the 1220s), among others, took many lives, destroyed much property and left deep scars. Hinduism found itself confronting a dynamic force animated by religious zeal in direct contradistinction to everything the faith stood for. Islam challenged the philosophic basis of Hinduism, questioned its social structure, denied its pantheistic beliefs, expressed contempt for its pluralist doctrines and coveted its treasures. It was a challenge of a very different order from that posed by Buddhism or Jainism. The impact of the Muslim invasions, and the proclivity of some Muslim warlords to attack temples for their treasures and demolish them in the process, as well as the inclination of some of the conquered peoples to adopt the religion of their conquerors, made the need for a renewal and revival of the Hindu faith all the more urgent after the eleventh century CE, when Ghazni's success had rung the alarm bells.

The looting of temples and their subsequent destruction—which occurred repeatedly, ranging from historic Somnath on the Gujarat coast to Mathura in the interior—was a direct assault on the Hindus and their faith, and an undeniable challenge to which Hinduism had to rise or succumb. For invaders like Mahmud of Ghazni the attacks had twin motives—the fabled wealth of India was mostly hoarded in its temples, which made them attractive targets, but there was also the zeal of the Muslim warrior to smash the seats of idolatry. The Hindus were left with a stark choice—revive or disappear.

Renewal was the Hindu response. This renewal occurred through a number of processes—the simplification and propagation of Brahminical doctrines; the adoption of some practices and beliefs from Buddhism and Jainism; the accommodation of popular folklore, local deities and regional forms of worship into the master faith; the greater emphasis on the worship of gods in easily accessible human form; the use of music, dance and theatre to propagate religious stories; the universal practice of daily worship at home, so that the temple was not the only locus of sustenance for the faith; and eventually, as I describe below, the rise of *bhakti* worship, in which an almost mystical devotion to a personal god became a hallmark of Hindu religiosity. In addition, there was Hinduism's very lack of a central organisational structure: the knowledge of the Vedas was preserved and perpetuated by being passed on from generation to generation within Brahmin families, or by individual sages or gurus to their disciples. Such a diffused pattern of dissemination was much more difficult to eliminate, or to subsume into a new faith. Another vital factor was the early truce between the spiritual and temporal powers in society: in response to the rise of Buddhism and Jainism, Brahmins (the priestly caste) and Kshatriyas (the warrior and ruling class) came to a mutual understanding that their interests would be best served in alliance, rather than in undermining each other.

All of these ensured that not only did India not turn into a fully Muslim country, as so many other Asian countries—from the Maldives to Malaya and Indonesia—were to do, but that Hinduism survived and thrived even in conditions of political dominance by rulers of another faith.

Indeed, the resilience of Hinduism throughout history is little short of remarkable. It has survived innumerable invasions, raids, attacks and outright conquest; each time, where lesser faiths in other places crumbled before the invader and most of the people adopted the conqueror's faith, Hinduism stood strong and bounced back. In the mid-nineteenth century, Karl Marx marvelled at this phenomenon and found it remarkable. Hinduism remained a non-aggressive faith, but it was extraordinarily strong in its own defence. Hinduism took the blows and battled on; and every time the invader withdrew, Hinduism arose again, sometimes bloodied but always unbowed.

RAMANUJA AND THE BHAKTI MOVEMENT

Key to this resilience was doctrinal openness and flexibility of practice. A thousand years ago in southern India, Ramanuja (said to have lived 1017–1137 CE to the age of 120), a great Vaishnava theologian, who headed the monastery at Srirangam, reinvented and revitalised Hinduism, following in Shankara's footsteps with a qualified form of Advaita. His doctrinal contribution was important: his commentaries on the Gita and on the Brahma Sutras contested Adi Shankara's interpretations of those scriptures. More important were the religious aspects of Ramanuja's teachings, to the effect that the burdens of *karma* can be overcome by Divine Grace, attained through the worship of a loving and just God—an alternative view to the recondite philosophical constructs of Shankara, and thus a vital contribution to Indian spiritual revival. Through this approach Ramanuja popularised worship and brought organisational energy into the faith, conducting daily *pujas* and annual temple festivals, allowing image-worship and more inclusive temple-based rituals at the Srirangam Mutth he headed and in other nearby temples. Strikingly, he permitted women and worshippers of the lower peasant castes (though not, it should be said, Dalits) to participate in temple worship, a privilege they had been denied. Ramanuja also allowed the chanting of the popular Alvar (or Azhvar) hymns, which were sung in demotic Tamil, the language of the people, rather than in the arcane Sanskrit of official temple liturgy. Ramanuja's reforms spread across southern India to other major Vaishnavite temples and can be seen in many ways as a reinvention of Hinduism, taking Shankara's work to the masses.

Ramanuja's innovations prefigured the popularisation of Hinduism in the Bhakti movement, which through prayer and song brought the esoterica of Hindu philosophy in simple language to the ears and the hearts of the common people. In some ways he could be said to be a pioneer of it. The Bhakti movement began in south India and swept northwards, creating a devotional theistic popular Hinduism that expressed itself vividly in the cult worship of different gods and goddesses and flourished across much of India between the twelfth and the eighteenth century CE. The movement started in Tamil Nadu between the fourth and the ninth centuries with the Nayanars and the Alvars, several of whom, notably the poetess Andal, were women. They sang in praise of Shiva and Vishnu respectively in Tamil, and as the Bhakti movement spread, brought more vernacular languages into a faith previously dominated by Sanskrit.

Ramananda, a Vaishnava *sanyasi* from Allahabad, travelled through much of the Indo-Gangetic plain, the land of Aryavarta, in the fourteenth century, preaching the doctrine of Bhakti, urging people to place their trust in, and surrender themselves to, a merciful God. The mysticism of his gospel, its offer of a refuge from the misery of human suffering, its assertion of equality of all before God and its depiction of God as a loving force in the lives of worshippers, gave Ramananda's teachings great appeal. He settled in Varanasi, where among the many disciples he acquired was the remarkable Muslim weaver Kabir, one of a dozen poet-sants (saints), both male and female, who took Ramananda's teachings to the masses.

Bhakti had its stars—poet-saints like Kabir (c. 1440–1510 CE), who wrote some extraordinarily compelling verses distilling the essence of Hindu philosophy, and who was singing in praise of religious harmony at a time when the West was conducting Inquisitions and burning witches and heretics at the stake; Lalleshwari or Lalla Rukh (c. 1317–1372 CE), the great Bhakti songstress of Kashmir, who sang passionately of her devotion to Shiva but as emotionally of her refusal to discriminate between Hindu and Muslim; mystic singers like Mirabai (c. 1498–1597 CE), whose songs transported the singer and her audience into a level of ecstasy reminiscent of some of today's Evangelical churches; the twelfth-century poet Jayadev, whose *Gita Govindam* revolutionised the worship of Radha and Krishna, and whose ideas were echoed in the lyrics of the blind bard Surdas (c. 1478–1583 CE), the man who helped establish the Vrindavan-Mathura area as Krishna's holy land; and the remarkable writer, poet and saint Tulsidas (c. 1532–1623 CE), author of two of the most popular Hindu texts even today, the *Ramcharitmanas*, retelling the story of Lord Rama, and the Hanuman Chalisa, forty-three devotional verses in praise of the powerful monkey-god. Tulsidas wrote in Avadhi (though initially in Sanskrit); Kabir's verse can still be understood by Hindi speakers today. Verse and song became vehicles for Bhakti ideas throughout India.

Mirabai's husband, the Rana of Udaipur, allegedly disapproved so much of her devotion to Lord Krishna that he tried to poison her, but miraculously the poison turned into honey as she drank it, and she danced in ecstasy before her adored Lord. As one of her hymns declares with the sense of abandonment and ecstatic devotion for which she is known:

> *Tying anklets upon her feet, Mira dances in ecstasy.*
> *People say Mira has gone mad.*
> *Her mother-in-law says she has disgraced the clan,*
> *The Rana sent her a cup of poison,*
> *Which Mira, laughingly, drank.*
> *I have myself become the eternal maid-servant of*
> *My Narayana.*
> *Mira's God is Giridhar, lifter of the mountain.*
> *O Indestructible One, meet me swiftly in your*
> *Eternal embrace.*[5]

Bhakti's creative effulgence was remarkable, and reached its peak, perhaps surprisingly, during the rule of the Muslim Mughal monarchs (1526 to the mid eighteenth century); the movement confirmed Hinduism's resilience in the face of Islamic conquest. But it was also much more than that: the Bhakti movement refreshed and strengthened Hindu society at a time when the state was in Muslim hands. It taught a staunch monotheism, shunned caste distinctions and rules, preached an absolute surrender to God and offered a religious experience that involved the direct realisation of God through devotion. To that extent, the Bhakti movement's reinterpretation of Hinduism resembled Islam's monotheism and egalitarianism; but its principles could also be found in the *Upanishads*, its personal gods in the *Puranas*, and its religious doctrine was anchored in that of the Bhagavad Gita, which summons the worshipper to surrender all and take refuge in *dharma*. The emotional connection of the worshipper to God that Bhakti expressed brought the devotee to a relationship of profound love for the divine, a love that, as the Gita expressed it, combined that of a father and a son, a devoted friend for another and a lover with their beloved.

The remarkable reach of Bhakti ideas ranged from the great poets, philosophers and preachers Narsi Mehta in Gujarat to Vidyapati in Mithila and Chaitanya Deva in Bengal (who founded the Vaishnava movement in Bengal through his kirtanas, devotional songs to Krishna), Jnaneswara, Tukaram, Eknath and Namdev in Maharashtra, Basavanna in Karnataka and Thyagaraja in Tamil Nadu. The Krishna devotee Shankara Deva, after travelling extensively across India, returned to his native Assam and led a major revival of Hinduism in the north-east of the subcontinent.

In Kashmir in the late tenth century, Acharya Abhinavagupta propounded the doctrines of Kashmiri Shaivism which have profoundly influenced the practice of the faith in that state. Some of the great *acharyas* from the south, like Ramanuja, in effect established their own sects, restoring strength to the religion while transforming its practice in their areas. Basavanna, also known as Basava or Basaveshwara (c. 1131–1167 CE), with his staunch rejection of the caste system, his emphasis on vegetarianism and his abjuring of temple worship, created a sect, the Lingayats or Veerashaivas, who are hugely influential in modern Karnataka. His challenge to caste was uncompromising. 'Loaded with the burden of the Vedas,' he said dismissively, 'the Brahmin is a veritable donkey.'[6] Though born a Brahmin himself, Basava shed his sacred thread at the age of eighteen and dismissed ideas of caste hierarchy: 'The higher type of man is the man who knows himself.' After all, as he pointed out: 'On the same earth stands the outcaste's hovel and the deity's temple. Whether for ritual or rinsing, is not the water the same?'[7] Members of all castes were the same; the Brahmin and the outcaste were born the same way. Or 'is there anybody in the world,' he asked, 'delivered through the ear?'[8]

Basava established a Hall of Experience (Anubhava Mantapa) where men and women from all castes could meet freely and discuss radical ideas. He shook off the established strictures against inter-dining and inter-marriage with 'Untouchables', provoking the social and political repression that extinguished his career; but his ideas, compiled in the form of *vachanas*, survived and have gained in strength to the present day. While the Jain influence is apparent in his establishment of monastery-like *mutths*, Basava's religious belief was in Vishishta Advaita, in which Shiva is equated with Brahman and the worship of Shiva leads to the Absolute. Another reformer, Madhvacharya (c. 1199–1294 CE), revived ideas of dualism and worship of the *saguna* Brahman in the form of Lord Krishna. His commentaries on the sacred texts, together with those of Sayana on the Vedas, are amongst the most significant contributions to Hindu philosophy after Adi Shankara's. Madhvacharya upheld dualism; in his theology the *atman* did not merge with Brahman but dwelt in close proximity to it. He also came closest to a theory of hell in Hinduism, suggesting that some souls were so weighed down by their bad deeds that they were unable to progress to salvation and had to suffer eternal damnation.

It is striking, too, that one offshoot of Bhakti contributed to the emergence of a wholly new religion, namely Sikhism. Its founder, Guru Nanak (1469–1539 CE), was also a poet and singer in the Bhakti tradition; the holy book of the Sikhs, the Guru Granth Sahib, includes large numbers of verses by Bhakti poets, most of all by Kabir. In its monotheism, and its emphasis on brotherhood and social equality, Sikhism derived much from Islam too, but its persecution by the later Mughals, notably Aurangzeb, turned Sikhism into a warrior faith, fighting to protect itself and the larger Hindu community. For many years in Sikhism's heartland, Punjab, Hindu families brought up one son as a Sikh, to fight for the faith.

Had Hinduism not acquired the demotic appeal to the masses that Bhakti provided it, many more might have converted to the religion of the rulers. But by offering an individual-centred path to the Divine, and by making spirituality accessible irrespective of one's caste, gender or circumstances of birth, Bhakti revived and rejuvenated the ancient Vedic traditions. Bhakti took Hinduism far away from the formalism of Vedic rituals, the austerity of asceticism, the abstractions of sages; it transformed the quest for *moksha* to a loving relationship between each individual and his or her personally chosen manifestation of God. Salvation became accessible to the lowest castes, to women and even to those formerly outside the Hindu fold, 'Untouchable' Dalits and Muslims. Bhakti brought vigour to the practice of faith by its conduct of shared religious services, collective *bhajan*-singing, community chanting of the names of the deity being adored, open (indeed sometimes extravagant) emotionalism in expressing love for the Divine, and the holding of festivals and pilgrimages. Much of what we regard as popular Hinduism today can trace its roots to the Bhakti movement.

Even something as basic as temple architecture served to reinforce faith in religion. Familiar legends from Hindu mythology are engraved or painted on the walls and pillars of most temples in the form of sculptures. Any available surface is used: the *shikharas* and *gopurams*, the outer walls of the sanctum sanctorum, and where possible on interior surfaces as well. As a result a Hindu temple becomes a permanent advertisement for its faith. Devotees who visit the temple recall and appreciate the visual representation of these tales and legends; this adds to their religious experience and reinforces their conviction.

It is clear from the foregoing that Hinduism has hardly been an unchanging religion. It faced major reform movements and embraced them whole—notably Buddhism, of which Swami Vivekananada said: 'Shakya Muni [the Buddha] came not to destroy, but he was the fulfilment, the logical conclusion, the logical development of the religion of the Hindus...the Buddhist cannot stand without the brain and philosophy of the Hindu, nor the Hindu without the heart of the Buddhist.' The *Matsya Purana* hailed the Buddha as an *avatara* of Vishnu, as did other texts and temple inscriptions. In Vivekananda's telling, both

Buddhism and Sikhism were variants of Hinduism that served to cleanse, purify and ultimately strengthen the mother faith.

The historical evolution of Hinduism testifies to its adaptability. The Vedas gave birth to an excessively ritualistic and formalistic religion; the *Upanishads* then lightened the practice of Hinduism through a spiritual movement based on philosophical enquiry. When the Upanishadic religion itself became mired in disputes over dogma, Buddhism preached a message of simplicity and morality that contrasted with a Hinduism mired in ritual and abstruse disputation. And then Adi Shankara travelled the length and breadth of the country, leading a moral and religious reawakening. Shankara and Ramanuja restored Hinduism to pre-eminence and popularity as the principal religion of India. Sages like Madhvacharya, Chaitanya, Ramananda and Basava (whose followers, the Lingayats, now want to be classified as a separate religion altogether, like the Sikhs); Kabir, Mirabai, Tulsidas, even Guru Nanak, who founded Sikhism, but whom many Hindus, notably Swami Vivekananda himself, see as a Hindu reformer—the names of those who rose to reform, revive and rejuvenate the beliefs of the people in this ancient land are legion. As early as the Gupta period, when Hindu religious revival first occurred in response to the rise of Buddhism, Hinduism came up with creative evidence of its adaptability through its emphasis on the doctrine of *avataras*. The doctrine is clearly stated in the Bhagavad Gita: 'When religion declines and evil-doers are to be destroyed, I shall be born at different periods,' says Krishna. Some *avataras* were worshipped as such even in the time of Panini, but it is with Krishna that we first have the idea of an *avatara* of God and not merely a deified human being, a doctrine that was handily adapted to the Buddha himself. Hinduism has never been uniform or unchanging, immovable or unalterable. It is a religion that has abjured the immutable revelation for the growth of human consciousness.

As we have seen, Islam was initially a threat, and the attacks of Muslim invaders on temples and Hindu treasures, as well as the rape and abduction of Hindu women, in a number of episodes in the five centuries from 1000 CE onwards, led to a defensive closing of the ranks and the adoption of protective practices that entrenched restrictions and prohibitions previously unknown in Hindu society. The protection of life, religion and chastity introduced rigidities into Hindu practice: restrictions on entry into temples (to safeguard their treasures from prying eyes), child marriages (to win protection for girls before they were old enough to be abducted by lustful invaders) and even the practice of *sati* (the burning of a widow on her husband's funeral pyre) were all portrayed as measures of self-defence during this turbulent period of Indian history, that devolved into pernicious social practices wrongly seen as intrinsic to Hinduism rather than as a reactions to assaults upon it.

But once Muslims went beyond invading and stayed on to rule, won adherents and made their peace with the country, Islamic precepts also played a part in the reshaping of Hinduism:[9] the Bhakti cults and the rise of Sikhism, both strongly influenced by Islamic ideas of equality and brotherhood, testify to that. Although conversion was not uncommon, forced or voluntary, whether of individuals who found it expedient to adopt the religion of the conquerors, or of entire communities (artisan sub-castes in north India, for instance) who were told that failure to convert would result in the loss of patronage for their products by the Muslim ruling classes, it was never universal, except in some pockets of the subcontinent (notably Kashmir, where most of the population, including many Brahmins, converted en masse to Islam, mostly under duress during the reign of Sultan Sikander [1389–1413 CE]).[10] The overwhelming majority of the populace stayed Hindu.

HINDUISM'S RESPONSE TO THE BRITISH

When the British came, with their peculiar blend of curiosity and contempt for the beliefs and practices of the land they had found so absurdly easy to conquer, Hinduism found itself sharing space with a fiercely monotheistic culture that (unlike its precursor, Islam) claimed the trappings of modernity and progress for itself. The British found a Hinduism which, in reaction to Islamic conquest, had in some ways retreated into a shell, adopting practices to shield it from the hostile faith and searching for security in insularity. Thus a civilisation which had historically sent envoys around the world, trading with the Roman empire and exporting its religious ideas across Asia, became so self-protective that it forbade travel 'across the black water', and insisted on excommunicating those who violated this proscription, or at least forced them to undergo purificatory rituals before they could be read-mitted into the Hindu fold. Most Britons in India sneered at a faith they saw as primitive and mired in superstition. (There were, of course, notable exceptions, but in general the colonial attitude to Hinduism was one of incomprehension and contempt.) The shock of contact inevitably had a catalytic effect, leading to some remarkable reactions on the part of Hindus, including another round of reform.

Some Hindus recoiled in disgust from the British, and retreated into the secure bunker of their faith as they had known it in practice, sealing themselves off from all foreign influence. But a few others looked at their faith in the light of the new intrusion, and were embarrassed by what they saw. The Hinduism they practised seemed, especially if seen through British eyes, mired in superstition and mumbo-jumbo; it was associated with idol worship, with incantations in a dead language, with caste hierarchy and iniquitous social practices. They craved a reformed Hinduism that could hold its own with Western Christianity and even earn the respect of the British.

The most interesting of those who felt this way was Raja Rammohan Roy (1772–1833 CE), an aristocratic Bengali from a prominent and wealthy family, educated in his mother-tongue as well as in Sanskrit, Persian and Arabic before being schooled in English. His view was in direct response to the disadvantageous position that Hinduism found itself in under early British rule. 'The present system of the Hindus is not well calculated to promote their political interests,' he argued shrewdly. 'It is necessary that some change should take place in their religion, at least for the sake of their political advantage and social comfort.'[11]

Accordingly, Roy promoted a rational, ethical, non-hierarchical, and modern Hinduism, committed to ending the worst Hindu social prac-tices of the day and streamlining Hindu theology. He founded a reform movement, the Brahmo Samaj, which was clearly a product of the interaction of his reformist ideas of Hinduism, emerging from a modernistic reading of Advaita Vedanta, with early-Victorian Christianity. The Brahmos rejected the idolatry that Hinduism had become synonymous with in British eyes and professed belief in a formless God, along with a monotheistic theology based on their reading of the *Upanishads* and of the Vedanta, Hindu sacred texts that credibly lent themselves well to such a 'modern' interpretation. Brahmos affirmed their belief in the existence of One Supreme God—'a God, endowed with a distinct personality and moral attributes equal to His nature, and intelligence befitting the Author and Preserver of the Universe.' Brahmos would worship Him alone, and not necessarily in temples or at specific holy days: 'We can adore Him at any time and at any place, provided that time and that place are calculated to compose and direct the mind towards Him.'

In creating the Brahmo Samaj, Roy was strongly influenced by Unitarianism, whose uncompromising monotheism posited the oneness of God (in opposition to the Trinity of the Father, the Son and the Holy Ghost). Roy's attitude to Hinduism was in many ways comparable to the Unitarians' to Christianity, paring the faith of unnecessary accretions and reducing it to its most basic affirmations of deism. (Today, it is impossible to read of the beliefs of the Unitarian Universalists without being struck by their similarities to the central tenets of Upanishadic Hinduism.) Some Hindu scholars refused to consider Roy to be a Hindu at all, seeing in the Brahmo faith a form of Christianity dressed in Indian clothes. Others saw Roy as a staunch reformist within the Hindu faith: he wore a sacred thread all his life. But it would take a Vivekananda, not a Roy, to preach, seven decades later, a robust, modernist and universalist Hinduism, anchored in its own precepts, that could look the rest of the world's religions in the eye and oblige them to blink.

Roy was motivated in large measure by a desire to impress his European acquaintances by proving, as he put it, that 'superstitious practices which deform the Hindu religion have nothing to do with the pure spirit of its dictates'. Accordingly, he combined precept with action. Social reform was crucial to his approach. Roy rejected those Hindu traditions that his education taught him to see as social evils, campaigning against caste discrimination, the denial of equal rights to women, sati, polygamy and child marriage, while arguing that none of these practices had sanction in the scriptures.

Roy passionately believed in modern, British-style education as an indispensable tool to transform society. The East India Company, busily engaged in sending back to England as much money as they could squeeze out of India, had no desire whatsoever to spend funds on creating educational institutions for Indians. So Roy realised an Indian would have to take up the challenge. In 1817, he set up the Hindu College at Calcutta in collaboration with a Scotsman not affiliated to the East India Company, David Hare, following it up with the Anglo-Hindu school in 1822 and the Vedanta College in 1826. Roy founded the Vedanta College to create an institution where his monotheistic doctrines could be taught alongside a contemporary Western curriculum. In a synthesis of Western and Indian learning. Roy maintained a frenetic pace of institution-building: in 1830, for instance, he helped the Revd Alexander Duff to establish the General Assembly's Institution (now known as Scottish Church College). Not only did Roy donate the land on which the institution was built, he personally recruited the first batch of Indian students to study there. He also campaigned for freedom of the press, which was hemmed in with various restrictions in his time.

Roy died, at the age of sixty-one, on a trip to England undertaken with a view to raising the stipend paid by the British to the Mughal Emperor, as well as in the hope of presenting a better account of his country to the British. He is buried in Bristol, amongst the people he had tried to impress, but far from the country he had worked so hard to transform. His influence outlasted him, though the Brahmo Samaj never acquired the prominence or the popularity that he might have hoped for and that he might have been able to give it had he lived a longer life.

Subsequent Brahmo thinkers included Debendranath Tagore, who questioned important Hindu precepts, challenging the authority of the Vedas and belief in reincarnation and *karma*, and Keshub Chandra Sen, who emphasised personal religious experience over doctrine and sought to make spirituality more accessible to ordinary people. Vivekananda's initial beliefs as a teenager were strongly influenced by these thinkers, whom he met and interacted with in his late teens, and the doctrines of the Brahmo Samaj. (But, as we shall see, he moved from the Brahmos as he learned new ideas at the feet of the mystic Ramakrishna Paramahansa.)

Brahmoism was not the only response to British Christianity in the colonial era. The brave and determined Ishwar Chandra Vidyasagar in Bengal led a social movement for widow remarriage, setting an example by marrying a widow himself. He also worked for the teaching of Sanskrit to be offered to all castes. The great Sanskrit scholar R. G. Bhandarkar set up the Prarthana Samaj in Bombay with M. G. Ranade to oppose the iniquities of the caste system. Half a century after Roy created the Brahmo Samaj, a dynamic Hindu sage, Swami Dayanand Saraswati (1824–1883), established the Arya Samaj as a pure but reformed version of the Hindu faith.

Unlike Roy, Dayanand asserted the infallible authority of the Vedas, while also affirming belief in one God and rejecting idol-worship as the Brahmos had done, along with other Puranic accretions to the pure Vedic religion. Arguing that idolatry and polytheism, which so attracted the contempt of the Christian missionaries, were not mentioned in the Vedas, Dayanand Saraswati called on Hindus to terminate these practices. (However, he opposed cow-slaughter, a debatable position for one anchoring himself in the Vedas, which is replete with stories of sacrificial offerings of animal, including at least one reference to the slaughter of cows.)[12] He established *gurukuls* (Vedic schools) as alternatives to English education; these schools emphasised Vedic values and culture, while teaching the Hindu precepts of devotion to, and the pursuit of, truth (*satyam*). The Arya Samajis saw their faith as Sanatana Dharma, and found their almighty Creator (known as Om, the primordial sound) in the *Yajur Veda*, rather than the Ishvaras of the Puranic age. Like some other Hindus, they regarded the text of the Vedas as itself divine, and reciting the Vedas as a sufficient act of worship.

But their belief systems were not purely of ancient origin. The reaction to Christianity in their doctrines is evident not only in the discarding of idol-worship but in the Arya Samaj doctrine that the Vedas are 'revealed' texts, while the other sacred books of the Hindus—the *Puranas*, the epics and even the Gita—are not. They are equally dismissive of the supposedly revealed texts of other faiths, such as the Bible and the Quran. In this respect the Arya Samaj departed from the principle of acceptance of other faiths as equally valid, the principle that characterises Swami Vivekananda's Hinduism.

As a reform movement, the Arya Samaj advocated the equality of all human beings and the empowerment of women; it opened its doors to all Hindus irrespective of caste or sect, performing simple marriages according to the prescriptions in the Brahmanas of the *Yajur Veda*. It also created a conversion ritual called *shuddhi*, complete with formal certification, for non-Hindus wishing to enter the faith, something which had never existed before and which seemed to have been inspired by Christian practices of baptism. In his *The Discovery of India* Jawaharlal Nehru describes the Arya Samaj as thus having introduced religious proselytisation to Hinduism. (Non-Hindus marrying Hindus have found that if they wish to adopt their spouse's faith, the only way they can do so is through the Arya Samaj's conversion route.)

These practices, however, have helped the Arya Samaj version of Hinduism appear more familiar to those exposed to the way the Semitic religions conduct their faith. Unsurprisingly, the Arya Samaj is strongly rooted in many Hindu expatriate communities, offering the equivalent of Christian 'Sunday school' classes in the principles of the faith to Hindu children in suburban America. Yet it remains little more than a sect in its own homeland, adhered to by a modest minority of Indian Hindus.

Greater local success was obtained by three nineteenth-century reformers (and contemporaries) in southern India, Sree Narayana Guru (1856–1928), Mahatma Ayyankali (1863–1941) and Chattampi Swami (1853–1924), whose lives and impact overlapped. Chattampi Swami, an upper-caste Hindu sage, opposed caste oppression and spoke up for the emancipation of women; Mahatma Ayyankali, from an 'Untouchable' community, fought successfully against the iniquitous discriminations that prevented outcastes from using certain roads and public spaces in

Travancore. But the greatest impact was that of Sree Narayana Guru, who overcame the disadvantages imposed upon the 'backward caste' Ezhava community by preaching a modern Hinduism of love, equality and universalism. 'One religion, one caste, one God for all mankind', was his dictum. 'Whatever a person's caste, it is enough that a human be good', he famously declared. He backed up his precepts by establishing educational institutions throughout South India and by setting up ashrams and spiritual retreats to advance his ideas. Mahatma Gandhi called on Sree Narayana Guru in 1925, three years before the latter's death; without a common language (the guru did not know English and Gandhiji had no Sanskrit), the two great souls communed largely in silence and through an interpreter, but the more famous man emerged awestruck from the experience. In 1999, Sree Narayana Guru was voted by the readers of the most popular Malayalam-language magazine the greatest Keralite of the twentieth century.

The mystic sage Ramana Maharishi (1879–1950), and the revolutionary-turned spiritual guide Sri Aurobindo (1872–1950), were two other remarkable contemporaries born in the nineteenth century. Ramana Maharishi's intense spirituality, his quest for self-realisation, his intuitive grasp of Advaita and Bhakti led to him being widely considered a Jivanmukta, one who had attained self-realisation in this life. One can see Ramakrishna as the exemplar of *bhakti yoga*, Vivekananda as the very model of *karma yoga*, and Ramana Maharishi as that of *jnana yoga*. His key question to aid the attainment of self-realisation was '*Who am I?*' Am I the body, the mind, the senses? Ramana Maharishi did not travel to disseminate a message, perform social service or establish a new order of monks, but the simple example of his spirituality made him an object of great popular veneration. It is said that on the night of his death, a comet passed across the sky behind his mountain abode at Arunachalam.

As for the Cambridge-educated Sri Aurobindo, he began as an extremist political revolutionary, and ended as an other-worldly spiritual giant. During his political phase (essentially 1905 to 1910), Sri Aurobindo evolved a philosophy of spiritual nationalism, writing passionately and evocatively of the divinity of the motherland, personified as a goddess, Bhavani Bharati (a forerunner in some ways of the Bharat Mata deified by the Hindutva movement). But during his incarceration in a bomb conspiracy case, Aurobindo realised his spiritual interests outstripped his political ones. He moved to the French enclave of Pondicherry and spent the last four decades of his life (1910–1950) there in spiritual contemplation, writing brilliant exegeses on aspects of Hinduism, including a magisterial commentary on the Gita, and establishing an ashram that thrives to this day. Rather than individual salvation, he was concerned with the spiritual evolution of the human race; his concept of Integral Yoga envisaged a threefold path that involved total surrender to the Divine, the raising of human consciousness to a 'supramental' level, and finally the transformation of the terrestrial human race into a wholly new order of being.

It was said of Sri Aurobindo that he could trace almost every modern Western idea to the ancient Hindu scriptures, and that if one could not find a specific reference upon examination, that was because one was reading the words literally and failing to comprehend that the ancient Hindu sages had elliptical and metaphorical means of conveying the ideas that today we consider modern. The French political scientist (and student of modern Hindu politics) Christophe Jaffrelot has labelled the process of adoption and acceptance of Western ideas, beliefs and values by Indian sages, masked by the claim that these were actually derived from the ancient Hindu texts, as 'strategic syncretism'.[13] Whatever one calls it, it was one more instance of how resilient Hinduism was in the face of Western colonial dominance, and how effectively it adapted to the demands of proving its viability and relevance in the modern era.

SWAMI VIVEKANANDA

Though Ramana Maharishi and Sri Aurobindo achieved their prominence after his death, Swami Vivekananda (1863–1902), who came of age at the culmination of all the developments I have earlier chronicled, was also heir to the grand, diverse and varied traditions of Hinduism, for he had drunk deeply from the well of a faith whose eclecticism he saw as a strength. As he put it, 'sect after sect arose in India and seemed to shake the religion of the Vedas to its very foundations, but [over the years]...these sects were all sucked in, absorbed and assimilated into the immense body of the mother faith. From the high spiritual flights of the Vedanta philosophy, of which the latest discoveries of science seem like echoes, to the low ideas of idolatry with its multifarious mythology, the agnosticism of the Buddhists and the atheism of the Jains, each and all have a place in the Hindu's religion.'

His initial beliefs were influenced by Brahmo concepts of a formless God and the rejection of idolatry, and anchored in a rationalised Hindu theology based on the *Upanishads* and reliant on Advaita Vedanta. But though Brahmoism was an influence, it was by no means the determinant influence; Vivekananda abandoned the Brahmos for the savant who became his guru, the mystic monk Ramakrishna Paramahamsa (1836–1886). Ramakrishna, who was subject to visions, trances and 'intense spiritual rhapsodies' (in the words of Dr Karan Singh), which brought him to purest consciousness, preached a religious universalism in which he urged the thousands who flocked to him to abandon all quarrels over religion and to look for God with a pure heart. He imparted his wisdom in simple parables that won him a devoted following among the masses as well as the elite of his day, as well as deep spiritual attainment that he imparted to his most illustrious devotee. From Ramakrishna, Swami Vivekananda acquired a more profound, as well as broader, familiarity with Hindu doctrines of the oneness of *atman* and Brahman, of the role of spirituality and the quest for self-realisation and liberation, as well as the stories and parables through which these beliefs could be propagated.

Vivekananda explained his sacred texts in terms his Western audience at the Chicago Parliament of the World's Religions could understand: 'The Hindus have received their religion through revelation, the Vedas. They hold that the Vedas are without beginning and without end. It may sound ludicrous to this audience, how a book can be without beginning or end. But by the Vedas no books are meant. They mean the accumulated treasury of spiritual laws discovered by different persons in different times. Just as the law of gravitation existed before its discovery, and would exist if all humanity forgot it, so is it with the laws that govern the spiritual world. The moral, ethical, and spiritual relations between soul and soul and between individual spirits and the Father of all spirits were there before their discovery, and would remain even if we forgot them.'

This led Vivekananda to the ringing affirmation that whereas many Westerners think of the self as a body that possesses a soul, Hinduism sees the self as a soul that possesses a body: 'The Vedas declare,' he said, that 'I am a spirit living in a body: I am not the body. The body will die, but I shall not die.' On the question of the existence of God, again an idea that would make his faith more comprehensible to foreigners, Vivekananda explained: 'at the head of all these laws, in and through every particle of matter and force, stands One, "*by whose command the wind blows, the fire burns, the clouds rain and death stalks upon the earth*".' (The 'One' was a carefully-chosen word; whereas to the Swami it implied the oneness of Brahman and atman, cosmic spirit and soul, it also embraced the idea of the One God of the Semitic faiths.) 'And what is His nature?' Vivekananda went on. 'He is everywhere, the pure and formless One, the Almighty and the All-merciful. "*Thou art our father, Thou art our mother, Thou art our beloved friend, Thou art the source of all strength; give us strength. Thou art He that beareth the burdens of the universe; help me bear the little burden of this life.*" Thus sang the Rishis of the Veda.'

A certain amount of mysticism inevitably came into the message, as his audience expected: 'the Hindu believes he is a spirit. Him the sword cannot pierce; Him the fire cannot burn; Him the water cannot melt; Him the air cannot dry. The Hindu believes that every soul is a circle whose circumference is nowhere, but whose centre is located in the body, and that death means the change of this centre from body to body.... The Vedas teach that the soul is divine, only held in the bondage of matter; perfection will be reached when this bond will burst and the word they use for it is, therefore, "*mukti*"—freedom, freedom from the bonds of imperfection, freedom from death and misery.'

But here Vivekananda had a little surprise up his sleeve for the listening Westerners, particularly for those who thought of their God as a distant vision, or an aged and forbidding figure in the clouds with a white beard. 'And how to worship Him?' he asked of his God. 'Through love. He is to be worshipped as the one beloved, dearer than everything in this and the next life. This is the doctrine of love declared in the Vedas, and let us see how it is fully developed and taught by Krishna whom the Hindus believe to have been God incarnate on earth. He taught that a man ought to live in this world like a lotus leaf, which grows in water but is never moistened by water; so a man ought to live in the world—his heart to God and his hands to work.' For Vivekananda this selfless love for God was implicit in the teachings of the Bhagavad Gita. 'It is good to love God for hope of reward in this or the next world, but it is better to love God for love's sake; and the prayer goes: "Lord, I do not want wealth nor children nor learning. If it be Thy will, I shall go from birth to birth; but grant me this, that I may love Thee without the hope of reward—love unselfishly for love's sake."'

To Vivekananda, the answer to the question 'What is Hinduism?' could be reduced to the idea of realisation, of the union of *atman* and Brahman, the *moksha* taught by Advaita Vedanta: 'the whole object of [Hinduism] is by constant struggle to become perfect, to become divine, to reach God, and see God; and this reaching God, seeing God, becoming perfect even as the Father in Heaven is perfect, constitutes the religion of the Hindus...' He explained: 'There is something beyond even this fine body, which is the Atman of man, which has neither beginning nor end, which knows not what death is...I am already joined—from my very birth, from the very fact of my life—I am in *Yoga* [union] with that infinite life....'

From there, having explained Hinduism in terms that Westerners could grasp, Vivekananda firmly parted from their basic assumptions. He argued that the Hindu religion 'means realisation and nothing short of that. "Believe in the doctrine and you are safe" can never be taught to us, for we do not believe in that; you are what you make yourselves...religion is to be realised, not only heard; it is not in learning some doctrine like a parrot.' This dismissal of Western catechisms enabled Vivekananda to argue robustly that Advaita was science rather than philosophy. Hinduism has always been free of the science versus faith conflicts that have bedevilled other religions. Indeed, in 1896, Vivekananda claimed that Advaita appealed to modern scientists: 'I may make bold to say that the only religion which agrees with, and even goes a little further than modern researchers, both on physical and moral lines is the Advaita, and that is why it appeals to modern scientists so much. They find that the old dualistic theories are not enough for them, do not satisfy their necessities. A man must have not only faith, but intellectual faith too.'

He also argued that 'there is no polytheism in India'. The idol worship one saw in India's temples should not be taken literally:

> By the law of association the material image calls up the mental idea and vice versa. This is why the Hindu uses an external symbol when he worships. He will tell you it helps to keep his mind fixed on the Being to whom he prays. He knows as well as you do that the image is not God, is not omnipresent.... To the Hindu, man is not travelling from error to truth, but from truth to truth, from lower to higher truth. To him all the religions from the lowest fetishism to the highest absolutism, mean so many attempts of the human soul to grasp and realise the Infinite, each determined by the conditions of its birth and association, and each of these marks a stage of progress.

And he added that it was not very different in the so-called monotheistic faiths: 'the images, crosses, and crescents are simply so many symbols—so many pegs to hang spiritual ideas on. It is not that this help is necessary for everyone, but those that do not need it have no right to say that it is wrong.' Idolatry in India 'is the attempt of undeveloped minds to grasp high spiritual truths'.

The Swami was certainly not seeking to downplay his own faith: far from it, he spoke proudly in 'the name of the most ancient order of monks in the world' and 'the mother of religions'. Vivekananda was contemptuous of what he called 'kitchen religion', the farrago of taboos and restrictions on diet and conduct that had come to constitute Hinduism for some. But he also made no distinction between the actions of Hindus as a people (embodied by their grant of asylum to people fleeing religious oppression, for instance) and their actions as a religious community (visible in their tolerance of other faiths). He spoke proudly of Hindu India offering refuge to Jews fleeing Roman persecution and Zoroastrians escaping Muslim rule in Persia: 'I am proud to belong to a country which has sheltered the persecuted and the refugees of all religions and all countries of the earth.' For him, there was no real distinction between Hindu believers accepting other faiths and Hindus extending asylum to people of other faiths, because Hinduism was as much a civilisation as a set of religious beliefs.

In a different speech to the same Chicago convention, Swami Vivekananda set out his philosophy in simple terms: 'Unity in variety is the plan of nature, and the Hindu has recognised it. Every other religion lays down certain fixed dogmas and tries to compel society to adopt them. It places before society only one coat which must fit Jack and John and Henry, all alike. If it does not fit John or Henry, he must go without a coat to cover his body. The Hindus have discovered that the absolute can only be realised, or thought of, or stated through the relative, and the images, crosses, and crescents are simply so many symbols—so many pegs to hang spiritual ideas on. It is not that this help is necessary for everyone, but those that do not need it have no right to say that it is wrong. Nor is it compulsory in Hinduism.'

Vivekananda was also, uncommonly for his time, a believer in gender equality: he related well to women, who numbered among his closest devotees, and worked with them to take his message to the world. It is no wonder then that he began those inspiring speeches to the Parliament of the World's Religions with the words, 'Sisters and brothers of America...' The first time he uttered them, it was reported, the phrase, and his voice, had an electrifying effect upon the audience.

In his book *Raja Yoga* Vivekananda introduced the 'four yogas', his interpretation of Patanjali's *Yoga Sutras*, as a practical means for each individual to work towards realising the divine force within himself. The four yogas were raja yoga (psychological and mystical practices as well as spiritual exercises), karma yoga (work and the way of action and social service in the quest for the divine), bhakti yoga (devotional worship and expression of love for the divine), and jnana yoga (the path

of knowledge and reason in the pursuit of self-realisation). The four
paths were distinct but could be pursued simultaneously or in parallel.
Vivekananda tried to combine all these in himself. He pursued his own
divinity by discipline and effort, deep study, reading and reflection, and
huge physical effort that included walking the length and breadth of
India with nothing but a staff, a water pot and his own charisma to
sustain him.

He was a profoundly moral figure, with none of the indulgences that
modern Indian 'godmen' have become known for; as Adi Shankara
preached, he lived by a code of truth, purity, celibacy and unselfishness
that anchored his *shraddha* (faith). Although many of his deeply committed followers were women, he treated them as sisters and daughters, irrespective of their age, and lived the celibate life of a *brahmach-
ari*, seeing intimate relations as incompatible with his mission of
spiritual service. In this he remained essentially a monk, but unlike his
preceptor Ramakrishna he was no other-worldly figure: a compelling
speaker and a magnetic presence, Swami Vivekananda was focused on
human behaviour in the real world he saw around him. He argued that
it is an insult to preach religion to a man with an empty stomach, and
for many in India, he said, God will only appear as a loaf of bread.

The Vedanta, interpreted in comprehensible contemporary terms,
became the vehicle for his preaching. As Vivekananda explained: 'Each
soul is potentially divine. The goal is to manifest this Divinity within by
controlling nature, external and internal. Do this either by work, or
worship, or mental discipline, or philosophy—by one, or more, or all of
these—and be free. This is the whole of religion. Doctrines, or dogmas,
or rituals, or books, or temples, or forms, are but secondary details.'

Vivekananda lived up to this precept himself: work, worship, mental
discipline and philosophy, he mastered them all. He believed that spiritual realisation needed the awakening of the human will; this required
him to adopt a path of pursuing spirituality through service. Worldly
success was important, but such success could only be the outcome of
focused thought and action. It is important to remember that Swami
Vivekananda—despite being a spiritual figure, despite being a disciple
of the immortal Ramakrishna Paramahamsa, despite being a *sannyasi*

who travelled throughout India and taught the message of Vedanta and the Gita, the message of religion and spirituality as he understood it—was also very much anchored in the real needs of India, of his people at that time and in the future.

Of the many angles from which the social problems of India could be analysed, he proceeded from the religious and spiritual perspectives. Therefore, the Swami founded the Ramakrishna Math, based on the twin ideals of self-realisation and service to the world, and named for his guru, Sri Ramakrishna Paramahamsa. But since a math (or matham or mutth) is essentially a place of contemplation, Vivekananda laid the foundation of the Ramakrishna Mission, also named for his preceptor, as a philanthropic, volunteer organisation to work alongside the religious monastic order to spread his teachings throughout the world. The Mission based its work on the principle of karma yoga, the path of selfless, altruistic service propounded by Vivekananda. Karma yoga preached an ethic of action and doing, not merely of the meditation and reflection that was all that spirituality had hitherto been identified with. Ever since its inception, the Ramakrishna Mission has stayed true to its motto of 'Atmano mokshartham jagat hitaya cha', which translated from Sanskrit means 'For one's own salvation, and for the good of the world'.

Vivekananda undoubtedly revolutionised the traditional image of the Hindu monk, the *sannyasi*, in India by setting the example and making social service an integral part of the *sannyasi*'s life. Initially, after the passing away of his guru, Sri Ramakrishna, he had thought of going on a pilgrimage to the holy places like Varanasi, Ayodhya, Vrindavan, and the ashrams of yogis in the Himalayas. However, after a couple of years spent on such visits, he turned his gaze to the common people for whom the only reality in life was their struggle for survival.

When, around Christmas of 1892, he travelled on foot to Kanyakumari, at the southern tip of India, he meditated on the 'last bit of Indian rock' jutting out into the ocean, on which now stands the Vivekananda Rock Memorial. It was at this juncture in his life that the Swami pondered over his experiences of observing the miseries of the poor in the various parts of the country, which culminated in his

'Vision of One India'. This has now come to be called the 'Kanyakumari resolve of 1892', about which he later wrote:

'At Cape Comorin, sitting in Mother Kumari's temple, I hit upon a plan: we are so many sannyasins wandering about, and teaching the people metaphysics? It is all madness. Did not our Gurudeva once say, "An empty stomach is no good for religion?" That those poor people are leading a life of brutes is simply due to ignorance... Suppose some sannyasins, bent on doing good to others, go from village to village, disseminating education and seeking in various ways to better the condition of all down to the Chandala...can't that bring forth good in time? ... We, as a nation, have lost our individuality, and that is the cause of all mischief in India. We have to give back to the nation its lost individuality and *raise the masses*...' Vivekananda wanted 'to set in motion a machinery which will bring noblest ideas to the doorstep of even the poorest and the meanest'.

These ideas galvanised his followers, in a country that had long been inured to the tyranny and oppression faced by a majority of the people. And thus began a new epoch in his life. Nationalism—not just in the sense of overthrowing the foreign ruler, but in the sense of national reawakening—became a prominent theme in Vivekananda's thought. He believed that a country's future depended on its people, and his teachings focused on what today we might call human development. Our modern systems of governance have a lot to learn from his teachings. His assessment of the social problems of India was realistic, rather than theoretical. He connected with the common man to a degree that would be the envy of most modern politicians, largely owing to the fact that he wandered all over the country with a few followers and a begging bowl in his hand.

What bothered the Swami, even more than poverty itself, was the gulf between the rich and the poor, between the high-placed and the low-born, and further, the ugly sight of the strong regularly oppressing the weak. 'This is our native land', he often bemoaned, 'where huts and palaces exist side-by-side.' Such was the dichotomy of the times that it seemed inconceivable to him that India could have the unity and brotherhood which are preconditions for national greatness. Born, as it were, a 'disunited mob', we could not combine: in our unity would lie the fulfilment of our nationhood.

But this would mean liberation from ourselves and not just from the British. Vivekananda was searingly honest in his criticism of the social practices that kept India backward. He denounced the oppression of the masses by iniquitous social practices, including caste discrimination. He propagated the idea that 'the divine, the absolute, exists within all human beings regardless of social status'. He also voiced his opposition against the manner in which women were kept, in conditions of servile dependence on men, which made them 'good only to weep at the slightest approach of mishap or danger'. He taught us values that actually mandated change in the arrangements of our society. He refused to accept that religion was cited in favour of iniquitous social practices like child marriage: he was a religious reformer as well as a social reformer. Child marriage, which Rammohan Roy had fought against, still persisted across India, since the British were reluctant to outlaw it. 'A girl of eight is married to a man of thirty and the parents are jubilant over it. And if anyone protests against it, the plea put forward is that our religion is being overturned', he lamented. His devotee Sister Nivedita, born in Britain as Margaret Noble, started a girls' school in Calcutta to advance his progressive ideas about the education of women. He wanted a fully educated India, an objective we have not yet fulfilled a century and a quarter later.

These practices, and the dissensions which divided Hindu society, pained Swami Vivekananda all the more because they were being adhered to in the name of religion. He preached that 'seeing the divine as the essence of others will promote love and social harmony', but he had no illusions about how prevalent such attitudes were. He was furious about those who claimed their beliefs were superior to anyone else's. 'Ask a man who wants to start a sectarian fight,' he declaimed, '"Have you seen God? Have you seen the Atman? If you have not, what right have you to preach his Name—you walking in darkness trying to lead me into the same darkness—the blind leading the blind, and both falling into the ditch?"'

Vivekananda helped create, in his own lifetime, a band of volunteers to work among the poor, the distressed and the marginalised. Many of these were young people, for Swami Vivekananda personified the eternal energy of Indian youth and awakened in many young people a restless quest for truth. One of his more famous exhortations to young Indians came from his lectures in *Raja Yoga*, in which he memorably said, 'Take up one idea. Make that one idea your life—think of it, dream of it, live on that idea. Let the brain, muscles, nerves, every part of your body, be full of that idea, and just leave every other idea alone. This is the way to success, that is the way great spiritual giants are produced'.

A spiritual giant himself, Vivekananda expressed his mission in disarmingly simple terms: 'What I want to propagate is a religion that will be equally acceptable to all minds; it must be equally philosophic, equally emotional, equally mystic and equally conducive to action'. His own teachings, as well as the work done by the Ramakrishna Math and Mission in the century after his passing, have made Swami Vivekananda a modern day apostle of the ideas that underpin the modern Hindu's conception of the world and of our place in it.

But the fact is that he never considered himself detached from the world; his spirituality was anchored in the world. Swami Vivekananda taught us that a true nationalism that was rooted in both spiritual yearning and a spirit of social service. 'Arise, awake, and stop not till the goal is reached' was his motto, citing a *sloka* (verse) of the *Katha Upanishad*. And that, to my mind, is the great lesson he leaves to those of us in public life: that we must have values, that we must join the quest for attainment of some knowledge of the Divine, for that is ultimately what all spirituality is about, but that spirituality is meaningless if it is not embedded in a genuine concern for the well-being of ordinary people in our country, and a willingness to act on it.

In multiple speeches around the world and in India, Vivekananda continually reiterated a basic message: that the Hindu recognises one supreme spirit that suffuses the universe. He worships the one God while recognising that others see and name Him differently. 'Ekam sat vipra bahudha vadanti': the Truth is One but sages call It by different names.

GREAT SOULS OF HINDUISM

AFTER THE SWAMI, TOWARDS THE MAHATMA

Two decades after Vivekananda's premature death at the age of thirty-nine, a very different figure, clad not in the saffron or ochre robes of the Hindu sage but in the cap and gown of the Oxford don, rose to explicate the Hindu religion to an audience of academics and theologians. Delivering the prestigious Upton Lectures at the age of thirty-eight, Dr Sarvepalli Radhakrishnan, then the youngest Fellow of All Souls' College, described 'the Hindu view of life' in contemporary terms. For the Hindu, Radhakrishnan explained, God is in the world, though God is not the world, and the world is not God; He is more than the Creator, he preserves, protects, destroys, remakes, and strives continuously, alongside human beings. The *Brihadaranyaka Upanishad* captures this idea beautifully, though Radhakrishnan did not cite it:

> *He who is abiding in the earth, yet different from the earth;*
> *He who is abiding in the water, yet different from the water;*
> *He who is abiding in the wind, yet different from the wind...*

> — *Brihadaranyaka Upanishad*, III.7.3–7[14]

In both places, the text uses the same Sanskrit word, '*antara*' which means both 'interior to (abiding in)' and 'different from'. There is no dualism between the natural (the reality we see around us) and the supernatural (the cosmic spirit); each is rooted in the other. As Radhakrishnan brilliantly put it: 'The Hindu spirit is that attitude towards life which regards the endless variety of the visible and the temporal world as sustained and supported by the invisible and eternal spirit.'[15]

Like Vivekananda in Chicago, Radhakrishnan had some startling news for his Western audience: the Hindu did not think in terms of good and evil. 'Evil has reference to the distance which good has to traverse. Ugliness is halfway to beauty. Error is a stage on the road to truth.' After all, he added: 'As every soul is unlike all others in the world, the destruction of even the most wicked soul will create a void in God's scheme.'[16] There was no notion of sin in this philosophy, nor of Heaven nor Hell. (And yet the idea of sin is not wholly absent from the Vedas; the notion that sins can be washed away in holy waters goes back to the *Rig Veda*.) Damnation was not God's way, since the sinner was himself part of the universal cosmic spirit. How could there be a hell, since it was impossible for there to be a place where God was not? Vivekananda had said years earlier that Hindus reject the idea of fear and the idea of sin: 'the Aryans threw it aside as a very primitive sort of idea and went further on... [for] a more philosophical and transcendental idea.' That idea Radhakrishnan expressed in almost poetic terms: 'The cure for error is not the stake or the cudgel, not force or persecution, but the quiet diffusion of light.'[17]

Radhakrishnan spoke as a professor of philosophy; Vivekananda declaimed as a preacher; but their message was the same, rendering the Hinduism of Advaita Vedanta comprehensible to the modern Western mind. It was, however, the charismatic Swami who had the more lasting impact. Vivekananda's overt respect for all other paths and religions was an integral part of what he preached. Part of his appeal lay in the way he combined ancient wisdom with contemporary insights, in spreading his profound message of interfaith harmony and spirituality married to rationalism.

Vivekananda had quoted the Bhagavad Gita to the effect that 'Whosoever comes to me, through whatsoever form, I reach him; all men are struggling through paths which in the end lead to me.' Vivekananda went on to denounce the fact that 'sectarianism, bigotry, and its horrible descendant, fanaticism, have long possessed this beautiful earth. They have filled the earth with violence, and drenched it often with human blood, destroyed civilisation, and sent whole nations to despair'.

His confident belief that the death-knell of these negative forces had been sounded was sadly not to be borne out. But his vision—summarised in the Sanskrit credo '*sarva dharma sambhava*'—all religions are equally worthy of respect—is, in fact, the kind of Hinduism practised by most of India's Hindus, whose instinctive acceptance of other faiths and forms of worship has long been the distinctive hallmark of Indianness, not merely in a narrow religious sense, but in a broader cultural and spiritual sense too.

The efforts of Swami Vivekananda and the other Hindu reformers and thinkers served to reassert their faith in the face of the racist notions of Christian superiority peddled by the colonial rulers. Far from the religion of superstitious idol-worshippers caricatured by the imperialists, they demonstrated that Hinduism was sophisticated, monotheistic and inclusive. It was a faith that had undergone several reformations and absorbed them all; the incorporation of Buddhist ideas, for instance, had made the Buddha—a figure familiar to, and respected by, many Westerners—a part of the Hindu faith. Hinduism had survived in even more sophisticated and cosmopolitan a form, and it would see off the threat of colonial modernity as well.

And yet, curiously enough, the nature and content of the Vedanta tradition meant that while it enabled Hindus to stand up with self-confidence against imperial rule, it did not generate a narrow Hindu nationalism. If Hinduism, as Advaita Vedanta taught, was an inclusive faith, the nationalism it animated must also be inclusive. Hindus thus agitated against colonial oppression, but they were happy to pursue the goal of *swaraj* or self-rule through collective action with other Indian religious communities.

MAHATMA GANDHI

The leader who most embodied this approach was Mahatma Gandhi, who called himself a follower of Advaita Vedanta. Swami Vivekananda had preached Advaita Vedanta as an inclusive universal religion; similarly Gandhi did not conceal his own staunch Hinduism, but presented it as a faith that respected and embraced all other faiths. He was immersed in Hindu beliefs and customs, and profoundly influenced by the Yamas of Adi Shankara, particularly *ahimsa* and *satya* to which he gave profound meaning when he applied them to the nationalist cause. But when Gandhi held prayer-meetings at which Hindu devotional bhajans were chanted, so also were songs, hymns and verses sacred to other religions. He actively promoted syncretism: *Raghupathi Raghava Raja Ram*, he chanted, *Ishwara Allah Tero naam*. This practice emerged from his Vedantic belief in the unity of God and all human beings; he believed staunchly that all beings have the same *atman* and therefore should be treated with equality. His conviction that all paths to God

should be seen as equally valid led him to respect the beliefs and practices of other faiths and to refuse to impose his own upon them (as he
explained when refusing to advocate a ban on cow slaughter that would
affect other communities).

Such behaviour did not endear him to every Hindu. Gandhi's assas-
sin, Nathuram Godse, denounced 'Gandhi's betrayal of Hinduism' during his trial. It was an odd charge, since many saw Gandhiji as the
quintessential Hindu leader in Indian politics, but it is true that his
Hinduism was not particularly religious in the conventional sense. He
died with the name of Rama on his lips but there is no evidence that he
ever believed in or worshipped a personal god. ('There is an indefinable mysterious power that pervades everything,' he wrote, implying
faith in an impersonal, undefinable power: 'I don't regard God as a
person.') Gandhi declared his faith in 'all that goes by the name of
Hindu scriptures' but, as the scholar K. P. Shankaran points out, he
'immediately qualified it by saying that he also believed in all other
religious texts in a similar way'.[18] He also took Hinduism's eclectic and
wide-ranging texts and belief structures literally, making it clear that
he retained the right to choose what tenets he believed in, to interpret
what they taught him, and to reject anything in them that he could not
agree with. His emphasis on the ethics of *satya* and *ahimsa*, elevating
them above almost any of the other principles of Hinduism, was distinctive: 'Truth for me is God.'

Gandhi was more a reinterpreter of Hinduism than a reformer of it;
by drawing from it to suit his beliefs and purposes, he redefined the
traditional vocabulary of Hinduism without ever departing from it. He
criticised many of the iniquitous social practices of Hinduism without
denouncing the faith from which they had emerged, and unlike his
contemporary Ambedkar, who denounced Hinduism's distortions and
cruelties and eventually left the faith, Gandhi always tried to change it
from within. According to K.P. Shankaran, Gandhi's rejection of the
vocabulary of the European Enlightenment and modernity (for the
reasons he had explained in his 1909 book, *Hind Swaraj*) forced him to
fall back on a vocabulary that he was familiar with, that of the Vaishnava
tradition of his parents. Gandhi's objective was to create an ethical

Indian state founded on *ahimsa* and *satya*, non-violence and truth, principles he found in Advaita philosophy. The national motto of independent India—*Satyameva Jayate* (Truth Alone Triumphs)—is from the *Mundaka Upanishad*, chosen by Mahatma Gandhi as his guiding credo. His own translation of the Bhagavad Gita portrays the text as a philosophy of Anashakti Yoga, meant for votaries of *ahimsa*. Gandhiji took a text that had traditionally been seen as extolling war and action, and transformed it into a paean to non-violence and truth. It was quite a feat (what some have seen as a creative 'misreading' of the text),[19] that located his Hinduism on a platform of *ahimsa* and *satya*, and at the same time anchored his political strategy in the Hindu faith of the masses.

And even while doing so, Gandhi took care to include Indians of other faiths in his capacious and agglomerative version of Hinduism. He noted that there is ample religious literature, both in the *astika* and *nastika* religious traditions, that supports a pluralistic approach to religious and cultural diversity. Gandhi found support for his Advaitist beliefs not only in the Vedanta but in the Jain concept of 'Anekantavada'—the notion that truth and reality are perceived differently by different people from their own different points of view, and that therefore no single perception can constitute the complete truth—from which he derived the axiom that 'truth is many-sided and relative'. Gandhi often expressed the view that the spirit of synthesis was the essential hallmark of Indian civilisation. This led him to declare once, in response to being classified a Hindu: 'I am a Hindu, a Muslim, a Christian, a Parsi, a Jew'. (To which the Muslim League leader Muhammad Ali Jinnah tartly riposted: 'Only a Hindu could say that.')

As a Hindu, I am proud to lay claim to the legacy of the tradition of thought and action that began with the Vedas and grew under Adi Shankara, flowered through Bhakti, embraced social reformers like Raja Rammohan Roy and Sree Narayana Guru, and has Swami Vivekananda and Mahatma Gandhi as two of its fountainheads.

PART TWO

POLITICAL HINDUISM

HINDUISM AND THE POLITICS OF HINDUTVA

When I was a columnist for *The Hindu*, which despite its name has been a secular, even left-inclined, newspaper throughout its existence, I received a number of letters from readers on the subject of Hindu ethics and *dharma*, prompted by some of my writings on the subject. One letter, from the retired Director-General of Police of Tripura State, Mr B. J. K. Tampi, made a challenging point. Arguing that *dharma* 'has a pre-eminently secular meaning of social ethics covering law-abiding conduct,' Mr Tampi sought for *dharma* its due prominence in Hindu life. 'In fact the four ends of human life,' he went on, 'dharma, artha, kama and moksha, are always mentioned in that order. The purport is that the pursuit of wealth and pleasure should be within the parameters of dharma and moksha (the final emancipation of the soul from rebirth through religious practices).' Mr Tampi adds, citing Swami Ranganathananda (1908–2005, the spiritual teacher who was the thirteenth and most famous head of the Ramakrishna Mission): 'the excessive Indian fear of rebirth has led to the neglect of true worldly dharma for the sake of an other-worldly moksha. It has made men unfit both in the worldly (secular) and spiritual spheres.'

Now I have never met the good Mr Tampi—whose theological learning is all the more impressive in one who served in the practical profession of a policeman—but his analysis gladdens my secular heart.

The fact is that, despite having done so much to attract the opprobrium of those who seek to politicise Hinduism, or the Hindutva brigade as I call them, I do believe that propagating *dharma*—and instilling deeply at all levels of society the need to live according to one's *dharma*—can be the key to bridging the present gap between the religious and the secular in India.

The social scientist T. N. Madan has argued that the increasing secularisation of modern Indian life is responsible for the rise of fundamentalism, since 'it is the marginalisation of faith, which is what secularism is, that permits the perversion of religion. There are no fundamentalists or revivalists in traditional society.'[1]

The implication is that secularism has deprived Indians of their moral underpinnings—the meaning that faith gives to life—and religious extremism has risen as an almost inevitable antithesis to the secular project. The only way out of this dilemma is for Hindus to return to the tolerant, holistic, just, pluralist *dharma* articulated so effectively by Swami Vivekananda, which embraces both worldly and spiritual duty.

After all, as Mr Tampi points out, the Hindu's secular pursuit of material happiness is not meant to be divorced from his obedience to the ethical and religious tenets of his faith. So the distinction between 'religious' and 'secular' is an artificial one: there is no such compartmentalisation in Hinduism. When you conduct your life by performing your duties ethically, are you 'secular' or (since you are fulfilling your *dharma* while adhering to a moral code) a 'good Hindu'?

There is also a terminological issue here. The secularism avowed by successive Indian governments, as Professor R. S. Misra of Banaras Hindu University has argued, is based on *dharma-nirpekshata* ('keeping apart from dharma'), which is impossible for any good Hindu to adhere to. BJP politicians like Rajnath Singh and Yogi Adityanath have argued that Indian governments cannot observe *dharma-nirpekshata* but should follow the precept of *panth-nirpekshata* (not favouring any particular sect or faith). In this they are not far removed from my argument—which I have made for several years before my entry into Indian politics—that 'secularism' is a misnomer in the Indian context of profuse religiosity, and what we should be talking about is 'pluralism'. I believe the roots of India's pluralism can be found in the Hindu acceptance of difference, which has become an article of faith for most of Indian society. But many critics of secularism are not terribly enamoured of pluralism either. To Professor Misra, for instance, the problem with *dharma-nirpekshata* is that an authentically Indian ethic would ensure that secular objectives are infused with *dharma*.

I find this view persuasive but incomplete. Yes, *dharma* is essential in the pursuit of material well-being, public order and good governance, but this should not mean turning public policy over to *sants* and *sadhus*, nor excluding any section of Indian society (for instance, minorities who reject the Hindu idea of *dharma* as irrelevant to their lives) from their rightful place in the Indian sun. If we can bring *dharma* into our national life, it must be to uphold, rather than at the expense of, the pluralist ideal of Indian-ness.

Hinduism has always acknowledged the existence of opposites (and reconciled them): pain and pleasure, success and failure, creation and destruction, life and death are all manifestations of the duality inherent in human existence. These pairings are not contradictory but complementary; they are aspects of the same overarching reality. So also with the secular and the sacred: a Hindu's life must involve both. To acknowledge this would both absorb and deflect the unsavoury aspects of the resurgence of Hindutva.

THE RSS AND SAVARKAR

India's current ruling party, the Bharatiya Janata Party, officially adopted Hindutva as its defining credo in 1989. It is the doctrine assiduously promoted by the Hindu nationalist volunteer organisation the Rashtriya Swayamsevak Sangh (RSS), founded in 1925, and its affiliated family of organisations in the 'Sangh Parivar', notably the Vishva Hindu Parishad (VHP, World Hindu Council), set up in 1964 with an avowed intention of protecting and promoting the Hindu religion. The word Hindutva is widely used by all of them, but what does the term actually mean?

The man largely credited with the invention of the concept of Hindutva—literally 'Hinduness'—is Vinayak Damodar Savarkar

(1883–1966), whose *Essentials Of Hindutva* (Bombay: Veer Savarkar Prakashan, 1st edn 1923) laid out the concept. Republished in 1928 as *Hindutva:Who Is a Hindu?*, it is in many ways the foundational text of the Hindu nationalist creed.

Savarkar chose the term 'Hindutva' to describe the 'quality of being a Hindu' in ethnic, cultural and political terms. He argued that a Hindu is one who considers India to be his motherland (*matrbhumi*), the land of his ancestors (*pitrbhumi*), and his holy land (*punya bhumi*). India is the land of the Hindus since their ethnicity is Indian and since the Hindu faith originated in India. (Other faiths that were born in India, like Sikhism, Buddhism and Jainism also qualified, in Sarvakar's terms, as variants of Hinduism since they fulfilled the same three criteria; but Islam and Christianity, born outside India, did not.) Thus a Hindu is someone born of Hindu parents, who regards India—'this land of Bharatvarsha, from the Indus to the Seas'—as his motherland as well as his holy land, 'that is the cradle-land of his religion.'

In keeping with the race doctrines of the times, Savarkar conceived Hindutva as an indefinable quality inherent in the Hindu 'race', which could not be identified directly with the specific tenets of Hinduism. Hindutva, he declared, 'is so varied and so rich, so powerful and so subtle, so elusive and yet so vivid'[2] that it defied such definition. But of course, the concept of Hindutva would have made no sense unless it was explained in relation to the religion of Hinduism. So Savarkar asserted: 'Hinduism is only a derivative, a fraction, a part of Hindutva.'[3] To him, the religion was therefore a subset of the political idea, rather than synonymous with it—something many of its proponents today would be surprised to hear. Savarkar, however, argued that: 'Failure to distinguish between Hindutva and Hinduism has given rise to much misunderstanding and mutual suspicion between some of those sister communities that have inherited this inestimable and common treasure of our Hindu civilisation… It is sufficient enough to point out that Hindutva is not identical with what is vaguely indicated by the term Hinduism. By an "ism" it is generally meant a theory or a code more or less based on spiritual or religious dogma or system. But when we attempt to investigate into the essential significance of Hindutva, we do not primarily—and certainly not mainly—concern ourselves with any particular theocratic or religious dogma or creed...'[4]

In other words, Hindutva is more than the Hindu religion, and as a political philosophy it does not confine itself to adherents of the Hindu faith. Despite this distinction, Hindutva would help achieve the political consolidation of the Hindu people, since Savarkar also argued that a Muslim or a Christian, even if born in India, could not claim allegiance to the three essentials of Hindutva: 'a common nation (*rashtra*), a common race (*jati*) and a common civilisation (*sanskriti*), as represented in a common history, common heroes, a common literature, a common art, a common law and a common jurisprudence, common fairs and festivals, rites and rituals, ceremonies and sacraments.'

Hindus, thus defined, constituted the Indian nation—a nation that had existed since antiquity, since Savarkar was explicitly rejecting the British view that India was just, in Churchill's notorious phrase, 'a geographical expression.... No more a single country than the Equator.' Savarkar's vision of Hindutva saw it as the animating principle of a 'Hindu Rashtra' (Hindu Nation) that extended across the entire Indian subcontinent, and was rooted in an undivided India ('*Akhand Bharat*') corresponding to the territorial aspirations of ancient dynasties like the Mauryas (320 BCE–180 BCE), who under Chandragupta and Ashoka had managed to knit most of the subcontinent under their territorial control. In the words of a later RSS publication, *Sri Guruji, the Man and his Mission*, 'It became evident that Hindus were the nation in Bharat and that Hindutva was Rashtriyatva [nationalism].'[5]

For Savarkar, Hinduness was synonymous with Indianness, properly understood. Savarkar's idea of Hindutva was so expansive that it covered everything that a scholar today would call 'Indic': 'Hindutva is not a word but a history. Not only the spiritual or religious history of our people as at times it is mistaken to be by being confounded with the other cognate term Hinduism, but a history in full... Hindutva embraces all the departments of thought and activity of the whole Being of our Hindu race.'[6]

In turn, the Hindu 'race' was inextricably bound to the idea of the nation. As Savarkar put it, 'We Hindus are bound together not only by the tie of the love we bear to a common fatherland and by the common blood that courses through our veins and keeps our hearts throbbing and our affections warm, but also by the tie of the common homage we pay to our great civilisation—our Hindu culture'. By definition, however, his idea of Hindutva, as mentioned above, excluded those whose ancestors came from elsewhere or whose holy lands lay outside India—thereby eliminating Muslim and Christians, India's two most significant minorities, from his frame of reference. What their place would be in Savarkar's Hindu Rashtra was not made explicitly clear, but the best they could hope for was a sort of second-class citizenship in which they could live in India only on sufferance.

In 1939 Savarkar wrote the foreword to a book by the Nazi sympathiser and European-born Hindu revivalist who called herself Savitri Devi. Savitri Devi (1905–1982), born Maximiani Portas of mixed Greek, French and English parentage, was a remarkable figure who, among other idiosyncratic beliefs, considered Adolf Hitler an avatar of Vishnu. Her book, prophetically titled *A Warning to the Hindus*, is a passionate polemic about the need for Hindu reassertion. Savitri Devi asserted that, 'Hinduism is the national religion of India, and there is no real India besides Hindu India'. Savarkar joined the author in arguing that:

> 'In all walks of life, for a long time, the Hindus have been fed on inertia-producing thoughts which disabled them to act energetically for any purpose in life, other than "moksha," that is to say escape from this world—where to? God knows. And this is one of the causes of the continuous enslavement of our Hindu Rashtra for centuries altogether'.[7]

Not for Savarkar the abstruse metaphysics of Advaita; what he and Savitri Devi were interested in was political power, here and now. For Savitri Devi, political power, defined as 'the power of law with organised military force' is 'everything in the world... We would like the Hindus to remember this, and to strive to acquire political power at any cost. Social reforms are necessary, not because they will bring more "humanity" among the Hindus, as many think, but because they will bring unity, that is to say power.'[8]

DEFINING NATIONHOOD: GOLWALKAR

This logic was taken even farther by M. S. Golwalkar (1906–1973), the *sarsangchalak* or head of the Rashtriya Swayamsevak Sangh (RSS) for three decades (1940–1973), who supplanted Savarkar as the principal ideologue of Hindu nationalism, notably in his 1939 screed *We, or Our Nationhood Defined*[9] and in the anthology of his writings and speeches, *Bunch of Thoughts*.[10] Golwalkar made it clear that India was the holy land of the Hindus. He writes: 'Hindusthan is the land of the Hindus and is the terra firma for the Hindu nation alone to flourish upon...'[11] According to him, India was a pristine Hindu country in ancient times,[12] a place of unparalleled glory destroyed in successive assaults by foreign invaders. He felt that a 'national regeneration' was necessary. He also contended that the national regeneration of this 'Hindu nation' (the 'motherland' for which the 'Hindu people' shed their blood)[13] could only come about through the revival of its Hinduness. Golwalkar rejected the concept of what he called 'territorial nationalism', the modern variant of nationalism which identified a state with its territory and bestowed equal rights of citizenship on all those who lived within it. That, to him, made no sense: a territory was not a nation, a people constituted a nation. Who were this people? In the Indian case, Hindus.[14] Golwalkar and the RSS became passionate advocates of 'cultural nationalism'.[15] This, of course, is directly opposed to the civic nationalism enshrined in the Constitution of India.

India's independence from colonial rule in 1947, Golwalkar argued, did not constitute real freedom because the new leaders held on to the 'perverted concept of nationalism' that located all who lived on India's territory as equal constituents of the nation. 'The concept of territorial nationalism,' he wrote, 'has verily emasculated our nation and what more can we expect of a body deprived of its vital energy? ...[and] so it is that we see today the germs of corruption, disintegration and dissipation eating into the vitals of our nation for having given up the natural living nationalism in the pursuit of an unnatural, unscientific and lifeless hybrid concept of territorial nationalism.'[16]

Golwalkar's *Bunch Of Thoughts* argues that territorial nationalism is a barbarism, since a nation is 'not a mere bundle of political and economic rights' but an embodiment of national culture—in India, 'ancient and sublime' Hinduism. In his tract, Golwalkar sneers at democracy—which he sees as alien to Hindu culture. He also writes approvingly of the Laws of Manu as the work of a 'great soul'; he talks of the high regard in which *Manu Smriti* is held around the world by referring to a statue in the Philippines bearing the inscription: 'The first, the greatest and wisest lawgiver of mankind'. (That Manu's legal prescription is condemned by many for its elitism and casteism, its gender prejudice, its implicitly authoritarian ethos and its disparagement of the lower castes never crosses Golwalkar's mind.) But in all fairness, Golwalkar was only echoing Nietzsche, who wrote of the *Manu Smriti*: 'This absolutely Aryan testimony, a priestly codex of morality based on the Vedas, of a presentation of caste and of ancient provenance not pessimistic even though priestly—completes my conceptions of religion in the most remarkable manner.'[17] For Golwalkar, therefore, salvation lies not in Indian democracy, but in the historian Manu S. Pillai's words, 'in embracing Hindu dharmocracy'.[18]

Pillai's phrase is not entirely tongue-in-cheek: Golwakar intends traditional Hindu practices to prevail in his Hindu Rashtra, including caste discrimination. 'We know as a matter of history,' he writes, 'that our north-western and north-eastern areas, where the influence of Buddhism had disrupted the caste system, fell an easy prey to the onslaught of Muslims.... But the areas of Delhi and Uttar Pradesh, which were considered to be very orthodox and rigid in caste restrictions, remained predominantly Hindu even after remaining the very citadels of Muslim power and fanaticism.'[19] So the more caste-ridden society was, the more robustly it resisted the encroachments of the foreign faiths that sought to erode it: to Golwalkar, 'the so-called "caste-ridden" Hindu Society has remained undying and inconquerable...(while) casteless societies crumbled to dust'.[20]

The alternative to territorial nationalism, to Golwalkar, was a nationalism based on race. In *We, or Our Nationhood Defined*, at the height of Hitler's rise, Golwalkar wrote: 'To keep up the purity of the Race and its culture, Germany shocked the world by her purging the country of the Semitic Races—the Jews. Race pride at its highest has been manifested here. Germany has also shown how well nigh impossible it is for Races and cultures, having differences going to the root, to be assimilated into one united whole, a good lesson for us in Hindustan to learn and profit by.'[21]

This marked an evolution from Savarkar's notion that saw Hindutva as principally a cultural identity and Hinduism as a part of a national Hindu culture. In an important respect, Golwalkar reversed Savarkar's logic: 'With us,' he wrote, 'culture is but a product of our all-comprehensive religion, a part of its body and not distinguishable from it.'[22] From Golwalkar onwards, Hindutva was seen as an ideology seeking to establish the hegemony of Hindus, Hindu values and the Hindu way of life in the political arrangements of India. In this he was building on Savarkar's derisive rejection of Gandhian 'universalism' and 'non-violence' which he considered delusionary opiates. Instead of Gandhi's moral lessons in favour of peace, Savarkar advocated the 'political virility'[23] of Hindutva, an idea which found full flower in Golwalkar.

Golwalkar made no bones about the principal targets of his race-hatred: 'Ever since that evil day, when Moslems first landed in Hindustan, right up to the present moment, the Hindu Nation has been gallantly fighting on to shake off the despoilers. The Race Spirit has been awakening'.[24] The association of Hindutva with an explicitly anti-Muslim agenda can be traced to its unambiguous avowal by Golwalkar. But 'race', fashionable though the term was when Golwakar wrote in the 1930s, especially in the context of Nazi ideology, was not an entirely accurate word for what he meant, not least since many, indeed most, of India's Muslims were descended from Hindu ancestors themselves and therefore were of the same race or ethnicity as the Hindus for whom Golwalkar was speaking.

According to the proponents of Hindutva, despite that common descent, Muslims had cut themselves off from Hindu culture: they prayed in Arabic, rather than the Sanskrit born on Indian soil, turned to a foreign city (Mecca) as their holiest of holies, and owed allegiance to a holy book, and beliefs spawned by it, that had no roots in the sacred land of India. Naipaul echoes this thought in his *Among the Believers*: 'It turns out now that the Arabs were the most successful imperialists of all time; since to be conquered by them (and then to be like them) is still, in the minds of the faithful, to be saved.'[25]

Golwalkar's answer was to seek the assimilation of Muslims and other minorities into the Hindu nationalist mainstream by forcing them to abandon these external allegiances (rather as the Jews were forced to adopt outward signs of adherence to Christianity during the Spanish Inquisition four and a half centuries earlier). The German notion of a volksgeist, a 'race spirit' to which everyone would have to conform, appealed strongly to Golwalkar. To remain in India, Muslims would have to submit themselves to Hindus. Recalling the parable of Muhammad going to the mountain, Golwalkar wrote: 'In the Indian situation, the Hindu is the mountain, and the Muslim population, Mohammed. I need not elaborate.'[26] A few paragraphs earlier I have quoted his approving words about Nazi theories of race. There is more in his writing that is even more chilling.

Golwalkar's hatred for non-Hindus was especially virulent when it came to Muslims and Christians; he regarded Parsis and Jews in India as model minorities who knew their place and did not ruffle any Hindu feathers. In his pungent view: '[H]ere was already a full-fledged ancient nation of the Hindus and the various communities which were living in the country were here either as guests, the Jews and Parsis, or as invaders, the Muslims and Christians.'[27] He added: 'They never faced the question how all such heterogenous groups could be called as children of the soil merely because, by an accident, they happened to reside in a common territory under the rule of a common enemy.'

Golwalkar strongly opposed all talk of a secular Indian state. As he wrote in *We, or Our Nationhood Defined*:

> 'There are only two courses open to these foreign elements', Golwalkar went on, 'either to merge themselves in the national race and adopt its culture or to live at its mercy so long as the national race may allow them to do so and quit the country at the sweet will of the national race. That is the only sound view on the minorities' problem... [The] foreign races in Hindusthan must either adopt the Hindu culture and language, must learn to respect and hold in reverence Hindu religion, must entertain no idea but those of the glori-

fication of the Hindu race and culture, i.e., of the Hindu nation and must lose their separate existence to merge in the Hindu race, or may stay in the country, wholly subordinated to the Hindu Nation, claiming nothing, deserving no privileges, far less any preferential treatment—not even citizen's rights.'[28]

Golwalkar acknowledged the reality of diversity within Hinduism, but argued that Hindus shared 'the same philosophy of life', 'the same goal' and 'the same holy samskaras',[29] which therefore formed a strong cultural and a civilisational basis for a nation. These values, aspirations and philosophy were not, however, in his view, shared by Muslims and Christians. Though the proponents of Hindutva would not welcome the comparison, Golwalkar's conception of Hindu India is not so very different from the prevailing ideology of a Muslim Pakistan.

While Hindutva has tended to reserve most of its virulence for Muslims, Golwalkar was openly suspicious of Christians too. In *Bunch of Thoughts* he describes how, though the Christians seemed 'quite harmless'[30] at a glance, with their missions, schools, and colleges, they were part of something more sinister. 'So long as the Christians here indulge in such activities and consider themselves as agents of the international movement for the spread of Christianity and refuse to offer their first loyalty to the land of their birth and behave as true children of the heritage and culture of their ancestors, they will remain here as hostiles and will have to be treated as such.'[31]

On the issue of these minorities, *Bunch of Thoughts* goes further than his earlier writings:

> 'We, in the Sangh, are Hindus to the core. That's why we have respect for all faiths and religious beliefs.... But the question before us now is, what is the attitude of those people who have been converted to Islam or Christianity? They are born in this land, no doubt. But are they true to its salt? Are they grateful towards this land which has brought them up? Do they feel that they are the children of this land and its tradition and that to serve it is their great good fortune? Do they feel it a duty to serve her? No! Together with the change in their faith, gone are the spirit of love and devotion for the nation.'[32]

These are sweeping generalisations that admit of no exception in Golwalkar's thinking:

> 'Whatever we believed in, the Muslim was wholly hostile to it. If we worship in the temple, he would desecrate it. If we carry on bhajans and car festivals, that would irritate him. If we worship [the] cow, he would like to eat it. If we glorify woman as a symbol of sacred motherhood, he would like to molest her.'

In a December 1947 speech, four months after Partition, Golwalkar, referring to Muslims, said that 'no power on earth' could keep Muslims in Hindustan. 'They should have to quit this country... If they were made to stay here the responsibility would be the Government's and the Hindu community would not be responsible. Mahatma Gandhi could not mislead them any longer. We have the means whereby [our] opponents could be immediately silenced'.[33]

Golwakar's alternative answer to this problem lay in reconversion. 'It is our duty,' Golwalkar offers, 'to call these our forlorn brothers, suffering under religious slavery for centuries, back to their ancestral home. As honest freedom-loving men, let them overthrow all signs of slavery and domination and follow the ancestral ways of devotion and national life'.[34] As Manu S. Pillai acidly observes, 'In other words, there is nothing a quiet *ghar wapsi* [reconversion to Hinduism] cannot solve when it comes to the building of a good dharmocracy.'[35]

The RSS's official understanding of Hindutva embraces this idea of Golwalkar's even today. In their reply to the tribunal constituted under the Unlawful Activities (Prevention) Act 1967 to hear a case on the RSS in 1993, the RSS made an official statement as follows:

> The term Hindu in the conviction as well as in the constitution of the RSS is a cultural and civilisational concept and not a political or religious term. The term as a cultural concept will include and did always include all including Sikhs, Buddhists, and Jains. The cultural nationality of India, in the conviction of the RSS, is Hindu and it was inclusive of all who are born and who have adopted Bharat as their Motherland, including Muslims, Christians and Parsis. The answer-

ing association submit that it is not just a matter of RSS conviction, but a fact borne out by history that the Muslims, Christians and Parsis too are Hindus by culture although as [adherents of different] religions they are not so.[36]

This statement, of course, elides the 'holy land' problem in Savarkar's famous tripartite formula: if you are a Muslim, Christian or Parsi, however 'Hindu' you may be culturally, India is not your holy land. Hindutva acolytes gloss over this contradiction by suggesting that the key lies in these minorities acknowledging their foundational Hindu-ness: if they see themselves as 'Muhammadan Hindus', 'Christian Hindus' and 'Parsi Hindus', India can accept them. Since few, if any, of the believers in those faiths are ready to see themselves in those terms, of course, it is logical to assume they remain unwelcome in Hindutva-led India.

It is striking how Hindutva's acolytes share so much formally with twentieth-century Muslim modernists in South Asia and the Middle East: their conception of the glorious past, their imagining of a fallen intermediary time (blamed on internal cultural failings and rapacious outsiders), their stilted conception of culture and cultural difference, their negative appraisal of 'Western' values and 'Westernisation', and their fervent desire for the political unity of a religious community as the essential requirement for the attainment or re-establishment of national glory. Golwalkar's views of nationalism continue to inspire his political followers nearly half a century after his death—except that, unlike when he expressed them, those who believe such things now hold power in India and are in a position to do something about them.

THE ADVENT OF THE BHARATIYA JANA SANGH AND DEEN DAYAL UPADHYAYA

It took a while to happen. While Savarkar and Golwalkar had attracted a lot of attention with their ideas in the 1920s and 1930s, the only political party willing to take them seriously was the Akhil Bharatiya Hindu Mahasabha, a fringe movement of which Savarkar became president in 1937. The Hindu Mahasabha fancied itself as a sort of Hindu answer to the Muslim League, but never enjoyed even a fraction of its support; indeed, the overwhelming majority of Hindu voters backed the secular Indian National Congress Party, rather than the party that claimed to be acting in the name of India's Hindus. The Mahasabha, however, openly advocated both 'Hindutva' and 'Hindu Rashtra', even as the Muslim League's call for Partition was tearing the country apart on communal lines. The Mahasabha's best-known leader, Syama Prasad Mookerjee, its president in 1944, was conscious of the limitations of Hindu nationalism as a political platform in such circumstances, and called for the membership of Hindu Mahasabha to be thrown open to all communities. Not surprisingly—since this would have vitiated the communal logic of the Mahasabha itself—his own members spurned his call, prompting Mookerjee to resign and to form a new political party in collaboration with the RSS. This was the Bharatiya Jana Sangh.

Mookerjee's choice of name for his new party was instructive. 'Bharatiya' literally meant 'Indian', 'Jana' the people, and 'Sangh,' in a genuflection to the RSS, which liked to refer to itself as 'the Sangh', stood for 'organisation'. Thus the Bharatiya Jana Sangh was the Indian People's Organisation. The Jana Sangh was openly viewed as a political emanation of the RSS, which had been banned after Mahatma Gandhi's assassination in 1948 and only allowed to resume functioning as a purely social and cultural, rather than political, association. The RSS could continue to advocate Hindu Samaj (Hindu society) but not a Hindu Rashtra—that would be a political objective which only a political party could pursue. And so a political party was born. The Bharatiya Jana Sangh was linked to the RSS, it was said, by an umbilical cord; its establishment of the Bharatiya Jana Sangh gave the RSS a political arm that would pursue Hindu interests within a national, as opposed to communal, framework. Hence 'Bharatiya' rather than 'Hindu'—but since Mookerjee subscribed to the Savarkar idea that all Indians, strictly speaking, were Hindus, there was no great contradiction there. To Mookerjee and his followers, Hinduism was a national identity rather than a communal one and the Bharatiya Jana Sangh in effect claimed the national mantle for its Hindutva agenda.

144

In the two and a half decades of its existence, the Bharatiya Jana Sangh impressed itself upon the nation's consciousness as a well-organised and effective opposition party with some able leaders, but it never came remotely close to power. Its best electoral performance was in 1967, when it won 35 seats in a right-of-centre 'Grand Alliance' with the liberal, pro-free enterprise Swatantra Party, which claimed 44—a total dwarfed by the 283 of the ruling Congress Party. This was the time when the concept of Hindutva received its fullest flowering under the leadership of party president Deen Dayal Upadhyaya, whose ideas, in particular his philosophy of Integral Humanism, I discuss below in some detail.

* * *

Pandit Deen Dayal Upadhyaya is undoubtedly the most significant ideologue of the contemporary Hindutva movement. Despite having served only one year (1967–1968) as president of the Bharatiya Jana Sangh, the precursor party of today's ruling BJP, before his life was prematurely cut short, Pandit Deen Dayal Upadhyaya (1916–1968) is enjoying something of a renaissance these days. The Narendra Modi government ruling India since 2014 swears by his life and work, and there has been a proliferation of seminars and conferences discussing and dissecting his philosophy of Integral Humanism. Numerous institutions have been named after him, from the Pandit Deendayal Upadhyaya Shekhawati University in Sikar (Rajasthan) to the Deen Dayal Upadhyaya Hospital, Delhi and the Pandit Deendayal Petroleum University, Gandhinagar, Gujarat. Millions of pounds of government funds have been spent on various schemes (*yojanas*) to perpetuate his name.[37] There are medical colleges, hospitals, parks and a flyover (in Bengaluru) that bear his name, not to mention the Pt. Deen Dayal Upadhyaya National Academy of Social Security, Janakpuri, Delhi. The Antyodaya scheme of service to the poorest of the poor is said by the government to have been inspired by him. The 'Make in India' scheme is dedicated to him, or more precisely, 'laid at his feet'.[38] The Mughalserai railway station, where he died in mysterious circumstances at the age of fifty-two, has been renamed for him. The Deen Dayal

Research Institute is reportedly 'a hub of frenetic activity', drowning under a 'flood of queries from government departments' trying to learn about Upadhyaya's ideas, which are now expected to animate their work.[39]

Upadhyaya's writings and speeches on the principles and policies of the Bharatiya Jana Sangh, his philosophy of 'Integral Humanism' and his vision for the rise of modern India, constitute the most comprehensive articulation of what might be described as a BJP ideology. The reverence in which he is held by those in power today and the near-deification of the man give him an intellectual status within the Hindutva movement second to none.

Upadhyaya saw his own thinking as flowing from that of Guru Golwalkar, the Sarsanghchalak of the RSS with whom he worked most closely. Golwalkar, in turn, was inspired by Vinayak ('Veer') Savarkar's ideology of Hindutva. But whereas Golwalkar, with his desire to learn from Nazi practices, was judged too extreme for most mainstream opinion, Upadhyaya, who couched his ideas in moderate language, enjoyed broader acceptability. Unlike many ideologues, Pandit Deen Dayal Upadhyaya was not just a theorist, but the leader of a growing political party and also its principal organiser. This created a curious paradox. As a political leader, it was imperative for him to respond to the day-to-day problems facing the party, critique government policies, issue and direct party propaganda, lead agitations, evolve the party's electoral strategy and negotiate coalitions. His philosophy was thus the animating spirit of a life of practical action. Upadhyaya's political role and values thus emerged from his philosophy, and the latter justified the former.

At the same time, the Jana Sangh of Upadhyaya's day was not a realistic contender for power. Upadhyaya thus saw himself in the longer term as a thinker whose role was, as one admirer put it, to project genuine nationalistic thought in the political sphere, well beyond the limited and short-term aim of the attainment of political office. One might even argue that had the prospects of power been more imminent, the president of the party might have spent his energies on more immediately attainable objectives, rather than abstract philosophical reflections divorced from his day-to-day tasks. It is possible to argue that the philosophy of Upadhyaya is the credo of man who does not believe he can ever have an opportunity to implement it.

But such a situation is in many ways preferable, because it means that the philosopher in question is not tailoring his thoughts to the expediencies of the political moment. In keeping with his circumstances, Deen Dayal Upadhyaya could afford the luxury—unavailable, say, to any of his counterparts in the ruling party—to develop his theoretical ideas in their pure and unalloyed form. Thus it is said by his admirers that Upadhyaya saw his political party as merely a vehicle to build a nation. Much of his philosophical thinking, therefore, focused on what constituted the Indian nation, and why, in his view, it had failed to become strong and unified. Upadhyaya saw this failure in moral terms—political corruption, the general public's lack of any urge to make India strong and prosperous, a 'degeneration' of society and the fading away of the idealism that had inspired the struggle for freedom. Indians had misled themselves into equating freedom with the mere overthrow of foreign rule; this negative view overlooked the need for something far more positive, a genuine and patriotic love for the motherland.

Like Savarkar and Golwalkar, Upadhyaya too deplored the concept of territorial nationalism, which saw the Indian nation as being formed of all the peoples who reside in this land. In his view reducing the idea of India to a territory and to everyone living in that space elided fundamental questions that needed to be answered:

Whose nation is this? What is freedom for?
What kind of life do we want to develop here?
What set of values are we going to accept?
What does the concept of nationhood really signify?

What does the concept of nationhood really signify? A territory and its inhabitants, as Westernised Indians seemed to believe, would embrace Hindus, Muslims, Christians and others under a common nationhood to resist British rule. This was a fallacy, according to Upadhyaya. 'A nation is not a mere geographical unit. The primary need of nationalism is the feeling of boundless dedication in the hearts of the people for their land. Our feeling for the motherland has a basis: our long, continuous habitation in the same land creates, by association, a sense of "my-ness".'[40]

The disappearance of the foreign power, Upadhyaya believed, had left a vacuum before a people accustomed to the 'negative patriotism' of anti-colonialism. Nationalism had to consist of far more than the mere rejection of foreign rule. Upadhyaya spurned the Western idea that nationalism as a political force was a product of the French Revolution and the situation created by it; he abjured the notion that a nation is made up of various constituent elements that can be itemised, such as a common race, religion, land, traditions, shared experience of calamities, means of transport, common political administration and so on. Such ideas, he believed, missed the essential ethos of nationalism— love for the motherland.

Since love for the motherland had never been inculcated in its inhabitants, their lives in independent India were now centred on money and greed—*artha* and *kama* in the classic quartet of human aspirations enumerated in the *Purusharthas*, at the expense of *dharma* and *moksha*. This modern materialism Upadhyaya saw as a major societal flaw. As he wrote in his book, *Rashtra Jeevan Ki Disha*:[41]

> All our ailments in today's political life have their origin in our avarice. A race for rights has banished the noble idea of service. Undue emphasis on the economic aspect of life has generated a number of lapses... Instead of character, quality and merit, wealth has become the measuring rod of individual prestige. This is a morbid situation... It must be our general approach to look upon money only as a means towards the satisfaction of our everyday needs: not an end in itself...this transformation in our attitude can be brought about only on the basis of the ideals of Indian culture.[42]

Dazzled by the material advances made by the so-called developed countries, Upadhyaya argued, India too had taken to aping the foreigners under the rubric of 'Five-Year Plans' and development projects. India had written a Constitution imitative of the West, divorced from any real connection to our mode of life and from authentically Indian ideas about the relationship between the individual and society. (In this he was echoing Golwalkar, who had lamented that our 'cumbersome' Constitution[43] was all the more deficient for incorporating 'absolutely nothing' from the *Manusmriti*). Upadhyaya thus felt the need for a Hindu political philosophy befitting an ancient nation like Bharat. This would have to be based on a positive concept of patriotism and a comprehensive vision of the nation as a complete entity—its security, its unity, its growth and development, the welfare of its entire populace and the full development of every individual—based on its inherent character, culture, spiritual underpinnings and permanent values that have, as he saw them, stood the test of time.

For Upadhyaya, India had a special personality distinct from that of other nations; it had an ethos of its own. Only a national philosophy that reflected this could be successful; only an authentic Indian approach would ensure happiness for Indians. Upadhyaya was convinced that independent India could not rely upon Western concepts like individualism, democracy, socialism, communism or capitalism; it had to reject these formulae and find its own approach. Unfortunately, in his view, India's polity after Independence had been built upon these superficial and feeble Western foundations rather than authentic Hindu ones.

To Upadhyaya, Western thought was predicated on ideas of conflict: it presumed a conflict between individual and society, between ruler and ruled, between the power of clergy and temporal power, between haves and have-nots. Indian thinking, on the other hand, laid emphasis on cooperation and synthesis, not conflict. But Upadhyaya went further in his exegesis. To the Western mind, he argued, the main theme of this conflict was over rights: rights of the individual and the groups he represented. This was where Hinduism was different. To Upadhyaya, the Bharatiya ethos emphasised duties, not rights; it required coordination and understanding, not conflict and hatred. All India needed to do, Upadhyaya averred, was to 'turn the searchlight inwards' and base its thinking on 'self-revelation', just as the Hindu seeker looked within himself for self-realisation. India's polity had to be anchored in the traditions and ethos of India's own ancient Hindu culture.

As we have seen, Upadhyaya was clear that reducing the Indian national idea to a territory and the people on it was fallacious. It was this sort of thinking, he argued sternly, that had led the nationalist movement, from the Khilafat agitation onwards, to turn towards a policy of appeasement of the Muslim community, a policy in turn sought to be justified by the need to forge a united front against the British. The RSS's founder leader, Dr K. A. Hedgewar (whose Marathi biography Upadhyaya translated) had pointed to the 'ideological confusion' this approach created. Muslim communalism, in his and Upadhyaya's view, had become more prominent and aggressive, while Congress leaders bent over backwards more and more to accommodate them.

The Partition of 1947 was undoubtedly a defeat for those who had wanted to preserve a united India, but it was not a failure of India's unity as much as it was the defeat of misconceived utopian efforts to embrace non-Hindus made in the name of national unity. It was not that our objective was wrong, in Upadhyaya's view; rather the methods to preserve India's unity through minority appeasement were wrong and so we were defeated.

'Every nation,' Upadhyaya said, 'wants to live a happy and prosperous life according to its own nature and that is the motive behind its intense desire for freedom. The nation that tries to follow a path of thought and action discordant with its own nature, meets with disaster. This is why our nation has been caught up in a whirlpool of difficulties.' India could and should contribute to the world 'in consonance with our culture and traditions.'[44]

That culture was, of course, Hindu. In India, 'there exists only one culture... There are no separate cultures here for Muslims and Christians.' Every community, therefore, including Muslims and Christians, 'must identify themselves with the age-long national cultural stream that was Hindu culture in this country.' His logic was that 'unless all people become part of the same cultural stream, national unity or integration is impossible. If we want to preserve Indian nationalism, this is the only way.' To him, 'the national cultural stream would continue to remain one and those who cannot identify themselves with it would not be considered nationals.'

To Upadhyaya, the national culture to which he was referring had to be Hindu; it explicitly could not be Muslim. 'Mecca, Medina, Hassan and Hussain, Sohrab and Rustom and Bulbul may be very significant in their own ways but they do not form a part of Indian national life and stream of Indian culture. How can those who are emotionally associated with these and look upon [the] Rama and Krishna tradition as alien be described as nationals? We see that the moment anybody embraces Islam, an effort is made to cut him off from the entire tradition of this country and connect him to the alien tradition.'[45]

Muslims, said Upadhyaya, even related differently to India's past: 'Some events involve triumph, some our humiliation. The memories of our glorious deeds make us proud; ignominies make us hang our heads in shame.'[46] But Hindus saw such historical events differently from Muslims.

> 'Aggressions by Mohammed Ghori or Mahmood Ghazni naturally fill us with agony. We develop a feeling of attachment to Prithviraj and other patriots. If instead, any person feels pride for the aggressors and no love for the Motherland, he can lay no claim to patriotism. The memory of Rana Pratap, Chhatrapati Shivaji or Guru Gobind Singh makes us bow down our heads with respect and devotion. On the other hand, the names of Aurangzeb, Alauddin, Clive or Dalhousie, fill us with anger that is natural towards foreign aggressors.'[47]

Only Hindu society, Upadhyaya underscored, felt this way about its heroes, supporting Rana Pratap over Akbar; therefore there was really no ground for doubt that Indian nationalism is Hindu nationalism.

Upadhyaya's conclusion was blunt: Muslims sought 'to destroy the values of Indian culture, its ideals, national heroes, traditions, places of devotion and worship', and therefore 'can never become an indivisible part of this country.' In Upadhayaya's vision, the inherent consciousness of unity, identical ties of history and tradition, relations of affinity between the land and the people and shared aspirations and hopes, made Hindustan a nation of Hindus. 'We shall have to concede that our nationality is none other than Hindu nationality. If any outsider comes into this country he shall have to move in step and adjust himself with Hindu nationality.'

But Upadhyaya did not adopt his mentor Golwalkar's ideas about dealing with India's Muslims as Hitler had dealt with the Jews. 'No sensible man will say that six crores of Muslims should be eradicated or thrown out of India,' he admitted in an article titled 'Akhand Bharat: Objectives and Means'.[48] '[B]ut then they will have to identify themselves completely with Indian life.' Muslims had to be accommodated within the Indian reality, but on what basis? 'This unity...can be established only among homogeneous cultures, not among the contrary ones. A preparation of various cereals and pulses mixed together can be prepared: but if sand particles find their way into it, the whole food is spoilt', he explained.[49] The way to eliminate these 'sand particles' was to 'purify' or 'nationalise Muslims'—to 'make Muslims proper Indians'. The Congress had wrongly tried to forge Hindu-Muslim unity against the British, but 'unless all people become part of the same cultural stream, national unity or integration is impossible... A situation will have to be created in which political aspirations of Islam in India will be rooted out. Then and then alone can a longing for cultural unity take root.'[50]

In demanding of Muslims and other minorities this subordination to, and total identification with, a Hindu Rashtra, Upadhyaya—while his reasons differed in both premise and approach—arrived at the same place as Savarkar and Golwalkar. But Upadhyaya went a few steps beyond them in developing more fully the concept of what a Hindu Rashtra might consist of.

In building his case for a Hindu Rashtra, Upadhyaya specifically disavowed the existing Constitution of India (which makes all the more curious the enthusiastic zeal with which his devotees today, from Prime Minister Modi on down, swear by it and celebrate every milestone in its adoption). As Upadhyaya put it in *Rashtra Jeevan Ki Disha*: 'We became free in 1947. The English quit India. We felt what was considered to be the greatest obstacle in the path of our effort of nation building was removed and were all of a sudden faced with the problem as to what the significance of this hard-earned independence was.'

Indian leaders tried to resolve this problem in the drafting of a Constitution. But in Upadhyaya's view, their failure to conceive properly of the nation led them into error. 'We aped the foreigners to such an extent that we failed to see that our inherent national ideals and traditions should be reflected in our Constitution. We satisfied ourselves with making a patchwork of theories and principles enunciated by foreign countries... The result was that our national culture and traditions were never reflected in these ideologies borrowed from elsewhere and so they utterly failed to touch the chords of our national being.'

Having rejected its premise, Upadhyaya was scathing about the Constitution's drafting and adoption: a nation, he argued, 'is not like a club which can be started or dissolved. A nation is not created by some crores of people passing a resolution and defining a common code of behaviour binding on all its members. A certain mass of people emerges with an inherent motivation. It is,' he added, using a Hindu analogy, 'like the soul adopting the medium of the body.'[51]

In the classic Hindu formula, a king must function according to his *raj dharma,* or code of governance, which is not defined by him, but is laid down for him by selfless unattached *rishis.* In contemporary language, Upadhyaya saw a Hindu king almost as one might a chief executive receiving his authority from the shareholders (in this case, the people), mediated through the vision of the board (in this case, the wisdom of the sages). Observing that the Constitution requires that any person holding a position of power has to take a pledge of loyalty to that Constitution, Upadhyaya asks three questions: were the people who framed the Constitution endowed with qualities of selflessness, an intense desire for public service and a deep knowledge of the rules of *dharma* as the rishis were? Or did they formulate this *Smriti* of a free India under the influence of the unsteady circumstances prevailing at the time? Did these people possess originality of thought or did they have a tendency to primarily imitate others?

Upadhyaya's implicit answers to these questions were in the negative: the Constitution-makers were not figures imbued with selflessness and *dharma,* they were overly in thrall to the turbulent politics of that era, and their minds had been colonised by Western ideas. The founding fathers of the Republic of India were largely Anglophile Indians schooled in Western systems of thought; their work revealed no Indianness, no *Bharatiyata*. The Constitution, therefore, was to him a flawed document, one incapable of guiding India towards the path of *raj dharma*. In fact it condemned Hindus to slavery: 'Self-rule and independence are considered to be synonyms. A deeper thinking will bring home to us the fact that even in a free country, the nation can remain in slavery.' The Hindu nation had been enslaved by inappropriate Westernisation.

Even the language in which the Constitution had been drafted betrayed this reality: 'If the original draft of the Constitution had been in Hindi or in any other Indian language', he felt, the 'un-Indian element' would not have been as dominant. But his concerns, of course, went well beyond language. The Constitution's core conception of the nation, in his view, was fundamentally not Indian at all: 'in the constitution, as it is now, it is the sentiments of the English that have found better expression than those of the Indians,' observed Upadhyaya. 'Thus, our constitution, like an English child born in India, has become Anglo-Indian in character, instead of purely Indian.'[52]

Upadhyaya thus questioned the very legitimacy of the Constitution and not just the process by which it was created. For Upadhyaya, the absence of the Hindu Rashtra idea in the Constitution was unacceptable. For him *dharma* had to be the central idea behind governance and nation-building. He categorically repudiated the secularists' view that *dharma* is an entirely personal matter, that it had nothing to do with society or nation. On the contrary, Upadhyaya argued that there is undoubtedly a supreme purpose to life, which transcended all differences and peculiarities of caste, sect, or language. This purpose is not a worldly one—it does not consist of seeking to erect a huge political empire or to dominate the world militarily. Indeed, militarism and temporal power, Upadhyaya wrote, were not a Hindu preoccupation. Hindus had never shed the blood of other peoples or perpetrated atrocities on other countries as Alexander, Genghis Khan, Mahmud of Ghazni—non-Hindu conquerors all—had done. Hindus had, instead, always given a warm welcome and shelter to refugee groups like the

Parsis and the Jews, who had become the victims of aggression and atrocities elsewhere and had fled to India.

In keeping with his distaste for foreign concepts and terms, Upadhyaya explicated his beliefs through the use of Sanskrit terms to which he ascribed specific contemporary meanings. A favourite word of Upadhyaya's is 'chiti', which he labels the 'soul power' of a nation. He describes this soul power through a homely analogy: a barber told his customer that his razor was sixty years old, and had been used by his father. Upon further scrutiny, the customer noticed that over the years the handle and blade had been replaced many times, but the barber still claimed that the razor was the same as used by his father. It was a point of pride and prestige for him: the essence of the razor was unchanged even if its physical trappings had been altered over the years. Every nation also had such an identity that did not change with circumstances and temporal alterations. Sadly, modern India—the democratic republic that had emerged under the Constitution—had no sense of its chiti.

One example of this was in the country's constitutional structure. Upadhyaya saw the seeds of division, for instance, even in the Constitution's decision to rename the provinces as 'states' as the Americans did; this reduced India to a federation of states, a dangerously divisive concept in his view. Upadhyaya acknowledged that, unlike the United States, every Indian state did not have its own constitution and that there was only one citizenship for the entire country, but he felt the formulation envisaged in the Constitution diluted the sacred idea of a unified Bharatvarsha (Indian sub-continent). The Constitution should have spoken of a unitary state rather than a union of states; the soul of Bharat was missing. He seemed unconscious of the argument that it was precisely because of these states and their linguistic basis that unity was achieved, for India was able to accommodate all its diversities and give them political expression without losing the bigger cause of united nationhood. Surely this was a way of preserving, not diluting, Bharat's chiti? Accompanying chiti is another force that Upadhyaya called 'virat shakti', literally immense strength or power, but more precisely 'a scientific term,' in his words, 'with a definite connotation. So long as the *chiti* is throbbing and pure, the Nation continues to prosper.' It is the spirit of *chiti* that creates *virat shakti*, the organised and unified fighting strength that protects the nation from aggression and dissension. While *chiti* is the soul of a nation, *virat shakti* is its life force. Of course, neither idea is even implicitly present in India's Constitution, underscoring, for Upadhyaya, its deeply flawed nature.

Upadhyaya worried that India's constitutional system had been created in negation of its true inherent national spirit and that if the modern Indian nation continued in this way, Hindu civilisation would perish. This is what had happened, after all, to Greece and Egypt, whose modern incarnations bore no relationship to the ancient civilisations from which they claimed descent. The same stock of people might be living in those countries, but they bore no resemblance to their glorious past civilisations or forebears. Indeed, the essence of their society, its identity, had changed. This was the fate that Upadhyaya feared would befall India if it continued down the secular Westernised path charted for it in its Constitution: it would lose its core identity (which lay in the form of its *chiti*) and in effect become something other than the continuing Bharatiya civilisation that could trace its origins back to the mists of time.

Deen Dayal Upadhyaya, contra Savarkar and Golwalkar, accepted that the India of which he was writing had to accommodate its Muslims and Christians too. He rejected the notion that the Hindu Rashtra would have to mean 'a theocratic State propagating the Hindu religion'. Upadhyaya was conscious that his critics associated the very establishment of such a Hindu state with a revival of the ritualism associated with the Hindu religion, notions of casteism and inflexible social hierarchy, and the return of discrimination and social inequality. No, he insisted: his Hindu Rashtra was not based on hatred against any community, nor was it reactionary. Rather, his Hinduism would be inclusive.

As a Hindu, Upadhyaya averred that he was not opposed to the Muslim and Christian modes of worship; indeed he never criticised the Prophets of either faith. He believed that how to worship God, and which God to worship, was each person's personal choice; the state had no role in such considerations. His quarrel, he explained, was not with any sect or mode of worship: it was purely political.

Upadhyaya said that he respected other religions, while arguing that the problem of Muslims and Christians was not religious. Gandhiji had tried religious syncretism, singing bhajans to the effect that Ishwar and Allah were the same, but political unity between the two communities had not followed. The issue therefore was one of political commitment to the country and its values, not with the practice of religious faith or with the goodness of any individual.

Every society, after all, has good and bad people. Upadhyaya reminded his listeners that Muslim generals had fought in the armies of Shivaji and the Peshwas. He had high praise for Muslim patriots among his contemporaries, singling out as examples Mohammed Currim Chagla, the highly cosmopolitan, secular jurist and diplomat, Hamid Dalwai, a crusader for reform within the Muslim community and the revolutionary Ashfaqulla Khan. But these men, Upadhyaya said, were individuals; their personal behaviour did not warrant any conclusions about the mind and attitudes of the Muslim masses. If all the people in the Muslim community were like Chagla, Upadhyaya once opined, then 'there would be no problem whatsoever'. But they were not, and quoting a few rare examples of good persons would not solve the problem.

This distinction between 'a few good Muslims' and a problematic 'Muslim community' was central to Upadhyaya's misconception of Muslims in India. He assumed a monolithic 'Muslim community' when in fact Muslim practices across the country were also hugely diverse and a pan-Indian Muslim identity of the kind he suggests did not exist. Still, in making these points, however tokenistically, Upadhyaya was undoubtedly going beyond the exclusively Hindu Rashtra advocated by the earlier Hindutva ideologues. He was willing to acknowledge that 'the inhabitants of this country included Hindus, Muslims, Christians, Parsis and others'. But he saw communal unrest in terms of the aspirations of various communities to establish their political domination in particular geographical areas, just as Jinnah had led the Muslims to the creation of a separate state hostile to India and venomous in its denial of India's historical nationalism. To fulfil these aspirations, Upadhyaya argued, each community sought an increase in its numerical strength to strengthen its hands. This is why these communities behaved as they did—Muslims rejected family planning and monogamy, while Christians, supported by foreign agencies and news media, carried on systematic conversion campaigns. Christian missionaries had undoubtedly, Upadhyaya wrote, made a determined effort, under the patronage of the British imperialist government, to wean away Hindus from their traditional culture, but their attempts at conversion were not as fanatical or violent as those of the Muslims. Still, such practices had to stop.

These problems could be contained if a Hindu Rashtra were established.

The critics of Hindu Rashtra, Upadhyaya argued, found that the term was inexpedient for them in the country's competitive politics: they were afraid of losing millions of Christian and Muslim voters. Their misconception was that the use of the term 'Hindu Rashtra' excluded Muslim and Christian communities. If both these communities became one with the national cultural mainstream—without any change in their modes of worship—they would be welcome in the new India. All they had to do was to own up to the ancient traditions of India, to look upon Hindu national heroes as their national heroes, and to develop devotion for Bharat Mata. Then they would be fully accepted as nationals of the Hindu Rashtra.

In affirming this view of India's political identity, Upadhyaya was in effect returning to the Savarkar-Golwalkar home base: his political inclusiveness was illusory, for the terms in which it was formulated, despite the seeming openness to other forms of religious worship, left no room for anything but submission to Hindu dominance. However, to be fair, in other aspects of his political philosophy, especially in relation to the economic needs of the underclasses, Upadhyaya demonstrated a more substantive inclusiveness.

Rather like Gandhi, Upadhyaya believed in *swaraj* ('self-governance'), visualising for India a decentralised polity and self-reliant economy centered on its villages. But there was a more profound consequence of this approach. He eschewed the label of socialism, but expelled seven of the nine MLAs his Jan Sangh party had in Rajasthan for opposing the Zamindari (big landowner) Abolition Act piloted by the Congress to cut large landholdings down to size in the name of socialism. Individual freedom in a democratic system, he argued, enabled the rich to monopolise production, gain economic power and influence government machinery. Upadhyaya deplored the fact that Indian villagers had lost their jobs to large factories. Socialism, he said, was an understandable response to the exploitation of the masses in the industrial age.

Still, he considered himself a political opponent of the socialists. Both socialism and capitalism, Upadhyaya argued, concentrated their attention on man's material aspirations and on the fulfilment of his gross desires. Both had implicit faith in modern science and technological progress. To Upadhyaya, the nature of production had come to be determined not by the needs or the welfare of human beings but by the nature and demands of machines. He wanted modern technology to be adapted to suit Indian requirements. In a centralised system of production, whether capitalist or socialist, whether under individual or state control, man's individuality is lost and he becomes a mere cog in the machine. Instead of bringing about human development by striking a balance between the material and spiritual needs, both systems have only created conflict. The answer lay in focusing on the human personality as a whole, and in creating a system that balanced competition with cooperation and harmonised material progress with spiritual advancement. This Upadhyaya dubbed 'Integral Humanism' (in contrast, it is suggested, with the former communist leader M. N. Roy's theory of 'Radical Humanism', but also, I imagine, borrowing from Sri Aurobindo's 'Integral Yoga').

The philosophy of Integral Humanism advocated the simultaneous and integrated functioning of the body, mind, intellect and soul of each human being. The philosophy of Integral Humanism was a synthesis of the material and the spiritual, the individual and the collective. It answered what Upadhyaya saw as the urgent need in India for a 'fresh breeze'.

He adumbrated this philosophy to some 500 party workers in 1964, developed it into an expanded version at the Jana Sangh party's plenary session in 1965, and expounded it finally and fully in the form of four lectures in Bombay, titled 'Integral Humanism'. The impact was strong, and lasting: Upadhyaya's Integral Humanism was adopted by the Jana Sangh as its official doctrine and has subsequently been inherited by the BJP, whose leaders treat it with the reverence a Lutheran accords to those famous theses nailed to the cathedral door.

Upadhyaya believed that humanity, in all its infinite diversity, had a common ethos or soul, which the ancient Hindu texts defined as *atman*. The apparent diversity is superficial; the essential unity is profound. This is the idea of Ekatmata or the unifying soul that pervades the world.

Man is a conglomerate of body, mind, intellect and soul: all four had to develop and thrive for society to progress. While material development was necessary, spiritual development was also indispensable. This was why Bharatiya culture had placed four objectives, *Purusharthas*, before every individual, which each of us was to pursue. The fulfilment of these goals occurred in society, since Ekatmata ensured that individual and society are mutually complementary. The desire for the welfare of humanity comes from that consciousness of unity. When an individual acts in the awareness that he and society are one *atman*, his actions will be conducive to the common good.

Systems that regard an individual as self-centered are defective, he argued, because they fail to take this into account. The ideal man, to Upadhyaya, views life through the four *Purusharthas* and works for their fulfilment; if everyone did so, in keeping with Bharatiya Advaita philosophy, whereby the good of the individual would coincide with the good of society, internal contradictions to achieve these ideals would be replaced by cooperation and compatibility. (This conviction required a leap of faith: the idea that the individual pursuing *artha* (material prosperity), for instance, would always do so selflessly in ways that would serve society collectively, did not seem grounded in practical experience.) Upadhyaya dissected what he saw as the failings of other prevailing systems before affirming the integral humanism of Bharatiya culture, which provided a unified view of the universe. The balanced pursuit of the *Purusharthas* would ensure that happiness was pursued across all four—man would not just gratify his senses but also seek mental, intellectual and spiritual happiness. Upadhyaya laid the greatest emphasis on the happiness of the soul: all other kinds of happiness, he believed, are derived from union with the soul.

Thus Upadhyaya took a stern view of those who saw *artha* as an end in itself. An excessive attachment to affluence, he felt, reduces man to a Mammon-worshipper who loses all sense of duty to his society, country and *dharma*. Similarly *kama* cannot be reduced to carnal pleasures at the expense of other priorities. *Dharma* is key since it ensures the maintenance and development of the people in harmony with the progress of society. *Dharma* went beyond the literal concept of religion and was not merely for Hindus: indeed, all places of worship, whether temples, churches, or mosques, should instil in the populace the practice of *dharma*.

All four Purusharthas are co-dependent, and together form a path to *moksha*. If a man is properly assembled as a function of the four Purusharthas, so will society be successfully constructed. When an individual starts on the path of fulfilling his *Purusharthas*, he comes into contact with a larger group of people, develops the willingness to work for others, and experiences shared joy and mutual understanding. Families, communities and nations are born of this. But the excessive individual freedom of the capitalist West and the collectivisation of the communist East had eroded this consciousness, which was now under threat in India.

For Upadhyaya, the Western theory of the social contract had to be rejected, for society is not a club that individuals can seek membership in. 'Society,' Upadhyaya writes (in terms similar to his conception of a nation), 'is not a institution created by individuals coming together. A society is born.... [T]he relation of a society to its individuals is the same as that of an organism and its limbs, or that of a tree and its branches, leaves and flowers. The question of who is more important of the two, society or individual, is not worth considering.'[53] In Bharatiya culture, we can neither ignore the individual nor lose sight of society's interests.

Society is a living organism, and has its own mind, intellect, and soul. Thus, it must have its own *Purusharthas*. The Samashti Dharma (*dharma* of society) embraces all that helps sustain the individual and

161

the society. When applied to Bharat, it involves guarding the bonds of affinity to the motherland—an amalgam of common history, culture, clothing, and creed. The Artha Purushartha of society should be against *prabhav*, social bifurcations through granting high social status to the rich, as well as against *abhav*, or dependence on other nations (thus self-reliance and egalitarianism are vital). The Kama Purushartha of society embodies the nation's desires, such as the restoration of an undivided Bharat, or the expulsion of China from Indian territory, and the protection and spread of Indian culture. The Moksha Purushartha of society would imply freedom from foreign domination, through cultural, economic and political freedom. This would make India a well-organised, powerful, and wealthy Hindu nation, based on Hindu values of non-violence, literature, and culture.

The Purusharthas are not just objectives, but constitute bonds between the individual and society, which are connected by education, work, enjoyment and *yajna* or sacrifice. A man's *yajna* requires that the work should not be done for himself, but for society; thus a farmer grows corn not just for himself but for society, and work done with a sense of duty and sacrifice becomes beneficial to society.

Society has obligations to the individual too. If society fails to provide an individual with a good education, and he or she is unable to get an adequate job to sustain himself, society has failed him. However, if after receiving a good education, the individual does not work for society, he would have neglected Samashti Dharma, the *dharma* of society, and been morally degraded. Society and the individual are therefore complementary, and stand together by following *dharma*. When this does not happen and the underlying unity is lost, conflicts arise between privileged castes and Untouchables, industrialists and workers and so on.

The greatest blunder our politicians make, Upadhyaya argued, is their assumption of the existence of inherently and basically different classes—social, political, linguistic—with different interests. The truth is Bharat is one country; its subjects are one and have to live as one people. *Antodaya*, service of the poorest and least fortunate in society, was a Hindu obligation. Minority appeasement (and for that matter class distinctions) has no place in such a vision.

Nor did Upadhyaya shy away from facing the challenge of Varna Vyavastha, which he translates not as the caste system but as the class system. Upadhyaya opposed both those who believed that Varna Vyavastha is God-made—that people are born into castes on the basis of their past lives—and those who pretend to use ideological opposition to caste to garner political power. Upadhyaya asserted that Varna Vyavastha was introduced to fulfil the needs of society, by requiring each individual to do what he can do best. In the past, the valiant came forward for defence, the studious for advanced knowledge and to teach: there was no superiority and inferiority in the system, merely capability. Varna Vyavastha was based on the view that a society is an organic whole; its purpose was to bring physical and spiritual happiness within everybody's reach.

Upadhyaya's philosophy did not stop there, but extended from Samashti to Parameshthi (society to God). Bharatiya culture, after all, does not end with humanity, but includes all naturally occurring things in creation—flora, fauna, air, water, sunlight, animals, rivers, planets. The Bharatiya Advaita philosophy begins at the family, encompassing humanity, the animal world, plant life, the inanimate world, and stops at nothing short of the Universe. Thus the philosophy of Integral Humanism envisages, in the words of an admirer, 'an ennobling expanse of human consciousness'.

Unlike Western social and political theories, Upadhyaya stressed, Integral Humanism did not emerge as a reaction to any particular circumstance and was based on 'positive' thinking. 'If by nature man is such that he does not mind fighting with others to enrich himself at the cost of others, then it is impossible to teach him to love others and live for them'.[54] But, in the Indian context of Bharatiya Advaita, it was clear that Integral Humanism was the only way forward. Upadhyaya advocated national reconstruction on the basis of this philosophy. However, the duty of Indians was not only to protect their culture, but to make it dynamic and efficient. 'If we march ahead,' Upadhyaya concluded, 'we will be able to place before the world ideals like nationalism, democracy, equality and world-amity in a balanced and integral form, along with permanent values in Bharatiya culture.'

When Deen Dayal Upadhyaya was expounding his political philosophy, he could not have foreseen the day that a political party claiming to be working in his name would govern with a crushing parliamentary majority. To what extent can they be said to have put his beliefs into practice?

The proliferation of Deen Dayal Upadhyaya institutions and schemes is misleading. The prophet of the BJP has so far been honoured in lip-service rather than literally.

In some senses, today's BJP leaders seem closer in spirit and conviction to the Hindu Rashtra of Savarkar and Golwalkar than to that of Upadhyaya. Not for them the partial generosity of acknowledging the place and role of the Muslims and Christians in the country; these are less tolerant men and women (one of the latter, after all, a Minister in the Modi government, divided the nation into Ramzaade, believers in Rama, and Haramzaade, bastards).[55] Where Deen Dayal harked back to ancient India's generosity in offering asylum to Parsis and Jews,[56] today's BJP government announces its determination to expel Rohingya Muslim asylum-seekers[57] because they happen to be Muslim, and therefore ipso facto are assumed to constitute a threat to India's security. Where Upadhyaya denounced materialism and embodied the virtues of a simple village life, preached the abolition of large landholdings and spoke up for the humble peasant, his followers in power swear by GDP growth and fiscal balance, subsidise the multi-billion pound ventures of capitalist cronies, sport imported designer sunglasses, wield Mont Blanc pens and wear the highest-quality tailored linens. Their slogans are not about the poor in India's villages, nor about the soul-force that animates this ancient civilisation, but about 'ease of doing business' and 'start-up India'. Where Upadhyaya deplored materialism and extolled self-reliance, the men ruling in his name exalt figures of GDP growth and clamour for Foreign Direct Investment; his injunctions against an excessive attachment to affluence and *prabhav* (or socio-economic distinctions) are ignored by rulers who crave the support of billionaires.

Upadhyaya believed that after Independence India lost its idealism, because by failing to create a Hindu Rashtra, it never recognised one grand uniting force to hold Indians together. It could be argued that for all its claims of supplying this force, Hindutva actually works by replacing hatred for the British with hatred for a minority—a formula that will result in division and destruction, not unity. I have often argued that we are all minorities in India, given our divisions of language, region, caste and cultural practices. Recognising and managing that diversity is a far better way of promoting unity than imposing one view on the rest—a method that will lead not back to a golden age but to certain disaster.

THE BJP AND HINDUTVA

Following Upadhyaya's death and its rout in the elections of 1971, the Bharatiya Jana Sangh merged in 1977 into the Janata Party, which was born from the resistance of all Opposition parties to Prime Minister Indira Gandhi's Emergency. But when the Janata Party won the national elections which followed, its internal contradictions soon surfaced. Foremost among these was the 'dual membership' issue, with many Janata Party members objecting to the continued involvement with the RSS of the former Bharatiya Jana Sangh politicians. The Janata Party split over RSS influence on its Sanghi elements, and the Bharatiya Jana Sangh members reconstituted themselves as the Bharatiya Janata Party (BJP) in 1980, vowing allegiance to 'Gandhian socialism' in an attempt to make themselves more appealing to the mainstream.

The experiment with moderate political messaging failed: the BJP won just two seats in India's 545-member Lok Sabha in 1984. Disillusioned with this unsuccessful attempt at seeking political respectability by tempering its core beliefs, the BJP remade itself into an explicitly Hindu party, stirring up Hindu sentiment.

The 1980s were a time of great ferment in Indian politics, with the Sikh separatist Khalistan movement at its peak, Assamese students rising in protest against Bangladeshi illegal immigrants who were transforming the demography of their state, Tamil separatism in neighbouring Sri Lanka drawing India into the maelstrom and a youthful but Westernised prime minister, Rajiv Gandhi, seemingly running the country from a great height, like the airline pilot he had once been. The BJP sensed an opportunity to carve out a distinctive space for itself as a defender of Hindu interests. In a resolution adopted officially at Palampur in 1989, it declared Hindutva as its ideology—while claiming that Hindutva represents 'cultural nationalism' and embodies 'Indian nationhood,' rather than a religious or theological concept. In the years following, the BJP established a distinctive Hindutva agenda in national politics, advocating 'Hindu' causes—some which manifestly went beyond religion, like the rights of Kashmiri Pandits brutalised by Islamist terrorists and driven from their homes in the Kashmir Valley to become refugees in their own land, and some which directly challenged other religions, such as the advocacy of a Uniform Civil Code to replace the personal laws of religious minorities.

The 'Muslim threat' presented itself in multiple ways—Muslim illegal migrants in Assam, reactionary Muslim conservatives opposing a liberal Supreme Court judgment in the Shah Bano Case (in which the court's award of alimony to a Muslim widow was then overturned by the government passing a law obliging her to seek support from the Waqf Board), and angry Muslim politicians denouncing Salman Rushdie's 'blasphemy' in his novel, *The Satanic Verses*. To those repelled by such developments, the BJP offered not just negative condemnation but a positive alternative cause dear to many Hindu hearts—a campaign to resurrect a legendary ancient temple to the birthplace of Lord Rama (the Ram Janmabhoomi) which had reputedly stood on the site of a disused sixteenth-century mosque, the Babri Masjid, in the north Indian holy town of Ayodhya.

The evidence for this claim is contested, though there is little doubt that some temple had indeed stood there, since in 1975, well before the mosque's destruction, the Archaeological Survey of India (ASI) unearthed fourteen pillar bases of kasauti stone with Hindu motifs in the foundations. Yet, very few details are available about the temple or whether it had indeed been destroyed to construct the masjid. But there is no doubt it is deeply entrenched in popular Hindu belief that this precisely was where Rama was born and where he must be worshipped. If this can be achieved without inflicting pain on Indian

Muslims, and while finding some way to make up for the barbarous destruction of the Babri Masjid, the nation will heave a sigh of relief, but a quarter-century after the demolition of the masjid, the case pends in the Supreme Court, and the temple remains unbuilt, its absence a potent symbol for the Hindutva movement and a perennial vote-winner for its acolytes.

The Ram Janmabhoomi campaign was incendiary politics, given the inflammatory potency of calls to replace a mosque with a temple; but for the BJP, it worked. The party's leader, L. K. Advani, rode across the Hindi heartland in a converted truck decorated to look like the chariot of an ancient Hindu warrior, making fiery speeches all the way. Hindu groups were exhorted to fire and consecrate bricks in every village in a Ram Shila Pujan (prayer ritual) and proceed with them to Ayodhya for use in the temple that would one day be built there. Pilgrimages were organised to Ayodhya to look at the spot where Hindus had to swallow the mortal insult of a holy site being occupied by a mosque. As emotions reached fever pitch, a howling, frenzied mob broke the 470-year old mosque apart in December 1992, levelling it to rubble while the police stood idly by.[58] The BJP had made its mark.

But while these two incidents tower above the others in the hall of infamy, the forces unleashed by Hindutva have led to numerous acts of violence in its name—and not only against non-Hindus. From the assassination of Mahatma Gandhi by Nathuram Godse in January 1948 for being too sympathetic to Muslims, to the murder of journalist Gauri Lankesh in September 2017 for her excoriating attacks on the Sangh Parivar, moderates, liberals and rationalists of Hindu background have also been targeted. It is distressing that there are BJP MPs who have publicly called for Gandhi's statues to be supplanted by those of Godse to commemorate his killing.

The catalogue of communal violence and riots, incited mainly by Hindutva organisations, is long and dismaying. Several erupted in 1964, 1965 and 1967, in places where Hindu refugees from the former East Pakistan were settled, notably Rourkela, Jamshedpur and Ranchi, where Hindu organisations exploited the refugees' tales of suffering to ignite communal passions and incite violence. The Bharatiya Jana

Sangh's resolution on the 'Indianisation of Indian Muslims' played a role in the Ahmedabad riots in 1969 while the Shiv Sena's ('Army of Shiva', a Mumbai-based Hindu right wing organisation supported by Marathi-speakers) communal agenda helped spark those in Bhivandi-Jalgaon in 1970. The 1980s saw thousands of Muslims being killed in riots, starting with Moradabad in 1980 and carrying on through the horrors of Biharsharif, Meerut, Bhiwandi and Baroda to the massacre at Nellie in Assam and a slew of riots around the 'Ram Shila Pujan' agitations to consecrate bricks in towns across northern India to rebuild the Ram Janmabhoomi. The 1990s, following the demolition of the Babri Masjid, witnessed what many have described as the worst riots of post-independence India—in Mumbai, Surat, Ahmedabad, Kanpur, Delhi and elsewhere. (And of course, unrelated to Hindutva, India also suffered the grotesque anti-Sikh riots of 1984, when mobs egged on by some leaders affiliated with the ruling Congress, and claiming to be revenging the assassination of Indira Gandhi by her Sikh bodyguards murdered 2,800 innocent Sikh civilians across India, including 2,100 in Delhi.)

Since the ascent of the BJP to power, the forces unleashed by the dominance of Hindutva have resulted in many incidents of violence. In one grim reckoning, more than fifty individuals have been killed in anti-minority acts of violence since mid-2014, and dozens of others stripped, beaten and humiliated. Particularly haunting is the story of fifteen-year-old Junaid Khan, returning home on a crowded train after buying new clothes for Id, who was stabbed repeatedly because he was Muslim and thrown off the train to bleed to death on the tracks. (Specific cases related to 'cow vigilantism' are discussed later.) Headlines have spoken continually of riots and killing, Hindu against Muslim, of men being slaughtered because of the mark on a forehead or the absence of a foreskin.

THE POLITICS OF DIVISION

There are essentially two kinds of politics in India: the politics of division and the politics of unity. The latter has increasingly been taken for granted and so the former has by far the greater momentum, as politicians seek to slice and dice the electorate into ever-smaller configurations of caste, language and religion, the better to appeal to such particularist identities in the quest for votes. But this resort to violence is a new low in our political life. The attacks on Muslim and (earlier) Christian families, the vandalism of their places of worship, the destruction of homes and livelihoods, and the horrific rapes, mutilations and burnings alive that have occurred, have nothing to do with religious beliefs—neither those of the victims nor of their attackers. They are instead part of a contemptible political project whose closest equivalent can in fact be found in the Islamist terrorism the Hindutva supporters claim to despise: the bomb blasts in Mumbai in January 1993 and the 'Indian Mujahideen' terrorist attacks in Delhi, Jaipur, and Ahmedabad, in which bombs were set to go off in hospitals, marketplaces and playgrounds.[59] The actions of both Hindu and Muslim terrorists are anti-national; both aim to divide the country by polarising people along their religious identities; and both hope to profit politically from such polarisation.

India must not let either set of terrorists prevail.

*　*　*

By 1996 the BJP had emerged as the largest single party in national elections, though the unwillingness of the 'secular' parties to ally with it had led to the collapse in thirteen days of its first attempt at forming a government. Two years later it was back, with an amiable conciliator, Prime Minister Atal Behari Vajpayee, heading a coalition government in 1998; though one more election intervened, this government lasted six years. The BJP, despite merely heading a coalition government, left no doubt about its ideological moorings, installing a plaque to honour Savarkar at the Andaman central jail where he had been imprisoned, while avoiding all mention of the obsequious letter of apology to the British that had won him his release. Describing himself as a 'prodigal son' longing to return to the 'parental doors of the government', despite the failure of his earlier letter of clemency in 1911 to obtain him a pardon, Savarkar wrote again on 14 November 1913:

'[If] the government in their manifold beneficence and mercy release me, I for one cannot but be the staunchest advocate of constitutional progress and loyalty to the English government which is the foremost condition of that progress. As long as we are in jails, there cannot be real happiness and joy in hundreds and thousands of homes of His Majesty's subjects in India, for blood is thicker than water; but if we are released, the people will raise a shout of joy and gratitude to the government, who knows how to forgive and correct, more than how to chastise and avenge.'[60]

Savarkar went on to add:

'Moreover, my conversion to the constitutional line would bring back all those misled young men in India and abroad who were once looking up to me as their guide. I am ready to serve the government in any capacity they like, for as my conversion is conscientious so I hope my future conduct would be. By keeping me in jail, nothing can be got in comparison to what would be otherwise. The Mighty alone can afford to be merciful and, therefore, where else can the prodigal son return but to the parental doors of the government.'

The parental doors of the BJP government were certainly thrown open to Savarkar; his behaviour towards the British rulers was airbrushed from official accounts of his life, a hagiographic biopic was released in 2001, and his portrait was even hung in Parliament's Central Hall, deliberately positioned to face that of Mahatma Gandhi.

During BJP rule at the head of a coalition government in Delhi, a purely BJP government, headed by a fiery and articulate ideologue, Chief Minister Narendra Modi, ruled Gujarat. It was on this government's watch that 1,000 to 2,000 people, mainly Muslims, were massacred in 2002, in a pogrom against that community that blighted the state's normally tranquil capital, Ahmedabad, and other places in Gandhi's homeland. The chief minister was accused of condoning the killings—or at the very least not taking prompt action to stop them—which ceased only after the Army was called in three days after they began. It was reported that Prime Minister Vajpayee wanted to dismiss him for his failure to prevent the massacre, but was dissuaded by the

Hindutva hardliners in his administration.[61] (Senior BJP leader Venkaiah Naidu confirmed this story on the record as an example of his party's democratic decision-making—according to Naidu, Prime Minister Vajpayee wanted Modi to resign as Gujarat chief minister after the 2002 riots, but had to give in to the party's 'collective decision' against the idea.) Be that as it may, the Gujarati public rallied behind him; Modi was re-elected as chief minister of Gujarat in elections later that year, 2002, and returned to office again with ever-larger majorities in 2007 and 2012. While his campaign rhetoric vehemently expressed Hindutva ideas, he also claimed to be governing effectively and promoting robust economic development, a message that resonated well beyond his state and gave him a credible national reputation for decisive and impactful leadership. This in turn propelled him to the position of the BJP's candidate for prime minister in 2014, and to a resounding victory in the general elections held across India that year.

Under Prime Minister Modi, the BJP has a sizeable parliamentary majority on its own that it had never enjoyed before; it is, therefore, not obliged to dilute its agenda to accommodate less Hindutva-minded coalition partners, since it does not need any of them to make up its majority. The BJP became the first governing party in the history of independent India to come to power without a single elected Muslim member of the Lok Sabha; the three Muslims who have served in its council of ministers are all appointees to the Rajya Sabha. Also, for the first time, Indian democracy finds itself facing the reality of its top three constitutional positions—president, vice president and prime minister—all being held by RSS members of the same ideological disposition.

It is difficult to escape the conclusion that this marks a significant step towards the Hindutva project of transforming India into a Hindu state, or at least a state with a distinctively Hindu identity. Many Hindutva ideologues have long deplored the fact that love for Hinduism had been, in India, a love that could not be acknowledged; officially promoted secularism, they argued, had made India a country where a Muslim could be proud to be Muslim, a Christian proud to be Christian, a Sikh proud to be Sikh, while a Hindu was proud to be...

secular. The groundswell of rage that anchors this perception takes in a host of factors: the uncritical acceptance by the Indian establishment of regressive practices among the Muslim community while demanding progressive behaviour from Hindus, the support for minority education while denying such aid to Hindus, the promotion of 'family planning' among Hindus but not among Muslims, the cultivation of 'vote banks' led by conservative Muslim leaders but the disparagement of their Hindu equivalents, and so on. The result is a widespread denunciation of the 'appeasement' of Muslims, which seems bizarre when one looks at the statistical evidence of Muslim socio-economic backwardness and the prevalence of discrimination in such areas as housing and employment. Muslims are under-represented in the nation's police forces and over-represented in its prisons. Yet Hindutva leaders have successfully stoked a perception that government benefits are skewed towards minorities, and thus justified their campaign for Hindu self-assertiveness. The unapologetic assertion of Hindutva, and its unabashed capture of the political pinnacle of authority in the land, thus represented a dramatic shift in India's political culture, whose implications are yet to be fully parsed.

Many Indian social scientists have described the Hindutva movement as fascist in the classical sense of the term. Marxist social scientist Prabhat Patnaik, for instance, is a prominent advocate of the argument that the Hindutva movement is 'classically fascist in class support, methods and programme'.[62] Patnaik and others find the following elements of classical fascism present in Hindutva: its attempt to create a unified homogeneous majority defined as 'the Hindus'; its sense of grievance against past injustice, especially by Muslim rulers; its sense of cultural superiority and affirmation of the timeless truths embodied in Hinduism; its interpretation of history in the light of its grievances against past oppressors and its faith in the superiority of its own tenets; its rejection of all arguments against such an interpretation of history; and its appeal to a religious and cultural Hindu majority articulated in terms of race and masculinity. (He could have added the frequent and easy resort to majoritarian mob violence against helpless members of minority faiths, occurring with increasingly troubling frequency in recent years.) Well before Modi became prime minister, the sociologist Ashis Nandy had described him as an archetypal fascist ('a classic, clinical case of a fascist').[63]

However, it must be said that Modi has not conducted himself in office in the manner Nandy's analysis would have suggested. He has repeatedly spoken of being a prime minister for all Indians; arguably his most effective slogan has been '*sab ka saath, sab ka vikas*'—'together with everyone, development for all'.

Nor can it be denied that the ascent of Hindutva supporters to the pinnacle of political power in India has occurred, significantly, under India's secular constitution, and through entirely democratic and legal means. The great question before us today is, therefore: Will constitutionalism tame Hindutva, or will Hindutva transform the workings of the constitution?

On 11 December 1995, a three-judge bench of the Supreme Court, headed by a famously liberal Chief Justice, J. S. Verma, declared that Hindutva was a 'way of life and not a religion'. The court explained: 'Ordinarily, Hindutva is understood as a way of life or a state of mind and is not to be equated with or understood as religious Hindu fundamentalism...it is a fallacy and an error of law to proceed on the assumption...that the use of words "Hindutva" or "Hinduism" per se depicts an attitude hostile to all persons practising any religion other than the Hindu religion... It may well be that these words are used in a speech to promote secularism or to emphasise the way of life of the Indian people and the Indian culture or ethos, or to criticise the policy of any political party as discriminatory or intolerant.'[64]

Unsurprisingly, this Supreme Court judgment found its way into the campaign manifesto of the BJP in the general elections of the following year, 1996. The party claimed the Supreme Court had 'endorsed the true meaning and content of Hindutva as being consistent with the true meaning and definition of secularism'. This could be said to mark the beginning of the constitutional acceptability of the concept of Hindutva—something that arguably is no longer in question, since on 2 January 2017, the Supreme Court of India declined to reconsider its 1995 judgment.

So the Constitution and its custodians have made their peace with Hindutva. But can Hindutva wholeheartedly accept the Constitution?

The more conformist of the two BJP prime ministers India has had, Atal Behari Vajpayee (in office from 1998 to 2004), took a moderate approach to constitutional change, arguing that 'even in the mightiest fort one has to repair the parapet from time to time' (while V. P. Singh cautioned that the 'tenants' should not go for 'rebuilding in the name of repairs').[65] His rule saw no dramatic change in India's constitutional arrangements, though his government did conduct a constitutional review that produced a 1,979-page report, universally unread. There has so far been no dramatic challenge to the Constitution under the second BJP prime minister, Narendra Modi, either, but here it is far less certain that the present approach will endure.

Deen Dayal Upadhyaya, who rejected the Constitution of India in conception, form and substance, would be astonished to find his supposed acolytes extolling its every line and holding special commemorations in Parliament with grandiloquent speeches to mark the anniversary not just of its adoption—which, after all, is Republic Day—but even of its passage by the Constituent Assembly in a newly anointed 'Constitution Day'. What would Upadhyaya have made, I wonder, of a prime minister, who swears by him, saying that this Constitution—the very document that Upadhyaya found fallacious, Westernised and devoid of *chiti* and *virat shakti*—is his 'holy book'?

It is, of course, difficult to know whether we should take the Hindutvavadis' claims to be admirers of the present secular, liberal, Western-influenced Constitution of India to be as sincere as their professions of devotion to Upadhyaya. Will Modi and his tribe, after consolidating their hold on both the Lok Sabha and the Rajya Sabha, and after taking over most of the state governments, feel emboldened to tear up the very Constitution to which they have so far so enthusiastically pledged allegiance?

There are already hints that the Constitution in its present form cannot long survive unscathed. Hindutva ideologue K. N. Govindacharya has declared that the Constitution must be transformed: 'Amendment is a short-term goal while rewriting is a long-term objective,' he stated.[66] His fundamental critique, expressed in interviews to leading Indian newspapers in 2017, is not far from Upadhyaya's of half a century earlier:

> 'Our Constitution is based upon the idea of individualism. It promotes individualism, which is against the Indian value system... while Indian civilisation is based upon family system, collectiveness. Other important components of our society such as caste system, panchayat system are not mirrored in the Constitution. Individualism is a western idea. It cannot be the basis of the Indian Constitution. A new Constitution should be written which would talk in favour of *Sarva* (all), not an individual.'

Aside from giving caste an honoured place in the Hindutva political system, 'We believe that Indian society and its cultural reality should be included in the Constitution.' For instance, 'in 'Bharatiya' society, family is the basic brick of society, and as in the Cuban Constitution, it is not the individual but family values that are crucial.'

Cuba as a model for India is a nice touch from a supposedly right-wing movement. But as in many communist systems, Parliament as we know it would cease to exist. 'The new Constitution would be based on the principles of collectiveness. In political terminology, you can call it a Guild System. Representatives of the different castes, professions, communities would be included in National Guild. Instead of the Upper House (Rajya Sabha) and Lower House (Lok Sabha) of Parliament, there would be only one National Guild in which 1,000 representatives from all over the country will discuss the problems of India. In the National Guild, 500 representatives would come through territorial representation, while 500 would come through functional representation.'

Human rights are another example of the Westernisation of the Indian constitutional system, according to Govindacharya: 'There cannot be any rights without checks and balances. If the Constitution gives us fundamental rights, it mentions fundamental duties too. But no one cares about that. Rights and duties should be seen in relation to each other. To exercise your rights, you should follow your duties. No one can exercise absolute freedom.' As Deen Dayal Upadhyaya had argued, 'fundamental duties, not just rights, must also be incorporated.' Secularism, like human rights, will have to go: it 'implies opposition of Hindus and appeasement of Muslims or other minorities. We should get rid of this word as soon as possible. It is completely irrelevant in the Indian context.'

Deen Dayal Upadhyaya's inspiration crops up again in the Hindutva rejection of the Western word 'socialism' in the Preamble of the Constitution. 'We have a better word—of Indian tradition—to express the spirit of socialism. It is [Upadhyaya's coinage] antodaya. Antodaya means antim aadmi (the last man).' Similarly democracy is a troubling term because it implies political contention. 'Instead of competitiveness, consensus and collectiveness should be the spirit of the democracy', says Govindacharya.[67] Shades of Cuba again!

The process of incorporating such Hindu concepts seems to have begun: 'We are doing it very silently. Discussions and debates have been taking place for some time. What I told you above are the initial outcomes of the debate', Govindacharya confirms. 'There may be many gaps which need deliberations, and a cool, calm, dispassionate discussion needs the right atmosphere and a mechanism. However, this is just not possible in the media glare.' Would a Hindutva-inspired revision of the Constitution, for example, move the issue of cow slaughter from the Directive Principles of the Constitution, where it is linked specifically to the preservation of milch-cattle and scientific principles of animal husbandry, to somewhere more binding, and anchored more explicitly to religious sanction? Govindacharya is clear: a Hindutva-drafted Constitution would provide for:

> 'eco-centric not anthropocentric development. I mean not just rights of the cow, but a holistic view of *zamin, jal, janwar, jungle* [land, water, animal, jungle]; for only in this protection lies the well-being of man. All the five must have sacred rights, and this should not just be rights-based but duty-based, and not just be components of state power. The cow is part of our civilisational past and it reflects those values, it should be a civilisational continuity in the preamble. The cow, environmental protection, all this requires constitutional protection. It is part of Hindu ethos, culture—like Bishnois who embrace death by

hugging those trees, this is all 'Bharatiya' culture. Instead of assuming man is conqueror of nature, it is the duty of humans to protect nature, and all this must be incorporated in the Constitution.'

Environmentalists may well approve, but the key question remains whether a Hindutva-modified Constitution, assuming that it ever comes to pass, will retain the core principle of independent India, that all adult Indians are deemed equal, irrespective of religion. Or would it consciously embrace the central theme of Hindutva, which would discriminate against non-Hindus? If it did so, it would be true to Hindutva as expounded by Savarkar, Golwalkar and Upadhyaya, but not to the Hinduism of Swami Vivekananda or Mahatma Gandhi, who did not define citizenship or Indianness in terms of the gods one worshipped, what one ate, the way one dressed or where one went for pilgrimage. But if it did not do so, it would betray a century's worth of political philosophising in the name of Hindutva, surrendering its tenets to the dominant nationalist stream it had long derided as 'pseudo-secular'.

This will be a crucial dilemma for the Hindutva ideologues. Do they take the opportunity given to them by their crushing political majority—which might not endure if they wait too long—to remake the Constitution as their principal thinkers had advocated? Or do they accept that the reality of ruling a multi-ethnic, multi-lingual and multi-religious polity makes the goal of 'Hindu, Hindi, Hindutva' unattainable?

Another litmus test would lie in whether a revised Hindutva Constitution would mandate a Uniform Civil Code for all the citizens of India. Leaders subscribing to Hindutva have long argued that differential laws based on religion—essentially the personal laws governing marriage, inheritance and divorce for Muslims, and also for other religious minorities—violate Article 44 of the Indian Constitution and have sowed the seeds of divisiveness between different communities; if we are all Hindus (albeit 'Hindu Muhammadans', 'Hindu Christians' and so on) why should we not all be subject to one civil code? Secular Congress leaders from Jawaharlal Nehru onwards have argued that while a Uniform Civil Code might be a desirable objective, it could only be adopted with the consent of the affected communities. This could not be obtained by pressure or by legal coercion; it required persuasion. Since minority leaders, especially Muslims, showed no inclination to be persuaded, seeing a uniform civil code as the imposition of majoritarian Hindu sensibilities, the idea needed to be deferred indefinitely, until the time was ripe. Hindutva leaders have long mocked this approach as caving in to minority prejudices; accepting Sharia law, they argue, violates the human rights principles of gender equality by discriminating against Muslim women and allows unelected and in some cases self-appointed religious personalities to interpret religious dictates and so 'lay down the law'. Could they now concede the permissibility of religious personal laws without losing credibility?

And would a Hindutva Constitution preserve the anomaly of Article 370, which grants a special status to the state of Jammu and Kashmir, to the extent that no law passed by the Parliament of India can apply to that state without being also passed by the Assembly of Jammu and Kashmir? Would the advocates of Hindutva allow the state to continue to restrict land-holding to 'state subjects', a status a woman would lose if she married a man from outside the state?

India's constitutionalists have long argued that it is a living document, susceptible to amendment in keeping with the evolving demands of time, subject of course to judicial interpretation, which has decreed that its 'basic structure' cannot be tampered with. Would transforming an egalitarian and secular Constitution into a document infused with the principles of Hindutva not violate its basic structure? And yet, can the advocates of Hindutva—the intellectual legatees of Savarkar, Golwakar and Upadhyaya—afford not to try?

A TRAVESTY OF HINDUISM

While not everything in the philosophy I have sought to summarise is objectionable—and there is much to admire, for instance, in Upadhyaya's humanistic thinking—there is much that is troubling too. By rejecting the territorial idea of the nation in favour of an abstract ethos of patriotism, it excludes many who belong on the territory of modern India and are loyal citizens but feel differently about Bharat

Mata (Mother India). In its emphasis on cultural authenticity and allegiance to ancient Indian traditions and beliefs, it risks alienating those who do not share these assumptions. While extolling the virtues of harmony and cooperation, it sows the seeds of further division by setting those who subscribe to these values against those who—for reasons of religion, politics or intellectual conviction—do not. And in dismissing minority appeasement but requiring minorities to accept Hindu ways of being as their own, it offers no real solution to the undeniable reality that 20 per cent of India's population are not Hindus and cannot be expected to conform to Hindu ideas of how they should live and what they should believe.

It also ignores, in its desire to portray a Hindu vision, the diversity within Hinduism itself. The faith is practised differently by people in different parts of the country, or worshipping different manifestations of the Divine, or adhering to different castes or sects. Even the Brahmins, who are spread throughout the country and are associated everywhere with learning, priestly functions and religious erudition, manifest diversity in their social practices: while the Malayali Brahmins grow their tuft of hair at the front, most orthodox Tamil Brahmins wear it at the back; where Iyengar Brahmin women regard white as the colour of widowhood, the Namboothiri Brahmin bride wears white at her wedding. As we have seen, Hinduism is not a totalising faith. Each Hindu may have a different conception of her own *dharma*. Integral Humanism undoubtedly emerges from a close and sustainable reading of Advaita philosophy, but Upadhyaya's is not the only way of being Hindu, and other sages and *rishis* may offer alternative approaches to the same conundrums. Upadhyaya's philosophy suffers the demerit of its own certitudes; it is unable to accommodate dissent.

Some have seen in his approach a reaction to Islam's assertiveness. In response to the suggestion that Hindus are behaving like Islamists, the one-time journalist and former BJP minister Arun Shourie commented tartly:

> 'In a word, three things are teaching the Hindus to become Islamic: the double-standards of the secularists and the State, the demonstrated

success of the Muslims in bending both the State and the secularists by intimidation, and the fact that both the State and the secularists pay attention to the sentiments of Hindus only when the Hindus become a little Islamic... [My] forecast: the more the secularists insist on double-standards, the more Islamic will the Hindus become.'

What does this 'Islamicised Hinduism' of the 'Sangh Parivar' consist of? The ideological foundations laid by Savarkar, Golwalkar and Upadhyaya have given members of the RSS a fairly coherent doctrine. It rests on the atavistic belief that India has been the land of the Hindus since ancient times, and that their identity and its identity are inter-twined. Since time immemorial, Hindutva advocates argue, Hindu culture and civilisation have constituted the essence of Indian life; Indian nationalism is therefore Hindu nationalism. The history of India is the story of the struggle of the Hindus, the owners and custodians of this ancient land, to protect and preserve their religion and culture against the onslaught of hostile alien invaders. It is true that the terri-tory of India also hosts non-Hindus, but these are invaders (Muslims, Christians) or guests (Jews, Parsis); they can be tolerated, depending on their loyalty to the land, but cannot be treated as equal to the Hindus unless they acknowledge the superiority of Hindus in India and adopt Hindu traditions and culture. Non-Hindus must acknowledge their Hindu parentage, or, better still, convert to Hinduism in a return to their true cultural roots.

Those political forces in India who are opposed to the Sangh's ideol-ogy are mistaken, the doctrine goes on, since they make the cardinal error of confusing 'national unity' with the unity of all those who hap-pen to be living in the territory of India, irrespective of religion or national origin. Such people are in fact anti-national, because their real motivation is the selfish desire to win minority votes in elections rather than care for the interests of the majority of the nation. The unity and consolidation of the Hindus is therefore essential. Since the Hindu people are surrounded by enemies, a polarisation must take place that pits Hindus against all others. To achieve this, though, Hindus must be unified; the lack of unity is the root cause of all the evils besetting the

Hindus. The Sangh Parivar's principal mission is to bring about that unity and lead it to the greater glory of the Hindu nation.

The problem with this doctrine, coherent and clear though it is, is its denial of the reality of what Hinduism is all about. What Swami Vivekananda would have seen as the strength of Hinduism—its extraordinary eclecticism and diversity, its acceptance of a wide range of beliefs and practices, its refusal to confine itself to the dogmas of a single holy book, its fluidity, the impossibility to define it down to a homogenous 'Semitic' creed—is precisely what the RSS ideologues see as its weakness.

The Sanghivadi quest for polarisation and unity is also a yearning to make Hinduism what it is not—to 'Semitise' it so that it looks like the faiths of the 'invaders': codified and doctrinaire, with an identifiable God (preferably Rama), a principal holy book (the Gita), a manageable ecclesiastic hierarchy, and of course a unified race and a people to pro-fess it. This is not the lived Hinduism of most Hindus. And so the obvi-ous question arises: must every believing Hindu automatically be assumed to subscribe to the Hindutva project? And since manifestly most do not, does the viability of the project require a continued drive to force the dissenters into the Hindutva straitjacket?

Whereas Hinduism is an inward-directed faith, focusing on Self-Realisation above all and the union of the soul with the Absolute, Hindutva is an outward-directed concept, aimed at creating social and cultural distinctions for a political purpose. Hindutva, therefore, is disconnected from the central assumptions and tenets of my Hinduism. Yet it piggy-backs on the faith, claiming to represent Hinduism, though it does so not as a set of doctrines or precepts but as a cultural marker. Hindutva adopts the Hindu religion not as a way of seeking the Divine but as a badge of worldly political identity. This has little to do with the Hinduism of Vivekananda, or of Adi Shankara; it is a twentieth-century idea, born of twentieth-century forms of political thinking that were already beginning to be dangerously out of date elsewhere in the world when they were propounded in India. Parties professing to speak for an entire people or 'volk' were discredited as well as destroyed in Europe in 1945; seven decades later, the idea flourishes in India, in the name of Hindutva.

Speaking for myself, any attempt to reduce my Hinduism—which sits comfortably with the Nehruvian notion of Indianness—to a sectarian notion of Hindutva is a travesty of what Hinduism really is. I too, as a Hindu, can say, when people tell me '*Garv se kaho ki tum Hindu ho*', that I am proud to be a Hindu, but in what is it that we are to take pride? I take pride in the openness, the diversity, the range, the lofty metaphysical aspirations of the Vedanta; of the various ways in which Hinduism is practised, eclectically, and of its extraordinary acceptance of differences.

Unfortunately, as I have noted, the votaries of Hindutva seem to take pride in Hinduism the way in which one might support a football team as a badge of identity, rather than as a set of values, principles and beliefs, and so Hinduism becomes reduced in their retelling to little more than a label on a T-shirt, a badge of allegiance rather than a way of relating to the cosmos.

My notion of Indianness and Hinduness is very much caught up in what Dr Radhakrishnan so memorably spoke of as a view of life. That view of life has very little room for intolerance, for dogma, for attacks on others because of what they do or do not believe. I am a Hindu, and I am a nationalist, but I am not a Hindu nationalist. My nationalism is unquestioningly, all-embracingly, Indian. The Sangh does not speak for Hindus like me.

BEYOND HOLY COWS

THE USES AND ABUSES OF HINDU CULTURE AND HISTORY

My own faith in religious pluralism is a legacy of my upbringing in 'secular' India. Secularism in India did not mean irreligiousness, which even avowedly atheist parties like the communists or the southern DMK, Dravida Munnetra Kazhagam (Dravidian Progress Federation) party found unpopular amongst their voters; indeed, in Calcutta's annual Durga Puja, the communist parties compete with each other to put up the most lavish *Puja pandals* (Hindu religious displays). Rather, secularism meant, in the Indian tradition, a profusion of religions, none of which was privileged by the state. I remember how, in the Calcutta neighbourhood where I lived during my high school years, the wail of the muezzin calling the Islamic faithful to prayer blended with the chant of the mantras and the tinkling of bells at the nearby Shiva temple and the crackling loudspeakers outside the Sikh gurudwara reciting verses from the Guru Granth Sahib. And just around the corner was St Paul's Cathedral.

As we have seen, the irony is that India's secular coexistence was paradoxically made possible by the fact that the overwhelming majority of Indians are Hindus. That acceptance of difference, which I have explored in this book and elsewhere, characterised the Hinduism propagated by Vivekananda and other visionary Hindu seers. This meant that it came naturally to Hindus to coexist with practitioners of other faiths. In a plural society, religious pluralism was merely one more kind of difference everyone accepted, just as we knew that around us were people who spoke different languages, ate different foods, dressed differently and had different shades of skin colour from ours.

SECULARISM AND SYNCRETISM

Secularism in India, therefore, did not mean separation of religion from state. Instead, secularism in India means a state that was equally indulgent of all religious groups, and favoured none.

Nor did it mean secularity in the French sense, or *laïcité*. The French concept keeps religion out of governmental institutions like schools and government out of religious institutions in turn, whereas Indian secularism cheerfully embraces financial support to religious schools and the persistence of 'personal law' for different religious communities. The Indian system has created incentives for various religious denominations to start and operate 'minority schools' and colleges with substantial government funding, impart religious education, and be exempt from various regulations and stipulations the Indian government imposes on non-minority institutions. (Critics, especially of the Hindutva variety, do not hesitate to point out that while government schools and colleges may not impart religious instruction, religious sects and charities affiliated to minority communities may open their own schools and receive state financial assistance even as they impart religious indoctrination.)

Under the Indian version of secularism, the government's financial largesse is extended to the Muslim Wakf Boards, Buddhist monasteries, and certain Christian religious institutions; and under a 1951 Religious and Charitable Endowment Law, state governments are empowered to take over, own and operate Hindu temples, collect revenue from offerings and redistribute that revenue to such purposes as it deems fit, including any non-temple-related ones. This may well be worth re-examination. Still, it came as a shock when, in 2016, the BJP government invited a Jain monk to address the Haryana state assembly, seating him in an exalted position above the Speaker of the House. Many Hindus saw this as a grave mistake. Religiosity is hardly unknown in our politics—there are several saffron-robed *sadhus* who have been elected to Parliament and one, Yogi Adityanath, serves as the chief minister of India's biggest state, Uttar Pradesh—but giving an *unelected* religious figure a position of prominence in an elected, representative democratic legislative body was fundamentally wrong, and crossed a line that had hitherto never been breached.

While the Haryana government's actions might have been unconscionable, there is no getting away from the fact that India is not secular in the commonly understood sense of the word. What it is, is pluralist: an overwhelmingly Hindu-majority country running political and governmental institutions that promote the survival, success and perpetuation of religious minorities. It is the idea that rather than distancing itself from religion (the idea of *dharma-nirpekshata* condemned by the critics of secularism), the state can embrace *all* religions.

My generation grew up in an India where our sense of nationhood lay in the slogan, 'unity in diversity'. We were brought up to take pluralism for granted, and to reject the communalism that had partitioned the nation when the British left. In rejecting the case for Pakistan, Indian nationalism also rejected the very idea that religion should be a determinant of nationhood. We never fell into the insidious trap of agreeing that, since Partition had established a state for Muslims, what remained was a state for Hindus. To accept the idea of India you had to spurn the logic that had divided the country.

In some ways, this kind of Indian secularism has ancient roots in our history. Admired monarchs from Ashoka, in the third century BCE, to Harsha, in the sixth century CE, gave their recognition and patronage to different religions. Ashoka's Rock Edict XII forbade people from honouring their own sects at the expense of others, and condemning the beliefs of others. Citizenship and political status in his state were never linked to one's religion. The coexistence of religions is evident from the fact that the Ellora Cave temples, some Jain, some Hindu and some Buddhist, were carved next to each other between the fifth and tenth centuries. While this traditional approach to secular or pluralist practice was not that of the Islamic kingdoms that established themselves from the twelfth century onwards, even Muslim rulers bound to uphold the less welcoming tenets of their faith had to reconcile themselves to ruling an overwhelmingly non-Muslim populace and accommodating prominent Hindus in government and the military. One monarch, the Mughal Emperor Akbar, went so far as to create his own syncretic religion, Din-e-Ilahi, to meld the best features of Islam, Hinduism and the other faiths of which he knew into a new 'national faith'. It did not outlast his reign, but the attempt was extraordinary.

The concept of *sarva dharma sambhava*—accepting the equality of all religions—was propounded by great Hindu sages like Ramakrishna and Vivekananda, as we have seen, and upheld by Mahatma Gandhi and the Indian nationalist movement. While it was an axiomatic tenet of the post-Independence India in which I grew up, *sarva dharma sambhava* has been increasingly rejected by some proponents of Hindutva who spurn the notion of religious universalism in favour of a more robust assertion of Hindu cultural identity and Hindus' political rights. The Hindutva ideologue David Frawley (Pandit Vamadeva Shastri), for instance, warns against *sarva dharma sambhava*, arguing that only Hindus are asked to practise this belief, which simply leads to confusion and 'does not convince the opponents but deludes the Hindus themselves'. Frawley asks: 'When have Christians or Muslims in India ever been criticised for violating Sarva Dharma Samabhava?... Under the guise of religious tolerance this idea of equality of religions is used to prevent scrutiny of [others'] religious dogmas'.[1]

Yet the lived reality of Indian syncretism is difficult to deny. Hindus who made the arduous uphill trek to the cave temple of Amarnath in northern Kashmir, where an ice lingam, a naturally-formed stalactite, is worshipped, would have known that a third of their offerings went to the family of Adam Malik, a Muslim shepherd who, it was said, found the cave four centuries ago and led a Hindu *sadhu* to see the astonishing sight. In my novel, *Riot*, I wrote of Syed Salar Masud Ghazi, popularly known as Ghazi Miyan, a Muslim warrior who is worshipped as a saint by Hindus in the Bahraich area of Uttar Pradesh. A number of

Muslim religious figures such as Nizamuddin Auliya, Moinuddin Chishti, Shah Madar and Shaikh Nasiruddin (alias Chiragh-i-Dilli) are also worshipped by Hindu devotees to this day. Even the richest Hindu temple, at Tirupati, has a Muslim connection. One legend has it that Lord Balaji's second wife is Muslim, Bibi Nanchira, the daughter of a sultan who was enamoured of the Lord, much to her father's dismay, until Balaji appeared in the Sultan's dreams and informed him that He wished to marry his daughter. The Sultan, overwhelmed, acquiesced and today Balaji's second wife is said to live in the town below, at His feet, while His first wife Padmavati resides on Tirumala hill, at the temple, in His heart.

Such stories are not uncommon in India. A Muslim goddess, Bonbibi, is worshipped in idol form as the protector of the mangrove forests adjoining the Bay of Bengal. The Nawabs of Oudh celebrated the annual Ram Leela and Krishna Leela; Nawab Wajid Ali Shah, who was to be deposed by the British, personally directed a Krishna Leela performance in which he asked his Begums to dance the parts of the gopis. The Nawabs of Oudh both established and patronised the Hanuman festival in Lucknow known as Bada Mangal. In Bengal, Muslim Patua painters specialised in painting the Hindu epics on long pieces of craft paper. And as I have mentioned earlier, Hindus are regular worshippers at Christian shrines like the Basilica of Our Lady of Good Health in Velankanni or Mount Mary Church in Mumbai; and in Kerala's Ambalappuzha, an image of St Thomas used to be carried in procession to the Krishna temple on festive occasions, alongside those of Krishna and associated Hindu divinities.

Stories abound of different communities habitually working together in pre-colonial times on issues that benefited principally one: for instance, Hindus helping Muslims to rebuild a shrine, or Muslims doing the same when a Hindu temple had to be reconstructed. Devout Hindus were sometimes given Muslim names and were often fluent scholars in Persian; Muslims served in the army of the Maratha (Hindu) warrior king Shivaji, as did Hindu Rajputs in the forces of the fiercely Islamist Aurangzeb. The Vijayanagara army included Muslim horseback contingents. At the village level, many historians argue that Hindus and

Muslims shared a wide spectrum of customs and beliefs, at times even jointly worshipping the same saint or holy spot. In Kerala's famous pilgrimage site of Sabarimala, after an arduous struggle up to the hill-top shrine of Lord Ayyappa, the devotee first encounters a shrine to his Muslim disciple, Vavar Swami. In keeping with Muslim practice, there is no idol therein, merely a symbolic stone slab, a sword (Vavar was a warrior) and a green cloth, the colour of Islam. Muslim divines manage the shrine. (In another astonishing example, astonishing since it is both anachronistic and syncretistic, a temple in South Arcot, Tamil Nadu, hosts a deity of Muttaal Raavuttan, a Muslim chieftain—complete with beard, kumkum and toddy pot—who protects Draupadi in the *Mahabharata*. Note, of course, that Islam did not exist when the *Mahabharata* was composed, but in post-Islamic retellings, a Muslim chieftain has entered the plot!)

Indians of all religious communities had long lived intertwined lives, and even religious practices were rarely exclusionary: thus Muslim musicians played and sang Hindu devotional songs, Hindus thronged Sufi shrines and worshipped Muslim saints there, and Muslim artisans in Benares made the traditional masks for the Hindu Ram-Leela performances. Northern India celebrated what was called a 'Ganga-Jamuni tehzeeb', a syncretic culture that melded the cultural practices of both faiths. The renowned scholar Romila Thapar has recounted how deeply devotional poetry was written by some poets who were born Muslim but worshipped Hindu deities, notably Sayyad Ibrahim, popularly known as Raskhan, whose *dohas* (couplets) and *bhajans* (hymns) dedicated to Lord Krishna were widely recited in the sixteenth century. The Mughal court, she points out, became the most impressive patron of the translation of many Sanskrit religious texts into Persian, including the epic *Mahabharata* (translated as the *Razmnamah*) and the *Bhagavad Gita*, with Brahmin priests collaborating on the translations with Persian scholars.

To Gyanendra Pandey, such tales, as well as parables of Hindu generals in Mughal courts, or of Hindu and Muslim ministers in the Sikh ruler Ranjit Singh's entourage, suggests there was 'fuzziness' about self-conscious identities and a lack of self-definition on the basis of religion (or even of caste), within both the Hindu and Muslim populations. These stories do not suggest mutually incompatible or hostile ideologies.

The reality of syncretism runs deep into social practice. Muslim artisans create the masks for the major Hindu festival of Dussehra in the holy city of Varanasi; the Ram Leela could not be performed without their work. Muslim Patachitra painters sing and paint *pats* (scrolls) about Hindu divinities. And among the most famous exponents of Hindu devotional music are the Muslim Dagar brothers—not to mention the Baul singers, a legacy of the Bhakti tradition, who sing Sufi-inspired folk songs in praise of a universal God. Muslim sociologists and anthropologists have argued that Islam in rural India is more Indian than Islamic, in the sense that the faith as practised by the ordinary Muslim villagers reflects the considerable degree of cultural assimilation that has occurred between Hindus and Muslims in their daily lives. The late Muslim reformist scholar Asghar Ali Engineer once wrote that 'rural Islam... [is] almost indistinguishable from Hinduism except in the form of worship....The degree may vary from one area to another; but cultural integration between the Hindus and Muslims is a fact which no one, except victims of misinformation, can deny.'

One of the most striking images of India that went around the internet in recent years was a photograph of a Muslim couple on Janmashtami day setting out on their scooter, the man with a beard and skullcap, the woman in all-encompassing burqa, taking their child to act in a school performance—and this Muslim boy was dressed as Krishna, complete with kiritam, peacock feather, blue-hued skin and flute.

Sadly, some Hindu chauvinists have distorted the basic tenets of their own religion—as described in the preceding chapters—to propagate a version of the faith in opposition to other religions, especially Islam and Christianity. Worse, this violent, extremist brand of Hinduism, which has no sanction in Hindu scriptures, theology or practice, appears to be gaining ground in recent times, with the covert or active assistance of many Hindutva-inclined politicians, religious leaders and groups. The two worst examples of these affronts to the spirit of Hinduism in modern times are undoubtedly, as I have mentioned, the demolition of the Babri Masjid in December 1991 by a howling, chanting mob of fanatics, and the massacre of innocents, mainly Muslims, in Gujarat in 2002.

What have we come to, that a land that has been a haven of tolerance for religious minorities throughout its history should have sunk so low? India's is a civilisation that, over millennia, has offered refuge and, more importantly, religious and cultural freedom, to Jews, Parsis, Muslims and several varieties of Christians. Christianity arrived on Indian soil, or so legend has it, with St Thomas the Apostle ('Doubting Thomas'), who is said to have come to the Kerala coast some time before 52 CE and was welcomed on shore by a flute-playing Jewish girl. He made many converts, so there are Indians today whose ancestors were Christian well before any European discovered Christianity (and before the forebears of many of today's Hindu chauvinists were even conscious of themselves as Hindus). One of the oldest mosques in the world outside the Arabian peninsula is also in Kerala, in Kodungalloor. The India where the muezzin's prayer and the pujari's mantra co-exist is an India of which we can all be proud.

But, as we know, there is also the India in which murderous mobs in Odisha sought to kill Christians and destroy their places of worship and homes, pulled down the Babri Masjid, conducted the pogrom in Gujarat and lynched Mohammed Akhlaq and Pehlu Khan more recently.

Tragically, the cycle of violence goes on, spawning new hostages to history, ensuring that future generations will be taught new wrongs to set right. We live, Octavio Paz once wrote, between oblivion and memory. Memory and oblivion: how one leads to the other, and back again, has been the concern of much of my writing. Today we are facing people who wish to wipe out memory, and supplant it with new 'memories' of their own invention. As I pointed out in the last words of my novel *Riot*, history is not a web woven with innocent hands.

But as this book is about Hinduism, what sticks in my craw is the claim of the perpetrators of such violence that they are acting in defence of my faith. Hinduism believes that there are various ways of reaching the ultimate truth. To me, the fact that adherents of this faith, in a particular perversion of its tenets, have chosen to take human life and destroy somebody else's sacred place in its name, to kill others because of the absence of a foreskin or lack of a mark on the forehead, this ultimately makes me, as a Hindu, deeply sorrowful and, in a very fundamental way, ashamed.

As I have shown throughout this book, how, after all, can such a religion lend itself to 'fundamentalism'? That devotees of this supremely tolerant faith have assaulted Muslims and Christians in its name is particularly galling. As we have seen, Hinduism has survived the Aryans, the Mughals, the British; it has taken from each—language, art, food, learning—and outlasted them all. Muslim invaders destroyed Hindu temples, putting mosques in their place, but this did not make India a Muslim land, nor did Hinduism suffer a fatal blow. Survival is the best revenge, rather than reprisal; undoing the wrongs of a different era through new wrongs in a different context only compounds the original sin ('an eye for an eye,' as Mahatma Gandhi famously said, 'makes the whole world blind'). Large, eclectic, agglomerative, the Hinduism that I know understands that faith is a matter of hearts and minds, not bricks and stone. 'Build Ram in your hearts' is what Hinduism has always enjoined: if Ram is in your heart, it would matter very little where else He is, or is not. How does it matter, then, what bricks or stones Ram can also be found in?

Living with people of various kinds of faith, Hindus developed their tradition of acceptance of difference, but also understood that in both principle and practice, religion and politics should be divorced. Our founding fathers, the majority of whom were Hindus, decided that India was not a Hindu Pakistan—and the vast majority of Indians took pride in that assertion. Where Pakistan reserved its top constitutional positions only for Muslims, and stamped 'non-Muslim' on the passports of its minority citizens in confirmation of their second-class status, Indians revelled in the prominence enjoyed by its various minorities in public life. Neither politics nor governance—and certainly not culture, sport or entertainment—was based on religious principles, and success in no field required a litmus test of faith.

Throughout the decades after Independence, the political culture of the country reflected these 'secular' assumptions and attitudes.

Though the Indian population was 80 per cent Hindu and the country had been partitioned as a result of a demand for a separate Muslim homeland, three of India's eleven presidents were Muslims; so were innumerable governors, cabinet ministers, chief ministers of states, ambassadors, generals, and Supreme Court justices. During the war with Pakistan in 1971, when the Pakistani leadership was foolish enough to proclaim a jihad against the Hindu 'unbelievers', the Indian Air Force in the northern sector was commanded by a Muslim (Air Marshal, later Air Chief Marshal, I. H. Latif); the army commander was a Parsi (General, later Field Marshal, S. H. F. J. Manekshaw), the general officer commanding the forces that marched into Bangladesh was a Sikh (General J. S. Aurora), and the general flown in to negotiate the surrender of the Pakistani forces in East Bengal was Jewish (Major-General J. F. R. Jacob). They led the armed forces of an overwhelmingly Hindu country.

That is India.

HINDU NATIONALISM

So the idea of India is of one land embracing many. As I have written before, it is the idea that a nation may endure differences of caste, creed, colour, culture, cuisine, conviction, costume and custom, and still rally around a consensus. That consensus is around the simple principle that in a diverse democracy you don't really need to agree—except on the ground rules of how you will disagree. The reason India has survived all the stresses and strains that have beset it for seventy years, and that led so many to predict its imminent disintegration, is that it maintained consensus on how to manage without consensus.

But the twentieth-century politics of deprivation has eroded Indian culture's confidence. As we have seen, Hindu chauvinism has emerged from the competition for resources in a contentious democracy. Politicians of all faiths across India seek to mobilise voters by appealing to narrow identities; by courting votes in the name of religion, caste and region, they have urged voters to define themselves on these lines. As religion, caste and region have come to dominate public discourse, to some it has become more important to be a Muslim, a Bodo or a Yadav than to be an Indian.

For Hindutva thinkers, the principles of tolerance and acceptance are emasculating. 'It is no longer enough for Hindus to be apostles of toler-ance with no clear principles or doctrines with which to sustain it', argues Frawley. 'They must stand for the truth, which cannot always be popular, and not simply seek to placate everyone'.[2] But their truth is built on the denial of the truths that Hindus have lived by for millennia.

This is why the development of what has been called 'Hindu funda-mentalism' and the resultant change in the public discourse about Indianness is so dangerous. The suggestion that only a Hindu, and only a certain kind of Hindu, can be an authentic Indian, is an affront to the very premise of Indian nationalism. An India that denies itself to some of us could end up being denied to all of us.

The reduction of non-Hindus to second-class status in their home-land is unthinkable. It would be a second Partition: and a partition in the Indian soul would be as bad as a partition in the Indian soil. But the roots of such thinking run deep in the ideology of Hindutva, and that is a cause for alarm for all concerned Hindus.

* * *

Hindutva (or as some would prefer to call it, *Sanghivad*—the beliefs and philosophy of the Sangh—to strip it of its religious connotations) is in many ways a distraction from the real issues facing the country: poverty and economic development, oppression and injustice, the evo-lution of our still-imperfect democracy. Identity politics becomes a diversion from the bread-and-butter (or dal-and-roti) issues that actu-ally affect most Hindus. As discussed in Chapter Five, the Hindutva project involves an attempt to create an overarching political ideology that would subsume all the adherents of a highly differentiated and eclectic religious faith. Accordingly, the idea of Hindu nationalism con-flates ideas of religion and culture with those of nation and state.

Nationalism is by definition indivisible, whereas religion and culture take on multiple manifestations. Culture, of course, contributes to national identity, yet culture alone cannot mould the nationalism of a country, let alone that of a plural land like India. In India during colonial rule, the reassertion of Indian culture was a nationalist project, which witnessed the revival of dance forms like Bharata Natyam and traditional classical music as well as modern literature in Indian languages, modern art (from Raja Ravi Varma to the Bengal School and painters like Husain who derived inspiration from the Indian epics) and what evolved into the gaudy cinema of Bollywood.

But an India confident in its own cultural diversity could celebrate multiple expressions of its culture. Hindutva sees culture differently; as Golwalkar wrote, culture 'is but a product of our all-comprehensive religion, a part of its body and not distinguishable from it'. For Hindutva's devotees, India's national culture is Hindu religious culture, and cultural nationalism cloaks plural India in a mantle of Hindu identity. Since Hindutva's conception of nationalism is rooted in the primacy of culture over politics, the historian K. N. Panikkar has pointed out, the Hindutva effort is to create an idea of the Indian nation in which the Hindu religious identity coincides with the cultural.

As David Frawley explains, after being ruled by Westernised Hindus for many decades after Independence, today, Hindus are rediscovering their roots. 'This movement is not simply a regressive return to medieval Hindu values, but a rediscovery of the validity and importance of Hindu culture and spirituality for both the future as well as the past. It includes discovering the importance of Hindu Yoga, Vedanta, Ayurveda, Vedic astrology, classical Indian art and culture, and the Hindu view of society and government'.[3]

What he calls 'the Bharatiya spiritual urge', he says, after extolling Yoga and meditation, 'did not arise from the suppression of other human urges but from a full flowering of human nature in all aspects, including the arts and the sciences. This we see lavishly embodied in Indian music and dance, mathematics and medicine'. This sounds reasonable enough, except when he adds that 'Hindus must learn to project a united front and reclaim the greater field of Hindu Dharma that covers all aspects of life and culture'.[4] This call for unity replaces variety with uniformity and dissent with dogma; a notion of Hindu *dharma* that is all-encompassing and covers 'all aspects of life and culture' has no room for difference or for heterodoxy, let alone for deviance.

But the Hindu religious identity exalted by Hindutva ideologues is defined in narrow terms. The inclusive Hinduism propagated by the thinkers whose views I explored in the first four chapters of this book is not the Hinduism of the Sangh Parivar. Vivekananda, Dayanand Saraswati, Aurobindo and Mahatma Gandhi are ostensibly revered, but their paeans to inclusivity are glossed over or ignored. The Hindutva premise, in Panikkar's words, is 'that national regeneration and resurgence would require the recreation of an authentic culture by reclaiming the indigenous and purging the exogenous. Hindutva's cultural project, encoded in the slogan "nationalise and spiritualise", therefore, is twofold: First, to retrieve and disseminate the cultural traditions of the "golden" Hindu past; and second, to eliminate all accretions that had become part of the heritage.'[5]

The former project, of digging up ancient glories of the past, is well under way; the latter is proceeding somewhat fitfully and episodically. We will examine both processes below, starting with the battles being fought over history.

One of the amusing, but nonetheless important, sidelights of the development of Hindutva theory has been the controversy about the origins of the Aryans. The Hindutva approach inevitably had implications for the commonly accepted narratives about India, including the idea that the Indo-Aryan people had migrated to northern India from the Central Asian steppes some time around 1500 BCE and authored the foundational texts of Hinduism, the Vedas. Golwalkar believed that was impossible; Hinduism, he was convinced, was an indigenous faith that grew from rather than put down roots in Indian soil, and so the Indo-Aryans could not possibly have come from elsewhere. His and Savarkar's idea of India being the *punyabhumi* of the Hindus required the Aryans to be indigenous to India, in contrast to India's Muslims, whose faith clearly originated in the Arabian peninsula. A veritable cottage industry was born of RSS-inclined historians debunking the Aryan migration theory, insisting that the Aryans, as the founders of Hinduism, belonged all along to India.

Some less-ideological scholars point out that the *Rig Veda* does not speak of any other land but northern India or Aryavarta. In her *Sacred*

Plants of India, Dr Nanditha Krishna shows how every plant and animal mentioned in the *Rig Veda* originates from this area. This leads some to the conclusion that the Aryans could not have come from anywhere else. But the same textual and vegetal evidence could also suggest that while the Aryans came from elsewhere, they only composed the Vedas after having created a settled civilisation in the Indo-Gangetic plains, which is why their allusions are all to India.

Unfortunately for the Hindutva ideologues, who seemed to be winning the historical battle, recent genetic research—published in a paper (in a peer-reviewed journal called *BMC Evolutionary Biology*) by Professor Martin P. Richards and fifteen other scientists, titled 'A Genetic Chronology for the Indian Subcontinent Points to Heavily Sex-biased Dispersals'—has confirmed that there were indeed significant migrations from the Central Asian steppes into the Indian subcontinent, starting from around 2000 BCE–1500 BCE.[6]

DNA studies show that the Indo-Aryan ethno-linguistic group has a higher signature of Central Asian genes than the corresponding Dravidian speakers; and given that Indo-Aryan languages have close affinities with the larger Indo-European linguistic family, it appears beyond dispute that a common proto-language was involved. The implications for the Savarkar-Golwalkar theory, though, are subversive, since they suggest that Hinduism or the Vedic religion may itself have originated with invaders from outside India, making it as 'un-Indian' in its origins as Islam or Christianity. The conclusions are sufficiently tentative to fall short of conclusive; one critical analysis concludes that 'it is difficult to deduce the direction of haplogroup R1a migration either into India or out of India, although the genetic data certainly show that there was migration between the regions'.[7] The advocates of Hindutva continue to insist the Indo-Aryans and their faith are indigenous to India, but DNA evidence may prove impossible to refute. Much of the dispute seems to centre not around whether there were infusions from abroad but as to whether they occurred 12,000 years ago or 4,000–3,500 years ago. If the first hypothesis is right, the resulting population was indigenous well before they composed the Vedas; the latter suggests a shorter gap between their arrival in India and the emergence of Hinduism.

To me this seems a distinction without a difference, but then I am much more comfortable with the idea that migrations into the subcontinent have been a permanent feature of Indian history than the Hindutva brigade is. In fact the Hindu Pallava kingdom even imported a monarch from Southeast Asia, when King Parameshwaravarman died without an heir in c. 731 CE.[8] A Pallava princess had been given in marriage to the Cham dynasty generations earlier and it was presumed one of her descendants could carry on the royal lineage. Accordingly, a delegation of nobles was sent to the Cambodia–Vietnam region and returned with a fourteen-year-old boy, who ruled for sixty-four years as King Nandivarman II (reigned c. 731–795 CE) and built a number of magnificent temples, including the famous Vaikuntha Perumal in Kanchipuram. Hinduism has been strengthened by its imports too.

HINDUISM AND SCIENCE

Similar battles are being waged over other kinds of intellectual terrain, with Hindu nationalists insisting upon recognising the glories of ancient Indian thought and long-neglected ancestral accomplishments, notably in science. There is definitely a case for enhancing the Indian public's awareness of the genuinely impressive accomplishments of their forebears (of which more below), rather than remaining schooled in a colonial-era Westernised view of the world. But the uncritical, indeed fantasy-laden, manner in which its Hindutva aficionados have advocated the cause has only discredited it.

The dominance of the BJP at the centre and in the states has propelled a number of true believers of Hindutva into positions of unprecedented influence, including in such forums[9] as the Indian Council for Historical Research, the University Grants Commission, and, it turned out, the programme committee of the Indian Science Congress, which scheduled a talk on 'Vedic Aviation Technology' in 2015 that elicited howls of protest from many delegates.

It has also given a licence to unqualified voices who gain in authority from their proximity to power. The 2018 statement by India's junior education Minister, Satyapal Singh, that Darwin's theory of evolution was "unscientific"—on the grounds that "no one has ever seen an ape turn into a man"—drew attention to the latest challenge posed to modern India by its current government. Earlier, another BJP stalwart, Rajasthan's education minister Vasudev Devnani, had dealt science another body blow by claiming that the cow is something of an obsession for the BJP, whose followers have assaulted human beings in the name of cow protection, but this was a step too far even for many of its sympathisers among the educated public.

The two Ministers are educated men: Satyapal Singh is a chemistry graduate, and Vasudev Devnani is a trained engineer. Whether their statements reveal the quality of science education in India, or merely confirm that Hindutva ideology trumps both scientific fact and common sense, neither learning nor governmental office appears to insulate either man from ignorance.

No greater proof of this can be found than the Prime Minister himself. Narendra Modi likes to be portrayed as a technology-friendly 21st century leader, but on 25 October 2014, Modi startled the world at the inauguration of a Mumbai hospital with the claim that the elephant-headed Hindu god Ganesh was proof of ancient India's knowledge of plastic surgery. He went on to cite the ancient epic, the Mahabharata, as confirming that "people then were aware of genetic science."

That the smallest imaginable elephant head cannot possibly fit into the largest available human neck does not appear to have occurred to the Prime Minister, whose fatuous claim discredited ancient India's genuine scientific accomplishments. Such ideas, because they are patently absurd, except in the realm of metaphor, have embarrassed those who advance them as well as those who cite them in support of broader, but equally unsubstantiated, claims to past scientific advances from genetic science to cloning and interstellar travel and the use of nuclear devices (by the philosopher-sage Kanada in the first century BCE). Petty chauvinism is always ugly but never more so than in the field of science, where knowledge must be uncontaminated by ideology, superstition or irrational pride.

India was indeed the world pioneer in plastic surgery; it produced the world's first known surgeon, Susruta, and archaeologists have found the world's oldest surgical instruments (dating from the 1st century) in India. There is evidence for rhinoplasty operations in the ancient texts. But the moment these historical facts were subsumed in a narrative about mythological transplated elephant heads, the actual facts were discredited.

This was not the Prime Minister's only offence. Before heading off for the Paris climate change negotiations, Modi told schoolchildren on Teachers' Day in 2014 that climate change was a myth because it was actually human beings whose capacity to cope with heat and cold has changed, rather than the environment. Global warming, he explained on national television, "is just a state of mind." What made it worse was that this came as an answer to a schoolchild's question about climate change. "That's because as you grow older you are less able to withstand heat and cold. The climate isn't changing." he said, "we are."

The disease is catching. On 31 May 2017, Justice Mahesh Chandra Sharma of the Rajasthan High Court, reportedly a science graduate himself, suggested to the Union of India that the cow be declared the national animal and that cow slaughter be punished with life imprisonment. In an interview to a television channel, Justice Sharma later told the nation that India's national bird, the peacock, "is a lifelong celibate" who "does not indulge in sex" but impregnates the peahen by shedding a tear. He cited Lord Krishna's use of a peacock feather as proof of its celibacy.

The idea of a peacock reproducing through tears may seem laughable, but there is nothing lachrymose about the ruling dispensation's dominant Hindutva ideology, which has helped propagate an astonishing amount of pseudoscience across the country. The gaggle of gurus who have made religion into a hugely successful business in India have inevitably joined the party. Modi associates like the yoga teacher and Ayurveda entrepreneur Baba Ramdev are regular offenders. Ramdev pronounces his pseudo-spiritual wisdom to the world, seeking, for instance, to sell medicines to "cure homosexuality".

Others assert, with some level of official encouragement, that the ancients had already discovered or invented every scientific accomplishment in the Vedic age, including jet aircraft (pushpak viman) and atomic weaponry. The underlying message is that ancient India had all the answers, and that traditional and indigenous practices and ways of life are vastly better than imported modern scientific ideas.

But the controversy also discredits the modern rationalists who, in their contempt for such exaggerated and ludicrous claims, also dismissed the more reasonable propositions pointing to genuine Indian accomplishments by the ancients. It is not necessary to debunk the genuine accomplishments of ancient Indian science in order to mock the laughable assertions of the Hindutva brigade. Separating the reasonable from the absurd is a necessary condition of well-founded criticism.

A BJP government choosing to assert its pride in yoga and Ayurveda, and seeking to promote them internationally, is, to my mind, perfectly acceptable. Not only are these extraordinary accomplishments of our civilisation, but they have always been, and should remain, beyond partisan politics. It is only if the BJP promoted them in place of fulfilling its responsibility to provide conventional healthcare and life-saving modern allopathic medicines to the Indian people, that we need object on policy grounds. But when the national manifesto of the BJP for the 2009 General Election claimed that in ancient times, rice yields in India stood at 20 tonnes per hectare—twice what farmers can produce today using intensive agriculture in the most fertile and propitious conditions imaginable—all one can do is to throw one's hands up in despair.

On the other hand, in asserting (in his own speech to the Indian Science Congress) that ancient Indians anticipated Pythagoras, Science and Technology Minister Dr Harsh Vardhan was not incorrect and should not have been ridiculed. In fact he could have added Newton, Copernicus, Kepler and Galileo as well, every single one of whom had been beaten to their famous 'discoveries' by an unknown and unsung Indian centuries earlier.

The *Rig Veda* asserted that gravitation held the universe together twenty-four centuries before the apple fell on Newton's head. Scholars working in Sanskrit anticipated his discoveries of calculus by at least 250 years. The Siddhantas are amongst the world's earliest texts on astronomy and mathematics; the *Surya Siddhanta*, written about 400 CE, includes a method for finding the times of planetary ascensions and eclipses. The notion of gravitation, or *gurutvakarshan*, features in these early texts. *Lost Discoveries*, by the American writer Dick Teresi, a comprehensive study of the ancient non-Western foundations of modern science, spells it out clearly: 'Two hundred years before Pythagoras,' writes Teresi, 'philosophers in northern India had understood that gravitation held the solar system together, and that therefore the sun, the most massive object, had to be at its centre.'[10]

Aryabhata was the first human being to explain, in 499 CE, that the daily rotation of the earth on its axis is what accounted for the daily rising and setting of the sun. (His ideas were so far in advance of his time that many later editors of his awe-inspiring *Aryabhatiya* altered the text to save his reputation from what they thought were serious errors.) Aryabhata conceived of the elliptical orbits of the planets a thousand years before Kepler, in the West, came to the same conclusion (having assumed, like all Europeans, that planetary orbits were circular rather than elliptical). He even estimated the value of the year at 365 days, six hours, 12 minutes and 30 seconds; in this he was only a few minutes off (the correct figure is just under 365 days and six hours). The translation of the *Aryabhatiya* into Latin in the thirteenth century taught Europeans a great deal; it also revealed to them that an Indian had known things that Europe would only learn of a millennium later.

The Vedic civilisation subscribed to the idea of a spherical earth at a time when everyone else, even the Greeks, assumed the earth was flat. By the fifth century CE Indians had calculated that the age of the earth was 4.3 billion years; as late as the nineteenth century, English scientists believed the earth was a hundred million years old, and it is only in the late twentieth century that Western scientists have come to estimate the earth to be about 4.6 billion years old.

India invented modern numerals (known to the world as 'Arabic' numerals because the West got them from the Arabs, who first encountered them in India). It was an Indian who first conceived of the zero, *shunya*; the concept of nothingness, *shunyata*, integral to Hindu and Buddhist thinking, simply did not exist in the West. Modern mathematics would have been impossible without the zero and the decimal system; just read a string of Roman numbers, which had no zeros, to understand their limitations.

Indian mathematicians invented negative numbers as well. The concept of infinite sets of rational numbers was understood by Jain thinkers in the sixth century BCE. Our forefathers can take credit for geometry, trigonometry, and calculus; the 'Bakhshali manuscript', seventy leaves of bark dating back to the early centuries of the Christian era, reveals fractions, simultaneous equations, quadratic equations, geometric progressions and even calculations of profit and loss, with interest.

The *Sulba Sutras*, composed between 800 and 500 BCE, demonstrate that India had Pythagoras's theorem before the great Greek was born, and a way of getting the square root of 2 correct to five decimal places. (Vedic Indians solved square roots in order to build sacrificial altars of the proper size.) The Kerala mathematician Nilakantha wrote sophisticated explanations of the irrationality of 'pi' before the West had heard of the concept. The *Vedanga Jyotisha*, written around 500 BCE, declares: 'Like the crest of a peacock, like the gem on the head of a snake, so is mathematics at the head of all knowledge.' India's mathematicians were poets too!

Hindus also invented the *Katapayadi* system (also known as Parralperru in Malayalam). In an age without paper and climatic conditions that tended to destroy records, this was a method where numbers could be transcribed as words or even verses. The idea that mathematical formulas could be written down as meaningful sentences helped preserve and perpetuate mathematical expertise in the country.

Indian numbers probably arrived in the Arab world in 773 CE with the diplomatic mission sent by the Hindu ruler of Sind to the court of the Caliph al-Mansur. This gave rise to the famous arithmetical text of al-Khwarizmi, written around 820 CE, which contains a detailed exposition of Indian mathematics, in particular the usefulness of the zero. It was al-Khwarizmi who is credited with the invention of algebra, though he properly credits Indians for it.

But the point is that, alas, India let this knowledge lapse. The reverence for the past that is integral to the ruling ideology is also reflective of a fear of rejecting the past, since the promotion of a faith-based communal identity is central to the Hindutva project, and faith is seen as emerging from the timeless wisdom of the past. Traditionalism benefits those who want to uphold the social order, ensure discipline and conformity, and prevent radical change. Science and rationality threaten such conformism.

This is why the ruling dispensation's political project of transforming secular India into a Hindu state requires the supremacy of religion over science. Religion is no longer just a question of your personal beliefs, a form of stretching out your hands to the divine; it is part of the assertion of a politics of identity built around faith. This requires an assault on science, since science challenges the established verities as religion does not.

When an Education Minister questions Darwin or asserts the miraculous powers of the cow, he is not merely offering a choice between a scientific theory and a faith-based one, he is reminding the public of their allegiance to a total worldview. That worldview embraces a larger political project that prescribes a set of beliefs and behaviours incompatible with science, skepticism and inquiry.

We had a glorious past; wallowing in it and debating it now will only saddle us with a contentious and unproductive present. Indians should take pride in what our forefathers did but resolve to be inspired by them rather than rest on their laurels. We need to use the past as a springboard, not as a battlefield. Only then can we rise above it to create for ourselves a future worthy of our remarkable past.

The BJP is still bent on creating a Hindu state in India. Sadly, this would not be the kind of Hindu state that has made India the scientific superpower of the ancient age, but one plunged in obscurantism and atavistic complacency. It is enough to make one shed a tear. One can only hope that there are no peahens around.

HINDUTVA AND HISTORY

Unsurprisingly, a later period of Indian history, following the Muslim conquests of north India, has become 'ground zero' in the battle of narratives between team Hindutva and the pluralists. When, with the publication of my 2016 book *Inglorious Empire: What the British Did to India*, I spoke of 200 years of foreign rule, I found it interesting that at the same time the Hindutva brigade, led by Prime Minister Modi himself, was speaking of 1,200 years of foreign rule. To them, the Muslim rulers of India, whether the Delhi Sultans, the Deccani Sultans or the Mughals (or the hundreds of other Muslims who occupied thrones of greater or lesser importance for several hundred years across the country) were all foreigners. I responded that while the founder of a Muslim dynasty may have well have come to India from abroad, he and his descendants stayed and assimilated in this country, married Hindu women, and immersed themselves in the fortunes of this land; each Mughal Emperor after Babar had less and less connection of blood or allegiance to a foreign country. If they looted or exploited India and Indians, they spent the proceeds of their loot in India, and did not send it off to enrich a foreign land as the British did. The Mughals received travellers from the Ferghana Valley politely, enquired about the well-being of the people there and perhaps even gave some money for the upkeep of the graves of their Chingizid ancestors, but they stopped seeing their original homeland as home. By the second generation, let alone the fifth or sixth, they were as 'Indian' as any Hindu.

This challenge of authenticity, however, cuts across a wide intellectual terrain. It emerges from those Hindus who share V. S. Naipaul's view of theirs as a 'wounded civilisation', a pristine Hindu land that was subjected to repeated defeats and conquests over the centuries at the hands of rapacious Muslim invaders and was enfeebled and subjugated in the process. To such people, independence is not merely British rule but an opportunity to restore the glory of their culture and religion, wounded by Muslim conquerors. Historians like Audrey Truschke, author of a sympathetic biography of the Mughal emperor Aurangzeb,[11] have argued that this account of Muslims despoiling the Hindu homeland is neither a continuous historical memory nor based on accurate records of the past. (For instance, it was a pious Hindu, Raja Jai Singh of Jaipur, who led Aurangzeb's armies against the Hindu warrior-hero Shivaji, just as the Hindu General Man Singh had led Akbar's forces against the Hindu hero Rana Pratap, whose principal lieutenant was a Muslim, Hakim Khan Sur.) But there is no gainsaying the emotional content of the Hindutva view of the past: it is for them a matter of faith that India is a Hindu nation, which Muslim rulers attacked, looted and sought to destroy, and documented historical facts that refute this view are at best an inconvenience, at worst an irrelevance.

Indeed, Truschke has disputed the widespread belief in India that Aurangzeb was a Muslim fanatic who destroyed thousands of Hindu temples, forced millions of Indians to convert to Islam, and enacted a genocide of Hindus. Though there is little doubt that he was indeed, in Jawaharlal Nehru's words, 'a bigot and an austere puritan'—he ended royal patronage of music, prohibited rituals of Hindu origin in his court, imposed the bigoted *jizya* tax on his non-Muslim subjects, withdrew land grants given to Hindus and introduced policies that favoured Muslims alone—none of the other propositions, she demonstrates in her work, was true, least of all the claim (made by many of those who fought successfully to remove his name from a prominent road in Delhi) that his ultimate aim was to eradicate Hindus and Hinduism. Historical evidence suggests that Aurangzeb did not destroy thousands of Hindu temples as is claimed and that the ones he did destroy were largely for political reasons; that he did little to promote conversions, as evidenced by the relatively modest number of Hindus who adopted Islam during Aurangzeb's rule; that he increased the proportion of Hindus in the Mughal nobility by co-opting a number of Maratha aristocrats from the Deccan; that he gave patronage to Hindu and Jain temples and liberally donated land to Brahmins; and that millions of Hindus thrived unmolested in his empire. History is a complex affair: Aurangzeb was undoubtedly an illiberal Muslim ruler, unlike his ancestors or the brother he decapitated on his ascent to the throne, Dara Shikoh, but he was not the genocidal mass-murderer and iconoclast many Hindus depict him as having been.

For Truschke, who concedes that Aurangzeb demolished a 'few dozen' temples, a 'historically legitimate view of Aurangzeb must explain why he protected Hindu temples more often than he demolished them'. Critics find this an insufficient excuse for his intolerance. One, Girish Shahane, no Hindutva apologist himself, retorts:

> 'Should we not criticise sportspersons who take money to fix matches unless they do so in most games they play? Should we

defend sexual predators on the grounds that the vast majority of their interactions with women are respectful? Should we object to a serial killer being called a psychopath because we can't be sure why he targeted particular victims but not hundreds of other people he met? It is important to push back against the Hindutvavadi idea of Muslim rulers as genocidal maniacs who destroyed shrines indiscriminately. But it is imperative we do it without explaining away Muslim religious prejudice where it exists.'[12]

A fairer assessment, in other words, might be to say that like many rulers of his time, whether Muslim or Hindu, Aurangzeb both protected and attacked Hindus and Muslims alike, though his religious bigotry was, of course, directed only at the former. But such nuanced accounts of Aurangzeb enjoy little traction amongst those who prefer their history in unambiguous shades of black and white. To quote Truschke once more, 'Aurangzeb is controversial not so much because of India's past but rather because of India's present... The narrative of Aurangzeb the Bigot, which crops up largely in polarising debates about Indian national identity, has more to do with modern politics than premodern history and is a byproduct and catalyst of growing intolerance in India.'

In this Hindutva-centred view, history is made of religion-based binaries, in which all Muslim rulers are evil and all Hindus are valiant resisters, embodiments of incipient Hindu nationalism. The Hindu nationalists believe, in Truschke's words, 'that India was subjected to repeated defeats over the centuries, including by generations of Muslim conquerors that enfeebled the people and their land...many in India feel injured by the Indo-Muslim past, and their sentiments [are] often undergirded by modern anti-Muslim sentiments.'[13] As K. N. Panikkar has pointed out, liberal and tolerant rulers such as Ashoka, Akbar, Jai Singh, Shahu Maharaj and Wajid Ali Shah do not figure in Hindutva's list of national heroes. (Indeed, where many nationalist historians extolled Akbar as the liberal, tolerant counterpart to the Islamist Aurangzeb, the Hindutva lobby has begun to attack him too, principally because he was Muslim, and like most medieval monarchs, killed princes who stood in his way, many of whom happened to be Hindu.)

Communal history continues past the era of Islamic rule. Among those Indians who revolted against the British, Bahadur Shah, Zinat Mahal, Maulavi Ahmadullah and General Bakht Khan, all Muslims, are conspicuous by their absence from Hindutva histories. And of course syncretic traditions such as the Bhakti movement, and universalist religious reformers like Rammohan Roy and Keshub Chandra Sen, do not receive much attention from the Hindutva orthodoxy. What does is the uncritical veneration of 'Hindu heroes' like Rana Pratap (portrayed now in Rajasthani textbooks as the victor of the Battle of Haldi Ghati against Akbar, which begs the question why Akbar and not he ruled the country for the following three decades) and of course Chhatrapati Shivaji, the intrepid Maratha warrior whose battles against the Mughals have now replaced accounts of Mughal kings in Maharashtra's textbooks. The Maharashtra Education Board's newly-revised class VII history book of 2017 has eliminated all mention of the pre-Mughal Muslim rulers of India as well, including Razia Sultan, the first woman queen of Delhi, Sher Shah Suri and Muhammad bin Tughlaq, who notoriously and disastrously moved India's capital south from Delhi to Daulatabad. (The educational system is the chosen battlefield for Hindutva's warriors, and curriculum revision their preferred weapon.)

THE STRUGGLE FOR FREEDOM

The debates over history are not confined to the distant past alone. Prime Minister Modi chose the anniversary of the Quit India movement in 1942 to launch a campaign called '70 Saal Azadi: Zara Yaad Karo Qurbani' ('Seventy years of freedom: remember the sacrifices'). The BJP which, led by the PM, has sought to drape itself in the mantle of nationalism, is now seeking to appropriate the freedom struggle for its cause. Ironically the Quit India movement is an occasion the BJP could well have chosen to criticise rather than celebrate, since it resulted in the jailing by the British of all the leaders and thousands of workers of the nationalist movement, giving the Muslim League the freedom it needed to build up a support base it had lacked in the elections of 1937, and thus, strengthened the hands of those who wanted Partition.

But the Modi government has no intention of repudiating Quit India as a Congress folly. It wants to make heroes of freedom fighters, by implication placing them on its own side in a contemporary retelling of history pegged to the seventieth anniversary of our independence. The complication is that the Sanghivadi political cause to which the BJP is heir—embodied in the Jana Sangh, the RSS, and the Hindutva movement—had no prominent freedom fighter of its own during the nationalist struggle for *azadi* (freedom). The BJP traces its origin to leaders who were not particularly active during the nationalist movement. The lack of inspiration for the people in the parent body of the BJP means they have to look for role models elsewhere.

The process had already begun, lest we forget, when then Chief Minister Modi moved aggressively to lay claim to the legacy of one of India's most respected founding fathers, Sardar Vallabhbhai Patel, before the 2014 election. In his quest to garb himself in a more distinguished lineage than his party can ordinarily lay claim to, Modi called on farmers across India to donate iron from their ploughs to construct a giant 550-foot statue of the Iron Man in his state, which would be by far the largest statue in the world, dwarfing the Statue of Liberty. But it will be less of a monument to the modest Gandhian it ostensibly honours than an embodiment of the overweening ambitions of its builder.

Modi's motives are easy to divine. His own image had been tarnished by the communal massacre in Gujarat when he was chief minister in 2002. Identifying himself with Patel—who is portrayed as the leader who stood up for the nation's Hindus during the horrors of Partition, stood up to Nehru in ordering the rebuilding of the ruined Somnath temple and was firm on issues like Kashmir—is an attempt at character-building by association: Modi himself as an embodiment of the tough, decisive man of action that Patel was, rather than the destructive bigot his enemies decry.

It helps that Patel is widely admired for his extraordinary role in forging India that gave him an unchallenged standing as 'the Iron Man'. Patel has both the national appeal and Gujarati origin that appeal to Modi. The Modi-as-latter-day-Patel message has been resonating well with many Gujaratis, who are proud to be reminded of a native son the nation looks up to, and with many of India's urban middle-class, who see in Modi a strong leader to cut through the confusion and indecision of India's messy democracy.

But Patel's conduct during the violence that accompanied Partition stands in stark contrast to Modi's in 2002. Both Patel and Modi were faced with the serious breakdown of law and order in their respective domains, involving violence and rioting against the Muslims. In Delhi in 1947, Patel immediately and effectively moved to ensure the protection of Muslims, herding 10,000 in the most vulnerable areas to the security of Delhi's Red Fort. Because Patel was afraid that local security forces might have been affected by the virus of communal passions, he moved army troops from Madras and Pune to Delhi to ensure law and order. Patel made it a point to send a reassuring signal to the Muslim community by attending prayers at the famous Nizamuddin Dargah to convey a clear message that Muslims and their faith belonged unquestionably on the soil of India. Patel also went to the border town of Amritsar, where there were attacks on Muslims fleeing to the new Islamic state of Pakistan, and pleaded with Hindu and Sikh mobs to stop victimising Muslim refugees. In each of these cases, Patel succeeded, and there are literally tens of thousands of people who are alive today because of his interventions.

The contrast with what happened in Gujarat in 2002 is painful. Whether or not one ascribes direct blame to Modi for the pogrom that year, he can certainly claim no credit for acting in the way Patel did in Delhi. In Gujarat, there was no direct and immediate action by Modi, as the state's chief executive, to protect Muslims. Nor did Modi express any public condemnation of the attacks, let alone undertake any symbolic action of going to a masjid or visiting a Muslim neighbourhood to convey reassurance.

One cannot imagine Patel saying to an interviewer, as Modi did, when asked how he felt about the killings of Muslims in Gujarat: "[if] someone else is driving a car and we're sitting behind, even then if a puppy comes under the wheel, will it be painful or not?"[14] There is a particular irony to a self-proclaimed 'Hindu nationalist' like Modi, whose speeches have often dripped with contempt for Muslims, laying

claim to the legacy of a Gandhian leader who would never have qualified his Indian nationalism with a religious label.

Sardar Patel believed in equal rights for all irrespective of their religion or caste. It is true that at the time of Partition Patel was inclined
to believe, unlike Nehru, that an entire community had seceded. In my
biography *Nehru: The Invention of India* (2003) I have given some examples of Nehru and Patel clashing on this issue. But there are an equal
number of examples where Patel, if he had to choose between what
was the right thing for many Hindus and what was the right thing morally, invariably plumped for the moral Gandhian approach.

An example, so often distorted by the Sangh Parivar apologists, was
his opposition to Nehru's pact with Liaquat Ali Khan, the prime minister of Pakistan, on the question of violence in East Pakistan against
the Hindu minority. The Nehru-Liaquat pact was indeed criticised by
Patel and he disagreed quite ferociously with Nehru on the matter. But
when Nehru insisted on his position, it was Patel who gave in, and his
reasoning was entirely Gandhian: that violence in West Bengal against
Muslims essentially took away Indians' moral right to condemn violence against Hindus in East Pakistan. That was not a Hindu nationalist
position but a classically Gandhian approach as an *Indian* nationalist.

History has often been contested terrain in India, but its revival in
the context of twenty-first century politics is a sobering sign that the
past continues to have a hold over the Hindutva movement in the present. While the Mughals will be demonised as a way of delegitimising
Indian Muslims (who are stigmatised as 'Babur ke aulad', the sons of
Babur rather than of the Indian soil), the arguments over Patel confirm
that he and other heroes of the freedom struggle will be hijacked to the
present ruling party's attempts to appropriate a halo of nationalism that
none of its forebears has done anything to earn.

HINDUTVA AND CULTURE

If the rewriting of the historical past is a vital first objective of the
Hindutva project, the second is the removal of what they see as the
various accretions to the Hindu idea that had arisen over the years.

These accretions, to the more rabid of the Hindutva brigades, include the acceptance of difference that Vivekananda and Radhakrishnan had celebrated. Indeed, the distinctive difference between what one might call the Nehruvian version of Indian nationalism and the Hindutva version of it is the latter's active rejection of different interpretations and the diversity of representations for which the Indian cultural tradition had become known, and which other Hindus portrayed as the strength of their culture.

One aspect of this is the relentless campaign being waged against heterodox interpretations of Hinduism itself—and this in the name of a faith which proudly includes no concept of heresy. Thus Hindutva mobs attacked and vandalised the invaluable Bhandarkar Oriental Research Institute's library in Pune to protest its co-operation with the research work of the historian James Laine, whose book allegedly cast aspersions on the parentage of Shivaji. The courts offer a less dramatic form of censorship, since Hindutva activists can invoke Section 295(a) of the Indian Penal Code, which criminalises insults to religious sentiments, though the intent was only to outlaw inflammatory writings published with deliberate and malicious intent. Under this provision, serious scholars like Wendy Doniger, who has authored several learned and brilliant studies of Hinduism, have been sued, and publishers, intimidated by the forces arrayed against them and reluctant to spend what it would take to defend their authors' freedoms, have usually caved in. One of Doniger's books on Hinduism was not only withdrawn from the marketplace by its publishers, but all existing copies pulped in order not to give offence to the Hindutva lobby.

The destruction and pulping of books, and the burning of libraries, is possible because the colonial-era law criminalises even accurate statements about Indian religion and history if these offend the sentiments of any community in India. Still, to see such actions being carried out in the name of the Hindu faith is profoundly disquieting. In the Hindu culture that I grew up with, books are revered. If I so much as accidentally touched a fallen book or even a magazine or newspaper with my foot, I was brought up to bend down, touch it again with my fingertips in apology and apply my fingers to my eyes and forehead to beg forgiveness from the Goddess Saraswati for my transgression, a practice I still perform in my seventh decade. This respect for the printed word can be found among Hindus of every part of the country. How can people who claim to be Hindu not just disrespect but actually destroy books?

The destruction of some people's books is inevitably accompanied by the promotion of other books. Foreign Minister Sushma Swaraj, not known to be an RSS sympathiser but aggressive in her cultural nationalism, proposed the adoption of the Bhagavad Gita as the 'Rashtriya Granth', or national holy book. There are four problems with Sushma Swaraj's advocacy of the Bhagavad Gita as our 'national holy book', of which the first is that, to cite no less a source than Prime Minister Modi himself, we already have a national holy book: it's called the Constitution of India.

The second is that we are a land of multiple faiths, each of which has its own holy books; on what basis would we pick any one of them in the capacity of a national holy book? Which Sikh would put the Gita ahead of the Guru Granth Sahib, for instance?

And if the answer to that question is, as Smt. Swaraj suggests, that it is the holiest book of the overwhelming Hindu majority of our population, the proposition is contestable, like most things in Hindu philosophy. As a practising (and reasonably widely-read) Hindu myself, I find many ideas in the *Upanishads* and the *Puranas* that are not in the *Gita*. I see Hinduism as a pluralistic faith of many holy books and many ways of worshipping the Divine. You don't have to agree with those Hindu scholars who argue that the *Gita*, being part of an *itihasa*, a subset of *smriti* (that which is heard and remembered, orally), ranks lower in the hierarchy of Hindu sacred texts than the Vedas and the *Upanishads*, which are *sruti* (seen, heard and recorded divine revelation). But such arguments apart, there is no doubt that there are many views of the relative merits of several Indian holy books.

Smt. Swaraj (like many before her, including Vivekananda and Gandhiji) may be inspired by the *Gita*, but other, equally devout, Hindus might have other preferences. As Dayanand might have asked: Why not the *RigVeda*, for instance, the primordial revelatory text of the

Hindu faith? Why not the *smriti* text known as the Srimad Bhagavatam, or Bhagavata Purana, which is recited for an entire week (*saptaham*) every year in many Hindu temples and homes? The quest to anoint a national holy book will not just divide Indians—it will divide Hindus as well.

But it's the fourth problem that's most relevant to a political discussion of the issue. For a government minister to raise the idea of a national holy book serves to ignite not just controversy, but fears—fears of a majoritarian project that will slowly but surely erode India's pluralist (officially secular) identity and replace it with an overtly Hindu one.

Signs of such inclinations have been accumulating since the BJP rode to power in May 2014. There has been the overt declaration by RSS leader Mohan Bhagwat that all Indians are Hindus,[15] and by implication that those who do not consider themselves Hindus aren't actually Indian, and don't belong here. There's the statement by a minister, Giriraj Singh, that those who don't vote for Modi should move to Pakistan,[16] and the one by another minister, Sadhvi Niranjana Jyoti, that people are either followers of Rama or bastards (*Ramzaade ya Haramzaade*). Neither of these offenders has been required to pay for their statements by relinquishing their seats on Prime Minister Modi's Council of Ministers.

There was the Shiv Sena MP, a member of the ruling coalition, shoving food down the throat of a fasting Muslim during Ramzan, and getting away without the slightest censure from the ruling party.[17] There have been numerous incidents of communal violence, instigated for political purposes no doubt, but instilling fear in the targeted minorities. And there was the faintly ridiculous episode of the mass conversion of fifty-seven bewildered Bengali Muslims in Agra, through a mix of intimidation and inducement, under the Sangh Parivar's long-dormant '*ghar wapsi*' scheme.[18] (Many of them, it seems, were illegal immigrants from Bangladesh, who thought that signing up would be an excellent dodge to regularise their status in India.)

The resultant uproar put '*ghar wapsi*' on the back burner, but the 'reconversion' to the parent faith of those Indians who are not Hindu remains a cherished Hindutva project. As Manmohan Vaidya of the RSS has explained: 'Ghar wapsi is a natural urge to connect to our roots.'

So Smt. Swaraj's declaration joins a long list of statements and actions by our Hindutva-inspired rulers that cumulatively have stirred disquiet across the country.

Is this wise? It is ironic that Prime Minister Modi keeps on emphasising the message of development and economic transformation, while his aides persist in raising bogeys that their leader has been attempting to lay to rest. There is little doubt that after the BJP rode to power on a mantra of inclusive development 'sab ka saath, sab ka vikas' its Hindutva core has begun to take advantage of its proximity to government to assertively push a sectarian agenda. As has been noted, Hindutva acolytes are being appointed to research professorships and vice-chancellorships; the Indian Council of Historical Research was headed for three years by a true believer whose Hindutva credentials reportedly outshine his historical ones, textbooks in BJP-ruled states like Maharashtra and Rajasthan are being rewritten to privilege ancient Hindu glories, and Sanskrit is being promoted. Some of this, one might argue, is inevitable in any democracy after a transfer of power from one ruling dispensation to another. But some, at least, distracts from the Prime Minister's central (and oft-repeated) message that economic growth is his faith, the Constitution is his holy book and Parliament is his temple.

Just as investors tend not to come to war zones—which is why peace on our borders is in our national interest—so too do investors prefer to risk their capital in harmonious societies that are focused on the future rather than divided by the past. The BJP and its Government should heed one simple dictum: leave religion to the personal space and preference of every Indian. Let us have no national holy book, just as our constitution forbids us from having a national religion. Our country was once divided over religion; let us not now promote a partition in the Indian soul that will be as bad as the partition we have already endured on Indian soil. Let us not awake demons that seven decades of secular Indian democracy have put to rest after the tragic horrors of 1947.

It is time to let sleeping dogmas lie.

NARROW-MINDED BIGOTRY

Hindutva takes a dully static view of India's cultural tradition, ignoring its capacity to react to and absorb foreign influences, and negating its inherent dynamism. In the name of this limited and narrow view of Hindu culture, and in addition to its threats to books, Hindutva activists have assaulted a film-maker for allegedly planning to shoot a love-scene between a Rajput princess and a Muslim conqueror (of which more later); vandalised exhibitions of M. F. Husain's paintings because he had depicted Hindu goddesses in the nude; disrupted the shooting of the Indo-Canadian Deepa Mehta's film on Benares widows for insulting an age-old Hindu practice; denigrated the Malayalam writer Kamala Das for her conversion to Islam as Kamala Suraiya; banned A. K. Ramanujam's classic text on the hundreds of versions of the *Ramayana* from the syllabus of Delhi University; and trashed a SAHMAT exhibition on the Ayodhya dispute. The politicisation of culture is truly complete under India's Hindutva government.

Of these, the assault on M. F. Husain and his works was typical of Hindutva intolerance. In 1996 a mob destroyed several paintings of the artist at an exhibition in Ahmedabad, outraged that a Muslim artist had portrayed Hindu goddesses in the nude. Husain had long been known to use Hindu iconography—goddesses and *apsaras* were among his favourite themes, and he had depicted Indira Gandhi as Durga, and the actress Madhuri Dixit as the *apsara* Menaka, to telling effect in the past, infusing his work with energetic reimaginings of the tales and legends of Hindu tradition. But rather than feeling flattered that a Muslim artist should draw so liberally from the Hindu ethos, the self-appointed custodians of Hindu culture were outraged that he had done so. An irate Hindutva cadre declared that no Muslim had the right to portray Hindu deities 'any way he wishes', going on to demand that Husain's paintings should all be immersed in the Ganga, so they might be simultaneously cleansed and destroyed.

At one time one could have said that this was not Hindu behaviour, and indeed the paintings objected to had been displayed for twenty years previously without any Hindu objecting to them. But this was not about Hinduism, it was about Hindutva politics: the Bajrang Dal and its ilk were practising a basic form of political me-too-ism. Having seen successive governments pandering to the offended sentiments of minority communities, they wanted to show they could be offended too, and thereby bend society to their will.

After the vandalism came the legal harassment of the nonagenarian artist by malicious lawsuits seeking his prosecution for allegedly having offended the petitioners' notions of morality by the use of nudity in his art, particularly in paintings of Hindu goddesses and in the depiction of the contours of India in the shape of a semi-nude female figure. The piling up of a number of cases motivated essentially by anti-Muslim bigotry drove Husain into self-imposed exile in Dubai and London and deprived India of a national treasure. So many abusive cases were filed against him that a court even went so far as to attach his home and his property—a decision later reversed by the Supreme Court. But Husain feared the harassment would not end there; the moment he set foot in Delhi or Mumbai, he said, he was sure to be dragged off to the lock-up, tormented by legal proceedings. He was nearly ninety-one when he fled the country, at an age when he should have been living as a beloved and honoured eminence in his native land. But he did not want to spend his last years battling the persecution of the petty hypocrites who had turned on him. So he stayed away, and passed away in exile.

Delhi High Court Justice Sanjay Kishan Kaul (later elevated to the Supreme Court) authored a magisterial judgment in 2007 disposing of several of these cases in a learned, closely-argued and meticulously-footnoted ruling that bears detailed reading and extensive citation.[19] Recalling the richness of India's 5,000-year-old culture, the judge noted:

'Ancient Indian art has been never been devoid of eroticism where sex worship and graphical representation of the union between man and woman has been a recurring feature. The sculpture on the earliest temples of (the) Mithuna image or the erotic couples in Bhubaneshwar, Konark and Puri in Orissa (150–1250 CE); Khajuraho in Madhya Pradesh (900–1050 CE); Limbojimata temple at Delmel, Mehsana (tenth century CE); Kupgallu Hill, Bellary,

Madras; and Nilkantha temple at Sunak near Baroda [are fine examples of this]... Even the very concept of (the) "lingam" of the God Shiva resting in the centre of the yoni, is in a way representation of the act of creation, the union of Prakriti and Purusha. The ultimate essence of a work of ancient Indian erotic art has been religious in character and can be enunciated as a state of heightened delight or ananda, the kind of bliss that can be experienced only by the spirit.'

But Husain's tormentors seemed to know nothing of these ancient Hindu traditions; instead, they professed to be defending their idea of the Hindu faith and the nation's cultural integrity. (In objecting to his use of nudity, they were in fact being far more Puritan, in the Christian sense of the term, than Hindu.) Instead of applauding the decision of a Muslim artist to derive inspiration from the ancient legends of his homeland, they accused him of desecrating a faith that was not his. Instead of honouring an artist who had revived worldwide appreciation of the richness and diversity of the sources of Indian culture, they attacked him for insulting Indian culture, reducing Indianness to the narrow bigotry of their own blinkers.

It is a disgrace that India allowed the most intolerant elements of its society to derail the life and work of such a great artist. These so-called Hindus had clearly never seen the inside of any of our ancient temples, had never marvelled at Khajuraho or seen a sunset at Konark. Theirs is a notion of 'Bharatiya Sanskriti' that is profoundly inauthentic, because it can be traced back no further than the Puritanism that accompanied the Muslim conquests.

The elderly artist had sought the dismissal of various cases filed against him for allegedly offending public decency and morality by his 'obscene' use of nudity in his paintings, particularly those of Hindu goddesses and of 'Bharat Mata'. While Justice Kaul's ruling took care of the legal aspects of the cases against Husain, his larger observations on the issue deserve the attention of every thinking Indian.

The most important of these, I believe, is the judge's rejection of the tendency of thin-skinned (or maliciously motivated) people across the country to claim to be offended by artistic and literary works. If you're easily offended, he argues, don't read the book, look at the painting or open the website that offends you, but don't prevent the artist or writer from enjoying his constitutionally protected freedom of expression. What is vital, according to Justice Kaul, is to look at the work of art from the artist's point of view—his or her intent rather than the hyper-sensitive viewer's reaction. Lest he be promptly denounced by the Hindutva brigade as a deracinated pseudo-secularist, the judge wisely cites Swami Vivekananda's words in defence of his approach: 'We tend to reduce everyone else to the limits of our own mental universe and begin privileging our own ethics, morality, sense of duty and even our sense of utility. All religious conflicts arose from this propensity to judge others. If we indeed must judge at all, then it must be "according to his own ideal, and not by that of anyone else". It is important, therefore, to learn to look at the duty of others through their own eyes and never judge the customs and observances of others through the prism of our own standards.'

But Justice Kaul goes even further in extending the boundaries of the permissible in India. Nudity and sex, he argues, have an honoured place in art and literature: 'In the land of the Kama Sutra, we shy away from its very name?' he asks in surprise. 'Beauty lies in the eyes of the beholder and so does obscenity… [In Hindu tradition], sex was embraced as an integral part of a full and complete life. It is most unfortunate that India's new "puritanism" is being carried out in the name of cultural purity and a host of ignorant people are vandalising art and pushing us towards a pre-Renaissance era.'

I am not disrespecting those of my Hindu readers who, while fully respecting Husain as an artist, and without expressing any of the communal bigotry that I found particularly distasteful about this affair, nonetheless expressed anguish at seeing representations of goddesses in the nude. They wrote to me at the time of their hurt that images they worshipped should have been so depicted; many asked why Husain has not depicted figures of other faiths, including his own, undressed. (He had once painted the Prophet's wife as a fully clad woman in a sari which even covered her head.) Several added that this was because Hindus are a pushover; other faiths are more robust in their self-defence, whereas Hindus like me are all too willing to accept being insulted.

There's a lot to be said about all this that go beyond the scope of this book. But some points must be made. First: I don't feel insulted by the paintings because (unlike the Danish cartoonists who caricatured the Prophet Muhammad) no insult was intended. Husain was, after all, a major artist, with a long record of being inspired by Hindu mythology as a vital source of inspiration for his work. His paintings of goddesses were consistent with fifty years of his paintings of other iconic Hindu images, clad and unclad. Husain, who grew up in Pandharpur, a major pilgrim centre, and spent all his formative years interacting with devout Hindus, watching Hindu festivals, and drawing nourishment from these influences, was fascinated by Hindu gods. More than the Prophet or any Muslim imagery, what fired his imagination was Hindu India, in which he was reared and which he sought to celebrate. I saw the paintings in that context; his critics saw them out of context (and judging by some emails I received, grossly exaggerated what the paintings depicted). Husain saw his paintings as being within a millennial Indian tradition in which nudity has been widely used in art, including on temple walls. So did I; in Thiruvananthapuram's annual Attukal Bhagavathy festival, the goddess is routinely portrayed topless in posters throughout the city.

Husain as an artist had long used form to suggest ideas beyond form; images in his works are both less and more than realistic depictions of what they portray. His paintings are full of metaphors and allusions; the body, he often said, is a representation of something formless, illusory (a form of *maya*). As a Hindu, I did not see his goddesses as literal depictions of the images I worship. I believe in the Upanishadic view that the Divine is essentially unknowable, and that all worship consists of human beings stretching out their hands to that which they cannot touch. But since we humans, with our limited minds, need something more specific to aid our imaginations, we visualise God in forms that we find more easily recognisable. Hinduism, in accepting that need, also gives its adherents an infinite variety of choices about how to imagine God. That's why there are 333,000 (or million) names and depictions of the Divine in Hinduism; each Hindu may pick the ones he wishes to venerate, and the form in which he wishes to venerate them. There's nothing more 'authentic' about a Raja Ravi Varma image of Saraswati than that of a calendar artist; each is imagining the goddess according to his own sensibility. As a Hindu, I had no difficulty in according Husain the same right.

The question of why Husain doesn't paint Muslim figures in the nude is a red herring. The Islamic tradition is a different one from either the Hindu or the Western. Islam, after all, prohibits any visual depiction of the Prophet, whereas visualising our gods and goddesses is central to the practice of Hinduism.

It is time all Indians, but especially Hindus, woke up to what is being done to our heritage in our name. To reduce the soaring majesty of an inclusive, free-ranging, eclectic and humane faith to the petit-bourgeois morality of narrow-minded bigots is a far greater betrayal of our culture than anything an artist can paint.

For where, in the Hindutva brigade's definition of '*Bharatiya sanskriti*', do the erotic sculptures of Khajuraho belong? Should their explicitly detailed couplings not be pulled down, as Fashion TV's cable signals were during the last BJP government? What about the *Kama Sutra*, the tradition of the devadasis, the eros of the Krishna Leela—are they all un-Indian now?

When the late, great Nobel Prize-winning Mexican poet Octavio Paz wrote his final ode to our civilisation, *In Light of India*, he devoted an entire section to Sanskrit erotic poetry, basing himself, among other things, on the Buddhist monk Vidyakara's immortal eleventh-century compilation of 1,728 *kavya* (poems), many of which are exquisitely profane. Are poets like Ladahachandra or Bhavakadevi, who a thousand years ago wrote verse after verse describing and praising the female breast, to be expelled from the Hindutva canon of 'Bharatiya sanskriti'? Should we tell the Octavio Paz of the future seeking to appreciate the attainments of our culture that the televised *Mahabharata* is 'Bharatiya sanskriti', but a classical portrayal of the erotic longings of the *gopis* for Krishna is not?

The televised *Mahabharata*, which broke a viewership record set by its predecessor the *Ramayana* series, has much to answer for. It would be unwise to underestimate the significant role of Ramananda Sagar's

Ramayana serial on Doordarshan in promoting Hindutva revival through a cardboard depiction of Rama as a Bollywood B-film hero, complete with crude special effects, melodramatic dialogue and theatrical acting. Encouraged by its success, B. R. Chopra offered similar treatment to the *Mahabharata*; both epics became the most widely-watched shows on television, attracting some 92 per cent of all television viewers to their weekly telecasts. A nation glued to its television sets in an era where there was only one channel, the public broadcaster Doordarshan, found itself alternately unified and exalted by seeing its collective national myths rendered simply and accessibly on the small screen. One of the many ironies of contemporary India is how a secular government and a materialistic Bollywood combined to produce the religious underpinnings for the rise of Hindu cultural nationalism in India.

(This has actually continued into the present day. There has been a proliferation of television channels, but several show hugely popular 'serials', the Indian version of soap operas, which embody and propagate conservative 'Hindu' values. Many Bollywood superstars are themselves Muslim, including five who sport the surname Khan, and they have all portrayed devout Hindu heroes and danced to devotional songs before Hindu idols. The portrayal of sympathetic Muslim characters in popular cinema, like the brave and patriotic Pathan in *Zanjeer* (1972) or the lovable Akbar in *Amar Akbar Anthony* (1977) has declined, subliminally reinforcing the notion of India as a land of Hindu ethos rather than pluralist culture.)

Hindutva hypocrisy is also much in evidence in relation to alcohol, deemed to be un-Hindu and officially banned in the prime minister's own home state of Gujarat (though, reportedly, widely available, at a price, under the table). Wide and frequent are the calls for Prohibition, and rare indeed the figure in Indian public life who would be willing to be photographed with a drink in his hand. And yet alcohol has a hoary history in Hindu literature. As I have mentioned earlier, Soma, or Som-Ras, was the favourite beverage of the Vedic deities and was offered in most of the sacrifices performed in honour of Rig Vedic gods like Indra, Agni, Varun, and others. The Vedic gods were no teetotallers, and drinking was an essential feature of these sacrifices: for instance, in one ritual (performed at the beginning of the Vajapeya sacrifice), the historian D. N. Jha describes a collective drinking ritual in which a sacrificer offered five cups to Indra as well as seventeen cups of soma and seventeen cups of sura to thirty-four gods.[20]

A large variety of some fifty intoxicating drinks are mentioned in ancient Hindu texts. Jha tells us that the use of alcohol by men was quite common, though sometimes discouraged among Brahmins, and instances of drinking among women were not rare. Sanskrit literature, including the plays of Kalidasa, and Buddhist Jataka texts, frequently mention alcoholic drinks. Ancient Hindus were far less puritanical than those who claim to be custodians of their legacy today. The prohibitionist instincts of Hindutva's shock troops find their sternest rebuke in the divine hedonism of their most ancient gods.

But the disapproval of alcohol as a sinful Western indulgence is of a piece with the assault on any cultural practice deemed to be insufficiently Hindu by the self-appointed guardians of Indian culture. The news from UP, telling us that Chief Minister Yogi Adityanath's anti-Romeo squads have questioned 21,37,520 people for being out with girls between 22 March and 15 December 2017, has offered a sobering reminder of how far moral policing has gone in today's India. Worse, it turns out that of those questioned, 9,33,099 have been officially "warned" and 1,706 FIRs issued against 3,003 persons. All this has happened in less than nine months.

So this is what a once-free society has been reduced to: multiple police squads, each consisting of a sub-inspector and two constables, patrolling Uttar Pradesh's university campuses, college yards, cinema theatres, parks and other public places, looking for "Romeos". The term seems to be loosely defined, entitling the cops to stop and question any young couple. While it may have once been intended to curb harassment by louts loafing in public places to "eve-tease" unwary women, the sheer numbers reported confirm that the harassment is now coming mainly from the authorities and not from their targets.

The term "anti-Romeo squad" is itself telling. It traces its origins to the "Roadside Romeos" of my own youth—raffish fellows in drainpipe pants, wavy locks and rakish moustaches, usually unemployed, who lounged about whistling at, or singing snatches of Bollywood film songs to, passing women. They were usually ignored, and mostly harmless. Today's UP police have a far broader target: a Romeo is any young man aspiring to woo his own Juliet. Shakespeare's Romeo, after all, defied convention and evaded his disapproving parents to pursue his love for a woman from the wrong family. That is precisely what Yogi Adityanath does not want Romeo's 21st century imitators to do.

The anti-Romeo squads are merely the latest sign of the continuing assault on any cultural practice deemed to be insufficiently Hindu by the self-appointed guardians of Indian culture. A new spurt of arrests is likely as the anti-Romeo squads double their vigilance for Valentine's Day. Until Yogi's victory, policing Valentine's Day lovers was a task undertaken by lumpen activists of assorted *senas* and *dals*; now, in a sort of reverse privatisation, it is a task that has been taken up by the BJP-run state.

And what of the freelance anti-romance troublemakers? After years of attacking couples holding hands on 14 February, trashing stores selling Valentine's Day greeting cards and shouting slogans outside cafes with canoodling couples, Hindutva activists changed tactics last year. The Hindu Mahasabha announced that it would send squads out to catch any unmarried couples out for a tryst on Valentine's Day and promptly cart them off to a temple to be married. (And, if the Hindutvavadi MP and Godse admirer Sakshi Maharaj has his way, they will be lectured on the virtues of producing between four and ten children forthwith, in order to give his fantasies a voting majority.)

The police-uniform-clad face of intolerance might be amusing if it weren't for the fact that all involved are deadly serious. The nativists argue that Valentine's Day is an imported celebration, which it is (but so is Christmas, or Id-ul-Nabi, or International Women's Day, for that matter, and they don't have the nerve to attack those). They also argue that it is un-Indian because it celebrates romantic love, and they're completely wrong. Historians tell us that there was a well-established Hindu tradition of adoration for Kamadeva, the lord of love, which was only abandoned after the Muslim invasions in medieval times. But then no one in the Hindu Mahasabha has any real idea of Hindu tradition—

their idea of Indian values is not just primitive and narrow-minded, it is also profoundly anti-historical.

In fact, what young people call 'PDA' or 'public display of affection' was widely prevalent in ancient India. As late as the eleventh century, Hindu sexual freedoms were commented on by shocked travellers from the Muslim world. Today's young celebrants of Valentine's Day are actually upholding India's ancient pre-Muslim culture, albeit in a much milder form than is on display, for instance, in Khajuraho. In a sense, 14 February is their attempt at observing *Kamadeva Divas*. How ironic that they should incur the disapproval of the self-appointed custodians of Hindu culture!

But let's face it: this is less about teenagers dating than about the ruling dispensation's political project of transforming secular India into their idea of a Hindu state. Tradition is sought to be upheld in the name of culture: Traditionalism benefits those who want to uphold the social order, ensure discipline and conformity, and prevent radical change. Love affairs, which may after all cross caste or religious lines, are to be disapproved of for threatening this social order. Worse still, they reflect the autonomy of the individual and her right to choose, which is anathema to those who would prefer to make faceless cow-worshippers of us all.[21] Would it have been better if the BJP government, with its fondness for rebaptising government schemes with new Sanskrit appellations, gave serious thought to just calling Valentine's Day *Kamadeva Divas*, to link it to ancient Hindu culture?

But it's in the 'self-appointed' part that the real problem lies. All this is being done in the name of a notion of Indian culture whose assertion is based on a denial of India's real rather than imagined past. India's culture has always been a capacious one, expanding to include new and varied influences, from the Greek invasions to the British. The central battle in contemporary Indian civilisation is that between those who, to borrow from Walt Whitman, acknowledge that as a result of our own historical experience, we are vast, we contain multitudes, and those who have presumptuously taken it upon themselves to define—in increasingly narrower terms—what is 'truly' Indian.

TARNISHING THE TAJ

The latest victim of this definitional exercise is India's most iconic monument, the Taj Mahal. In a country whose toxic politics has led to everything—from festival firecrackers to animal husbandry (the care and protection of cows, of which more anon)—taking on a 'communal', religious colouring, it shouldn't be too much of a surprise that its most famous monument hasn't been exempt.

The Taj Mahal is India's most magnificent piece of architecture. Built nearly four centuries ago by the Mughal Emperor Shah Jahan as a mausoleum for his beloved wife, who had borne him thirteen children and died in the process of producing the fourteenth, it attracts tens of millions of tourists and is by far the country's most-photographed building. The exquisite marble monument to love was hailed by India's only winner of the Nobel Prize for literature, Rabindranath Tagore, as 'a teardrop on the cheek of Time'.

But the Taj now has other reasons for tears. Its gleaming white surface is yellowing as a result of rampant air pollution from factories and small businesses around it, as well as the Mathura refinery not far way. Repairs are needed so frequently that scaffolding often obscures its famous minarets. There has been a 35 per cent drop in foreign tourists from the 743,000 who went there in 2012 to the 480,000 tourists who came in 2015.[22] The crowded and grimy town of Agra in Uttar Pradesh, which hosts the Taj, puts visitors off: American basketball player Kevin Durant sparked a row with his graphic descriptions of the awful conditions around the Taj Mahal after a visit there in the summer of 2017.

And worst of all, the new ruling party in Uttar Pradesh, the BJP, has decided that far from being proud of its most famous edifice, it wants as little to do with it as possible.

Yogi Adityanath, the chief minister, began the controversy by deploring the fact that his government used to give models of the Taj as gifts to visiting foreign dignitaries. Declaring that the monument did not 'reflect Indian culture', the Yogi announced the government would be handing out copies of the Hindu holy book, the Bhagavad Gita, instead.[23]

It got worse. The Uttar Pradesh Tourism Department issued a brochure listing the state's principal attractions—and omitted the Taj

225

Mahal altogether. The state's (and the country's) biggest tourism draw was denied any cultural heritage funding in the allotments for the current fiscal year.

Domestic tourists have also decreased significantly. Indian tourists reportedly prefer the attractions of the holy city of Varanasi in the same state, Uttar Pradesh. This mirrors and reinforces the monument's neglect by the state government in favour of Hindu religious tourism.

But the objection to the Taj is more basic. One extremist BJP legislator labelled the tomb 'a blot' on the fair name of his state, a relic that had been 'built by traitors'. The Taj Mahal 'should have no place in Indian history,' he said, demanding that India's history be 'changed' to remove it.[24]

The ruling party's campaign against the Taj Mahal might seem bizarre; after all, why would anyone undermine a universally admired architectural marvel that is such a revenue generator? But those familiar with the tortured prejudices of the ruling BJP would be less surprised. The attacks on the Taj are part of their politics of hate towards anything associated with the history of the centuries of Muslim rule in India.

As we have seen, to many in the BJP, this was a period of slavery and discrimination against the Hindu population, conducted by foreign invaders who had despoiled a prosperous land, destroyed temples and palaces, assaulted Hindu women and converted millions of Hindus. In their telling, this sordid saga culminated in the vivisection of the motherland in the 1947 Partition of India by the British, which created Pakistan.

That this is an unduly simplistic black-and-white rendition of a complex history, in which there was far more assimilation and co-existence than religious conflict, is irrelevant to Hindu chauvinists who constitute the bulk of the BJP's support base. To them, the Taj is an enduring symbol not of love, but of conquest and humiliation.

Resentment that a monument built by a Muslim emperor is Hindu-majority India's most recognisable monument was, in the past, a fringe obsession of the 'loony' Hindu right. But the fringe is now in power in Uttar Pradesh and its enablers rule the roost in Delhi.

Before becoming chief minister in a surprise appointment by his party, Yogi Adityanath was best known for his incendiary, anti-Muslim speeches, laden with toxic rhetoric, and for leading a volunteer squad of hoodlums who specialised in attacking Muslim targets. Adityanath spent eleven days in jail in 2007 for fomenting religious tension through hate speech, earned notoriety by calling India's most beloved film star (the Muslim Shah Rukh Khan) a terrorist,[25] and has urged his party's government in New Delhi to emulate Donald Trump's travel ban on Muslims.

But even he has been obliged by public and political opinion to surrender to national outrage over the latest controversy. After stoking it in the first place, the chief minister was forced to visit Agra officially to assure an anxious public that his government was committed to protecting the Taj. 'What is important,' he conceded grudgingly, 'is that it was built by the blood and sweat of India's farmers and labourers.'[26]

This acknowledgement is only partly reassuring. It opens the door to another divisive fringe view of the Taj, that of the chauvinist historian P. N. Oak, who argued that the monument was originally a Shiva temple named 'Tejo Mahalaya'. Some misguided Hindutva elements have already been caught trying to perform a Shiva puja in the mausoleum. The RSS, the parent body of the Hindu 'family' of organisations that includes the BJP, has called for Muslims to be prohibited from praying there as well.

To many Indians, in these circumstances, the BJP's newfound love for the Taj might be as alarming as its well-expressed hate for it. (Meanwhile, while the Yogi was busy criticising the Taj, it was the Kerala government far away in the south that brought out an ad 'saluting' the Taj for its role in helping tourists discover India!)

The Taj Mahal is merely the latest victim of a political campaign over Indian history that seeks to reinvent the idea of India itself. Whereas for seven decades after Independence, Indianness rested on faith in the country's pluralism, the ascent of the Hindu-chauvinist BJP has brought with it attempts to redefine the country as a Hindu nation long subjugated by foreigners. This 'cultural nationalism' by the Hindu right, stoking long-buried resentments and promoting hatred for the Muslim minority, is not just deeply divisive; it undermines the country's global soft power and fragments its domestic political and social discourse. As the author Nayantara Sahgal wrote: 'Vast slices of our multi-religious, multi-cultural heritage—which includes our literature, architecture, language, food, music, dance, dress and manners are being dishonoured and disowned, leaving us shrunk into a monoculture which is not only not Hinduism, but the antitheses of all that India has stood for, worked for, and safeguarded as a proud and cherished inheritance.'[27]

At almost the same time as the Taj controversy came one over a film on the Rajput queen Padmavati, who is said to have immolated herself, together with 16,000 other Rajput women, rather than be captured alive by the invading Delhi Sultan Alauddin Khilji. The historicity of the incident is somewhat in doubt: no contemporary account of Khilji's attack on Chittorgarh, including by historians accompanying his forces, mentions the queen. But Padmavati became legend more than two centuries later, when the Sufi mystic poet Malik Mohammed Jayasi devoted his lyrical epic *Padmavat* to her story. It has been suggested that Jayasi did not intend his tale to be taken literally, and that he had chosen Khilji's attack on Chittor because its name included the word 'chit' (consciousness); his poem is said to have been an allegory for the union of mind and soul, under attack from external forces, with the man-woman story a standard trope of the Persian mystic poetry tradition.

But literature, once published, acquires a life of its own. The tale was picked up and retold with enthusiasm—by Bengali bards, Rajasthani folk-tellers, and even the English Colonel Tod, who included Padmavati's tale in his compilation, *Annals and Antiquities of Rajputana*. In countless retellings, Padmavati was soon deified: she became the symbol of Rajput female honour and purity, nobly resisting the lustful Muslim, her self-immolation (*'jauhar'*) the epitome of sacrificial Hindu womanhood. The reputed site of her suicide became a tourist attraction. The legend grew, with one colourful figure, the head of a Rajput organisation, the Karni Sena, claiming to be directly descended from her. (When confronted with the theory that she was fictional, he replied, 'I am 37th in her direct line of descent. Am I a ghost?')

The controversy confirmed once again that to some Hindus, the difference between historical fact and cultural myth matters not at all; what is remembered and believed is as important as what is verifiable.

No less an ardent secularist than India's first Prime Minister, Jawaharlal Nehru, had written seven decades earlier: 'Facts and fiction are so interwoven together as to be inseparable, and this amalgam becomes an imagined history, which may not tell us exactly what happened but does tell us something equally important—what people believed had taken place, what they thought their heroic ancestors were capable of, and what ideals inspired them... Thus, this imagined history, mixture of fact and fiction, or sometimes only fiction, becomes symbolically true and tells us of the minds and hearts and purposes of the people...'[28] This, in a nutshell, explained Rajput passions over the depiction of a cultural heroine who may or may not have existed.

With so much riding on Padmavati's image, the Bollywood filmmaker who set out to make a film of her story found himself treading unwittingly on the newly-roused passions about the past. The Karni Sena trashed his film set, at Jaigarh Fort in Jaipur, and disrupted further shooting in a new (less 'authentic') location at Kolhapur, accusing him of filming a love scene between the Hindu queen and the Muslim invader. Though he denied this, the Rajput community then successfully delayed the release of the film, claiming that it 'distorted history'—the fact that they had not actually seen it before making this claim was apparently irrelevant to the protestors (as well as to four BJP chief ministers, who pre-emptively announced a ban on screening the yet-unreleased film in their states). When the film was eventually released on the orders of the Supreme Court, violent protests by hoodlums, including an attack on a school bus, successfully intimidated theatre owners, so that the film was not shown in several states even though they were free to screen it.

'Taking offence' is the name of the game these days; 'hurting the sentiments of a community' is the name of the crime. The old Hindu boasts of expansive tolerance are wearing thin. (But the film-maker should well have been warned by the experience of another film a decade ago, this time unconnected to any religious community. The threat of protests and possible prosecution had caused a Bollywood star and producer to retitle a film originally named *Billoo Barber* without the second word, because the hairdressers' community absurdly protested that the term 'barber' was an insult to their profession.)

It may not seem to matter very much what some lumpen elements think of a Bollywood film, or of Valentine's Day, for that matter. But it is precisely this kind of narrow-mindedness that also led to the notorious 'pulping' of Wendy Doniger's erudite study of Hinduism. If these intolerant bullies are allowed to get away with their lawless acts of intolerance and intimidation, we are allowing them to do violence to something profoundly vital to our survival as a civilisation.

Pluralist and democratic India must, by definition, tolerate plural expressions of its many identities. To allow the self-appointed arbiters of Bharatiya sanskriti to impose their hypocrisy and double standards on the rest of us is to permit them to define Indianness down until it ceases to be Indian.

But I am not optimistic about the prospects for any such development. My late father, Chandran Tharoor, used to tell me more than five decades ago that India is not just the world's largest democracy, it is also the world's largest hypocrisy. The wisdom and accuracy of his perception was again on display when my two attempts to introduce a Private Member's Bill to amend Section 377 of the Indian Penal Code (which criminalises homosexuality) were comprehensively defeated in the Lok Sabha by homophobic bigotry in the name of Hindutva.

Here was the spectacle of a parliamentary democracy refusing to entertain debate—the ruling party using its brute majority to defeat a motion without even a discussion. How can a deliberative legislature in what claims to be the temple of democracy dismiss an issue out of hand without even hearing the arguments in its favour or against it?

And to add to the hypocrisy, nowhere in over two thousand years of recorded Hindu texts is there any evidence that the Indian ethos was intolerant of sexual difference or gender orientation. Ours is a culture that embraces Shikhandi in the *Mahabharata*, the homoerotic sculptures (mixed in with the rest) in Khajuraho, and the very concept of the Ardhanarishwara, the half-man half-woman embodiment of divinity. No historical records reveal the persecution or prosecution of sexual deviancy in India. Now we have the spectacle of the party of Hindutva, the self-appointed guardians of Bharatiya Sanskriti, betraying a Hindu history of tolerance in order to uphold (without debate) an iniquitous law from the British colonial era. It is a new low in the annals of Indian democracy and a triumph for Indian hypocrisy.

In proposing to amend Section 377, I had explained that we shouldn't have a law on the books that can be used to oppress and harass innocent people conducting their personal lives in private. What two people do to express their love and desire for each other should be strictly between them. The government has no place in India's bedrooms.

But equally important, I had tried to explain (though alas, I was not allowed to do so in Parliament) that my Bill was not about sex but about freedom. Section 377 violates the constitutional rights of dignity, privacy, equality and non-discrimination (Articles 14, 15 and 21) guaranteed to all Indian citizens. It is a British relic, drafted in 1860 and based on outdated Victorian morals rather than authentically Indian values. It has no place in twenty-first century India.

To compound the ironies, within half an hour of the defeat of my amendment, I was rising in the same Lok Sabha to speak in favour of the Rights of Transgender Persons Bill, which had already been passed earlier in the Rajya Sabha. The passage of this progressive bill would have the indirect effect of nullifying the application of Section 377 to transgenders, while leaving it on the books to be used to harass and oppress homosexuals and straight people. How's that for both democracy and hypocrisy taken to their extreme?

Ironically, the one source of hope for a progressive outcome in keeping with the long-established Hindu tradition rests with a secular institution—the judiciary. The Supreme Court's willingness to conduct a curative review of Section 377, and their assertion in a separate case that Indians enjoy a right to privacy, may well signal a return to that tradition. It is ironic that where a Hindutva-inclined majority renders our elected legislature a bastion of illiberalism, it is the unelected judiciary that remains the last repository of hope for the timeless values of our civilisation.

THE COW BELT AND BEEF POLITICS

Indian politics, in all its manifestations, continues to both amaze and appal. The latest example of both lies in a uniquely Indian phenomenon, one which has begun to flourish under the current government—cow vigilantism.

Many orthodox Hindus, particularly in the northern Indian states irreverently dubbed 'the cow belt', not only do not eat beef, but worship the cow as Gaumata, the mother of all, a provider of nourishment and sustenance. Several Indian states have passed laws outlawing cow slaughter; some go farther and neither permit the possession nor the consumption of beef. These are, for the most part, barely enforced; the police have better things to do than to check people's kitchens.

But following the BJP's victory in the 2014 elections, a wave of Hindu triumphalism has swept India. In its wake have come new laws to protect cows and vociferous demands for their strict enforcement. Gaurakshak or cow protection societies have been revived, and many have taken it upon themselves to compel compliance. In the process, not only have they taken the law into their own hands, but they have perpetrated grave crimes, including murder, in the name of the cow. Seventy cases of cow-related violence have been reported in the last eight years, of which 97 per cent (68 out of 70) have occurred during the three years of BJP rule and a majority of these have occurred in BJP-ruled states. 136 people have been injured in these attacks and 28 killed: 86 per cent of the victims were, of course, Muslim.[29]

Many of the incidents are well known: the case of a dairy farmer, Pehlu Khan, transporting cattle legally with a licence, being beaten to death on 1 April 2017 while his tormentors filmed his pleas for mercy on their mobile phones, is particularly egregious. A cattle-herder in Haryana, Mustain Abbas, was murdered and mutilated a year earlier for doing his job, herding cattle. Truckers, cattle traders and alleged cow smugglers have also been killed by 'cow protection' groups. A sixteen-year-old Kashmiri Muslim boy was murdered for having hitched a ride on a truck that was transporting cattle.

In 2015, when a Muslim, Mohammed Akhlaq, father of a serving Indian Air Force serviceman, was lynched by a mob in Uttar Pradesh on suspicions of having killed a cow, the authorities launched a forensic investigation into whether the meat in his refrigerator was beef (it was not). The fact that the man had been killed and his son nearly beaten to death was equated with an unfounded allegation of beef consumption, as if the latter 'crime' could extenuate the former. Worse, when a man who was part of the lynch mob died of natural causes a few weeks later, his coffin was draped with the Indian flag and a serving union minister who attended his funeral hailed him—an unspeakable act, and coming from a high office-holder of the secular Indian state, an unacceptable one.

Muslims have not been the only targets of the cow vigilantes. In addition, the lynch-mobs have linked their cause to another staple of Indian society—violence against Dalits. Many Dalits still make a living performing tasks that other Hindus are unwilling to take on. Upper caste Hindus may worship the cow, but cows, alas, are not immortal, and when they die (ideally of natural causes), their carcasses need to be disposed of. This task has traditionally been left to Dalits, who for centuries and more have skinned the animal to sell its hide to tanners and leather-makers, disposed of its meat to Muslim butchers in the few states where it is legal, and buried or cremated the rest. It is a distasteful task to many caste Hindus, and most are happy to let willing Dalits do it. In turn, dead cows have become a source of livelihood for many Dalits and Muslims.

But several recent incidents have shaken the foundations of this arrangement. Four Dalit youths caught skinning a cow were stripped, tied and beaten with iron rods in the state of Gujarat by cow vigilantes who accused them of killing the animal (they had not).[30] Two Dalit women were assaulted in BJP-ruled Madhya Pradesh for carrying cow meat (which turned out, upon inspection, to be buffalo meat and therefore not illegal).[31]

Such incidents have heightened the sense of vulnerability felt by many who do not necessarily share the reverence the vigilantes feel for cows. Yet, for the first time, India has a central government that refuses to disapprove of cow vigilantism. The Minister for Social Justice, whose principal responsibility is to promote the welfare of India's Dalits, regretted not the vigilantes' violence but the fact that they had perpetrated it on the basis of ill-founded rumours.[32] In other words, their mission was so transcendently just that their misbehaviour could be condoned if their targets really had killed or eaten a cow.

The atmosphere of cow fundamentalism enforced by the vigilantes has caused immense economic complications. Many farmers look after their cows with respect, but once they are too old to produce milk, they find it unaffordable to maintain them and quietly sell their cows to butchers (or to those who could transport them across state lines to states where cows could legally be slaughtered). With this option now foreclosed in the present climate, many farmers are being driven into debt by the expense of maintaining unproductive and uneconomic cattle. And the country's population of cows is proving increasingly unsustainable.[33]

It is not a coincidence that 63 per cent of atrocities against Dalits because of cow vigilantism occur in just four states—U.P., Bihar, M.P. and Rajasthan, in order of magnitude. The rise of Hindu chauvinism, unchecked by government, has given rein to assorted petty bigotries.

There are signs of an incipient Dalit backlash against the injustice of being obliged to do unpleasant work to make a living and then being assaulted for doing it. After the Gujarat incident one group of Dalits in the state has flatly refused to continue with its traditional profession of disposing of dead cows. 'If the cow is your mother,' they asked upper-caste Hindus, 'why don't you bury her?'

The irony is that, as a commentator on the Dharmashastras points out, though the cow was sacred in Vedic times, it was this that allowed for beef to be consumed.[34] There are references in the *Rig Veda*, in the Dharmashastric literature, the *Taittiriya Brahmana* ('Verily, the cow is food') and the *Vajasaneyi Samhita* that support the contention of beef being eaten at the time.[35] The historian D. N. Jha has pointed out dozens of examples to prove that the *Rig Veda* is full of allusions to the slaughter and consumption of cows. Ancient lawgivers, Manu included, appear to grant sanction for the slaughter and consumption of cow meat. The great sage and law-giver Yajnavalkya (of the Upanishads) is quoted as saying, on the subject of whether beef should be eaten: 'I, for one, eat it, provided that it is tender'.[36]

Ambedkar theorised that the worship of the cow emerged from the struggle between Buddhism and Brahmanism; by making the cow a sacred animal and beef-eating a sacrilege, he argued, Brahmanism sought to establish its supremacy over Buddhism. Be that as it may, the ruling dispensation's relentless drive to promote its ideology of Hindutva has latched on to the cow as its current instrument of choice. Cow protection has become the façade for a broader agenda, and is being resisted precisely for that reason.

There is no doubt about the veneration of the cow across India, and the respect for it as a source of milk and nourishment for all and, after its death, of meat and nourishment for some. Calls during the Constituent Assembly deliberations to ban cow slaughter, opposed by a vocal minority, were finally reduced to a 'directive principle' anchored in economics and not religion: Article 48 of the Constitution says that 'the State shall endeavour to organise agriculture and animal husbandry on modern and scientific lines and shall, in particular, take steps for preserving and improving the breeds, and prohibiting the slaughter, of cows and calves and other milch and draught cattle.' So this 'endeavour' (stopping well short of a ban) was related specifically to the needs of agriculture and animal husbandry, not of worship.

Mahatma Gandhi himself said that though he did not eat meat and was personally opposed to cow slaughter, in a multi-religious country like India he could not justify imposing his Hindu views on the many who did not share his faith. Many Hindus feel the same way; I am vegetarian myself, and abhor the idea of consuming the corpses of animals, but I do not judge those who, for cultural or other personal reasons, do so. I only ask that animals be treated decently and without cruelty, and that even their slaughter, for purposes of consumption, be conducted humanely and with minimal pain and suffering for the poor creatures.

The furore that accompanied the new Prevention of Cruelty to Animals Act (Regulation of Livestock Markets) Rules, 2016, rolled out by the Ministry of Environmental Affairs in Delhi, polarised opinion across the country, especially in beef-eating states like Kerala. There it produced a strong reaction from an indignant chief minister, invited condemnation across the local political spectrum, forced the state to drag the centre to court, united warring student union factions to organise beef festivals across the state and even gave Twitizens a field day with #PoMoneModi (Go Away Modi), used last when the PM compared Kerala to the African nation of Somalia, resurfacing as a popular hashtag.[37]

Though the new rules do not directly impose a beef ban, they contrive to make cow slaughter all but impossible through the back door, by making it impossible to transport or sell cattle for slaughter. In the process, they have raised fundamental questions the government cannot escape, even as it tried to shift the focus to the misbehaviour of a few young men who misguidedly slaughtered a calf in public as a form of protest.

The first issue is constitutional—the decision to institute the full prohibition of cow slaughter is a prerogative of the states, not the government at the centre. Entry 15 of the State List of the Seventh Schedule of the Constitution provides for the 'Preservation, protection and improvement of stock and prevention of animal diseases, veterinary training and practice', empowering the state legislatures to legislate the prevention of slaughter and preservation of cattle. Different states have different approaches to cow welfare. Some states like Uttar Pradesh, Madhya Pradesh and Delhi have strict laws while others such as Kerala, Tamil Nadu, West Bengal, Manipur, Mizoram and Nagaland have milder rules or no rules governing the welfare of cows. The blanket new rule is clearly an infringement on the rights of the states, undermining the federal rights guaranteed by our Constitution.

The second objection is practical. The Constitution rightly speaks of milch and draught cattle. Cows produce milk for about eight years, at which point they are too old for either milch or draught purposes. But they go on to live another eight years. Farmers have to spend large sums of money on their food and fodder requirements and other maintenance costs of a cow, a fortune for agriculturalists who often live barely above subsistence level. This is why they sell non-lactating cows, normally for slaughter. Even our highest courts, despite their variety of views on the matter, have recognised that 'a total ban on [cattle slaughter] was not permissible if, under economic conditions, keeping useless bull or bullock be a burden on the society and therefore not in the public interest.'

India is already home to nearly 512 million cows, according to the 19th National Livestock Census 2012. Aside from maintaining them decently, India would also have to deal with deforestation and over-grazing, as well as the problems caused by abandoned cattle, who stray onto the streets and in many cases die of malnutrition in old age. The previous policy recognised that banning cow slaughter would impose an economic burden on farmers, who, given the paucity of resources at their disposal, would struggle to maintain these animals. As a result, India is or was the largest exporter of buffalo meat in the world—a multi-billion-dollar business. Since the sale and transfer of animals is integral to keep this going, the new rules are likely to severely cripple the meat export, dairy, leather and other allied businesses, which provide employment for over one million individuals within the country, mainly from minority communities. The state of Maharashtra's 2015 beef ban had already destroyed the livelihoods of a million Muslim butchers and truckers in that state; a nationwide ban would push more people into poverty who are currently leading economically productive lives.

Where beef was legally available, it was consumed not just by Muslims and other minorities, but also by a section of Hindus, as a vital source of protein for those who cannot afford other kinds of meat. Statistics suggest that just 2 per cent of the Hindu population consume beef, but this 2 per cent translates to 12.5 million individuals, making them the second largest consumers of beef in the country. And in reality many others do so who do not admit to the practice. Scheduled castes and tribes (SC/ST) comprise the overwhelming majority (more than 70 per cent) of the beef-eating Hindu population, while 21 per cent hail from the OBC community. The government decision is therefore socially discriminatory, since it specifically and disproportionately harms the poorer and less privileged sections of Indian society.

But the real concern about the government's rules is not just about beef or the welfare of the cow, but about freedom. For most of India's existence, the default approach has essentially been 'live and let live'—make your own choice about beef, and let others do the same. Like many Hindus, I have never considered it my business what others eat. Indians have generally felt free to be themselves, within our dynamic and diverse society. It is that freedom that the BJP's followers are challenging today.

The Hindutva lobby, emboldened by the BJP's absolute majority, seek to impose their particular view of what India should be, regardless of whom it hurts. This is why the reaction has been so visceral, even from non-beef eaters like myself. Our resistance is to the way India is being changed into something it never was—an intolerant majoritarian society.

THE QUESTION OF CONVERSION

An issue that erupted in the past, has been simmering for a while and is waiting to explode is the issue of conversions of Hindus to other faiths, notably Islam and Christianity. In the case of Islam, the issue has been complicated by allegations of 'love jihad', the alleged entrapment of unwary Hindu girls by Muslim men with the sole intent of conversion to their faith. In the case of Christianity, the existence of missionary societies with an avowed intent of harvesting souls for the Lord has created suspicion among Hindu groups. Some states have already outlawed conversions without the specific permission of the government; the use of inducements or threats to convert is already illegal across much of the country.

Hindu leaders known for their liberality have tended to be less accommodative on the question of conversions. Swami Vivekananda memorably told his American listeners a century and a quarter ago: 'Christian brethren of America, you are so fond of sending out missionaries to save the souls of heathens. I ask you: what have you done and are doing to save their bodies from starvation? In India, there are 300 million men and women living on an average of a little more than 50 cents a month. I have seen them living for years upon wild flowers. During the terrible famines, thousands died from hunger but the missionaries did nothing. They come and offer life but only on condition that the Hindus become Christians, abandoning the faith of their fathers and forefathers. Is it right? There are hundreds of asylums, but if the Muslims or the Hindus go there, they are kicked out. There are thousands of asylums erected by Hindus where anybody is received. There are hundreds of churches that have been erected with the assistance of the Hindus, but no Hindu temples for which a Christian has given a penny.'

To Vivekananda, it was a case of misplaced priorities. 'Brethren of America, you erect churches all through India, but the crying evil in the East is not religion', he declared. 'They have religion enough, but it is bread that the suffering millions of burning India cry out for with parched throats. What they want is bread, but they are given a stone. It is an insult to a starving people to offer them religion; it is an insult to a starving man to teach him metaphysics. Therefore, if you wish to illustrate the meaning of "brotherhood", treat the Hindus more kindly, even though they are Hindus and are faithful to their religion. Send missionaries to them to teach them how better to earn a piece of bread and not to teach them metaphysical nonsense.'

And he recalled the non-proselytising instincts of his own faith: 'Do I wish that the Christian would become Hindu? God forbid. Do I wish that the Hindu or Buddhist would become Christian? God forbid... The Christian is not to become a Hindu or a Buddhist, nor a Hindu or a Buddhist to become a Christian. But each must assimilate the spirit of the others and yet preserve their individuality and grow according to their own law of growth.'

Similarly, Mahatma Gandhi considered religious conversion harmful. He wrote, 'If I had power and could legislate, I should certainly stop all proselytising... In Hindu households the advent of a missionary has meant the disruption of the family coming in the wake of change of dress, manners, language, food and drink.'

At the same time, Hindus like me accept that every individual's spiritual needs are different, and if some wish to find salvation through another faith, that is surely their prerogative. Certainly, episodes of anti-missionary violence in Odisha and Gujarat some years ago do not speak well of those who perpetrate it: a self-confident faith like Hinduism, secure in its own broad-minded liberality, has no need of gangster-like violence in its defence. When, at the time of such violence, specifically the brutal murder in 1999 of Australian missionary Graham Staines, and his two sons in Odisha, I wrote a column passionately denouncing it, I was gratified by the large number of readers (including several describing themselves as believing Hindus) who were as outraged as I was at the anti-Christian thuggery that had been perpetrated in the name of Hinduism. Killers of children have no right to claim the mantle of Hinduism, even if they insist they are acting on behalf of their faith: it is as simple as that. Murder does not have a religion—even when it claims a religious excuse.

Of course, it is easy enough to condemn anti-Christian violence because it *is* violence, and because it represents a threat to law and order as well as to that nebulous idea we call India's 'image'. But an argument that several readers made needs to be faced squarely. In the words of one correspondent: could the violence 'be a reaction to provocations from those religions that believe that only their path is the right path and the rest of humanity are infidels?' He went on to critique 'the aggressive strategy being pursued by some interests in the US to get people in India converted en masse to Christianity, not necessarily by fair means.' In his view, 'aggressive evangelism directed against India by powerful church organisations in America enjoying enormous money power, has only one focused objective—to get India into the Christian fold, as they have succeeded, to a considerable extent, in South Korea and are now in the process of conquering Mongolia.' Arguing that 'mass conversions of illiterates and semi-literates—and they also happen to be poor, extremely poor' is exploitative, he concluded: 'powerful organisations from abroad with enormous money power indulging in mass conversion' are 'a destabilising factor provoking retaliation'.

Such concerns, which are widely shared, including by people in responsible positions in government, must be heeded; but at the same time I cannot accept any justification for the thugs' actions, nor am I prepared to see behind the violence an 'understandable' Hindu resistance to Christian zealotry. Put simply, no non-violent activity, however provocative, can ever legitimise violence. We must reject and denounce assaults and killings, whatever they may claim to be reacting to. Our democracy will not long survive if we condone people resorting to violence in pursuit of their ends, however genuine and heartfelt their grievances may be. The whole point about our system of governance is that it allows all Indians to resolve their concerns through legitimate means, including seeking legal redress or political change—but not violence.

Staines himself had devoted his life to the care of leprosy patients; his widow continued this work after his murder, and was awarded a Padma Shri, a major national honour, by the previous government of India. But let us assume, for the purposes of argument, that Christian missionaries are indeed using a variety of inducements (development assistance, healthcare, education, sanitation, even chicanery—though there is only anecdotal evidence of missionary 'trickery') to win converts for their faith. So what? If a citizen of India feels that his faith has not helped him to find peace of mind and material fulfilment, why should he not have the option of trying a different item on the spiritual menu? Surely freedom of belief is any Indian's fundamental right under our democratic constitution, however ill-founded his belief might be. And if Hindu zealots suspect that his conversion was fraudulently obtained, why do they not offer counter-inducements rather than violence? Instead of destroying churches, perhaps a Hindu-financed sewage system or *pathshala* (village school) might reopen the blinkered eyes of the credulous.

Freedom of conscience is not a negotiable right. An India where an individual is not free to change his or her faith would be inconceivable. Some have been citing Gandhi's criticism of conversions, but his view was based on an eclectic, all-embracing view of religiousness that is a far cry from the narrow bigotry of those who today quote him in opposing conversions. Gandhi's point was that there was no need to convert from one religion to any other because all religions essentially believed the same thing.

The fact is that many faiths do tend to see theirs as the only true path to salvation, and their religious leaders feel a duty to spread the light of a supposedly superior understanding of God to those less fortunate. As Gandhians or as rationalists we are free to decry their views, but the Indian Constitution gives each Indian the right to 'propagate' his religion—and to challenge that right would, in the most fundamental sense, be unconstitutional.

So let each religion do its thing, and let each Indian be free to choose. At the same time, let conversion be an issue of individual conscience and not mass delusion. I would have no difficulty in considering, in principle, the idea of a democratically-elected legislature deciding that the constitutionally-protected right to convert to another faith can only be exercised by an individual, rather than by an entire clan, tribe or village. An end to ceremonies of mass conversion (often suspected to be achieved by inducements) might not be a bad thing: let each individual who believes he or she has seen the light go through an individual act of conversion—one in which he or she must affirm that they know what they are giving up and what they are entering into.

Of course, the debate is not merely a religious one—it is profoundly political. The devotees of Hindutva let me know in no uncertain terms what they thought of me when I expressed such views in three columns in the *Times of India* in September and October 2008. But I reject their presumption that they speak for all or even most Hindus. Hinduism, we are repeatedly told, is a tolerant faith. The central tenet of tolerance is that the tolerant society accepts that which it does not understand and even that which it does not like, so long as it is not sought to be imposed upon the unwilling. Of course, it is true that, while Hinduism as a faith might privilege tolerance, this does not necessarily mean that all Hindus behave tolerantly. But one cannot simultaneously extol the tolerance of Hinduism and attack Christian homes and places of worship.

In one of those columns I argued that the premise behind much of the criticism of conversions is troubling because it seems to accord legitimacy to the argument that conversions are inherently antinational. I made the point that India is founded on the rejection of the very idea that religion should be a determinant of nationhood, and cautioned that the distinction between Hindu nationalism and Indian nationalism could be all too easily blurred. Your Indianness has nothing to do with which God you choose to worship, or not.

In any case, as we have discussed, Hinduism teaches *ekam sat vipra bahudha vadanti* (The Truth is one thing though the sages call it by different names). Why, then, are any of my co-religionists unhappy about some tribal Hindus becoming Christian? If a Hindu decides he wishes to be a Christian, how does it matter that he has found a different way of stretching his hands out towards God? Truth is one, the Hindu believes, but there are many ways of attaining it.

As we have seen, Hinduism has never claimed a monopoly on spiritual wisdom; that is what has made it so attractive to seekers from around the world. Its eclecticism is its strength. So the rejection of other forms of worship, other ways of seeking the Truth, is profoundly un-Hindu, as well as being un-Indian. Worse, the version of Indianness propagated by the opponents of conversion—the presumption that to be Hindu is more authentically Indian, and that to lapse from Hinduism is to dilute one's identification with the motherland—resembles nothing so much as the arguments for the creation of Pakistan, of which the nationalism of Gandhi, Nehru and Azad is the fundamental repudiation. In many Muslim countries it is illegal for a Muslim to convert to any other faith; in some, such apostasy is even punishable by death. India has no room for such practices. There is no such thing as a Hindu heresy. Yet, ironically, it is the most chauvinist of the Hindutva brigade who seek to emulate this Muslim convention.

They are therefore being untrue both to Hinduism and to Indian nationalism. The nationalist movement rejected the belief that religion was the most important element in shaping political identity. In India, our system recognises the diversity of our people and guarantees that religious affiliation will be neither a handicap nor an advantage. By challenging that right, the advocates of Hindutva are undermining the very basis for Indian citizenship and the constitutional basis of the Indian state.

To say that conversions are somehow inherently wrong would accord legitimacy to the rhetoric of the Bajrang Dal and its cohorts—who declare openly that conversions from Hinduism to any other faith are anti-national. Implicit is the idea, as I've noted, that to be Hindu is somehow more natural, more authentically Indian, than to be anything else, and that to lapse from Hinduism is to dilute one's identification with the motherland.

As a Hindu, I reject that notion utterly. To suggest that an Indian Hindu becoming Christian is an anti-national act not only insults the millions of patriotic Indians who trace their Christianity to more distant forebears, including the Kerala Christians whose families converted to the faith of Saint Thomas centuries before the ancestors of many of today's Hindu chauvinists even learned to think of themselves as Hindu. It is an insult, too, to the national leaders, freedom fighters, educationists, scientists, military men, journalists and sportsmen of the Christian faith who have brought so much glory to the country through their actions and sacrifices. It is, indeed, an insult to the very idea of India. Nothing could be more anti-national than that.

One reader, Raju Rajagopal, writing 'as a fellow Hindu', expressed himself trenchantly in describing 'terrorism' and 'communal riots' as 'two sides of the same coin, which systematically feed on each other.' The only difference, he added, is 'that the first kind of terrorism is being unleashed by a fanatical few who swear no allegiance to the idea of India, whereas the second kind of terror is being unleashed by those who claim to love India more dearly than you and I, who are part of the electoral politics of India, and who know the exact consequences of their actions: creating deep fissures between communities, whose horrific consequences the world has witnessed once too often in recent decades.'

That is the real problem here. Nehru had warned that the communalism of the majority was especially dangerous because it could present itself as nationalist. Yet Hindu nationalism is not Indian nationalism. And it has nothing to do with genuine Hinduism either. A reader bearing a Christian name wrote to tell me that when his brother was getting married to a Hindu girl, the Hindu priest made a point of saying to him before the ceremony words to the effect of: 'When I say god, I don't mean a particular god.' As this reader commented: 'it's at moments like that that I can't help but feel proud to be Indian and to be moved by its religiosity—even though I'm an atheist.'

The real alternatives in our country are between those who believe in an India where differences arising from your birth, language, social status, mode of worship or dietary preferences shouldn't determine your Indianness, and those who define Indianness along one or more of these divisions. In other words the really important debate is not about conversions, but between the unifiers and the dividers—between those who think all Indians are 'us', whichever God they choose to worship, and those who think that Indians can be divided into 'us' and 'them'.

It is time for all Hindus to say: stop the politics of division.

We are *all* Indians.

PART THREE

TAKING BACK HINDUISM

7

TAKING BACK HINDUISM

If Hindutva is resisted by the vast majority of liberal Hindus, it is hardly paradoxical to suggest that Hinduism, India's ancient homegrown faith, can help strengthen Indianness in ways that the proponents of Hindutva have not understood. In one sense Hinduism is almost the ideal faith for the twenty-first century: a faith without apostasy, where there are no heretics to cast out because there has never been any such thing as a Hindu heresy. A faith that is eclectic and non-doctrinaire responds ideally to the incertitudes of a post-modern world.

So it was hard for a Hindu, proud of his faith's and his country's liberal traditions, not to be mortified, in 2015, when the visiting US President, Barack Obama, felt obliged to deliver a speech in New Delhi urging the government to live up to India's own values—and did it again in a post-Presidential visit in 2017.

'India will succeed so long as it is not split along the lines of religious faith,' Mr Obama said in 2015 in an implicit rebuke to the Hindutva brigades. The president was, of course, polite, couching his praise of religious diversity as a mutual strength of both India and the US, and speaking of his own challenges as a politician with the middle name of Hussein in a country increasingly hostile to Muslims. Many Obama critics in the US had alleged that he is a Muslim, not a Christian, the President acknowledged. 'There have been times when my faith has been questioned by people who don't know me...they said that I adhered to a different religion, as if that were somehow a bad thing,' he said.[1]

The president could hardly have been unaware, of course, that India's Hindutva-leaning prime minister had had a long track record of implying that belonging to a different religion than his own is indeed a bad thing—and that he depends for his political success on the support of people who have variously wanted all non-Hindus to convert 'back' to the mother faith or be driven out of the country. And he did it again on a visit to New Delhi in December 2017: 'A country shouldn't be divided into sectarian lines and that is something I have told Prime Minister Modi in person as well as to people in America,' Obama declared. 'For a country like India where there is a Muslim population that is successful, integrated and considers itself as Indian, which is not the case in some other countries, this should be nourished and cultivated.'

Obama's message on both occasions was pointed: if India did not resolve the problems of bigotry that are dividing the country, Mr Modi's proclaimed ambitious development plans would be thwarted. It was a message many of us in the political Opposition had also been giving Mr Modi and his colleagues. But coming from a US president, whose visit was being hailed by the government as a diplomatic triumph and whose 'bromance' with the Indian PM had seen first names being used and much friendly banter, it was a pointed reminder of the fundamental contradiction at the heart of Modi's regime.

As I had spelt out in my 2014 book *India Shastra*, Mr Modi's speeches and rhetoric appeared to recognise, and harness, a vital shift in our national politics from a politics of identity to a politics of performance; yet he had risen to power at the helm of a party, the BJP, which is ill-suited to the challenge of delinking India's polity from the incendiary issue of religious identity on which it had built its base.

Of course, Indians don't need an American visitor to tell them to uphold the ideal of freedom of religion, when our history is one of coexistence, the acceptance of religious diversity is deeply embedded in our culture and our Constitution reflects our pluralism. It's a great pity that a foreign leader is obliged to recognise that some Indians do not share the values on which India is built and which are reified in our

Constitution. As I have long argued, Indian democracy is all about the management of diversity, and if we don't respect our diversity we will no longer be the India that Mahatma Gandhi fought to free.

But for the first time, India has elected a prime minister who was himself named for 'severe violations of religious freedom' in reports by the US State Department from 2002 onwards, refused an American visa and was banned from entering the United States before he became prime minister. Mr Modi wasn't elected PM for condoning violence against minorities, but to fulfil an aspirational development vision he effectively articulated. Mr Obama's speech was a way of telling him he can't do that without abandoning his old religious intolerance that earned him those American strictures.

The problem is that the dominant strand in the ruling party cares far more about asserting Hindu chauvinism than it does about the economic reforms and investments that Mr Modi trumpeted—and which won him the support of voters who did not share his 'Hindutva' agenda. A party dependent on people who urge Hindu women to have four children—'no, ten!', as the Shankaracharya of Badrikashram said—not only shows profound disrespect to Hindu women[2] (who have to endure the labour to fulfil the Hindutva brigade's political fantasies) but proves itself out of touch with the real values and priorities of the Hindu masses in whose name it claims to speak.

The fact remains that the Modi regime has given free rein to the most retrograde elements in Indian society, who are busy rewriting textbooks to glorify Hindu leaders, extolling the virtues of ancient science over modern technology, beating the drums over 'love jihad', extolling *ghar wapsi*, and asserting that India's identity must be purely Hindu. Majoritarian communalism, as Nehru had long recognised, is a fundamental threat to our pluralist democracy. But throughout his life as an RSS *pracharak*, Modi has devoted himself to the very worldview that is undermining India's harmony.

TOLERANCE AND ACCEPTANCE

As a believing Hindu, I cannot agree with the followers of Hindutva. Indeed, I am ashamed of what they are doing while claiming to be acting in the name of my faith. The violence is particularly sickening: it has led hundreds of thousands of Hindus across India to protest with placards screaming, 'Not In My Name'. As I have explained throughout this book, and would like to reiterate, I have always prided myself on belonging to a religion of astonishing breadth and range of belief; a religion that acknowledges all ways of worshipping God as equally valid—indeed, the only major religion in the world that does not claim to be the only true religion. As I have often asked: How dare a bunch of thugs shrink the soaring majesty of the Vedas and the *Upanishads* to the petty bigotry of their brand of identity politics? Why should any Hindu allow them to diminish Hinduism to the raucous self-glorification of the football hooligan, to take a religion of awe-inspiring tolerance and reduce it to a chauvinist rampage?

Hinduism, with its openness, its respect for variety, its acceptance of all other faiths, is one religion which has always been able to assert itself without threatening others. But this is not the Hindutva that destroyed the Babri Masjid, nor that is spewed in hate-filled diatribes by communal politicians. It is, instead, the Hinduism of Swami Vivekananda, whom I have quoted at such length in this book. It is important to parse some of Swami Vivekananda's most significant assertions. The first is his assertion that Hinduism stands for 'both tolerance and universal acceptance. We believe not only in universal toleration, but we accept all religions as true.' He had quoted a hymn I have already cited, to the effect that as different streams originating in different places all flow into the same sea, so do all paths lead to the same divinity. He repeatedly asserted the wisdom of the Advaita belief that Truth is One even if the sages call It by different names. Vivekananda's vision—summarised in the credo *'sarva dharma sambhava'*—is, in fact, the kind of Hinduism practised by the vast majority of Hindus, whose instinctive acceptance of other faiths and forms of worship has long been the vital hallmark of our culture.

Of course it is true that, while Hinduism as a faith might privilege tolerance, this does not necessarily mean that all Hindus behave tolerantly. Nor should we assume that, even when religion is used as a mobilising identity, all those so mobilised act in accordance with the tenets of their religion. Nonetheless it is ironic that even the Maratha warrior-king Shivaji, after whom the bigoted Shiv Sena is named, exemplified the Hindu respect for other faiths. In the account of a critic, the Mughal historian Khafi Khan, Shivaji made it a rule that his followers should do no harm to mosques, the Quran or to women. 'Whenever a copy of the sacred Quran came into his hands,' Khafi Khan wrote, Shivaji 'treated it with respect, and gave it to some of his Mussalman followers'.[3] Other sources confirm Shivaji's standing orders to his troops that if they came across a Quran or a Bible they should preserve it safely until it could be passed on to a Muslim or Christian.

It is this doctrine of universal acceptance that has been increasingly called into question by the acolytes of Hindutva. Vivekananda had given his fellow Hindus a character certificate many of them no longer deserve. 'The Hindus have their faults,' Vivekananda added, but '...they are always for punishing their own bodies, and never for cutting the throats of their neighbours. If the Hindu fanatic burns himself on the pyre, he never lights the fire of Inquisition.'[4] These words have a tragic echo 125 years later in an India in which Hindu fanaticism is rising, and adopting a form that Vivekananda would not have recognised as Hindu.

The economist Amartya Sen made a related point in regretting the neglect by the votaries of Hindutva of the great achievements of Hindu civilisation in favour of its more dubious features. As Sen wrote about Hindu militants: 'Not for them the sophistication of the *Upanishads* or Gita, or of Brahmagupta or Sankara, or of Kalidasa or Sudraka; they prefer the adoration of Rama's idol and Hanuman's image. Their nationalism also ignores the rationalist traditions of India, a country in which some of the earliest steps in algebra, geometry, and astronomy were taken, where the decimal system emerged, where early philosophy—secular as well as religious—achieved exceptional sophistication, where people invented games like chess, pioneered sex education, and began the first systematic study of political economy. The Hindu militant chooses instead to present India—explicitly or implicitly—as a country of unquestioning idolaters, delirious fanatics, belligerent devotees, and religious murderers.'[5]

To discriminate against another, to attack another, to kill another, to destroy another's place of worship, is not part of the Hindu *dharma* so magnificently preached by Vivekananda, nor the Hinduism propagated

253

in twenty-first-century India by popular spiritual leaders like Sri Sri Ravi Shankar (founder of the Art of Living) and Sadhguru Jaggi Vasudev (founder of the Isha Ashram), who preach a humane, practical faith using techniques of meditation and yoga as well as spiritual advice anchored in the ancient texts. Why, then, are the voices of Hindu religious leaders not being raised in defence of these fundamentals of Hinduism against those who would violently pervert it?

I reject the presumption that the purveyors of hatred speak for all or even most Hindus. The Hindutva ideology is in fact a malign distortion of Hinduism. It is striking that leaders of now-defunct twentieth-century political parties like the Liberal Party and the pro-free enterprise Swatantra Party were unabashed in their avowal of their Hinduism; the Liberal leader Srinivasa Sastry wrote learned disquisitions on the *Ramayana*, and the founder of Swatantra, C. Rajagopalachari ('Rajaji'), was a Sanskrit scholar whose translations of the Itihasas and lectures on aspects of Hinduism are still widely read, decades after his death. Neither would have recognised the intolerance and bigotry of Hindutva as in any way representative of the faith they held dear. Many leaders in the Congress Party are similarly comfortable in their Hindu beliefs while rejecting the political construct of Hindutva. It suits the purveyors of Hindutva to imply that the choice is between their belligerent interpretation of Hinduism and the godless Westernisation of the 'pseudo-seculars'. Rajaji and Sastry proved that you could wear your Hinduism on your sleeve and still be a political liberal. But that choice is elided by the identification of Hindutva with political Hinduism, as if such a conflation is the only possible approach open to practising Hindus.

I reject that idea. I not only consider myself both a Hindu and a liberal, but find that liberalism is the political ideology that most corresponds to the wide-ranging and open-minded nature of my faith.

A REFLECTION OF INSECURITY

The irony is that Hindutva reassertion is a reflection of insecurity rather than self-confidence. It is built on constant reminders of humiliation and defeat, sustained by tales of Muslim conquest and rule, stoked by stories of destroyed temples and looted treasures, all of which have imprisoned susceptible Hindus in a narrative of victimhood. Hindutva is an answer to a perception of failure and defeat, rather than a broad-minded story of a confident faith finding its place in the world. Looking back towards the failures of the past, it offers no hopes for the successes of the future.

This seems to be conceded even by one of the foremost voices of contemporary Hindutva, the American David Frawley. Hindus, he writes in his foundational screed *Arise Arjuna!* (1995), 'are generally suffering from a lack of self-esteem and an inferiority complex by which they are afraid to really express themselves or their religion. They have been beaten down by centuries of foreign rule and ongoing attempts to convert them'. Frawley's answer is for Indians to reassert Hindu pride, but his diagnosis calls that prescription into question.

As a Hindu and an Indian, I would argue that the whole point about India is the rejection of the idea that religion should be a determinant of nationhood. Our nationalist leaders did not jump to the conclusion that a Partition-formed Muslim state dictated an equivalent one for Hindus. To accept the idea of India you have to spurn the logic that divided the country in 1947. Your Indianness has nothing to do with which god you choose to worship, or not. We are not going to reduce ourselves to a Hindu Pakistan.

That is the real problem here. As I have mentioned earlier, Nehru had warned that the communalism of the majority was especially dangerous because it could present itself as nationalist. Yet, Hindu nationalism is not Indian nationalism. And it has nothing to do with genuine Hinduism either.

I too am proud of my Hinduism; I do not want to cede its verities to fanatics. I consider myself a Hindu and a nationalist, but I am not a Hindu nationalist. To discriminate against another, to attack another, to kill another, to destroy another's place of worship, on the basis of his faith is not part of Hindu *dharma*, as it was not part of Swami Vivekananda's. It is time to go back to these fundamentals of Hinduism. It is time to rescue Hindu *dharma* from the fundamentalists.

* * *

The misuse of Hinduism for sectarian minority-bashing is especially sad since Hinduism provides the basis for a shared sense of common culture within India that has little to do with religion. Bestselling authors like Amish Tripathi have achieved spectacular success by reinventing characters from Hindu mythology and the epics in stories accessible to modern readers, without surrendering to the prevalent chauvinism and bigotry of the Hindutva reassertion. Hindu festivals, from Holi to Diwali and of course Kerala's Onam, have already gone beyond their religious origins to unite Indians of all faiths as a shared experience (the revelry of Holi, the celebratory gift-giving of Onam, and the lights, firecrackers, mithais and social gambling of Diwali, have made all three into 'secular' occasions). Festivals—utsavas, melas, leelas—all 'Hindu' in origin, have become occasions for the mingling of ordinary Indians of all backgrounds. Religion lies at the heart of Indian culture, but not necessarily as a source of division; religious myths like the *Ramayana* and the *Mahabharata* provide a common idiom, a shared matrix of reference, to all Indians, and it was not surprising that when Doordarshan broadcast a fifty-two-episode serialisation of the *Mahabharata*, the script was written by a Muslim, Dr Rahi Masoom Raza. Hinduism and Islam are intertwined in India; both religions, after all, have shared the same history in the same space, and theirs is a cohabitation of necessity as well as fact.

To some degree, India's other minorities have found it comfortable to take on elements of Hindu culture as proof of their own integration into the national mainstream. The tennis-playing brothers Anand, Vijay and Ashok Amritraj all bear Hindu names, but they are Christian, the sons of Robert and Maggie Amritraj, and they played with prominent crosses dangling from their necks, which they were fond of kissing in supplication or gratitude at tense moments on court. But giving their children Hindu names must have seemed, to Robert and Maggie, more nationalist in these post-colonial times, and quite unrelated to which god they were brought up to worship. I would not wish to make too much of this, because Muslim Indians still feel obliged to adopt Arab names in deference to the roots of their faith, but the Amritraj case (repeated in many other Christian families I know) is merely an example of Hinduism serving as a framework for the voluntary cultural assimilation of minority groups, without either compulsion or conversion becoming an issue. Keralites almost unanimously consider the Christian singer Yesudas (whose very name is derived from Jesus!) to be the greatest-ever singer of Malayalam devotional songs and bhajans; for decades his songs were played at and around the Guruvayur temple while, as a Christian, the singer himself was not allowed in. (In September 2017 it was, however, announced that were he to make a formal request, he would be permitted entry as a confirmed *bhakt* of Lord Krishna).

HINDUISM AS CULTURE

It is to a great degree possible to speak of Hinduism as culture rather than as religion (a distinction the votaries of Hindutva distort in extolling Savarkar's enunciation of a similar view). The inauguration of a public project, the laying of a foundation stone or the launching of a ship usually start with the ritual smashing of a coconut, an auspicious practice in Hinduism but one which most Indians of other faiths cheerfully accept in much the same spirit as teetotallers acknowledge the role of champagne in a Western celebration. Interestingly, similar Hindu customs have survived in now-Muslim Java and now-Buddhist Thailand. Islamic Indonesians still cherish the *Ramayana* legend, now shorn (for them) of its religious associations. Javanese Muslims bear Sanskrit names. Hindu culture can easily be embraced by non-Hindus if it is separated from religious faith and treated as a heritage to which all may lay claim. I have often argued that the *Mahabharata* and the *Ramayana* should be taught in our schools just as the *Odyssey* and the *Iliad* are in Western ones, not as religious texts but as towering accomplishments of our culture and the source of so many legends and cultural references.

Amartya Sen is right to stress that Hinduism is not simply the Hindutva of Ayodhya or Gujarat; it has left all Indians a religious, philosophical, spiritual and historical legacy that gives meaning to the civilisational content of secular Indian nationalism. In building an Indian nation that takes account of the country's true Hindu heritage, we have to return to the pluralism of the national movement. This must involve turning away from the strident calls for Hindutva that would privilege a doctrinaire view of Hinduism at the expense of the minorities, because such calls are a denial of the essence of the Hinduism of Vivekananda. I say this not as a godless secularist, but as a proud Hindu who is mortified at what his own faith is being reduced to in the hands of bigots—petty men who know little about the beliefs, the traditions and the history of the faith in whose 'defence' they claim to act. They have distorted a pluralist religious philosophy in the process of instrumentalising it as a political ideology.

The way in which history and cultural memory informs contemporary attitudes varies from family to family. My mother's prosperous Nair family in Palakkad, for instance, lived in mortal terror of imminent attack by Tipu Sultan and lost most of its wealth in a foolish attempt to protect it from him by burying their treasures in an unknown location—they never found them again! But despite the stories that have been wryly and ruefully told and retold and passed down the generations over the two centuries since, my family and I never extended our dislike of Tipu and his marauders to a rejection of 'Muslims' as a whole, and certainly not to any Muslims of today. While we have no illusions about past attacks on temples by Muslim raiders, we did not bring up our children to use the past to justify bigotry in the present. One can appreciate history and leave it where it belongs.

Indians today have to find real answers to the dilemmas of running a plural nation. Nationalists often define their nation in terms of a cohesive group of people, held together by a common enemy. The common enemy of Indians is an internal one, but not the one identified by the Hindutva fanatics and their ilk. The common enemy lies in the forces of sectarian division that would, if unchecked, tear the country apart—or transform it into something that most self-respecting Hindus would refuse to recognise.

In many ways, the fundamental conflict of our times is the clash between, no, not civilisations, but doctrines—religious and ethnic fundamentalism on the one hand, secular consumerist capitalism on the other. The clash is taking place amidst a paradox. Thanks to globalisation, the world has been coming together into a single international market, just as it is simultaneously being torn apart by civil war, terrorism and the breakup of nations. Today there is a backlash, or more accurately two kinds of backlash: one a widely-noted current of economic anti-globalisation, as the 'losers' rebel against the elites who have been exporting their jobs to faraway lands; and the other what one can call cultural anti-globalisation, whose proponents seek the comforts of traditional identity. In many places in the West the two backlashes overlap, but in a country like India they do not; India's government seeks to be part of globalisation while rejecting the cultural diversity it implies. The Hindutva movement in India is part of this latter backlash against cosmopolitanism, multiculturalism and secularism in the name of cultural rootedness, religious or ethnic identity and nationalist authenticity.

In India this claim to authenticity and rootedness has taken on a majoritarian Hindu colouring under the BJP. It has sought to reduce Indians to a singular identity framed around their religious affiliation. Each individual, as I pointed out in my 1997 book *India: From Midnight to the Millennium*, has many identities. Sometimes religion obliges us to deny the truth about our own complexity by obliterating the multiplicity inherent in our identities. Religious fundamentalism, in particular, does so because it embodies a passion for pure belonging, a yearning intensified by the threatening tidal wave of globalisation as well as by the specificities of the devotees' politics. And it feeds on the inevitable sense among its adherents of being wounded, whether real or imagined. In this way, Hindutva reassertion draws from the same wellsprings as Islamist fanaticism and white-nationalist Christian fundamentalism.

What is to be done? We cannot delegitimise religion, and indeed there is something precious and valuable in a faith that allows a human being to see himself at one with others stretching their hands out towards God around the world. But can we separate religion from identity? Can we dream of a world in which religion has an honoured place but where the need for spirituality will no longer be associated with the need to belong? If we want religion to stop feeding fanaticism, terror and ethnic wars, we must find other ways of satisfying the need for identity. If identity can relate principally to citizenship rather than faith, to a land rather than a doctrine, and if that identity is one that can live in harmony with other identities, then we might still escape the worst horrors that the doomsayers (like Samuel Huntington, who two decades ago foretold a 'clash of civilisations') can conceive. A domestic 'clash of civilisations' would destroy India, which has survived and thrived as a civilisational medley.

Thanks, in many ways, to the eclectic inclusiveness of Hinduism, everything in India exists in countless variants. There was no single standard, no fixed stereotype, no 'one way'. This pluralism emerged from the very nature of the country; it was made inevitable by India's geography and reaffirmed by its history. There was simply too much of both to permit a single, exclusionist nationalism. When Hindutva's cadres demanded that all Indians declare 'Bharat Mata ki Jai (Victory to Holy Mother India)' as a litmus test of their nationalism, many of us insisted that no Indian should be obliged to mouth a slogan he did not believe in his heart. If some Muslims, for instance, felt that their religion did not allow them to hail their motherland as a goddess, the Constitution of India gave them the right not to. Hindutva wrongly seeks to deny them this right.

We were brought up to take this for granted, and to reject the sectarianism that had partitioned the nation when the British left. I was raised unaware of my own caste and unconscious of the religious loyalties of my schoolmates and friends. Of course, knowledge of these details came in time, but too late for any of it to matter, even less to influence my attitude or conduct. We were Indians: we were brought up (and constantly exhorted) to believe in an idea of nationhood transcending communal divisions. This may sound like the lofty obliviousness of the privileged, but such beliefs were held not only by elites: they were a reflection of how most Indians lived, even in the villages. Independent India was born out of a nationalist struggle in which acceptance of each other which we, perhaps unwisely, called secularism was fundamental to the nationalist consensus.

It is true that Hindu zealotry—which ought to be a contradiction in terms—is partly a reaction to other chauvinisms. As I have pointed out, the unreflective avowal by many Hindus of their own secularism has provoked the scorn of some Hindus, who despise the secularists as deracinated 'Macaulayputras' (sons of Macaulay) or 'Babur ke aulad' (sons of Babur). They see such Hindus as cut off from their own culture and heritage, and challenge them to rediscover their authentic roots, as defined by the proponents of Hindutva.

HINDUISM IS NOT A MONOLITH

But Hinduism is no monolith; its strength is found within each Hindu, not in the collectivity. Defining a 'Hindu' cause may well be a political reaction to the definition of non-Hindu causes: the Hindutva idea originated around the same time as the rise of a separate Muslim consciousness in the polity in the early twentieth century, and the resentments that spilled over into the destruction of the Babri Masjid in the century's last decade were largely articulated in opposition to the imagined 'appeasement' of India's minorities. The rage of the Hindu mobs is that of those who feel themselves supplanted in this competition of identities, who think that they are taking their country back from usurpers of long ago. They want revenge against history, but they do not realise that history is its own revenge.

The Hindutva fanatics seek to reinvent Hindu identity with a new belief structure and a new vocabulary. They seek to make Hinduism more like the Semitic religions they resent but wish to emulate: to pick fewer sacred books, notably the Gita, and exalt them would produce a less 'baggy', tighter version of the faith; to focus on fewer gods, notably Shiva, Rama and Krishna, with Ganesh and various forms of Devi thrown in, would sharpen Hindu divinity; to standardise religious practices around specific familiar festivals, rituals and gatherings, would provide a greater sense of community. Their associated efforts include a desire to control and restrict what Hindus eat, so their rejection of beef (even though several castes did eat it in the past) would itself become a marker of identity; to promote Hindi as a national language (though it is quite foreign to nearly half the country) so as to ensure that the vocabulary of Hindudom can be more easily transmitted; to mouth the same slogans ('Bharat Mata ki Jai!') and chant the same songs ('Vande Mataram' is a must), even though some Muslims are uncomfortable with both, in order to promote conformity. This invented Hinduism has much more to do with an era of political and cultural insecurity and a faltering new sense of aspiration than with the Vedas, the *Puranas* or the Bhakti movement: it denies the lived history of Hinduism even while claiming to speak in its name.

The central challenge of India is the challenge of accommodating the aspirations of different groups in the national dream. The ethos of Hinduism—inclusionist, flexible, agglomerative—helped the nation meet this challenge. The doctrine of Hindutva prefers uniformity to accommodation. The struggle for India's soul will be between two Hinduisms: the 'secularist' Indianism of the nationalist movement and the particularist fanaticism of the Ayodhya mob. It is a battle that rages still.

* * *

The inevitable backlash to my writings about Hindutva excesses, from the Babri Masjid demolition to the Gujarat horrors, has largely taken the form of belligerent emails and assorted social media fulminations from the less reflective of the Hindutva brigade. I have been excoriated as 'anti-Hindu' and described by several as a 'well-known leftist', which will no doubt amuse those of my friends who knew me in college thirty years ago as one of the very few supporters of Rajaji's conservative Swatantra Party—in those consensually socialist times. And from time to time a Hindutvavadi, reminding me of the religion that has been mine from birth, succumbed to the temptation to urge me predictably to heed that well-worn slogan: '*Garv se kaho ki hum Hindu hain*' (Say with pride that we are Hindus).

All right, let us take him up on that. I am indeed proud that I am a Hindu. But of what is it that I am, and am not, proud?

I am not proud of my co-religionists attacking and destroying Muslim homes and shops. I am not proud of Hindus raping Muslim girls, or slitting the wombs of Muslim mothers. I am not proud of Hindu vegetarians who have roasted human beings alive and rejoiced over the corpses. I am not proud of those who reduce the lofty metaphysical speculations of the

Upanishads to the petty bigotry of their own sense of identity, which they assert in order to exclude, not embrace, others.

I am proud that India's pluralism is paradoxically sustained by the fact that the overwhelming majority of Indians are Hindus, because Hinduism has taught them to live amidst a variety of other identities.

I am proud of those Hindus, like the Shankaracharya of Kanchi, who say that Hindus and Muslims must live like Ram and Lakshman in India. I am not proud of those Hindus, like 'Sadhvi' Rithambhara, who say that Muslims are like sour lemons curdling the milk of Hindu India.

I am not proud of those who suggest that only a Hindu, and only a certain kind of Hindu, can be an authentic Indian. I am not proud of those Hindus who say that people of other religions live in India only on their sufferance, and not because they belong on our soil. I am proud of those Hindus who realise that an India that denies itself to some of us could end up being denied to all of us.

I am proud of those Hindus who utterly reject Hindu communalism, conscious that the communalism of the majority is especially dangerous because it can present itself as nationalist. I am proud of those Hindus who respect the distinction between Hindu nationalism and Indian nationalism. Obviously, majorities are never seen as 'separatist', since separatism is by definition pursued by a minority. But majority communalism is in fact an extreme form of separatism, because it seeks to separate other Indians, integral parts of our country, from India itself. I am proud of those Hindus who recognise that the saffron and the green both belong equally on the Indian flag.

The reduction of non-Hindus to second-class status in their own homeland is unthinkable. As I have pointed out here, and elsewhere, it would be a second partition: and a partition in the Indian soul would be as bad as a partition in the Indian soil. For Hindus like myself, the only possible idea of India is that of a nation greater than the sum of its parts. That is the only India that will allow us to call ourselves not Brahmins, not Bengalis, not Hindus, not Hindi-speakers, but simply Indians.

How about another slogan for Hindus like me? *Garv se kaho ki hum Indian hain* (Say with pride that we are Indian).

* * *

There is an old Puranic story about Truth. It seems a brash young warrior sought the hand of a beautiful princess. Her father, the king, thought he was a bit too cocksure and callow. He decreed that the warrior could only marry the princess after he had found Truth.

So the warrior set out into the world on a quest for Truth. He went to temples and monasteries, to mountain tops where sages meditated, to remote forests where ascetics scourged themselves, but nowhere could he find Truth.

Despairing one day and seeking shelter from a thunderstorm, he took refuge in a musty cave. There was an old crone there, a hag with matted hair and warts on her face, the skin hanging loose from her bony limbs, her teeth yellow and rotting, her breath malodorous. But as he spoke to her, with each question she answered, he realised he had come to the end of his journey: she was Truth.

They spoke all night, and when the storm cleared, the warrior told her he had fulfilled his quest. Armed with his knowledge of Truth, he could go back to the palace and claim his bride.

'Now that I have found Truth,' he said, 'what shall I tell them at the palace about you?'

The wizened old creature smiled. 'Tell them,' she said, 'tell them that I am young and beautiful.'

So Truth exists, but is not always true. That subtle insight is typical of the wisdom of the ancient Hindus. It gives the lie to the petty bigotries, the glib certitudes, the righteous fanaticism of those who advocate Hindutva.

The tragedy for many Hindus is that the Hindu nationalists, often ironically referred to by their critics as *bhakts* (the 'devout'), are betraying daily the values of the very faith to which they claim to be committed. Since the original Bhakti movement began in Tamil Nadu in the sixth century, Hindu thought has stressed the personal nature of religion and emphasised the inclusive philosophy and all-embracing syncretism of the faith that Adi Shankara and Vivekananda taught to the world as Hinduism. The traditional Hindu texts, starting with the Vedas, were imbued with a sense of philosophical wonder, raising questions about creation, the nature of being and the meaning of life, and treating nothing as too sacred to interrogate. It is an act of treason to Hinduism to take this faith of mystery and doubt and reduce it to brazen certitudes, to shun diversity and extol dogma and to claim that it is the only authentic Hinduism.

The political project of Hindutva is nothing less than an assault on the religion; but where Hinduism has for millennia proved its resilience to external attacks, it is now revealing its vulnerability to attack from within. That is why Hindutva politics must be resisted; in presenting a view of Hinduism that is at odds with everything Hinduism has sought to stand for, it seeks to refashion Hinduism as something it has never been. Indeed, as the economist Kaushik Basu has argued, it reveals the insecurity of Hindutva's cheerleaders that they want to remake their country and religion in the very image of the countries and religions they claim to detest.

Hinduism attaches importance to *pramana* (instruments of warranted inference) in the pursuit of *jnana*, or knowledge. As long as you can demonstrate the validity or rigour of your *pramana*, you are entitled to the specific belief structure you wish to adhere to. It is this feature, unlike other traditions that rely on revelation as claims to truth, that ensures Hinduism is more open to diversity of belief. My friend Keerthik Sasidharan suggested to me, in twenty-first-century terms, that Hinduism is analogous to an open-source operating system on top of which others can build applications to be deployed in the receptive hardware of human brains. All Hinduism demands before the formation of any belief is analytical and logical consistency. Even the existence of God is subject to this test. The Nietzschean formulation that God created Man and Man returned the compliment is anticipated more than a millennium ago in this verse by Udayanacharya, the tenth-century logician, addressed to the deity Jagannatha of Puri:

> You're so drunk on wealth and power
> that you ignore my presence.
> Just wait: when the Buddhists come,
> your whole existence
> depends on me.[6]

(Yet it should be said that Udayanacharya is the very sage credited with so roundly trouncing Buddhists in debate that Buddhism never dared to challenge Hinduism in India thereafter.)

A RELIGION WITHOUT FUNDAMENTALS

When I stood for the post of UN Secretary General in 2006, journalists quizzed me about the role my Hindu faith played in my worldview. I conceded that it was true that faith can influence one's conduct in one's career and life. For some, it is merely a question of faith in themselves; for others, including me, that sense of faith emerges from a faith in something larger than ourselves. Faith is, at some level, what gives you the courage to take the risks you must take, and enables you to make peace with yourself when you suffer the inevitable setbacks and calumnies that are the lot of those who try to make a difference in the world. So I had no difficulty in saying openly that I am a believing Hindu. But I was also quick to explain what that phrase means to me. I'm not a 'Hindu fundamentalist'. As I have explained in this book, and said often in the past, the fundamental thing about Hinduism is that it is a religion without fundamentals. My faith in global diversity emerges from my Hindu beliefs as well, since we have an extraordinary diversity of religious practices within Hinduism, a faith with no single sacred book but many. Mine is a faith that allows each believer to reach out his or her hands to his or her notion of the godhead. I was brought up in the belief that all ways of worship are equally valid. I relished pointing out that my father prayed devoutly every day, but never used to oblige me to join him. In the Hindu way, he wanted me to find my own truth. And that was precisely the manner in which I brought up my own sons.

Finding my own truth gave me a truth that admits of the possibility that there might be other truths. I therefore bring to the world an attitude that is open, accommodating and tolerant of others' beliefs. Mine is not a faith for those who seek unquestioning dogmas, but there is no better belief-system for an era of doubt and uncertainty than a religion that cheerfully accommodates both.

The misuse of religion for political purposes is of course a sad, sometimes tragic, aspect of our contemporary reality. As UN

Secretary General Kofi Annan once said, the problem is never with the faith, but with the faithful. All faiths strive sincerely to animate the divine spark in each of us, but some of their followers, alas, use their faith as a club to beat others with, rather than a platform to raise themselves to the heavens. Since Hinduism believes that there are various ways of reaching the ultimate truth, as a Hindu I fully accepted the belief systems of others as equal to my own. That is why I cannot and do not accept the Hindutva fanatics' interpretation of the values and principles of my faith.

But what does it mean to me to be a practising Hindu? As I mentioned above, I have never been a frequent visitor to temples, though I do believe in praying every day, even if only for a couple of minutes. Many Hindus who can afford the space have a place for puja within their homes; at minimum, a picture, a little statue, or several. I too have maintained a little puja alcove at my homes where I try to reach out to the divine spirit. Yet, I believe in the Upanishadic doctrine that the Divine is essentially unknowable and unattainable by ordinary mortals. All prayer is an attempt to reach out to that which we cannot touch. While I do occasionally visit temples, and I appreciate how important they are to my mother and most other devout Hindus, I believe that one does not need any intermediaries between oneself and one's notion of the Divine. If God is in your heart, it matters little where else He resides.

So I take pride in the openness, the diversity, the range, the sublime philosophical aspirations of the Vedanta. I cherish the diversity, the lack of compulsion, and the richness of the various ways in which Hinduism is practised eclectically. And I admire the civilisational heritage of tolerance that makes Hindu societies open their arms to people of every other faith, to come and practise their beliefs in peace amidst Hindus. It is remarkable, for instance, that the only country on earth where the Jewish people have lived for centuries and never experienced a single episode of anti-Semitism is India. That is the Hinduism in which I gladly take pride.

Hinduism's suitability for the modern world lies in many ways in its recognition of uncertainty and its pragmatic non-dogmatism. The religion of 'maybe He does not know' is a faith for the non-dogmatic, one which looks beyond the blacks and whites, the grim certitudes of lesser mortals, to the acknowledgement of the scope for doubt, for different points of view on the great questions of life and death. Vivekananda's immortal 'We believe not only in universal toleration but we accept all religions as true' is a prescription for peace and coexistence among competing dogmatisms in a world full of too many dogmas. This is why it was perhaps the ideal faith for a candidate for United Nations Secretary General to profess. (And when I lost the race, my faith offered me consolation too, in the Bhagavad Gita's dictum that one did what was one's *dharma* to do, regardless of the consequences.)

Hinduism does not see the world in terms of absolutes. Blacks and whites are largely absent from its ethos. It sees competing notions of good and evil, duty and betrayal, everywhere, and seeks wisdom in finding the right approach suited for each specific circumstance. Vivekananda used to tell a parable of the frog in the well: 'I am a Hindu. I am sitting in my own little well and thinking that the whole world is my little well. The Christians sit in their little well and think the whole world is their well. The Muslims sit in their little well and think that is the whole world.' To Vivekananda, the world was one where each frog had much to learn from the others, if he would only look beyond his well.

Hinduism is not a totalising belief system; it offers a way of coping with the complexity of the world. It acknowledges that the truth is plural, that there is no one correct answer to the big questions of creation, or of the meaning of life. In its reverence for sages and rishis, it admits that knowledge may come from an exchange between two or more views, neither of which necessarily possesses a monopoly on the truth. The greatest truth, to the Hindu, is that which accepts the existence of other truths.

Hinduism sees life as an evolving dynamic, not a contest that can ever be settled once and for all. It is open to negotiation on ways of being and believing; it permits negotiation even with God. It offers rites and rituals, but leaves it up to each individual to choose which ones he wishes to adhere to. Each Hindu must find his own truth. Each individual achieves his own salvation and self-fulfilment.

At the same time Hinduism is also anchored in the real world. A superficial view of Hinduism sees its other-worldly 'timelessness'. But in fact the religion is anchored not in a world-denying spirituality, as Raimon Panikkar points out; in his words, it is not the timeless, but the 'time-full', which wins Vedic approbation. Time is depicted in hymns in the *Atharva Veda* as perpetually replenishing itself from a full vessel which, in spite of all efforts, can never be emptied. Since time transcends time, it is without beginning or end, without limit; and in that sense it is like God. 'Time am I, world-destroying,' says Krishna in the Bhagavad Gita, stressing 'I am imperishable Time'. As a verse in the *Maitreya Upanishad* puts it:

From time all beings emerge
From time they advance and grow
In time, too, they come to rest.
Time is embodied and also bodiless.

The harm religion does when it is passionately self-righteous—wars, crusades, communal violence, jihad—is arguably greater than the benefits religion produces when it does well (teaching morality, answering prayers, providing balm to troubled souls). In its long history, Hinduism has never launched an apocalyptic war of religion or tried to impose one correct answer on all of life. Hindus like to speak of theirs as a religion of peace, but then so do other faiths. Still, the Hindu scriptures are replete with hymns to peace, and are infused with the idea that human beings must seek peace within themselves and peace with all other human beings. Many Vedic mantras set out to achieve these ends; of these the Shanti Mantra is the most famous, and prays for peace in heaven, on earth and in the human heart. The words 'Om Shantih! Shantih! Shantihi!' are uttered three times at the end of every sacred action or after the recitation of a sacred text—three times because the Hindu seeks peace in all three realms. Humans cannot enjoy personal peace in the absence of peace on earth, but equally there cannot be peace in the world if there is no peace in the inner hearts of the human beings in the world. A verse of the *Yajur Veda* (xxxvi, 17) chants:

To the heavens be peace, to the sky and the earth,
To the waters be peace, to plants and all trees,
To the Gods be peace, to Brahman be peace,
To all men be peace, again and again—peace also to me![7]

The speaker of the Sixteenth Lok Sabha, the Lower House of the Indian parliament, the first in that office from the BJP, introduced the practice of uttering 'Om Shantih! Shantih! Shantihi!' after the otherwise ritualistic reading of obituary notices during each session. Though this implied the introduction of religious language into a secular Parliament, her words were echoed by many MPs, and not only those of her party. While as a liberal I was initially dismayed by her doing this, I soon came around to the view that as long as no one was obliged to follow her, calling for peace was hardly objectionable. A Hindu could be overtly Hindu, I felt, if in the process she was being all-embracing in her expression of her faith, while not imposing it on others.

Hinduism is a life-affirming religion of joy and play (*leela*). It sees the world as suffused with radiance rather than darkness; as the Bhagavad Gita says, 'That splendour which is from the sun, which illumines this whole world, which is in the moon and in fire—know that splendour is also mine.' In turn this refulgence is Man's, since he is enjoined by the *Upanishads* to see all beings in himself and himself in all things; he therefore radiates in his person the splendour of the Universe. Yes, the Hindu scriptures acknowledge the existence of human sorrow and suffering, but see them as part of an awakening to the transcendent. The Vedas do not ask why we suffer; they take human sorrow as a given, an affliction to be dealt with and overcome. The *Upanishads* are more questioning of suffering; they use a word, *dukha*, sadness and existential distress, a word not found in the Vedas. Ideally one must be detached from such suffering, as the Gita teaches, and by eliminating sorrow in oneself through self-realisation, help remove it from others. This seems impossible for most ordinary people, and so the easier solution is to take refuge in the Lord.

Similarly, the Hindu scriptures speculate about the mystery of what lies beyond human life, but they are not obsessed with death; as Panikkar brilliantly put it, 'they seem to describe an existential attitude that takes cognisance of the phenomenon of death but denies to it any character of ultimacy... It is by integrating the fact of death into life, by reabsorbing, as it were, death into life...by finding a ground that is common to both death and life, that we can find the proper Vedic perspective.' This notion of the continuity between life and death is a particularly Hindu idea, with death, as it were, inbuilt into life. Panikkar again: 'The beyond is the unfathomable ocean which makes the beaches on this side worth walking and playing on.'

Hindus believe that, at most, religion can create a platform upon which the beautiful things in life can be attained. Destiny, knowledge, reflection and prayer may equip you to achieve fulfilment. The Hindu is a seeker, but the holy grail he seeks is within himself. Hinduism urges you to explore your own mind and heart to discover the truths about life. The model of the ideal questing Hindu may be found in a description of the sage Narada in the Valmiki *Ramayana*: 'Dedicated to self-learning, fully in control of the senses, seeker of the truth'. Yoga, meditation, prayer, social service are all means to that end, but not the only ones. You have to work hard yourself to achieve those things that are worth achieving. The doctrine of *karma yoga* preached by both Vivekananda and Mahatma Gandhi is a doctrine of action, not of passivity or fatalism. There is no lassitude in the pursuit of the Purusharthas.

The wise Hindu can hold two or more opposing ideas together in her mind at the same time. That is the way the world is. For the Hindu texts uniquely operate from a platform of scepticism, not a springboard of certitude. The *Rig Veda* verse that says 'maybe He does not know' about the Creator is not an invention of post-modernism, but the wisdom of a timeless text that has lasted for three and a half millennia and will always be valid.

Most faiths prioritise one identity, one narrative and one holy book. Hinduism recognises that everyone has multiple identities, accepts diverse narratives and respects several sacred books. Indeed, the folk Hinduism of multiple beliefs cannot be forced into the Abrahamic framework of One Book, One Deity and one way of doing things. The more the Hindu grapples with the great questions, the more she understands how much is beyond our understanding.

271

Yet the Hindu lives in reality, in the here and now, conscious that on the way to renunciation and liberation from the world, there are worldly duties and responsibilities to family, community and nation that must be performed without regard to their rewards. Hindus do not shelter from the besieging forces of life behind the safety of their doctrinal battlements, the omniscience of their dogmas, the fatwas or encyclicals of their priests. They are unafraid to face the cross currents, acknowledging how little they know. Indeed Hindus are not awed by the complexity of the world, because they accept the world is complex, and much passes their understanding.

A RELIGION FOR THE 21ST CENTURY

In the twenty-first century, Hinduism has many of the attributes of a universal religion—a religion that is personal and individualistic, privileges the individual and does not subordinate one to a collectivity; a religion that grants and respects complete freedom to the believer to find his or her own answers to the true meaning of life; a religion that offers a wide range of choice in religious practice, even in regard to the nature and form of the formless God; a religion that places great emphasis on one's mind, and values one's capacity for reflection, intellectual enquiry, and self-study; a religion that distances itself from dogma and holy writ, that is minimally prescriptive and yet offers an abundance of options, spiritual and philosophical texts and social and cultural practices to choose from. In a world where resistance to authority is growing, Hinduism imposes no authorities; in a world of networked individuals, Hinduism proposes no institutional hierarchies; in a world of open-source information-sharing, Hinduism accepts all paths as equally valid; in a world of rapid transformations and accelerating change, Hinduism is adaptable and flexible, which is why it has survived for nearly 4,000 years.

In 1926, Professor Clement Webb suggested that Hinduism, with its tradition of openness, tolerance and acceptance of the Divine in the most diverse forms imaginable, 'could perhaps more easily than any other faith develop, without loss of continuity with its past, into a universal religion...' This remains true almost a century later. Universalism comes easily to Hinduism. Hindus respect the environment because it embodies the unity of all creation, and in this, too, theirs is a faith for the twenty-first century.

Dr Karan Singh, the former maharaja of Kashmir and Indian politician who is also a superbly readable scholar of Hindu philosophy, identifies five major principles in Hinduism that lend relevance and validity to the faith in today's world. At the risk of inadequate paraphrase, these are, according to him: the recognition of the unity of all mankind, epitomised in the Rig Vedic phrase '*vasudhaiva kutumbakam*', the world is one family; the harmony of all religions, epitomised in that Rig Vedic statement that was Swami Vivekananda's favourite, '*ekam sat vipra bahudha vadanti*'; the divinity inherent in each individual, transcending the social stratifications and hierarchies that have all too often distorted this principle in Hindu society; the creative synthesis of practical action and contemplative knowledge, science and religion, meditation and social service, in the faith; and finally, the cosmic vision of Hindu philosophy, incorporating the infinite galaxies of which the Earth is just a tiny speck. In Dr Singh's own words: 'such is the grandeur and mystery of the Atman that it can move towards a comprehension of the unutterable mystery of existence. We, who are children of the past and the future, of earth and heaven, of light and darkness, of the human and the divine, at once evanescent and eternal, of the world and beyond it, within time and in eternity, yet have the capacity to comprehend our condition, to rise above our terrestrial limitations, and finally, to transcend the throbbing abyss of space and time itself.' This, Dr Singh says, is the message of Hinduism, and it is a message that can and should resonate throughout the world.

Yet such a universal creed can only be the Hinduism described in this book, rather than the petty intolerant Hindutva being propagated by bigots in a travesty of the majesty of their faith. Swami Vivekananda had, as usual, put it best:

'if there is ever to be a universal religion, it must be one which will have no location in place or time; which will be infinite like the God it will preach, and whose sun will shine upon the followers of

Krishna and of Christ, on saints and sinners alike; which will not be Brahminic or Buddhistic, Christian or Mohammedan, but the sum total of all these...and still have infinite space for development; which in its catholicity will embrace in infinite arms, and find a place for every human being from the lowest grovelling savage, not far removed from the brute, to the highest man towering by the virtues of his head and heart almost above humanity, making society stand in awe of him and doubt his human nature. It will be a religion which will have no place for persecution or intolerance in its polity, which will recognise divinity in every man and woman, and whose whole scope, whose whole force, will be centered in aiding humanity to realise its own true, divine nature. Offer such a religion and all the nations will follow you.'

I am a Hindu who is proud to offer such a religion to the world. I do so conscious that Hinduism does not seek to proselytise, only to offer itself as an example that others may or may not choose to follow. Unlike the Abrahamic faiths it manifests no desire to universalise itself; yet its tenets and values are universally applicable. But first it must be revived and reasserted, in its glorious liberalism, its openness and acceptance, its eclecticism and universalism, in the land of its own birth. As the Hindu hymn (from the *Brihadaranyaka Upanishad*) says, in words that resonate with meaning for every human being on the planet:

Asato ma sad gamaya!
Tamaso ma jyotir gamaya!
Mrityor ma amritam gamaya!

Lead me from Untruth to Truth,
Lead me from darkness to light,
Lead me from death to immortality.

NOTES

PREFACE AND ACKNOWLEDGEMENTS

1. Right down to spellings, I have throughout eschewed the scholarly Romanised spellings of Sanskrit words favoured by the classic texts for simple versions that approximate the way the words are pronounced. This has led me to invent one spelling, 'mutth', for the Hindu monastery more frequently spelt '*mutt*' or '*math*', both of which might confuse or mislead the average English-speaker.

1. MY HINDUISM

1. Derived from Nanditha Krishna, *Hinduism and Nature*, New Delhi: Penguin Books, 2017, p. 5–6.
2. Debiprasad Chattopadhyaya and M. K. Gangopadhyaya (eds), *Carvaka/Lokayata: An Anthology of Source Materials and Some Recent Studies*, Indian Council of Philosophical Research, 1990, p. 352.
3. Mahatma Gandhi, *Hindu Dharma*, Ahmedabad: Navajivan Publishing House, 1950, p. 6.
4. Quoted in Sri Swami Sivananda, *All About Hinduism*, The Divine Life Society, 1947.
5. '[A] man can be as truly a Hindu as any without believing in the Vedas as an independent religious authority', V. D. Savarkar, *Hindutva: Who is a Hindu?* (originally published under the title *Essentials of Hindutva*), Bombay: Veer Savarkar Prakashan, 1923, p. 81.
6. Quoted in Jawaharlal Nehru, *The Discovery of India*, 1946.

275

7. Sarvepalli Radhakrishnan, *The Hindu Way of Life*, London: Geo. Allen & Unwin Ltd., 1927.
8. Swami Vivekananda, *The Complete Works of Swami Vivekananda*, Chennai: Manonmani Publishers, 2015.
9. Ibid.
10. Ibid.
11. Adapted from Friedrich Max Müller, *The Upanishads: Part II*, Oxford: Clarendon Press, 1884.
12. Raimon Panikkar, *The Vedic Experience: Mantramañjarı: An Anthology Of The Vedas For Modern Man*, Berkeley: University of California Press, 1977.
13. I am indebted to Dr Nanditha Krishna for this insight.
14. Robert L. Brown, *Ganesh: Studies of an Indian God*, New York: SUNY Press, 1991, p. 21.
15. 'Milk-drinking deities unleash mass hysteria', quoted in *Great Mysteries of the 20th Century*, Reader's Digest, 1999.

2. THE HINDU WAY

1. Shakunthala Jagannathan's translation.
2. François Bernier, *Travels in the Mogul Empire*, Manchester: Archibald Constable & Company, 1670.
3. S. Radhakrishnan, *The Hindu View of Life*, London: Geo. Allen & Unwin, 1926.
4. Diana L. Eck, *Encountering God: A Spiritual Journey from Bozeman to Banares*, Boston: Beacon Press, 1993, p. 76.
5. Herbert Risley, *The People of India*, Simla: Thacker, Spink & Co, 1915, p. 244.
6. Juan Mascaro, *The Upanishads*, London: Penguin Books, 1965.
7. The temple's riches are truly staggering. Donations from the public, the value of the thousands of kilos of hair they donate to the Lord through tonsuring their heads at the temple, the price of entry tickets, the specific fees paid for particular rituals and offerings, the sale of prasadam (usually in the form of the famous and patented Tirupati laddoo (milk sweets) and the cash deposited in the donation-urns or hundis within the temple itself. Tirupati's budget for 2015–2016 was c $392 million, compared to the Vatican's budget of c $274 million in the same year.

Since Lord Balaji is a particular favourite of those who pray for wealth, their gratitude for answered prayers is also munificent.

8. The ancient Indian science of Ayurveda groups foods into three categories, satvik, rajasik and tamasik, each category producing effects on the body of the consumer. Foods that grow under the ground, like onion and garlic, fall into the unhealthy tamasik category, along with meat, alcohol, coffee and tobacco.

9. In Tvastar's dwelling Indra drank the Soma, a hundredworth of juice pressed from the mortar, translated by Ralph T. H. Griffith.

10. Rutvij Merchant, 'Answering the ultimate question: who is a Hindu?', Firstpost.com, 24 September 2014.

11. See page 253.

12. K. Balasubramania Iyer, *Yaksha Prasna*, Bombay: Bhavan's Book Company, 1989.

13. I am indebted to Dr Nanditha Krishna for this insight.

14. Since the precise dates are impossible to establish, some authorities prefer a later date for the commencement of their composition.

15. Upinder Singh, *Political Violence in Ancient India*, Cambridge, MA: Harvard University Press, 2017, p. 236.

16. 'Having taken the bow furnished by the *Upanishads*, the great weapon and fixed in it the arrow rendered pointed by constant meditation and having drawn it with the mind fixed on the *Brahman*, hit, good looking youth! at that mark the immortal *Brahman*'. www.wisdomlib.org

17. Raimon Panikkar, *The Vedic Experience*, p. 66.

3. QUESTIONING HINDU CUSTOMS

1. Radhakrishnan, *The Hindu Way of Life*, London: Geo. Allen & Unwin, 1927.

2. Manu S. Pillai, 'Women, Lingayats and "the Hindus"', *LiveMint*, 25 September 2017.

3. Manu S. Pillai, 'The Kerala of the past and present', *LiveMint*, 2 September 2017.

4. Seema Chishti, 'Biggest caste survey: One in four Indians admit to practising untouchability', *Indian Express*, 29 November 2014.

5. A scholar friend finds the figure for Christians surprisingly low. In Tamil Nadu, she tells me, many churches have separate pews and burial

grounds for different castes, and some even make Dalits sit outside the church.

6. Amit Thorat, 'Mapping Exclusion', *Indian Express*, 3 December 2014.

7. Tejaswini Tabhane, 'No Mr Tharoor, I Don't Want to Enter Your Kitchen', www.roundtableindia.co.in, 16 September 2017.

4. GREAT SOULS OF HINDUISM

1. Michael Comans, *The Method of Early Advaita Vedanta: A Study of Gaud. apada, S'aṅkara, Sures'vara, and Padmapada*, Delhi: Motilal Banarsidass, 2000.

2. Raimon Panikkar, *The Vedic Experience: Mantramañjarı: An Anthology Of The Vedas For Modern Man*, Berkeley: University of California Press, 1977.

3. Adapted from Swami Vivekananda, *The Complete Works of Swami Vivekananda*, Chennai: Manonmani Publishers, 2015.

4. Friedrich Max Müller, *The Upanishads*, Oxford: Clarendon Press, 1884.

5. Dr Karan Singh, *Essays on Hinduism*, New Delhi: Ratna Sagar, 1987, p. 25.

6. Karigoudar Ishwara, *Speaking of Basava: Lingayat Religion and Culture in South Asia*, Boulder, Colarado: Westview Press, 1992, p. 212.

7. Manu S. Pillai, 'Basava and the Emergence of Lingayat identity', *LiveMint*, 28 July 2017.

8. Ibid.

9. In turn Sufism shows the influence of Hindu mysticism on Islam, but that is another story.

10. The period of Muslim conversions in the north saw the migration of several communities of Hindus southwards, bringing their religion and skills to other parts of India.

11. Gauri Shankar Bhatt, 'Brahmo Samaj, Arya Samaj, and the Church-Sect Typology', *Review of Religious Research*, 10, 1968, p. 24.

12. See page 253.

13. Christophe Jaffrelot, 'Hindu Nationalism: Strategic Syncretism in Ideology Building', *Economic and Political Weekly*, Vol. 28 No. 12/13, 20–27 March 1993.

14. Raimon Panikkar, *The Vedic Experience: Mantramañjarı: An Anthology Of The Vedas For Modern Man*, Berkeley: University of California Press, 1977.

15. S. Radhakrishnan, *The Hindu View of Life*, London: Geo. Allen & Unwin, 1926.
16. Ibid.
17. Ibid.
18. K. P. Shankaran, 'In Good Faith: Gandhi's radical Hinduism', *Indian Express*, 4 December 2017.
19. Ibid.

5. HINDUISM AND THE POLITICS OF HINDUTVA

1. T. N. Madan, 'Secularism in its place', *The Journal of Asian Studies*, vol. 46, No. 4, November 1987, pp. 747–759.
2. V. D. Savarkar, *Hindutva*, p. 3.
3. Ibid.
4. Ibid., pp. 3–4.
5. Quoted in M. J. Akbar, *India: The Siege Within: Challenges to a Nation's Unity*, New Delhi: UBSPD, 1996.
6. V. D. Savarkar, *Hindutva*, p. 3.
7. www.savitridevi.org/hindus-foreword.html
8. www.savitridevi.org/hindus-06.html
9. 3rd edition, Nagpur: Bharat Prakashan, 1945.
10. 4th impression, Bangalore: Vikrama Prakashan, 1968.
11. Golwalkar, *We, or Our Nationhood Defined*, pp. 52–53.
12. Ibid., p. 42.
13. Golwalkar, *Bunch of Thoughts*, p. 123.
14. Ibid., pp. 142–143.
15. Ibid., p. 22. ('Our concept of Hindu Nation is not a mere bundle of political and economic rights. It is essentially a cultural one.')
16. Ibid., p. 156.
17. Nietzsche in a letter to his friend Peter Gast, cited by Koenraad Elst in 'Manu as a weapon against egalitarianism: Nietzsche and Hindu political philosophy', paper presented at the annual conference of the Friedrich Nietzsche Society, Leiden, 2006.
18. Manu S. Pillai, 'Decoding RSS ideologue MS Golwalkar's nationalism', *Livemint*, 15 July 2017.
19. Ibid.
20. Ibid.

21. Golwalkar, *We, or Our Nationhood Defined*, p. 22.

22. Ibid.

23. Savarkar, *Hindutva*, p. 20.

24. Golwalkar, *We, or Our Nationhood Defined*, pp. 15, 16.

25. V. S. Naipaul, *Among the Believers: An Islamic Journey*, London: Penguin Books, 1982.

26. *Organiser*, 3 June 1979.

27. Golwalkar, *Bunch of Thoughts*, p. 142.

28. Golwalkar, *We, or Our Nationhood Defined*, pp. 104–105.

29. Golwalkar, *Bunch of Thoughts*, p. 102.

30. Ibid., p. 179.

31. Ibid., p. 186.

32. Golwalkar, *Bunch of Thoughts*, pp. 156.

33. Ramachandra Guha, 'They Too Wrote Our History', *Outlook*, 22 August 2005.

34. Golwalkar, *Bunch of Thoughts*, p. 131.

35. Manu S. Pillai, 'Decoding RSS ideologue MS Golwalkar's nationalism', *Livemint*, 15 July 2017.

36. Murad Ali Beg, 'Hindutva', *Frontier*, 6 June 2017.

37. Debapriya Mondal, 'Budget 2017: FM Jaitley announces Rs 4, 814 crore for Deen Dayal Upadhyaya Gram Jyoti Yojana, *Economic Times*, 1 February 2017. 'Budget 2016: Rs 200 cr for events on Deendayal Upadhyaya', *Times of India*, 29 February 2016. Deeptiman Tiwary, 'BJP going all out to resurrect Deen Dayal Upadhyaya's legacy', *Times of India*, 3 October 2014.

38. Jyoti Malhotra, 'New pedestal for a saffron pioneer', *India Today*, 14 October 2015.

39. Bhavdeep Kang, 'Who is this man who features in every Modi speech?', Grist Media, 6 October 2014.

40. K. S. Bharathi, *The Political Thought of Pandit Deendayal Upadhyaya*, New Delhi: Concept Publishing Company, 1998, p. 86.

41. Bhishkar, C. P., *Pt. Deendayal Upadhyay Ideology & Perception—Part 5: Concept of The Rashtra*, New Delhi: Suruchi Prakashan, 2014, p. 4.

42. The Direction of National Life, Lucknow: Lohit Prakashan, 1971.

43. Golwalkar, *Bunch of Thoughts*, p. 227.

44. Quoted in V. V. Nene, *Pandit Deendayal Upadhyaya: Ideology and Perception*, trans. by M. K. Paranjape and D. R. Kulkarni, New Delhi: Suruchi Prakashan, 1988, pp. 10–11.

45. C. P. Bhishkar, *Pt. Deendayal Upadhyay Ideology & Perception—Part 5: Concept of The Rashtra*, New Delhi: Suruchi Prakashan, 2014, p. 156.

46. Ibid., p. 17.

47. Ibid., p. 18.

48. Ibid., p. 155.

49. Ibid., pp. 109–110.

50. Ibid., p. 157.

51. Ibid., p. 87.

52. Ibid., p. 179.

53. Dattopant Bapurao Thengadi, *Pandit Deendayal Upadhyaya: Ideology and Perception*, Vol. 2, New Delhi: Suruchi Prakashan, 1988, p. 50.

54. V. V. Nene, *Pt. Deendayal Upadhyay Ideology & Perception—Part-2: Integral Humanism*, New Delhi: Suruchi Prakashan, 2014, p. 77.

55. 'Ramzada vs haramzada: Outrage over Union Minister Sadhvi's remark', *Indian Express*, 2 December 2014.

56. Bhishkar, C. P., *Pt. Deendayal Upadhyay Ideology & Perception—Part 5: Concept of The Rashtra*, New Delhi: Suruchi Prakashan, 2014, p. 93. ('[Bharat] has always given a warm welcome and shelter to social groups... like the Parsis and Jews.')

57. Suchitra Mohanty, 'Rohingya refugees "threat to national security", Centre tells Supreme Court', *LiveMint*, 14 September 2017.

58. Dilip Awasthi, 'Ayodhya, December 6, 1992: A nation's shame', *India Today*, 31 December 1992.

59. The militant violence in Kashmir, and the terror attacks of 26/11 in Mumbai, which have been planned and directed from across the border by Pakistan, are beyond the scope of this book.

60. Akshaya Mukul, 'Savarkar had begged the British for mercy', *Times of India*, 3 May 2002.

61. 'Vajpayee wanted Modi to quit over Gujarat riots, but party said no: Venkaiah Naidu', *India Today*, 9 March 2014.

62. Prabhat Patnaik, 'The Fascism of Our Times', *Social Scientist*, Vol. 21 No. 3/4, 1993.

63. Ashis Nandy, 'Obituary of a Culture', *Seminar*, 2002.

64. *Dr. Ramesh Yeshwant Prabhoo vs Shri Prabhakar Kashinath Kunte & Others*, 1996 SCC (1) 130.

65. Manu S. Pillai, 'Why the BJP wouldn't have risen the way it did with Vajpayee', *Livemint*, 28 January 2017.

66. Vishwadeepak, 'We should remove secularism, socialism from the Constitution: Govindacharya', *National Herald*, updated on www. nationalheraldindia.com, 2 October 2017.
67. Ibid.

6. BEYOND HOLY COWS: THE USES AND ABUSES OF HINDU CULTURE AND HISTORY

1. Vamadev Shastri, 'Sarva Dharma Sambhava: Unity or Confusion of Religions?', www.hinduhumanrights.info, 18 August 2013.
2. David Frawley, *Awaken Bharata: A Call for India's Rebirth*, New Delhi: Voice of India, 1998, p. xxv.
3. David Frawley, *Arise Arjuna: Hinduism and the Modern World*, New Delhi: Voice of India, 1995, p. 15.
4. David Frawley, *Awaken Bharata: A Call for India's Rebirth*, New Delhi: Voice of India, 1998, p. xxv.
5. K. N. Panikkar, 'In the Name of Nationalism', *Frontline*, 13 March 2004.
6. K. Thangaraj and G. Chaubey, 'Too early to settle the Aryan migration debate', *The Hindu*, 13 July 2017.
7. Ibid. Also see Michael Danino, 'Aryans and the Indus Valley Civilization: Archaeological, Skeletal and Molecular Evidence' in *A Companion to South Asia in the Past* edited by Gwen Robbins Schug and Subhash R. Walimbe, Oxford: John Wiley & Sons, 2016; and Danino's response ('The problematics of genetics and the Aryan issue', *The Hindu*, 29 June 2017) to Tony Joseph, 'How genetics is settling the Aryan migration debate', *The Hindu*, 16 June 2017.
8. P. L. Kessler, 'South East Asia–Cambodia, www.historyfiles.co.uk.
9. This is not to imply that all the recent appointees to such bodies are Hindutvavadis, merely that some with Hindutva credentials have been placed in key positions.
10. Dick Teresi, *Lost Discoveries: The Ancient Roots of Modern Science from the Babylonians to the Maya*, New York: Simon & Schuster, 2002.
11. Audrey Truschke, *Aurangzeb: The Man and the Myth*, New Delhi: Penguin Books, 2017.
12. Girish Shahane, 'Aurangzeb was a bigot not just by our standards but also by those of his predecessors and peers', *Scroll.in*, 1 November 2017.

13. Audrey Truschke, '"Some of the hate mail is chilling": Historian Audrey Truschke on the backlash to her Aurangzeb book', *Scroll.in*, 25 May 2017.

14. Ross Colvin and Sruthi Gottipati, 'Interview with BJP leader Narendra Modi', Reuters, 12 Juy 2013.

15. '"All Indians Originally Hindus", RSS Chief Mohan Bhagwat Says Hinduism's Door Open To All', *Outlook*, 12 September 2017.

16. 'Giriraj Singh wanted to send PM critics to Pakistan. Now, he is a minister', www.NDTV.com, 10 November 2014.

17. 'Shiv Sena MP Force-Feeds Man Who Was Fasting for Ramzan', www.NDTV.com, 23 July 2014.

18. Pheroze L. Vincent, 'Bengali slum dwellers caught in crossfire' *The Hindu*, 10 December 2014.

19. Full text of the judgment at: Sanjay Kishan Kaul, 'There should be freedom for the thought we hate', *Outlook*, 8 May 2008.

20. D. N. Jha, 'What the Gods Drank', *Indian Express*, 29 July 2017.

21. 'UP CM Yogi Adityanath's anti-Romeo squads: "Moral policing", "Taliban-like", international media has its say,' *Indian Express*, 3 April 2017.

22. Annie Gowen, 'Is India neglecting the Taj because it was built by Muslims?', *Washington Post*, 3 October 2016.

23. 'Adityanath: Foreign dignitaries are now being gifted the Gita and not 'un-Indian' Taj Mahal replicas', *Scroll.in*, 16 June 2017.

24. 'Taj Mahal is a "blot on Indian culture", was built by traitors, says BJP leader Sangeet Som', *Scroll.in*, 16 October 2017.

25. 'Yogi Adityanath slams SRK, compares him with Hafiz Saeed', *The Hindu*, 4 November, 2015.

26. Sowmiya Ashok, 'Don't get into why Taj Mahal was built, when or how… Taj a gem, will protect it: Yogi Adityanath', *Indian Express*, 27 October 2017.

27. Nayantara Sahgal, 'A Hindu Speaks', www.indiancultureforum.in, 11 October 2017.

28. Jawaharlal Nehru, *The Discovery of India*, Calcutta: The Signet Press, 1946.

29. Alison Saldanha, 'Cow-Related Hate Crimes Peaked in 2017, 86% of Those Killed Muslim', *thewire.in*, 8 December 2017.

30. '4 Dalits stripped, beaten up for skinning dead cow', *Times of India*, 13 July 2016.

31. Siddharth Ranjan Das, 'Muslim Women Beaten Over Beef Rumour, Spectators Film Attack, Cops Watch', www.NDTV.com, 27 July 2016.

32. Amulya Gopalakrishnan, 'We Are All Gau Rakshaks: Whether or not we care about cows, we certainly don't mind vigilantism', *Times of India*, 1 August 2016.

33. Venkitesh Ramakrishnan, 'The Cow Menace', *Frontline*, 10 November 2017.

34. 'It was not that the cow was not sacred in Vedic times, it was because of her sacredness that it is ordained in the *Vajasaneyi Samhita* that beef should be eaten.' From *Dharma Shastra Vichar* (Marathi) by Panduranga Vaman Kane, quoted in B. R. Ambedkar, *The Untouchables: Who Were They and Why They Became Untouchables?*, 1948. Accessed via www.ambedkarintellectuals.in on 15 December 2017.

35. Jha, D. N., *The Myth of the Holy Cow*, London: Verso Books, 2004, pg 139. ('The Vedas mention about 250 animals out of which at least 50 were deemed fit for sacrifice, by implication for divine as well as human consumption. The *Taittiriya Brahmana* categorically tells us, "Verily the cow is food" (atho annam vai gauh) and Yajnavalkya's insistence on eating the tender (amsala) flesh of the cow is well known.')

36. 'Nevertheless Yagnavalkya said, "I, for one, eat it, provided that it is tender."' In *The Satapatha Brahmana According to the Text of the Madhyandina School* translated by Julius Eggeling, Oxford: Clarendon Press, 1885, p. 11.

37. Nandagopal Rajan, '#PoMoneModi: Angry Kerala responds to PM Modi's Somalia comparision', *Indian Express*, 13 May 2016.

7. TAKING BACK HINDUISM

1. Suhasini Haider, 'India will succeed if it is not splintered along religious lines: Barack Obama', *The Hindu*, 28 January 2015.

2. Sandeep Joshi, 'Hindu women should have 10 children: Shankaracharya', *The Hindu*, 19 January 2015.

3. Percival Spear, Vincent Smith (trans.), *The Oxford History of India*, 4th edn, London: Oxford University Press, p. 412.

4. Makarand R. Paranjape (ed.), *Swami Vivekananda: A Contemporary Reader*, New Delhi: Routledge, 2015.

5. Amartya Sen, 'Threats to Secular India', *Social Scientist*, Volume 21, 1993.

6. http://prekshaa.in/story-verse-udayanacharya-nyaya-tarka-vaisheshika-shastra-buddhism-puri-jagannath/
7. Raimon Panikkar, *The Vedic Experience*.

BIBLIOGRAPHY

Agrawala, Vasudev Sharan, *Padmavat: Malik Muhammad Jayasi krit Mahakavya (Mool Aur Sanjeevani Vyakhya)*, Jhansi: Sahitya Sadan, 1955.

Ananthamurthy, U. R., *Hindutva or Hind Swaraj*, New Delhi: HarperCollins, 2016.

Andersen, Walter K. and Damle, Shridhar D., *The Brotherhood in Saffron: The Rashtriya Swayamsevak Sangh and Hindu Revivalism*, New Delhi: Vistaar Publications, 1987.

Basham, A. L., *The Wonder That Was India*, London: Picador, 2004.

Chinmayananda, Swami, *The Holy Geeta*, Mumbai: Chinmaya Mission Trust, 1992.

Coomaraswamy, Ananda, *A New Approach to the Vedas: An Essay in Translation and Exegesis*, New Delhi: South Asia Books, 1994.

Deshpande, C. R., *Transmission of the Mahabharata Tradition*, Simla: Indian Institute of Advanced Study, 1978.

Doniger, Wendy, *On Hinduism*, New Delhi: Aleph Book Company, 2013.

————, *The Hindus: An Alternative History*, New Delhi: Penguin Books, 2009.

Eck, Diana, *India: A Sacred Geography*, New York: Harmony Books, 2013.

Elst, Koenraad, *Bharatiya Janata Party Vis-a-vis Hindu Resurgence*, New Delhi: Voice of India, 1997.

Embree, Ainslie T., *Sources of Indian Tradition, Vol. 1: From the Beginning to 1800*, New York: Columbia University Press, 1958.

Gambhirananda, Swami, trans., *Eight Upanishads with the Commentary of Sankaracarya*, Second Revised Edition, vols I and II, Kolkata: Advaita Ashrama, 1989 and reprinted 2006.

Ganeri, Jonardon, *Artha: Meaning (Foundations of Philosophy in India)*, New Delhi: Oxford University Press, 2011.

287

BIBLIOGRAPHY

Golwalkar, M. S., *Bunch of Thoughts*, Fourth imp, Bangalore: Vikram Prakashan, 1968.

————, *We, or Our Nation Defined*, Third edn, Nagpur: Bharat Publications, 1945.

Guru, Nataraja, *The Word of the Guru: The Life and Teaching of Guru Narayana*, New Delhi: DK Printworld, 2003.

Jaffrelot, Christophe, *Hindu Nationalism: A Reader*, Princeton: Princeton University Press, 2007.

————, *The Hindu Nationalist Movement and Indian Politics: 1925 to the 1990s*, London: Hurst, 1996.

Jagannathan, Shakunthala, *Hinduism*, Bombay: Vakil, Feffer and Simons, 1984.

Jha, D. N., *The Myth of the Holy Cow*, New Delhi: Navnayana Books, 2009.

————, 'What the gods drank', *Indian Express*, 29 July 2017.

Khan, Ansar Hussain, *The Rediscovery of India: A New Subcontinent*, Hyderabad: Orient Longman, 1995.

Krishna, Nanditha and Jagannathan, Shakunthala, *Ganesha: The Auspicious... The Beginning*, Bombay: Vakil, Feffer And Simons, 1992.

Kumaran, Murkkoth, *The Biography of Sree Narayana Guru*, Sivagiri: Sivagiri Madom, 2011.

Lannoy, Richard, *The Speaking Tree: A Study of Indian Culture and Society*, New York & London: Oxford University Press, 1971.

Mandeville, John, *The Travels of Sir John Mandeville*, Moseley, C. (trans.), London: Penguin Books, 2005.

Mascaro, Juan, *The Upanishads*, London: Penguin Books, 1965.

Menon, Ramesh, *Bhagavata Purana*, New Delhi: Rupa Publications, 2007.

Nehru, Jawaharlal, *The Discovery of India*, Calcutta: The Signet Press, 1946

Pandey, Gyanendra, 'Which of Us are Hindus?' in *Hindus and Others: The Question of Identity in India Today*, New Delhi: Viking, 1993.

Panikkar, Raimon, *The Vedic Experience: Mantramañjari: An Anthology of the Vedas for Modern Man*, Berkeley: University of California Press, 1977.

Parthasarathy, Swami A., *Vedanta Treatise: The Eternities*, Bombay: Vakil & Sons, 1978.

Prakashan, Bharat, *Shri Guruji: The Man and His Mission, On the Occasion of His 51st Birthday*, Delhi: Bharat Prakashan, 1955.

Prasad, Swami Muni Narayana, *The Philosophy of Narayana Guru*, New Delhi: DK Printworld, 2003.

Radhakrishnan, S., *The Hindu View of Life*, London: Geo. Allen & Unwin Ltd., 1927.

BIBLIOGRAPHY

Ramachandran, R., *A History of Hinduism: From the Origins to the Present* (unpublished manuscript), 2017.

Saraswati, Swami Satyananda, *Four Chapters on Freedom: Commentary on the Yoga Sutras of Patanjali*, Munger: Yoga Publications Trust, 1976.

Savarkar, V. D., *Essentials of Hindutva* (available only on PDF) & *Hindutva: Who Is a Hindu?*, 1928, reprint Gorakhpur: Gita Press, 1993.

————, *Hindutva: Who is a Hindu?*, Bombay: Veer Savarkar Prakashan, 1923.

Sen, K. M., *Hinduism*, London: Penguin Books, 1978.

Singh, Dr Karan, *Essays on Hinduism*, Delhi: Ratna Sagar, 1989.

Singh, Upinder, *The Idea of Ancient India: Essays on Religion, Politics, and Archaeology*, New Delhi: Sage Publications, 2016.

Swami, Shri Purohit, *The Geeta: The Gospel of Lord Shri Krishna*, London: Faber and Faber, 1935.

Thapar, Romila: *The Penguin History of Early India from the Origins to AD 1300*, New Delhi: Penguin Books, 2003.

Tharoor, Shashi, *India: From Midnight to the Millenium and Beyond*, New Delhi: Penguin Books, 2012.

————, *Inglorious Empire: What the British Did in India*, London: Hurst, 2017.

————, *India Shastra: Reflections on the Nation in our Time*, New Delhi: Aleph Book Company, 2015.

————, *The Great Indian Novel*, New Delhi: Penguin Books, 1989.

The Life of Swami Vivekananda by his Eastern and Western Disciples, 2 vols, Kolkata: Advaita Ashrama Trust, 1999.

Upadhyaya, Deendayal, *Rashtra Jeevan Ki Disha*, Lucknow: Lokhit Prakashan, 1976, 2010.

Viswanathan, Ed, *Am I a Hindu?*, New Delhi: Rupa Publications, 1993.

Vivekananda, Swami, *The Complete Works of Swami Vivekananda*, Chennai: Manonmani Publishers, 2015.

Zaehner, R. C., *Hinduism*, London: Oxford University Press, 196.

INDEX

Adi Shankara xiii, 6, 46, 56,
68–69, 74, 83, 87, 89–95, 98,
102, 104, 118, 125, 127, 181,
264
atman and Brahman 91–93
idea of Purusharthas 93
philosophy 74, 89–95
Upadeshasahasri 92, 93
Vivekachudamani 90
Adityanath, Yogi 132, 185, 222–
223, 225–227
Advaita Vedanta 56, 87, 89, 91–92,
93–95, 107, 113, 115–116, 124,
125, 127
Akhil Bharatiya Hindu Mahasabha
143–144, 223
Ambedkar, Dr B. R. 66, 126,
234–235
Arya Samaj 109–110
Aryabhata 201
Aryan migration theory 195–197
Ashoka 135, 185, 206
astika Hindu 7, 10, 127
Atharva Veda 47, 64, 269
atman 7, 40, 63, 83, 91–93, 102,
113–115, 121, 125, 160
Aurangzeb 102, 151, 187, 204–206

Babri Masjid demolition 261,
262 Basava (Basavanna or
Basaveshwara) 68, 101–102, 104
Bhagavad Gita 4, 13, 41, 50, 57,
89, 101, 124, 188, 212, 225,
269
Bhakti movement 98–103, 207,
262, 264
Bharatiya Jana Sangh 143–146,
160, 165, 208
Bharatiya Janata Party (BJP) 132,
144–146, 160, 164–171, 173–
174, 184, 197–200, 207–208,
213–214, 220, 224–227, 229,
232, 233, 237, 250, 259
Brahman 16, 31, 33, 34–37, 40,
42, 54, 63–64, 69, 83–84,
91–93, 102, 113–115, 270
Brahmin 32, 39, 40, 42, 60,
66–67, 71, 73, 75, 96, 97, 101,
105, 179, 188, 205, 222, 263
Brahmo Samaj 59, 106–109
Buddhism 7, 22, 59, 90, 95–97,
103–104, 125, 138, 184, 185,
201, 234, 265

caste 5, 10, 24, 51, 79, 80, 94, 98,

100, 101–103, 106, 109–11,
121, 162, 169, 192, 233, 237,
260
discrimination 67–69, 73–75, 93
108, 121, 138, 156
identity 59, 69–71, 189
in Hinduism/Hindu society 11,
65, 67, 85, 103, 110, 139, 175
reservations 69–70, 72
Christian missionaries 58, 59,
109. 141, 158, 238–240

Dalit 42, 66, 68, 69, 71, 72,
74–75, 79, 98, 103, 233
Dera Sacha Sauda 78–80
dharma 17, 34, 35, 42, 43, 46,
50–53, 75, 82, 85, 88, 89, 93,
101, 131–133, 148, 154, 194,
255, 268
Dharmashastras 49, 50, 53, 66
Dvaita 12, 56

Eck, Diana L. 6

Gandhi, Mahatma 10–11, 41, 53,
70, 74, 93, 111, 125–127, 139,
142, 144, 157, 158, 167, 170,
177, 186, 191, 195, 212, 235,
243, 251, 271
criticism of conversions 239, 241
Ganesh 18, 23–29, 38, 54, 198,
261
ghar wapsi 142, 213, 251
Golwalkar, M. S. 146–155, 164,
177, 194
Bunch of Thoughts 137–138,
141–142
hatred for non–Hindus 140–142
views of nationalism 137–143
Guru Nanak 102, 104, 143

Hedgewar, K. B. 150
Hindu Rashtra (Hindu Nation)
135–138, 144, 152, 154,
156–158, 164
Hindu–Muslim unity 152, 185,
256
Hindutva xi, xiv, 139, 141, 145–
146, 166–168, 172–173, 180,
184, 193, 196–197, 203–207,
210, 214, 215, 221–224, 227,
249–250, 256, 258
conception of nationalism 135,
143, 166, 171, 194, 243
distinction from Hinduism 135,
181–182, 195, 216, 251–254,
261–263, 273
Hindutva–modified Constitution
174–178, 212
RSS's official understanding of
142
contemporary movement 133,
165, 170–172, 173, 186, 190,
214, 217, 221, 230, 235, 253,
259
Savarkar's idea of 11–12, 134,
139, 146, 257
as a political philosophy 172,
193, 265
Husain, M. F. 194, 215–220

idol worship 11, 54–55, 96–97,
106–110, 113, 116, 125
Indian Council of Historical
Research xiv, 214
Indian National Congress 144, 145,
150, 168, 177, 254
Indian Penal Code 211, 230
Indus Valley Civilization 88
Integral Humanism 145–146,
159–160, 163, 179

INDEX

Ishwar Chandra Vidyasagar 109
Islam 9, 22, 44, 96, 101, 102, 104,
    105, 134, 141, 151, 152, 179,
    188, 189, 196, 205, 220, 238,
    256
    Itihasas 47, 50, 52–53, 254

Jainism 7, 22, 59, 95–97, 102,
    113, 127, 134, 143, 185, 202,
    205
Jews 33, 117, 138, 140, 152, 155,
    164, 180, 190
Jha, D. N. 222, 234
Judaism xiii, 9, 44

Kabir 59, 74, 99–100, 102, 104
Kama Sutra 35, 218, 220
Karma yoga 111, 117, 119, 271
Kaul, Justice Sanjay Kishan 216
Kena Upanishad 9, 36, 95
Khalistan movement 165
Khilafat agitation 150
K. N. Govindacharya 174–176

Mahabharata 20, 24, 26, 40,
    46, 50–52, 56, 88, 188, 198,
    220–221, 230, 256, 257
Mahavira 22, 89, 95
Maitreya Upanishad 14, 269
Mahmud of Ghazni 96, 97, 154
Manusmriti 46, 47, 149, 301

Mirabai xv, 47, 99, 100, 104
Modi, Narendra 145, 152, 164,
    170–174, 204, 207–209, 212,
    213–214, 235, 250–251
moksha 34, 83–85, 90, 92–93,
    94, 103, 115, 131, 136, 148,
    161–162
Mookerjee, Syama Prasad 144

Muslim 5, 11, 16, 35, 41, 44, 47,
    57, 59, 63, 69, 72, 78, 96–97,
    99, 100, 103, 104–105, 117,
    127, 135, 136, 138, 139–144,
    147, 150–152, 156–158, 164,
    166–169, 170, 171–172, 176,
    177–178, 180, 184, 185, 186–
    192, 193, 195, 203, 204–207,
    209–210, 213, 215–221, 223,
    224, 226–229, 232–233, 237,
    238, 243, 249, 250, 253, 254,
    255, 256, 257, 258, 260, 261,
    262, 263, 268

Naipaul, V. S. 82, 139, 204
Nehru, 12, 74, 110, 177, 182, 205,
    208, 210–211, 243, 244, 251,
    255
nirguna Brahman 15–16, 54

Obama, Barack 249–251
Onam 38, 60–61, 256
Other Backward Classes (OBC)
    70, 79, 237

Padmavati 187, 228–229
Panikkar, K. N. 194, 206
Panikkar, Raimon 4, 9, 269
Patanjali 88, 117
Patel, Sardar Vallabhbhai 208–210
    pilgrimages 6, 12, 37–38, 62,
    94, 103, 119, 167, 177, 188
polytheism 109, 116
Prevention of Cruelty to Animals
    Act (Regulation of Livestock
    Markets) Rules, 2016 235

Puranas 47, 53–55, 57, 74, 81, 88,
    101, 103, 110, 212, 213, 262
Purusharthas 34, 83, 93, 148,
    160–162, 271

Quit India movement 207–208

Radhakrishnan, Dr Sarvepalli 4, 6, 12, 123
Raja Ravi Varma 75, 194, 220
Ram Janmabhoomi 166–168
Ramanuja 74, 98–99, 101, 104
Ramayana 20, 50–52, 67, 88, 215, 220–221, 254, 256, 257, 271
Rashtriya Swayamsevak Sangh (RSS) 133, 135, 137, 142–144, 146, 150, 165, 171, 180–181, 195, 208, 212, 214, 227, 251
Rig Veda vii, 8, 16, 31, 40, 46–48, 66, 124, 195, 200, 212, 234, 271
Roy, Raja Rammohan, 106–108, 121, 127

saguna Brahman 17, 54, 102
Sanatana Dharma 5, 11, 42–45, 57, 109
Sangh Parivar 133, 167, 180, 181, 195, 210, 213
sannyasi 40, 91, 95–96, 118–120
Sarva Dharma Sama Bhava 124, 186, 252
Savarkar, V. D. 11–12, 133–136, 137, 139, 143, 144, 146, 147, 152, 156, 158, 164, 169–170, 177, 178, 180, 195, 196, 257
secularism 132–133, 171, 173, 176, 183, 184–185, 259–261
Semitic religions 9, 44, 110, 114, 138, 181, 261
Sen, Keshub Chandra 108, 207
Shad Darshanas 7, 56, 89
Shaivites 33, 43, 54
Sikhism 59, 79, 102, 104–105, 134
Smritis 49–50

Sree Narayana Guru 68, 74–75, 110–111, 127
Srutis 47–48, 50
Swami Dayanand Saraswati 109, 195, 212

Taj Mahal 225–227
territorial nationalism 137–139, 147
Tulsidas 52, 100, 104
Truschke, Audrey 204–206

Uniform Civil Code 166, 177–178
Untouchables 66–67, 69, 85, 102, 103, 110, 162
Upadhyaya, Deen Dayal 143, 145–165, 174–177
  against Western concepts 148, 154, 161
  Hindu political philosophy 146–147, 175–176, 178
  Hindu Rashtra 150–153, 157, 164–165, 174–175
  ideal man 160
  India's political identity, 147, 149, 155–156, 158–159, 162
  Respect for religions 156–157
Upanishads xiii, 9, 11, 12, 14, 40, 48, 56, 63, 68, 74, 84, 87, 88, 89–90, 104, 107, 113, 212, 219, 234, 252, 253, 263, 267, 270
upper castes 68, 72, 73, 74, 85, 233

Vaishnavites 43, 54, 98
Vedanta School 56, 87, 89–95, 107, 113, 115, 118, 124, 125, 182
Vedic civilization 17, 201

INDEX

Vivekananda, Swami 4, 31, 53, 56,
87, 104, 107, 109, 111, 112–
125, 127, 177, 184, 186, 195,
212, 238–239, 271
on Buddhism and Sikhism 103
on Hinduism 13, 57, 110, 113,
115–118, 181, 252–253, 258,
264, 268, 273–274
about spirituality 31, 33, 114,
122–124, 132, 218, 273
sannyasi's life 118–119
on nationalism 120, 211

criticism of social practices 74,
116–117, 121

Western thought xiv, 45, 112–115,
123–125, 147–149, 153–154,
156, 161, 163, 175

Yajnavalkya (Upanishads) xiii, 31,
88, 234
Yajnavalkya (smriti) 46, 49
Yajur Veda 47, 48, 109, 110, 269
Yoga Sutras 88, 117–118

The Committee

By Walter Goodman

THE CLOWNS OF COMMERCE

ALL HONORABLE MEN

The Committee

The extraordinary career of the House Committee on Un-American Activities

★ ★ ★ ★ ★ ★ ★ ★ ★ ★ ★ ★ ★ ★ ★ ★

by Walter Goodman

FOREWORD BY RICHARD H. ROVERE

Farrar, Straus and Giroux

NEW YORK

For my sons, Hal and Bennet

Foreword

Walter Goodman's accomplisment is a large and salutary one—very much *pro bono publico,* very much what the age demands, or at least requires. It is the work of a man who knows and loves this country and has a deep understanding of its political processes, the noble ones as well as those that are ugly and despicable. The prose is elegant, often eloquent; the mood, as befits the matter, ironic and at times comic.

My tribute, I feel, should be taken not merely at face value but at somewhat more than face value, for I must explain that I approached this book with about as much resistance as sympathy. To read it was, of course, a professional responsibility, even an act of civic virtue. But virtue, as all the virtuous know, cannot buy happiness. I could not approach a volume of formidable bulk on this particular subject without a certain amount of self-pity. It so happens that the House Committee on Un-American Activities and I are, in professional terms, exactly of an age. We both set up shop just thirty years ago. The Committee has had its ups and downs, as have I. By and large, though, my legitimate grievances have been few in number and of no great magnitude. But a recurring chore that I have found odious in the extreme has been keeping abreast of the doings of this preposterous and often vicious product of American democracy. I would hate to see an accounting of the number of hours I have spent, or misspent, attending its open hearings, reading its zany reports, and writing about the people who have served on it or been victimized by it. The rewards of diligence have been meager, for, with few exceptions, the investigators and the investigated have seemed richly to deserve each other—though, of course, poetic justice is never to

be equated with that of the blindfolded goddess with the true
scales. In any case, I have always found the Committee a disagreeable subject to write about, and I could not help feeling
somewhat put upon as I faced the prospect of reading a long
book about it. Others, I thought, might benefit from a study of
what the Committee had been up to for thirty long years, and
it might be a good thing for me to commend such an exercise
to them and explain wherein the profit might lie. But for me a
recitation of this history could only be coals to Newcastle all
the way—a journey of whose squalor I already knew too much.

Mr. Goodman did not allow me to feel dutiful or self-pitying
for more than a few moments. I was almost immediately swept
up by the freshness of his narrative, impressed by the display
of intellectual toughness, delighted by his instinct for the sar-
donic. More than that, I learned, almost at the outset, a lesson
I hope not to forget about the frailty of memory and the need
for humility. I had thought that Mr. Goodman could not tell
me anything about the Committee that I did not already know.
This was arrogance of a sort, and I have, I hope, been purged
of it. Mr. Goodman has told me a great deal I either never
knew or had forgotten. (The distinction is trivial; if a fact has
fled my mind, I am as ignorant as if I had never known it.) At
all odds, the pathetic role of the anti-Nazi Samuel Dickstein in
fathering the Committee was news to me—and a valuable addition to my collection of boomerang effects in politics. I was
also, until I read this book, unaware of the extent to which the
Committee, in its early days, was as racist as it was anti-Communist and anti-New Deal. In all probability, I was aware of
this a quarter of a century ago—I put in more time covering the
Committee in its earlier years than in its middle and later ones
—but it was an aspect of its being that, in retrospect, was not
part of my knowledge. I think I understand why. In the years
since 1948, the cold war has dominated the thinking of everyone—liberal journalists and heresy-hunters not excluded. (Some
liberal journalists, alas, became heresy-hunters.) Also, in this
period, we have seen the death of anti-Semitism as an important motivating force in American politics. In the early years
of the Committee's existence, overt anti-Semitism among Con-

gressmen was no more disreputable than overt anti-Negro sentiment is in certain Southern legislatures today. There are no
doubt anti-Semites in Congress at present, but any open expression of the bias today would be so widely regarded as "un-
American" as to make it politically dangerous. The day of anti-
Semitism's respectability is far enough in the past that some of
us have difficulty in recalling it. I like to think that this kind
of history will repeat itself—that bigotry in every form will become politically disreputable.

The Committee is far more than a history of the Committee.
It is a work that contributes greatly to our understanding of the
American Left in the mid-twentieth century and also, to a
slightly lesser extent, of the American Right. Mr. Goodman
deals sharply with both these movements—or, better perhaps,
tendencies, since neither was ever any more than a cluster
of factions—and I suspect that some of his younger readers
will be impatient with him for the even-handedness of his contempt for the Stalinist Left and the yahoo Right. The fashion
now, in many intellectual circles, is to be intolerant of those
who are not indiscriminately tolerant of radical "dissent." This
modishness has no appeal for Mr. Goodman. Though plainly
more Left than Right in his own sympathies, he does not accept
the view that the Communists whom the Committee harassed—
along, of course, with many non-Communists—were undeserv-
ing of any form of investigation or political censure. The excesses of the cold war, particularly in the years of McCarthyism
rampant, and the increasing impotence of orthodox Communists have led many to think that no one ever had a legitimate
cause for apprehension over the political power of the Communist Party of the United States. Mr. Goodman thinks otherwise and so, emphatically, do I. It is, to be sure, easy to
exaggerate the influence of Communists in America—J. Edgar
Hoover has been doing this for going on half a century—but
underestimation is equally easy and equally fatuous. If one
wishes to understand the weakness and fragmentation of the
Left in the 1960's, one must know something of the strength
and character of the Left in the 1930's. There was, as I see it,
then a chance for an indigenous radical movement of sufficient

force and integrity to have endured into the present and to
have played a part in strengthening American democracy. It is
often said that the New Deal stole all the thunder of the Left
and institutionalized it inside the Democratic Party. This is
partly true—the New Deal gave some scope to radical theorists
and even to radical activists. But the New Deal cannot be
blamed for the political disarray and intellectual shoddiness of
the American Left today. Nor can the Communists be held
altogether responsible. But a great deal of damage was done by
Communist bureaucrats who feigned a concern for the future
of American society when what in fact concerned them above
all other things was the national interest and foreign policy of
the U.S.S.R. Discovering what the Communist Party had really
been up to was, for many American radicals, far more traumatic
and destructive than the later discovery of some that they had
served the interests of the Central Intelligence Agency. Though
individual Communists may have been men of a rather simple-
minded integrity, the Party was a totalitarian wrecker. Mr.
Goodman has a solid appreciation of this basic truth, and this
lends added force to his indictment of the Committee. He is
no less anti-Communist than Martin Dies or any of Dies's successors. To some, such a statement may seem not faint praise
but downright condemnation. I will stand by it. What distin-
guishes Mr. Goodman from most of those he writes about on
both sides of the hearing-room table is his own liberal and
humanistic intelligence, his commitment to democratic values
—a commitment shared neither by the Committee nor by most
of its victims.

The Committee goes on—it may survive the century, if America survives the century, and outlast most of us now alive. It
has never been quite the same since Joe McCarthy muscled in
on the territory eighteen years, but it nevertheless survived
McCarthy and the specific virus we called McCarthyism. It is
something of an anachronism, rather like the heraldry units
that are rumored still to be found in Robert McNamara's Pentagon. Yet there are authentic historical reasons for its survival.
Once more running counter to the conventional wisdom of today's liberalism, Mr. Goodman writes that "there is nothing

un-American about the Un-American Activities Committee."
In liberal and intellectual circles, it has long been the custom
to mock the very notion that such ungainly words as "Americanism" and "un-Americanism" could have any real meaning
or content. Behind the mocking, there was a romantic idealism
—a picture of this country as so diverse, so committed to
Thomas Jefferson's dream of the open marketplace of ideas that
no specific dogma and no specific heresy could be labeled
"American" or "un-American." But this, as Mr. Goodman says,
is nonsense. Ours "is not the land exclusively of Lincoln and
Jefferson." Martin Dies, Joe Pool, Joe McCarthy, Barry Goldwater, George Wallace are every bit as American as Jefferson,
and it is for their America that the Committee has spoken and
will continue to speak. It is not an attractive thought, but it is
an inescapable conclusion and one we shall have to live with
and adjust to. Those of us who want Jefferson's America to
survive and perhaps in time prevail will find guidance and a
fortifying good humor in this admirable book.

Richard H. Rovere

NEW YORK CITY
NOVEMBER, 1967

Preface

IF the House Committee on Un-American Activities had not been invented, there would be no good reason for it to exist. But exist it does, and this chronicle is designed neither as polemic nor, emphatically, as apologetics. That is not to suggest that I am lacking in opinions about the Committee and all that it has represented for three decades; the reader will have to go no great distance before he can clear me of that crime at least. But while I would be dismayed at a charge of indifference, it was never my principal intention to produce a document for service in the fitful campaign for abolition. Such documents have been produced, on both sides of the case, and whatever their individual merits, all are hobbled by constraints endemic to the form.

Still, a reader approaching a book on so controversial a subject is entitled to know something of the author's stance. As a liberal—I confess it, though I fear to think what the word may convey to any given reader—I find myself fraternally troubled by the dilemma which the Committee has from the first constituted for liberals in this country. The Communists, despising us, have exploited our good names for their own interests. The hunters of Communists, despising us, have offended our dearest beliefs and attacked our cherished causes. We can, it seems to me, do nothing but bear up—continue to oppose the Committee, continue to champion the political freedoms of persons who, we know, mock us for soft-headedness, and make clear that we are doing so not out of misplaced affection for totalitarians of the left but out of reverence for liberty.

How liberals have reacted to the Committee's recurrent challenges is one theme of this book, but not *the* theme. That is

[xiii]

not so readily summarized. I began my research in the belief that the Committee's activities have a good deal to tell us about the nation that has endured them for thirty years, the system that has sustained them, and the times to which they have lent inimitable color. I complete the writing with the hope that some of this may be found in these pages.

W. G.

GREENBURGH, NEW YORK
NOVEMBER, 1967

Contents

FOREWORD *by Richard H. Rovere*   vii
PREFACE   xiii

1 DICKSTEIN'S MONSTER   3
Fish Committee • McCormack-Dickstein Committee • Martin Dies

2 1938: THE DIES COMMITTEE   24
John Frey and Walter Steele • J. B. Matthews • Federal Theatre • Harry Bridges • Frank Murphy

3 1939: DISARRAY ON THE LEFT   59
General Moseley • Fritz Kuhn • Earl Browder • William Z. Foster • American League for Peace and Democracy • Joe Curran • American Youth Congress • Consumers Union

4 1940: POPULARITY AND POWER   89
William Dudley Pelley • Raids on Communists • Smith Act • Mike Quill • Carl Byoir • Nazis • F.D.R. • Jerry Voorhis

5 1941–1944: END OF THE TETHER   118
Institute for Propaganda Analysis • American Peace Mobilization • O.P.A., F.C.C., B.E.W., etc. • Watson-Dodd-Lovett • Japanese-Americans • Walter Winchell • C.I.O.-P.A.C.

6 1945–1946: RANKIN'S COUP 167

John Rankin • Joint Anti-Fascist Refugee Committee • Gerald L. K. Smith • Louis Budenz

7 1947: THE THOMAS COMMITTEE 190

Gerhart Eisler • Southern Conference for Human Welfare • Hanns Eisler • Hollywood Ten

8 1948: VINTAGE YEAR 226

Mundt-Nixon Bill • Edward Condon • Elizabeth Bentley • Harry Dexter White • Alger Hiss and Whittaker Chambers • Laurence Duggan • J. Parnell Thomas

9 1949–1950: IN CONTEMPT 272

John Wood • Atomic Scientists • G. Racey Jordan • William Remington • Lee Pressman • Internal Security Act

10 1951–1952: MANY ARE CALLED 297

Hollywood Revisited • Oliver Clubb • Herbert Philbrick • United Electrical Workers

11 1953–1954: THE VELDE CAPERS 321

Harold Velde • Schools and Colleges • Bishop Oxnam • Truman Subpoenaed

12 THE FIFTH AMENDMENT 351

Dean Griswold and Professor Hook • John Watkins • Lloyd Barenblatt

13 1955–1956: THE WALTER COMMITTEE 367

Francis Walter • John Gojack • Edward Corsi • Broadway • Fund for the Republic • N.L.R.B. • Otto Nathan • Arthur Miller

Contents

14 1957–1960: OPERATION ABOLITION   399

Musicians and Artists • Boris Morros • Air Force Manual • Mitchell and Martin • Legislation • J. Edgar Hoover • Cyrus Eaton • Frank Wilkinson and Carl Braden • Contempt Cases • James Roosevelt • San Francisco

15 1961–1966: THE LEAN YEARS   435

Women Strike for Peace • Travelers to Cuba • Russell Nixon, Dagmar Wilson, Donna Allen • Dr. Stamler and Mrs. Hall • Ku Klux Klan • Vietnam

16 1967...: UN-AMERICAN?   482

APPENDICES   497
NOTES   523
BIBLIOGRAPHY   549
INDEX   551

Illustrations

All *photographs from Wide World Photos*

FOLLOWING PAGE 204

The Dies Committee; J. B. Matthews
Samuel Dickstein; Earl Browder
Fritz Kuhn; Martin Dies
Mrs. Eleanor Roosevelt
Joe Curran and Harry Bridges; Mike Quill
John Rankin
The Eisler case; Two of the Hollywood Ten
J. Parnell Thomas and friends; Elizabeth Bentley
Harry Dexter White

FOLLOWING PAGE 428

Alger Hiss; Whittaker Chambers
Robert Stripling and the microfilm; Richard Nixon
Chambers and family; Hiss on his way to prison
Chairman Velde and Bishop Oxnam
Rep. Walter and Matthew Cvetic
Hearings on show business
In San Francisco
Mrs. Dagmar Wilson; Robert Shelton
Arthur Kinoy; Rep. Joe Pool

THE United States, to my eye, is incomparably the greatest show on earth. It is a show which avoids diligently all the kinds of clowning which tire me most quickly—for example, royal ceremonials, the tedious hocus-pocus of haute politique, the taking of politics seriously—and lays chief stress upon the kinds which delight me unceasingly—for example, the ribald combats of demagogues, the exquisitely ingenious operations of master rogues, the pursuit of witches and heretics, the desperate struggles of inferior men to claw their way into Heaven.

H. L. MENCKEN

The Committee

1

Dickstein's Monster

IN THE RANKS of those public men, from Pyrrhus forward,
who have striven and striven and at last succeeded, only
to have their triumph turn shortly to gall, a place must be set
aside for Samuel Dickstein. He served in the House of Representatives for twenty-two years, from 1923 to 1944, and during
that whole time no cause took more of his energies or his passions than the creation of a committee to investigate subversive
activities. Assigning political paternity is a speculative game,
but if any man deserves the title of Father of the Committee,
it is Representative Dickstein. He earned the distinction by
relentless trying from 1933 to 1938 and had the rest of his life
to regret it.

There was nothing unnatural in Sam Dickstein's growing
passionate over what he, with many others, viewed as seditious
behavior in the nineteen-thirties. Germany was on the march
in Europe, and at home Nazi sympathizers were openly rallying, goose-stepping, and reviling Jews. Congressman Dickstein's New York City district, running along the East River
from Chatham Square to East Houston Street, was the home
of immigrants from Eastern Europe. Like his own parents, who
had carried him to America at the age of three, these thousands
and tens of thousands had run away from the pogroms of the
Old World only to find that the New World was not able to
repeal their history. In their East Side ghetto, their beards were
pulled, their wives insulted, their sons beaten. That much was

[3]

acceptable, but now in Germany torment of the Jew had become not just an entertainment but an expression of political faith, and all that the East Side immigrants had ever learned told them that their adopted home was not immune to the madness.

Sam Dickstein, who started his career as a special deputy attorney general in New York State and would end it, in the tradition of loyal city-machine Democrats, as a state Supreme Court justice, sought to strike at the danger not with the legislative arm of the Congress but with its investigative arm. It was difficult in a free country to pass laws against individuals joining together in Teutonic fellowship to drink beer and rail at Jews, but nothing in the Constitution prohibited investigating them. In demanding an investigation of the German-American Bund, the New Yorker was merely availing himself of a weapon which the national legislature had used, with notable effect, since its beginnings. The exigencies of ordinary politics often led legislators to peep into odd corners of the executive establishment and elsewhere, and there was no requirement that they produce a law to justify the time and money they spent; the public enlightenment that presumably attended their revelations together with the *possibility* that a law might actually emerge at some future time or other was justification enough. Unrestricted, for practical purposes, as to the subject matter of their inquiries or the manner in which these were conducted, uncommitted to tangible results, each committee chairman might allow his inclinations generous sway.

Congressional investigations were particularly in vogue after World War I, as indeed they always are after a war, when our political parties shake off an enforced unity and return to their natural life of mutual recrimination. In the nineteen-twenties and thirties, there were investigations into the conduct of the war, into the Teapot Dome scandal, into banks, lobbies, railroads, the munitions industry, strike breakers, the stock exchange. The nation's moneyed interests were the defendants in nearly all these inquests, and so the hearings were attacked by conservatives as Star Chamber proceedings and defended by liberals as legitimate expressions of the people's right to know. In the same year that Andrew W. Mellon protested to President Coolidge that "government by investigation is not government," Felix Frankfurter told the readers of *The New Republic*: "The procedure of Congressional investigations should remain as it is. No limitations should be imposed by Congressional legislation or standing rules. The power of investigation should be left untrammeled." Professor Frankfurter did, however, add the caution that it depends on the Congress itself, on the press, and on the good sense of the people to keep this large power from degenerating into partisan advantage. Nearly thirty years later, when Senator McCarthy was abroad in the land, Mr. Justice Frankfurter would raise his voice in concern over the use of the power he had once championed.

As for subversive doctrines and activities, they had occupied the attention of Congressional investigators, off and on, since the Armistice. In February 1919, the Senate, unnerved by the Bolshevik ascendance in Russia, took the occasion of two pro-Soviet rallies in Washington as the starting point for an investigation of "any efforts being made to propagate in this country the principles of any party exercising or claiming to exercise authority in Russia . . . [and] any effort to incite the overthrow of the Government of this country, or all governments, by force or by the destruction of life or property or the general cessation of industry." Hearings were held by a committee originally set up to look into "the brewing industry and German propaganda" and a report was issued. In March 1919 the New York legislature established a joint committee, under Senator Clayton R. Lusk, to investigate seditious activities. The Lusk Committee would be a beacon to Communist-hounders still unweaned, but it was not yet the time of the investigator in the land. Even the great Red Scare of 1919–1920, complete with strikes, bombings, Attorney General Palmer's raids on radicals, and the expulsion from these shores of 246 men and three women aboard the S.S. *Buford*, popularly known as the Soviet Ark, passed smoothly into the euphoria of the Harding-Coolidge decade.

It was not until after the stock-market crash that the House of Representatives decided that the domestic menace of Bolshevism was worthy of formal study by a proper committee of the House. Their decision followed hard upon a revelation in May 1930 by Grover Whalen, lately of Wanamaker's Department Store and at that moment New York City's police commissioner,[1] that he had seven documents which connected the Soviet Amtorg Trading Corporation with the dissemination of Communist propaganda in this country. Commissioner Whalen's charges would never be proved; indeed, as Fiorello La Guardia demonstrated in one of his last acts as a U. S. Congressman, the documents were forgeries—the commissioner had been put upon. But this was not yet certain when the Committee on Rules acted. It reported a resolution that it had killed two months earlier which provided for an investigation not only of Communist propaganda, the Communist Party and all affiliated organizations, the Communist International, the Amtorg Trading Corporation and the *Daily Worker*—but of "all entities, groups or individuals who are alleged to advise, teach or advocate the overthrow by force or violence of the Government of the United States, or attempt to undermine our republican form of government by inciting riots, sabotage or revolutionary disorders."[2] Hamilton Fish of New York, original sponsor of the ambitious proposal, explained to his colleagues: "It is not the purpose of this resolution to interfere with any group except the Communists in the United States, and we propose to deport all alien Communists." In response to Representative Ramseyer of Iowa, who suggested that Congress ought to be doing something about unemployment, Fish pointed out that after deporting "every single alien Communist", one could "give those jobs to honest, loyal American

[1] Those who lived in New York during the thirties will remember the robustly elegant Mr. Whalen not as police commissioner, a title he held for only seventeen months, but as the town's official greeter, splendidly mustached, a smile on his heavy face, a flower in his buttonhole, a big hand at the ready for shaking; it was a position that satisfied his particular gifts better than detective work.

[2] When in the course of the House debate on the resolution, Representative Huddleston of Alabama brought up the question of investigating fascism, Representative Snell, chairman of the Rules Committee, replied that he didn't know what that was, but he guessed the resolution covered it "if it is something wrong."

citizens who are unemployed." Thus counseled, the House established the Committee by a vote of 210 to 18, the first in a not yet ended series of lopsided votes in favor of such investigative bodies, and Fish was named chairman.

In the demonology of the liberal press of the time, Ham Fish was a throwback to the Salem witch hunters (who could resist a joke about the Fish-ing expedition?), but with the advantage of three inquisitorial decades behind us, we can see now that the New York aristocrat, though no less of a Communist-hater than the chairmen who would follow him, was more of a gentleman. Edmund Wilson, then entering his brief Communist phase,[3] reported that Fish looked like "a Hannibal turned tailor's dummy or a blank-eyed vacuous Bashan bull," and, considering the fellow's size, was the more impressed with his manners. But although Fish may not have been as rude as some, he equaled any man in the House in his ignorance of the subject he was investigating. (Except, possibly, his fellows on the Committee, who had difficulty with unfamiliar words such as "bourgeoisie" and "liquidate.") The prevailing ignorance in Congress about Communism reflected that of the national electorate, and the hearings served as a display case for all sorts of foolishness. "What?" exclaimed Fish to Peter A. Bogdanov, chairman of the board of Amtorg. "You were a prisoner under the Czar and you don't know how many political prisoners there were in Siberia?" Mr. Bogdanov chuckled and his interpreter replied, "He says that the Czar didn't send him to Siberia to count the number of prisoners." Nor did it

[3] The Un-American Activities Committee would for many years be much involved with persons who were drawn to radical movements by the same dismal vision of America that troubled Wilson at the start of the thirties: "There are today in the United States, according to the census director, something like nine million men out of work; our cities are scenes of privation and misery on a scale which sickens the imagination; our agricultural life is bankrupt; our industry, in shifting to the South, has reverted almost to the horrible conditions, before the Factory Acts, of the England of a hundred years ago, and the fight of the unions there for recognition is all to begin again; so many banks are failing that the newspapers do not dare to print the truth about them. And when we look to South America or to the European countries west of Russia, we see only the same economic chaos, the same lack of capacity or will to deal with it, and the same resultant suffering. May we not well fear that what has broken down, in the course of one catastrophic year, is not simply the machinery of representative government but the capitalist system itself?"

help the Committee's reputation for seriousness when it discovered a case of vegetables in a Baltimore warehouse where it had expected to find a case of bombs.

In his exchanges with Communist Party leaders, like William Z. Foster, Chairman Fish was operating under a joint disability. Not only didn't he know much about matters that Foster, though far from an intellectual, had taken pains to absorb,[4] but he was so steeped in his own old-American, upper-class, private-school values—values that would ultimately bring him to leadership of the most perverse element of the America First movement—that he could not credit these people with really believing what they said they believed. William Foster may have drawn his strength from a sense of history moving implacably toward the destruction of Hamilton Fish and all his sisters and his cousins and his aunts, but Hamilton Fish had a no less powerful sense of history as name, family, and Harvard. It was narrow but powerful, and there was no place in it for the eccentricities of the unwashed. In the committee room, Fish was like a schoolmaster faced with a class from Hell's Kitchen who were doing their nasty darndest to put one over on him. His strategy was to trip the witnesses up, make them admit that really, at bottom, they did too believe in God and capitalism just as all the Fishes had down the years.

The hearings, carried on in fairly haphazard style, took six months, from July to December of 1930, at the end of which time the Committee produced a report. It credited the Communist Party with a dues-paying membership of about 12,000 and little noticeable influence despite an estimated half-million sympathizers. It attacked the Civil Liberties Union for its defense of Communists and noted that Grover Whalen's charges against Amtorg had not been supported by the evidence. Out of these mild ingredients, the Committee managed to distill thirteen hearty recommendations, which included declaring the Communist Party illegal, deporting alien Communists, enacting federal laws to prevent Communists from

---

[4] Foster put his lifetime ideology in a nutshell in 1925: "I am for the Comintern from start to finish . . . and if the Comintern finds itself criss-cross with my opinions, there is only one thing to do and that is to change my opinion to fit the policy of the Comintern."

spreading false rumors that might cause runs on banks, and considering an embargo on all articles imported from Russia. Its most intoxicating proposal called on the Department of State to get permission for Treasury agents to go to Russia— the government of which we had yet to recognize—and study the use of forced labor in the timber industry to determine whether we should stop importing Red timber. The want of diplomatic relations between America and the U.S.S.R. also interfered with Fish's dream of sending all the Reds back where they came from.

Doctors who recommend major surgery for a case of heartburn leave themselves open to the suspicion that they simply like to cut, and the Fish Committee's recommendations were taken in this spirit. In a calm minority report, Representative John E. Nelson of Maine pointed out that Communists did exist, unfortunately, but even granting that their intentions were frankly subversive, the problems they presented were related to the country's larger economic and social problems and these did not lend themselves to solution by criminal statute. Of the numerous bills put forward in 1931 and 1932 to deport alien Communists—and most C.P. members at the time were aliens, with East European Jews particularly noticeable among them—only one, introduced by the young representative from Orange County, Texas, Martin Dies, managed to get through the House, and it was never called to a vote in the Senate.

Although Samuel Dickstein did not take a starring role in these events, he was a featured player. In 1930 he joined Hamilton Fish in condemning religious persecution in Russia. In 1932 he brought Martin Dies's anti-Communist bill to the floor of the House. In 1933, after the assassination attempt on President-elect Roosevelt, he called for a Congressional investigation of anarchists. A few months later, as chairman of the House Immigration Committee, he conducted his own unofficial inquiry into Nazi propaganda, featuring secret letters, smuggled papers, and a witness named Mr. X, who wore spats. He predicted, in words that soon became a refrain, that his revelations would "shock the country."

It was not his revelations that did most to forward his plans, however, but the rise of Adolf Hitler. On the return of Congress to Washington in January 1934, Dickstein offered a resolution to investigate Nazi activities in the United States, and other forms of subversive propaganda. It was supported by Hamilton Fish and after a lively debate, in which a Congressman from Nebraska suggested that the whole thing was a scheme by Jews to offend German-Americans like those in his state who admired the Führer, the Dickstein resolution was authorized by 168 to 31; appointed to the chairmanship of the Committee was John McCormack of Massachusetts, destined to grow old as Speaker of the House. Samuel Dickstein made it known that he had been passed over in deference to his own feeling that a non-Jew should conduct this particular inquiry. Perhaps that was only a rationalization, but he accepted the position of vice chairman along with the gratification of hearing people speak for years thereafter of the "Dickstein Committee."

The McCormack-Dickstein or Dickstein-McCormack hearings began in the summer of 1934 and continued off and on into the fall. For the most part they were based on competent investigation and were fairly respectful of witnesses. The majority of the hearings were held in executive session, and the few public sessions, at which witnesses were permitted counsel, were conducted in a relatively orderly way—when Chairman McCormack was present. When the more emotional Dickstein was on his own in two days of hearings he conducted in New York as a subcommittee of one, he kept getting into arguments with the editor of *Healey's Irish Weekly,* who insisted on making cracks about the "radical Jewish minority influence in Washington." "Don't give me that junk," the Congressman told the anti-Semite. "Don't let you and I get into an argument, because I am not looking for any unless you want some. I am prepared for you." He left little doubt of that. In a thesis on investigating committees written in 1937, a Ph.D. candidate at Syracuse University observed:

> Much of the investigation into Nazi propaganda activities may be classified into two parts: first, the counsel usually questions the

witnesses upon the facts of his activities ("What have you done?") and presents exhibits accordingly and, second, one of the committee, nearly always Mr. Dickstein, then proceeds to explore the witness' opinions ("Why did you do it?" "Is it right?" "Is it American?") and to bait him further if it can be found that he has not taken out his second citizenship papers or if he has allowed the first ones to lapse. A large number of the Nazi sympathizers were found to be between the receipt of their first and second papers and this gave Mr. Dickstein an opportunity to explore the witness' opinion upon what was right and proper for an American citizen or a prospective American.

It was one of Sam Dickstein's boasts that at the beginning of his career he defended, without compensation, 30,000 New York City tenants against landlords, and one can readily imagine him going after landlords or anarchists or Nazis in the same hot temper. Chairman McCormack's coolness as an inquisitor could only have exasperated Vice Chairman Dickstein (asked at the conclusion of the hearings whether the Nazis were a threat, McCormack replied, "The movement is nowhere near as strong as it was"), but the New Yorker found means of drawing attention to his case. He emerged from a closed one-man session on the establishment, by the Friends of New Germany, of a *Wille und Macht* children's camp in New Jersey, to tell reporters: "I would not keep a dog there. The camp is full of poison ivy, and there are unsanitary conditions. They goose-step all day." A few days later, the camp leader sent the children home. At the final hearings of the Committee, held in the New York City Bar Association building, several hundred German-Americans helped satisfy Mr. Dickstein's taste for excitement and publicity by packing the hearing room, cutting radio wires, chanting "Down with Dickstein," and bringing the meeting to a disorderly climax with Nazi salutes and shouts of "Heil Hitler!"

In the Committee's report, submitted in February 1935, we hear the voice of McCormack. It cited examples of pro-German propaganda paid for by German diplomats, and reported that the youth camps were pro-Hitler. It noted the existence of other anti-Semitic organizations such as William Dudley Pelley's Silver Shirts, and concurred in the Fish Committee's conclusion that the Communist Party was a branch of the Third International. Two of McCormack's recommendations, a far more moderate assortment than that of Ham Fish, were actually destined to become law—the compulsory registration of foreign agents distributing propaganda in the United States, and an extension of subpoena powers to Congressional investigating committees holding hearings outside of the District of Columbia.

It is tempting, from a distance of three decades, to be patronizing about the political nightmares of the thirties, but in fact there were fascists in America and there were Communists, both groups at their peaks of strength and both possessed by dreams that could not thrive in our frustrating democracy. One might sneer away the Red-baiting of the Hearst press and shrug off the ceaseless cries of "Fascist!" from the left, and yet be uneasy about the future. As Arthur Schlesinger, Jr., was to comment twenty years later, "For a moment in 1935, intelligent observers could almost believe that the traditional structure of American politics was on the verge of dissolution."

Whether a Congressional committee was equipped to shore up the structure, however, was another matter. One of the earliest and still popular charges against Congressional investigations in general, and those into subversion in particular, is that they are not motivated by any real legislative intent and produce few laws worth mentioning. Years after the Fish Committee concluded its work, critics were still pointing out that it took testimony from 225 witnesses in fourteen cities, produced a voluminous report, and passed at once into obscurity. Yet a lack of legislative progeny by itself is not sufficient to prove a committee of Congress sterile. Before the turn of the century, Woodrow Wilson wrote what would stand among his most quotable lines in the twenties and thirties—"the informing function of Congress should be even preferred to its legislative function"—and whatever their shortcomings of intelligence, organization, and good intentions, both the Fish and McCormack committees undoubtedly carried out an informing function. But it was early recognized that in the course of publicizing Communist and fascist techniques, committee members might yield to a craving for personal publicity, might make careless charges or engage in common politicking. Neither Representative Fish nor Representative Dickstein was able to resist temptation altogether. Thoughtful defenders of Congressional investigations like the young Felix Frankfurter and thoughtful critics like the young Walter Lippmann came to much the same conclusion about them. In Lippmann's words: "Essentially, the case is one in which good precedents must be made by the legislative bodies themselves . . ." And Frankfurter wrote: "The safeguards against abuse and folly are to be looked for in the forces of responsibility which are operating from within Congress . . ."

In practice, as the contrast between the methods of the irascible Dickstein and the reserved McCormack demonstrated, the conduct of a Congressional investigation generally proceeds from the temperament and objectives of the committee chairman—unless he is an unusually weak figure, in which case a more forceful member can be counted on to fill the breach. The chairman's prerogatives are a cherished part of our Congressional tradition. Within wide limits, he sets his own rules of procedure, and his personality as much as his conscious intention determines how witnesses will be treated. The rules of the courtroom do not here prevail. They neither restrain the prosecutor nor shield the defendant. A forceful exercise of the chairman's power was a disturbing feature of Senator Thad Caraway's 1930 investigation of lobbyists as well as of Ham Fish's 1930 investigation of Communists and would remain an acute source of trouble during the innumerable hearings into subversion that lay ahead.

The word "subversion" itself, particularly as understood by men like Fish, Dickstein, and Dies, could only compound the difficulty of holding an orderly inquiry. In January 1937, Dickstein, whose inquisitorial passions had been choked rather than slaked by the McCormack hearings, introduced a resolution in language that opened up spectacular new investigative vistas. In the previous year he had asked, unsuccessfully, to be allowed to investigate the Black Legion, an insignificant anti-Semitic gang. Now he wanted to probe all organizations "found operating in the United States for the purpose of diffusing within the United States of slanderous or libelous un-American propaganda of religious, racial or subversive political prejudices which tends to incite the use of force and violence or which tends to incite libelous attacks upon the President of the United States or other officers of the Federal Government, whether such propaganda appears to be of foreign or domestic origin." Dickstein promised that his resolution—with its evocative term, "un-American," destined for so long and famous a life—would permit the investigation not merely of Nazis, but of "Everybody!"

When the resolution came to the floor of the House in April, it found almost no support. Representative Johnson of Minnesota asked a question—"What is meant by un-American activities?"—which was to echo down the decades without ever receiving a much better answer than it received that day, when it was ignored. Civil libertarians opposed the resolution as a witch hunt, and Maury Maverick of Texas cautioned Dickstein that it could "start a wave of anti-Semitic propaganda all over this country." The pro-German contingent was opposed because the gentleman from New York had made it abundantly clear that what he meant by "un-American activities" were pro-German activities. Even so confirmed a subversive-hunter as Hamilton Fish—perhaps taking personally the reference to libels on the President—came out against Dickstein, warning in the very language of his enemies: "This bill sets up an un-American check-up, nothing more or less, and restores the Alien and Sedition laws." J. Parnell Thomas of New Jersey, a freshman already winning a reputation for being able to spot Communist subversion in the fall of any sparrow, mocked the Dickstein resolution as inviting the investigation of soldiers parading in kilts and playing bagpipes.

Sam Dickstein must be forgiven if he suspected that it was not so much the language of his resolution that offended men like Fish and Thomas, as its sponsor. He, Sam Dickstein, was the main obstacle to his own ambitions. The entire House

understood whom Representative Lindsay C. Warren of North
Carolina had in mind when he observed that "investigations
of this nature, and the membership of the House knows it,
are generally for the self-glorification and advertisement of
those who conduct them and who have an itch and flair for
publicity and advertisement in the papers of the nation rather
than in the sober forum of the committee rooms." In truth,
Dickstein had asked for it. In a few years he had succeeded
in making a national reputation for himself with his campaign,
in and out of Congress, against pro-Nazi groups. He spoke
incessantly of fascist plots, of "Nazi rats, spies and agents . . .
recruiting and drilling uniformed and armed groups . . . I will
name you one hundred spies . . ." He proclaimed that there
were 50,000 fascists in Connecticut alone, and held aloft pictures of goose-stepping youths in New Jersey. He brought the
name of Fritz Kuhn, leader of the native Nazi movement, to
the attention of the country, and began an extended exchange
of epithets with the recently naturalized Ford Motor Company
chemist over which of them was a better type of citizen. (Kuhn
said that Dickstein was a spy for Soviet Russia.) It was in vain
that the New Yorker now assured the House that he had no
itch for personal glory, and did not even want to be appointed
chairman of his proposed committee. No pretense of rationality
could conceal his obsession. Despite the calm support of
Representative McCormack, the resolution was tabled by a
vote of 184 to 38. Only two Republicans supported Dickstein,
and most members of his own party refrained from declaring
themselves. "It is a vote," he told the House, with his accustomed flourishes, "which gave aid and comfort to all the
enemies of America and all subversive organizations plotting
to destroy our form of government."

The House voted down another resolution that day—this
one the child of Martin Dies, for an investigation of sit-down
strikes, an epidemic of which, he reported, "is sweeping the
nation and threatening the very foundations of orderly government." One among several investigations unavailingly proposed by the young Texan in 1937, it was frankly designed
to counteract the Senate's Civil Liberties Committee, headed

by Robert M. La Follette, which, with the blessing of F.D.R. and the C.I.O., was effectively exposing labor espionage and violent union-busting tactics in the steel and automobile industries. Dies, who had recently helped lead the opposition to the wages and hours bill, identified himself as a friend of labor, which caused some merriment in the chamber, and after a noisy debate, supporters of the Administration turned him back. But three months later, Martin Dies, with the encouragement of Vice President Garner, Speaker Bankhead, and Majority Leader Rayburn, and with the assured support of the Southern bloc, put forward a new version of the Dickstein resolution—and the two men, the small, dressy unpopular New York New Dealer and the big, rowdy popular Texan who had already made an imposing place for himself among the restive conservatives of both parties, joined in the cause of a committee to investigate "subversive and un-American propaganda."[5] The fact that a victory for the Dies resolution could only be taken as a personal rebuff to himself could not have been lost upon Sam Dickstein, yet he became its most fervent advocate. Whereas Dies had modestly requested merely a special committee, Dickstein declared: "There should be a standing committee of this House known as the Committee on Un-American Activities, which should watch every subversive group in this country." He would live to see his dream realized by a Jew-hater from Mississippi.

In the months leading up to the House debate on the Dies resolution, Dickstein's campaign of exposure was abetted by Germany's heightening pressures on its European neighbors and by the behavior of those thousands of Germans in this country who were caught up in the old country's madness. They held larger rallies, flew greater numbers of swastikas,

---

[5] The resolution, as passed, read as follows: "Resolved, that the Speaker of the House of Representatives be, and he is hereby, authorized to appoint a special committee to be composed of seven members for the purpose of conducting an investigation of (1) the extent, character, and object of un-American propaganda activities in the United States, (2) the diffusion within the United States of subversive and un-American propaganda that is instigated from foreign countries or of a domestic origin and attacks the principle of the form of government as guaranteed by the Constitution, and (3) all other questions in relation thereto that would aid Congress in any necessary remedial legislation."

made more arrogant speeches, and took to behaving like the advance contingent of an already triumphant faith. Herr Kuhn called on his fellows to form a bloc "to deepen the German-conscious attitude" in the United States. A Stuttgart newspaper had the poor judgment to extoll the German-American camps as places where boys and girls could "learn to harmonize their duties as American citizens and their national and racial mission as Germans." White Russians, Italian fascists, and members of organizations with names like the American Gentile League came to drink beer with their Teutonic brothers. Dickstein made the most of their celebrations. In Detroit, he reported, "many thousands of little tots, ranging from four to six years of age" were "parading around in the Youth Movement uniforms crying 'Heil Hitler' and swearing by the Nazi Government." He told of 25,000 men and women in Nassau County "going crazy, dressed in uniforms and goose-stepping their way for miles at all hours of the night . . . disturbing the peace of the community and defying the police . . ." Even the neighborhood of Westchester was contaminated. So advanced among its adherents was the illusion of Nazi power that when American Legion posts, aroused by Dickstein, began to growl threateningly, the head of Camp Nordland in Andover, New Jersey, warned that if any Legionnaires trespassed upon his property, "they would not get out alive."

When six Bundists from Camp Yaphank on Long Island went on trial for failing to register as members of an oath-bound organization as required by a 1923 anti-Klu Klux Klan law, the courtroom was filled with uniformed veterans and Bund members in regalia, all hoping for trouble.[6] In April 1938, the ill will between Legionnaires and Bundsmen burst into riot at a meeting at the Yorkville Casino of 3,500 admirers of Adolf Hitler on the occasion of his forty-ninth birthday. When a speaker commended the German seizure of Austria as a "birthday gift by Chancellor Hitler" to Greater Germany, a man in the audience rose to inquire, "Is this an American or a

[6] At a Yorkville rally to protest the convictions of the Bundists, a speaker from Ohio asked the five hundred German-Americans before him whether they wanted a government by Hitler in the United States. "Yes!" they chorused back with lusty good will. "You should have said 'No,'" chided the speaker.

German meeting?" As uniformed storm troopers converged on him, several dozen Legionnaires also rose and donned their blue overseas caps. They were, unhappily, no match for the *Ordnungsdienst*, who were equipped with blackjacks and heavy-buckled belts. However, an unfriendly crowd soon gathered outside the casino, and police reserves had to be called to protect the Germans as they made their way home.

So successful were the native Nazis in provoking distaste for themselves that the F.B.I. opened an investigation of the Bund camps and the American Civil Liberties Union joined with the nonlibertarian Hamilton Fish in proposing a ban on private military groups. The weeks before the Dies resolution came up in Congress were troubled by the Sudeten crisis in Europe and a German spy trial in New York. Dickstein capitalized untiringly on every incident and every fear. "You can find almost 200,000 men of the Bund ready to put on uniforms and to use a gun," he warned. "There are 200,000 people in this country who should have their citizenship papers canceled because they are a burden and a threat to the country." He told of millions of dollars being taken out of the United States by the "secret Nazi police" and of millions more being sent in for subversive purposes. He reported that Bundists were setting up their camps suspiciously close to arms factories, and forecast bloody battles on the streets of America as aroused patriots took action.

As part of his campaign, Dickstein began inserting into the Congressional Record the names of suspect firms, organizations, and individuals—"expert spies," "smugglers," "Nazi aides," and "agitators." Most of the names came from the files of the McCormack Committee, which, out of regard for ordinary rules of evidence, had been sealed to the public. On being asked for documentation to back up his charges, Dickstein explained that putting all his mass of evidence into the Record would be a frightful drain on the Government Printing Office but that any colleague who wished to pay a visit to his office might have a look at it. When Representative Cochran of Missouri produced affidavits from six of eighteen persons in St. Louis named by Dickstein, swearing they had never been Nazis, the

New Yorker declined even to place their denials in the Record. He had no apologies to make: ". . . if out of these hundreds of names that I have buttonholed as fascists and Nazis or whatever I have called them, only six filed a protest, I think I have done a pretty good job."

In this aggressive defense, made in December 1937, and in the reply of Maury Maverick we find ourselves at the center of an enduring debate. Maverick argued that when the names of individuals "whose honor and patriotism are questioned" are put in the Record, "it should only be after an investigation, with the witnesses under oath. I do not think people should be libeled through the country by mere rumor. It is unfair." Dickstein was unmoved, just as later investigators would be unmoved by the remonstrances of those whom Joe McCarthy called the "bleeding hearts." There was a threat abroad; there was a threat at home. Was this an hour for legalistic niceties?

No man worked harder or more effectively than Samuel Dickstein to rally support for the Dies resolution. And it was support of a kind that the Texan could not attract on his own. The veterans' organizations were primed to back any investigation of practically anybody, Communist, fascist, or osteopath. The perfervid anti-Communists were of course with Martin Dies. But the affections of single-minded anti-fascists would never go out to the swaggering Congressman from Orange County. To them, Dickstein's voice and intentions were comforting. Among the organizations that came through with an endorsement of an investigation which they believed would be directed primarily at Bundists were the Federal Council of Churches, the Non-Sectarian Anti-Nazi League, the New Jersey C.I.O., and the American League for Peace and Democracy. All would have reason to rue the day.

For the coalition of Republicans and Southern Democrats in the House, who had perforce been growing closer since Roosevelt's 1936 sweep, Martin Dies was a David come to judgment on the New Deal. John Rankin of Mississippi opposed the creation of an un-American activities committee until he was assured that it would be headed by the Texan, Dies, and not by the Jew, Dickstein. The country was still deep in depression, and disturbing currents were running through the land. Radicals of many varieties, some taking inspiration from the Soviet experiment, roamed freely among the discontented, making up in vehemence and foolhardiness what they lacked in numbers. Major sections of American industry were in turmoil as industrial workers organized and struck and fought their bloody battles. To heirs of an older America, where economic and political power resided in the propertied man, the owner of a business, the farmer, the shopkeeper, it was as though some subterranean monster were breaking through the shell of the earth and overturning all the dear landmarks. To them, Samuel Dickstein, the rabbi's son from Russia via the Lower East Side, was irredeemably alien. As Representative Shannon of Missouri explained with nice delicacy, "Many members of Congress felt that an investigation of this kind should not be headed by a foreign-born citizen." But Martin Dies was one of their own. His father, Congressman from Texas from 1909 to 1919, mistrusted immigrants, despised Bolsheviks, and broke with President Wilson over the League of Nations. Big, boyish Martin, an impetuous lock of hair complementing his smooth boyish features, often included a proud reference to Dad in his juicy back-country speeches. With the patronage of Vice President Garner, the young man had found a place on the House Rules Committee, where he was able to assist in holding up the Administration's wages and hours bill, which the South viewed as a discriminatory measure. As representative of the hill people of east Texas, more than ninety percent of them of undiluted Anglo-Saxon stock, he epitomized an entrenched, embattled suspicion of big cities, big capital, big labor, and big government as well as of foreigners, big and small, whom he perennially proposed to deport, and foreign ideologies. His first bill, introduced the day after he took his seat in Congress in 1931, would have suspended immigration to the United States for five years. America's unemployment problem, he agreed with Ham Fish, had been caused by the flooding of the land by foreigners, and would not be solved until they were sent back home. Here was a man who could be trusted with an investigation of "the extent, character and object of un-American propaganda activities in the United States."

And Martin Dies wanted very much to lead an investigation —practically any investigation. Impressed with the success of Senate committee chairmen like Nye and La Follette in getting their names in the papers, he proposed looking into, among other things, Administration restrictions on freedom of press and radio, the resignation of government officials to take lucrative jobs in private industry, charges that America was controlled by sixty families, and the sugar lobby. Finally, on the verge of success, young Martin the Populist appeared before the House for the calling up of his resolution on May 26, 1938, like the rehabilitated slum boy at the end of the B-movie, combed, scrubbed, and ready for prep school. "I am not inclined to look under every bed for a Communist," he assured his listeners. He was concerned over the photographs he had seen of Bundists saluting the swastika, and over the danger that President Roosevelt might be assassinated by one of the 480,000 Nazis in the United States. He was aware of the peril to "fundamental rights far more important than the objective we seek," in any legislative attempt to prohibit un-American activities. He acknowledged that a committee composed of publicity seekers could do more harm than good: "I believe all depends on the way the committee is handled." He did not favor a lavish expenditure of money on such investigations, and he did favor free speech. When Representative Warren said that seven months was "long enough to investigate any subject on earth," Dies agreed and at once accepted an amendment that the Committee conclude its business and issue its report by the end of that very session of Congress.

It was left to supporters of the investigation, like Taylor of Tennessee, to go to work on the Communists. Taylor, who had favored an investigation of the sit-down strikes because most of the Detroit agitators did not have American names and who took public pride in having helped to write the first restrictive immigration law ever placed on the statute books, told the House that "Communist radicals recently for the second time had the unmitigated audacity and depravity to desecrate that hallowed shrine to every red-blooded American—Plymouth Rock—by enveloping it in red paint. The miserable wretches who committed this dastardly deed ought to be hunted down, like rattlesnakes, and kicked out of the country." He was applauded. Robison of Kentucky asked: "Now why should we permit a lot of Communists from Russia or elsewhere who hate religion, who hate this government, and desire to see it overthrown and a Communist dictatorship established to organize on American soil, march under the red flag of Communism and engage in subversive propaganda and activities for the purpose of destroying our government?"

The opposition, led by Maury Maverick, warned that the resolution gave "blanket powers to investigate, humiliate, meddle with anything and everything . . . from the German Saengerfest to B'nai B'rith . . ." When Patrick of Alabama asked yet again, like the chorus in an Edward Lear rhyme, "But what is un-Americanism?" Maverick could barely hold himself in: "Un-American! Un-American is simply something that somebody else does not agree to." Representative Boileau of Wisconsin predicted that Dies would be investigating the wages and hours bill and Thomas would be investigating the whole New Deal before they were through, and several Congressmen made the point that the nation's real problem was its millions of unemployed. "Whenever a parliamentary body in any country of the world has found itself unable to deal with the economic problems that face the people," said O'Malley of Wisconsin, "they go on a witch hunt."

But the Dies-Dickstein strategy had been well conceived. There was anxiety in the country over the parading Nazis and the incendiary radicals, and an investigation that promised to expose subversives on the left as well as on the right was bound to command popular support. As Representative Cochran observed, the resolution had gone too far to be turned down now. And he added in words that many Congressmen have repeated, though not so openly, since that momentous day: "I do not want to be accused of refusing to vote for legislation to investigate un-American activities."

The Dies resolution was approved by a vote of 191 to 41, and when the freshly victorious Representative Dickstein rose to request permission to speak for three minutes, he was unceremoniously turned down. A week and a half later, the Chair appointed the members of the new Committee. Sam Dickstein, who had labored with all his heart for this day, was not among them.

2

1938: The Dies Committee

THE company from which Representative Dickstein had been excluded was a conservative one. It contained one unflaming New Dealer, John J. Dempsey of New Mexico; one wavering New Dealer, Arthur D. Healey of Massachusetts; two old-school Democrats, Joe Starnes of Alabama and Harold G. Mosier of Ohio; and two Republicans of the distant right wing, Noah M. Mason of Illinois and J. Parnell Thomas. Thomas, born Feeney, of Allendale, New Jersey! The pudgy, belligerent bond salesman and insurance broker made a home with the Committee. Here his disposition could find expression, his animosities find scope, his politics find fellowship. Alone of the six, he would stay with his chairman until the end—and after, until the day of his due reward. When J. B. Matthews, soon to be established as chief Committee investigator, wrote his autobiography, *Odyssey of a Fellow Traveler,* he dedicated it to but five of the Congressmen—"Three Democrats, Two Republicans: Five Americans"—pointedly leaving out the unfraternal Dempsey and Healey. The Committee on Un-American Activities would suffer the usual goings and comings over the next thirty years of political wars, but it would hold its conservative cast. Liberals who joined it with intimations of reform invariably gave up after a while, missionaries turning from a fatally damned congregation to more hopeful work.

The Committee on Accounts allotted Chairman Dies $25,000 instead of the $100,000 he had requested. Although the sum was more than the Fish Committee spent and only $5,000 less than that given to the McCormack Committee, it was a painfully small allocation, considering the expansive language of the resolution. This led in the following months to an intragovernmental charade that hinted at a rupture to come. Dies asked for the loan of investigators from the Departments of Justice and of Labor, a favor to which he was entitled by the terms of the resolution ("The head of each executive department is hereby requested to detail to said committee such number of legal and expert assistants as said committee may from time to time deem necessary"), and which he knew that his arch nemesis, the La Follette Civil Liberties Committee, had received. The executive departments turned him down. "Ho-hum," commented the President on being informed of Dies's complaints. When the La Follette Committee, as a sort of practical joke, offered the loan of two of its investigators, Dies questioned the men, convinced himself that "they were either Communists or Communist sympathizers," and declined. As several staff members of the Civil Liberties Committee were later pronounced Communists by Senator La Follette himself, Dies's suspicion may have been sound. In any case, the limited funds available to the Committee obliged it to make do with two stenographers, four investigators, three of whom would quickly be dismissed, and a youthful clerk named, haply, Robert E. Stripling, whom Dies had brought to the capital from Texas to be assistant sergeant of arms of the House and who would stay on with the Committee for a long time. The shortage of staff reinforced the chairman's predilection for witnesses from groups such as the American Legion's Americanism Committee. Their voluntary testimony would become a characteristic of the Committee's first months of operation and a point of dispute for years thereafter.

The opening of hearings in mid-August 1938 was preceded by two fanfares. At the end of July, J. Parnell Thomas demanded a sweeping investigation of the W.P.A.'s Federal Theatre and Writers Project. On the basis of "startling evidence" in his possession, he concluded that the project was "a hotbed for Communists," "infested with radicals from top to bottom," and "one more link in the vast and unparalleled New

Deal propaganda machine." Observers acquainted with the language and learning of Parnell Thomas would find nothing out of the ordinary in this announcement, but it was the beginning of the end for the government's first and only venture into subsidized theater.

In August, Dies himself swept on to the stage where he would star for many seasons to come. He announced to the press that he had issued a subpoena to the pro-German propagandist, George Sylvester Viereck, upon learning that Viereck was about to pay a call on Adolf Hitler. Viereck explained that he was indeed going to Europe—but it was to see his old friend the Kaiser and other prominent persons, and not Hitler, whom he doubted would have time for him. Nevertheless, he canceled his passage. Having thus found his way on to page 1 —DIES OPENS WAR ON PROPAGANDISTS—the Congressman lost interest in the case, and Viereck sailed for Europe a week later without appearing before the Committee. This apparently unproductive gesture of the new chairman had two useful results, not counting that of inconveniencing the friend of the Kaiser. It alerted newspaper readers to the imminent opening of an investigation into subversion, and prolonged for another hour the hopes of those of Mr. Dickstein's persuasion as to the Committee's intentions. It also showed Martin Dies at his most engaging, when at the press conference called to publicize his pass at Viereck, he expressed his disdain for "the old kind of investigation that would go after somebody only for cheap publicity." The ability to divorce one's mind from one's actions is, enlightened persons recognize today, a symptom of psychological aberration, but it is also a cherished political talent.

In a radio speech three days before the start of hearings, Dies again promised that there would be no three-ring circuses, that he would not "permit any individual or organization to use the Committee as a sounding board to obtain publicity or to injure others." And on August 12, as hearings—from which the public was at first excluded—were about to begin in the air-cooled caucus room on the second floor of the Old House Office Building, he laid aside his cigar and delivered a statement that might have been written by Roger Baldwin:

... this Committee is determined to conduct its investigation upon a dignified plane and to adopt and maintain throughout the course of the hearings a judicial attitude. The Committee has no preconceived views of what the truth is respecting the subject matter of this inquiry ... We shall be fair and impartial at all times and treat every witness with fairness and courtesy ... This Committee will not permit any "character assassination" or any "smearing" of innocent people ... It is the Chair's opinion that the usefulness or value of any investigation is measured by the fairness and impartiality of the committee conducting the investigation. Neither the public nor the Congress will have any confidence in the findings of a committee which adopts a partisan or preconceived attitude ... It is easy to "smear" someone's name or reputation by unsupported charges or an unjustified attack, but it is difficult to repair the damage that has been done ... when any individual or organization is involved in any charge or attack made in the course of the hearings, that individual or organization will be accorded an opportunity to refute such charge or attack.

He concluded by cautioning the assembled reporters and photographers against calling people un-American just because of "an honest difference of opinion with respect to some economic, political or social question."

In the days that followed, observers began to wonder whether the lady of breeding who had made such a dignified entrance into town was in fact setting up a bawdy house. The Dies Committee established itself on the nation's front pages at once and stayed there for most of August. *The New York Times* accorded it more than five hundred column-inches of space in its first month and a half of life, and other newspapers were even more accommodating. This triumph with the press was generally attributed to the chairman's shrewdness in opening hearings in mid-August when the capital is no fit place to be; F.D.R. was away and news was scarce. One pair of analysts suggested that Dies was fortunate in having a name that came to only three and a half characters in the count of headline writers. But there was no need to strain for explanations. The reason that the Dies Committee received such extensive coverage in its first weeks was simply that it provided such good copy.

It all started off fairly quietly with a set of witnesses discussing the activities of the German-American Bund. They were led by John C. Metcalfe, a German-born former reporter for the Chicago *Daily Times* who had been assigned in 1937 to infiltrate the Bund. He joined the Astoria, Queens, chapter under the name of Hellmut Oberwinder, became a storm trooper, and won the confidence of Fritz Kuhn himself. Metcalfe, who had served the McCormack Committee and was now working as a kind of voluntary investigator for Representative Dies, told of the Bund's direction by the German Auslands Bureau in Stuttgart, of its plot to establish "a vast spy network" and a "powerful sabotage machine" among the German minority in America. There were 500,000 Nazis and Nazi sympathizers in this country, he said. His report was not startling to anyone who had been paying attention to Samuel Dickstein for the past several years, and indeed it provided one of the few bits of satisfaction that Dickstein would be able to draw from the Committee's work. At odd moments in the ensuing weeks, Metcalfe would reappear with further news of Nazi plottings, like the comic who pops out between burlesque skits with a broom and sets diligently to sweeping up the stage until he is kicked off so that the show may proceed.

It proceeded on August 13 with John P. Frey, president of the Metal Trades Department of the American Federation of Labor. *The New York Times* gave him a two-column headline on its Sunday front page:

COMMUNISTS RULE THE C.I.O.

FREY OF A.F.L. TESTIFIES;

HE NAMES 284 ORGANIZERS

Just two days before, the La Follette Civil Liberties Committee had held its final hearings on anti-union activity at General Motors. Now it was the turn of the anti-C.I.O. forces. The Administration had feared just such an attack on its political and ideological allies, and had employed Representative McCormack to urge Dies to restrain himself. "From this intramural Congressional struggle," as one historian has observed, "emerged a facsimile in microcosm of the battle between the New Deal and its political enemies."

Frey was a blunt witness. He told the Committee that the Communists had made no progress in the United States until the C.I.O. was organized, but "since then the Communist Party had become a definite factor in the American labor movement." The C.I.O. program of sit-down strikes and mass picketing had the "hearty endorsement of the Communist Party," since it trained Party members "for the day when the signal for revolution is given." Already they were infiltrating the Democratic Party and nudging the Administration to the left. Frey charged that the La Follette Committee, darling of the liberal community,[1] was cooperating with the Communists, and in his three days of testifying, hardly a major industrial union escaped the charge of Communist influence.

One of the many names uttered by Frey was that of Harry Bridges, the Australian-born head of the West Coast longshoremen, a most aggressive and effective union chief with a pronounced affinity for Communist causes. On August 14, while Frey was still testifying, Dies released to the newspapers a report from the Committee's main investigator, Edward F. Sullivan, who had been out surveying the Pacific Coast. He wrote that Harry Bridges was responsible for 60 per cent of the labor strife in that area, and that he was being protected from deportation by "an outstanding official" in the Department of Labor. Sullivan also observed that Communism was rampant in the movie industry—the start of a long-lasting fascination with Hollywood on the part of the Committee—and in the schools. As for Nazi activities, Jewish organizations "were naturally concerned," but this concern was "not shared by any other agency."

On August 16 it was the turn before the Committee of Walter Steele, editor of the fiercely conservative *National Republic*, as well as chairman of the American Coalition Committee on

[1] Under a headline, SAVE THE CIVIL LIBERTIES INQUIRY, in November 1939, *The New Republic*'s editors used the language of Congressional inquisitors of all periods: "Nothing holds the forces of darkness in check like a Senatorial searchlight always in readiness to be turned upon their activities."

National Security, an organization that took in 114 other organizations of a patriotic nature. Thus, as Steele conceded, he spoke for some twenty million people. He was an experienced witness, having testified before both the Fish and Dickstein committees, and would perform yet again for the Thomas Committee. In his two days of testimony in August, he named hundreds of infested organizations, from the American League for Peace and Democracy, with which the Committee would wrestle for months to come, to the American Civil Liberties Union to the Camp Fire Girls, who were in danger of being misled by persons who claimed they were interested in forwarding international understanding.

The Frey and Steele hearings established a tone and a mode of operation for the Dies Committee in its first year. Samuel Dickstein promptly denounced his child, but Hamilton Fish, the grandparent, said, "I love the Dies Committee for the enemies it has made." The *Daily Worker,* possessed of a limited stock of invective, called the Committee an "outfit of storm troopers," and the non-Communist liberals running *The Nation* and *The New Republic* thoroughly agreed. Catholic diocesan papers, on the other hand, complimented the Committee for its "distinguished service to the country," and so did the *Chicago Tribune*. Chairman Dies was the "Man of the Week" for Father Coughlin's *Social Justice* in September 1938, and by 1939 the anti-Semitic priest from Royal Oak was promoting the Protestant Fundamentalist from Texas for President. And in between Dies's allies and enemies were many newspapers which were impressed by some of the testimony but disturbed by the rough-and-ready rules of procedure.

For Martin Dies the surge of newspaper attention was one of those crucial events in the life of the young child which, we are told, makes it so difficult to shake off bad habits later. It was not that the reporters were uncritically accepting of all that went on in the caucus room; on the contrary, in a poll taken in October 1938 by a pair of New York *Daily News* columnists, of the eighteen reporters who regularly covered the proceedings—and were the only outsiders who had the privilege of viewing them at first-hand—only two, from conservative newspapers, thought they were fair, while eleven thought they were unfair; the others either straddled or declined to commit themselves. The problem before the newspapermen was that the charges being made day after day were newsworthy in themselves, whereas the observation that the Committee allowed charges to be made without asking for supporting evidence verged on editorial comment. Denials came late and were relegated to back pages and ends of columns.

It was a well-advertised secret that major C.I.O. unions such as the Auto Workers, the Maritime Workers, and the Transport Workers harbored Communists in important positions and that Ben Gold, the head of the Fur Workers, was a genuine, deep-dyed Red. John L. Lewis needed their organizing skills and their physical courage in the mid-thirties, and they reciprocated by using the growing C.I.O. power for their own ends. Zygmund Dobrzynski, a former national director of the U.A.W. organizing drive at Ford who appeared before the Committee in 1938, gave an illuminating and typical instance of Communist tactics:

> During the first organizational days, when the U.A.W. was formed, and the men were beginning to recognize that unionism was the thing they needed, they came in by the hundreds; the automobile industry was made up of men, primarily, who had never been in any union before, and who were completely inexperienced, not knowing even how to make a motion on the floor . . . the members of the Communist Party knew how to speak; some of them had extensive soap-box experience . . . It is very simple for a man who understands public speaking and parliamentary rules to control a meeting of uninitiated people . . . By preparing motions ahead of time, having discussions ahead of time, and then dividing up in various sections of the hall [the Communists] would give the impression that the particular policy they were trying to have the meeting adopt was generally supported throughout the membership.

But did the evidence support Frey's indictment of the C.I.O. as a tool of Moscow? Particularly when the indictment was issued by an old-line craft-union chieftain, a delegate from the Iron Molders, who looked upon the unorganized unskilled in much the way a Southern sheriff looked upon the voteless Negro, and who had led the effort to kick the C.I.O. out of the A. F. of L. It was his dictum that "Unskilled labor must become skilled before it can gain its rights." A few weeks after Frey's appearance, another witness, in the course of testifying quite convincingly about Communist influence in Mike Quill's Transport Workers Union, remarked: "I would not have joined if the A. F. of L. had done its job." It was a critical point for understanding the Communist intrusion into the C.I.O., but it was of no interest to the Committee.

After Frey left the stand, newspaper reporters speculated on his batting average. How many of the hundreds of persons he had named were actually under Communist Party direction? How many were dupes? How influential were the C.P. members? Did membership mean the same thing to all of them? And what did it mean for the labor movement? The reporters could only wonder. Considering the numbers of persons implicated in the first weeks of testimony, it would have been impossible within the space of a Congressman's lifetime to give every one of them an opportunity to defend himself; a study of the 1938 hearings published by *Public Opinion Quarterly* noted that "of the hundreds or perhaps thousands of persons who were accused of being "Communists' or (infrequently) 'Nazis' . . . with a single possible exception not one of the accused has been called to the stand . . ." Nor did the Committee make any effort at cross-examination. Dies lounged back and smoked his cigar or chewed his gum and watched reporters taking notes about the C.I.O., the American Civil Liberties Union, or the Farmer-Labor Party, about John Dewey, Paul H. Douglas, or H. L. Mencken. When he or Starnes or Mason or Thomas broke in, it was usually to spur a witness on to more stimulating charges: "Do you not think," Thomas inquired of one man, "that the many steps taken by our government in recent years such as the reorganization bill and the Supreme Court bill constitute a prelude to dictatorship in this country?" (The Democrats present, in a rare exercise of loyalty to the Administration, objected and the question was not answered.)

Attempts to get supporting evidence for the deluge of charges were desultory. When, for example, investigator Metcalfe told of a Nazi scheme to plant spies in American munitions plants, shipyards, and airplane factories, Dies asked: "How do you know this?" Metcalfe replied: "We have checked our sources and find them absolutely reliable," and went on as though he had answered the question. Investigator Sullivan's report on Harry Bridges was certified by nothing more than the investigator's remark that it was "based upon the statements of persons in all walks of business, industrial and agricultural life on the West Coast." As an informal preliminary and private report to the Committee, his conclusions about Bridges's affinity for the Communist Party might have been useful and appropriate, but the chairman released them to the press as written and then a day later, after they had been widely circulated, commented that while he thought it was "advisable that the public should have the benefit of the report," the Committee did "not now vouch for its accuracy."

Dies did, however, vouch for the accuracy of Frey. At the close of the A. F. of L. leader's time before the Committee, the chairman said: "I am convinced of the reliability of those sources"—which Frey had said that he could not "openly give." When John Brophy, the most prominent of the dozens of C.I.O. officials named by Frey, took exception to being labeled a Communist consort (and produced two priests to affirm that he was a thoroughgoing Catholic with a son in training for the priesthood, the ultimate defense in cases of this sort), Frey replied: "The Communist connection was not mine. I quoted the official journal of the United Mine Workers Union, and they charged him with being tied up with Communism and endeavoring to sell the Miners Union. It is the testimony of the U.M.W. and not mine. I merely introduced their testimony." He did not add that the U.M.W. charge was based on a statement made by John L. Lewis in the mid-twenties when he was contending against Brophy, who did have Communist support for a time but was never one of their own, for leadership of the union—

or that Brophy might have won had not the Communists deserted him in a typical shift of Moscow-directed policy. A rare instance of the chairman rousing himself to chide one of his volunteer witnesses came during a discussion of education when one of the pieces of evidence cited of John Dewey's radicalism was that he had been attacked by Matthew Woll of the A. F. of L. Dies interjected that "the mere fact that somebody denounced him is no particular proof." It was an unusual nod to courtroom amenities, and it did not stop the witness for very long.

The Committee's decision to welcome volunteer witnesses as the Fish Committee had, made partly because it had not been granted enough money to do its own investigating, was in itself a guarantee that the proceedings would be diverted into irregular byways, by volunteers like the pastor of a Washington Congregational Church who was upset that James Roosevelt's published income tax returns for five years listed no church contributions. The best people do not offer themselves for such work, and the volunteers of 1938 turned out to be a gamy bunch. Walter Steele, the representative of twenty million patriots, was on the advisory board of the Paul Reveres, an active anti-Semitic group of the political fringe. His credentials as an expert on un-Americanism, as he had explained at the Fish hearings, was that he read Communist publications and collected names from them. His magazine, the *National Republic,* was emphatically anti-Communist, but it was also emphatically anti-labor, anti-alien, and pro-Franco. Edward Sullivan, the Committee's preeminent investigator, was dropped from the small staff in September—for financial reasons, the chairman explained—after the La Follette Committee reminded the press that he had been identified in its hearings as a labor spy of standing for the Railway Audit and Inspection Company of Pittsburgh, with a history of Jew-baiting and Catholic-baiting. Sullivan, who had worked and shared an office with James True, inventor of the "Kike Killer," an instrument for bashing in the heads of Jews, found employment after his release from the Committee with the Ukrainian Nationalist Federation, whose mission it was to annex the Ukraine to the Third Reich.

Along with witnesses from the ranks of the ultra-right and a few ordinary criminals came a number of persons with conspicuous axes to grind, like Alice Lee Jemison who accused the Indian Bureau of the Department of the Interior of trying to spread Communism and paganism. "The Jemison dame," as Secretary Ickes ungallantly spoke of her, had been going around for years trying to get the government to pay $3,500 to every Indian from whom she had collected one dollar in dues. Ickes, whose feud with Dies began early and lasted to the end, charged, without offering any more evidence than Miss Jemison did, that Nazi agents had collaborated in her testimony so that they could attack the United States for treating Indians worse than the Germans treated Jews. The lady had never been able to get any publicity for herself, he observed, "until the accommodating Congressman Dies came along intent on smearing the New Deal whenever he could." Later on, the pleasures of 1938 having receded, Dies himself would grant, in one of his periodic nods to critics as appropriation time approached, that his Committee had had some "screwball witnesses" before it and that, unfortunately, some decent American may have been "smeared."

But that was later. In mid-August, the Congressmen were still splashing around like kids in a new swimming hole, with no particular direction and only the vaguest notion of a future that would call them home to supper. It was all quite hit and miss. Then, on August 20, arrived Joseph Brown Matthews. Where the Committee knew nothing about Communism except what it did not like, J. B. Matthews, who had been recommended to Dies by the columnist George Sokolsky, knew everything, and gave freely of his knowledge. Soon he would put much of it into an illuminating book, *The Trojan Horse in America*, published under the by-line of Martin Dies. The Committee would cling to Matthews for years to come, like ladies to the interior decorator who is able to dignify their tastes and bolster their pretensions with the jargon of the expert. "The nation owes him [Matthews] a debt of gratitude which will not be paid or even acknowledged in this genera-

tion," wrote Dies in his 1963 autobiography. That is a controversial assessment, but of Martin Dies's own debt there can be
no question.

The howlers committed by the members of the Dies Committee were something special even for Congressional committees. Having heard something about the John Reed clubs, Dies
asked a witness if a Michigan labor leader named John G.
Reid was the fellow who founded them. Starnes had the misfortune to mix up a British Laborite, Tom Mann, with Thomas
Mann, the writer—an understandable mistake, as it turned out,
since both men were opposed to fascism. And it was Starnes
too, class of '21 at Alabama U. and a former schoolteacher in
Guntersville, who on hearing a witness mention the name
Christopher Marlowe, demanded, "You're quoting from this
Marlowe. Is he a Communist?"

J. B. Matthews was above such gaffes. He spent his boyhood
in Kentucky, where he was born in 1894, and his young man-
hood in Malaya as a Methodist missionary and student of exotic
languages. On his return to this country in the early nineteen-
twenties he became imbued with the social gospel. His gift was
for preaching, in the piss-and-vinegar mode of Kentucky Methodism; his two main themes were racial equality and pacifism;
for a dozen years he gave himself unstintingly to these and related causes.

> I moved from religious fundamentalism to the social gospel. From
> the social gospel with its earnest humanitarianism, I went to po-
> litical reform à la La Follette the Elder. I moved to pacifism.
> After pacifism came socialism of the Norman Thomas brand. I
> went, finally, from socialism to communism.

There were a handful of men and women in the thirties, not
members of the Communist Party, whose names on a letterhead
constituted a kind of imprimatur for the board of a radical
organization, the rally of protest, the appeal for justice, the
petition for redress of grievances: Reinhold Niebuhr, Harry F.
Ward, Roger Baldwin, Robert Morss Lovett—and J. B. Matthews. Such associations, Carlyle discerned, are the "surest
symptom of Social Unrest: in such a way, most infallibly of all,

does Social Unrest exhibit itself, find solacement and also nutriment." Matthews was abundantly solaced and richly nourished during the nation's parlous time. It was not mere boasting when he wrote of himself: "No other person in the United States had such an impressive united front record." During his years of faith he wrote for, spoke for and lent his name to more than sixty organizations and publications active in the service of peace, race relations, labor solidarity and anti-fascism. He held official positions with fifteen of them, and gave more than a hundred speeches before audiences mass and select. "*What* we join," he wrote, "may be and, indeed, often is un-American, but the *act* of joining is typically American." If that is so—and the excuse was rarely extended by Matthews to unrepentant joiners—no more typical American ever breathed. Matthews covered the spectrum of radical life—Socialist, Stalinist, Lovestoneite, Musteite, Trotskyite, I.W.W., Socialist Labor Party— without favoritism. "The catholicity of my radicalism," he wrote, "is in the record beyond dispute."

The instinctive reaction on the left after his appearance before the Dies Committee was to deny his credentials, which were stunningly authentic (Earl Browder said Matthews was merely secretary of the American League Against War and Fascism for a while, when everyone knew he was its first national chairman); to give the lie to his charges of Communist domination of united front organizations, which were in the main convincing; to argue that non-Communists could work profitably with Communists where the liberal, anti-fascist community was united—a hotly disputed position on the left at that time; and to impugn the motives behind Matthews's startling reformation.

What made his reformation so very startling was that unlike many who had disengaged themselves from the Popular Front dream of the thirties, he had for years been the least questioning of fellow travelers. He wanted, he claimed, symphony not cacophony in the leftist orchestra. It is true that he resigned the chairmanship of the American League Against War and Fascism (later the American League for Peace and Democracy) in 1934, after the Communists broke up a Madison

Square Garden memorial meeting called to honor the Austrian Social Democrats defeated by the Dollfuss regime,[2] but he remained on the organization's board. In 1932, on one of his annual trips to the Soviet Union, he saw the ravages of famine in the Ukraine. Three years later, when the Hearst press ran an accurate series of articles on the famine, he wrote a rebuttal in the *Daily Worker,* condemning as a betrayal of the working class the thought that there could be famine in the Socialist Fatherland. When at a meeting of the Student Congress Against War in 1934 Jane Addams made a speech denouncing all wars, Matthews, although a pacifist of long standing, took issue with her in accord with the Stalinist line of the period and reminded the students that there were differences between imperialistic wars and non-imperialistic wars. The congress, under the skilled control usual at such gatherings, voted its agreement with him. The Socialist Party, already vigilantly anti-Stalinist, suspended Matthews for his attendance on Communist needs, and he was dismissed from his post as executive secretary of the pacifist Fellowship of Reconciliation because he took the position that a pacifist should support the workers in a hypothetical class war.

When it came to fellow traveling, Matthews was a prodigy. But for a man who had spent so much of his life among ideologies, he had only a scant acquaintance with politics or economics. His fervor for pacifism and racial equality was certainly sincere, but they seem to have been fired by a need to be fervent about something—a common enough need, particularly among performing orators—when the heat of rural methodism could no longer warm him. But this fuel would run out too, and he would grow old tending the fires of anti-Communism. In 1935 he was warning that big business, government officials, and blind liberals were opening the way to fascism. Three years later he was warning that labor unions, government officials, and blind liberals were opening the way to Communism. Fi-

---

[2] This riot caused great indignation on the left. Such names as Edmund Wilson, John Dos Passos, Lionel Trilling, John Chamberlain, and Clifton Fadiman were signed to an open letter denouncing "the culpability and shame of the Communists" for their "disruption of working-class action in support of the Austrian worker."

nally, after an hour of renewed glory with Senator McCarthy's Investigation Subcommittee, he became a private consultant on Communism to Hearst, whom he had denounced to the cheers of his comrades in his earlier incarnations.

Replying, in his post-reformation autobiography, to the Socialists who accused him of having been an agent provocateur, he wrote: "Communists and Socialists have difficulty in understanding the obvious; they incline toward suspicions of conspiracy." Indeed they do, and Matthews was not free from the inclination. Again and again, in his charges of Communist control of this organization or that, he presented as proof positive a Communist boast that it was so controlled: "Nor is it necessary for us red-baiters to formulate accusations of Communist leadership; we need only quote the Communists themselves who had affirmed it over and over again." Because Earl Browder took credit at a Moscow meeting for the formation of the American League Against War and Fascism, which was to become the leading united front group of the thirties, that settled the matter for Matthews: "This could dispose, once and for all, of the question of whether or not the American League was launched by the Communist Party." He quoted Browder incessantly and without a hint of skepticism. "In the center, as the conscious moving and directive force of the united front movements in all its phases, stands the Communist Party," boasted Browder, and for Matthews this was a compelling item of proof.

In Matthews's time of grace, as in his period of sin, the columns of the *Daily Worker* were a prime source of truth, and would remain so for his successors. When he found, however, that the *Worker* had listed his name on a committee he had never heard of, or on a report he had never signed, he commented, "There is nothing extraordinary about Communists using the names of persons without their permission." He demonstrated convincingly how the front organizations inflated their membership figures; then he used the inflated figures as evidence of the national peril. He never appreciated the contradictions in which he was entangled, or the humor of them. He was a man of so little humor that he could allow himself to

mention Shirley Temple in his testimony as having unwittingly
served the interests of the Communist Party by sending greetings to the French Communist paper *Ce Soir* and then be outraged with Harold Ickes, Frances Perkins, and other antagonists
who made fun of him for it.[3]

Not being anything of an ideologist, Matthews made few distinctions between the feuding elements of the radical left when
he belonged to it, and forgot even those as soon as he departed.
In 1934 he was reprimanded by the Socialists because "I believed wholeheartedly in the united front of all radical groups
and accepted their invitations without regard to the bitter en-
mities which separated them." In 1938 his message was that
the philosophy of every group on the left would lead equally
and surely to a reaction which would bring on fascism. He
accorded each of them, from the biggest front to the tiniest
splinter, the same importance that each accorded itself. And
just as every group was of immense consequence, so every
member was either a conspirator or a dupe.

Despite all of his experience, Matthews had no perspective
on the times that produced the fronts and small insight into
the motives that drew people to them. If it ever occurred to
him that there were differences between Heywood Broun and
Reinhold Niebuhr, he never paused over them. As for the
fronts he had served so faithfully, his error was not so much
that he overestimated the power of the Communists within
them, as liberals of the time protested, but that he overestimated the significance of the organizations themselves. They
were, as Murray Kempton has observed, "structures of enormous pretension and pathetic foundation." They would not
long survive.

In his confessions, *Odyssey of a Fellow Traveler*, Matthews
explains that he left the radical cause when the scholarly Dr.
Jekyll in his nature won the battle with the Marxist Mr. Hyde.

---

[3] Liberals, understandably but unjustly, would never let the Shirley Temple
incident die. Ickes commented: "They've gone into Hollywood and there discovered a great red plot. They have found dangerous radicals there, led by
little Shirley Temple. Imagine the great committee raiding her nursery and
seizing her dolls as evidence." Madame Perkins said it was fortunate that
Shirley was born an American citizen or Dies would have tried to get her
deported.

This occurred in 1935. Some time before that glad triumph, Matthews had become an executive of Consumers Research, an organization dedicated to protecting the citizenry from hazardous, poisonous and shoddy goods foisted upon it by big business abetted by minions in advertising. As with all organizations that he touched during this period, C.R. attracted numbers of Communists, and when, in 1935, the organization's employees went on strike after three of their number had been fired for union activities, Matthews felt that he had observed Communist maneuverings long enough to recognize a play for power when he saw one. What he saw now were such prominent fellow travelers as Vito Marcantonio and Heywood Broun leading the Town Hall rally called to damn him.

Matthews was a vice president and member of the Board of Directors at Consumers Research, the most respectable position he had held in years, and he was even trying to get the Democratic nomination to run for the New Jersey Assembly; he took his stand against the strikers. "I cannot name the precise day on which I became a socialist or the precise day on which I ceased to be one," he wrote, but the second event seems to have occurred precisely at this time. The strike was bitter; Matthews refused arbitration because he was convinced the Communists would rig the results, and he held fast against an N.L.R.B. decision that would have reinstated the fired workers. The employees never returned to Consumers Research—which would soon begin leavening its analysis of merchandise with assessments of the Wagner Act ("the greatest piece of legislative chicane") and the Social Security Act ("the most dishonest piece of legislation ever devised")—but went off to form the rival and more successful Consumers Union. Now J. B. Matthews was no longer a suitable attraction for left-wing rallies. By 1936 he was out of radical politics, and in mid-1938, having studied and found that he was, after all, "a political and economic conservative," he enlisted with the armies of the right and was given a bodyguard by Chairman Dies. Soon he was employing his oratorical powers on behalf of organizations like American Patriots, Inc., and the League for Constitutional

Government, and having his work printed in Father Coughlin's *Social Justice*.

It was J. B. Matthews's curse to be unable to survive except in extravagant company. He looked at America and saw nothing between Earl Browder and Martin Dies. "Seven generations of American ancestry," he confessed, "were not enough despite even their Northern European derivation, to save me from heeding the appeals of a collectivism which is at war with every basic concept that has made America great." Nor were all those North European-derived generations able to give him any sense of the realities of American politics in the nineteen-twenties and -thirties. He knew that the Communists were conspirators—and in denying this many liberals would hurt their own cause. ("A twentieth century American 'liberal,'" Matthews observed only too accurately for the period, "would rather face the charge of slapping his grandmother than to be accused of 'red-baiting.'") But he also believed that the conspiracy was working; he shared the Communists' own severe delusions.

The Dies Committee prized Matthews for his delusions, for his simplifications, and, most especially, for his supply of names. His files, consisting mainly of mailing lists, letterheads —"To me the letterhead of a Communist front is a nugget"— and back copies of radical magazines, were the richest store of names Dies had yet happened on, of particular delight because they included so many individuals associated in one way or another with the Administration. The Dies Committee was from the outset on the track of the New Deal and all its works. That Mr. Roosevelt did not see this is unthinkable—there was only a perfunctory effort at concealment—but it would take a little time before the President correctly estimated the Committee's potential for political damage.

The attack on the W.P.A.'s Federal Theatre and Writers Project, anticipated by J. Parnell Thomas in July, struck the Administration where it was especially vulnerable. Subsidized theater was not a program that the Democrats could count on the nation to support with passion. Its record in some ways was impressive enough—more than a thousand productions in twenty-two states in a few years, most of them given free to school and community groups. The quality varied, but the enthusiasm was remarkably sustained. The W.P.A. shows ranged from hits like *Swing Mikado,* presented in New York at a $1.10 top, and *Run Little Children,* which ran for forty-two weeks in Chicago, to *Twelfth Night* and *Dr. Faustus,* from tawdry comedies to the Negro *Macbeth* to *Murder in the Cathedral.* The greater part of its audience had never seen live theater before; the W.P.A. brought *She Stoops to Conquer* to remote reaches of Florida and invaded the Dakotas. But among the W.P.A. projects, Federal Theatre was always something special, a somehow frivolous enterprise when so many were out of work and hungry. The fact that the performers were paid only $22.73 a week plus $3 a day living expenses on the road could hardly justify, in the popular mind, an endeavor that was so far removed from the urgent concerns of the country. Moreover, the notion of singling out for subsidy several thousand writers and actors strained the generous impulses of many Congressmen. Even if Federal Theatre had been operated in a condition of absolute ideological purity, it could not have held out against the anti-New Deal forces who were regrouping in 1938 and dreamed of destroying the W.P.A. altogether; if they could not have hung Federal Theatre on a charge of radicalism, they would have done it on a charge of using dirty words. But ideological purity was not one of Federal Theatre's strengths.

"Practically every play presented under the auspices of the Project," charged Thomas before any hearings had been held, "is sheer propaganda for Communism or the New Deal." The Project, he said, was dominated by Communists, working through the short-lived Workers Alliance,[4] a sort of labor union for people on relief that was put to such uses as helping Congressman Vito Marcantonio get elected. Although the testi-

[4] At one point a major Committee witness, in the course of listing Workers Alliance officials who were Communists, mentioned one "radical socialist" who was related to "an attorney for the Civil Liberties Union, prosecuting the case in Jersey City against Mayor Hague." Thomas thereupon interjected: "In other words, that is the second connection, then, that you have made between the Communists and the Federal Writers Project in New York City and the Jersey City Civil Liberties Union?"

mony before the Committee contained the usual proportion of oddities (There was the slightly anti-Semitic witness, later employed as a Committee investigator, who identified herself as secretary of an organization called the Committee of Relief Status Professional Theatrical Employees of the Federal Theatre Project, to which practically nobody belonged, and there was the small blond actress who disclosed that a colored man named Van Cleve had called her for a date and her superiors had not taken her complaints about it seriously), the plain fact was that Communists were exceedingly active in the W.P.A. Theatre and Writers Project; they did all they could to get their own people into it and to turn the whole enterprise into an agitprop machine.

Ellen S. Woodward, assistant administrator of the W.P.A., and Hallie Flanagan, director of the Theatre Project, were the first aggrieved persons accorded the privilege of testifying before the Dies Committee. They managed to maintain a fair degree of dignity in the face of severe heckling from Committee members, a contrast to the placid acceptance of the testimony of those who had come bearing charges.[5] But their cause was hopeless. Mrs. Flanagan, who had arrived at Federal Theatre after an outstanding career at Vassar, had had the bad luck to have co-authored a play which was described by the *New Masses* as the "best revolutionary play yet produced in America." She said that only ten per cent of the plays presented by Federal Theatre dealt with social and political problems, in the manner of *Triple-A Plowed Under, One Third of a Nation,* and *It Can't Happen Here,* but she must have known that such questions were not susceptible to measurement by percentages. How, after all, was one to measure the inspiration of the Brooklyn W.P.A. Theatre, where *Julius Caesar* was staged "to emphasize the dictator angle and show Brutus as the defender of the rights of freedom"? The revolutionary

---

[5] MRS. WOODWARD: You know, it seems to me the capitalistic press would certainly say so if we were doing that [spreading Communist propaganda].

    THOMAS: What press did you say?
    STARNES: She said the capitalistic press.
    THOMAS: What do you mean by capitalistic press?
    DIES: That is a Communistic term.

dream was the literary catalyst of the time, the great generative impulse of the depression. Little that came out of it would endure, but for young writers of that era, with no stake in a business society, infected still with the excitement of the Soviet experiment, there was small appeal in drawing room comedy or melodrama. They loaded their works with Social Seriousness and passed heavy, sometimes indigestible portions on to their audiences, thereby bringing about what persons with a casual interest in letters, such as Earl Browder, would believe was a renaissance of American drama and literature. The cultural tone they established, as Richard Rovere has observed, was "deplorable because it was metallic and strident. Communist culture was not aristocratic; it was cheap and vulgar and corny." The left-wing writers of the thirties sought their heroes among working stiffs and bloodied Negroes and their plots in ghettos and slums. Those with genuine talent shook off the ailment sooner than the others, who continued to use their social consciousness as a substitute for genius until the movement ran out on them and they settled down in their advertising agencies or Hollywood studios. Their spirit thrived for nearly a decade and naturally flourished in the W.P.A. Theatre, which brought together writers, performers, and directors with the least to lose.

In July 1939, a month after the Federal Theatre's brief existence had been ended by Congress, a critic proposed that a tombstone be put up, with the words KILLED BY THE COMMUNISTS OF NEW YORK. Certainly the Communists participated in the murder—although for men like Thomas, Dies, and Starnes, who judged plays by their titles and were never accused of having actually witnessed any of the productions that outraged them, virtually all theater of the time was subversive.[6] The

---

[6] During the Federal Theatre debate in the House on June 16, 1939, Everett Dirksen, then at the start of his own long histrionic career, entertained his colleagues with a list of plays, none of which he had seen, that the Federal Theatre had presented: "I have one here—*A New Deal for Mary*, which is a grand title. Then there is *The Mayor and the Manicure* and *Mother Goose Goes to Town*. Also, *A New Kind of Love*. I wonder what that can be. It smacks somewhat of the Soviet. Then there is *Up in Mabel's Room*. There is an intriguing title for you . . . Here is another, *Be Sure Your Sex Will Find You Out* . . . Then there is *Cheating Husbands*. That would be well for the front page of some Washington daily. Next we have *Companionate Maggie*, and this

Communists used Federal Theatre as a patronage tool in their little conspiracies as well as a weapon in their endless ideological wars. They were especially arrogant in the New York bastion, where they busied themselves in collecting for China, recruiting for Spain, and stirring things up in any way they could. When it came to art, the Communists were by no means un-American; they cared as little for it as the Committee did, as little as the nation did. With the pressure on after the rebuff of the 1938 elections, the Administration chucked Federal Theatre. Emmet Lavery, its program director, later blamed W.P.A. Administrator Harry Hopkins for not rising to the defense, for trying to prevent Mrs. Flanagan even from testifying before the Dies Committee in his concern over getting his W.P.A. appropriation through a resistant Congress. Corrupted from within, belabored from without, dependent on a public and an Administration with more important things on their minds, Federal Theatre never lived to realize its promise. Its career presents both a caution and an inspiration to those who are enthusiastic about federal subsidies to the arts, but for Thomas and Dies, its death was taken as a personal victory in a continuing vendetta.

Another assault on the Administration began very early in the Dies Committee hearings with the report of investigator Sullivan that "an outstanding official" of the Department of Labor was protecting Harry Bridges. Dies translated "outstanding official" to mean Secretary of Labor Frances Perkins herself, and in a series of public attacks—culminating in a gesture at impeachment instigated by Thomas in January 1939— charged her with refusing to enforce the law and deport the Australian-born unnaturalized Bridges, whom Dies certified to be a Communist.

---

great rhetorical and intriguing question, *Did Adam Sin?* Another one that they have dished up is *Go Easy, Mabel,* and still another that would strike the fancy of anybody—*Just a Love Nest.* Here is one that is surely adapted to the temple of the modern age, *Lend Me Your Husband.* And then this very happy title, *Love 'Em and Leave 'Em.* Also we have *Mary's Other Husband.* Now, if you want that kind of salacious tripe, very well, vote for it, but if anybody has an interest in decency on the stage, if anyone has an interest in real cultural values, you will not find it in this kind of junk . . ." A few minutes later, an amendment to save Federal Theatre was voted down, 56 to 192.

Many Labor Department employees at the time doubtless had kinder feelings toward Harry Bridges than toward Martin Dies, but even if they had shared the latter's distaste for the former, deportation would still have been something of a problem. There was no question that Bridges, then West Coast regional director of the C.I.O. and president of the International Longshoremen and Warehousemen's Union, was a tough labor leader; he had proved that in the 1934 West Coast maritime strike when he displaced the old waterfront bosses. (As the Dies Committee hearings began he was leading a warehouse strike that was threatening the West Coast with a severe pickle shortage.) Nor was there much question that, like numbers of other C.I.O. officials of the period, he had only the friendliest feelings for Communists; if anything his feelings were friendlier than most. It was a large question, however, whether anyone could prove that he was a member of the Communist Party. Moreover, even if an old Party card of his had been unearthed, the Department of Labor would have faced difficulties in evicting him. As Madame Perkins repeatedly explained through the latter part of 1938, the U.S. Court of Appeals had recently ruled that "Membership in the Communist Party is not ground for deportation." The Labor Department had suspended proceedings in the Bridges affair while this ruling, made in the case of a man named Strecker, was being appealed before the U.S. Supreme Court. Strecker had actually admitted past Party membership, and so the case against him was that much stronger than the one against Bridges. Strecker would finally win his case when the Supreme Court ruled that an individual could not be deported because he had at some time in the past belonged to the Communist Party, but nothing could persuade Dies that there was not a high-level conspiracy afoot to keep Harry Bridges safe and well in this country.

The Bridges case occupied our courts for years. James M. Landis, liberal dean of the Harvard Law School, who was delegated to study the case, ruled in 1939 that on the basis of the evidence against Bridges, he was not a Communist, but J. Edgar Hoover reported that he was, and periodically the controversial union organizer found himself on the verge of being shipped back to Australia by the Justice Department—under continual pressure from Congress—only to be rescued in the nick by a higher power, like the girl in the Saturday serials. Finally, in 1945, the Supreme Court overturned his deportation order for once and all. "Seldom, if ever, in the history of this nation," wrote Justice Murphy in a concurring opinion that owed less perhaps to a judicial mind than to a generous heart, "has there been such a concentrated and relentless crusade to deport an individual because he dared to exercise the freedom that belongs to him as a human being and that is guaranteed to him by the Constitution."

Sorties such as those against Frances Perkins and the W.P.A. were annoying to the Administration but bearable. The elections of 1938, however, gave Dies an opportunity to show that he could be a severe threat to New Deal candidates involved in close races. California, Minnesota, and Michigan were the three states that enjoyed the Committee's attention that fall. No incident in its history demonstrates more clearly the Texan's aims or the methods he was prepared to use to achieve them.

From California in the latter part of October came Harper Knowles, described as chairman of that state's American Legion Radical Research Committee, and Ray E. Nimmo, a Los Angeles attorney, to testify in duet, first, that Frances Perkins was guilty of "gross malfeasance of office" for "coddling" Harry Bridges, and, climactically, that the Democratic candidates for governor, lieutenant governor, and senator (Culbert Olson, Ellis Patterson, and Sheridan Downey, respectively) were in the pockets of the Communist Party. Knowles was at once disowned by the commander of the State Legion Department and was revealed to be on leave as secretary of the Associated Farmers, a West Coast organization dedicated to preventing the spread of unionism and headed by the Republican candidate for the Senate. (Knowles showed his colors when he complained that a wage of three dollars a day for farm workers would bankrupt California's fruit growers and packers. When he appeared before Dean Landis in connection with the investigation of the Bridges case the following year, Landis found him to be "neither candid nor forthright.")

From Minnesota came seven persons, for whom the chairman had cordially supplied invitations in the form of blank subpoenas issued via a former Republican mayor of St. Paul. They reported that the Farmer-Labor Party had been taken over by Communists and that Governor Elmer A. Benson had not repudiated an endorsement by Earl Browder in his election campaign against young Harold Stassen, that he had led a New York City parade of the American League for Peace and Democracy in August 1937, and that he had allowed himself to be photographed standing next to a C.P. official. "Where Communism goes, that's where we will go," proclaimed Dies in defense of his election-time hearings, which he conducted without the participation of most members of his Committee, who were out campaigning. "We're not going to let questions of political expedience stop us from getting at the facts."

And from Michigan, where Governor Frank Murphy was caught up in an exceedingly hard election fight, came a Republican Circuit Court judge, Paul V. Gadola, and a former city manager of Flint, John M. Barringer, to accuse the governor of a "treasonable attitude" in condoning Communist-led sit-down strikes against General Motors in 1937.

The Michigan case was the critical one. Frank Murphy, a particular friend of the President, was campaigning under two serious handicaps: he was a Catholic and his term as governor had been shaken by the most dramatic labor conflict in the country's history. When he came to office in January 1937, C.I.O. organizers in the automobile industry had grown bold enough and desperate enough to begin taking over the plants. From November 1936 to July 1937 there were 147 sit-down strikes in Detroit, and Murphy found himself between union militants, including Communists and their allies like the Reuther brothers, and men of vigilante disposition, such as Barringer and his supporters in the American Legion. If Murphy had been a stronger personality, blood would probably have run in Detroit, and in that sense his weakness was a blessing to the nation. Moreover, he had sympathy for the strikers; when they took over the Fisher body plants in Flint and held them for several weeks, he resisted pressure to send in the

National Guard, which had been assembled in the city to dislodge them. In this he had the support of the White House. On being informed that the governor desired an adjournment of hearings on a writ to evacuate the two seized plants, Judge Gadola, no friend of the C.I.O. or the New Deal, replied: "To hell with the governor!" and issued the writ anyway. Whereupon Murphy prevented the sheriff from executing it. These actions won him the support of the Communist Party in his 1938 campaign.

Murphy's plausible defense was that "a civil war was imminent in Flint in February of 1937" and that any attempt to eject the workers would have provoked a riot. Less plausible was his claim to have honored the order of the court. But his strongest point was that in the end a quarter of a million men went back to their jobs and "not a single human life had been lost, not a liberty had been suppressed, even though we had passed through the most terrifying industrial strike in history." A few years later, according to Dies, Frank Murphy, then a Supreme Court Justice, apologized to him in private for his behavior as governor and urged Dies to carry on his work and get the Communists out of government. "Mr. Dies," he is supposed to have said, "I know you have no reason to like or respect me, but I was under terrific pressure from the President and many of my political friends, and I let them pressure me against my better instincts." Whatever the Justice's remorse in 1940, what his political enemies could not forgive in 1938 was that the peaceful settlement which he hailed signaled the triumph of the C.I.O. in the automobile industry.

The attack on Murphy wounded Mr. Roosevelt much more deeply than the attacks on Madame Perkins or Federal Theatre. He had already remonstrated privately with Dies for giving John Frey a platform upon which to campaign against the New Deal's friends in the C.I.O., and now he vented his pain by issuing the first formal criticism of a committee of Congress ever made by a President. In a lengthy statement, he called the hearings "a flagrantly unfair and un-American attempt to influence an election" and warmly defended Murphy. He anticipated the sensitivities of future administrations by asking that the Committee "abandon the practice of merely providing a forum for those who for political purposes, or otherwise, seek headlines which they could not otherwise attain." And he concluded, somewhat unfortunately, by comparing Murphy's achievement in the Detroit strikes to the recent agreement at Munich: "People may properly differ as to the results of such negotiations but the fact remains that bloodshed was averted." Representatives Healey and Dempsey, themselves busy campaigning in their home districts, wired Dies asking for a recess in the hearings until after the election. The chairman, whose victory in the Texas primaries weeks earlier saved him the bother of campaigning in October, spiritedly rebuked both his colleagues and the President and pledged in words that would serve him as a peroration for years to come that "I wish to make it plain that I shall continue to do my duty undeterred and unafraid."

Frank Murphy's defeat in Michigan in 1938 was accounted by the Administration as the most serious loss in a year of Democratic losses. The Republicans gained eighty seats in the House and eight in the Senate and deposed eleven Democratic governors. For Dies, that amounted to a famous victory. The New Deal won in California but lost in Minnesota; as for Michigan, the results there would stand as one of the Congressman's proudest accomplishments. The memory of the sit-down strike, freshly awakened by the Committee hearings a few weeks before the election, hurt Murphy badly. His plurality in Flint, center of much of the strife, dropped from 13,000 in 1936 to 1,396 in 1938, while the incumbent sheriff, bitterly opposed by the auto workers, led all candidates.

But the election of 1938 represented more than a reaction to the sit-down strikes, frightening as they were. The nation had absorbed many changes, and deep ones, in the foregoing six years, and had given the New Deal its enthusiastic mandate for three elections in a row; now the time had come to take stock. Insofar as there had been a radical temper in America in the first half of the decade, by 1938 it was pretty well spent. The New Deal had not turned the corner to prosperity, but it had brought the Depression under control, and now there was time for native conservatism, particularly in the South and the Midwest, to catch its breath and reassert itself. Arthur Krock could rejoice:

> As the final returns are counted the New Deal has been halted; the Republican Party is large enough for effective opposition; the moderate Democrats in Congress can guide legislation . . . the sit-down strike and the Democratic-C.I.O. alliance have been emphatically rebuked; the country is back on a two-party system . . .

Even if the Dies Committee had never existed, 1938 would have been a dark year for the New Deal, but it was Martin Dies's good luck to be part of, to speak for, a significant national feeling. "When Roosevelt was elected he had no more enthusiastic and sincere advocate than myself," Dies wrote in 1963. That was something of an overstatement, but certainly he was no enemy to the Administration during his first terms in Congress. He took pride in the fact that F.D.R. gave orders to admit him to the Presidential office by a side door. The only reference to the young Texan in the initial volume of Harold Ickes's diaries had to do with his appearance among a group of Congressmen "in full sympathy" with the Public Works Administration. Ickes would find no kinder word for him thereafter than "ass," "moron" and "fascist."

In April 1936—months after F.D.R.'s discernible move to the left—Dies was calling on the country to "keep in the White House that great leader of the plain people, the Jefferson and Jackson of the twentieth century, our present and future president, Franklin D. Roosevelt." A year later, by which time Southerners had become painfully aware that their concept of the Democratic Party was different from that of their nominal allies in Northern cities and in the industrial unions, and the President's court-packing plan had resulted in a stalemated session of Congress, Dies was still able to josh with F.D.R. at a June "harmony outing" on the shores of Chesapeake Bay. In his self-created role of Supreme Shouter, Dies inducted F.D.R. into the "Demagogue Club" after pledging him never to do anything that would injure his chances of election, to appropriate generously but not to tax and never to be consistent. "I wish to caution you," intoned the Supreme Shouter, "upon penalty of being ejected from the Club, not to embarrass the Congress with any more legislation of a controversial nature." It was great fun, but weak salve for the wound in the Democratic Party. To Martin Dies, even before he became a specialist on Communism, the people who descended upon Washington with the New Deal seemed an alien bunch—all those "idealists, dreamers, politicians, professional 'do-gooders' and just plain job-hunters." In Dies's home district, there were no big cities, not many college graduates and hardly any foreign-born voters. The New Deal harbored big-city types, alumni of Eastern colleges, second-generation Americans, Jews, persons who would support the C.I.O.'s organizing drives of oil refinery workers in Texas and hold unsettling ideas about the condition of the Negro. The South had not turned Democratic for them.

If Dies needed further confirmation that he was on the right track after the November elections, it came in December in the form of a Gallup Poll. Of the three out of five voters who had heard of the Committee, 74 per cent were in favor of continuing the investigations. Republicans were substantially more in favor than Democrats, and the investigations had left the best impression in the Midwest and the South. "He is publicity mad," wrote Harold Ickes, "and the unfortunate Gallup Poll will make him worse than ever." Public support for Dies ranged from the wholehearted embrace of the far right to the friendly but slightly exasperated acceptance of the center. The editors of *Colliers*, in a good example of a popular position, wrote:

> Not that Dies runs a top-notch show, nor is he the ideal man for the job. Obviously he is not impartial. Anything but. Most of the witnesses he has produced to date have been funny-looking phonies whom, we surmise, he dug up under wet stones, and most of their yarns about Fascist and Communist activities in this country have been fantastic. Seemingly, the man has no judgment about such things, no sense of perspective, no instinct for effective showmanship.

Thereupon, *Colliers* asked that he be given more money for the new year. Whatever critics thought of his showmanship,

Dies had produced the outstanding political show of 1938, and he was almost as annoyed by the quibblings of the conservative press as by the outright damnation of the liberals.

The election results and the Gallup Poll, meat for the Dies Committee, was food for thought for New Dealers. Ickes confided to his diary in December that the Cabinet agreed that Dies was becoming "a hair shirt for the Administration . . . because apparently his chief object in life is to smear the Administration, incidental of course to getting publicity for himself"—but the Cabinet was divided over tactics. Ickes, like Madame Perkins and W.P.A. Administrator Harry Hopkins, served Dies as a major target, and so wanted to make an all-out fight of it. When Dies placed him in the company of Browder and Stalin as a "purveyor of class hatred," Ickes retaliated by telling a press conference that Dies was "the outstanding zany in our political history."[7] Shortly before he was due to make a speech to a Washington convention of the American League for Peace and Democracy entitled, "Playing with Loaded Dies," Ickes received a message from Roosevelt, via White House Press Secretary Steve Early, telling him "for God's sake not to do it," lest it antagonize Congress. Across the Cabinet table from the explosive Secretary of the Interior sat Vice President Garner, a patron of Dies, and Postmaster General Farley, the ultimate politician, who proposed that Harry Bridges be deported for the good of the Democratic Party.

The President, informed by Congressmen returning to the capital for the new session that sentiment back home made it impossible to vote against continuance of the Committee, took a middle course. He directed Frank Murphy, his newly appointed Attorney General, to have agents of the Department of Justice investigate all charges of Communist activity raised

[7] In his autobiography written when the Dies Committee was still in flower, Ickes gave free play to his feelings for the chairman as well as to his feeling for invective: "For his unmitigated gall, for his long-winded yammerings that seemingly go 'babbling' on forever, and for the strange power that he appears to have over Congress, I christen him 'Bubble Dancer' Dies who cavorts lumberingly on the Congressional stage with nothing but a toy balloon with which to hide his intellectual nudity. To my mind, the most contemptible human being in public life is the one who will recklessly smear another's character and then wrap himself tightly in his Congressional immunity."

by the Dies Committee. His hope was that some of the Committee's funds and functions might thereby be diverted to the executive branch. When in January, F.D.R. denied reappointment on the National Labor Relations Board to Donald W. Smith, a member who had been criticized by the A.F. of L. and by Dies for giving undue aid and comfort to the C.I.O., it was interpreted as a further gesture of conciliation. But Dies was too far gone in triumph to be responsive to conciliation. The first report of his Committee, issued January 3, 1939, led off with a criticism of the Administration for its lack of cooperation. It attacked the Federal Theatre and Writers Project, the National Labor Relations Board, Frank Murphy's behavior during the sit-down strikes, and the Department of Labor's indulgence of Harry Bridges. Along with the report Dies brought in a resolution asking for $150,000 and a two-year extension. A few weeks later, Thomas offered a motion of impeachment against Secretary Perkins and two other Labor Department officials for failing to rid the land of Bridges. The proposal came to nothing, but it put the Administration on notice that the Committee's most aggressive members were feeling their political muscle. In February the House, responding to mail in support of the Committee, voted 344 to 35 to give Dies $100,000 for his work in 1939—"a complete falling down of the so-called Democratic leadership of the House," complained Ickes somewhat unjustly. The Administration's faithful Sam Rayburn was closer to the mark when he said: "Martin Dies could beat me right now in my own district."

Representative Rayburn and Speaker Bankhead were sent by Roosevelt to bring the light to Dies early in 1939. They explained, in case it had escaped his notice, that his accusations against Cabinet members were hurtful to the Democratic Party. Bankhead did not exercise himself over this mission, but relations between the fellow Texans, Rayburn and Dies, deteriorated from this time. When Dies returned to Washington in 1953 for his second tour of Congressional duty, Rayburn, that "Democrat without any prefixes or suffixes," would barely speak to him. The major result of the January 1939 negotiations was that Jerry Voorhis, a young, well-to-do liberal hope from California, was named to replace Representative Mosier, defeated in the Ohio primaries to the glee of that state's C.I.O. A Yale Phi Beta Kappa, Voorhis had been in Congress since 1936 and was one of the small group who voted against continuation of the Dies Committee in 1939. Rhea Whitley, a thirty-five-year-old former F.B.I. agent who had reputedly helped get John Dillinger, became Committee counsel, and J. B. Matthews was given the job of chief investigator.

Whereas the Administration dealt with the Dies Committee as an unfortunate incident in the political game, a nuisance on the way to becoming a threat, the liberal community was unable to deal with it at all, except through jeremiads. As the nineteen-thirties drew to a close, the nation's liberals were still going through their great crisis of conscience with regard to Communism, and the Dies investigation, with all of the attendant publicity, was aggravating their condition. Revolution in Russia, depression in America, fascism in Italy and Germany, the ruin of the beginnings of democracy in Spain—these events had drawn America's liberals into alliance with the Communists, and it would not be easy for many to disengage themselves despite purges in Moscow and machinations in New York. They saw that the attack by Dies was aimed as much at them as at the Communist Party and they sprang to the barricades. Had they been less committed to the united front, less bemused by the Soviet experiment, or had Dies and Thomas been somewhat less disposed to random attacks, the liberals might have been spared some heartache. As it was, the major organs of our liberal intelligentsia responded to Dies with cries of "Fascist!" and statements of principle that give off a sickly glow in the unsentimental light of history.

"When the Communists come to the aid of what we regard as a worthy cause," wrote the editors of *The New Republic* in June of 1938, "we propose to welcome their help as we would that of anyone else. If they advocate what we consider wrong, we shall attack them as we would anyone else." And a few months after John Frey's testimony they assured their readers and themselves that if John L. Lewis and Sidney Hillman countenanced "a few" Communists, "it is because the persons in question are able and conscientious trade-unionists who do not allow party politics to interfere with their jobs." Paul Y. Anderson, the newspaperman who covered the Dies Committee for *The Nation*, headed his first dispatch: FASCISM HITS WASHINGTON. An editorial in that issue declared:

> It is hardly news that Communists participate, with varying degrees of influence in a host of left organizations, with whose aims their own party politics coincide. Why shouldn't they? And why should the fact of their participation make such movements untouchable for other anti-fascists inside the government or outside?

The most amiable assessment of our domestic Communists was made early in 1939 by a group of prominent lawyers who petitioned the House of Representatives to abolish the Dies Committee. Having examined the Party, the lawyers found no proof of its domination by Moscow. "A reasonable construction of language," they reported, "compels the conclusion that the members of the Communist Party of the U.S.A. have the right, power and authority to make their own decisions precisely as members of any other American organization." Furthermore, there was nothing to show that the Party had failed to work in the "traditions of Jefferson, Paine, Jackson and Lincoln." When a group of liberals, led by John Dewey and Sidney Hook, formed the Committee for Cultural Freedom in 1939, and issued a manifesto calling for the "clearest differentiation from Stalinism together with all its fronts, stooges and innocents," Freda Kirchwey, editor and publisher of *The Nation*, responded:

> To advocate a policy of "clearest differentiation" on the left is a counsel of disruption. With all their faults, the Communists perform necessary functions in the confused struggle of our time. They have helped to build up and to run a string of organizations known as "fronts" by their opponents—which clearly serve the cause not of "totalitarian doctrine" but of a more workable democracy. And the value of these organizations lies largely in the energy and discipline and zeal of their Communist elements.

Martin Dies held no illusions about the possibilities of cooperating with the Communists for any but Communist goals.

But such wisdom came easier to him than to those who shared many of those goals."In instance after instance," as *The New Republic's* editors kept reminding themselves, "the Communists have fought and are fighting for civil liberties, for union principles, for social legislation." Representative Dies, whose passions did not include civil liberties, union principles, or social legislation, was above temptation. He detested the Reds not in spite of their devotion to such causes but on account of them. Nineteen thirty-nine, the year of the outbreak of war in Europe and of the Hitler-Stalin pact, was traumatic for the American liberal's attachment to Soviet Communism. Some non-Communists learned early; many learned late; a few will never learn. But in matters of the heart, there is always the question of who calls forth the greater sympathy—those who have been led up blind alleys by their infatuations, or those who never fell in love at all.

3

★ ★ ★ ★ ★

1939: Disarray on the Left

IT WAS a running source of irritation to liberals for the whole life of the Dies Committee that its chairman was more readily aroused by seditionists of the left than by those of the right. While the Nazis marched in Europe, at home Bundists rallied, Christian Fronters conspired, anti-Semites howled on street corners—and Dies was scarcely moved. Every whisper on the left, however, set his blood racing. He was prone to declarations like "We are going to investigate and expose the Nazi and fascist movements in this country as thoroughly as we do the Communist movement." But his heart wasn't in it.

Yet in May 1939 the Dies Committee suddenly announced that it was investigating a plot that involved friends of fascism. It also involved Jews. That much could be gathered from the first announcements, but not much more than that. The announcements were accorded the generous newspaper attention to which Dies was by now accustomed, but in this case the publicity received was a function of the secrecy invested. It was all very secret. Nameless and closely guarded witnesses, hidden one from the other, were led to the Committee room along devious routes. The members of the Committee had pledged themselves to secrecy. It was reported that Dies had requested and received special permission from the Messrs. Rayburn and Bankhead to undertake this special investigation. A letter was made public from George Van Horn Moseley, a retired major general in the U.S. army, to a captain in the army reserve; it contained the stimulating sentences, "If the Jews bump me off, be sure to see that they get the credit for it from coast to coast. It will help our cause." On the basis of the first reports out of Washington, a careful newspaper reader could be sure only that the Committee was about to investigate either a Jewish plot or a plot against the Jews.

It turned out to be a little of both. As Dudley Pierrepont Gilbert, a Manhattan socialite, dilettante anti-Semite, and organizer of American Nationalists, Inc., explained it—a waiter at New York's Harmonie Club, organized by and for well-to-do Jews of the city, had been conveying to him (Gilbert) reports of plottings on which he (the waiter) had eavesdropped. Gilbert forwarded the eavesdroppings to James Erwin Campbell, an army reserve captain in Kentucky, who mimeographed them and distributed them to American Legion posts. It was a Legion official in the South who brought them to the Committee's attention. Most of the reports were never made public by Dies because they were so viciously anti-Semitic, but the gist was that rich Red Jews were planning to take over the government in August. With the help of a force of 150,000 mercenaries from Spain and elsewhere, who were being smuggled into this country through Mexico, they were going to seize eight of the army's eleven arsenals. Simultaneously, with their tentacles among both capitalists and the proletariat, the Jews were going to depress the value of stocks and bonds and foment strikes.

Headline writers tended to play the story nearly straight. New York *Post*: 'RED ARMY PLOT' TO SEIZE GOVERNMENT IS BARED. Baltimore *Sun*: FANTASTIC PLOT TO SEIZE NATION BARED BY DIES. New York *Daily News*: 'RED ARMY PLOT' TO TAKE OVER NATION STIRS U.S. PROBERS. St. Louis *Star Times*: DIES HEARS OF 'M-DAY' PLOT TO SEIZE U.S. An exception was Hearst's New York *Journal-American*, which reported: ANTI-SEMITIC PLOT EXPOSED BY DIES. The *Journal-American*, it developed, had gotten the story right. Two main figures called before the Committee were General Moseley and George E. Deatherage, national commander of the Knights of the White Camelia. Deatherage, who described himself as a construction engineer whereas reporters referred to him as a house painter, had a plan to save the nation from the Jewish plot and had selected General Moseley, who combined an estimable military record with open disgust for the New Deal, to mount the white horse. Lacking the genteel inspiration of a Cliveden, such was the most elegant strategy that America's fascists could work out.

At the first reports that the Jewish plot was being investigated, Deatherage wired Dies "a great big kiss" from "all the boys," but by the time he came before the Committee he had lost his amiability. His appearance, behind a small mustache and dark glasses, befitted his sinister name, and he was truculent from the start. When Dies told him not to volunteer information, he said "I don't know about that"—and stood up. "You sit down," ordered Dies. "You come over here and make me sit down," returned Deatherage. He threatened to "pop" a man in the audience who he believed was "sneering and smiling" at him. As he explained later, he was "of a rather nervous disposition." Most of the Knight's testimony concerned his efforts to mobilize the anti-Semites of the country against the Jewish international bankers and Communists who were conspiring to take things over. Dies was put in the unaccustomed position of defending the President and Mrs. Roosevelt from slanders, as he exhorted Deatherage to mend his ways. "All American citizens have rights," the chairman reminded the witness. "That is right," Deatherage countered, "except I am bigoted enough to believe in white supremacy in the South." "With that exception," Dies allowed, "you agree with the statement?" "Yes," said Deatherage.

General Moseley, who had retired as commander of the army's Fourth Corps in September 1938, after nearly forty years of service in the Philippines, in Mexico, with the A.E.F. in France, and against Depression mobs or what were imagined to be mobs in this country, preceded his appearance before the Committee with a call to the American people "to save our republic now before it is too late." Secretary of the Army Woodring attributed Moseley's politics to pique over not being named army chief of staff, but his anti-Semitism seems to have been in earnest. He liked the idea of sterilizing all refugees disembarking on these shores. A speech he made in Springfield, Illinois, a few weeks before being summoned to Washington gives a fair example of his approach to the Jewish problem:

> The problem of the Jew in America must be studied and solved without further delay. We cannot expect to escape the experience of every other nation in the world which has been faced with the very same problem. Jewish refugees from abroad are entering this country in large numbers, lawfully and unlawfully, from those parts of the world where anti-Semitism is growing. That same feeling is growing rapidly in America from coast to coast. The problem should be recognized before further tragedy overtakes the Jews who live in the United States of America . . . Over two thousand years of recorded history shows very clearly that those traits which have made the Jew unwelcome every place he has been domiciled cannot be bred out.

Moseley was attended in the hearing room by a loyal cadre, including freshman Representative Thorkelson of Montana, who had just been described by William Dudley Pelley, the nation's leading Jew-baiter, as a "new statesman rearing high above the miasma of skulduggery," and by an aide who rushed forward to snatch a cup of drinking water from the general's reach and refill it from the cooler in the corner of the room in order to save him from being poisoned. Voorhis, Healey, and Dempsey enjoyed getting the general to say silly things, and his performance together with that of Deatherage and their associates exposed our native fascists as a ragtag bunch whose delusion it was that if they acted as mad as Adolf Hitler they too might become führers or friends of führers.

After its muddled beginning, the Committee handled the case with surprising efficiency, but there was still dissatisfaction on the left. It was charged that Dies had not followed through on this investigation, though it was difficult to see what could have been gained by giving the clownish head of the White Camelias further opportunity for display. A major proposition of the Popular Front period—the years between 1935 and 1939 when Moscow found it beneficial to cooperate with mere liberals—was that It Could Happen Here—indeed that It Was Happening. Those under its spell belittled any suggestion that the U.S. followers of Stalin were not devoted to democracy, but were insistent on the black menace of fascism. Communists were profligate with the word "fascist"—the Party press would have been in serious trouble for copy without it—and many non-Communists joined them in hurling it at Martin Dies. Yet despite their unbending antagonism, even these critics could find little to complain of in the opening weeks of the Committee hearings, which resumed in mid-August, when Dies returned to Washington after one of the lengthy illnesses that would keep him at home in Texas during a good part of his tenure as Congressman.

First in the witness chair was Fritz Kuhn, another aspiring führer. Under Rhea Whitley's questioning, a good deal of information was brought out on the Bund's structure, its relations with like-minded groups, its ties to Hitler's Germany, and its free and easy financing, for which Kuhn would quite soon be sent to jail. The Bund president had been arrested a few weeks before for drunkenness, profanity, and grand larceny; the temperature in Washington was in the nineties; and he was in an atrocious humor. The high point of his appearance occurred in an exchange with Representative Starnes, who with cotton-patch subtlety, was attempting to refute Kuhn's contention that the Bund was a thoroughly patriotic American institution, with minimal ties to the old country.

STARNES: Is not Mr. Hitler against the Communists?

KUHN: Aren't you against the Communists?

STARNES: Is not Mr. Hitler anti-Semitic?

KUHN: Aren't you anti-Semitic?

STARNES: I am asking you the question. Is not Mr. Hitler anti-Semitic?

KUHN: I suppose so, from what I hear.

STARNES: Has he not driven hundreds of thousands of those unfortunate people out of the country?

KUHN: Have not the Communists driven hundreds of thousands of people out of Russia?

STARNES: I am asking you the question with reference to the treatment of Jews in Germany.

KUHN: That is up to Mr. Hitler, not to me. What do I have to do with Mr. Hitler? Subpoena Mr. Hitler here.

STARNES: You want to establish a party with the same position in this country, do you not?

KUHN (*banging on the table*):   That is absolutely a lie!

STARNES: Don't you call me a liar!

Whereupon Representative Starnes leaped up and plunged through a line of photographers toward Kuhn. Two Capitol policemen intervened; the chairman said, "Sit down, Joe"; and the hearings proceeded.

Other witnesses were produced who told of the Bund's pro-Nazi indoctrination courses, and a nineteen-year-old former Bundist maiden provided a peek into the sexual play at Bund camps. When Kuhn was brought back a few weeks later, after the Wehrmacht had overrun Poland, he was free on bail of $50,000, having been indicted for misusing Bund funds; now he was accompanied by two lawyers and was still in bad humor. His career was sinking fast.

The second star witness of mid-summer 1939 was Earl Browder, the Kansas-born secretary of the U.S. Communist Party, who was to enjoy the paeans of his comrades until 1945, when he would be abruptly toppled by order of the Kremlin and made fit subject for vilification, an early fatality of the cold war. But in 1939 he was still the beloved leader.

On August 24 the U.S.S.R. signed its non-aggression pact with Germany. As August Raymond Ogden, that diligent chronicler of the Dies Committee, observes, the pact was a "godsend" to the Committee and would keep it on the front pages despite competition from the outbreak of World War II and a special emergency session of Congress. The summer's hearings had been rambling along with stray anti-Semites, persons of tiny followings and of no consequence in themselves, who had the pleasure of explaining in the hearing of newspapermen why they detested Jews. Now the domestic Communist Party, trying clumsily to get into a different pair of ideological trousers, stood exposed as a total creature of Moscow. Just a few weeks before, Browder had been fiercely condemning the speculation of "reactionaries" that the U.S.S.R. might join hands with Hitler: "There is as much chance of agreement," he told an audience in Charlottesville, Virginia, in July, "as of Earl Browder being elected president of the Chamber of Commerce." He was at the Committee's mercy.

There were satisfactions for everyone at the hearings. Browder's admission that he had traveled on false passports, which would send him to prison from 1940 to 1942, the interval between the end of the Popular Front and the start of the U.S.–Soviet alliance, served Dies as a major accomplishment for the rest of his career. Browder's pioneering refusal to respond to questions about his forgery on the grounds of possible self-incrimination would light the way for Communists yet unsung. Matthews, ever in search not of information but of confirmation and equipped with his endless lists of names, drew from Browder a definition of a Communist "transmission belt" —"a technical term referring to the tactics whereby the Communists establish their relations with the masses of the people"—broad enough to be applied as anyone cared to apply it. Thomas observed that Mrs. Roosevelt and Secretaries Ickes and Wallace had addressed or sent greetings to a number of the organizations that fitted Browder's definition, and concluded: "It seems as though the New Deal was hand in glove with the Communist Party." He took offense when Representative Dempsey called his statement "a cheap political speech." Starnes, too, participated in his manner. "The greatest authorities on the theory of Communism are Marx, Engels, Lenin and Stalin," said Browder. "Who was the second?" interjected Starnes. "I did not get the second name." A few minutes later Starnes found himself arguing that there had been no killing in the American Revolution, unlike in the Russian Revolution.

Despite such passages, this was one of the Committee's better hearings. Whitley's conduct of the examination, except for a moment when he somehow got off on the activities of some of Browder's relatives in Russia, was straightforward and not argumentative. In contrast to Matthews, he was not bent on scoring points. Browder made a pleasant witness. There were the necessary evasions and lies, but he was considerably more responsive than Kuhn. The most revealing parts of his testimony, on his Party's *volte face* after the Nazi-Soviet pact, came in colloquies with Voorhis, assisted by Representative Joseph E. Casey of Massachusetts, a liberal who had recently been named to the Committee to replace Healey. Browder conceded that there had never been a fundamental disagreement between the U.S. Party and the Communist International; he defended the outlawing of political parties in the Soviet Union; he explained to the bewildered Starnes that the Trotskyites, those scoundrels, had no purpose in life other than to wreck the work of virtuous Communists—they are "all bad," he said; he stated with no glint of humor that "The *Daily Worker* is completely free to develop and conduct the paper in any way in which the editorial staff in America desires . . ." And he praised the German-Soviet nonaggression pact as a "very big concession by Hitler" which was entirely in the interests of America because it broke up the Axis, relieved the Japanese pressure on American interests in the Far East, and "dissolved the threat to the Monroe Doctrine" by Spain. The pact, he affirmed, "was an act of friendship between these [German and Russian] peoples and in no way an alliance between governments."

Browder was living proof of all that old-time radicals had been saying about the Stalinists for years. Long before this demonstration, an astute former Communist, J.B.S. Hardman, wrote that the Communist Party went on the rocks in America "because of the inability of its leadership to read developments and trends in American reality and to measure up to the possibilities of the situation." He continued:

> There undoubtedly is room in the United States for a realistically aggressive labor movement, but obviously such a movement will not thrive on a foundation of canonized truths and canned reasoning, and under the tutelage of political puppets manipulated from a distance of seven thousand miles.

The explanations by Party functionaries of their startling twists of policy had been a source of hilarity to ex-Communist radicals like Hardman for years; now a wider audience could enjoy them. The Soviet Union, explained Browder, "in the interest of stopping this whole drifting into war, and this conspiracy of hiding the realities of the situation had to demonstrate before the world that it was not bound by any compact to go to war."

Even those who were most impatient with Chamberlain and Daladier for balking at an agreement with the U.S.S.R. would be struck by the instantaneousness and thoroughness of the American Party's embrace of Stalin's tactics. Alfred Kazin recalls in his autobiography that he followed the *Daily Worker* diligently during this period "with savage joy at its confusion as those who had been eloquent about the Oakies, the unemployed, the victims of fascism now tried to explain the secret contribution that the noble Stalin, the great Stalin, the all-wise and far-seeing Stalin, had made to the cause of world peace." For a Party member to take issue with the Hitler-Stalin pact, explained Browder, "would be a demonstration of a most serious lack of understanding of politics, and a serious disregard of the national interests of America which have been helped by the pact."[1] Soon the Communists and the more adjustable fellow travelers would be charging F.D.R. with using the Dies Committee to whip up war hysteria.

Other Communist officials and former officials were called—notably Benjamin Gitlow, twice the Communist candidate for vice president, who broke in 1929 after his faction was rebuffed by Stalin and was now setting out on the path of professional anti-Communism walked by J. B. Matthews. Gitlow provided interesting information on Party operations and finances in the twenties, filling in some of the gaps left by Browder's selective recollections; Walter G. Krivitsky, a former general in Soviet

---

[1] One exchange with Voorhis made the C.P.'s position as clear as it would ever be.

VOORHIS: Have you any doubt as to who the aggressor is?
BROWDER: I have no real doubt.
VOORHIS: And, as you expressed previously, you said the Soviet Union was against aggressor nations?
BROWDER: Yes.
VOORHIS: And you think this pact with Germany, an aggressor nation as you determine it, is being against the aggressor?
BROWDER: Yes.
VOORHIS: It is consistent with their being against it, to make a pact of non-aggression?
BROWDER: Absolutely.

military intelligence who had fled the purges in 1937[2] and was to die in New York under mysterious circumstances in 1941, told of the world-wide activities of the O.G.P.U.; but Committee members had their most fun in trying to get current C.P. officials to say whether they would fight for this country in a hypothetical war against Russia.

William Z. Foster, who owed his place as the Party's national chairman to the Moscow decision that rejected Gitlow, testified on September 29, after the U.S.S.R. had marched into Poland. Foster said that the Soviet Union was "one hundred per cent justified in thereby extending its protection over the former Russian people."

"Have you ever settled any question regarding the Party line independent of the Comintern?" asked Dies.

FOSTER: Tens of thousands.

DIES: Independent of the Cominform?

FOSTER: Independent of course; every day; every day, on every question that comes along, we make settlements.

DIES: Every day—can you cite a single instance where any decision of the Communist Party finally taken has conflicted with the decision of the Comintern?

FOSTER: Well, no, I cannot—no major decision.

When Foster was done testifying, spectators cheered Dies's proposal, to be raised innumerable times thereafter, that the Communist Party be disbanded.

It was a difficult period for the C.P., and the Dies Committee must be granted the credit it claimed for making it more difficult. The membership was in turmoil; the Russian-born Jews who were so large a part of the small Party fled from an alliance with Hitler, and even those intellectuals who had been able to reconcile themselves to the amenities of dictatorship had trouble adapting to such a pact. Granville Hicks, the Party's preeminent academic adornment in its united front manifestation, now departed the fold, with more candor and less anguish than many. A few weeks after Browder, a squire speaking of a prize bull, described Hicks as "one of our most distinguished

2 "General Krivitsky, you are Smelka Ginsberg!" announced the *New Masses*.

Communist educators," the writer and critic issued his melancholy farewell in a communication to *The New Republic*. (The *New Masses* had declined to print it.) He wrote:

> If they had only admitted their ignorance, the Communist Party of the United States would be intact today. But instead they insisted that the Soviet-German nonaggression pact was the greatest possible contribution to peace and democracy and offered anything that came into their heads as proof. They rushed into print with apologies completely devoid of clarity and logic. Only one conclusion could be drawn: If the Party leaders could not defend the Soviet Union intelligently, they would defend it stupidly.

The stupidity was what most annoyed Hicks.

> The leaders of the Communist Party have tried to appear omniscient, and they have succeeded in being ridiculous. They have clutched at straws, juggled sophistries, shut their eyes to facts . . . They have shown that they are strong in faith—which the future may or may not justify—and weak in intelligence.

As the U. S. Communist Party made its conversion from collective security to isolationism, front groups found themselves in a barely tenable position. Having become adept at holding to the necessary line by the tips of their fingers, they were now called on to do so by the skin of their teeth. The photograph of that smiling group in the Kremlin—Stalin, Ribbentrop, Molotov—as J. M. Cameron, an English leftist of the period would write, "gave visible substance to the reality that lay behind the fictitious account of Soviet affairs that we took to be a true account in that age of faith." It made things very difficult. For the fellow travelers to continue to be of use to the Party, they had to become isolationists, but that would expose their want of independence to their densest friends, and so terminate their usefulness anyway.

The largest and most important of the front organizations of the period was the American League for Peace and Democracy —though its claim to represent upwards of seven million people was typically generous; the League at no time had more than 20,000 individual members, nearly half of them in New York City. It was formed in 1933, as the American League Against

War and Fascism, an outgrowth of a 1932 Congress Against War, organized in Amsterdam by Henri Barbusse and Romain Rolland, who had been aroused by Japan's conquest of Manchuria. J. B. Matthews was its first national chairman, and from the beginning it was controlled by Stalinists through the various organizations that constituted the bulk of its membership. The only people who took the seven-million membership figure straight were Dies, Matthews, and boosters on the left. In 1934 Dr. Harry F. Ward, a Methodist clergyman and professor of Christian Ethics at Union Theological Seminary, became chairman, and three years later, in an early bow to the power of the positive slogan, the organization became the American League for Peace and Democracy. Its influence grew through 1938. The name of Earl Browder, who had been a vice president at the outset, was scratched from the letterhead—though the C.P. continued to be a major financial contributor—and such prominent New Dealers as Harold Ickes, Elmer Benson, and Robert Jackson sent warm greetings to its congresses. Newspapers treated it with respect; *The New Republic* commissioned its officials to write of its high purposes; and it had advocates in Congress.

Dr. Ward came before the Dies Committee on October 23, 1939, during an unresolved dispute over the behavior of Committee agents while taking records from the League's Washington and Chicago offices. Ward was the model of a model fellow traveler—"a distinguished divine," as the New Deal's Representative Coffee described him, "one of the leading and most learned scholars in America." Under the questioning of his A.L.W.F. predecessor J. B. Matthews, Ward explained that he was neither for nor against Communism. "My position on Communism is that of a critical student, sir." In his five years as chairman of the League, he had never noticed any attempt at domination by the Communist Party. He emphasized that the League had policy differences with the Communists, but his main example—"we never stood for collective security as a broad policy. We stood only for concerted action to prevent aggression, that is, aggression of the fascist powers, by withholding economic aid to them from the democracies"—

was not overpowering. As for the Nazi-Soviet pact, he had lately observed "an increasing recognition . . . that the action of the Soviet Union in regard to Hitler has given him more of a check than it has helped him." From his study of Soviet society Ward had concluded that Soviet workers "have a better opportunity than the unorganized workers in this country and just about the same as effectively organized workers," and he was at pains to point out that "there is a vital difference between Communism and fascism so far as war and dictators are concerned . . . they are not the same kind of dictators." Pressed by Voorhis, he explained that the difference lay between the "collective dictatorship of the Soviet Union" and the "personal dictatorship of Hitler."

It was an exemplary performance. In staging it, Dies did a service for the nation's liberals. But that was not sufficient satisfaction. Now, as throughout his captaincy of the Committee, he needed blood, and organizations do not bleed. Its members do, however, and virtually the entire membership of the League's Washington, D.C., chapter was made up of government employees, including a number of high officials. Here was an opportunity to get at the New Deal and at individual New Dealers. The temptation was, as always, irresistible. The League's Washington list (whether it was the membership list or just a mailing list nobody seemed certain) was made public on October 25, at the insistence of Mason and over the mild objections of Voorhis. It contained the names of 563 federal employees, the great majority in positions paying under $3,000 a year, but a few of greater consequence. The featured names were Oscar Chapman, then Assistant Secretary of the Interior; Louis Block, a member of the Maritime Labor Board; Mordecai Ezekiel, an influential official in the Agricultural Adjustment Administration; Edwin S. Smith, a member of the National Labor Relations Board, whose partiality toward the C.I.O. had already been the subject of Committee testimony; and Nathan Witt, the N.L.R.B.'s executive secretary.[3]

[3] A year later the Communist Witt and the fellow traveler Smith would lose their places in the N.L.R.B. and their power to nudge the American labor movement along Communist lines. We shall come across their names again in this history.

For the League itself, the publicity was only another bump on the road to the graveyard. It was fast expiring, strangled in the twists of Soviet policy. Under pressure to make some statement on the Nazi-Soviet pact and the partition of Poland, its national board announced: "We neither condemn nor approve the actions of the Soviet Union. Our members will have their own opinions on these matters and will express and implement them in their political organizations outside the League."[4] Their members did indeed have their own opinions; they quit by the thousands. Roger N. Baldwin, who had worked closely with Ward at both the League and the American Civil Liberties Union, was one of those who resigned. He denied to the end, however, that the League had been "controlled" by the Communist Party, explaining: "We were, of course, prevented from taking any position in opposition to Communist policy, for they would have withdrawn and thus wrecked the united front. But the area of conflict was comparatively slight. When it became acute, after the Nazi-Soviet Pact, it killed the League." Baldwin said on resigning that he was still willing to collaborate with Communists on domestic matters, but he gave up on them where the interests of the U.S.S.R. were concerned. Thousands of other non-Communists came to a similar or harsher conclusion, and within four months the American League for Peace and Democracy, bereft of members and of money and of reputation, dissolved itself.[5] "There was no middle way, no fence that could be straddled," lamented its ex-director of religious work in an ingenuous postmortem. "The toleration fundamental to a broad united front has disappeared." The Reverend Dr. Ward, ever strong in

---

[4] The position is much the same as that adopted nearly twenty years later by the remnant U.S. Communist Party, confronted by the Soviet repression in Hungary: "We do not seek to justify the use of Soviet troops in Hungary's internal crisis on November 4 [1956]. Neither do we join in the condemnation of these actions . . ."

[5] One of its final actions was to urge friends of the League to buy Christmas cards at 5¢ apiece, containing this greeting:

> Peace on earth, good will toward men
> Our wish to you before Congressman Dies decides
> That Peace, good will and Christmas are
> Un-American.

faith, went on to become honorary co-chairman of the Civil Rights Congress.

Criticism of the Committee for making public the Washington A.L.P.D. list swelled beyond the usual dimensions. Representative Dempsey, annoyed that Dies and Mason had refused to wait for him to finish a telephone call and had issued the list in his absence, complained of inaccuracies. The Committee should have taken the time to do some checking, he protested, and cited the case of a Washington schoolteacher who found herself listed as a member of a Communist front with which she had had no connection whatever. In reply, Mason adopted a remarkable line of reasoning: "If there were mistakes of names being on the list that were not members it was not the mistake of the Dies Committee, it was the mistake of the records and the local chapter of the League. Please, therefore, do not blame the Dies Committee if there were names on that list that should not have been on it." Coffee charged that the list's release was "obviously for the purpose of intimidating government employees." Mason preferred to call it the "culmination of a campaign of 'moral suasion.'" He and Dies pointed out that the Committee had listed the League as a Communist front in its first report, early in 1939; hence its members had had plenty of time to see the light and withdraw. If the League were not a Communist front, adherents of the Dies position asked, why should its members be ashamed of being identified with it? If it were, why, having been put on notice, did they continue to belong?

The liberal press was annoyed partly on principle and partly because its editors and writers rather admired the League; they would surely have been little disturbed had the Committee published a membership list of the Silver Shirts. In November, the editor of *The Nation* was still able to write that the League's members "represent a wide variety of points of view" and "if it has been 'controlled' by its Communist members their influence has been singularly moderate." The League itself issued a statement whose rhetoric was sufficient to damn it as a front group without further evidence:

Long after Mr. Dies' name has been forgotten the six hundred names of the members of the American League for Peace and Democracy in Washington will stand as a testimonial to the courage of Americans who refuse to be intimidated by this twentieth century inquisition. No American is safe so long as the Dies Committee is permitted to defy the American Bill of Rights. The American League for Peace and Democracy will continue to expose the enemies of peace and democracy in the United States.

The publication of the list was an outburst of that vigilanteeism that Dies and his man Matthews could never repress for very long. "The real job this Committee has to do," said Voorhis in his civilized way during the debate on the floor, "is not that of questioning individuals or obtaining and publishing lists of individuals but determining as near as it can the facts about organizations." But Matthews, brimming with the passions of the apostate, and Dies, with his flair for page-one copy, would be satisfied with nothing less than public repentance or public retribution. The published list contained many inaccuracies. ("The remedy is simple," observed Congressman Gifford. "Those on the list can explain whether or not they ought to be on it. Their character is not assassinated except for a moment.") Like all membership (or mailing) lists of large organizations, it contained the names of persons who had only the remotest connection with the League and the vaguest idea of what the commotion was about. Some of those listed were Communists; the majority were not; many were merely foolish or careless. To most of them, deeply worried over the continuing triumphs of fascism, it must have seemed, as it seemed to *The New Republic* in 1938, that "the Communists today are not acting as a revolutionary group; they are so committed to the policy of cooperation with all democratic forces that one can hardly tell them from New Deal Democrats." The Communists *were* acting that way—numbers of them quite sincerely—in the late thirties. By its act of mass exposure, the Dies Committee had obliterated all distinctions. It had used its powers to punish, en masse, hundreds of persons innocent of any known crime whose motives for being in the League were diverse and whose actions while in it, never investigated, were by no means *per se* subversive of America's interests. After a few good weeks, the Dies Committee had returned to the bad old ways of 1938.

Mr. Roosevelt, not unattuned to the political reverberations of the list publication, termed it a "sordid procedure." Dies replied, on the C.B.S. network, that he was "grieved and pained" by the comment, but that he was determined to carry on his high task despite all obstacles. Although neither seemed eager to resume their feud of the year before, they could not help rubbing one another the wrong way. When Dies announced that the Administration had asked the Justice Department to begin "purging" 2,850 "known Communists" in key government positions, Roosevelt replied that he was waiting for Dies to let him in on the source of his information. When Thomas attacked Attorney General Murphy as being "strangely indifferent and listless in the case of Browder," shortly before the Communist leader was indicted for passport forgery, Dies unpredictably called his statement "most inappropriate"; then he began badgering Murphy to indict the entire League for Peace and Democracy. The mild Murphy could not find anything to indict the League for, but he expressed his gratitude to the Dies Committee for all its help. (Ickes wrote in his diary that Dies had the Attorney General "buffaloed," and added dryly that fighting back did not seem to fit in with Murphy's disposition.)

In its remaining public hearings of 1939, the Committee entered two other areas which, like the peace groups, gave America's Stalinists vast illusions of success for a time but finally ended in irrelevance and futility. Dies and Matthews saw and made much of Communist influence in the labor movement as represented by Joe Curran's Maritime Workers, and in youth groups such as the American Youth Congress and the American Student Union. Like the Stalinists, they made too much of a limited and short-lived influence. Under Matthews's tutelage, Dies learned to share the Communists' own enchantment with their conspiratorial string-pullings, and long after the strings were frayed to tatters, he would still be sawing away at them.

Joseph Curran, president of the National Maritime Union, owed his ascendancy over the sailors in the thirties to the Communists; it was with their brain and muscle that he built up a powerful union machine. Disaffected N.M.U. members identified him to the Committee as a Communist figurehead, and indeed he was obliging to his various *eminences rouges*. During the Hitler-Stalin pact, his men picketed the White House with signs reading NO CONVOYS!, but once Russia was at war, he became anti-fascist to the point of strike-breaking. Yet, as he would prove, it was an oversimplification to write him off as another stooge of Moscow.

Before being selected for union leadership by the Communists, Curran, the bucko boatswain's mate, was known among the men who sailed with him as "No-Coffee-Time Joe" because he would not give them fifteen minutes off for a cup of coffee. "He was strictly a company man at that time," recalled a former shipmate. In his bellowing appearance before the Committee—"What a circus!" he yelled—Curran gave his own explanation of his relations with the Communists:

> . . . my stomach, when it comes to looking for a pork chop in it and I am out on the picket line, does not know whether a dollar bill is red or green, as long as it buys a pork chop. And our respectable citizens would not give us anything and I did not question the character of each individual which offered me the price of a meal when I was on strike to better my conditions. And it seems to me that those people that fed us at that time were so-called Communists.

His speech, though disingenuous, was not without a portion of truth. In the desperate early thirties the A.F. of L.'s International Seamen's Union was more concerned with taking rake-offs from shipowners than in assisting the sailors. It was destroyed in the bitter seamen's strike of 1936–37 which lasted for ninety-nine days and from which emerged the N.M.U., headed by Joe Curran and his palace guard of Communists. From 1938 to 1945 he was their man, but then in 1945, as the cold war took form and Communist allies were neither an indispensable support nor an unmitigated blessing, he threw them out. In the nineteen-sixties he would be a booster of the war in Vietnam.

Curran was innocent of Marxism-Leninism. He found in the Communist Party a ladder by which he could ascend, and when it had served its purpose, he kicked it over. Neither the Communists nor Matthews could fathom a union leader like Curran—not because he was so deep but because he cared so little for the strange world on which their minds were centered. As Murray Kempton wrote of the case, "Curran was only a sailor. There had been a time when he was hungry, and the Communists had fed him when no one else would. But it had been enough for him, as for most of the other seamen, to be fed and to win for himself a place in the here and now." Curran was too devoted to the here and now to thrive on dreams of the millennium, too self-serving to give himself for long to any outside cause, and too tough to allow any cause to take what he saw no advantage in giving.

At the end of November, the Committee, chaired by Starnes, began taking testimony from the officers of two youth groups which had been repeatedly labeled Communist fronts by volunteer witnesses, beginning with Walter Steele. The three days of rather inconclusive hearings were distinguished by the presence of Mrs. Eleanor Roosevelt, a supremely tolerant patron of the American Youth Congress and good friend of Joseph P. Lash, national secretary of the American Student Union. Declining the invitation of Representative Starnes to take a place at the Committee table, the First Lady showed solidarity with the young folks by sitting beside them in the hearing room, to the delight of press photographers, and taking seven of them back to the White House for lunch each day in official cars.

In 1939, the American Youth Congress, yet another fruit of the Popular Front clime, claimed four and a half million members. These were not individuals, however, but persons who belonged to some sixty affiliated groups, ranging from the Y.W.C.A. to the American League for Peace and Democracy, from the Esperanto Association of North America to the Association of Lithuanian Workers. How many of the four and a half million knew that they were counted on the membership rolls of the congress is moot. Still, numbers of New Dealers, particularly in the National Youth Administration, took the A.Y.C. at its own estimate and listened attentively to the recommendations of its leaders on what should be done to help the nation's young people with employment and education. Their recommendations for federal aid in these areas no longer seems revolutionary. When it came to international affairs, however, the congress was another of those organizations, like the C.P. itself, whose passport for protest was good only up to the borders of the Soviet Union. It was made indignant by events in Mississippi and Mongolia and Madrid, but Moscow was Moscow's business. Although, as Congress leaders repeatedly emphasized, avowed Communists represented but a small minority on its governing body, they were invariably joined by fellow travelers to give the party line certain victory when the occasion demanded. The mechanics of Communist control have been set forth by Irving Howe and Lewis Coser:

> Let us suppose that a local branch of a Methodist youth organization, numbering a thousand, affiliated with the A.Y.C. Generally this would happen after one member—he might be a young Communist who had "colonized" or, better yet, a Methodist with "progressive" leanings—took the floor to propose affiliation to a Congress representing all of American youth. What, after all, could seem more reasonable? And naturally it would be the member who had made the proposal that would probably be sent as delegate to the A.Y.C. Soon most of the other young Methodists turned back to their Methodism and forgot about the A.Y.C. while their delegate continued to "represent" them. Thus, to control the bloc of votes he held, the A.Y.C. leadership needed to deal only with him and, more often than not, could ignore the members of his organization. It was neat.

As the hearings started, the presence of Mrs. Roosevelt and the absence of Mr. Dies seemed to have a calming effect on everyone. Whitley conducted the questioning of the A.Y.C. leaders politely and after being permitted to offer the Committee a petition for its abolition, they responded politely. They denied "absolutely" that they were Communist-dominated, and noted that their last congress had passed a resolution condemning "all forms of dictatorship" whether Communist, fascist or Nazi. They did not add that a resolution condemning Communism more directly had first been rejected, which placed the youngsters in a position of either voting for the second resolution or embarrassing themselves in public. Mrs. Roosevelt, ever largehearted in such matters, told reporters that she had conducted her own investigation long before the Dies Committee and found nothing "to indicate any outside control . . . nothing that was not within the actions which any American citizen could take with propriety." The young folks had simply lied to her, and she had believed them.

By one of those unhappy strokes that kept shaking front groups during these months, the Russians chose to invade Finland bare hours before the Youth Congress leaders proclaimed their independence to the Dies Committee. A few weeks later, more than 4,000 A.Y.C. delegates assembled in Washington for a Citizenship Institute. They sang their songs in a drenching February rain before the South Portico of the White House to the tune of *I Can't Give You Anything But Love, Baby:*

> We've been getting nothing else but love, Franklin.
> That's the thing youth has plenty of, Franklin.
> Dies has said that we're "red"; don't be misled.
> Lies are spread, when instead
> Jobs for Youth is where we're head-in'.

Then they stood silent as the President, who in 1937 had written them that they had "the good will and the best wishes of all who are concerned with the future of American democracy," strongly denounced the U.S.S.R. for its aggression. The only youthful cheers came when F.D.R. referred to a vote by their New York affiliate against a U.S. loan to Finland. At their congress early in 1940, the A.Y.C. refused to take a stand on the Soviet invasion just as the A.L.P.D. had refused to take a stand on the Nazi-Soviet pact, and shouted down a resolution

to bar from their organization all supporters of totalitarian organizations. For the rest of the year, the A.Y.C. denounced
the "war hysteria" in this country, termed the Administration's
defense program an effort to "Hitlerize" America, and opposed
aid to England, the sale of arms to belligerents, compulsory
military training and conscription. They favored strict neutral-
ity in any European war, and picketed the White House where
they had once been guests. "Don't lease or lend our lives!" was
their slogan in early 1941. By now even Mrs. Roosevelt had
given up on them, and refused to speak at their meetings. They
had to settle for Paul Robeson as their guest of honor. Then came
the German invasion of Russia and the peace-loving, sturdy-
lunged representatives of American youth demanded cooperation "with the peoples of the world to protect our national
interests and our security which are menaced by fascism." It
must sometimes have seemed to fellow travelers between 1939
and 1941 that the course of world affairs was directed to no
other end than to embarrass friends of the Soviet Union.

Where the leaders of the A.Y.C. would go down the line
into political eccentricity on the Stalinist train, singing about
Joe Hill, Joseph Lash was a more interesting case. His questioning by Matthews, who had been hastily summoned back from
New York by Starnes for the purpose, made for a less decorous
scene than Whitley's questioning of the lads from the A.Y.C.
Representative Rankin, sitting in on the proceedings, thought
Matthews did fine, but Mrs. Roosevelt disagreed. His "whole
attitude, tone of voice and phraseology," she observed in one
of her *My Day* columns, "made one feel that a prisoner, considered guilty, was being tried at the bar." Lash responded in
song: "If you see an un-American lurking near/ Why, alkalize
with Martin Dies and he will disappear." He was applauded,
and the session broke up amid a flurry of excitement when
Matthews charged abruptly that the previous day's denials of
Communist tendencies by A.Y.C. leaders were "false." "That's
not true!" cried one of them, jumping to his feet. Starnes told
him to sit down, and they all adjourned for lunch.

Lash was a young Socialist who split with his anti-Stalinist mentors in 1937 and succumbed to the dream of the united front. He wrote at the time: "Under the vigorous leadership of the Soviet Union (whom we are quick to berate but slow to praise) the world labor movement is rallying around the concept of collective action against the aggressor." In that year, the Oxford Peace Pledge, a personal renunciation of all wars, sponsored by the American Student Union, was abandoned in favor of a pledge against "imperialist" wars, in accord with the "collective security" line then coming into its own. Lash acknowledged that Communist influence within the A.S.U.— which had been created in 1935 by a merger of Communist and Socialist youth groups and never had more than a few thousand members—was strong. He had opposed the original merger and, when he came before J. B. Matthews, he had taken to heart the lesson of the Nazi-Soviet pact and was close to getting a divorce from his Communist associates—but he could not bring himself to do so under the auspices of the Dies Committee. "I tried not to answer questions," he explained a couple of years later, "because the more I answered questions here the more difficult it made my work in trying to get the Communist influence out of the A.S.U." Instead, he delivered speeches that he seemed to have saved from a junior high school play:

> I know that there are young Communists and I have had a great many disagreements with them, but I say if I am honest and can stand up against others in the light of day that they will have to give way, and that they are sincere and honest people and that it is the job of those of us who believe in democracy to talk with them, to work with them and to show them how democracy works.

Hardly had he finished telling the Committee that he believed that the Russian invasion of Finland should be condemned, then more than one hundred leaders of A.S.U. college chapters in New York City adopted a resolution defending the invasion of "a puppet state created and maintained by imperial powers from abroad." At the A.S.U. annual meeting in Madison, Wisconsin, Lash spoke against "those who are prepared to justify any policy of the Soviet Union," whereupon his comrades rejected a resolution condemning the attack on Finland by 322 to 29. Lash did not seek reelection.

Early in 1942, still under the patronage of Mrs. Roosevelt, Lash was given a second hearing by the Dies Committee, this time behind closed doors. Now he was seeking absolution from Dies so that he might obtain a commission in Naval Intelligence. He apologized for singing his song during his previous visit, and spoke much more frankly about the extent of Communist domination of both the A.S.U. and the A.Y.C. during their green years. Now the thirty-two-year-old Lash, whom Dies enjoyed calling "a perennial student", was general secretary of the International Student Service and was trying to keep his former collaborators out of positions of influence. He refused to become a source of names for the Communist-hunters, however, and instead of giving him clearance for a commission, the majority of the Committee, with Thomas as spokesman, judged that he ought to be drafted right away. Dies, on the other hand, felt that this would imperil U.S. security: "Anyone who has been active in Communist or Nazi movements should not be taken into our armed services." Lash, who had never requested deferment but had been placed in a 1-H classification because he was over twenty-eight, declared, in the language of A.S.U. platforms, that he "would be glad to serve with the millions of other young Americans in this great struggle for human freedom," and he wound up in the army.

The progress of men like Joseph Lash from a flirtation with Stalinism to marriage with the New York *Post* was not rare. The radical movement of the thirties was the training ground for many liberal warriors of the fifties. It nurtured a great deal of foolishness, but at the same time strained out the easy enthusiasms of youth and left the grownups politically more mature, in closer touch with America. But for Dies this was small progress indeed. In 1954 he still thought of Lash as a Communist, or at best a former Communist:

I submit that Mr. Lash's admission before our Committee that he had associated closely with the Communists and was in substantial agreement with the Communists was a confession that he was a Communist. It was not necessary for Joseph Lash to be a card-holding member of the Communist Party of the United States to be a Communist. It has been clearly established that some Communists do not hold a formal membership in the Party for strategic reasons.

Dies had, predictably, missed the whole meaning of Lash's experience. He saved his absolution for the repentant radical who chose to go the way of J. B. Matthews.

In the weeks preceding the turn of the year, as the time approached for the Committee's annual reckoning and reestablishment by Congress, Dies's normal hunger for publicity grew acute. It was now that he could be counted on to announce that Leon Trotsky and Diego Rivera were coming up from Mexico to testify and to promise on one of his frequent radio addresses that, given one more year, his Committee would see to the "deportation of no less than seven million aliens employed in American industries while Americans go without employment." Trotsky did not come (owing to Administration resistance, Dies charged); the seven million did not go; but the Committee carried on.

The public hearings of 1939 ended with testimony on Communist tactics by Jay Lovestone, who had been deposed as U.S. C.P. chieftain by Stalin in 1929, but that did not end the Committee's work for the year. On Sunday, December 10, in time to make the lean Monday newspapers, Dies released to the press a report written by J. B. Matthews on consumer groups. Matthews charged that all the major national consumer organizations, except for his own alma mater, Consumers Research (where his wife was still employed), were Communist transmission belts. He charged that many of their leaders, particularly the renegade founders of Consumers Union, were Communists in fact or at heart, and that all were engaged in a plot "to sabotage and destroy advertising, and through its destruction to undermine and help destroy the capitalist system of free enterprise." The Communists believed, he explained, that this was "a revolutionary tactic worthy of a great deal of attention."

That Communists were influential in consumer organizations such as the League of Women Shoppers was a reasonable surmise, but Matthews's report—riddled with inaccuracies, straining after incriminating clues, and relying heavily on mere assumption—was not a persuasive document. In one place he mentioned that an official in the Department of Agriculture had investigated *Good Housekeeping* magazine, and he went on: "While there is no record of the findings of the investigation being used as a basis for action against the magazine, it may be assumed that such was the intention." He quoted Arthur Kallet, one of the founders of Consumers Union, as saying that "cooperation does provide a splendid escape for participants in the day-to-day struggles against the capitalist system . . ." Matthews commented: "The politically informed person will have no difficulty in recognizing the strictly Communist phraseology of the foregoing statement." The exegesis told at least as much about Matthews as about Kallet.

As a preliminary indictment in preparation for an investigation of consumer groups, the Matthews report might have had some utility. But it was made public without benefit of any hearings whatever, and without the participation or even the knowledge of the other members of the Committee. Dies, Matthews, and two staff members held a brief and secret meeting at 6 p.m. on a Sunday evening; security was so tight that two weeks later other Committee members still did not know where the meeting had taken place. Wherever it was, Matthews presented the report and it was immediately released to the press. Voorhis complained that the work was "purely and simply the opinion" of Matthews, and post-publication protests kept it from ever being printed in the Committee record.

The union of Dies and Matthews had never been more productive. The staff director's vendetta against Consumers Union and all its allies mated perfectly with the chairman's quest after support from businessmen for his political ambitions. A few weeks before the issuance of the report, Dies promised the annual convention of the Associated Grocery Manufacturers

of America that he was about to give the consumers movement
the once-over, in appreciation of the fact, as *Business Week*
noted, that "Some businessmen have never been able to look
at the consumer movement without seeing red."

The activities of Matthews and certain friends leading up
to the report were equally unedifying. In August the Federal
Trade Commission had issued a complaint against the Hearst
Corporation's *Good Housekeeping* magazine, charging it with
"misleading and deceptive acts and practices in the issuance
of Guarantys, Seals of Approval and the publication in advertising pages of grossly exaggerated and false claims of products
advertised therein." Richard Berlin, executive vice president
of the Hearst magazines, retorted that subversive elements
such as Consumers Union were out to harm advertising in general. Shortly thereafter, Matthews attended a dinner at the
home of George Sokolsky, the conservative columnist and
sometime employee of the National Association of Manufacturers. Present were representatives of several big manufacturers of consumer goods as well as F. J. Schlink, Matthews's
former partner at Consumers Research. There the strategy was
developed to attack the competing consumer groups as anti-
advertising and Communist. The Dies Committee's report was
released to the New York papers by the Hearst organization,
at which time vice president Berlin, who had seen the report
before most of the members of the Committee, gave it his
personal seal of approval.[6]

The New Dealers on the Committee—Voorhis, Casey, and
Dempsey—whom Dies had efficiently ignored in his release of
both the A.L.P.D. names and the Matthews report, were
aroused yet again by a draft of the Committee's second annual
report. Presumably written by Matthews and destined never
to be made public, it charged that Communists had from the
beginning wielded "the dominant influence" in the C.I.O. and
reiterated the "shameful and alarming" finding that hundreds
of employees of the federal government belonged to the

---

[6] Relations between Matthews and *Good Housekeeping* had improved spectacularly since 1935, when the former was attacking the latter for having
reached "the nethermost depth of vulgarity on the subject of toilet tissue."

A.L.P.D. But now the liberal Democrats had a bargaining point; they threatened to issue a minority report and so emphasize the dissension within the Committee if the Matthews-Dies draft were not rewritten.

Dies gave in and the result, issued early in January 1940 was a sober statement, evenly divided between fascist and Communist activities, which began, unexceptionally:

> Every modern democratic nation is confronted by two pressing problems. The first is the preservation of the constitutional liberties which their people have gained through years of struggle; the second is the problem of adjusting the economic life to the difficulties of the machine age . . .

This was no longer the language of Matthews. Of the C.I.O. it reported mildly that while ten or twelve unions were "more than tinged" with Communism, the leadership had been trying to clean up the situation and "most of its largest organizations are free of Communist control, domination or even serious influences.[7] It listed only eleven organizations as Communist fronts, including the American Student Union but excluding the American Youth Congress, which it merely chided for permitting Communists to affiliate; and it did not mention consumer groups at all. It even warned against loose usage on the right of the epithet "Communist," and went so far as to remind the nation that during its united front phase the C.P. "was deliberately refraining from preaching Communism in any real sense of the term." The Committee's sternest critics had difficulty in faulting a report that *The New York Times* called "an astonishingly able and balanced document." As a further show of repentance, Dies decided not to make public a report of two Committee investigators on Communist activities in Hollywood.

---

[7] Voorhis, Casey, and Mason each expressed his regrets to the House later for the listing in the "more than tinged" category of the United Electrical, Radio and Machine Workers. They explained that James Carey, the union's president, had protested the slur. Some years later Carey would explain to another Congressional committee how he had discovered at just about this time that he was "isolated" in his own union: "It was now easy to spot the Communists because of their flip-flop on the war, and as months passed I discovered that they were in complete control of the national office; they dominated the executive committee, ran the union paper and were strongly entrenched in the locals and districts. All the organizers were Party-liners."

Flushed with this victory, Voorhis drew up a four-point recommendation for the improvement of Committee procedures and presented it to the Rules Committee. He called for a regular executive meeting at least once a week; an end to the issuance of public statements, press releases or reports which had not first been submitted to the entire Committee; efforts to call accused persons as soon as possible after the accusation had been made; and no public utterances by Committee members about ongoing investigations. There were smiles at the Rules Committee at the thought of Martin Dies being bound by such a table of etiquette, and the recommendation was set aside.

The House debate over continuing the Committee followed the previous year's pattern. Although a Gallup Poll, released in mid-December, showed a perceptible decline in support of the Committee following the release of the A.L.P.D. list, still three-quarters of the population appeared to favor its continuance. Some newspaper editorials again lamented the fact that Martin Dies had to be the one doing the job, but the majority agreed it was a job that had to be done. The House again heard Fish, Thomas, and Starnes defend the Committee as the bastion of our way of life and Coffee and New York City's Vito Marcantonio damn it as a corrupter of our liberties. Voorhis and Casey, while supporting continuance of the Committee, offered reasoned criticisms of their chairman's methods of operation. Dies himself, ill in Texas as he had been for much of the year, was not present to stand in his own defense—though he did muster the strength to deliver a radio talk criticizing the apathy of the Department of Justice in going after subversives, attributing his illness to his labors in behalf of America and warning that "Our government cannot survive unless Christianity remains firm in the hearts of our people." Mail in favor of the Committee was heavy, and many of the 344 Congressmen who voted for a third year's continuance (only 21 voted Nay) must have shared the feeling of Representative Eberharter:

> The House today is confronted with the choice of two evils. On the one hand, to adopt this resolution is to seemingly approve the

un-American procedure of the Special Committee to Investigate Un-American Activities. On the other hand, to defeat the resolution is to seemingly approve of a continuation of subversive activities.

The majority made peace with its doubts by cutting Dies's appropriation back to $75,000 for the new year.

4

★ ★ ★ ★ ★

1940: Popularity and Power

LIBERALS of all degrees were necessarily troubled by Martin Dies's outbreaks of vigilanteeism and by his unmistakable political intent. Those who had reveled in the Popular Front and still harbored soft feelings for their late allies, the Communists, were especially aroused, and some of them chose to reply to Dies in his own language. As he had labeled them Communists, they labeled him fascist. As he had placed them in the company of Earl Browder, they placed him in the company of Fritz Kuhn. Like Dies, the liberals who took this line were abiding by the Stalinist principle of "objective truth"— *viz.*, if a man's actions forward the cause of fascism (or Communism) then he is, objectively speaking, a fascist (or Communist) even if he is not literally a fascist (or Communist). A perilous form of reasoning which would lure the anti-Dies forces into a humiliating trap.

A leading voice in the long campaign against Dies belonged to *The Nation*, not Communist, never Communist, but displeased by anti-Communists. The burden of its charge, reiterated many times, was that the Texan was collaborating with the "reputable" periphery of the Christian Front and was avoiding an investigation of people such as Father Coughlin and Gerald L. K. Smith who, unlike Communist fronters, really warranted being investigated. There was good basis to the charge; even so thoroughgoing an anti-Communist as Westbrook Pegler commented: "The Dies Committee should have treated Coughlin just as it treated Earl Browder, but tiptoed around him for fear that he would cry up a holy war." Dies's critics on the left went much further, however, not hesitating to convict him of fascist proclivities. Certainly the small-town Texas lawyer felt more comfortable in the company of Legionnaires than of professors, and the people who cheered him at rallies where he said things like "God gave us America and the Marxists shall not take it away" did not represent the intellectual cream of American life. But if Dies could be convicted because he had spoken at a luncheon that Fritz Kuhn happened to attend; if it was proof of his fascism that he was praised by Joseph P. Kamp of the far-right Constitutional Educational League and had dealings with Merwin K. Hart of the far-right New York State Economic Council—both of whom in turn had dealings with a still shabbier class of patriots—then by a like syllogism the editors of *The Nation* and of most other liberal organs could without further ado be hung as Communists. They argued that Dies must have a warm spot for William Dudley Pelley of North Carolina, head of the frankly Jew-hating Silver Shirts, because the Committee hadn't been able to track him down for questioning. But those whom Sidney Hook has called our "totalitarian liberals" had for years been far more closely attached to Earl Browder—and Pelley's influence was hardly impressive beside that of the Communist leader's in his lionized days. Moreover, although Dies's claim to credit for the arrest on charges of sedition of seventeen Christian Fronters in New York[1] was merely humorous, he had spoken much more harshly about Nazism and fascism than such liberals as *Nation* editor Freda Kirchwey had spoken about Communism. Even loyal readers of *The Nation*, who were prepared to believe anything ill of the Congressman, however weakly grounded, must have wished that the evidence of a link between Dies and Pelley was a little more palpable, a little less conjectural . . . and suddenly, for a few days in January 1940, it seemed that their case was made.

On January 22, during the Rules Committee's perfunctory

---

[1] The subsequent acquittal of the Christian Fronters was used by champions of the Committee in Congress to show that Dies had been right not to bother about them.

hearings on the continuance of the Dies Committee, Congressman Frank E. Hook of Michigan, a ferocious opponent of Dies, announced that he possessed written evidence of an "understanding between Dies and Pelley." When Representative Starnes started to defend his absent chairman, Representative Cox of Georgia remarked, "He doesn't need any defense before this committee." Hook thereupon inserted in the record of the House excerpts from what he maintained were letters between Pelley and David Mayne, the Silver Shirt leader's representative in Washington. *The Nation* had evidently been given access to the evidence at the same time as Hook or even earlier, for its issue dated January 27 carried an article by assistant editor James Wechsler, who had outgrown the American Student Union and the Young Communist League, which contained portions of the alleged Pelley-Mayne correspondence. Written on stationery of "The Silver Shirt Legion of America," one of these letters referred to "the understanding that Dies will not go out of his way to embarrass us—True—Fr. Coughlin —George or the Legion." In another letter, Pelley explained that a booklet he had issued in 1939 attacking the Dies Committee for harassing Gentile patriots instead of finding out "whether there is any Jewish conspiracy against constitutional forms of government" was intended only "to create the general impression that there existed between Dies and myself a personal 'gripe' sufficient to keep us apart from any form of cooperation . . . and was actually intended . . . to offset any rumors —in the event of suspicion—that he and I through mutual contacts had an understanding." Wechsler delighted in the scoop. But within a week these letters were shown to have been part of a hoax; it was a case of the desire to believe sending respectable men headlong into a slough of gullibility.

The innocent strategist behind the anti-Dies plot was Gardner Jackson, legislative representative of Labor's Non-Partisan League, an indefatigable worker for the underdog, whose name had naturally found its way onto many of J. B. Matthews's lists. Jackson was no Communist, and he had earned, by earnest works, a reputation for integrity as well as for courage and good will, but the thought of the Dies Committee clouded his

nobler faculties. He set a young associate named Harold Weisberg on the track of Dies. Assisted by Drew Pearson, Weisberg
made contact with Mayne, who obligingly turned over the
letters—to put Jackson "out on a limb," he later explained.
Weisberg paid Mayne $105 and promised him a job in the
Department of Agriculture.

With this material in hand, Jackson held a dinner party in
mid-January for a few New Deal Congressmen to discuss how
the letters might be used against Dies as the debate over continuing his Committee approached. Most of Gardner's guests
were skeptical of the letters, and advised against using them,
but Hook, a New Dealer whose mind could not keep apace of
his temper, was . . . yes, hooked. As Pelley himself would later
interpret the event to reporters, "I think he was just played for
a sucker, don't you?" Mayne, who had previously been employed by the Committee to try to get Pelley to testify, had set
as a condition of his handing over the letters that he would be
notified before they were used; Weisberg so notified him,
whereupon, according to some reports, Mayne notified the
Committee counsel, Rhea Whitley. The Committee, it was later
suggested by mortified liberals, had actually hired private detectives to sell false documents to Congressmen who craved
them. This was never proven, but whatever the Committee
staff's part in the initial plotting of this comedy-mystery, they
rubbed their hands at the denouement. Mayne unresistingly
admitted his forgery at once to Dies's young friend, Committee
investigator Robert Stripling, who from then on took credit
for breaking the case. Mayne was eventually brought to trial
for his prank; he pleaded guilty and received a suspended
sentence.

Hook's response, as it dawned upon him that he had been
most grievously taken in, was that of the captain who attempts
to sustain his sinking ship by blustering back at the hurricane:

> If there is any question of forgery then the Dies Committee is
> guilty of conspiracy to bribe a person to commit forgery to cover
> up their past nefarious acts. It is typical Dies Committee smear-
> ing to befog the real issue of collaboration with those closely
> connected with the Christian Front . . . There was only one real

effort to overthrow the government of the United States, and that came from below the Mason-Dixon line. It looks as if another effort is coming from that source.

Hook made much of an affidavit from Mayne to the effect that the signatures on the letters were those of Pelley, and he refused to apologize for entering them into the Record—though he relented to the extent of agreeing to withdraw them, a concession that the defenders of Dies, overjoyed at the way the case had developed, would not accept without an accompanying apology. Hook continued to rant, demanding that the Department of Justice investigate the "charges of forgery, collusion and conspiracy."

At an open meeting of the Committee on February 6, where Mayne testified that he had simply traced the signatures, leaving out the second "e" in Pelley on purpose, Hook, according to an eye-witness account, stood over him "trembling with rage" and "roared his questions until he was requested to stand at the other end of the Committee table." Only then did the choleric gentleman from Michigan finally apologize—"If the House feels its integrity impugned or if any member is aggrieved, I do not hesitate to apologize"—and the forgeries were expunged. A year later he would still be exorcising his embarrassment, blaming everything on "investigators who cooperate and collaborate with men to mislead and entrap a Member of Congress for the purpose of smearing him before the public because he had the courage of his convictions . . ." *The Nation* dealt with the unfortunate fate of its scoop by making light of the letters that had seemed so dramatic to its editors a week or two before. The emphasis on the forgeries, they now protested, was designed to obfuscate the evidence of Dies's hobnobbing with Christian Fronters. Martin Dies, still at home in Orange, Texas, recovering from influenza and a ruptured appendix, was all at once, and most strangely, martyr as well as prosecutor and judge.[2]

[2] In his autobiography Dies claims that the incident of the letters was but one of repeated low efforts to destroy his work. These included, he writes, a New Deal conspiracy to slander him as an income tax evader, an attempt to kidnap his son Bobby, and a plot, which he only narrowly escaped, to entrap him with a pretty girl in her room at the Mayflower Hotel.

At the climax of the affair, William Dudley Pelley, whom the Committee had supposedly been seeking for months to no avail in the back alleys of North Carolina, suddenly appeared in Washington. The Committee, lacking the services of Whitley whose resignation had gone unnoticed in the furor over the Mayne letters, hastily called Pelley before it, for the first, and completely unplanned, public hearing of the year. Stripling would claim credit for this accomplishment too, but it did nothing to enhance the Committee's glory. Starnes presided and obtained little from the long-sought witness other than vagueness as to the Silver Shirts's financial arrangements and compliments—"God bless this Committee"—that could only be compromising from such a source. "I'm giving Martin Dies an absolutely clean bill of health," Pelley told reporters outside the hearing room. "I admire the work he's done." He expressed particular fondness while testifying for Representative Thomas, whom he commended fulsomely for demanding the impeachment of Mme Perkins. "I may say I have yet to admire any action of yours," retorted Thomas. "I am sorry," replied Pelley with fine North Carolina grace, "because I think your work is splendid, splendid." Starnes finally dismissed him with a denunciation of his evil principles, and he was afterward arrested for violating the good behavior proviso in a suspended sentence he had received some years before in a stock fraud case.

William Dudley Pelley was one of those slightly cracked, slightly crooked characters who provided handfuls of followers and a much larger number of opponents with a bit of stimulation in the years of fascism's victories. The rabidity of his anti-Semitism was certified by the stream of pamphlets from his publishing operation in Asheville. "I don't hold any hatred toward any Jews in the United States," he told the Committee, and a few minutes later added, "I feel exactly as the Nazi Party in Germany felt in regard to Germany, regarding the Jewish element in our population, yes sir." The menace he inspired he owed mainly to the fears of the times and the desire on the left to locate and put on display un-Americanism elsewhere than in the Communist Party; Pelley took their attention as a tribute to his effectiveness and made as much of it as he could. That was not much, but today, as yesterday, there is no group in the land so trivial or so lunatic that it cannot arouse anxiety among the anxiety-prone and be exposed in press and from podium to its own boundless satisfaction.

As the stir over Pelley subsided, a recuperated Dies returned to Washington and the leadership of his Committee. His sights were set now on the middling Communist Party functionary: "We're going to try to get all the Communist leaders to come before our Committee, and they will be asked to supply the names. If they don't we will institute contempt proceedings against them. The law will permit the government to keep them in jail if they don't talk." In the first spring weeks of 1940, Dies exhibited a rather private understanding of what was permitted the chairman of a Congressional committee by the laws on which he was relying to keep Communists in jail. At his direction, Committee investigators carried out a series of raids on C.P. offices in the East, climaxing with an assault on the Philadelphia headquarters of the Communist Party and the International Workers Order. On April 12, two investigators, assisted by eight Philadelphia detectives and a squad of motorcycle police, broke into the offices, filled a two-ton truck with books, pamphlets, and files, and sped away across the Delaware River Bridge into New Jersey.

When Federal Judge George A. Welsh angrily ordered the arrest of the raiders and asked Dies not to use his captured documents until the court could pass on a C.P. petition to recover them, the chairman replied that it was too late; he had already placed them in the official record. Fourteen years later, in a magazine interview, Dies was still chuckling over this coup:

> Once I got a big haul in Philadelphia. I knew there was a federal judge there who was going to give us trouble so I had it timed and grabbed the stuff about four o'clock and rushed it to a secret place. I had a photostat machine set up and we spent all night making copies of this stuff. The next morning the federal judge issued an injunction. He ordered all the records to be returned, arrested two of my investigators, and so I hid out in a blind office

until we completed the photostating. Then I came out and announced we were going to honor and obey this injunction.

In May, Judge Welsh ruled the Committee raids illegal, as violations of the Fourth Amendment, and his eleven-page decision was a ringing defense of the civil liberties of unpopular minorities. The Communists, he observed, are "very much in the minority in our country, but their rights which they claim were invaded are rights that are sacred to us all." Dies could not share this view. He replied: "If we can't obtain legally records of a revolutionary group, records that show seditious activities, then there is no way to defend democracy." For all the dash of their abduction, the Philadelphia records never proved of value to anyone, so far as is known, and certainly they revealed nothing in the way of subversive activities. But the case did provide a view into Dies's conception of the Constitution—which he once described as "simply different words for the Sermon on the Mount." He expressed outrage at the court's defense of "agents of foreign dictators who claim constitutional rights and shirk constitutional duties"—and began a campaign—more oratorical than legislative—for laws to set matters straight.

Dies, as always, wanted names, but the C.P. officials he called up in late March and early April refused to provide them. A Pittsburgh man refused to tell the Committee the real name of the member who used the pseudonym "Franklin Delano Roosevelt" in his Party dues book. (A *Daily Worker* editorial, in its usual spirit of fun, declared that any suggestion that the warmonger Roosevelt was a C.P. member was an insult to the Party.) The C.P. secretary for western Pennsylvania yelled: "I will not give you any names of any people because you are trying to build up a blacklist." The secretary for the District of Columbia and Maryland was defiant: "To answer these questions would assist the Committee in the establishment of a general blacklist of Communists which would make it difficult and uncomfortable for those named to hold jobs and only because of their beliefs." The president of the Massachusetts Young Communist League would not give the names of his fellow members at Harvard on the grounds that they would be subjected to economic persecution in violation of the due process amendment of the Constitution. And the executive secretary of the New England C.P., a particularly obstreperous witness, refused flatly to answer any questions until the Committee allowed him to read a statement from "ten thousand citizens of Boston." "Throw him out!" yelled the audience.

These five persons were cited for contempt by the Committee; there was no question of the readiness of the House to approve the citations—indeed, as it turned out, to approve them unanimously. But again, Dies, impatient with the ordinary course of the law in contempt cases, which called for House approval followed by a grand jury hearing, took a shortcut in getting at the two New England Communists. Without placing the matter before the House, he had them jailed in Washington on warrants obtained directly from a U.S. commissioner. They were promptly freed on a writ of habeas corpus, and a few days later a court ruled that their constitutional rights had been violated by the abbreviated procedure.

Four of the five cases hung fire for the duration of the war. (The C.P. secretary for western Pennsylvania pleaded *nolo contendere*, settling for a six-month suspended sentence and a fine of $150.) The Pittsburgh man was finally acquitted because of the use of coercive tactics by the Committee. The indictment against the man with the petition from Boston was dismissed in 1947 on a motion of the government. The Party official from the District of Columbia and the Young Communist League president were found guilty and sentenced, respectively, to a thirty-day suspended sentence and a fine of $250, and a one-to-six-month suspended sentence and a fine of $150.

A few years after these first contempt-of-Committee cases were mildly resolved, there arose a spate of constitutional challenges to the Committee's powers which would define somewhat the rights of recalcitrant witnesses, but in 1940 a readily resistable force had apparently met a temporarily immovable object, and the result was a standoff. Having been rebuffed in his efforts to increase the efficiency of the law and, incidentally, his own powers, Dies was left with the alternative of continuing to call up Communists who would continue to refuse to testify even though they might wind up in jail in due course. This rigmarole was not in the chairman's style. As Ogden notes, "Even the publicity was lacking, as witnesses who refuse to speak do not make good newspaper copy save on the first or second occasion." So impatient was Dies that several Party officials were dismissed without contempt proceedings despite their refusal to name names.

Dies fired off a final salvo for the benefit of page-one scanners when he sent out subpoenas to ninety leaders of Communist and fascist groups to come to Washington and bring their records with them, but, like so many of his announced campaigns, it never went beyond the gesture. He satisfied himself with predicting that the Communists' tactics would bring legislation requiring all political organizations with international affiliations to register with the Secretary of State and to keep their records open. He never did much about this either—the rigors of drawing up laws and of trying to get them passed seemed to weary him—but in June 1940 the Congress did pass an expanded version of the Smith Act which called for the registration and fingerprinting of all aliens over fourteen, the deportation of the criminals and subversives among them (especially, its sponsors hoped, the detested Harry Bridges), and, in the spacious language of the final bill, defined it a crime "to teach and advocate the overthrow of the United States Government by force and violence." (Representative McCormack specially wished it to be remembered that the "teach and advocate" provision was his contribution to the measure.) A version of this bill had already passed the House over the opposition of a small number of liberals in July 1939, as war jitters began to afflict the nation, and although it would have cleared the Senate easily even without benefit of the Dies Committee's spring hearings, these did undoubtedly whet the appetites of alien-eaters around the land. As Representative Celler said when the bill returned to the House from the Senate in June 1940: "Candidly, I am informed that if we do not accept this bill, we will get one far worse. Any bill containing dreadful provisions against the alien would pass this House with no substantial opposition. In common parlance, it would go through 'like a dose of salts.'" And indeed, it went through by a vote of 382 to 4, with only Marcantonio speaking against it.[3]

A child, frustrated in carrying out an adventure in which he has invested an hour's dreams, will often seek comfort in a retreat to the proven pleasures of yesterday. So, in the weeks following his unprofitable encounter with the lesser Communists, Dies went to the Spanish Civil War, to the C.I.O., to Hollywood, in search of the satisfactions he had been denied elsewhere. And although none of these brief hearings carried the punch that he liked, each was in its way instructive.

The testimony on the Abraham Lincoln Brigade from volunteers and their relatives provided a taste of an especially bitter part of the bitter war in Spain: the use by the Stalinists of their control of the international brigade to carry on their own vendetta against anti-Stalinists. It would always be hard for Loyalist sympathizers in America to face up to this aspect of the Spanish tragedy, and the last person in the world they could take instruction from on so sensitive a matter was Martin Dies, who had never been heard to utter an unkind word about Franco. Yet the story of the war in Spain and of the traumas of American liberalism are not complete without a chapter on the brutalities of the commissars behind the Loyalist lines. The Dies Committee, for its part, showed no interest in any of the other chapters.

The union leaders to whom Dies devoted himself in April and May—Harry Bridges, Mervyn Rathbone of the American Communications Association, and Michael J. Quill of the Trans-

---

[3] Marcantonio, the tough, hard-working demagogue from East Harlem and Washington's exemplary fellow traveler, warned about the Smith Act taking us "with seven-league boots toward establishing in America, in free America, the slavelike institutions of Nazi Germany." But when the "teach and advocate" law was first used against Trotskyites during the war, the *Daily Worker* supported the prosecution, with an argument that might have been quoted from Martin Dies: "The American people can find no objection to the destruction of the Fifth Column in this country. On the contrary, they must insist on it." When, after the war, the C.P. leaders themselves were brought to trial for violating the Smith Act, Communists discovered again that a question of civil liberties was involved and hastened to defend our free institutions.

port Workers Union—had all been charged with Communist affiliations and sympathies innumerable times before, and the latest witnesses, former members of their unions, only added a few more instances of Communists-at-work to an already substantial body of testimony. Rathborne, who had recently been honored by the President with a position on the board of the National Youth Administration, came before the Committee attended by Vito Marcantonio as his counsel, and politely denied everything. Quill put on a much livelier show. He referred to his predecessor as head of the Transport Workers, Thomas Humphrey O'Shea (who told the Committee he was ejected from the leadership by Communists so that Quill could take over) as "your stool pigeon" and when Representative Thomas demanded that the designation be struck from the record, Quill agreed to change it to "lunatic."

Quill, the former subway station agent, was fresh from having been refused the nomination of the American Labor Party for reelection to the New York City Council. The A.L.P., then attempting to cleanse its ranks of Communists, disowned him when he could not bring himself to criticize the Nazi-Soviet pact. "They are digging up some phoney idea about the Soviet-German pact," Quill explained to the Committee. "I don't know what it had to do with building sewers in Bronx County, New York, but they wanted me to take a stand in it and support the war policy of Chamberlain. We don't support that by anybody. We in the labor movement are against war and anybody who causes war." In this latter group he included the Dies Committee. "You are trying to bring about a war hysteria to stampede the American people into war." He made an impossible witness, loud, gross, and about as responsive as an opposing left tackle; he exasperated even the tolerant Voorhis. When the chairman said, "He came here for the purpose of insulting this Committee," no one could challenge the observation. Finally, when Dies was unable to quiet him down and stop him from hollering about "sabotage" on the subways, he was forcibly ejected from the hearing room, crying "Labor will live!" all the way out.

The lumpy leader of the subway and trolley drivers was very

much the professional Irishman, regaling anybody who would gather round with his purported experiences in the I.R.A. as a boy, but only the politically color-blind could believe that his favorite color was green. His Communism never went deep, however, and as the fashion in political cosmetics changed around 1948, he was able to kick his comrades out and forego ideological coloration entirely. Many Communists of the thirties, wrongheaded and brutal though they frequently were, showed considerable courage when the pressure was on. "Red Mike" Quill never cared that much. The great achievement of his thirty-year career as ruler of the T.W.U. was his tenacity in holding to power with the collusion of New York City's Democratic Party machine; his Marxism was blarney from the start, and some months before his death in 1966, the former radical was demanding that a policeman be installed on every bus in New York to save his bourgeois drivers from the depredations of the downtrodden.

In July, Dies, sitting as a one-man committee in executive session, took testimony from a John L. Leech who identified himself as an ousted member of the Hollywood Communist Party. Leech was like those Slavonians described by Rousseau who spent their lives wandering about and submitting to be baptized where they found it worth their while. In addition to revealing that Young Communist Leaguers in California were luring soldiers and sailors to Red socials, he named forty-two actors, actresses, writers, producers, and directors as C.P. members, sympathizers, or contributors. In an unaccustomed show of restraint, Dies did not make public their names, but a few weeks later a Los Angeles grand jury, which for some unaccountable reason had also taken testimony from Leech, released a score of them to the press. It turned out to be a mixed bag— containing both flaming devotees of the Party and persons who had merely lent their names or their money to some apparently worthy cause in which the C.P. had a hand. Leech was habituated to making strong charges against well-known individuals and then backing down when pressed for evidence or confronted by the accused. Most of his testimony dribbled away like sand. Still the nation was treated to the odd experience of reading that the great stars in whom it had invested so much of its emotional life, those near-mythical figures, were appearing one by one before a Congressman from Orange, Texas, for absolution. Dies, sitting alone, received, heard, and issued his clearances to James Cagney, Humphrey Bogart, and Fredric March, to Franchot Tone, Luise Rainer, and Francis Lederer. Neither he nor they gave any sign that they recognized some presumption in these proceedings. (Years afterward, Representative John Rankin of Mississippi, annoyed at Fredric March for his participation in the Independent Citizens Committee of the Arts, Sciences and Professions, would remind the House that the actor had been "identified as a member of the Communist Party by a Party member who testified under oath before the Tenney Fact Finding Committee of the State of California." Such are the uses of the Leeches among us.) [4]

The nervousness of the Hollywood community when faced with the kind of attack at which Martin Dies was expert would be exhibited on a wider screen in 1947. But already in 1940, mere liberals among the actors and directors were being outmaneuvered on both right and left. In response to one of Dies's periodic pledges to investigate subversive influences in Hollywood, the town's fellow travelers organized a meeting in Philharmonic Hall. A skit, *When Martin Comes,* written by Donald Ogden Stewart, a scenarist of comedies and pillar of fellow traveldom, was performed by the author and Dorothy Parker, who had mislaid her renowned wit for the occasion. Every line betrayed the sources of its inspiration, and the production helps

[4] Witness Leech also brought up the name, in the closed hearings in Beaumont, Texas, of a California Congressman, Franck Havenner. Leech claimed to have met Havenner at gatherings where only Communists were *persona grata,* and although he confessed to a lack of documentation on the matter, he allowed that it was his "understanding" that the Congressman was a member of the Communist Party. Nothing of this was made public until the 1944 campaign, when an anti-Havenner advertisement in the San Francisco *Chronicle,* sponsored by "a group of citizens who believe in good government and the American way of life", carried selected portions of the testimony. None of the members of the Dies Committee, with the exception of the chairman, had been aware of its existence, but the mystery of its release was lifted somewhat when it was learned that before the 1944 campaign James H. Steadman, a Committee investigator who took part in the Leech interview, went to work for Albert C. Mattei, president of the Honolulu Oil Company, a major financial supporter of the Republican cause in northern California and the chief backer of Havenner's opponent in 1944.

us to recall how funny were Hollywood's serious movies of the period. Here is an excerpt from Miss Parker's entirely unsatiric climactic speech:

> . . . The people want democracy—real democracy, Mr. Dies, and they look toward Hollywood to give it to them because they don't get it any more in their newspapers. And that's why you're out here, Mr. Dies—that's why you want to destroy the Hollywood progressive organizations—because you've got to control this medium if you want to bring fascism to this country . . . We're grateful to Hollywood for our jobs and we're grateful for the opportunity it gives us to speak for American democracy . . .

We shall hear again from those Hollywood voices who, in their next encounter with the Un-American Activities Committee, will tell us in equally hapless prose that our choice in America rests between fascism and them.

The Committee was called upon to sit as judge in yet another case at about this time: a dispute between Representative Wright Patman, a relic of populism from Texas, and Carl Byoir, the preeminent public relations man. While serving the Great Atlantic and Pacific Tea Company, Byoir had helped defeat an effort by Patman to restrict the operations of chain stores. Now Patman charged that Byoir was a German agent, retained by Adolf Hitler through George Sylvester Viereck, "to sell Hitlerism to America." As he warmed to his subject, Patman added that Byoir was supposed to set up "the greatest spy organization in the history of the world" and was unfit to wear the uniform of a lieutenant colonel in the U.S. army reserve.

The nature of the public relations craft does not allow of superfluous fastidiousness in the choice of clients and Byoir, as the McCormack-Dickstein hearings had disclosed years before, had indeed served the German Tourist Bureau at a fee of $6,000 a month from 1933 to 1935, but beyond that he seemed to be as clean as the requirements of his profession permitted. Patman came before the Committee with much more indignation than evidence. The F.B.I. had already cleared Byoir; a subcommittee of the Dies Committee had also cleared him; in September the full Committee cleared him; and again, in August of the following year, for once and all, it "fully exonerated" Byoir "of any charges reflecting on his Americanism or loyalty to the government of the United States." Congressman Patman, having made his accusations while wearing the cloak of Congressional immunity, could not be fitted with a libel suit. It was a passing incident for the Committee, an engagement which, for a change, it had not sought, and which it performed with a sense of fairness that it did not always exert in the cases of persons accused of being hirelings of Moscow, but it raised a question that would prove troublesome in years to come: What is an appropriate tribunal for adjudicating public charges against a man's loyalty? The fact that the job could have fallen to a body like the Dies Committee indicated how far we were in 1940 from a sensible answer.

Dies made passes at other national threats that spring and summer—propaganda in textbooks and conspiracies in Mexico, the T.V.A.,[5] and the W.P.A.—but he was an impatient fisherman. His eye was readily caught, his net quickly cast, but if the game did not jump in at once he moved on. And in these latter months of 1940 there was an inviting place for him to move. Suddenly that spring the war in Europe had turned real; the German blitzkrieg swept through the Low Countries; Mussolini joined Hitler; France fell. In this country attention turned to the rush build-up of war industries, and for the quasi-official hunters of subversion this was taken as an opportunity to cry sabotage. Their cause was abetted by the Communist union leaders, still opposed to aiding Britain, who were bent on creating as much industrial turbulence as they could. As Congress debated the problem of what to do about aliens, particularly those in the defense program, Dies won the standing applause of the House with a half-hour speech on the Trojan Horse in our midst. He reported that he was swamped with "new leads,"

[5] The entirely unincriminating T.V.A. hearings would be exhumed in 1947 by Senator McKellar of Tennessee in an attempt to block the nomination of Gordon Clapp as T.V.A. administrator and of David Lilienthal as chairman of the Atomic Energy Commission. Legislators and publicists of all political hues have found that selected excerpts from transcripts can be useful even when the hearing taken in its entirety does not prove what they wish it had proved.

including an unconfirmed one that the Germans were building air bases in Mexico, and he asked for another $100,000 for his Committee.

Soon he was warning that "Foreign governments have placed agents and saboteurs in every key industry, and unless the government acts within thirty days I predict a series of actual sabotage that will cripple the whole national defense program." A chemist told a subcommittee of Starnes, Voorhis, and Mason of three instances of suspected sabotage at his Pennsylvania shipbuilding firm—such as the stuffing of pieces of a sweater into the oil pressure system of a ship, which he attributed to Communists and Nazis in the vicinity. Starnes warned that there were hundreds of Bundsmen, Communists, and aliens employed in defense plants. Dies improved on this, declaring that there were 5,000 in Detroit alone, and he was planning to publish industry-by-industry lists of all workers with Communist, Nazi, or fascist connections. In this group he included not only Bundists and C.P. card holders, but members of suspect unions such as the N.M.U. and the T.W.U. When the Hercules powder plant in New Jersey blew up in September, killing fifty-one persons and threatening to throw an uneasy nation into a proper panic, Dies proclaimed it was the very incident of sabotage that he had predicted the year before, when federal officials had just "laughed at us."

A few weeks after the Hercules explosion, Congress voted an additional $35,000 to carry the Committee through the end of the year. This brought its total appropriation to $235,000—the largest amount ever appropriated for a special investigating committee in the experience of the chairman of the Committee on Accounts—and it pepped up Dies's attack on federal security measures. "Employers say they cannot fire some of these saboteurs because of the National Labor Relations Board," he protested, and delivered a Texas threat—"We may have a showdown on that." He announced that he had been sending material on the activities of foreign counsulates to the State Department, and threatened to make his information public if the government didn't crack down. He kept demanding an "early answer" from Roosevelt and the Republican Presidential candidate Wendell Willkie, both of whom had criticized the Committee's work, to the question he first put to them in August: "Whether or not, you will advocate, favor and support legislation which will outlaw the Communist Party, the German-American Bund, the fascist organizations and, in fact, all political organizations that are shown to be under the control of foreign governments or the agencies of foreign governments." When, on November 12, three powder plants in the east were blown up within one hour of each other, Dies was ready with a warning that "the acts of sabotage in the past twenty-four hours are only a beginning." He promised to ask Congress for four or five million dollars in order to "close in" on subversive elements throughout the country. Thomas took the occasion of the mysterious explosions to demand "a shake-up in our government so that there will be no more coddling of subversive groups or activities. The federal government should cooperate with the employers so that they can get tough about whom they hire and fire." In particular, he wanted them to be tough on aliens in defense work: "If these men want to work in these industries and these plants, why aren't they patriotic enough to become American citizens?"

Dies offered little evidence to support his riot of charges, and did not stay to see if his predictions would come true. (When he spoke of imminent sabotage in West Coast airplane factories, California's Governor Olson humorously asked him for additional details so that preventive measures might be taken.) But events in Europe made his warnings seem far from incredible. The fifth column was a popular dramatic subject, and even F.D.R. conceded that the Dies Committee had provided the government with some information about its doings. The suspicion of aliens which had resulted in the patriotic excesses of World War I was visible again, with anti-alien legislation being much advocated in the Capitol by men like Thomas and a group of Southern representatives, led by Smith of Virginia, Cox of Georgia, and Rankin of Mississippi.[6] It was a frighten-

[6] Among the alien-baiting laws proposed in the House during these years (F.D.R. commented in 1940 that they were coming through at the rate of three a minute) were bills to deport aliens considered "inimical to the public

ing time; there was no reason to doubt that potential fifth columnists were at large and everyone was agreed that something ought to be done about them. What is surprising is not that Dies's hazily substantiated charges should have been taken as evidence of anything besides showmanship, but that despite all the tough talk in Congress, the final results were so mild. We did succumb to the Smith Act, but faced with a far greater threat than in 1917, the nation behaved with far more dignity. In part this was due to less provocation—there was not the kind of opposition among radicals to our participation in World War II that there had been to World War I; but, more important, Franklin Roosevelt proved in this test a sturdier bulwark of civil liberties than Woodrow Wilson.

It took much less political shrewdness than F.D.R. possessed to see that the constant assailing of aliens was merely one more way that his Congressional opponents had found of shooting at their favorite targets—the C.I.O. and the National Labor Relations Act and, through them, at the whole New Deal and all its hated progeny. The twelve-day Vultee aircraft strike in November 1940 was for the New Deal's enemies an opportunity to launch a particularly strong attack on the N.L.R.B. which, they charged, was preventing employers from firing the hoards of subversive aliens in defense plants. The Vultee strike was led by U.A.W. organizers who had been called Communists by John Frey at the start of the Dies Committee hearings, and an F.B.I. investigation of the strike confirmed that it was Communist-directed. Within a year, the U.S.S.R. having entered the war, America's Communists would be patriotic to the point of strike-breaking, but in 1940 they were opposed to the U.S. defense effort and were doing what they could to impede it. Vultee was at the time the only firm producing training planes for the army; to the anti-C.I.O. nativists, the strike bore out all their premonitions of Red subversion, and they were not disposed to suffer their anxieties in silence. "We have coddled that bunch of cutthroats long

---

interest," to deport aliens who did not take out their citizenship papers within three months, to deport all aliens and prohibit all immigration, and, from Representative Howard Smith, to ban aliens from the practice of optometry.

enough!" proclaimed Representative Sumners of Texas, chairman of the House Judiciary Committee, in a debate on the Vultee strike, aliens, and subversives in general:

> They respect just one thing and I am in favor of giving them a double dose of their own medicine. They preach force. The time has come when America has got to subject them to the only sort of argument that they pay any attention to, and that is all there is to it . . . They come over here, a lot of them do, driven from the countries of their nativity, and they do not more than get to this country until they begin to try to tell Americans how to run this government. We have had enough of it.

His remarks, applauded by his audience, were not the most intemperate of the day—Representative Smith proposed punishing sabotage in defense industries with life imprisonment—and Voorhis pardonably dramatized the temper of his colleagues when he said, "I think the House at the present time is in a completely totalitarian state of mind."

Dies was very much a part of the nativist group, but what brought him into open conflict with the Administration was not the treatment of aliens, about whom he and the Department of Justice definitely differed, but the treatment of pro-German propagandists about whom they quite agreed. Dies had promised to hold no public hearings during the 1940 election campaign, and although he abided by the letter of his pledge, his spirit was not subdued. His calls in speeches and news releases for immediate dismissal from defense plants of workers "suspected of subversive activities" never flagged, and his book *The Trojan Horse in America*—in large part a review of J. B. Matthews's testimony on front groups involving New Dealers—came out in time for the campaign. But Attorney General Robert Jackson, whose distaste for Martin Dies was not classified material—did not pick up the gauntlet until late in November. F.D.R. had been awarded his third term, the Democrats were in secure control of Congress, and Dies had, by issuing with great fanfare a White Book on German operations in this country, opened himself to the charge of interfering with the work of our official law-enforcement agencies.

The Committee's White Book, a collation of correspondence gathered in a series of raids by Committee investigators, presented evidence that organizations such as the Transocean News Service, the German Library of Information, and the German Railroad Office[7] were subsidized by German consulates in this country, and in addition to preaching appeasement were trying to fix up useful business arrangements for the Third Reich. A *New York Times* editorial gave a fair assessment of the report, finding it of value but somewhat anticlimactic after the advance build-up. (Dies had announced that the work of Nazis in the United States would be "destroyed" as a result of his exposé, which was "unique in American history.") The *Times* wrote:

> To anyone who knows the structure of the German Reich, there is nothing surprising in the evidence that German consuls have helped to subsidize a Nazi propaganda service, or that German businessmen have been planning trade conquests in the hemisphere. The Dies "White Book" seems to tell chiefly of little schemes and little men, and of techniques as clumsy as Von Papen's in the days of the World War.

Dies's conclusion that he had uncovered an espionage ring was a leap of imagination; the German representatives came through as more human creatures than the journalism of the day gave them credit for being. Particularly touching in the published correspondence were the pleas for money to the German Embassy in Washington of poor Manfred Zapp, who had been sent to this country in 1938 to run the Transocean News Service: "My postage stamp supply is sufficient for four days, thanks to your remittance of August 1 . . . Berlin has just now sent us $934. That is merely a drop in the bucket. From this I was able to pay immediately the rent, telephone and telegraph bills of last month and the wages . . . I already am dunned from every side and keep away from my office as much as possible." To a German minister in South Africa,

---

[7] The German Railroad Office was surely one of the most feckless covers for subversion ever conceived by the Aryan mind. It was ostensibly in the business of encouraging Americans to come visit the romantic castles of Germany while the war was going on.

he wrote steadfastly: "Almost all New York is enraged against the German barbarians. That is the atmosphere in which I must spread Transocean. However, I believe that I will still succeed in handling the local press." His success was not stunning. When a representative of a Cleveland newspaper expressed interest in taking his service, Zapp told him all about what he was offering, only to have the man publish the whole story in the New York *World Telegram*. ". . . We cannot co-operate with people who are so dishonorable," Zapp decided.

Two days after the White Paper was issued, Attorney General Jackson, in a statement to the press, accused Dies of interfering with the work of the F.B.I. The Committee's prime source, one Fassbender, was, Jackson said, "known as a professional and unreliable informer," of no value in court. (Dickstein, who had had occasion to throw Fassbender out of his office, was left with the impression that the man was "hungry and starving. He would have sold his mother for a dollar and a good meal.") The F.B.I. had been investigating the German representatives for many months, noted Jackson, and the Committee paper would make the building of a legal case that much more difficult. Because of its release, the Justice Department was compelled to bring charges against Manfred Zapp before a grand jury at once although its case was not yet complete. Jackson's statement concluded:

> The F.B.I. has gone about its task in an efficient and workmanlike manner without alarmist tactics and without sensationalism. It will continue to supply the proper agencies and government authorities with reliable, thoroughly sifted evidence as to subversive activities in this country. Efforts to arouse public sentiment or emotion, if that is desirable, will have to come from other sources.

By pitting Dies against J. Edgar Hoover instead of against F.D.R. and by choosing Nazis rather than Communists to fight over, the Administration had gotten the best possible odds for itself, and Dies tried at once to shift the grounds of the quarrel back to tried territory. He attacked "Jackson's record of encouraging Communist organizations in America." He reminded the nation once again that Jackson had endorsed the League for Peace and Democracy, which "openly advocated sabotage against the United States in the event of war," and had spoken before the Consumers National Federation and had written for the League of American Writers. In the following days Dies lumped Nazis and Communists together in the kind of broad-spectrum attack on the virus of un-Americanism which he relished:

> I sincerely trust that immediate steps will be taken by the government to end Communist instigated strikes. The only effective measure that will prevent the agents of totalitarian powers from stifling our national defense program through strikes and acts of sabotage is to expel from national defense industries all Communists, fascists and Nazis.

He said there were at least six million people in the United States who belonged to organizations controlled by Germany, Italy, and Russia, and he was going to publish all their names. Late in November the Committee issued a 938-page document which it described as a report of Communist plans for sabotaging American industry in the event of war. This Red Book was, in fact, a compilation of the writings of eminent Communists from Karl Marx to Earl Browder, evidently everything Matthews could lay hands on at short notice regarding the violent overthrow of capitalism. It contained no information on any current plans for sabotaging American industry.

At about the same time, Dies sent a telegram to the President, asking him to coordinate activities against fifth columnists and so avoid "misunderstanding and conflict" between the Committee and the Departments of Justice and State. He held out an olive branch—or was it a sword? "There is plenty of work for all of us to do without indulging in unprofitable dispute and childish rivalries." Whether branch or blade, Dies's ambition to sit with the Administration as a co-equal law enforcement body was rebuked by return wire; F.D.R. reiterated Jackson's warning that the Committee's methods might "defeat the ends of justice." Pressing Dies on his vulnerable spot, Roosevelt pointed out that the administration of justice lay with the executive department, whose plans "may be severely handicapped or completely destroyed by premature disclosure of facts or suppositions to the public, or by hasty seizure of evidence which might with a little patience be obtained in a manner to be admissible in court . . ."

However, F.D.R. relented to the extent of inviting the Congressman in for a visit. A meeting was set up, and on November 29 Dies appeared at the White House, where he was obliged to wait in an anteroom while the President chatted with his old friend Gardner Jackson, instigator of the Pelley affair. Dies took this small joke of F.D.R.'s hard; he would complain of the indignity twice on the floor of the House, the waiting time rising from thirty minutes to forty-five minutes as his memory worked on it. Nor were his feelings assuaged when upon being admitted to the President's office after the half or three-quarters of an hour, he found in addition to the Roosevelt charm a stenographer waiting to make a record of the conversation. No transcript was ever released (the President, grumbled Dies, did not live up to his promise to send him a copy), but the report at the time was that Roosevelt spent the greater part of their fifty minutes together giving the Congressman a dressing down. In the recollection of Dies, published years after F.D.R.'s death, the President told him that day that Josef Stalin was a great leader and that some of his (F.D.R.'s) best friends were Communists. He said further, according to Dies, that the Communists were no threat to America and joshed the chairman with seeing a Red under his bed every night.

We have only Martin Dies's word for what passed between them, but it would not have been out of keeping with Roosevelt's attitude toward the anti-Communist investigations to express sentiments like those—or, more exactly, sentiments that sounded like those to Dies. Mr. Roosevelt was not one to brood about the internal Communist menace; indisputably, some of his best political friends had been, until the Nazi-Soviet pact, assiduous fellow travelers; and although he had sharply denounced Russia's invasion of Finland and was now high on the Communist hate list, he would believe until the end of his life that he could somehow handle Uncle Joe. Moreover, it was abundantly clear by the end of 1940 that the Administration could expect no kindness at the hands of Martin Dies, and secure in his recent election victory, F.D.R. could afford to be lighthearted about the Congressman's crusade. Whatever their conversation, Dies emerged from the meeting to take advantage of the fact that there were reporters waiting for him by calling for a two-year extension of his Committee and one million dollars. A few days later he told a radio audience that termination of his investigation "would bring to me a deep sense of personal relief" but that "it would mean an important victory for the fifth column in America" and so, despite opposition, obstruction, and untold tribulations, he had determined not to spare himself.

The entire Dies-Administration interchange took place in the shadow of the extension vote. The Committee's franchise was due to run out early in January, and as in prior years, the question was only how much money Dies would get this time. His popularity throughout the country was higher than ever; only 7 per cent of Dr. Gallup's sample felt that the life of the Committee should not be renewed, and 57 per cent favored giving Dies the million dollars he wanted. His staunchest support came again from patriotic groups; his opposition on the left was less vocal than in other years, partly because of the dissolution of the Popular Front, partly because he had lately been busy raiding the offices of Nazis instead of Communists. Dies was in a strong position, but he recognized that there has never been any political profit to be garnered in picking a fight with J. Edgar Hoover—"I certainly have no intention of interfering in any way with the work of the F.B.I. If a conflict arises between us, and the F.B.I. is watching a possible law violator, we will leave the case to them"—and he assigned Voorhis, a friend of the Administration, to work out some sort of public *quid pro quo* with the Department of Justice. In mid-December, after Jackson had again rebuked Dies for prematurely implying that an agreement had been reached whereby F.B.I. materials would be placed at his disposal, the attorney general set down in a letter to Voorhis—that carefully avoided all reference to the chairman of his Committee—the mutual understanding that the Justice Department would

secretly give the Committee information on fifth column activities not fit for prosecution, and the Committee would furnish
the department with material on prosecutable activities. It was
a paper agreement with little meaning, but a success for Dies;
to the general reader it established him as a recognized force
in the anti-subversive campaign, an authorized co-worker of
J. Edgar Hoover.

A few days after the agreement, Hoover issued a report of
his own, which agreed with the findings of the Committee
that Harry Bridges was a Communist, but made a point of
disagreeing with Dies on the whole question of sabotage which
for months had provided the fuel for his anti-alien campaign.
Just two weeks earlier Dies had spoken dramatically of "five
separate acts of sabotage" committed on "a most important
experimental plane," and now Hoover reported that an F.B.I.
survey of 1,200 war plants had uncovered no evidence of
organized sabotage in American industry. He went so far as to
reprimand Dies for his generalized criticisms of the F.B.I.
Hoover's report was open to no interpretation other than that
the Congressman was careless with the facts he broadcast
abroad so persistently—not a novel suggestion and one which
Dies was always quick to quarrel with when it came from the
mouths of others. But even Martin Dies could not bring himself
to call J. Edgar Hoover a tool of the Communist Party. The
mass of his Committee's supporters, after all, revered the F.B.I.
and Dies prudently allowed this slap to go unacknowledged.

The Committee ended its third year with three reports. On
the first day of 1941, Dies released a translation of an "official
confidential manual" of the German-American Bund which,
according to the Committee, proved that the Bund was "an absolutely militarized organization patterned after the ruthlessly
efficient military set-up which characterizes Hitler's machine
in Germany." Unexpectedly, the document lived up to the
Committee's description. Concerned mainly with the O.D. or
Ordnungsdienst, the Bund's police, the manual clearly took
as its model the chain of command of the Nazi storm troopers.
It extolled the O.D. men as representatives "of the Fuehrership

of American Germania"—their mission "to exterminate with all their power the stinking poison of red Jewish infection in America." The manual was obtained from Gerhard Wilhelm Kunze, the jailed Fritz Kuhn's replacement as national leader of the Bund. Kunze, unlike Kuhn, was born in this country, and he took pains in his appearance before a subcommittee to display his facility with the native tongue. Explaining that the Bund's use of the swastika was not to be construed as a tribute to Nazi Germany, he said:

> We recognize that symbol over there and elsewhere in the world as a symbol of Christian nationalism in contradistinction to atheistic internationalism, and we use it because it happens to be that form most generally used by races of the world closely related to us, but it has no connection whatsoever with the political philosophy of national socialism.[8]

A few days after the release of the Bund manual came a report on how the Axis countries were exploiting our international postal agreements to distribute their propaganda in this country by courtesy of the U.S. Post Office.

And in between these reports Dies made public his official report to Congress on his Committee's activities during 1939 and 1940. It was accompanied by one more of the chairman's sensational announcements: the Committee was investigating the transfer of at least $15 million in the past two months from the Central Bank of the U.S.S.R. to Germany and the other Axis powers. This news might have meant anything, or nothing, and it was to be another of those page one flurries that subsided as the ink dried. The official report, in addition to reviewing the Committee's endeavors and characterizing them without excessive modesty—"Our work has been a type of public education whose importance cannot be exaggerated"—for the first time put forward recommendations for legislation. Most of

---

[8] In August, some weeks before Kunze's appearance, the Bund held a joint rally with the Ku Klux Klan and the Protestant War Veterans of America at Camp Nordland, which prompted the Committee to call up its first witnesses from the K.K.K. One of them, an elderly minister and former Grand Kaliff from New Jersey, put the organization's essential principle as succinctly as it has ever been put: "I say it and I say it again that this is a free country and it gives me the right to attack . . . any group of people or any race, and I still hold that right."

these proposals Dies and his fellows in Congress had already called for many times: the deportation of alien spies and saboteurs as well as of "aliens who advocate any basic change in the form of government," and an end to immigration from countries that refused to accept the return of their undesirables; the outlawing of all organizations under the control of a foreign government and restrictions on totalitarian propaganda; making the statutory period for revocation of citizenship papers at least ten years and extending the statute of limitations on fraudulent passports to seven years. Voorhis took exception to the recommendation that federal financial support be withheld from educational institutions that permitted faculty members to advocate Communism, fascism or Nazism.

The proposals were in their way perfect, true to the spirit of the Committee and to an irrepressible spirit of America itself. The suspicion of the foreigner and nervousness over foreign ideologies, the mistrust of intellectuals, the impulse toward a show of toughness—powerful forces throughout our history—were primed for bursting in the anxious year of 1940, which began with the democracies beleaguered and ended with Britain standing alone. It was a good year for Martin Dies. He had tracked down no spies and he would not follow through on his legislative proposals, but a large part of the nation looked to him as a guardian of some essence of Americanism against all varieties of imported peril. In addition to exposing Nazis in 1940, his Committee had exposed cases of fraud in Communist Party nominating petitions, which resulted in the Party being taken off the ballot in several states.

The Congressional opposition of previous years was routed by his popularity. In the 1940 election Coffee of Washington, one of the earliest and most forceful critics of the Committee, used as a slogan "The Dies Committee endorses John Coffee's reelection," and when it came time for extending the Committee's life in February 1941, Coffee voted aye. "There is hardly a handful of the House today," said Hamilton Fish, leading the easy way to extension, "that will speak or vote against the continuation of the Dies Committee. Some of those who spoke against it only a year ago are not back in the House."

For the opposition, the debate was a catastrophe. Representative Marcantonio, allowed one minute, inveighed, as was his custom, against the coming of fascism. Representative Hook, allowed one minute, asked what the Dies Committee had uncovered that hadn't been known before, which gave Representative Cox an opportunity to reply, to the vast amusement of his colleagues: ". . . the Committee exposed the fact that there was a half-witted fool around town here that was selling forged materials to members of Congress . . ." Representative Dickstein, allowed five minutes, quickly ruined his day by charging "that one hundred and ten fascist organizations in this country had the back key and have now the back key to the back door of the Dies Committee." Whereupon Rankin of Mississippi immediately obtained an hour's time to attack Dickstein for maligning a member of the House, a parliamentary maneuver that silenced the blustering New Yorker. "I do not want any such man to . . . pretend to speak for me or for those old-line Americans that I have the honor to represent," said Rankin, lest anyone forget that Dickstein was born in Russia and was a Jew to boot. Rankin turned most of his time over to Dies, who used it mainly to defend his extra-Congressional activities, the lectures he had been giving around the country and the articles he had been writing, and to tell of the sacrifices he had endured in the line of duty. He was accorded another standing round of applause when he finished on the verge of collapse. Even some liberals could join in, recalling how much of the year had been taken up with German agents and Bundists. A few weeks later, by a vote of 354 to 6, the Special Committee was given an unprecedented fourth year of life, and was granted the sum of $150,000, the largest yet, to carry it along until April 1942.

A triumphant hour—yet its high promise would not be realized. Dies was only midway through his career as Committee chairman; he now had a thirty-man staff and brave battles lay ahead; but in the coming months political rebuffs at home, dramatic changes in the war, and his uncontrollable animus toward the Administration would conspire fatefully against his ambitions.

5

★ ★ ★ ★ ★

1941-1944: End of the Tether

THE Committee began 1941 with a change of personnel.
Harry P. Beam, an unmemorable Democrat from Illinois,
replaced Representative Dempsey, who did not stand for reelection. It was of small moment. Dies had always gone where
his temper, public attention, and J. B. Matthews directed without waiting upon his colleagues, and they would play a progressively lesser part in his adventures in the years ahead. As the
careful Ogden notes:

> Somewhere between the fall of France and 7 December 1941
> the Committee, as far as the public record indicates, had dis-
> appeared. Its place had been taken by a one-man agency which
> could not properly be called administrative and yet could not be
> called legislative. The information gathered by the investigators
> was utilized by the chairman who, to all intents and purposes,
> had become the Committee.

From the summer of 1940 to the end of the life of the Dies
Committee, Chairman Dies never appeared at a public hearing.

The first affray of the new season was set off by J. B.
Matthews. In a tactic that recalled his 1939 assault on consumer
organizations, the Committee's chief of staff issued a statement
to the press that an investigation was under way into the Institute for Propaganda Analysis. The I.P.A. had been set up a
few years before by a group of educators with the announced
purpose of "assisting the public in detecting and analyzing
propaganda." (As Edward L. Bernays tells the story, the Institute was conceived at the end of a meeting at the Columbia

University Club called by E. A. Filene, the Boston department store owner. It was a dull, unprofitable meeting, and Filene, ever bent on getting people to buy his ideas as well as his merchandise, finally said to Clyde Miller of Teachers College— who would lose his post because of his political proclivities before the decade was done— "You there—here is ten thousand dollars for the first year. I don't care how you spend the money.")

By 1941 I.P.A. teaching guides were being used by a million children in three thousand public and private high schools around the country, and dozens of textbooks made reference to its work—which treated U.S. institutions and slogans with heavy skepticism. The National Association of Manufacturers was moved to hire an assistant professor of banking at Columbia University to make a survey of textbooks; he read six hundred of them and found that a substantial number "tended to criticize our government and hold in derision or contempt the system of private enterprise." The N.A.M.'s scholar objected strenuously to what he regarded as a program of making children critical without giving them a foundation for criticism: "Let's teach the pupils something about the principles of democracy or private enterprise before we start to tell them it is all run by a bunch of crooks and is no good."

The I.P.A. composed a reply which spoke disparagingly of the role of the N.A.M. in education, and Matthews's statement came out on the very February day that it was published. To support his description of the I.P.A. directors as "frankly left wing," Matthews noted that the president, Kirtley Mather of Harvard, had gone on record as criticizing the Dies Committee, had raised objections to throwing the Communist Party off the ballot, and had asked aid for anti-fascist refugees from Spain. Matthews also noted that in January 1940 I.P.A.'s official bulletin had carried an unflattering survey of his own methods of operation. Entitled *Mr. Dies Goes to Town*, it analyzed Matthews's attack on consumer groups and concluded:

It seems evident, after studying Mr. Matthews' report, that his charges against the consumer movement are wholly unfounded. Of course, the Communists in any group can be expected to exert an influence far beyond their numbers; organized minorities always do. Still, to indict an entire movement, involving hundreds of thousands, if not millions of people, just because three or four of the leaders *may* be Communists is hardly justifiable. They may be Communists, but Mr. Matthews cannot be said to have proved it: his evidence is sparse and flimsy, at best. Moreover, suppose they are Communists: what is Communistic about wanting to make your purchases as economically as possible?

Despite its ingenuous air, the I.P.A. study did pinpoint the weaknesses of the report on consumers, and its criticisms of Matthews's techniques on that occasion could be applied to his report on the I.P.A. itself. Its directors, along with most of the nation's educators, had small use for the Dies Committee; they leaned rather to the left than to the right, and as the resignations the following month of Paul H. Douglas of Chicago University and Eduard C. Lindeman of the New York School for Social Work—both interventionists—would reveal, they disagreed among themselves on whether to oppose Administration policies toward the war in Europe. (In October the I.P.A. bulletin would be suspended "for the duration of the international crisis.") But that it was a Communist voice, Matthews did not exert himself to demonstrate. His release, presumably having gratified the N.A.M. as much as his report on consumers had gratified the Hearst Corporation, was the beginning and the end of his battle with I.P.A. In March its directors wrote Dies to ask that he either carry out a real investigation or announce that the entire indictment had been abandoned.

Dies did neither. His attention had been drawn yet again to a subject dear to him—Communists in the C.I.O. His particular target this March was the Steel Workers Organizing Committee; he inserted a charge into the Congressional Record that at least twenty-seven persons, whom he named as having been identified as Communists before his Committee, were involved with S.W.O.C. As Dies undoubtedly anticipated, this drew blood from Philip Murray, the steel union chief who had recently taken over from John L. Lewis as head of the C.I.O. Murray retorted that of the twenty-seven names, eleven had never been associated with S.W.O.C., fifteen had been gone for at least three years, and only one remained.

Dies's rejoinder, in a long telegram which he read to the House, skipped over his apparent errors of fact and asked Murray what he planned to do about the numerous Communists still leading unions within the C.I.O.: Curran, Quill, Bridges, Gold, and the others whose names had been popping up in Committee hearings since 1938. Murray, in his reply, followed Dies's example. Instead of answering the question, he accused Dies of labor-baiting. Whereupon the chairman, an old hand at this kind of brawl, answered it for him: "You are unwilling or unable to rid your organization of Communist influences . . ." Whatever the inadequacies of Matthews's researches into S.W.O.C., the estimate of Murray's position was, for the time, close to the mark. As Dies told the House: "Communists have obtained such a stranglehold on many of the unions in the C.I.O. that it is now beyond the power of Mr. Philip Murray or anyone else in the organization's leadership to do anything about the matter." In 1941 Murray did not have the strength to confront the Communists around him—including so intimate an advisor as Lee Pressman, the union's tough counsel. A struggle against them was already building up within the C.I.O., but Murray could not admit to an enemy like Dies that the species even existed. During the war years, when the Communists cooperated enthusiastically with the forces of light, there would be no sense in upsetting arms production with an internecine battle. But soon after the war the Communists in the C.I.O. would be beaten, and thoroughly —some ousted, some reformed, some merely grown too tired to fight in a cause which the Soviet Union's aspirations in Europe was making untenable at home. Martin Dies deserves some credit for the defeat of labor's Communists in America, but Josef Stalin deserves more.

From the time when, as a novice Congressman, Dies was elevated to the House Rules Committee, he was looked upon as a coming man in Democratic politics. His remarkable number of citations on page one, his busy schedule of appearances around the country (160 speeches between August 1938 and February 1941), his magazine articles (*Liberty* was his favored outlet) and newspaper interviews about menaces internal and external—all these stirred speculation about his future. So, when Senator Morris Sheppard of Texas died in April 1941, Dies was a foremost candidate for the vacant seat, and he devoted himself that spring to campaigning for the Democratic nomination, on the basis of his Committee's performance.

There were twenty-five aspirants for the job, including another young Congressman, Lyndon B. Johnson, who was a friend of F.D.R. and of the New Deal. The representative from Orange later complained, undoubtedly with justice, that "Word was spread in the right quarters that the election of Dies would mean that Texas would expect much less in federal handouts." To counter this appeal, Henry Ford offered Dies financial support from industrialists to wage an all-out patriotic campaign, with brass bands and movie stars, but there were strings attached and the deal was not consummated. Dies's own explanation of why he rejected the money will not satisfy all students of his career: "Somehow I couldn't bring myself to accept the offer. It went against my grain to thus make a spectacle of patriotism."

The Senate seat went to Governor W. Lee O'Daniel, who beat out Lyndon Johnson by 1,311 votes. Dies came in fourth, behind the state's attorney general, and complained that the "C.I.O. and fifth column organizations poured hundreds of thousands of dollars" into the state to defeat him. But there was no particular need to look to sinister elements to explain his defeat. "Pappy" Lee O'Daniel, who went around campaigning with a hillbilly band and a troop of ballad singers, was a great favorite in rural counties, and Johnson, an all-out New Dealer whose slogan was nothing less than "Johnson and Roosevelt," carried the big cities. Liberal commentators who chose to find in Dies's defeat evidence that his game was up were engaged in wishful thinking, yet his political career never did advance. For all his popularity in the polls, he was no match for the likes of Lyndon Johnson in a major campaign. He was vigorous at attack when he was attacking a target that few cared to defend, but sustained effort of a more complicated, not to say constructive, sort seemed to tire him. He had ruined himself with the Administration, with much of labor, and with many regular Democrats, including some of the most important politicians in his own state, and he never again reached out toward any office beyond the honorable one of U.S. Congressman.

As Dies was campaigning in Texas, in Washington a subcommittee of Starnes, Voorhis, and Mason returned to the ever-sustaining wells of Communist frontism. Hazel Huffman, who had told the Committee years before that the Federal Theatre Project was a Red nest, had been assigned to infiltrate the American Peace Mobilization, and now returned to say what everyone knew: that it was Communist-dominated. She made her case, but the hearing was only a shadow of past Committee glories because the A.P.M. was only a shadow of past Communist glories. The organization was set up in September 1940, at an "Emergency Peace Mobilization" held in Chicago Stadium under sponsorship of a body called the Committee to Defend America by Keeping Out of War. The Socialist Party, with its trained nose for such matters, at once branded the event "Communist inspired and controlled from end to end." A Presbyterian minister from Norman, Oklahoma, was rung in to chair the proceedings, but the main haranguers were circuit standards like Joe Curran who shouted that industrialists and bankers were behind the conscription bill; Mike Quill, who shouted that American labor "will fight only on American soil"; and the hard core leaders of the remnant American Youth Congress. Senators Nye and Clark, isolationist spokesmen, took back their acceptances of invitations to the rally upon being informed of its auspices. The A.P.M. did everything in the manual. It staged demonstrations against the draft, opposed lend-lease, and protested against the no-strike bill. There was a lot of folk singing at their meetings, lyrics like:

> I'd rather be at home, even living in a hollow log
> than go to the Army, be treated like a dirty dog.

And:

> Wendell Willkie and Franklin D.
> seems to me they both agree
> they both agree on killin' me.[1]

In April, three hundred A.P.M. members picketed the Pennsylvania Avenue entrance of the White House and sent a statement to the President telling him that "our foreign policy should seek to prevent the spread of war by establishing genuinely friendly relations with the Soviet Union." In May the A.P.M. started a perpetual Peace Vigil in front of the White House in protest against aid to Britain; it lasted for forty days. Its leaders chose June 21 to issue a call for a National Peace Week. This event was rained out when, on June 22, Germany marched into the Soviet Motherland, and shortly thereafter the American Peace Mobilization became the American People's Mobilization, its new slogan "For Victory Over Fascism!", its new platform "U.S. aid to all peoples fighting Hitler!" War, recently horrendous, had regained its virtues.

For those fellow travelers who still had the strength and will to travel, adjustment to the needs of the U.S.S.R. was second nature by now, and the June 1941 adjustment came easier than most since it permitted them to return from outermost political Siberia. For Dies, on the other hand, the violent break between Germany and Russia offered nothing in the way of profit. He predicted that Hitler would be in control of the U.S.S.R. within thirty days and that "All of those gullibles and fellow travelers in America who aided the Communist cause prior to the alliance may be expected to resume their activities in behalf of Moscow." He was nearer the truth about America than about Russia, but the subject of Communist

---

[1] Another A.P.M. favorite was *Washington Break-Down*:

Franklin D., listen to me, you ain't a-gonna send me 'cross the sea; you ain't a-gonna send me 'cross the sea;
You may say it's for defense, it's that kinda talk that I'm against; I'm against, I'm against, that kinda talk ain't got no sense.
Lafayette, we are here, we're gonna stay right over here; we're gonna stay right over here.
Marcantonio is the best, but I wouldn't give a nickel for all the rest; I wouldn't give a nickel for all the rest.

subversion could not very well sustain him as long as the U.S.S.R. remained in the fight. For the next four years fellow traveling would be one of the lesser offenses in our national life; far from seeking to subvert the defense effort or, in a few months, the war effort, the entire left would be lashing us on to ever greater exertions, particularly in relief of the heroic Soviet people. Dies would be driven to cry in open frustration that ". . . our present foreign policy of all-out aid to Russia is one that makes it very easy for Communists and their sympathizers to pose as the most ardent patriots."

But all was not over yet. As the country moved onto a war footing, Dies was presented with new opportunities for attacks on old targets. Among the men being appointed to responsible positions in Washington's burgeoning bureaucratic establishment were quite a number that Matthews had on his lists, as having been in the thrall of one or more front groups during the thirties. Not only were they suspect in themselves, but they were now going to work for agencies whose purposes were a source of deep suspicion to most Republican Congressmen and to many Democrats. It was only in the nature of things, therefore, that when the far-reaching price- and rent-control bills came up for debate in the House in the summer and fall of 1941, Dies took the occasion to assail Leon Henderson, the President's choice to head the Office of Price Administration and Civilian Supply. While Henderson testified before the Banking and Currency Committee, Dies protested to the House that the new administrator had belonged to five Communist-controlled organizations, in particular the Washington Friends of Spanish Democracy: "I wouldn't put him in charge of dog catchers." In a letter to F.D.R. a few weeks later, Dies accused Henderson, four of his principal subordinates, and fifty unnamed lesser employees of his agency of having Communist-front records. Henderson, no man to remain silent before such an assault, said he would pass along all evidence to the Civil Service Commission but refused to take "funny letters to the President as a basis for firing anybody." He also declared himself ready "to eat on the Treasury steps any Communist organization to which I belong."

As the fight against price-control legislation, pressed earnestly by business and agricultural interests, continued into November, Dies returned to the attack. On the eve of a vote in the House, which watered down the bill significantly before passing it, Dies delivered a long address in which he complained that the four high O.P.A. employees he had exposed in August were still O.P.A. employees: ". . . I demand that before any price-fixing bill is passed we have definite assurance that those charged with the administration of this act shall be loyal, patriotic Americans who believe in our system of free enterprise and who will seek to preserve it." His strongest case was against Robert A. Brady, head consultant to Henderson. In a book published in 1937 by the Left Book Club, a principal organ of England's Marxist establishment, Brady described the business enterprise under capitalism as "centralized, autocratic, intolerant . . . the most completely amoral and materialistic single-purpose institution the human mind has yet devised." He foresaw a choice only between "the triumph of reaction and a new lease on life for capitalism, or else a victory for socialism and the extermination of the rich and powerful of bank, factory, bivouac and cloister." This was heady stuff, coming from a government consultant. "Think of that, my colleagues!" exclaimed Dies. "Here is a man who frankly advocates socialism and the destruction of the church!" If that were not enough, Brady had belonged to the American League for Peace and Democracy and the Harry Bridges Defense Committee, and was among the signers of a manifesto issued in August 1939 in praise of the Soviet regime. Even discounting some of Dies's more vivid language, Brady was an unpolitic choice for an agency with the delicate job of controlling prices in an economy where government controls would be strenuously resisted, and soon afterward the Civil Service Commission recommended that he and his wife, also in the O.P.A. service, be discharged.

While the O.P.A. fight was being resolved, Dies opened a second front—the Federal Communications Commission, which had recently hired Goodwin Watson as a broadcast analyst. Without Committee hearings or consultation with his colleagues, Dies wrote a letter to F.C.C. Chairman James L. Fly, designating Watson as a "propagandist for Communism and the Soviet Union." When ten days passed with no answer from Fly, Dies repeated his charge to the House. He read excerpts from a book of Watson's on the "failure of gradualism" among the Austrian Socialists. The material was not nearly so rousing as that of Robert Brady, exterminator of cloisters, and Watson's record, as recited by Dies, indicated that he was merely a run-of-the-mill fellow traveler. A faculty member at Columbia University for sixteen years and a distinguished social psychologist, he had been associated with the Workers Alliance, Consumers Union, and the League of Women Shoppers, had supported the reelection of Vito Marcantonio, had protested the ban on Communists in the Civil Liberties Union, and had publicly opposed William Randolph Hearst and the Dies Committee. In a letter to *The New York Times* Watson contended that he had actually belonged to only one of the thirteen groups cited by the Congressman—Consumers Union—and had written only two articles on the U.S.S.R. in his entire life.

F.C.C. Chairman Fly held his peace officially, but in January a story appeared in *Newsweek* to the effect that Martin Dies was being praised by Axis propagandists. When Chairman Dies asked Fly what it was all about, the latter explained that in August, September, and October, according to the F.C.C.'s monitoring service, the Congressman from Orange, Texas, had been the beneficiary of "as many favorable references in Axis propaganda as any living American public figure." Representative Marcantonio made much of this piece of news, which owed something to J. B. Matthews's technique of sizing people up on the basis of lines of type in the *Daily Worker*, and the House, angered by this affront to one of its own, voted an amendment to the F.C.C. appropriation which deleted Goodwin Watson's salary. It was turned back by the Senate, but two years later, when another appropriation bill came up for passage, Watson would find himself the center of a constitutional *cause célèbre*.

In January Dies stepped again into the well of the House to inform members that Malcolm Cowley, long the book editor for *The New Republic* and recently hired by Archibald Mac-Leish as chief information analyst of the Office of Facts and Figures at a salary of $8,000 a year, was "one of the chief Communist intellectuals of this country." He noted that his Committee's files gave Cowley seventy-two connections with the Communist Party and its fronts, and the Hearst press, to which the report was leaked, publicized the charges with gusto. Cowley's record as literary wheelhorse for the Stalinists throughout the thirties, up until the Hitler-Stalin pact, could not bear extensive scrutiny, and in March he resigned.

When in February the Congress was debating an appropriation for the newly created Office of Civilian Defense, Dies came forward with the news that in this seemingly harmless agency too, Communists were "trying to take things over." Here he found himself up against several old antagonists. The executive director of O.C.D. was James M. Landis, former dean of the Harvard Law School, who after eleven weeks of hearings in 1939 had judged that there was no proof that Harry Bridges, may we be protected from the evil eye, was affiliated with the Communist Party. The assistant director was no other than Mrs. Roosevelt herself, lately the patroness of radical students, and among the friends and protegés whom the largehearted First Lady had brought with her into the agency were the actor Melvyn Douglas, who had an off-screen affinity for left-wing causes, and, ultimate affront, none other than the celebrated leader of youth, Joseph P. Lash. But this skirmish was lost in a larger controversy as the scourge of un-Americans took time out from meeting the threat of the New Deal to meet the threat from Japan.

Just three days after Pearl Harbor, Martin Dies let reporters know that he had had fifty-two witnesses ready to testify in August on the subject of Japanese espionage on the West Coast and the Pacific islands, but the Department of Justice had withheld approval of hearings—presumably out of delicacy for the feelings of the Japanese, with whom negotiations were then in progress. From this kernel quickly sprung up an enormous tree. A few weeks later, while arguing unsuccessfully for an amendment to the foreign agents registration bill to compel the Communist Party, the German-American Bund, and the Kyffhauserbund to furnish the names of their members, Dies told the House he was convinced that if his hearings had gone off according to schedule, "the Pearl Harbor tragedy never would have occurred because we would have made public the plans of the Japanese to seize control of the Pacific."[2] He now predicted that if the government did not become more alert to the activities of subversives, the West Coast was in for "a tragedy that will make Pearl Harbor sink into insignificance." Some days after this speech he charged that 15,000 Japanese nationals were involved in espionage and he promised to issue a Yellow Paper containing "impressive evidence," which had been turned over to the several intelligence departments in the fall of 1941, that the Japanese had planned to attack where indeed they did attack—Pearl Harbor. Following a number of such handbills, the 285-page Yellow Paper—one quarter of it given over to a Justice Department list of Japanese treaty merchants—made its appearance. It told a moderately interesting story of Japanese espionage efforts, but did not live up to the advance promotion. As Voorhis observed, none of the information in the Committee's possession that he had seen "was anywhere near definite enough to show that a Japanese attack would take place in Hawaii on December 7 or to predict when such an attack might be made."

Freshman Representative Thomas Eliot of Massachusetts, then coming into leadership of the sparse anti-Dies forces, pointed out that contrary to what Dies had told the newspapers (or, anyway, what the newspapers had printed, since Dies claimed frequently that he was a victim of the misquote), the Department of Justice had done nothing to prevent the issuance of his Japanese report, though it had relayed the feelings of the Secretary of State and the President that they were "unable to

---

[2] In his excitement, he may have forgotten that at the end of October, midway between his scheduled hearings and the bombing of Pearl Harbor, he had assured the New Orleans Association of Commerce: ". . . The Japanese policy was just a bluff—and not too good a bluff at that. A lot of Americans like myself would like to see them bring their coal burners out for a good licking, but they won't."

approve" open hearings in August. Eliot also disclosed that when Attorney General Biddle wrote to Dies for the evidence—that supposedly had already been turned over to his department—of the "elaborate sabotage plot . . . uncovered by agents of your Special Committee," the chairman merely wrote back that his agents on the West Coast would be willing to cooperate with Mr. Biddle's agents. "I assume," wrote Dies to Biddle, "that with the hundreds of agents which you have you would have no difficulty getting the facts." Pressed on these points by Eliot in a debate early in March, Dies raised the issue of personal privilege on the grounds that Eliot had called him a liar, and expatiated upon Comunists in the C.I.O., upon his record of exposing Nazis, upon the dignity of the Congress, upon the need for patriotism in so parlous a time, and upon his father's service in the House: "Let me say to the gentleman that whether he serves here a long time or a short time the first thing is to learn to love and respect the Members of this House."

Eliot, who would be merely a short-timer but who could hold his genealogical own with Dies by reminding the House that *his* great-grandfather had served there ninety years before, did not love his colleague from Texas sufficiently to halt his attack. Much of the Japanese report, he disclosed, had been "lifted without benefit of quotation marks." In particular, the famous Pacific strategy map which Dies said gave "clear proof of the intentions of the Japanese to make an assault on Pearl Harbor" and which the Committee's agents claimed to have obtained "under extraordinarily difficult circumstances," in the first place did not show, as billed, "in great detail positions of battle formations around Pearl Harbor," and in the second place, had been published in 1935 in a large-circulation Japanese magazine named *King*, which also ran love stories and a picture of Lou Gehrig. Another major item in the Yellow Paper was a Japanese handbook of the U. S. Navy: "It was with great difficulty that the agents of the Committee were able to obtain a copy of the volume." Eliot picked up the book, published in the early nineteen-thirties, in the Library of Congress. Marcantonio pitched in and showed that the remainder of the report owed a great deal, none of it acknowledged, to a weekly news-letter published in Los Angeles and sold at ten cents a copy. So scrupulous were the anonymous writers of the Committee report in adhering to the language of the newsletter that where the latter had "(illustration on this page)," the report had "(illustration on this page)," only, in the case of the report, there was no accompanying illustration.

The argument about the Yellow Paper ran directly into the annual debate over whether to continue the Committee through 1942. No one expected anything other than a fourth overwhelming extension, but our alliance with Russia against the Axis combined with Dies's persistent assaults on the Administration's emergency agencies gave his opposition a record number of votes against renewal—46 nays to 331 yeas. The minority directed their fire mainly at the Committee's failure to exert itself against Nazis and fascists, while the defenders played variations on Thomas's refrain that "The Dies Committee may turn out to be the last remaining safeguard against the dictatorship of the proletariat in America." Voorhis, fair-minded as always but rather plaintive by now, asked once again that the Committee function as a committee, with regular hearings, decisions by majority, and like amenities. Not a single meeting had been held since the previous extension. The Committee's appropriation was not voted on until late April owing to the unavailability of the chairman, who was at home in Texas; it was granted $110,000 but now the opposition was up to sixty-four members. The reason for the surprising increase in just a few weeks was that in between the two votes Dies had again been active.

In the closing days of March, skipping consultation with the other members of his Committee, Dies sent an "open letter" to Vice President Wallace, charging thirty-five officials of the Board of Economic Warfare, which Wallace headed, with Communist-front affiliations—again the League for Peace and Democracy—and calling for their resignation or dismissal. The letter, which Wallace received in his morning newspaper, named ten of the thirty-five; mostly it had to do with an economist, Maurice Parmalee, who in 1939 had published a book with pictures called *Nudism in Modern Life,* which was ruled obscene by a district court judge. "At least," lectured the proper Dies, "there is no place in such an agency for an outstanding advocate of nudism." Wallace issued a strong rejoinder, complaining that the Congressman had not taken the trouble to bring the charges, "which might as well have come from Goebbels himself," to his attention before publicizing them, and he promised that the F.B.I. would check all of the named employees. He noted that Dies had neglected to mention that the district court's ruling on Parmalee's book had been reversed by the U.S. Court of Appeals, which, on the precedent of the *Ulysses* case, decided that "the book as a whole is not obscene" despite some questionable photographs. In the style of Marcantonio, the Vice President estimated that the letter's effect "on our morale would be less damaging if Mr. Dies were on the Hitler payroll."[3]

What, in particular, bothered Dies and other opponents of the New Deal about the B.E.W. was that in addition to having the tasks of controlling exports, stimulating imports of strategic raw materials, and engaging in economic warfare, it was supposed to be contemplating postwar economic problems. Congressmen on the right, already unhappy over the wartime restrictions on business, feared that the odd types then entrenching themselves in the emergency agencies would not readily relinquish their powers after the war. "I have reliable evidence, which I am not at liberty to disclose at the present time," Dies warned the House, "that some of those who hold key positions in our defense agencies consider themselves strategically placed for purposes of revolutionary change in our form of government and economics if and when the great crisis engulfs us." In the meantime, nudism was sufficiently naked subversion for the House, and the Congressmen had a high time with it. "I hold in my hand two of Mr. Parmalee's books," announced Repre-

---

[3] The most surprising people were wrapping themselves in the flag during these years. Moved by Dies's attack on the B.E.W., *The New Republic* commented: "There will presently be many American fathers and mothers of sons dead on the battlefield who may begin to ask themselves why Mr. Dies doesn't ever, not ever, do anything to help our war effort instead of hurting it."

sentative Cox, "and if I have ever seen anything that is filthy and dirty it is in these books." If a weakness for nudism were not enough, Parmalee had also written pamphlets with titles like *Farewell to Poverty* and *Bolshevism, Fascism and the Liberal-Democratic State*. The Administration was embarrassed, and in April he was dismissed, on the pretext of "reorganization."[4] Another of the ten, a specialist on Australian affairs, resigned after Voorhis accused him of Nazi sympathies because of his attacks on U.S. foreign policy in 1940. Voorhis later apologized when it became evident that the gentleman was no Nazi at all but simply a fellow-traveling pacifist during the Hitler-Stalin alliance.

All of the named officials, including the departed, were cleared by the F.B.I., and the balance of the thirty-five to whom Dies had originally referred were forgotten among the hosts of anonymous accused. But the name of one of the ten lingered, to the embarrassment of the chairman. In a speech soon after the release of the open letter, Voorhis complained about the unilateral method of operation and about the technique of listing the names of nine persons and surrounding them with "quite lurid material" having to do with a tenth, the scandalous Parmalee. Voorhis pointed out that, by definition, a Communist-front organization was composed partly of persons who were not Communists, and he directed attention in particular to the B.E.W. official named David B. Vaughn. Vaughn denied ever belonging to the A.L.P.D., and, indeed, there seemed to be a mistake somewhere. Sure enough, it turned out that the Vaughn employed by the B.E.W. was a Kentucky banker, and not the Boston University professor with whom the Committee's researchers had confused him. In May banker Vaughn sued Dies for $750,000. In July, Dies made public apology for the mistaken identification, agreed to pay Vaughn's legal fees, and hastened to submit to the House Accounts Committee a bill for $611 to cover costs in the Vaughn case and in a lesser suit that had been brought against

---

[4] The B.E.W. may have deserved its bohemian reputation. A second economist was later discharged after Dies reported that he conducted "rhythmic ritual services" in his off hours.

him for a similar reason. "There is a clear intention to sabotage the Committee through the filing of suits," he complained, as the House paid his court costs.

The Committee's next accusatory flurry, a mere entr'acte in its anti-Administration marathon, came in June when, employing the Matthews manner, it attacked the Union for Democratic Action as "an organization composed chiefly of individuals who have been a significant part of the interlocking directorate of the Communist movement in the United States." The U.D.A. was further charged, along with the *Daily Worker*, the *New Masses*, and *Time* magazine, with being the spearhead of a plot to discredit Congress and alter our form of government— a theme that would occupy Dies more and more in his final years. There had been no hearings on the matter; no U.D.A. representative had been invited to present his side of the case; and no specific accusations of Communism were made against any individual.

The U.D.A. had in fact been formed in April 1941, before the Nazi-Soviet rupture, for the main purpose of supporting Administration moves to intervene in the war in Europe, and had been assailed by the *Daily Worker* as "the fifth column of Wall Street empire." Its first chairman was Reinhold Niebuhr and its founders hoped to develop a strong anti-Communist voice on the left. It had remained staunchly pro–New Deal in this Congressional election year of 1942 and a few weeks earlier had aroused pique on the right by collaborating with *The New Republic* to publish a supplement entitled *A Congress to Win the War*, which graded senators and representatives by their agreement with Administration proposals and had no good marks for Representative Dies or his closest political friends. Among the Congressmen singled out as "obstructionists" were Representatives Starnes ("Never has he voted for the domestic legislation of the New Deal, except the T.V.A. which is so popular in his district that he dare not oppose it"), Thomas ("has a clear record as a reactionary isolationist"), and Dies himself ("clearly acting in the best interests of the Axis governments"). In addition, it had only hard words for such supporters of the Committee as Fish, Rankin, and Mundt.

The Committee report, gotten up in retaliation for this provocation, defined U.D.A. policy as proposing that "the sole remaining function of Congress is to ratify by unanimous vote whatever wish is born anywhere in the whole vast structure of the executive branch down to the last whim of any and every Administration official." The U.D.A. did not, in truth, show any great independence or discrimination when it came to Roosevelt's policies; still the Committee report was a campaign document pure and simple. Voorhis, the one-man minority, dissented from it, defending the "right of loyal American citizens to disagree politically with a majority of the Dies Committee without being branded as subversive and un-American." There was not a single Communist in the U.D.A., he stated, and the Committee did not stoop to pick up this gauntlet; the demand for a hearing by U.D.A. President Frank Kingdon went unacknowledged.

The Committee's aims had never been more clear, and the Administration was preparing a counterblast in time for election day. In the spring of 1941, Congress had allocated $100,000 to the Department of Justice to investigate federal employees suspected of belonging to subversive organizations. The job was not one that Attorney General Biddle craved; it was forced on him by a Congress goaded continuously by Dies during the period of the German-Soviet pact. In many and diverse forums Dies demanded that "at least one thousand government employees sympathetic with totalitarian ideology must be discharged." It took several months for him to draw up a list of suspects for Biddle, but finally, in October, he sent along 1,121 names, accompanied by his trade mark: "The evidence which I am submitting to you, Mr. Attorney General, indicates that there is a new influx of subversive elements into official Washington." While Dies was complaining that subversives were running amok through the federal bureaucracy, liberals were complaining that charges against low-level employees were being made and acted upon without sufficient care: they were denied hearings, the names of their accusers remained secret, and they were sometimes dismissed without being told why, although there was reason to believe it was for nothing more sinister than working for the abolition of the poll tax or for aid to Loyalist Spain.

The attorney general's report to Congress on the uses to which he had put the $100,000 constituted a rebuttal to both sides in this dispute, but more emphatically to Chairman Dies. With the investigation largely completed, only two persons on the Dies list had been dismissed and a third had been subjected to some lesser disciplinary action. Most of the names submitted, it was evident, had simply been culled from mailing lists of fellow-traveling organizations like the National Federation of Constitutional Liberties and its capital chapter, the Washington Committee for Democratic Action, and, commented Biddle tartly, "never should have been submitted for investigation in the first place." He concluded with the observation that sweeping charges of disloyalty in the federal service were unjustified and that the results of the investigation were "utterly disproportionate to the resources expended"; he recommended that thereafter investigations of federal employees be restricted to cases where there were substantial reasons for suspecting a violation of the law. (Congress showed its appreciation by giving his department another $200,000 to proceed with the investigations Biddle strenuously opposed.)

Dies was roused to customary fury by the attorney general's report, and he used a point of personal privilege, now becoming his favorite parliamentary device, to denounce Biddle for ignoring the mandate of Congress. The Congressional directive, he pointed out, had ordered the attorney general "to investigate the employees of every department, agency and independent establishment of the federal government who are members of subversive organizations or advocate the overthrow of the federal government, and report its findings to Congress." What this meant, explained Dies, was that Biddle was supposed to supply Congress with "the names of the members of the organizations, tell who the subversive organizations are . . ." instead of presuming to make an investigation on his own, in cahoots with agency heads who were themselves on one or more tainted lists. It was the Congressman's simple desire that the Department of Justice lend its authority to publicizing the names of government employees whose affiliations may at one time have been misguided but whose loyalty to this country was not seriously in doubt. Biddle refused to turn his department into a certifying agency for the Dies Committee, and the battle went to him.[5] But the war was far from over.

A substantial part of the Committee's round-up report for 1941 and 1942 was given to complaints against Biddle, Henderson, Fly, and Wallace for not showing due fervor in pursuit of deviant federal employees. Devoted in the main to celebrating previously publicized accomplishments of the Committee—it now had 135 file cabinets containing more than a million cards—the report owed its newsworthiness to the inclusion of a dissent by Jerry Voorhis. Voorhis refused to sign for a number of reasons: Committee members had not been given a chance to discuss the report, but had had it presented to them on a "take-it-or-leave-it" basis; the charges of subversion, leveled against persons whose politics the majority found distasteful, were not adequately supported by evidence; the claim in the report that Japanese relocation was "a direct result" of the Committee's investigation of Japanese espionage was "extravagant"; in its discussion of the 1941 strikes, the report did not give sufficient credit to the over-all loyalty of American labor. Most important to Voorhis, the report contained little that might guide citizens on how to "identify, avoid and combat the propaganda activities of agents and friends of enemy nations of the United States in the current war"; he complained that the Committee had delayed for months the release of a study on Axis-front movements that he had helped to develop. Behind the delay of the Axis-front report was the Committee majority's dislike of a complimentary reference to the Administration in Voorhis's introduction. For Thomas it was "nothing more than

[5] It was in such skirmishes that Mr. Biddle earned the tribute that Professor Robert E. Cushman paid him in his study *Civil Liberties in Wartime,* published in 1943: "Congress had included in the Alien Registration Act of 1940 the most drastic law directed against sedition since the Sedition Act of 1798, and the Department of Justice might have embarked on a campaign of drastic repression, but this the Attorney General refused to do."

a whitewash of the New Deal." A report on Nazi activities was issued a few months later, without the complimentary reference, and did not make startling reading beside newspaper accounts of the government's arrest and indictment of dozens of native fascists for sedition. But by then Voorhis had resigned from the Committee.

During his four years in the company of Martin Dies, Jerry Voorhis was a disappointment to the nation's more truculent liberals as well as to those whose best friends were Communists —"wobbly as usual," commented Ickes. Although he exercised a restraining influence on the chairman's vigilante inclinations, he believed to the end that there was a place for such a committee in Congress—and not solely for the purpose of exposing oddities on the right. He believed that the Un-American Activities Committee had rendered a service to progressives by analyzing the workings of Communist fronts and to labor by exposing Communists in unions. For fellow travelers, this was a sign of lamentable weakness: in a special supplement published by *The Nation* in October 1942, the Dies Committee was attacked as "a camouflaged pill box in the fascist fight for control of our democracy." Editor Freda Kirchwey fired the troops: "It needs to be stormed and overthrown, not reformed." But Voorhis's only real weakness was that of a rational, fair-minded, and courteous man thrown into the company of men who were irrational, unfair, and discourteous and who had the power to satisfy their rudest passions. He was like a graduate student in sociology trying to talk sense to the drunkards in a skid-row bar. Again and again he asked that Committee rules be put in order to keep the chairman within bounds, and, as he conceded shortly before his resignation, he had been "one hundred per cent unsuccessful."

After each rebuff he considered quitting but, like an outmatched boxer with too many trainers in his corner, he allowed friends to persuade him to stay on and do what he could. Until, at last, when the Committee came up for a two-year extension on February 10, 1943, Voorhis cast his vote against it. It had become, he said, "more and more a political instrument of definite conservative bias, and less and less a dignified, important and effective Congressional committee." Ninety-four members, a record, voted against extension this time, but 302 voted for it. The opposition was composed largely of big-city Democrats. Other Democrats, though they might make nasty remarks about Dies in private, would not risk the disfavor of the Legionnaires and the Hearst and McCormick press with a nay, and Republicans, who had done surpassingly well in the 1942 elections, appreciated the Texan's value as an anti-Administration ally. The Committee was allotted $75,000, which included payment for David Vaughn.[6]

It was at this time, fortified by the conservative victories in the off-year voting, that Dies chose to launch his climactic attack on the Administration. This last major performance of his career gave full airing to the presumptions of the forces in Congress dedicated to resisting the executive branch. On February 1, 1943, Dies took the floor of the House for an hour and a half on another question of personal privilege. He was offended this time by the National Lawyers Guild, which had that morning placed on the desk of every representative a manifesto opposing renewal of the Special Committee: "Martin Dies and his Committee is the secret weapon with which Adolf Hitler hopes to soften up our Nation for military conquest." Dies used his ninety minutes to berate an assortment of enemies, such as *The New Republic* and Marshall Field, publisher of *PM*, to defend himself against accusations of anti-Semitism and anti-Negro sentiments, and to make patriotic periods. He was applauded at frequent intervals, which encouraged him to ever higher flights of eloquence:

> How would you like to go back to your constituents, to that father and mother who have just received word that their dearly beloved son has given his life in defense of America, how would you like to stand up there on the stump, Democrat or Republican, and attempt to defend the appointment by bureaucracy of a man

[6] Vacancies caused by the departures of the prudent Casey, the anonymous Beam, and the disheartened Voorhis were filled by Wirt Courtney of Tennessee, John M. Costello of California, and, as resident liberal, Herman R. Eberharter of Pennsylvania. A Republican, Karl E. Mundt of South Dakota, was added in acknowledgment of the election results.

who does not believe in the system these boys fought and died to preserve?

The substance of his remarks was yet another list of names— thirty-nine government employees whose ouster he demanded. Most of them worked in the recently created wartime agencies and had figured in his previous attacks on the Board of Economic Warfare, the War Production Board, and the Federal Communications Commission. Most had belonged to the League for Peace and Democracy and like groups on the left. Dies accused none of them of being C.P. members or of disloyalty to America; he attacked them as "irresponsible, unrepresentative, radical and crackpot," and issued an ultimatum to the Administration that, as the event turned out, was not mere bluster: "If you do not get rid of these people, we will refuse to appropriate money for their salaries." When he had done, Will Rogers, son of the late humorist and a new representative from California, rose to make his maiden address. He said: "I should like it to be known that I disagree with the sentiments expressed, the flamboyant manner of expression used and the use of this great forum as a means of what we in Hollywood would call personal publicity." But the critical gentleman was in a minority. The Republicans and Southern Democrats cheered Dies, and three days later Joe Hendricks of Florida rose to press the advantage.

The occasion was a billion-dollar Treasury–Post Office appropriation bill. Hendricks offered an amendment that no part of the appropriation should go to pay the salaries of any of the individuals named by Dies. Only one of these, William Pickens, a Negro economist, actually worked for the Treasury Department, but Hendricks proclaimed his intention to add his amendment to every appropriation bill that came up because, in the past, several persons on Dies's list had been ousted from one agency only to reappear in another. He was especially upset that Maurice Parmalee, the B.E.W.'s student of nudist habits, had found his way onto the Railroad Retirement Board. Hendricks was aiming at a state of things where "there will be no place else for these men to hedge hop."

There was precedent of sorts for Hendricks's proposal. In January 1942, as we have noted, during Dies's give-and-take with the F.C.C., the House deleted the salary of Goodwin Watson from the agency's appropriation, but the Senate killed the amendment. In a similar case, David Lasser, former head of the Workers Alliance, was discharged from his W.P.A. job after the House added an amendment to the 1940 Relief Appropriation Act forbidding him a salary; the provision was omitted from the 1941 appropriation bill, and Lasser turned up on Dies's 1943 list, this time as an employee of the War Production Board. Still, the idea of exempting from payment by the Treasury Department thirty-eight persons who did not work for that department, struck representatives on both sides of the aisle as far-fetched. Ludlow of Indiana called it "one of the most peculiar pieces of legislation ever presented to the House." It was natural that Voorhis would find danger in Dies's standard of whether or not an official "fell into a certain category which the gentleman categorized as 'crackpot,'" but even conservative voices like those of Dirksen of Illinois, Bender of Ohio, and Case of South Dakota—all destined for the Senate—were troubled by the wholesale blacklisting. Case said: "I am not willing to condemn thirty-eight men and women in thirty minutes on ex-parte presentation without even a specific statement on each one of the individuals concerned." The amendment was rejected by a vote of 146 to 153, whereupon Hendricks offered an amendment that barred payment to Pickens alone, and this was passed, 163 to 111.

Pickens, a Phi Beta Kappa from Yale, former teacher and dean at Negro colleges and officer of the N.A.A.C.P., was in charge of a small section of the Treasury Department's War Savings staff, his assignment to promote the purchase of war bonds by Negro organizations. Dies took exception to him because over the years he had been, among other compromising things, a vice chairman of the American League Against War and Fascism, a member of the American Committee for the Protection of the Foreign Born and the United American Spanish Aid Committee, and a contributor of articles to the *New Masses*. In a statement to Representative Ludlow, the

Treasury Department noted that it had "long been aware" of the charges concerning Pickens and was "convinced that they were without any substantial foundation . . . we are satisfied that Mr. Pickens is completely loyal to the government of the United States." The action against him by an agitated House alerted the Administration to difficulties to come with subsequent appropriation bills, and F.D.R. sought to head them off by issuing an executive order setting up an interdepartmental committee to handle complaints of subversive activity within the executive branch. It was the tactic of the school principal who invites a bunch of teenage toughs into the gym for a display of calisthenics in order to get their minds off breaking the building's windows. The haters of the New Deal were enjoying their romp too much to be so easily distracted. Clare Hoffman of Michigan, who bore to the native fascist fringe approximately the same relationship that Vito Marcantonio bore to native Communists, voiced their high spirits: ". . . last November by a majority of more than a million the American people told candidates for Congress that the waste, the extravagance, the muddling and the confusion, the crackpot plans and schemes of the starry-eyed New Deal dreamers should be brought to an end." And what surer way to do this than by eliminating the dreamers themselves?

On February 8 the House of Representatives enjoyed one of its rowdier days as the Administration, much on the defensive, attempted to do away with the Pickens amendment and substitute for it a resolution delegating to a subcommittee of the Appropriations Committee the task of investigating all charges of subversive tendencies among government employees and taking prompt action against them if the charges were sustained. The victors of the previous day were out for a kill, but passage of a billion-dollar appropriation bill was in jeopardy, and Speaker Rayburn, Majority Leader McCormack, and Minority Leader Martin conferred hurriedly at the rear of the chamber on tactics. Their great hope of success was Pickens's race. Overnight it had dawned upon the Republican leadership that many people might not understand that Pickens owed the misfortune of being singled out for execution not to any accident of birth but to the accident that he alone of Dies's thirty-nine was on the payroll of the Treasury Department at the moment when its appropriation was before the House. Hendricks assured his colleagues that he had had no idea at the time he offered his amendment that the fellow was a Negro. Hadn't he called him "*Mister* Pickens" all the previous day, when the entire world knew that "a Southerner does not refer to a colored man as 'mister' "? To guard himself against any semblance of prejudice, Hendricks never called Pickens "mister" again. The inimitable Rankin with excellent logic declared: "I voted to strike him off when I thought he was a white man, and I shall certainly not vote to put him back on because he is a Negro." But Congressmen from north of Mississippi could not afford so much logic: ". . . One poor colored man . . . ," intoned Knutson of Minnesota. "My God, that is almost lynch law." If so, it was the first time in our history that a man was saved from being lynched *because* he was a Negro.

On the next day the forces of propriety were rallied, debate was more orderly, and the nativists were indignant but not hopeful. "Somebody is playing to the Negro vote," charged Colmer of Mississippi. And Hoffman interpreted the approaching reversal as part of a conspiracy against the Dies Committee:

Being unable to kick the Dies Committee out the front door of the Congress, the Administration and a few others, including the C.I.O. and the Communists, propose to do the job by taking over the duties of the Dies Committee and giving those duties to other committees and so get rid of the Dies Committee by kicking it out the back door.

There was truth in his argument, but even Hamilton Fish was concerned about people back home concluding that Congress had come down hard on a poor lone Negro, and the resolution to appoint a new committee was adopted by an overwhelming vote. Then, by 267 to 136, the House struck out the anti-Pickens amendment which it had inserted barely a weekend before. It also passed an amendment of Representative Dirksen, barring payment by the Treasury Department and the Post Office to any persons excluded from any other appropriation bill, a method of discouraging transfers of objectionable individuals such as David Lasser. Appointed to the new subcommittee were three Democrats and two Republicans: John H. Kerr of North Carolina as chairman, Clinton P. Anderson of New Mexico, Albert Gore of Tennessee, Frank B. Keefe of Wisconsin, and D. Lane Powers of New Jersey.[7] Dies at once promised to supply them with his complaints not merely against the thirty-nine but against the hundreds or thousands of other employees who to his mind had not been satisfactorily investigated by the attorney general.

The Kerr Committee selected for its first defendants six names from among the thirty-nine. Three of them—Goodwin B. Watson, William E. Dodd, Jr., and Frederick L. Schuman—came from the F.C.C., specifically the branch that monitored foreign broadcasts and so was the source of the report that Martin Dies was a pet of Axis commentators. The other three—Robert Morss Lovett, Jack Fahy, and Arthur Goldschmidt—were in Harold Ickes's Department of the Interior. William Pickens was left in peace. Each of the suspects was called before a closed session of the committee and questioned, on the basis of his Dies-Matthews dossier, about his undesirable associations and his opinions of Communism and capitalism. The hearings went smoothly, unimpeded by additional witnesses, counsel for the defense, observers from the accused's agencies, or any form of cross-examination. In April came the judgment. A cruel month for Watson, Dodd, and Lovett. Why the other three, including the confirmed Soviet apologist Schuman, were let off was never explained, beyond such unilluminating phrases as "not sufficient evidence to support a recommendation of unfitness." The convicted three, declared "unfit for the present to continue in government employment," were not charged with being or having been members of the Communist Party or with failing to perform their jobs satisfactorily.

[7] Investigating the executive branch was popular in the seventy-eighth Congress. Along with the Kerr Committee went the Cox Committee to investigate the F.C.C.—"the nastiest nest of rats to be found in the entire country," in Representative Cox's view—and the Smith Committee to investigate untoward behavior by the executive. Both were dominated by the Republican–Southern Democrat coalition then in its ascendance.

They were found guilty because of their association with organizations deemed subversive by the attorney general, their articles and speeches criticizing U.S. policies, capitalism and the profit system, and their support for causes, such as Loyalist Spain, which seemed suspect to the Congressmen.

Dodd, an assistant news editor at the F.C.C. with a salary of $3,200, had the lowest function and the briefest record of the three. He had been a paid employee as well as a member of the A.L.P.D.; had had the audacity to continue his membership in the Washington Bookshop after the Justice Department ruled it subversive; had spoken in behalf of such causes as Spanish relief and China relief; had written in 1938, after a trip to the U.S.S.R., that "here is a nation which carries the future of our civilization. Here there is hope, justice and progress"; and, most shocking to the tribunal, had been host at a cocktail party for the Harry Bridges Defense Fund while deportation proceedings were under way against the abominable Australian. As Representative Powers preferred to describe the occasion, he had "opened his home to Harry Bridges." (Martin Dies would not fail to note in his autobiography that years later Dodd's sister, Martha and her husband, Alfred Stern, defected to Czechoslovakia.) Dodd told the Committee that he believed in private enterprise, the capitalistic system, and the Christian religion, particularly the Baptist branch, and tried to pass some of his alleged activities off onto his late father, the former U.S. ambassador to Germany, but it availed him not.

Goodwin Watson, chief analyst for the Foreign Broadcast Information Service, had a more extensive history of rote radicalism and cooperation with leftward-leaning groups, and apologized for some of it. He had been enlightened by the Soviet-Nazi pact as to the real nature of bodies like the American Student Union. He attributed the fiery declarations of his past—including such titillating thirtyish slogans as "there is no safe compromise with capitalism"—to the depression, and explained that his views had been changed by the good works of the New Deal and his disillusionment with Soviet totalitarianism. True, he had never spoken or written as strenuously against the U.S.S.R. as he had for it, but now, he emphasized, he was a member of the *right wing* of the American Labor Party. His protestations went for nought. Representative Keefe of Oshkosh could not forgive him for sympathizing with "the Loyalist Government of Spain, which was in fact the Communist Government, was it not?"

Robert Morss Lovett was yet another case—and an extraordinary one; he challenged even the record of J. B. Matthews as a joiner. Lovett's social consciousness developed late. In 1917, when he was forty-six years old, with a long career as professor of English at the University of Chicago behind him, he became outraged by the excesses of war patriots against radicals and conscientious objectors. From then on, there was no liberal or radical cause anywhere that needed to get along without him: Sacco-Vanzetti, birth control, Mother Bloor, the abolition of capital punishment, Hull-House, Tom Mooney, industrial unions, Loyalist Spain, the Russian Revolution. "My old mother used to say to me when I was a little bit of a kid," reflected Representative Powers, faced with Dr. Lovett's record, " 'Sonny, you will always be judged by the company you keep.' " Even in his role as professor of English, Lovett could not resist finding social significance wherever he looked: "I like to read *King Lear* as having a reference to King James's proclivity for giving away the royal demesne to his favorites"—a predilection that gave him a better reputation among reformers than among literary critics. Pressure from the Illinois state legislature nearly got him thrown off the University of Chicago faculty in 1935 because he had been arrested for watching Chicago cops push around Negro girls on strike at an apron factory. The legislature was especially disturbed, as the Kerr Committee would be a decade later, at his comment to a former student that all governments, including his own, were "rotten." In 1939 the elderly fighter for good causes was appointed government secretary to the Virgin Islands, and it was of this post that the Kerr Committee decided to dispossess him.

In Lovett's defense, Harold Ickes wrote to Representative Kerr:

He has for the seventy-three years of his life found it difficult to think ill of any man, and so far as I know has never questioned the motives of anyone who sought a good objective. If the sub-committee will appreciate this essential goodness of Mr. Lovett, it will find the answer to why this man, who obviously is not a Communist, has frequently associated himself with them in one non-political enterprise or another.

The estimate was just, but the understanding of even the Secretary of the Interior had been taxed when in June 1941 his friend and subordinate signed his name to the call to the annual conference of the Communist-run League of American Writers, then still pursuing an isolationist course. Secretary Ickes was obliged to reprimand him:

> In view of the international situation and the announced and deliberate policy of the Administration, of which you are a part, to give all possible aid to the nations that are resisting Hitler and Nazism, your signature to this call represents an indiscretion of a high order and is embarrassing to this Department.

(A few days after the League denounced war against Hitler as imperialistic, Russia was invaded, and the writers reversed themselves.)

Robert Morss Lovett, like his old chum Harry F. Ward, who had led him into the paths of social service, made a career of being used by the Communists. "I am not ashamed of any action that I have ever taken in defending the Soviet Union," he told the Kerr Committee in 1943, and he told the Dies Committee that he didn't recognize the term "Communist-front organization"; his alliance with the Communists was an effort to further objectives which he and they had in common: "So far as Communists are concerned, I have viewed them as human beings, capable, like the rest of us, of giving aid to humane and generous causes." In the recurrent splits on the left, he stood always, like the early J. B. Matthews, for "minimizing differences." Much of his interrogation was given over to his views of capitalism, socialism, and collectivism; he shocked the Congressmen by parroting all the pulse-quickening propositions he had picked up in the thirties. "Mr. Lovett," interrupted Representative Keefe, the group's bully boy, "did I understand you to say that human greed is the motive of the profit system?" He stayed with the Communists through their twists and turns of 1939, 1940, and 1941—from A.L.W.F. to A.L.P.D. to both appearances of A.P.M.—but by 1948, when he wrote his autobiography, a doubt seems to have stirred in his mind.

> I still believe that liberals and Communists can work together for good in local causes, and both are deeply concerned with civil liberties in the United States, but after the League for Peace and Democracy and the League of American Writers, I am suspicious of organizations which enjoy their existence on sufferance and depend on the variable policies of a foreign power.

His suspicions were not only very late, they were also very small.

In its condemnation of Lovett, the Kerr Committee expressed the fear that he would "propagate his subversive philosophies through control of government money spent in the Virgin Islands." (One of the difficulties under which the committee labored was that it had not been supplied with a foolproof definition of the word "subversive.") No evidence whatever was produced that Lovett had done any such thing during his years there, and to judge by the nearly unanimous defense he received from the people of the Virgin Islands, this gentle and humane man seems to have been doing an exemplary job; Mr. Ickes had taken a chance on him and, despite his indiscretion in the case of the League of American Writers, he had done nothing to betray the trust. But the issues that now arose from his case, and from the cases of Watson and Dodd, had nothing to do with their professional competence and not much to do with their opinions. The three men were pawns in a political test of strength that would finally be decided by reference to the U.S. Constitution.

In May the House Appropriations Committee added an amendment to the $134 million deficiency appropriation bill which stipulated that not a penny of it or of any other supply measure was to be used to pay the salaries of Watson, Dodd, and Lovett. Debate in the House was stormy. Marcantonio delivered his standard harangue: "Hitler used the Reichstag trial, he used the Communist bogey, the same pattern that we employ here for the present restriction and subsequent destruction of democratic rights." To Representative O'Connor's question, "Whether any member of the committee, or the committee, found anything in these men's records as public servants that indicates they are not performing their duty working for the government . . . ," Representative Kerr replied, "I do not think we looked into that . . . Nobody asked us to see whether these men were conducting themselves properly." No Congressman rose at this point to remind the House that even during the September bloodletting of the French Revolution, when men were slaughtered for the cut of a coat, the judges commented, "We are not here to judge opinions, but to judge the results of them." The House supported Kerr by a vote of 318 to 62, without having been given an opportunity to read the testimony in the case, and the bill went to the Senate, which rejected it unanimously. Three times more the Senate turned back the amendment, but the House remained adamant and finally, in July, a "compromise" was reached that required the President to appoint the three men and have them confirmed by the Senate before November 15 in order for them to keep their jobs. Senator McKellar explained when he first brought the demands of the House back to the Senate: "The Senate conferees have most reluctantly felt obliged to yield to this unjust provision in order to get the appropriation bill out of Congress and enacted into law."

The deficiency measure was but one of a half dozen major appropriation bills that were being delayed by strong anti-Administration forces in Congress bent on restricting the President's expanding emergency powers. Representative Dirksen put the case candidly in his defense of the rider:

We are gradually getting to the fruition of an issue that has been growing for a long time, the issue between the bureaus that seek to branch out beyond the intent of Congress on the one hand, and the Congress on the other hand in the determination of the policies of government . . . You had better meet this issue now, because bureaucracy will grow to a point where it will lick you if you do not.

The issue was met. The Crop Insurance Program was ordered liquidated from the Department of Agriculture supply bill. The National Youth Administration was struck out of the Labor Department supply bill, and the N.L.R.B. was ordered to keep away from jurisdictional disputes. Appropriations for the Office of Price Administration and the Office of War Information were sharply cut in the war-agencies bill. Roosevelt had to bow before each of these challenges, and he had to accept the urgent-deficiency bill, too, which contained the funds for millions of dollars in overtime pay and past-due wages for thousands of federal employees. He signed the bill in July, with an angry statement that described the rider, Section 304, as unconstitutional, unwise, and discriminatory. It was, he said, an "unwarranted encroachment" on the executive branch which he would have vetoed if he could have done so without imperiling essential wartime appropriations. He added that he did not consider it binding.

Those who rejoiced in the victory over Watson, Dodd, and Lovett and the philosophies that they represented acknowledged no constitutional barriers; to them the only question was whether an employer has the right to fire an employee. Control of the purse strings, they reasoned, made Congress an employer and all federal officials were its employees, with no property rights in their jobs. Since when had the firing of a worker been construed as a judicial proceeding? Representative Hoffman stated the position in a vivid way: "We have the right to say we do not want a certain class of people or certain individuals on the payroll. It may be because their hair is red or because they are bald, or because they wear it down over their coat collars. It makes no difference at all." Representative Cannon added: "We can lop off the salary of any person as we see fit."

Their opponents argued that in depriving the three officials of their jobs, Congress had passed a bill of attainder—a legislative act inflicting punishment without a judicial trial—as well as an ex post facto law, imposing punishment for an act that was not punishable at the time it was committed. And if this were not enough, by singling out three federal employees by name, the Congress had infringed on the powers of its coequal branches of government. Secretary Ickes and the F.C.C. commissioners kept the condemned at work, without pay, beyond the November 15 deadline in order to establish grounds for a test case by the three; in fact, Lovett stayed on until the following March when Ickes had to ask for his resignation out of concern for the upcoming Interior Department appropriation. Attorney General Biddle notified Congress that it would have to find a lawyer for itself since the solicitor general was occupied in supporting the plaintiffs .

In November 1945 the U.S. Court of Claims awarded the three their back pay, which came to $2,158, on the grounds that the Congressional rider was an attempt to tie the hands of the federal disbursing officer, thus making the appropriation measure contradictory and invalid. It was a narrowly construed decision that avoided the question of the act's constitutionality: Section 304, stated Chief Justice Whaley, "constituted a mere stoppage of disbursing routine, nothing more." But the concurring opinions of three of his four colleagues were strongly critical of Congress. Judge J. Warren Madden viewed the rider's purpose as "a shocking and outrageous injustice, unique in our history." The following June the Supreme Court unanimously supported the lower court's finding and, with Frankfurter and Reed dissenting, went further. Speaking for the majority was Justice Black:

> When our Constitution and Bill of Rights were written, our ancestors had ample reason to know that legislative trials and punishment were too dangerous to liberty to exist in the nation of free men they envisioned. And so they proscribed bills of attainder. Section 304 is one.

Justice Frankfurter argued that since no offense was specified in the rider and no declaration of guilt was made, it could not be regarded as a bill of attainder. "If Congress chooses to say that men shall not be paid," he reasoned, "or even that they shall be removed from their jobs, we cannot decide that Congress also said that they are guilty of an offense." The majority, however, was more concerned with the amendment's effect than with its wording, and the effect, wrote Black, "was to inflict punishment without the safeguards of a judicial trial." Administrations to come were in this manner saved from a harassment technique of surpassing potential.

As these matters were being resolved, the Un-American Activities Committee embarked on its first public hearings in nearly two years—and the last hearings of any consequence in its status as a special committee. In June 1943 Representatives Costello, Mundt, and Eberharter began taking testimony in Los Angeles on the relocation of the West Coast Japanese-Americans who had been put into "protective custody" after Pearl Harbor. Some 112,000 people, two-thirds of them born in this country, had been compelled by an executive order, implemented by the army, to evacuate their homes in California, western Oregon and Washington, and southern Arizona. About 3,000 of them, deemed dangerous to the security of the region, were placed in internment camps; the others were divided into those who refused to take a pledge of loyalty to the United States and so found themselves in "segregation centers," and the rest, the majority, who were transported—with little in the way of lock, stock, or barrel—into desert camps, in theory until they could be placed elsewhere. The program was administered by the War Relocation Authority, a new agency which owed its creation to the resistance of Western communities to resettlement of the Japanese. Given the haste with which these thousands of families were forced to dispose of their businesses, property, and possessions; the barracks into which they were jammed—seven in a room measuring 20' by 25', without running water; the awareness on the part of the better educated among them that Japanese citizens in other parts of the country had not been put behind barbed wire and that German and Italian aliens had not been interned by the carload on the basis of nationality; given all this, it is astonishing that the troublemakers among them did not act up more violently or have a greater effect on the rest, that the army had to be called into the camps only twice to keep order.

The subcommittee event was, as usual, well heralded: DIES COMMITTEE SAYS INTERNED JAPANESE AMONG BEST-FED CIVILIANS IN THE WORLD. Chief investigator Stripling supplied the Denver *Post,* which was waging its own campaign against the W.R.A., with the fiction that Japanese trained in espionage were among those being released at the rate of 10,000 a week, while those still in the camps were being pampered. But nervousness over the threat of espionage was not the only, or the major, reason for America's exercise in mass punishment. For years the Hearst newspapers, the American Legion and its California cousins in patriotism such as the Sons and Daughters of the Golden West, and the area's farmers, businessmen and A. F. of L. unions, irritated by Japanese success in commercial ventures and by the very existence of their tightly knit, conspicuously foreign, but eminently peaceable communities, had been inveighing against the Yellow Peril. Pearl Harbor afforded these groups an opportunity to spend their passions and stock their pocketbooks by booting out their Japanese neighbors. The patriots were especially fortunate in the appointment of General John DeWitt to take charge of defense measures on the West Coast. Said the general: "I don't care what they do with the Japs, as long as they don't send them back here. A Jap is a Jap." The sentiment would not go without amen in Congress, as long as John Rankin still served there: "I am in favor of shipping them back to Japan when this war is over. The way to tell which ones ought to be shipped back to Japan is, I would take a blood test." Representative Thomas brooded over the report that the interned Japanese were enjoying excellent food and wine: "Are we to release this fat-waisted Jap while our boys on Guadalcanal are barely receiving enough food with which to keep alive?" In the Senate, meanwhile, the Military Affairs Committee was pressuring the Administration to give over control of the relocation camps to the military.

Costello, the Californian, opened his Los Angeles hearings with a procession of witnesses who could be counted on to express the most implacable sentiments toward the Japanese. They complained of the inscrutable Oriental temperament, cited instances of coddling and waste in relocation centers (where the daily food bill sometimes went as high as forty-five cents a person), mocked the teaching in the camps of Japanese pastimes such as judo and goh, instead of baseball, and warned that their fellow citizens would not be restrained from violence if the Japanese were permitted to return to their homes. They objected to the whole concept of relocation unless it meant relocating the people to someplace east of Okinawa, and they urged that the army take over from the W.R.A., which they suspected of harboring good intentions.

The mayor of Los Angeles explained that he didn't want the Japanese back because their appearance of faithfulness in their work made it so difficult to "tell who is loyal and who is not." The sheriff of California's Orange County described the perils for the Japanese in his neighborhood, as U.S. Marines returned from the South Pacific. An official of the Orange County Farm Bureau expressed dismay over the Japanese reluctance to work for white people, and noted that the state had been driven to force them to sell their property by law. An official of the Native Sons of the Golden West, which had brought suit to cancel the citizenship rights of persons of Japanese descent, called for bills that would make it mandatory that land and boats in Golden California be owned by American citizens. A representative of the Los Angeles County American Legion observed that the release of the Japanese would fill the country with "potential saboteurs and spies." The president of the Salt River Valley Water Users' Association in Arizona (where an unconstitutional law had recently been passed requiring any-one who wished to sell anything to a Japanese to give ten days' notice of his intention in a newspaper and file a declaration of intent with the governor) reported proudly that the folks in his area "have always been against them [the Japanese] coming into the community, and restrictive laws have been passed." An American Legionnaire from Phoenix wanted it plainly understood that between Arizona Japs and California Japs he played no favorites: "They are all the same. We don't want any of them." The secretary of the Los Angeles Central Labor Office said it worried him that "the Japanese all look alike," and declared that "the labor movement is positively opposed to any Japanese being allowed freedom of movement anywhere in the United States . . ." The deputy sheriff of Yuma County, Arizona, reported that the Japanese from a nearby relocation center were upsetting townspeople by monopolizing the stools at the drugstore fountain.

These spokesmen were received more warmly by Chairman Costello than the ministers and members of the Fellowship of Reconciliation who held that the great majority of Japanese were loyal to this country and ought to be released. Asked by Representative Mundt whether it was not advisable for the government to keep the Japanese out of an area where bodily harm might be done to them, a vice chairman of the Fellowship replied, "No, I would say that what we ought to do is deal with the people who would do them bodily harm." It was a stunning thought in the circumstances. Costello himself enunciated the principle behind the mass evacuation in his questioning of A. L. Wirin, the American Civil Liberties Union representative, who noted that there had been no act of sabotage on the Pacific Coast before, during, or after Pearl Harbor, and called for the immediate return of the great majority of Japanese to their homes. "Don't you think," asked Costello, "that the justification of the placing of Jews in Germany, by the Hitler regime, in concentration camps, was pretty much that the Germans did not understand the Jewish mind and therefore they thought the best thing to do was to get them out of the way?" There was no trouble understanding Costello's mind.

The hearings were carried forward in Washington, where the director of the War Relocation Authority, Dillon S. Myer, defended his wards against the previous witnesses. Myer, succeeding Milton Eisenhower in the post, was attempting to do a distasteful and difficult job (particularly difficult was the sorting out of loyal from disloyal Japanese and keeping anti-American feeling at a minimum) with a barely adequate staff drawn largely from the Indian Service, Japanese experts being busy elsewhere at the time. He made small impression on the Committee majority. Thomas saw the whole affair as another New Deal plot—"It is just a silly social experiment you are conducting." The Committee report, issued in September, though not so bluntly composed, was critical of W.R.A. practices and personnel to the point of calling for Myer's ouster. Some of the criticisms of W.R.A. methods were well taken, but the Congressmen showed no patience for the civil liberties issues that had been raised by our treatment of 85,000 citizens. This was left to Representative Eberharter, replacing Jerry Voorhis as the Committee's voice of enlightenment. In his dissent, Eberharter discussed the legal ambiguities, criticized the majority report as prejudiced and unsubstantiated, and commended the W.R.A. for doing as well as it had done, all things considered. A few months later the Committee released another report on Japanese activities in the United States; here it complimented itself on seeing to it that the Japanese were removed from the West Coast and warned against their release from relocation camps without thorough investigation. America's treatment of the Japanese among us during the war remains the darkest page in an otherwise remarkably clear civil-liberties record. It is not the fault of the majority of the Dies Committee that the page is no blacker.

Martin Dies did not play a leading part in the investigation of the relocation camps, and indeed was rarely heard from during 1943. The Detroit race riots in June brought him forward for a moment, like a beloved star making a quick duty appearance at an actors' benefit; he announced his intention to investigate. The city's mayor pleaded with him to stay away from Detroit—life was burdensome enough just then. Whereupon Dies enlarged his plans; now he proposed to make an exhaustive, nationwide study of racial hatred, which he ascribed to "a combination of un-American propaganda activities and the coddling of races by politically minded people in this country who ignore the vast differences between the protection and the coddling of a race." Having relieved himself of this diagnosis, he troubled the subject no further.

Nineteen forty-four was the last year of the Dies Committee, and the chairman used part of it to join with Clare Hoffman and other foes of F.D.R. in a slanging match against Walter Winchell. For several weeks the columnist and radio commentator was the most popular subject for argument in the House of Representatives, to such a degree that, what with the yelling of the members and the demonstrating in the galleries, Speaker McCormack was unable to keep order. Winchell had over a period of weeks been attacking anti-Administration Congressmen for hampering the war effort, charging them with hobnobbing with the fascist-minded. He did not reach for elegance: "Many of Hitler's American pals have been arrested, but too many have been renominated." He called Congress the "House of Reprehensibles" and said it included "some of the sorriest stumblebums in the nation." Winchell's support of the Dies Committee in its first years had won him the chairman's kindest feelings. "I shall always have a warm spot in my heart for you," he wrote to the columnist in December 1940. But affections cool, and now, rising on one of his points of personal privilege, Dies called Winchell a liar for linking him with rightist Joseph Kamp, hinted he might investigate his sponsor and the N.B.C. Blue Network, and threatened to pass a law of some sort if he wasn't granted equal time.

Winchell's sponsor, the Andrew Jergens Company, manufacturer of lotions, attempted to spread balm over Dies's feelings by offering him fifteen minutes immediately following one of Winchell's Sunday evening broadcasts. Dies accepted and spoke from 9:15 to 9:30 on March 26. He told Mr. and Mrs. America and All the Ships at Sea that Winchell, "a peddler of bedroom keyhole scandal to the American people," was the tool of a clique that was impugning public officials and trying "to destroy the prestige of Congress in the interest of setting up an all-powerful central executive." He promised to expose the brains and the money behind this nefarious business and begged Winchell to "remember that those who expect tolerance in others should extend tolerance to others." Winchell responded with a challenge to Dies to sue him. The two met briefly in the reception room of Station WMAL in

Washington after the broadcast. "Let's get together and tell some more lies about each other," snapped Winchell. "I'd have to go some to get even," snapped Dies. The exchange was on the level of the entire debate, and although Mr. and Mrs. America's decision of who came out on top depended on how much they liked or hated F.D.R., on one point the evidence was conclusive: the Congressman and the commentator thoroughly deserved one another. (A few years later Winchell, whose political tastes were fashioned mainly at the Stork Club, would be a cheerleader for Joe McCarthy.)

The Winchell altercation was only an interlude for Dies in this last year; his preoccupation was with the C.I.O. Political Action Committee. He had every reason to detest the P.A.C. Had it not been brought into being by what its founders called the "deplorable record of the 78th Congress"? Did it not have as its incessantly proclaimed goal the removal from Washington of those representatives who, since the Republican gains of 1942, had frustrated Administration plans regarding taxes, incomes, and price control, and had passed the Smith-Connally anti-strike bill? Did it not list among the scores of Congressmen ripe for purging seven of the eight members of the Dies Committee and all of its champions in the House, including Smith of Virginia, Cox of Georgia, and Rankin of Mississippi? Were not the dossiers of its prime movers thick with the titles of front organizations against which the Committee had done famous battle, and, indeed, did not the C.I.O. itself still harbor its twenty-one Communist unions? Was the P.A.C. not working hammer in sickle with the Administration to get a fourth term for F.D.R., and was not its chairman, Sidney Hillman of the Amalgamated Clothing Workers, so formidable a political figure that he would hold veto power in 1944 over the Democrats' choice of a candidate for the vice presidency?

Dies's campaign against the P.A.C. began in January 1944, when his Committee received its final $75,000 from the House, and lasted clear up to election day. It was accompanied by only the gesture of an investigation. Hillman turned down the Committee's demand for the P.A.C.'s financial records—which the F.B.I. had already scrutinized and which would be made available later to the Committee on Congressional Expenditures—on the grounds that the Un-American Activities Committee had no authority to investigate a political group. A subpoena was issued for him, but he was never called to testify. The charges against the P.A.C. were mighty edifices teetering on a fragment of a foundation. Dies, supervising the proceedings from his ranch in Jasper, Texas, charged that the organization had raised a slush fund of $2 million to defeat members of Congress in 1944—$250,000 to defeat him alone— in violation of the Smith-Connally law which prohibited unions from making political contributions. He charged that government officials were cooperating with the P.A.C. in violation of the Hatch Act. On a visit to Washington he notified the House that "Sidney Hillman will soon succeed Earl Browder as head of the Communists in the United States." Stripling compiled a record of telephone calls and telegrams between the P.A.C. offices and a number of high Administration officials, not omitting Mrs. Roosevelt; he concluded that the P.A.C. was "the political arm of the New Deal Administration." When Dies told him to release this report at once to any syndicated columnist he wished, he gave it to Westbrook Pegler. Dies called on the attorney general to prosecute seventy-two government officials with alleged ties to the P.A.C. If Biddle didn't act at once, then he, Dies, would demand legislation "divorcing the government from the C.I.O." J. B. Matthews pored over his lists and found that 82 of the 141 members of the National Citizens Political Action Committee, an offshoot of the C.I.O.–P.A.C., had cooperated with twenty-five Communist fronts; the P.A.C., he certified, was now the major front organization in the land, representing the Communist Party's "supreme bid for power in the twenty-five years of its history." A week before election day a three-man subcommittee—humorously composed of two Democrats, Starnes and Costello, who were still warm from defeat in their respective primaries (for which the P.A.C. took some credit), and the dependable Thomas—issued a report, an echo of the year's charges. The P.A.C. was a "rallying point for the Communist

Party and its allied groups and organizations to rise to power by taking control of a major political party." (The last official publication of the Dies Committee, acting through Costello, consisted of 2,000 pages worth of material which it had collected over the years and put hurriedly between covers at the end of 1944 lest the fruits of Matthews's labors be lost to posterity. It was, according to a staff member in 1950, "a fair cross-section of our files today." Entitled *Communist Front Organizations with Special Reference to the National Citizens Political Action Committee* and published in seven volumes, this "Appendix Nine" contained 22,000 names—some Communists, many not—and was distributed to numerous government agencies before it was ordered restricted and destroyed by the full Committee in 1945. Copies of this catch-all, which contained no hint that some of the thousands of persons listed might not be subversive, reside still in the files of our security agencies and are available to Congressmen through the Library of Congress for whatever use they may care to make of the contents.)

Once again, as so often in the Committee's essays, it was not possible to take its charges straight, yet impossible to dismiss them altogether. Its purposes were blatantly partisan, yet there was some fire within the billows of smoke. Major C.I.O. unions were still in Communist hands—though their hours were numbered—and they were influential in the P.A.C. Far from being political pariahs, in 1944 our Communists and fellow travelers in the unions and out wanted only what all liberals wanted: a fourth term for F.D.R. and the unconditional surrender of the Axis powers. Their pretensions to patriotism had never seemed more genuine, and every victory on the Eastern front added to their prestige. As for Hillman, the "Russian pantsmaker" as John L. Lewis sourly titled him, he had not somersaulted with the Communists during the Nazi-Soviet pact, but he had joined with the likes of Marcantonio, Quill, and Curran to take the New York State American Labor Party out of the hands of anti-Communist unionists. And although his eminence in Democratic politics was never what the Republican campaign cry, "Clear it with Sidney," implied, the P.A.C. did constitute a power play by left-wing union leaders ambitiously contemplating the shape of things in postwar America.

On May 12, in the middle of his battle against the P.A.C., Martin Dies announced from Texas that he would not seek reelection. He had been in ill health, with a throat ailment, for several weeks; he was wearied after fourteen years in the House; he wanted to go into private business—"I have always had a dread of becoming a professional politician, dependent upon the public for my livelihood." Moreover, as many were quick to point out cheerily, he faced a hard campaign in 1944. A few days earlier a Democratic convention in his home county, influenced now by recently organized oil refinery workers, had labeled him a demagogue. Later, he would charge that as part of its assault on him the Administration gave large contracts to industries along the Gulf Coast section of his district in order to bring in thousands of workers from other states, and that Internal Revenue agents were sent down from Baltimore in 1943 to foster innuendo in his district about his financial dealings. The steel workers, in convention at the hour of Dies's announcement of retirement, paused to celebrate what Philip Murray called "the most outstanding contribution made by Dies to our national welfare." Before the year was over, Murray and his steelworkers, Hillman and his pantsmakers, and the entire C.I.O.–P.A.C. would have a great deal more to celebrate. Not only did Roosevelt win his fourth term, but the Democrats substantially increased their majority in the House of Representatives. As sauce to the banquet for unregenerate New Dealers, the grandfather of the Dies Committee, Hamilton Fish, was retired by an independent Republican.

So there was a satisfying formal design to the career of the Dies Committee. It ended, as it began, in an election year, with an attack on C.I.O.–Communist–New Deal interlocking subversion. Having won his spurs in rides against sit-down strikers and left-wing unionists, Dies retreated before the vigor, short-lived, of the C.I.O.–P.A.C. Would his Committee be continued without him? The question did not weigh heavily in those halls where private sentiments are not always reflected by public votes. It was not quite a case of good riddance, not quite; but Dies, having said "So long, Doc" to Matthews, was gone, Mason had retired, Starnes had been defeated, and the halls of Congress were unshaken by any swell of reluctance to let their creature drift away with them into oblivion. Still, one loyal voice was raised. A day after the announcement of the chairman's intent to leave the field, one voice urged that the Un-American Activities Committee not merely be extended, but that it be made a permanent standing committee of the House: ". . . the weapon of exposure which has been so effectively used by our Committee must be maintained . . ." So, dimly intimating his own future glory, spoke J. Parnell Thomas.

Martin Dies returned to Washington in 1953 as Congressman at large from Texas and he served until 1959, bringing to twenty years his career in the House of Representatives. The Republicans were in charge in 1953, and he was received politely enough. When a Senate subcommittee was formed to suggest rules for the improvement of Congressional investigations, then in one of their more uproarious phases, the veteran investigator was invited to give expert testimony. He advised the senators: "Primarily, if you get a good chairman and a good committee you will have a good investigation. Outside of that, all you need is a few general rules to see that the witness and the public get a fair break." No one laughed openly, but his time had run out. The leaders of his party, whose memories were as long as their tenure, refused him a position on his own Committee when they took control of Congress in 1955, and he was like an aging actor returned to the stage of past triumphs only to find that other performers had won the matinee-goers' hearts. The returned's only moment came in the summer of 1954 when the Congress passed the Communist Control Act, but even that was not as punishing to the Reds as he and his odd ally in this cause, Senator Hubert Humphrey, proposed.[8]

[8] Mr. Humphrey's leadership of the Senate liberals in an attempt to add penalties against individual Communists to the 1954 bill was a transparent

It is easy for us, removed from the sound and fury of the thirties, to see that neither J. B. Matthews nor Vito Marcantonio defined the nature of the struggle that roared about the big and blustering figure of Martin Dies. It was not a struggle of Communism versus the Republic, even though some of the union chiefs and federal officials whom Dies attacked aspired to nothing grander than to function as bureaucrats in a Sovietized America. Nor was it a struggle of democracy versus fascism, even though the hearts of men like Hoffman and Rankin went out to the Christian Fronters. What Dies represented was an aching nostalgia for pre–World War I America. He stood for the small town populated by a few hundred neighborly descendants of early settlers and against the big cities with their polyglot masses. He stood for a style of life that was being shaken by industrial unions, by the Negro awakening, by revolutionary currents of every sort. He stood for fundamentalist enthusiasm against the radical enlightenment. He stood for Western insularity and against Eastern cosmopolitanism, for a strong legislature and against a strong executive, for the old verities and old slogans and against the new slogans and new demands. He stood, practically alone, he rapidly persuaded himself, for capitalism and the Constitution and God, and these were under attack from Pennsylvania Avenue and from New York City as much as from Moscow.

But Dies, unlike the Marxist ideologues, could not subsist on theories; he needed flesh, and of a certain kind. The pleasure of helping to send Earl Browder to jail was slight beside the pleasure of drawing blood from Frances Perkins, Harold Ickes, or Henry Wallace. Politics was a street brawl for him; one hit out and hoped that more blows landed on the other gang than on bystanders. Since in New Deal Washington nearly everybody belonged to the other gang the odds were in his favor. It was a severe strain for New Dealers to keep fair minds and equable tempers while being mauled—though Voorhis did re-

effort to erase the "soft on Communism" taint from their party in an election year and embarrass the Republican Administration, which had the good sense to oppose the measure, into a veto. The effects of Senator McCarthy's crusade have been somewhat exaggerated in the telling, but this strange legislative exhibition was one of them.

markably well—and the flamboyant chairman's windy demagogy, unflagging opportunism, and casual cruelties strained
their objectivity. He called on sinners to repent—on condition
that they repent not only the sins of Communism and those of
fellow traveling, but the multitudinous sins of liberalism as
well; he wanted them groveling or not at all.

The trouble was that Dies, having sat at the feet of Matthews, was more often than not right about the organizations
he labeled Communist fronts. He did not understand much
more about them or about what drew thousands of non-
Communists into them, and certainly he understood nothing
about the unknown individuals he condemned because he
came upon their names on a list—but on the single, crucial
point of Communist control he was right. He was right about
the American League for Peace and Democracy. He was
right about the unions he charged with Communist leadership.
He was right about the primary allegiance of the Communist
Party. And because he was right and because so many liberals
of the time found it so difficult to confess even to themselves
that a Martin Dies was closer to a central truth about Communism in America than a Harry Ward and a Robert Morss
Lovett, many resorted to foolish defenses and transparent
rationalizations that would plague them for years to come. It
was flagrantly dishonorable to throw selfless men, with whom
one had stood in worthy causes from Sacco and Vanzetti
forward, to vicious benighted inquisitors, and so liberal spokesmen found themselves arguing that Communists were pretty
much like Masons and the C.P. was like the G.O.P. The outrage
they roared at the Committee's free and easy methods would
have turned to purrs had only the methods been directed at
Father Coughlin and Gerald L. K. Smith.

Thirty years later we can see that those on both sides who
honestly believed or honestly feared that America's future
belonged to fascism or to Communism shared a great mis-
judgment; they underestimated the resilience and endurance
of our institutions. Our economic and political arrangements
were rife with inequalities; compared to other systems they
lacked theoretical underpinning and aesthetic satisfaction;

they offered little in the thirties to match the dynamism of the fascist countries or the ferver of the U.S.S.R. But they would confound both those who called for their overthrow before sunset and those, like Dies, who believed they were defending the institutions by resisting all change. Our body politic, it turned out, was like a peculiar patient who can survive the most extensive surgery and shed astonishingly little blood in the process. There are no guarantees that this will always be the case, that every operation will cost little and end happily, but experience does allow the hope that the radicals of the sixties, like those of the thirties, will make their contributions within the system and not only, as they enjoy protesting, in spite of it. It also suggests that those who wish to crush the noisy young people today will tomorrow, when their extravagances have become picturesque memories, live contentedly with the changes they have goaded us into accepting.

But not Martin Dies. He went back to Texas in 1959 and in 1963 he published his autobiography. He was sixty-two years old; the world was awry, and he uttered dry words in a dry season. The recognition of the U.S.S.R. was "a colossal blunder." The "pink fringe around the Red core of Communism . . . really headed America for disaster." We lost World War II to the Communists. Newspapers had treated him unfairly and the liberal establishment in book publishing had conspired against him. Aliens had poured into the land. The drive for civil rights was forwarding Communist purposes. The direct election of U.S. Senators was a mistake. "Ultra-liberals" had betrayed the invasion of Cuba. Why hadn't the American Civil Liberties Union been investigated? Liberals had inflicted an unsound fiscal policy on the country. The tax-exempt foundations were worrisome: "To realize the inherent dangers we need only recall that Alger Hiss was president of the Carnegie Fund." The United Nations was a "reservoir of espionage agents." Liberals had the same goals as Communists, and responsibility for our present peril must be laid at their feet.

The memories of his battles against subversives in the government are still green for him, oases in the political desert he sees all around. His hatreds—of F.D.R., Mrs. Roosevelt, Francis Biddle, and all the rest, most of them shades now— have grown more virulent with the decades, but that is a kind of comfort too. Because there are not many trophies left him of his important years. He cannot hope for the national eulogies which Henry Wallace and Frances Perkins and Gardner Jackson received, which all the old New Dealers have received, and will receive. America is in the hands of past antagonists, Lyndon Johnson and the Reuther boys, and Martin Dies has ended up in the same accommodating boat as Earl Browder, unhonored even by his heirs and successors.

6

★ ★ ★ ★ ★

1945-1946: Rankin's Coup

O PENING DAY of a new Congress is not ordinarily a productive occasion. It is short on time, long on formalities and
fellowship. Such was the expectation on Wednesday, January
3, 1945, as members of the seventy-ninth Congress took their
places and listened to their chaplain call on God for assistance
in building "a future altogether worthy of our traditions." The
future of this Congress held the end of World War II, an
explosion of challenges around the globe and the resumption
of unsettled political battles at home. Large matters, but one
man present that day had something more homely in mind.
There was a misunderstanding about John E. Rankin among
those who relied for their news on the columns of *PM* or even
of more objective journals. He was classed with all the other
haters down South: rude, ignorant fellows not much different
in nature from the farm animals which the more affluent of
them owned. That he despised Negroes, Jews, aliens, and
liberals was, to be sure, his foremost claim to Americanism—but
along with his extensive hates and vaunted ignorance went
a canny mind, an energetic temperament, and an excellent
grasp of parliamentary procedure. He was not an elegant
debater, but he enjoyed the sport and could be counted on to
turn any sparring match into a rough and tumble and often as
not to land a mean blow or two. On this Wednesday he bided
his time while Minority Leader Martin introduced Speaker
Rayburn and while Speaker Rayburn spoke about national
unity—until Chairman Sabath of the Rules Committee made

the customary proposal to adopt the rules of the previous Congress. Then Rankin arose and offered an amendment to the rules—to make the Committee on Un-American Activities a standing committee of the House, with great latitude as to what it might investigate and how it chose to go about its investigating.

The move took the House leadership by surprise, not only because it was in itself unorthodox, but because an understanding had been arrived at that any effort at reincarnating the Dies Committee would be given over to the mercies of Sabath's group. By offering his amendment now, before the Rules Committee itself had been reestablished, the forewarned gentleman from Mississippi was attempting an end run. Rankin's main argument, besides the rhetorical one that the Dies Committee had "performed a duty second to none," was that if the House did not act with dispatch, the files so assiduously collected by J. B. Matthews might be removed by unnamed persons and thrown into the Potomac River. Rankin took care to remind his colleagues that the American Legion, whose political potential loomed very large indeed as the war neared its end, had lately asked Congress to continue the Committee and make it permanent.

The leaders of the House had no inclination on this opening day to affront patriots by an insult to the memory of Martin Dies. On the other hand, they had no enthusiasm for adopting his offspring as their own unto eternity. So they entrusted their cause to Representative McCormack, who explained in his passion-quelling way that he was certainly in favor of continuance of the Special Committee, but wanted the matter taken up in proper order, via the Rules Committee. He urged a vote against "the procedure that in 150 years of Constitutional history, no Congress . . . has ever followed to establish a permanent committee of this kind." In a division on the question, Rankin's amendment was defeated by 134 to 146. Whereupon the Mississippian, with the experience of nearly a quarter of a century in the House, knew he had won. He asked for a roll call, and now the vote was 207 for the Committee and 186 against. Forty members, including the young man from Texas, Lyndon B. Johnson, voted a neutral "present." "I caught 'em flat-footed and flat-headed," Rankin rejoiced. A few minutes later, at 3:28 p.m., the House adjourned, having to its own astonishment and at some cost to its traditions, created a permanent Committee on Un-American Activities.

The majority vote of January 3, made up of 137 Republicans and 70 Democrats, 63 of them from the South, put the Administration on notice that despite F.D.R.'s success in November, the conservative coalition in Congress which had proved such a nuisance during the past two years was still very much alive. As if to still any doubts on this point, Representative Hoffman, recent victor over a strong C.I.O.–P.A.C. campaign in his Michigan district, rose on January 4 like the spirit of things past, present, and future, to carry forward Martin Dies's attack on New Dealers, parlor pinks, and left-wingers. After Hoffman had thanked God for the Un-American Activities Committee, Voorhis, who had been in the minority the day before, offered once again his outline of how to make a decent woman of her, thus prompting Rankin to declare himself against any muzzling of the new group. But Rankin added, in an unusual bow to propriety, "I do not believe, and I have never believed in smear campaigns."

Rankin's opinions were of more than ordinary interest because, as progenitor of the new Committee, he was entitled to become its chairman. This honor he let pass since he did not wish to relinquish the chairmanship of the Veterans Affairs Committee, whose future in 1945 was extremely promising, but the issue was merely nominal. The Dies Committee had in fact become the Rankin Committee. Appointed as chairman was a delegate from the Jersey City Democratic machine, Edward J. Hart, whose qualifications for the role were that he had during ten years in Congress managed to give offense neither to the C.I.O. nor to the South. He had voted against the Rankin amendment but took no part in the debate. "I am glad such a thoroughgoing American will be in charge of that

Committee," said Attorney General Biddle, with crossed fingers.[1]

Karl Mundt started the Committee on its way by sending out letters to a hundred prominent Americans, inviting them to set down their notions of what constituted "un-American activities." Walter Winchell, Eleanor Roosevelt, the Knights of Columbus, veterans' organizations, the nation's governors, Drew Pearson, Henry Wallace, Harold Ickes—all were solicited. "Unless it is held that there is no such thing as un-American activity," reasoned Mundt, "Americans should be able to agree on what it is and our Committee could then expose it." *Life* magazine called this venture "very serious and public spirited." About half of the sample replied and some weeks later the Brookings Institution, to which the replies had been turned over, submitted a monograph that was very like one of Jerry Voorhis's speeches. The Committee was reminded that its object was not to prosecute, persecute, or punish anybody—just to present the facts. The whole very serious and public-spirited study vanished at once, like a Quaker tract beneath the heels of fans pressing toward the fights.

Certainly the realistic Rankin paid it no mind. He now had his Committee; a few weeks later he had $50,000 to sustain it—"merely the beginning," he informed the House; he had a Committee counsel, Ernie Adamson, who shared his philosophy and style; and he had a chairman who could be voted down or ignored as the occasion seemed to require. (He also had the pleasure, in March, of seeing Aubrey Williams, former administrator of the National Youth Administration and a favorite target of the Dies Committee, refused confirmation by the Senate to head the Rural Electrification Administration, a victory for the spirit of Martin Dies.)

[1] The other Democrats, in addition to Rankin, were Herbert C. Bonner of North Carolina, J. Hardin Peterson of Florida, John R. Murdock of Arizona, and J. W. Robinson of Utah; though Murdock and Robinson would show displeasure at some of the Committee's doings, none of these men would play much of a part in the business of the next two years. On the Republican side, Gerald W. Landis of Indiana was named to keep company the reappointed Representatives Mundt and Thomas. And a Georgia-born lawyer, Ernie Adamson, became chief counsel.

As the spring of 1945 turned into summer, the Committee, over the objections of its chairman, embarked upon its first open hearings. At the bar once again was the Office of Price Administration. The agency, which many businessmen saw as the New Deal incarnate, was in trouble. Up for renewal in Congress, it was met with bitter attacks, and, as Hart discerned, the Committee hearings, which opened on the very day that the agency's fate was scheduled to be taken up in the House, were Rankin's contribution to the anti-O.P.A. cause. The gentleman from Mississippi made no secret of his conviction that the O.P.A.—along with the Wagner Act, the wages and hours bill, and similar novelties—was at the root of most of the nation's ills. "It is about time we got rid of the O.P.A.," he announced periodically. "I am tired of those commissars attempting to tell the American people how naked they shall go."

The hearings in June, under Adamson's direction, centered on an O.P.A. radio program, *Soldiers with Coupons,* that was being presented for fifteen minutes a week over several stations around the country. The program featured dramatic skits entitled *Black Market in Meat, Nylon Black Market,* and *Rent Control,* and the cost of the time on the New York station where it originated was borne, as a wartime public service, by Standard Brands, makers of Chase and Sanborn coffee, Fleischman's yeast, and other popular staples. The shows, written by a man of allegedly questionable political tendencies, were peopled with good guys named Tony, Sam, Nick, Irving, and Mom, who talked to landlords named Bolton or Allen or White like this: "You won't paint. You won't fix nothing. You chisel on the heat and now you want to raise the rent." The deus ex machina was always Your O.P.A.: "Sure thing, Joe, the O.P.A. was set up for little guys like you and me." These efforts did owe something to the Union Square school of dramatic literature, but to call them subversive was stretching a point. To Rankin, however, the O.P.A. was from start to finish a tool of bureaucratic subversion, and Chairman Hart was hard put to keep the hearings from straying into the policy matters then being argued over in the House. Representative Murdock helped him by persistently asking the counsel for specific evidence of wrongdoing. Thus inhibited and with no real charge against the agency except for the fact that it existed, Adamson thrashed around for three days, hinting at some sort of plot between Standard Brands and the White House, with O.P.A. Administrator Chester Bowles serving as sinister broker, to defame American business. The hearings produced nothing more spectacular than another twinge of discomfort for a severely ailing agency.

Having done what he could to advance the evisceration of the O.P.A., which represented the kind of economic order that some on the left dreamed of continuing in a peacetime America, Rankin turned West. He announced that his Committee was about to search out "one of the most dangerous plots ever instigated for the overthrow of the government . . . the greatest hotbed of subversive activities in the United States." The plot and hotbed were in Hollywood. "We're on the trail of the tarantula," said Rankin, "and we're going to follow through."

The decision to investigate the movies, long on the agenda of Martin Dies and just then under scrutiny by the Tenney Committee of the California state legislature, was made at a meeting of six of the Hart Committee's members, not including its chairman. Such a flouting of authority, not to say Congressional courtesy, would have been unthinkable during the Dies stewardship, but from the first days of Hart's appointment, it was evident that he had neither the votes nor the personality nor the heart to control his committee. One member explained to reporters how they got started on the tarantula's trail: "Mr. Rankin offered a motion to send investigators to Hollywood. We don't know what information he has but the motion was agreed to on the theory that we ought to find out whether our acting chairman is having nightmares or whether there really is something that ought to be investigated."

For Ed Hart that was the end. Two days later, he notified the Speaker that he was resigning as chairman of the Committee—"My physician has given me definite instructions to diminish substantially my activities for an indefinite time." In response to speculation that some intra-Committee dissension lay behind the withdrawal, Representative Mundt assured the House that it was strictly a question of health; he gave Hart A-1 clearance as a good American who "exemplified a fearless courage and a devotion to principle which won him the admiration of our entire Committee." Rankin, for his part, spared no more thought for the departure of the admired chairman than he had for his presence, and replying to charges of a witch hunt from Walter Winchell and Drew Pearson, reiterated his determination "to expose those elements that are insidiously trying to spread subversive propaganda, poison the minds of your children, distort the history of our country and discredit Christianity . . ."

No sooner had John S. Wood of Georgia been named to the Committee chairmanship than five California Democrats met with him privately and attempted to impress upon him the political uses to which previous investigations in their state had been put. Rankin's reply to this piece of impertinence was the revelation that 191 paintings, "loathsome paintings" by contributing artists of the *New Masses,* were at that moment hanging in the homes of film celebrities. "I am sure," he said, "that some of them got into the home of Charles Chaplin, the perverted subject of Great Britain who has become notorious for his forcible seduction of white girls . . ." The source of Rankin's animus against Hollywood—and he made no particular effort to conceal it—was the large number of Jews eminent in the film industry. "I have no quarrel with any man about his religion," he explained after a Committee investigator was reported to have warned some liberal Jews to "watch their steps" lest the fate of Germany's Jews overtake them. "Any man who believes in the fundamental principles of Christianity and lives up to them, whether he is Catholic or Protestant, certainly deserves the respect and confidence of mankind." In Rankin's mind, to call a Jew a Communist was a tautology. His convictions led him to attribute all the horrors of the Russian revolution to Trotsky and to see Stalin as a kind of reformer, a seminary student who opened the churches, got rid of the commissars, and drove the local Reds to America. "Communism is older than Christianity," he would explain from time to time. "It hounded and persecuted the Savior during his earthly ministry, inspired his crucifixion, derided him in his dying agony, and then gambled for his garments at the foot of the cross." In the halls of Congress he called Walter Winchell "a little slime-mongering kike" and he took glee in baiting his Jewish colleagues, particularly Sabath and Celler. One day he referred to the latter as "the Jewish gentleman from New York." When Celler protested, Rankin asked, "Does the member from New York object to being called a Jew or does he object to being called a gentleman? What is he kicking about?"[2]

The Committee went forward with its Hollywood investigation, but except for periodic hints by Rankin and Counsel Adamson of dreadful findings, "so hot" that they could not even be released, it bore no fruit. The movie industry was not fated to undergo its test of fire quite yet. Hollywood was not the only media of communication in enemy hands, however. In fact, they all were, and the Committee, under the generalship of its chief counsel, found time a few months later to cast a fleeting glance at radio, when Ernie Adamson "requested" the scripts of seven commentators in New York City, all of a leftward bent.[3] Adamson did not trouble to make nice political distinctions among them. It was sufficient that one or another had reportedly praised the Soviet army, criticized Congressmen and Chiang Kai-shek, was foreign-born or spoke English with an accent. Adamson's initiative had not been sanctioned by a Committee vote, and engendered a vigorous debate on the floor of the House, but Wood and Rankin backed him up. "Do you know the reason we called for the scripts?" asked Rankin, and replied: "Some of those scripts ought not to be drummed into the ears of the American people." Two of the broadcasters were hastily dropped by their stations, and Wood introduced a bill which would have required, among other things, that news programs be clearly distinguished from

[2] "Upon analysis," wrote Rankin's admirer Westbrook Pegler, "the worst offense charged to Rankin of Mississippi is that he has the sort of manly personal temper that most Americans respect in their friends and fellow men."
[3] They were Cecil Brown, William S. Gailmore, Hans Jacob, Johannes Steel, Raymond Gram Swing, J. Raymond Walsh, and Sidney Walton.

opinion programs and that the commentator's name, place of birth, nationality, and political affiliation be open to public inspection. "The time has come," an unidentified Committee spokesman told reporters, "to determine how far you can go with free speech." To emphasize the point, when a full-page advertisement featuring cartoons of gagged couples, headed YOU CAN'T TALK . . . IT'S UN-AMERICAN and signed by Citizens to Abolish the Wood-Rankin Committee (many of them familiar signatories from united front days), appeared in *The New York Times*, Thomas hastened to New York to question not only its sponsors but the head of the advertising agency which had placed it as well as a representative of the newspaper's advertising department.

By such efforts, the Rankin Committee after six months left no more doubt of its intentions than the Dies Committee had, and there was nothing it could do short of investigating the Daughters of the American Revolution for denying Constitution Hall to Negro performers that could placate its critics. But neither Rankin nor his talkative chief counsel Adamson were of a placating spirit; they could not open their mouths without incensing spokesmen of the various organizations, ranging from genuine civil libertarian to mere Communist, who allied themselves with a handful of Congressmen in the endless and unrewarding effort to abolish the Committee.

By the fall of 1945, when the Committee turned its attention to the Communist Party, the radical left in America was in distressed circumstances. The year began sunnily for our Communists, led by Earl Browder and nourished by the victorious alliance against the Germans. It ended under the cloud of cold war, with Browder, "the man from the heart of America," as C.P. warhorse Elizabeth Gurley Flynn liked to speak of him in better days, in disgrace and William Z. Foster carrying the proletarian banner. A few weeks after the Yalta Conference of February 1945, where it became evident that Stalin on the one hand and Roosevelt and Churchill on the other had conflicting hopes for the political future of Western Europe, Browder, personification of the wartime era of good Russian-

American feelings, promoter of the suddenly anachronistic line of "peaceful coexistence" between capitalism and socialism, was rudely cast down. The sentence was delivered in April by the French Communist chief Jacques Duclos, reprinted in May by the *Daily Worker,* and accepted by former comrades and sycophants with the customary beating of breasts. In July Browder and Browderism were denounced at a special convention, and the Communist Political Association became once again the Communist Party. It would not be very long, promised Foster at a rally in September, before the United States would be nationalizing its banks. In February 1946, Browder was expelled from the Party as a "social imperialist." The 1945 events naturally invited the attention of the Committee, and several C.P. leaders were summoned to Washington. But it was the Ham Fish experience all over again. Browder was terse and antagonistic. Foster was garrulous and antagonistic. Adamson, the interrogator, was antagonistic and inept. And an opportunity to show the extent of the American Communists' servitude to Moscow was lost as Mundt and Rankin used the hearings to exhibit their patriotic detestation of Communism and all its works.

Following tradition, the Committee moved at the end of 1945 from the Communist Party proper to groups which it was convinced were fronts: the National Council of American-Soviet Friendship, the National Federation for Constitutional Liberties and, most especially, the Joint Anti-Fascist Refugee Committee. Its attention was drawn to the last-named by a Madison Square Garden rally in September to raise money for the maintenance of some 200,000 Spanish refugees in France. The rally, whose slogan was "Break Off Relations With Franco!," was very much in the old Popular Front vein, with the acting head of the Soviet embassy, Nikolai Novikov, there to assure everyone that "Now as before the Soviet Union is the leading power in the task of protection of democracy in the whole world." Especially upsetting to numbers of people in this country was the talk by British Laborite Harold Laski, transmitted from England and broadcast to American radio listeners outside of the Garden. Laski, whom neither Rankin nor Adamson had ever heard of up to this time and whom Thomas described as the "Red fascist leader of England," shared the wishful thoughts of those who believed that Franco might actually be toppled by the displeasure of the West over his services to Hitler during the recent war. He suggested in his speech that the footdragging of America and Britain in this cause might be due to fear of hostility from the Vatican. Catholic organizations mounted a campaign of protest, and in a few weeks the Committee received thousands of postcards demanding an investigation. Rankin and Adamson, like children commanded to eat a lollypop, responded without delay.

The "Joint" in Joint Anti-Fascist Refugee Committee had reference to the fact that it was created in 1942 from a merger of three organizations, each of them qualified candidates for the Dies Committee lists: The American Committee to Save Refugees, the United American Spanish Aid Committee, and the League of American Writers. Its function was ostensibly to provide medical care and other services to Spanish refugees in France, and for this purpose it had been licensed by the President's War Relief Control Board and granted tax exemption. The Spanish refugees, for whom the world victory over fascism was a bitter irony while Franco remained in power, unquestionably needed assistance and needed it sorely, but friends of the Anti-Fascist Refugee Committee were being disingenuous when they compared the group to agencies like the Red Cross and U.N.R.R.A. Having selected its beneficiaries on political grounds, its every plea for funds constituted an attack on Franco; it could not have avoided becoming an anti-Franco propaganda source if it had wanted to, and it didn't want to. Its board of directors was sprinkled with Communists, the most prominent being Howard Fast, writer of popular novels, and the entire board was strenuously and unapologetically anti-fascist. To Rankin, Adamson, and Wood, being anti-Franco was a symptom of anti-Americanism, and they charged that the Anti-Fascist Refugee Committee was "engaged in political activity in behalf of Communists" and that it was disseminating propaganda of "a subversive character." In searching for documentation of these charges, Wood had to reach back to the

Spanish Civil War, when Dr. Edward K. Barsky, the committee's chairman, ran a hospital in Spain "organized on the model of the Soviet Republic. He [Barsky] referred to himself as the commissar and the employees of that organization were required to address each other as comrades."[4]

But the question of what the Anti-Fascist Refugee Committee had done was lost in the commotion over what it would not do. It refused to turn over the records subpoenaed by Chairman Wood "in the interest of saving time" after Adamson had asked the War Relief Control Board to revoke the group's license. Barsky claimed that he had no authority to hand over the records, since such authority was vested in the executive board. The members of the executive board, coached by their collective attorney, claimed that they had voted to give over this authority to their executive secretary, a young woman named Helen R. Bryan. Miss Bryan claimed that, "as custodian of the books and records," she had been left with "the responsibility of determining, after consultation with counsel, what action to take, within the limits of my legal rights, to protect its records from unlawful search and seizure," and she had concluded that the subpoena was invalid. It was not, she contended, pertinent to the Congressional inquiry; she doubted the constitutionality of the Un-American Activities Committee; she objected to the catch-all subpoena on the grounds that it would prevent her organization from operating; and she feared that disclosure of the records would put the families of refugees in jeopardy.

This buck-passing was designed not only to annoy Wood and Rankin and to establish a legal defense, but to feed a debate in Congress, led by Marcantonio, over the Un-American Activities Committee, and to launch a public campaign against its existence. Barsky was cited for contempt by the House at the end of March. "We are going to have a roll call on this

4 The Committee's case against J.A.F.R.C. took up most of its report, issued June 7, 1946, which also ridiculed the Department of Justice for its sedition trial of a batch of native fascists and attacked a 1945 army pamphlet for the statement: "In the United States, native fascists have often been anti-Catholic, anti-Jewish, anti-labor, anti-foreign born." The Committee commented: "If a person is anti-white or anti-Gentile, or anti-white man, under the Army teachings, he is quite all right."

resolution," said Rankin, "and I am sure the American people will be interested in the vote." There were only four nays. And a few weeks later, after a bitter debate which pitted Rankin, Mundt, and Thomas against Celler, Marcantonio, and Helen Gahagan Douglas, the Committee set a record by obtaining contempt citations against all sixteen members of the executive board and Miss Bryan. Each of them had appeared before the Committee and, in identical language, refused to abet the investigation.

Other contempt citations were obtained that summer, on similar grounds and amid similar angry debate, against Corliss Lamont, chairman of the National Council of American-Soviet Friendship, whom the Dies Committee had, with fair accuracy, called "probably the most persistent propandist for the Soviet Union to be found anywhere in the United States"; Richard Morford, the Council's director; and George Marshall, chairman of the National Federation for Constitutional Liberties.[5] Being tested in each of these cases was the power of the Committee to demand that documents be produced for its inspection. All of those cited, with the exception of Corliss Lamont, who had not exactly refused to produce his group's documents but had merely said they were under Morford's control, were indicted, found guilty, and rebuffed by appelate courts.

The power of Congress to punish for contempt is an old one. Since 1857 it has been a misdemeanor, carrying a sentence of from one month to one year in jail and a fine of from $100 to $1,000, to fail to appear before an arm of Congress or to answer any pertinent questions. The procedure in these cases—

[5] The citing of Marshall delayed adjournment of Congress since each time that Rankin rose to bring his Committee's resolution to the floor, Marcantonio or an ally would suggest the lack of a quorum. When a majority of the members were rounded up by the ringing of the House bell, Rankin moved to "dispense with proceedings" so that he might go ahead with his contempt citations. One of the Marcantonio group—Biemiller, Hook, and De Lacy—thereupon asked for a roll call, which showed that a quorum was no longer present, the Congressmen having left the chamber. The procedure was repeated eight times and exhausted an entire July afternoon. When Rankin protested that it constituted "a dilatory tactic," there was laughter in the House since it was he who had taught Marcantonio the trick during the debate on setting up a Fair Employment Practices Commission.

which Martin Dies, as we have seen, attempted to circumvent
—is rather complicated: After a committee of either House
votes to cite a witness for contempt, the case is brought before
the respective House, which almost invariably accedes to the
desires of the committee. The U.S. attorney is thereupon instructed to prepare a bill of indictment; a grand jury does the
indicting; and the trial takes place in federal court. The Un-
American Activities Committee, whose resolution grants it the
broad franchise "to hold such hearings, to require the attendance of such witnesses and the production of such books,
papers and documents, and to take such testimony as it deems
necessary," holds the record, with no near competitor, for
instituting contempt citations, and scores of witnesses have
learned the truth of the lesson that District Judge Holtzoff
delivered in turning down a plea by five defendants in these
early cases: "A person who declines to comply with a direction
of the Committee on the basis of a claim that the resolution
creating it is invalid, or that the Committee is exceeding its
jurisdiction, acts at his peril."

Marshall was given three months and $500; Morford, three
months and $350. Five of the members of J.A.F.R.C. resigned
and expressed a wish to purge themselves and so were let off
with a fine of $500 and three-month suspended sentences. The
others, with the exception of Chairman Barsky, were made to
serve their three months, and Barsky was given six months
along with a $500 fine. In turning back the appeal of Barsky
et al., the Court of Appeals laid down a thoroughgoing affirmation of the Committee's legitimacy and practices. Judge Edger-
ton wrote a blunt dissent, in words very like those the
Committee's opponents had been uttering for nearly a decade
and would still be uttering two decades later: "In my opinion
the House Committee investigation abridges freedom of speech
and inflicts punishment without trial." But he was in a two-
to-one minority. Judges Clark and Prettyman strenuously
affirmed the right of Congress to inquire into potential threats
to the national security even if it could not be shown that
these threats were clear and present. The remedy for unseemly

conduct by a committee of Congress, declared the judges, lay with the Congress or the people, not with the courts. When the Supreme Court refused to review the case, Howard Fast, bound for jail, announced "the beginning of fascism in America."[6]

In his study of these events, Professor Carl Beck summarizes the points of law which were developed out of the contempt citations of the seventy-ninth Congress:

> It was held that the existence of a quorum of the Committee could only be challenged during the hearings, not upon trial; it was held that testimony taken during investigations was admissible in the trial even though it was to be used to incriminate the witness; it was held that a trial jury may be composed of government employees even though their freedom of decision may be restricted by government loyalty oaths and security programs; it was held that the Committee could subpoena documents, particularly where there existed some evidence of subversive activities; it was held that a member of the board of directors of an organization was responsible for corporate decisions; it was held that the witness cannot decide what is pertinent and not pertinent because he might well challenge all questions; it was held that freedom of speech was not unduly impinged by an investigation into political associations; and finally, it was held that the resolution establishing the Committee on Un-American Activities and the subpoenas issued by the Committee did not suffer from the vice of vagueness.

The Committee thus emerged from its encounters with Barsky, Marshall, Morford, and the rest in a stronger position than its supporters could dare have hoped.

In January 1946, while the contempt cases were in process, the Committee devoted a day to taking testimony from Gerald L. K. Smith, the country's noisiest anti-Semite, whose past associations included William Dudley Pelley, Huey Long, Francis Townsend, and Father Coughlin and whose current vehicle was the America First Party. The summons to Smith

[6] Meeting Fast on the street shortly before he went off to serve his time, Lillian Hellman tells us, Dashiell Hammett remarked, "It will be easier for you, Howard, if you first take off the crown of thorns."

was designed to show that, despite slanders to the contrary, the Committee was as troubled by un-Americanism on the right as on the left, and an invitation was issued to every member of Congress to come and assist in the questioning. The only response this brought was an unfriendly statement from Representatives Celler, De Lacy, Marcantonio, Patterson, and Savage, which conveyed their doubts that the Committee would give Smith the same going-over it gave Communists. The doubts were amply justified by the event. Rankin acted as Smith's advocate, Thomas as his straight man—"Would you say that [the New Deal] was more fascist or more Communist?" Chairman Wood succumbed as usual, and before the hearing was half over, Smith was being drawn out on his opinions concerning Communists in government, the armed services, unions, and the movies—"I am convinced that Frank Sinatra is not a naïve dupe." The Committee's partisans would from this time use the fact that Smith had been questioned as evidence of its impartiality in seeking out subversion, but rarely, even in the most exuberant days of Martin Dies, had it given a more open display of ideological bias.

With no perceptible plan to guide it, the Committee tended in these two years to seek inspiration in headlines, and so when a Soviet spy ring was discovered which had obtained atomic secrets with the assistance of officials in the Canadian government, it was only natural for Counsel Adamson to announce that Chairman Wood was making a secret trip which had something to do with evidence of attempts to obtain information on the atomic bomb. "We are not on a cold trail by any means," said Adamson, and when a Russian naval lieutenant was arrested by the F.B.I. in Portland, Oregon, in March, the counsel, who had no particular information about the case but was growing increasingly impressed with his own expertise in such matters, informed newspapermen that it seemed to him the fellow might be a courier. Rankin announced from time to time that there were spies in this country trying to steal the secrets of the atom bomb. Later events would support the conjecture, but neither at the time he made his charges nor ever after did he produce any evidence to back them up.

As debate over the McMahon bill, which vested control of atomic energy in a civilian board ("one of the most dangerous pieces of legislation ever to come before Congress," in the opinion of Rankin), reached its height in the House in the summer of 1946, Thomas made public a report by Adamson warning that scientists at Oak Ridge had formed societies that favored world government: "These societies are definitely opposed to Army supervision at Oak Ridge and are just waiting for the day when military administration will be thrown out." In one of the cruder Committee efforts to influence legislation which it had not studied and which was none of its authorized business, Ernie Adamson advised the country that he personally had concluded that "the Army should exercise permanent control over the manufacture of atomic energy." A version of the McMahon bill was approved despite this unsolicited advice, and some weeks later Wood reported that a year's investigation had failed to bring to light any evidence of a foreign atom-bomb spy ring at work in the United States. The atom-spy charges would remain quiescent until 1948.

In the middle of May the Committee's sponsors came before the House to ask for $75,000 more to carry out their duties. The debate took the usual form. Hatton W. Sumners of Texas, chairman of the Judiciary Committee, gave an incoherent speech on the Anglo-Saxon form of government, which the Un-American Activities Committee was laboring to preserve. Mundt read statements by J. Edgar Hoover and reminded his colleagues, "This is an election year and that roll call on the Committee appropriation should become an index which will be widely quoted in many Congressional districts . . ." Coffee criticized the Committee's coddling of Gerald L. K. Smith and its indifference to the right of free speech. Sabath asked for an investigation of the Ku Klux Klan and other rightist groups. When Marcantonio prophesied that the additional funds would go to investigate the C.I.O.'s Political Action Committee, Rankin began applauding; the Republican side of the House joined in, and the New Yorker's speech was lost in laughter.[7] Rankin ended up the debate with a denunciation of the Communist practice of raping women in Eastern Europe—"Christian women, if you please . . ." The Committee got its money, by a vote of 240 to 81, with young Lyndon B. Johnson of Texas in the minority, and spent the next several months trying to find ways to use it up.

Its random essays here and there—a power strike in Pittsburgh, the Unitarian Service Committee's assistance to Spanish refugees in France—came to naught, until the middle of October, when Thomas reached out and grasped the life buoy of Louis F. Budenz. Budenz, preeminent example of the fervent Communist turned fervent Catholic anti-Communist, was like a tourist who is drawn to the shabbiest sections of all the towns he visits. As a Communist, he was managing editor of the *Daily Worker;* as an anti-Communist since his break in 1945, he became a star performer for the passionate right. It was his inclination to melodrama that brought him to the Committee's attention in the fall of 1946. On Sunday, October 13, he delivered a radio talk in Detroit, in which he said that American Communists took their orders from a secret agent of the Kremlin. The disclosure was made in the language of *The Shadow:* "This man never shows his face. Communist leaders never see him, but they follow his orders or suggestions implicitly." On Tuesday Thomas announced that Budenz would testify before the Un-American Activities Committee. By Thursday the name of the alleged secret agent was no longer secret. A New York newspaper printed and Bundenz confirmed that it was Gerhart Eisler, also known as Hans Berger, Austrian-born Communist who had come to this country from Germany in 1941, was known to the F.B.I., and was then living with his wife in an apartment in Long Island City. The Eislers were due to leave America on Friday, on a Russian ship bound for Leipzig—"It is very strange they started to move him away as soon as I identified him," said Budenz—but the exit permit

[7] That summer, with Congressional elections approaching, Rankin, as acting chairman of the Committee, did his best to confirm Marcantonio's prophesy by ordering his investigators to begin a "thorough" inquiry into the C.I.O.– P.A.C. But nothing developed, except for a newspaper story or two.

was canceled. On being subpoened, Eisler said he was "very glad" for the chance to "defend myself against the accusation of having misused the hospitality which the great American people and its government granted me, a German anti-fascist." The *Daily Worker* wrote the whole thing off as a "provocation," a "Hitlerite Kremlin agent fable."

The questioning of Budenz was delayed until November 22 at his own request. On appearing, he reviewed his ten years in the Communist Party, apologized for his infatuation, and discussed, in an informed way, the C.P.'s subservience to Moscow and the tactical nature of the nominal disbanding of the Communist International early in the war. Rankin, Mundt, and Thomas, like handlers of a skilled but insufficiently bloodthirsty boxer, did their best during most of their three and a half hours together to free him of what inhibitions he may have had over turning the hearings into an anti-Communist rally. "I think the distinction you are trying to make, Mr. Budenz," Mundt drew him on gently, "is that what they actually have in Russia is not the Communism of Marx and Engels but a dictatorship, and Communism under which people are denied a great many things under the concepts of Communism." And Rankin, less gently—"Regarding these over-run countries, are you familiar with the rape of innocent women, the murder of innocent men, the plunder of the peasants and the robbery of the helpless people in those areas by the Communist regime?"

As for Eisler, it soon appeared that Budenz had no hard evidence of his charge that the German émigré was the representative of the Communist International in this country. That Moscow did have such a person here, however, strained credulity less than Eisler's statement at a meeting in his behalf that "there never was a Communist Party in the world that would allow anyone, even a foreign Communist, to run its business." That Eisler was Moscow's mouthpiece was quite possible; but no one could have been convicted on the basis of the speculative case made by Budenz. Eisler, in the audience, had grounds for his complaint that the Committee preferred not to question him. When he finally was called more than two months later, after the Committee had managed to round up additional evidence, his pleasure at the prospect of defending himself against misuse of the national hospitality had, as we shall see, diminished.

On November 6, about two weeks before the Budenz hearing, the country went through its off-year Congressional elections, and gave a great victory to the Republican Party. The G.O.P. won most of the governorships, a narrow majority in the Senate, and a substantial majority in the House. It was a momentous event, a rebuff to those who had hoped to bring America out of the war with a planned economy, and a stunning blow to the political pretensions of the C.I.O.–P.A.C. It also bespoke a stiffening of the nation's feelings toward our late ally, Russia. For the Un-American Activities Committee, it meant Republican control for the first time in its history—not in itself of overriding significance since Democratic administrations which had endured Dies and Rankin had little worse to fear from the blackest Republicans. But differences there would be. In California, Jerry Voorhis, who had left the Committee in sadness and disgust, lost to the unknown Richard M. Nixon, who would leave it in triumph, for the Senate and beyond. (Joseph R. McCarthy, meanwhile, took his seat in the Upper House.)

Less than three weeks after the election, President Truman delegated to an interagency committee the job of testing the loyalty of more than two million government employees. To what extent the Truman loyalty order represented a real concern over pinkish tendencies of officials in the State Department and elsewhere, to what extent it was designed to head off more ferocious attacks from Republican-controlled committees in the new Congress, even the men who concocted it could not say. But insofar as the latter reasoning was involved, the Administration tactic was futile. "The Committee," promised Rankin, "will intensify its drive and its efforts to remove from the federal payroll every Communist and every other subversive individual." A day after the loyalty order was issued, Thomas, soon to be the Committee's chairman, made it clear that Administration purge or no Administration purge,

he took the Republican sweep as a mandate to ferret out and
expose Communists and Communist sympathizers in government, unions, Hollywood, the schools, and in groups "trying
to dissipate our atomic bomb knowledge for the benefit of a
foreign power." During his ten years in the House and his
eight years on the Un-American Activities Committee, Thomas
had made it his special mission to expose the New Deal as
a Communist project and New Dealers as subversive *per se*.
Whatever else may be said of him, he was not secretive about
his intentions toward liberal Democrats, and the Administration
was amply forewarned.

In the final weeks of the seventy-ninth Congress, Rankin and
Adamson gave way to the kind of frenzy that turns under-
graduate beach parties into riots as the weekend ebbs. On
November 14 Harlow Shapley, director of the Harvard College
Observatory and officer of the Independent Committee of the
Arts, Sciences and Professions—major political arm of the
Russophile left—was summoned to an executive hearing for his
group's audacity in trying to defeat the new Republican Speak-
er of the House, Joe Martin, Jr., during his campaign in
Massachusetts. Rankin, the only Committee member present,
cut loose. He tore a statement from Shapley's hands, ordered
the police to eject his lawyer, former Congressman Thomas
Eliot, yelled a good deal, and threatened contempt proceedings.

In December Rankin called on veterans' organizations to
assist him in investigating "pink teachers," and Adamson, in
Hollywood during a violent A.F. of L. strike against the studios,
declared that it was "not open to debate" that the Communist
Party was trying to gain domination of the movie industry.
In the last days of the year the counsel, altogether carried away
by now, released a report which he had not taken the trouble
to have approved by the Committee. It told of a conspiracy to
promote a Communist revolution through a general strike that
would wreck the U.S. economy; of seventeen C.I.O. unions
dominated by Soviet agents; of the Library of Congress being
turned into "a haven for aliens and foreign-minded Americans"
—at a time when "many native-born and naturalized scholars
are looking for such jobs"; of improper activities by U.N.

representatives; of the danger that Communists might paralyze the Panama Canal. Adamson had managed to surpass even J. B. Matthews for sheer enterprise.

This was not the first time that Adamson had let himself go. His most curious private campaign had occurred some months before, when he took to writing letters to groups such as the Veterans Against Discrimination, in which he pointed out that their circulars in support of the F.E.P.C. bill "refer to democracy several times." He advised them that "this country was not organized as a democracy" and that the Constitution guarantees a republican form of government. Having established this much, he put the question: "Is it your purpose to conduct a propaganda campaign against the administration of the provisions of the Constitution?" When he wrote such a letter to Drew Pearson to question the closing line of the columnist's Sunday evening broadcasts, which included the offensive words "make democracy work," Pearson suggested a padded cell for the Committee counsel.

The issuance of the unauthorized conspiracy report was Adamson's last official act in behalf of a nondemocratic way of life. Rankin, the only member of the Committee to have been given an advance look at the report, found it to his taste and defended him, but Thomas announced, "Adamson will not draw one more day's pay if I become chairman of the Committee." Adamson replied that Thomas was sore because the report had not been held back for a week so that he could have put his name on it—as chairman. "Anyway," said Adamson, sounding very much like Martin Dies in his moments of self-pity, "I'm tired of the whole thing. There's lots of cussing and very little commendation attached to a job like mine." He was replaced by Robert Stripling, who had come at last, through a long apprenticeship, to his reward.

Early in January a well-expurgated version of the Adamson report was adopted and released by the Committee. All of the most colorful of the chief counsel's charges, such as the conspiracy to foment a general strike and the capture of the Library of Congress, had been dropped, and the report now contented itself with a general statement about Communists "entrenched" in government, labor, education, and "a number of" C.I.O. unions. It also recommended a batch of curbs on foreign agents and on aliens, including one to bar second-class mailing privileges to any organization distributing "un-American propaganda." It proposed further the creation of a new, independent commission in Washington with the power to discharge any government employee "whose loyalty to the United States is found to be in doubt." Not many weeks would pass before Mr. Truman acted upon such cold-war recommendations.

Measured even against the special standards established by Martin Dies, the Rankin Committee did not do very well. Even Dies's man, Stripling, was dissatisfied; referring to the detection by a staff member of a similarity between the words Kreml (the hair tonic) and Kremlin, Stripling called it an "all-time low in investigations." The antic viciousness and abiding bigotry of Rankin along with the outright silliness of Adamson were guarantees against any sort of accomplishment, but for opponents of the Committee, within the Administration and without, the replacement of Wood by Thomas was no blessing. Rankin remained, and the new chairman had backed Martin Dies for six years with unmatched consistency and glee. With Republicans in charge of the Congress, the Administration could no longer work on vestiges of party loyalty to keep the Committee subdued—not that it had had much success with its appeals to its Southern cousins anyway. In two years there would be a Presidential election, and not even the most wishful Democrat could imagine that Thomas and the G.O.P. leaders would, like ladies making believe they do not see the buffet table, delicately resist the temptations of the occasion. A long time had passed since the last G.O.P. banquet and there was hunger in the ranks. It was with such exhilarating prospects that the House Un-American Activities Committee entered what was to be the grandest period of its existence.

7

1947: The Thomas Committee

THE first business of the new Committee was old business. The five Republicans—Thomas, Mundt, McDowell of Pennsylvania, Vail of Illinois, and Nixon of California—and four Democrats—Wood, Peterson, Bonner, and Rankin—gathered on February 6 to resume hearings into the suspended Eisler affair. "Mr. Gerhart Eisler, take the stand," called Robert Stripling. "I am not going to take the stand," replied Eisler, and the relationship never improved. Eisler, who had recently been taken into custody by the Immigration authorities, refused to be sworn unless he was permitted to deliver three minutes' worth of remarks; Chairman Thomas promised him that privilege, but said that he would first have to be sworn and questioned. "That is where you are mistaken," retorted Eisler, whose soft round face and rimless glasses were incongruous with his fierce manner. "I have to do nothing. A political prisoner has to do nothing." He and Thomas yelled at one another for a quarter of an hour without getting anywhere. He was cited for contempt on the spot, and escorted back to his cell on Ellis Island while his attorney handed out to reporters his three minutes' worth of remarks, twenty legal-sized pages of them, an ideological rejoinder to Louis Budenz.

But now there was more evidence against Eisler than the surmises of Budenz. According to an F.B.I. report, Eisler had taken an extremely active role in Party work, apparently as a liaison man between the Comintern and the C.P.–U.S.A., since his arrival on these shores. His means of support were obscure, but under a false name he had been receiving a monthly check of $150 from the Joint Anti-Fascist Refugee Committee, presumably a channel for C.P. funds. A former Party member told of meeting Eisler while taking a course in conspiracy and more academic subjects at the International Lenin School in Moscow in 1931. Budenz reappeared to give further details on Eisler's role in laying down Comintern discipline to straying functionaries. And Eisler's sister, Ruth Fischer (her mother's name), who had not been on speaking terms with Gerhart since her expulsion from the German Communist Party in 1926 for anti-Stalinist sentiments, called him "the perfect terrorist type." She charged that he had helped carry out purges in China in 1930 and had had a hand in the deaths of numerous comrades, including the eminent Russian theoretician Nikolai Bukharin.

The resolution to cite Eisler for contempt was presented to the House on February 18 by Richard Nixon, making his maiden speech. The young man from California took some liberties with the facts, referring to a supposed connection of Eisler with a Canadian atom-spy ring and giving him credit for conspiratorial powers which still wanted documentation. But there was no doubt that Eisler—"the murderous little Moscow agent," as McDowell titled him—had been a hardworking Comintern emissary for years under various names, had lied his way into this country, and had traveled, in behalf of the Party, on a forged passport. Nor was there any doubt that he had been in contempt of the Committee, and the resolution to cite him was passed by the House with only one dissenting vote—Marcantonio saw the affair as "a smokescreen behind which reaction advances to trample ruthlessly over the liberties of the American people."

A few days later Leon Josephson, a former lawyer for the International Labor Defense, who, according to handwriting experts, had assisted Eisler in faking a passport application, came before the Committee. He refused to testify on the grounds that the Committee did not have authority to question him and that, anyway, the presence of Rankin, who had been elected without benefit of Negro suffrage, rendered the proceedings unlawful. Stripling charged that Josephson was "involved in an elaborate system of possible espionage in which fraudulent passports were used," and he, too, was expeditiously cited for contempt.[1]

The third contempt citation of 1947 was awarded to Eugene Dennis, general secretary of the C.P., U.S.A. Dennis, whose trim mustache and wavy hair gave him the look of the fellow who used to lose the girl in B-movies, came before the Committee of his own volition during hearings on two bills to outlaw his Party. No sooner had he taken the stand then it became evident that he and the Committee were in perfect accord; he had no intention of answering questions and they had no particular interest in asking any; he was courting a contempt citation and they were ready to oblige. He refused to give his real name—which everybody knew was Francis Xavier Waldron; when Stripling asked for it, he turned to Thomas: "Mr. Chairman, the underling, this secretary, does not dictate what I say or don't say." Voices rose, and Thomas finally ordered the guards to "Take him out!" When Stripling handed him a subpoena to return in two weeks, Dennis, playing the role to the hilt, hollered, "Who the hell do you think you are?" and cast the document to the floor. "I hold this Committee in contempt!" he roared as he was hustled away. In lieu of responding to the subpoena when the two weeks came round, he sent along a Party attorney with the message that the Committee was not a body that might lawfully subpoena witnesses to appear before it. In the House, Nixon reviewed Dennis's behavior without undue emotion—which Mundt supplied by calling the C.P. figurehead a "political Rhett Butler trying to create chaos and destroy and wreck our free civilization." Mundt demanded stiffer penalties for contempt of Congress and accused the Department of Justice of dragging its feet about prosecuting the growing numbers of the contemptuous.

Eisler, Josephson, and Dennis, all of whom would have faced more severe indictments if they had chosen to testify about

[1] In fact Josephson was cited twice—once for not appearing before the Committee when first summoned and once for not answering any questions when he finally did appear. The government did not press the first case.

their passport finaglings, were found guilty of contempt and given the maximum sentence—$1,000 and one year in jail. Their appeals to a higher court met sharp rejections. Dennis's attacks on the Committee's legality were dissmissed by a unanimous Court of Appeals as "sheer nonsense."[2] To Josephson the Court of Appeals explained that since he had refused to answer any questions at all, he could not base a defense on the grounds that he was refusing to answer only nonpertinent questions. Justice Chase, speaking for the two-man majority, commented dryly: "The only real basis for the appellant's contention seems to be that in some way the First Amendment in protecting freedom of speech guarantees such privacy in speaking as the particular speaker may desire, and this privacy is violated by whatever disclosure occurs incidental to an investigation for legislative purposes."

Despite a strong dissent by Justice Clark of the Court of Appeals, which condemned the Committee for misusing its powers, subverting the Constitution, and jeopardizing American liberties, the Supreme Court declined to review the Josephson case. (Justices Douglas, Rutledge, and Murphy were in favor of a review.) The Court did review the Dennis conviction—but only a narrow aspect of it, the question of whether the presence of government employees on the jury deprived the defendant of his rights to a fair trial. The decision, with Black and Frankfurter dissenting, was that it did not. Eisler's case was in process of being argued before the highest court when the defendant, who had been advertising himself as "a victim of a witch-hunting hysteria in this country," fled to East Germany.

The reluctance of the judiciary in these early cases to set limits on the Committee even when the justices were plainly disconcerted by some of its procedures, derived both from respect for the investigatory powers of Congress and for that body's exclusive jurisdiction over the manners of its com-

[2] In the light of subsequent developments, "sheer nonsense" does not quite settle the charge that the election practices of the state of Mississippi were unconstitutional.

mittees. As Justice Jackson, an old adversary of the Dies Committee, wrote regarding the Eisler case:

> I should not want to be understood as approving the use that the Committee on Un-American Activities has frequently made of its powers. But I think it would be an unwarranted act of judicial usurpation to strip Congress of its investigatory power, or to assume for the courts the function of supervising Congressional committees. I should . . . leave the responsibility for the behavior of its committees squarely on the shoulders of Congress.

Thomas used these cases as yet another springboard for his unending attacks on the Administration. "Where has the Department of Justice been for the past twelve years?" he asked. "What were they doing when these comrades were traveling throughout the world on fraudulent American passports in furtherance of their foreign-directed conspiratorial activities?" For his Committee, untrammeled by the courts and secure in the support of the House, the string of successes in sending Communists and fellow travelers to jail stood as an affirmation of its powers and an invitation to proceed apace with its mission.

The anti-Communist mission was being pursued with mounting fervor in other quarters, too, in 1947. A determination to contain Russia's designs for hegemony in Europe had been growing in Washington since before the end of the war, and now it had come to a testing point in Greece and Turkey. The fortunes of the Un-American Activities Committee were always inflenced by the stars of international conflict, and not since the days of the Nazi-Soviet pact had the stars been more propitious. For veteran loathers of Communists like Thomas, the Truman Doctrine was an acknowledgment from the very bosom of softhearted liberalism of their rightness down the years. We had to be tough—internally no less than externally— and the chairman barraged the attorney general with demands for action against the Communist Party and all its accessories and accomplices. The Soviet-oriented left understood what Thomas was about and found relief in sponsoring "Free

Gerhart Eisler" rallies where our unkindness toward the U.S.S.R. abroad and toward its devotees at home could be whipped in tandem. At one such rally in March, Marcantonio called for "a people's political party throughout these United States." Gideon's Army was a-gathering.

Late that month, as the Committee was beginning its hearings into two bills to outlaw the Communist Party, the President issued a sweeping executive order designed to cleanse Washington of suspected Communists and sympathizers. Under its provisions an elaborate system was set up for checking on the purity of government workers without the nuisance of legal forms. Now not only membership in or affiliation with a group judged subversive by the attorney general was grounds for dismissal; "sympathetic association" with a "movement" or with a "group or combination of persons" might do it. The files of the Un-American Activities Committee were designated as a source of information on suspect employees. Even Rankin was moved to commend the President, asking only that he go one step further and put an end to the "pernicious activities" of the Anti-Defamation League. Thomas drew attention to the fact that he had put forward a bill for a loyalty commission that was "almost identical" with Mr. Truman's order, and Mundt flatly took credit unto the Committee for getting the executive branch to act. Once again, an effort by the executive to take the play away from Congress, to put the testing of loyalty into more responsible hands than those of the flag-waving legislators, was interpreted as a victory for the flag-wavers. This Truman Loyalty Order had a base in reality; with Russia and America in direct confrontation, Communists and their hangers-on could not be trusted in sensitive posts, a conclusion that would be heavily accented by the revelations of 1948. Yet the postwar fears of internal subversion would never be entirely justified by experience, and the Administration's forced reaction to a moderate threat would in the coming months and years help to fuel a national mania for loyalty tests of all sorts which, with the unfailing assistance of the Un-American Activities Committee, would cling for a decade.

After paying their several compliments to Mr. Truman, the Congressmen turned to bills before them. This was the first time that the Committee had actually set out to grapple with legislation; unfortunately for this maiden effort, the proposed laws had no virtue except as redundant affirmation of their sponsors' hatred for Communism. One of them, the creation of Rankin, would have made it unlawful, at the risk of a $10,000 fine and ten years in jail, "in any course of instruction or teaching in any public or private school, college or university to advocate or to express or convey the impression of sympathy with or approval of, Communism or Communist ideology" or to send through the mails any publication "any part of which expresses or conveys the impression of sympathy with or approval of Communism or Communist ideology."

For five days in March, the Committee listened to an assortment of witnesses selected not for their legal acuity but for their known abhorrence of Communism. But even they proved a disappointment to Rankin. Only the representatives of veterans' groups and the Daughters of the American Revolution favored the bills. All of the most prestigious witnesses—William C. Bullitt, former ambassador to the Soviet Union and to France; William Green, president of the A. F. of L.; Eric Johnston, head of the Motion Picture Producers Association; and, of greatest consequence, J. Edgar Hoover—opposed outlawing the Party. Hoover came before the Committee like the archbishop paying a call on a group of lay brothers. He patronized them; they fussed over him. When after awing them with the proportions of the Communist threat—including the statistic that in 1917 there was only one Communist for every 2,777 persons in Russia whereas in 1947 there was one Communist for every 1,814 persons in the United States—he warned mildly against making martyrs of the Communists, that was a death knell for the legislation. The Committee voted five to three against reporting the bills, as the legislators, particularly Nixon, turned their thoughts to a law for compulsory registration of Communists.

Rankin, of course, was in the minority in this vote, and indeed his position on the Committee had deteriorated notice-

ably under the new regime. His manner was as rowdy as ever—
"Would you say that Stalin is the Genghis Khan of the twentieth century?" he asked a legionnaire. During the questioning of Ambassador Bullitt, he gave a little talk on what the Communists had inflicted on the people of the Ukraine, "the white people of Russia," and inquired of the ambassador whether it was not a fact that 75 per cent of the C.P. members in this country were Jews. But Thomas made a much tougher chairman than Wood, and the Mississippian found himself repeatedly being called back from his excursions into racism. As Rankin's influence waned, that of the young Nixon began to shine. Beside men like Thomas and Mundt, he was indeed a bright spark. Though he managed to make it clear that he was as patriotic as the next fellow, he never ranted; his questions were lucid and to the point and he had an orderly influence on the proceedings.

Still, he did not entirely inhibit the entertainment; the friendly witnesses were allowed to perform pretty much as they pleased and the hearings provided good newspaper copy. George Earle, a former governor of Pennsylvania, announced, "I don't think there is better than an even chance that five years from today ten per cent of us in America will be alive." He rambled on for a time about the perils of atomic attack from Russia until even Thomas, no skeptic on this subject, broke in to remark that he didn't quite understand what that had to do with the particular bills up for discussion. The chairman himself, however, assured a commander of the V.F.W., "I am one hundred per cent with you on the transfer of the atomic bomb development back to the military. If we put the atomic bomb in the hands of a group of milktoasts we can be certain that we can just hurry the day when the bomb is going to be used against us."

Victor A. Kravchenko, a former Soviet army captain and official of the Soviet Purchasing Commission who had defected in 1944 and set down his experiences in the book *I Chose Freedom*, made the front pages by declaring that "every responsible representative of the Soviet Union in the United States may be regarded as a possible economic, political or military spy."

There was no reason to dispute this observation, and his suggestion that the outlawing of the Communist Party would not be in accord with America's traditions of freedom was relevant to the subject at hand. But with the encouragement of Committee members, Kravchenko, who testified through an interpreter and behind an outsized pair of dark glasses that covered the entire upper half of his face, ventured the opinion that Marshall Field, publisher of the Chicago *Sun* and *PM*, was more dangerous to America than the Communists; that if you cut off the roofs of Russia one dark night, you'd discover that 75 per cent of the people were opposed to the regime; that the death of Stalin would mean no change in Soviet policies; and that Molotov would probably take over. "Horse radish is no sweeter than parsley," he reminded the Committee. This awakened the Slavic muse in Andrei A. Gromyko, then becoming well known for his *nyet*-saying as the U.S.S.R.'s representative on the U.N. Security Council. Gromyko commented: "When a dog has nothing to do, it licks its underbelly. Sometimes that attracts spectators." To which Kravchenko replied: "When the dog barks, the wind carries the dog's bark."

Walter B. Steele, still representing the American Coalition of Patriotic, Civic and Fraternal Societies, as he had when he helped to launch the Dies Committee, was permitted to read off hundreds of names, old and new, Communists and associates of Communists, fellow travelers and associates of fellow travelers, members of organizations, sponsors of meetings, writers of articles, signers of petitions—a thoroughly indigestible mass of names, names, names, for which Thomas congratulated him effusively. One cannot improve on Professor Robert K. Carr's description of this full day's testimony as possibly "the most irresponsible ever presented to the Un-American Activities Committee."

The thread of the Committee's long-standing interest in Hollywood ran through these hearings. Eric Johnston, doing his job, said that "The Communists hate and fear the American motion picture. It is their number one hate." But to Nixon's question of how many anti-Communist films Hollywood had produced in the past five years, he had to concede there hadn't been any. Nixon was also concerned about *The Grapes of Wrath* being shown in Yugoslavia. J. Edgar Hoover described *Mission to Moscow,* the film version of Ambassador Joseph E. Davies's book "explaining" the Moscow purge trials, as "a prostitution of historical fact." And Jack B. Tenney, the inquisitorial state senator from California, testified that Charles Chaplin, Fredric March, John Garfield, Edward G. Robinson, and Frank Sinatra were abetting Communism. The Committee was working up to its spectacular investigation of the movies.[3]

Although 1947 must bo down in the history of the Committee as the year of Hollywood, the investigators found time and cause to expose yet once again the presence of Communists in the leadership of important unions. In February, the ten-month-long strike at the Allis-Chalmers Company drew attention to the United Auto Workers, then in the throes of a battle for control between R. J. Thomas and Walter Reuther. Former members of the Allis-Chalmers local told how the Communists were using the strike to help Thomas. In July, it was the turn of a local of the Food, Tobacco and Agricultural Workers, then striking against the Winston-Salem factories of the Reynolds Tobacco Company, and a Bridgeport, Connecticut, local of the United Electrical Workers involved in a fight against the national union's Communist leaders. No revelations were forthcoming from these hearings, but they called attention to the continued presence and latest activities of Communists within the C.I.O. and may have hastened their expulsion.

Four reports were issued in 1947, with the usual ado. Their subjects were the Communist Party, the American Youth for Democracy, the Southern Conference for Human Welfare, and the Civil Rights Congress. All were prosecutor's briefs. All contained kernels of truth; it was difficult to quarrel in 1947 with the observation that the Communist Party was an agency of

[3] It would be negligent to leave these hearings without noting that while they were going on one morning, a freshman senator entered the hearing room and was invited by Thomas to participate in the questioning. He declined, saying, "I just came over to watch the very excellent job that you gentlemen are doing. I am here merely to listen, and not to ask questions." Thus spoke Joseph R. McCarthy.

Moscow or that the Civil Rights Congress, conceived in 1946 by a merger of the International Labor Defense and the National Federation for Constitutional Liberties with such godparents as Paul Robeson, Vito Marcantonio, Lee Pressman, and the ubiquitous Harry F. Ward, was a Communist front engaged in "a campaign of vilification against the American government."[4] But all the reports were marred by an unfastidious use of evidence, sloppy organization and writing, rampant emotionalism, and wild charges. The report on the A.Y.D., one of the least effectual pieces of C.P. machinery ever created, opened with the announcement that "the specter of Communism stalks our college campuses . . ." The organizations attacked cried "Fascist!" and one was carried back to the early days of Martin Dies.

The weakest of the reports, the one on the Southern Conference for Human Welfare, was gotten together in great haste in mid-June in order that it might be released on the Sunday before a scheduled Monday evening rally at Washington's Water Gate sponsored by the Conference and featuring Henry Wallace. It was at this meeting that Wallace made it plain that there would be a third party in the 1948 elections, dedicated to the proposition that the Russians earnestly wanted peace. Thomas's announcement was timed to scare off government employees from attending the rally, which was garnished with investigators making notes.[5]

The Southern Conference for Human Welfare was formed in 1938 by united-fronters for the expressed purpose of improving the economic lot of the South in general and the Negro in particular. The Committee charged that it was "perhaps the most deviously camouflaged Communist-front operation," and

[4] In a pamphlet, entitled *America's Thought Police*, issued shortly after it had been pilloried by the Committee, the Civil Rights Congress charged, typically: "The activities of the Committee present a deadly parallel with the pattern that Hitler applied in Continental Europe."

[5] Thomas's press release was preceded by the news that he and Rankin had received death threats which they had turned over to the F.B.I. The one to Thomas was in the form of a poem:

> My little butterball
> You're due for a fall.
> Sometime in June
> There will be a boom.

showed just how well camouflaged it was by presenting a completely unconvincing batch of alleged evidence about its subversive nature. The report was a hodgepodge—heavily slanted
from beginning to end, and filled with inaccuracies and irrelevancies. The major points of the indictment—that the Conference showed "unswerving loyalty" to Soviet foreign policy, that
it never took issue with the policies of the C.P., that it "maintained in decisive posts persons who have the confidence of the
Communist Party"—were not out and out falsehoods, but they
were too broadly framed and too sketchily developed to be
taken as proved. Remotely relevant items were snatched from
the air and tossed into the stew. One such paragraph, a favorite
ever since with the Committee's critics, indicates the lengths
to which lack of hard evidence led the concocters of this report. "Entertainer at the Washington meeting [of the Confer-
ence] was Susan Reed, employed by Café Society, a night club,
owned by Barney Josephson, brother of Leon Josephson, leading Communist, Soviet Secret Service operative, charged with
passport frauds. Mrs. Leon Josephson also owns an interest in
the enterprise. Barney Josephson has been a supporter of the
New York branch of the Southern Conference."

All the tricks of the Dies days were employed: meaningless
quotes from the *Daily Worker*, carefully selected extracts from
resolutions, a box score of individual affiliations of sixty-two
members of the Conference which could have meant anything
or nothing. In a critique of the report, Professor Walter Gellhorn of the Columbia University Law School paused to explain
the box-score technique:

> This device involves, first, seeking to establish a tie, however
> tenuous, between an unpopular individual or organization and
> some person connected with the Southern Conference; second,
> ascribing to that person all the undesirable qualities of the indi-
> vidual or organization with whom he has been momentarily
> linked; and finally, attributing to the Southern Conference the
> qualities which have been acquired by infection, as it were,
> by those intermediate persons.

Unquestionably there were individuals in the leadership of
the Southern Conference who attempted, with some success,

to steer it along the Communist line on specific issues. In 1940 they beat down pro-allied liberals who sought support for the Administration's preparedness policy. There were others, led by Dr. Frank P. Graham, president of the University of North Carolina, who resisted. The Committee indictment, as usual, made no distinctions. Its argument that the Southern Conference's "professed interest in Southern welfare is simply an expedient for larger aims serving the Soviet Union and its subversive Communist Party in the United States" had the effect of simplifying complicated motives; though Rankin could not credit the possibility, one might be a fellow traveler and yet be sincerely distressed at the lynching of Negroes. But in 1947 the cold war was creating the same kinds of difficulties for a liberal-Communist alliance as had the Nazi-Soviet pact, and by the end of the year, the Southern Conference had faded away.

Thomas promised in June that he was arranging "an all-inclusive program of investigations and hearings on fascism" and McDowell, turned into a subcommittee for the purpose, said that he was devoting "hundreds of hours" to the matter. But by the spring of 1947 the call of Hollywood was strong, and Thomas had no intention of tying his shipmates to the mast and stuffing his ears with cotton. An investigation of the movie industry was a project dear to the heart of Martin Dies; he spoke of it as early as August 1938 and, with the aid of witness Leech, made gestures westward now and then in the ensuing years. Shortly before Pearl Harbor, when Charles Lindbergh was titillating Midwesterners with the specter of Jews propagandizing America, Senate isolationists made a pass at Hollywood for its pro-British, anti-Nazi films. But it remained for Thomas to engage the movie industry. To Rankin, Hollywood was Semitic territory. To Thomas, it was New Deal territory. To the entire Committee, it was a veritable sun around which the press worshipfully rotated. And it was also a place where real live Communists could readily be found.

A sneak preview was held in May at the Biltmore Hotel in Los Angeles, Thomas and McDowell, their quest after fascists laid to rest, presiding. The hearings were closed, but each afternoon the chairman and investigator Stripling took care to inform newspapermen of the charges issued by the witnesses whom they had chosen to hear. Robert Taylor told them that government officials had prevented him from entering the navy in 1943 until he had completed *Song of Russia* for M.G.M., a film that Thomas identified as "Communist propaganda that favored its ideologies, its institutions and its ways of life over the same things in America." Mrs. Lela Rogers, mother of Ginger, told them, according to Stripling, that Ginger had stalwartly refused to speak the line, "Share and share alike—that's democracy," in the film *Tender Comrade*, written by Dalton Trumbo, whom she classified with Clifford Odets as a Communist. Thomas said that Adolphe Menjou said that "Hollywood is one of the main centers of Communist activity in America." Speaking on his own, the chairman announced that the Screen Writers Guild was "lousy with Communists" and "the government had wielded the iron fist in order to get the companies to put on certain Communist propaganda." Committee investigators meanwhile visited Hollywood offices, warning producers to clean their houses of Communists before they were compelled to do so by Congress or public opinion.

Two weeks after their Los Angeles visit, the Thomas-McDowell subcommittee issued an indictment, based on what their fourteen friendly witnesses had told them: the N.L.R.B. was abetting the effort of Communist organizers to take control of the industry; scores of highly paid screen writers were injecting propaganda into movies; White House pressure had resulted in the production of "some of the most flagrant Communist propaganda films"; subtle techniques were used for glorifying the Communist Party, while the Communists prevented the production of films which glorified loyal American citizens; the heads of the studios had done nothing to prevent all of this. Exposure was essential; public hearings were promised. Not one of the above charges would ever be substantiated, but the publicity which these coming attractions received bespoke high success for the feature event.

The summer was given over to research, and in the early fall the case of Hanns Eisler, younger brother of the recently convicted Gerhart, was taken up by the Committee. Hanns, who wrote music for the movies, had come to America during the war, and it was the mechanics of his entry that aroused Thomas. Summoned before the Hollywood subcommittee in May, Eisler had been dismissed after an hour, with satisfaction to neither side. Thomas told reporters that the witness "sought to evade and confuse the issues." Eisler told them that he was "offended as a scholar, a scientist and a composer."

On Hanns Eisler's return in September, it became evident that Thomas was out for larger game than the pudgy and rumpled composer of *The Comintern March.* The Committee's investigators had discovered that early in 1939 when Eisler, a German refugee in this country on a temporary visa, was seeking permanent status, Eleanor Roosevelt wrote two notes bringing the case to the attention of her old friend, Undersecretary of State Sumner Welles. The First Lady's compassion for Germany's persecuted Jews was as famous as it was abundant— and it had been tapped in this instance by an acquaintance who had assured her that Eisler was no Communist. Mrs. Roosevelt was not the only one to ask the State Department for sympathetic consideration of Eisler's case in 1939 when his temporary visa was running out. Malcolm Cowley of *The New Republic,* Freda Kirchwey of *The Nation,* Russell Davenport of *Fortune,* the columnist Dorothy Thompson, and the commentator Raymond Gram Swing were among those who made representations. During the composer's stay here, a place had been found for him on the faculty of New York's New School for Social Research so that, being a titular professor, he might in time qualify as a nonquota immigrant. His supporters were moved by the plight of a homeless man of talent suffering from State Department red tape, and some of them were more moved than they might otherwise have been because of his reputation as "a progressive musician." One State Department official wrote to another at the time: "If this alien [Eisler] obtains an immigration visa and enters the United States, we are likely to hear from the anti-Communist organizations in

The Special Committee on Un-American Activities poses for its first meeting: (left to right) Joe Starnes, John Dempsey, J. Parnell Thomas, Chairman Dies, Harold Mosier, Noah Mason, Arthur Healey.

Soon they would be joined by J. B. Matthews, the man with the telephone.

Whatever their philosophical differences, the four orators pictured here shared at least one major political principle—that of the raised fist. They are (clockwise, beginning top left) Samuel Dickstein, Earl Browder, Fritz Kuhn, Martin Dies.

Mrs. Eleanor Roosevelt joined members of the American Youth Congress at their appearance before the Committee. Here she shares grins with the A.Y.C. chairman, Jack McMichael.

The Committee's three least favorite personages from the labor movement during the early years were (left to right) Joe Curran, Harry Bridges, Mike Quill.

The anti-Semitic John Rankin might have been taken for an orthodox Jew after he wrapped himself in a tallis of petitions signed by Californians who supported the Committee's plan to investigate the movies.

Dear Sumner:

All these papers were brought to me yesterday by a friend of Mr. Eisler. The man who brought them is a perfectly honest person and very much disturbed. He thinks the State Department has really told the Cuban Consul that they do not wish to admit him and he is perfectly sure that the Eislers are not communists and have no political affiliations of any kind. He is sure that they believe our form of Government is "heaven" and would be entirely agreeable without reservation to take an oath of allegiance.

I believe that the Labor Department did not examine the case carefully enough. Why not do it all over again and bring it out in the open and let the Eislers defend themselves?

Cordially,

Eleanor Roosevelt

MEMORANDUM FOR HON. SUMNER WELLES

See Mrs. Roosevelt's note:

"Dear Sumner - This Eisler case seems a hard nut to crack. What do you suggest?

Sincerely,

E.R."

The 1947 Hollywood hearings began with an investigation of Mrs. Roosevelt's efforts to assist Hanns Eisler. They ended with ten writers, including Dalton Trumbo and John Howard Lawson, at right, being cheered off to jail.

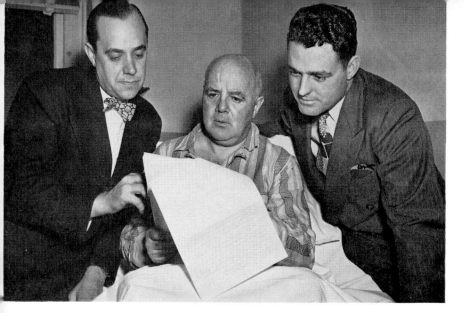

Photographers were invited into the room occupied by J. Parnell Thomas at Walter Reed Hospital, so that the Congressman, assisted by Robert Stripling (left) and Committee investigator William Wheeler, could produce an impromptu report that called Dr. Edward Condon "one of the weakest links in our atomic security."

Joining Elizabeth Bentley before the start of her momentous testimony were (left to right) Committee members John McDowell, Richard Nixon, Karl Mundt, John Rankin, F. Edward Hébert, J. Hardin Peterson, Chairman Thomas.

Harry Dexter White made a dramatic defense against Miss Bentley's charges. He died soon after this appearence, but his case lived on.

this country. Of course, if he is refused an immigration visa, there will also be some repercussions among the so-called liberal elements in this country."

The Committee's case, as conveyed to the press, was that Eisler owed his final acceptance here in the fall of 1940, despite evidence of Communist activity and affiliations in his State Department folder (Stripling called him "the Karl Marx of Communism in the musical field"), to "influence and pressure exerted by certain prominent persons." That he had been at least a nominal C.P. member in Germany in the nineteen-twenties Eisler finally admitted to the Committee, amid persistent disclaimers, evasions, and parryings which soon turned comical. One of his songs, translated by the eminent American Communist, V. J. Jerome, contained the stanza:

> The Comintern calls you,
>
> > Raise high Soviet banner,
> > In steeled ranks to battle.
> > Raise sickle and hammer;
> > Our answer: Red Legions.
> > We raise in our might;
> > Our answer: Red Storm Troops.
> > We lunge to the fight;
> > Our answer: Red Storm Troops.

Confronted with this number, Eisler shrugged, "I am not responsible for literary translations."[6]

That Mrs. Roosevelt had taken an active, though by no means overbearing, interest in Eisler's plight was readily documented. That the pleas in his behalf had had some effect was evident and that Eisler did indeed succeed in gaining permanent admission to the country, despite his various services to the Red legions, was indisputable. But the course of things was not nearly so smoothly sinister as the Committee sought

---

[6] Representative McDowell was especially affronted by a song that Eisler wrote which ridiculed the law against abortion. This prompted Rankin to describe the body of his work as "filth," and the gentleman from Mississippi set forth credentials for this critical judgment which astounded those who had listened to him in Congress over the years: "I suppose that I am as familiar with American poetry and with English poetry generally as any member of either House."

to convey. Sumner Welles, correct and convincing in the witness chair, showed that he had replied to Mrs. Roosevelt that there were laws on the subject of admission to this country and even chided her a bit: "These friends of Mr. Eisler . . . seem to think that there is some special consideration or treatment which can be given him which is not provided for in our law or that perhaps certain liberties could be taken with the law." He passed the First Lady's notes along to the appropriate assistant secretary, a State Department veteran named George Messersmith, who had been on the receiving end of the other importunings in Eisler's behalf.

The warm feelings which Messersmith felt for any refugee from Hitler were made warmer by the mild intervention of Mrs. Roosevelt. Messersmith wrote to the counsel general in Havana, the port through which Eisler hoped to enter this country, that although the composer was "a man of very liberal views" he [Messersmith] found it difficult to believe that he was a Communist or ought to be excluded—"It would seem to me that, unless there is definite and convincing proof that Mr. Eisler does hold opinions which would exclude him, his case can be favorably considered from that point of view." As it turned out, Messersmith's humane indiscretion was not strikingly successful. It was nearly two years before Eisler managed to gain permanent entry—not from the representative in Havana, but from a consular official in a Mexican border town who, accidentally or on purpose, failed to heed the "Stop" on the Eisler file. No sooner had the composer crossed over to this side of the border than the permit was withdrawn and it was not restored until the case was heard by the Labor Department's Immigration Board, which ruled in his favor in October 1940. Although the Committee vested him with the title of "international Communist agent," it produced no evidence that he did anything more subversive during his years in this country than write music for Hollywood movies.

Eisler swore at the Mexican border that he had never been affiliated with the Communist Party and had never cooperated with the Soviet regime: "My political belief is—I admire very much the United States. I hate fascism in every form and I hate Stalin in the same way as I hate Hitler." He wanted it understood that he was not a political creature. "My whole life is devoted wholly to music." He had thus not been altogether frank in entering the country, and a few days after the end of the Committee hearings, he was arrested and deportation proceedings were instituted aaginst him. He then took to repeating his brother's comparisons between the United States and Hitler Germany, and in 1948—a year in which Mr. Truman's Justice Department undertook a vigorous deportation campaign against Communist aliens as a means of demonstrating that Democrats could be just as tough on such people as Republicans—Hanns Eisler was permitted to leave the country voluntarily. Consigning Rankin, Thomas, and McDowell to the garbage heap of history, he and his pretty wife set off for Czechoslovakia.

In October 1947 the Committee had reason to be content: it had puffed up an innocuous effort to assist a victim of Hitler, albeit a Communist, into a plot against the national security, had passed off a low-budget film as a mighty extravaganza, and was ready to go to work in earnest on Hollywood.

The Hollywood hearings began on October 20 before a subcommittee of Thomas, Vail, and McDowell. It was a gala premiere. There were batteries of floodlights, microphones and cameras—one of them a TV camera, still a novelty at the time; more than a hundred newspapermen; a promised cast of dozens, featuring several of the industry's great names; and an audience of hundreds, mainly middle-aged women crushing for a glimpse of Robert Taylor, too many even for the spacious Caucus Room of the Old Office Building.

The first witnesses, most of whom had appeared before Thomas and McDowell in the spring, were all cooperative in their fashion. Jack L. Warner, head of the studio with the most liberal reputation in Hollywood, producer of *Mission to Moscow*, extolled his own patriotism, boasted of firing a host of writers whom he deemed Communists (including several, like Clifford Odets and Irwin Shaw, who, it turned out, he had not fired at all), liberally gave the names of suspects without any accompanying evidence, pausing now and then to withdraw some names which he had given in his first appearance, and offered, on behalf of himself and his brothers, to set up a fund to ship to Russia people who didn't like the American system. Nixon, sitting in with the subcommittee, led Warner on to larger and firmer declarations of his Americanism, then put the question of how many anti-Communist films his studio had produced. Warner replied, lamely, that one was being worked on. In the businessman's testimony, defensive of himself, careless of the reputations of others, the experienced moviegoer could sense the denouement to come.

The remainder of the week was given over to even friendlier witnesses than Jack Warner, collected mostly from the membership of the Motion Picture Alliance for the Preservation of American Ideals, a conservative band which director Sam Wood had formed in 1944 to counter what he believed to be a Communist effort at a takeover of the industry. (When at the onset of their testimony, an attorney for several of the figures named as Communists by members of the Alliance rose to ask for the privilege of cross-examination, Thomas ordered him ejected from the Caucus Room.) Walt Disney, a paternal employer, told angrily of the indignities he had been made to suffer in the great studio strike of the nineteen-forties. The most plausible testimony came from writers, such as Morrie Ryskind, who had had firsthand experience with Communists in the Screen Writers Guild and gave details of their machinations for gaining power, maintaining it, and putting it at the service of causes close to the Soviet heart. (Dalton Trumbo, one of the named Communists, would later charge, with the charity for the motives of others he showed throughout the affair, that the friendly witnesses were seeking the jobs of the unfriendly ones.) The silliest testimony came, again, from Mrs. Rogers, who reported that she had saved Ginger from appearing in pictures like *None But the Lonely Heart* and *Sister Carrie* which conveyed a depressing idea of life under capitalism. She also said that she believed Clifford Odets was a Communist because she had read so in some column and had never come across a denial. The most pointless testimony came from Gary Cooper, who had been invited to Washington for show, and whose appearance (in double-breasted suit, light blue silk necktie, and white shirt) brought sighs from the spectators. Gary remembered reading some un-American stuff in scripts and rejecting them, but he couldn't call to mind the names of the scripts because he did most of his reading at night. On the issue of Communism he said, "From what I hear, I don't like it because it isn't on the level." Robert Montgomery, George Murphy, and Ronald Reagan gave calm statements of Communist activity in the Screen Actors Guild; all had been active in Guild affairs and were agreed that the Communists hadn't gotten anywhere. They declined to be drawn by Stripling into the question of whether the Communist Party should be outlawed, pointing out that they were not experts in that line. Other witnesses proved more amenable. Adolphe Menjou presented himself as a student of Marxism, Fabian Socialism, Communism, Stalinism, "and its probable effects on the American people if they ever gain power here," mentioned his friendship with Senator Taft and J. Edgar Hoover, stated unequivocally that the Communist Party should be outlawed and that universal military training should be instituted, and fully satisfied both the subcommittee and the audience, which gave him a good hand when he was done.

In their efforts to build a case against the film industry, Thomas, Vail, and Stripling spurred the first week's witnesses on to ever more fevered denunciations of Communists—in Hollywood and everywhere else. They indulged the witnesses in rumor, speculation, and surmise, allowed them to enter numerous names of alleged Communists into the record without pressing for documentation, and invited their views on matters well beyond their ken, listening soberly as the mother of Ginger Rogers declared, in response to a leading question, that the Communist Party was an agent of a foreign government and ought to be outlawed. In part, this was normal Committee treatment of friendly witnesses, but as the days drew on it became clear that Thomas needed whatever bits of support he could get to bolster a badly sagging indictment.

His original charges that Hollywood films were a trove of subversive propaganda, stocked by Washington, remained mere charges. The first five days of hearings served only to confirm what had been common knowledge in Hollywood for years: Communists were playing a significant part in the long, violent, and unsuccessful jurisdictional strike that had been troubling the film industry since 1945—an effort to form one industrial union out of the several craft unions—and C.P. members had by customary stratagems managed to turn the Screen Writers Guild to their various purposes. The Communists had been riding high during the war, and now their opponents were gleefully taking advantage of this grand opportunity to balance the accounts.

The second week was given over mainly to the accused. Most of them were writers whose names, accompanied by epithets, had recurred in the testimony of the friendly witnesses and who had reputations in Hollywood as Communists. Two of them—Emmet Lavery, president of the Screen Writers Guild, and Bertolt Brecht said that they were not members of the Party—but the others would neither deny nor confirm.[7] The confrontation between the subcommittee and the group that came to be known as the Hollywood Ten was unedifying in the extreme.[8] The ten had been advised by their attorneys, the most prominent of whom was Robert Kenny, former attorney general of California, to counter the question, "Are you now or have you ever been a member of the Communist Party?" with a rejection of the Committee's right to pose it. Moreover, they decided to be most aggressive about doing so. Thomas replied in kind; the audience applauded and booed;

[7] According to that foremost Brechtien Eric Bentley, one of the attorneys for the subpoenaed writers advised Brecht to say that he *was* a Communist on the reasoning that otherwise the Committee would forge a C.P. card in his name and charge him with perjury. Brecht, never a screen writer, was summoned because he had collaborated with Hanns Eisler on several works. His questioning by the determinedly unliterary Stripling, an exercise in aimlessness and near incoherence, is available to posterity on a record, *Bertolt Brecht Before the Committee on Un-American Activities.*

[8] Nineteen unfriendly witnesses were scheduled by the Committee: twelve writers, five directors, one producer, and one actor. The ten who took the First Amendment were: Alvah Bessie, Herbert Biberman, Lester Cole, Edward Dmytryk, Ring Lardner, Jr., John Howard Lawson, Albert Maltz, Samuel Ornitz, Adrian Scott, Dalton Trumbo.

and one after another they were dismissed, hollering, from the witness chair.

"It is the orthodox procedure of Communists," wrote Edmund Wilson after covering the Fish hearings of 1930, "to use public appearances of all kinds as pretexts for propagandist speeches . . . This practice has its value; it enables the Communist to cut out the ground from under the assumptions on which the charges against him rest, to substitute his own version of the case for the version of the society which is trying him." As if to demonstrate what Wilson meant, John Howard Lawson, Grand Old Man of Hollywood Communism and the first of the unfriendly witnesses to appear, told Thomas: "I am not on trial here, Mr. Chairman. This Committee is on trial before the American people. Let us get that straight." Thus inspired, the normally overbearing Thomas outdid himself. He turned down attorney Kenny's attack on the Committee's constitutionality, suggesting that he seek remedy in the courts, and later called Kenny back to question him about the advice he had given his clients. He gaveled down attorney Bartley Crum's demand for permission to cross-examine the first week's witnesses. He refused to allow Lawson to read a prepared statement denouncing the Committee as a fascist tool. ("Rational people don't argue with dirt," wrote Lawson and devoted most of his statement to declaiming upon his own integrity.) Thomas pounded his gavel and threatened Lawson with contempt when the writer reminded him that the friendly witnesses had been allowed to talk to their heart's content. Lawson, hamming it up, kept yelling that the Committee was trying to invade the rights of Protestants, Jews, Catholics, Democrats, and Republicans—"You are using the old technique, which was used in Hitler Germany, in order to create a scare here!" He was finally pulled away from the stand in the middle of still another proclamation of his Americanism. A few minutes later, his calm restored, he was smiling for photographers.

And so it went for four days, as the witnesses worked hard to provoke Thomas into some legal misstep which could be used in the court proceedings that lay ahead. Albert Maltz addressed Stripling as "Mr. Quisling" and complained, "Next you are going to ask me what my religious beliefs are." Thomas said he wasn't going to ask that at all, but Maltz continued with the rehearsed text: "And you are going to insist . . . that since you do not like my religious beliefs I should not work in such industry." Dalton Trumbo brought a pile of twenty scripts along with him and offered to read them; he also offered to read a statement which compared Washington to Berlin on the eve of the Reichstag fire. "This is the beginning . . ." he yelled after being dismissed from the witness chair, ". . . of an American concentration camp." "This is typical Communist tactics," Thomas yelled back, gaveling furiously. When Edward Dmytryk, a relatively subdued witness, said he felt there was a constitutional issue involved in the Committee's question regarding his C.P. membership, Thomas thundered, "Where did you learn about the Constitution? Tell me where you learned about the Constitution?" Twice the chairman, quite beside himself, ordered a witness to leave the stand before Stripling had had an opportunity to pose the crucial question about his C.P. affiliation. A rare moment of humor in this inelegant script came when Ring Lardner, Jr., observed as Thomas, gaveling away, ordered him to depart, "I think I am leaving by force."[9]

After each uproarious interlude, a staff investigator read into the record a list of Communist credits of the reluctant witness, including the numbers of their C.P. cards. The evidence was persuasive; all had been openly active in their faith (though Lardner and Dmytryk were less noisy about it than Trumbo and Lawson), and their records were nicely in accord with their performances before the Committee. The fortunes of the dozen or two Communist writers who enlivened Hollywood's studios during the nineteen-thirties and -forties varied from Dalton Trumbo, who had come into wealth with such major screenplays as A *Bill of Divorcement, Kitty Foyle,* and *Thirty Seconds Over Tokyo,* to Alvah Bessie, who merely eked out a living, by Hollywood standards, with *Objective Burma* and

---

[9] Thirteen years later Lardner, the best-humored of the bunch, would concede in a *Saturday Evening Post* article that he had been a C.P. member, of an undependable sort, in 1948.

The Very Thought of You, to Samuel Ornitz, who specialized in B-films for Republic Pictures. The only name among them whom critics reckoned with was that of Clifford Odets. The others were craftsmen, more or less adept at setting down on paper the ideas in a producer's head. It was not arduous work, except to the spirit; they were paid very well (the skilled Trumbo earning more than $100,000 a year) and these revolutionaries could mock in comfort the hands they kissed in conference. They busied themselves with all the authorized causes of their time—neutrality before June 1941, Russian war relief and a second front afterward, the beginnings of the Progressive Party. With the help of C.P. members and admirers elsewhere in the studios, they recruited comrades to join them in manipulating the Screen Writers Guild. They petitioned incessantly, rallied at the hint of an exploitable injustice, and held endless cocktail parties for the raising of funds; they ground out polemics and manifestos for the Communist press; they cudgeled their brains over theological matters. In February 1946, Albert Maltz, one of the more talented of the cadre, contributed an article to the *New Masses,* in which he took mild issue with the hard cultural line of the cold war period. The occasion for the article was an attack by the Communist writer John Wexley on Scott and Dmytryk for cutting out of their film *Cornered* some long propagandistic speeches which Wexley had inserted. "I have come to believe," wrote Maltz, "that the accepted understanding of art as a weapon is not a useful guide, but a strait jacket." He recalled that *Watch on the Rhine,* Lillian Hellman's anti-Nazi play, was attacked by the *New Masses* in 1940 and praised in 1942 solely because of political changes in Europe. He had a good word for such unreliable writers as Steinbeck and Farrell—"Writers must be judged by their work and not by the committees they join." The Party hierarchy, having just expelled Earl Browder, had no patience for such quibblings, and Maltz was smothered with doctrinal truths. Bessie and Biberman damned him with particular fervor at a night-time meeting of their cell. In print, Bessie, who could show not a fraction of Maltz's talent, proclaimed, "We need writers who will joyfully impose upon themselves the discipline of understanding and acting upon working-class theory." Maltz, writer of such muscular screenplays as *The Pride of the Marines* and *Destination Tokyo*, succumbed at once. In April he recanted in the *Daily Worker*, berating himself for his "one-sided nondialectical treatment of complex issues," for his "distorted view of the facts, history and contribution of left-wing culture to American life." His article read as though it had been translated direct from the Russian, and it was evident that there was no brighter dream in Albert Maltz's constellation than to be a defendant at a Moscow trial.

For such men, a call to the Un-American Activities Committee was an opportunity to broadcast upon a national stage the stimulating messages which they had never been able to put into their movies. "The attack on the motion picture industry," Lawson told several thousand Progressive Citizens of America, "marks an entirely new phase of the drive toward thought control in the United States." Maltz told the Civil Rights Congress that if the Committee got the right to burn films "the result will be that they will get the right to burn the people who made the films." Hollywood's Communists saw themselves much as they saw Josef Stalin—honorable, tough-minded progressives beleaguered by fascistic brutes and betrayed by pansy-like liberals. How else, being writers after all and radical writers at that, could they interpret their peculiar position? How else come to terms with careers that parodied the writer's craft and a radicalism that one toasted in champagne? In charging that these men had corrupted Hollywood, Thomas had the facts of the case backwards. In Hollywood you wrote to order, and the Communists, despising what they were ordered to write, labored to maintain the illusion that, substantial salaries notwithstanding, they would always be outsiders; that whatever capitalist frivolity might emerge from their typewriters, they formed the last bastion of integrity in a corrupt trade. "Always, in Hollywood," wrote Alvah Bessie, veteran of the war in Spain and co-author of *The Very Thought of You*, "the honest writer attempts to improve on the frequently shoddy material given to him to adapt for films; he frequently succeeds—and this is sometimes called 'subversion.' "[1]

Lawson was the coach of the Hollywood team, the only one of them who had any ties of consequence with the Party chieftains in New York. "As for myself," he wrote in a left-wing magazine before his troubles came upon him, "I do not hesitate to say that it is my aim to present the Communist position and to do so in the most specific manner." A non-Communist minor writer who had been enticed into the fringes of the group told the Committee that he had heard Lawson exhort his teammates to get five minutes of Party doctrine into every film, and to place such moments in expensive scenes so that they would not be cut by the producer. Lawson was also purported to have advised sympathetic extras to behave like slobs if they were playing rich characters and to look downtrodden if they were playing poor ones.

The trouble was that despite a noble Negro here, a nasty banker there, the locker room plays never quite came off on the field. Lawson's main accomplishment was *Blockade,* his 1936 film about the Spanish Civil War; it contained not a word about Franco or fascism, and audiences might be pardoned for leaving the theatre a bit uncertain about which side they had been rooting for. The Scott-Dmytryk film *Crossfire* was a simple attack on anti-Semitism, notable only because it had taken Hollywood's Jewish producers so long to get around to the subject; it was about as subversive as the National Conference of Christians and Jews, which, to be sure, was subversive enough for John Rankin. Lester Cole put La Pasionaria's line about it being better to die on one's feet than live on one's knees into a movie about a boy's school, a fairly safe insertion since only the dedicated would recognize the source or what it *really* meant. Alvah Bessie's finest moment came when he wrote into the wartime film *Action in the North Atlantic* a scene of a Soviet plane—"its red star plainly on the fuselage"—

---

[1] In 1966 Bessie contributed to the world of letters a novel entitled *The Symbol,* based on the life of Marilyn Monroe. If there were anything to be said for a blacklist, Bessie's work would say it.

dipping a wing in salute to a U.S. merchant ship. "It's ours!" cried Dane Clark.

Thomas, who kept promising to show up Hollywood movies as a fount of Marxism, at length rested his case on three war-time films: *Mission to Moscow, North Star,* and *Song of Russia.* There was no doubt that all were pro-Russian—James Agee wrote that *Mission to Moscow* was "almost describable as the first Soviet production to come from a major American studio . . . a great, glad two-million-dollar bowl of canned borscht . . ."—and even more misleading about life in the U.S.S.R. than most movies were about life at home. (The Russian-born novelist, Ayn Rand, one of the Committee's expert witnesses, pointed out that *Song of Russia* showed people smiling and didn't show any bread lines.) But Thomas could not support his charge that this propaganda had been engineered by New Dealers in Washington—though they certainly did not oppose such gestures to our ally in the East. Robert Taylor apologetically took back in the fall the impression of government interference with his military life which he had left in the spring. As an M.G.M. script supervisor, a member of the Motion Picture Alliance for the Preservation of American Ideals, observed, the pro-Russian movies were "a form of intellectual lend-lease." Battles were, after all, raging on the Eastern front, and it would have been odd if among all the war films of the time there had not been one or two boosting the Soviet Union.

As the hearings proceeded, it seemed that the movie industry, which had girded for its Stalingrad, was emerging relatively unbruised from the encounter with Thomas. While former Secretary of State James F. Byrnes, still an influential figure among Southern conservatives, lent his counsel and weight in private, Paul V. McNutt, former governor of Indiana and high commissioner to the Philippines, pressed publicly and cease-lessly for Thomas's alleged list of the allegedly tainted movies. "What pictures are on such a list?" he demanded. "What lines and what scenes contain Communist propaganda?" This in-formation Thomas, who grew indignant at such requests, never supplied, and even Representative McDowell was led to observe toward the end of the first week that he had heard no evidence of Communist propaganda, except that bankers were sometimes cast as villains.

Eric Johnston, president and spokesman for the Motion Picture Producers Association, adopted a strategy of making broad attacks on the Committee's unexpressed intentions as well as on its unconcealed techniques. He put Thomas on the defensive with warnings against censorship, and called on the leaders of Congress to overhaul the procedures of Committee investigations. The open-handed flinging about of names by the first week's witnesses, not excepting his employers, gave point to Johnston's charge: "Too often individuals and institutions have been condemned without a hearing or a chance to speak in self-defense; slandered and libeled by hostile witnesses not subject to cross-examination and immune from subsequent suit or prosecution." At the very time that this civil libertarian text was being composed, however, Johnston was suggesting to the producers that they agree not to employ "proven Communists." The producers did not, for the moment, accept this recommendation, on the technicality that such a pact might constitute a conspiracy to deprive persons of a livelihood. Instead, they put it up to Congress to rule on whether Communists were in fact agents of a foreign government.[2]

In private meetings of attorneys for the producers and the writers on the eve of the opening of the Hollywood hearings, Johnston, renowned for his winning manner, gave his personal assurances that there would be no blacklist: "Tell the boys not to worry. We're not going totalitarian to please this Committee." Even Jack Warner, who strained to bursting in his effort to please the Committee, told Thomas: "I can't, for the life of me, figure where men could get together and try in any form, shape or manner to deprive a man of a livelihood because of his political beliefs." By November he was able to figure it. At the end of the month, fifty leading motion picture

[2] Stripling digressed during his questioning of Johnston to press him about a trusted assistant of his who once belonged to the Communist Party. It was the same diversion that Senator McCarthy would use, to his sorrow, against Joseph Welch in the Army-McCarthy hearings of 1954.

executives held a secret two-day meeting at the Waldorf-Astoria and emerged with the announcement that they had unanimously decided to "discharge or suspend without compensation" the unfriendly ten, whose "actions have been a disservice to their employers and have impaired their usefulness to the industry." No one would be rehired until he had purged himself of contempt or been acquitted or declared under oath that he was not a Communist. ". . . A constructive step . . ." commented Thomas.

The producers had fought back the besiegers of their town only to bend their knee to the foreign gods anyway. Sam Goldwyn, Walter Wanger, and Dore Schary were against the decision; the brothers Warner, Spyros Skouras of Twentieth Century-Fox, and Nicholas Schenck of Metro-Goldwyn-Mayer favored it. But the decisive pressure came from the New York financial interests upon which the studios relied. The brawling exhibition of the unfriendly witnesses, in addition to being an embarrassment to everyone, had apparently left some moviegoers with the idea that Hollywood was a nest of Red agitators, and it was feared that box office receipts might be affected. Even newspapers critical of the hearings were put off by the writers' performances, while the Hearst press, ever partial to the Committee, had given the proceedings lavish coverage and were clamoring for restrictive laws—"The need is for FEDERAL CENSORSHIP OF MOTION PICTURES. The Constitution PERMITS it. The law SANCTIONS it. The safety and welfare of America DEMAND it!" The dismissal of a few politically obnoxious employees seemed a cheap price for the protection of an entire industry.

A three-man delegation, led by Dore Schary, a former writer whose studio, R.K.O., had produced *Crossfire* and who had defended Scott and Dmytryk before the Committee, was sent to bear the producers' decision to a meeting of the Screen Writers Guild.[3] Schary explained to the assembled writers,

---

[3] Like Bertolt Brecht, Schary had been advised by an attorney for the writers to join his clients in pleading the First Amendment, with the warning that the Committee had forged a C.P. card in his name. If the attorneys for the Communists truly believed this, it may be written off as a case of hysteria.

who included six of the unfriendly ten and a number of others who faced quick dismissal, that unrepenting Communists would no longer be considered suitable for employment in the movies. "We do not expect you to condone this," he said, but added the hope that all survivors would pitch in with a new "council of unity" to help improve the industry's image. Invited shortly thereafter to accept an award for *Crossfire* by a reputable Philadelphia organization, Schary, whose studio had just fired Scott and Dmytryk over his dissent, had the grace to decline, but Eric Johnston went to Philadelphia, accepted the award, and gave a talk on the virtues of tolerance. Johnston had shown in this difficult time the qualities that had brought him to eminence with the Chamber of Commerce early in life. They were the qualities that Demosthenes showed when he wrote an oration for Apollodorus to use against Phormion and, in the same case, an oration for Phormion to use against Apollodorus —"having simply," Plutarch tells us, "furnished two adversaries out of the same shop with weapons to wound one another." It was a sorry cause indeed on which Eric Johnston could not put a noble construction.

So began the blacklist, which would torment the entertainment industry for more than a decade. Whatever the defects of Mr. Truman's Loyalty Order, it had as its justification the premise that Communists do not make trustworthy public servants. No such justification was available to the movie industry or, later, to the yet more anxiety-prone television industry. Dependent utterly on the whims of public pleasure, the moguls in Hollywood and New York, then at the height of their powers, were like those mothers who fear pneumonia in every draft. It would not have taken much courage or sacrifice to hold out against blacklisting, but they had grown flabby on a diet of public relations and collapsed before empty threats.

The particular irony of the producers' submission lay in the fact that the hearings had not gone well from Thomas's point of view. Few newspapers shared Hearst's enthusiasm for

---

If they did not believe it but were trying simply to frighten Schary and Brecht into noncooperation, that suggests that their main interest was in churning up a *cause célèbre*.

federal censorship, even of so distant a cousin as the movies. The weightiest editorial pages—*The New York Times*, the *Herald Tribune*, the Washington *Post*, the Detroit *Free Press*— roundly condemned the Committee for airing unsubstantiated charges and denying accused persons basic means of defending themselves.[4] Eminent film personalities, joined in the Committee for the First Amendment, took out full-page advertisements attacking the hearings, delivered coast-to-coast broadcasts entitled *Hollywood Fights Back*, and chartered a plane called Star of the Red Sea for a very well publicized flight to Washington, with well-publicized stopovers along the way. Thomas also took to the air—the A.B.C. network—to attack these "glamor flights" of the actors and actresses. The ogre of publicity that affrighted the producers was an old pal to the protesting stars. The newspaper reader's eye might skip over the protests of the Progressive Citizens of America, full of prophecies of the rise of fascism, but it could hardly fail to be attracted by such names, most of them untainted by Communism, as Spencer Tracy, Katharine Hepburn, Myrna Loy, Judy Garland, Gregory Peck, James Stewart, Rita Hayworth, Ava Gardner, Frank Sinatra, Humphrey Bogart, and Lauren Bacall. (After seeing the Communist writers perform, some of the actors would lose their enthusiasm for the defense.)

Attendance in the Caucus Room dropped off after the witness-stars had gone home, and a Gallup Poll taken in November indicated that as many people disapproved of the hearings as approved of them. Thomas did not have these figures at hand in the last days of October, but he sensed that his show was falling somewhat flat, and he was on the defensive. He proclaimed on October 29 that his Committee had "not been swayed, intimidated or influenced by either Hollywood glamour, pressure groups, threats, ridicule or high-pressure tactics on the part of high-paid puppets and apologists for the motion picture industry." A day later he abruptly

---

[4] Governor Earl Warren of California, not yet the leader of a civil libertarian Supreme Court and looking toward a possible Republican Presidential nomination in 1948, skirted the dispute. He contented himself with assuring his constituents that "for every Communist or fellow-traveler in your industry there are literally thousands of men and women who abhor Communism."

adjourned the hearings, immediately after Committee investigator Louis Russell told the interesting if scarcely relevant story of how in 1942 the Soviet vice counsel in San Francisco asked a physicist friend named George Charles Eltenton to to see what he could find out about the radiation work then under way at the University of California; Eltenton approached Haakon Chevalier, an assistant professor of romance languages and friend of the eminent physicist J. Robert Oppenheimer, who was subsequently put in charge of the Los Alamos atomic project; Chevalier put the request to Oppenheimer and was turned down flat.[5] Having thrown out this intriguing bit to the press, which had been growing sated on unresponsive witnesses, Thomas called a halt, pledging to resume his investigation in a few weeks. There were still sixty-eight Communists on his list and he was determined to expose them. Moreover, his staff, with the help of "expert analysts," was making an exhaustive study of Communist propaganda in movies, and that too would be exposed. He reiterated these intentions in the following weeks, but made no move to act upon them. The hearings, in Stripling's estimate, had taken on "the overtones of a broken record." Besides, there were ten contempt citations pending, and it was to these that Thomas now turned his energies.

The citations were brought before the Congress in November at a special session called partly for the purpose of appropriating funds to resist Communist advances in Europe, and Committee members did not let the circumstance go unnoted. McDowell read out the roster of countries that had fallen to the Communist conspiracy, starting with Russia, then informed the House that Albert Maltz, the first witness up for citing, "is a colonel in the conspiratorial, political army of Soviet Russia"—a sudden promotion for the luckless Maltz. The handful of representatives who opposed the citations—Eberharter, Holifield, Javits, Klein, Mrs. Douglas, as well as the indefatigable Marcantonio who saw the affair as another plot of

[5] Years later Dr. Oppenheimer, a favorite target of the right wing, would be stigmatized as a security risk by the Atomic Energy Commission and deprived of clearance largely because of his past association with Communists and his attempt to protect Chevalier by withholding his name from security officials when he told them of the incident in California.

monopoly capitalism—based their opposition on the way the hearings had been conducted and the motives of the Committee in conducting them. Javits granted that the Committee had ample power to allow loose charges to be made in public and then call upon the accused persons to deny them, but argued that such a procedure was nonetheless improper. In attempting to place the burden of controlling the Un-American Activities Committee on Congress itself, Javits was following the import of the Court of Appeals decision in the Barsky case, but the parent wished for no such responsibility over its child. Nixon delivered a brief, unemotional lecture to the effect that there were only two issues before the Congress: The first, a matter of fact—had the witnesses refused to answer the Committee's questions? The second, a matter of law—did the Committee have the power to ask those questions? To both Mr. Nixon answered aye, as did the Congress by a succession of overwhelming votes—347 to 17 in the case of Colonel Maltz. Where the courts had deferred to the Congress, the Congress now deferred to the courts, like two gentlemen bowing each other through a door which neither wishes to enter. The courts had ruled that they could not control unseemly conduct by Congressional committees; the Congress had showed that it would not control it. The authority of committee chairmen to pursue their own goals in their own ways was left unimpaired.[6]

The Hollywood Ten, whom Henry Wallace, beginning his campaign for the presidency, described as "most adept at carrying truth to the people," all waived trial by jury and were all found guilty. Eight of them received the maximum sentence of one year in jail and $1,000; Biberman and Dmytryk were given six months and $1,000. Lawson and Trumbo appealed their sentences in behalf of the entire group, which was feeling

[6] Rankin, who was annoyed that he had not been included on the Hollywood subcommittee, had a few words to contribute during this debate. He disclosed that the names of many of the signers of a petition condemning the Committee had been changed from the original—Eddie Cantor having been born Edward Iskowitz; Edward G. Robinson, Emanuel Goldenburg; Danny Kaye, David Daniel Kamisky; Melvyn Douglas, Melvyn Hesselberg; and so forth.

pressed for funds now,[7] on the grounds that their right of free speech included the right to remain silent and was impinged upon when they were forced under threat of punishment to disclose their political opinions and affiliations. In 1949 the U.S. Court of Appeals upheld their convictions. The unanimous decision was phrased forcefully and unambiguously, emphasizing that the Barsky, Eisler, and Dennis decisions "leave it no longer subject to the slightest doubt that the Committee was and is constitutionally created, that it functions under valid statute and resolution which have repeatedly and without exception been upheld as constitutional, that the 'question under inquiry' by the Committee was proper, that the power of inquiry includes power to require a witness before the Committee to disclose whether or not he is a Communist, and the failure or refusal of a witness so to disclose is properly punishable . . ." In a tribute to himself published soon after this decision, Trumbo wrote, "All effective communication upon any subject . . . becomes as of June 13, 1949, the legitimate object of government regulation." The Supreme Court denied certiorari, with Justices Black and Douglas dissenting, and the Hollywood Ten went to jail, an action which Ring Lardner, Jr. told a rally of the Civil Rights Congress against America's participation in the Korean War elevated him to the company of Socrates and St. Paul.

When they got out, they were blacklisted. American Legion posts and local chambers of commerce were cooperating with newly formed and sometimes moneymaking vigilante groups in guaranteeing the purity not only of the movies but of radio and the lusty, if neurotic, infant television as well. The Committee's files and its good will were at their disposal for the infliction of misery on dissenters, and they reveled in the cowardice of show business. The blacklists flourished for years after, a blemish on the nation which has not yet been entirely removed. Hollywood turned out a number of anti-Communist

---

[7] The Screen Writers Guild voted against contributing to their defense and, as their incomes had tumbled precipitously, the Unfriendly Ten had to depend on outside contributions.

films such as *The Red Menace* and *The Iron Curtain* and *I Married a Communist* but found uses for the more useful of the convicted writers like Trumbo, permitting them to contribute screenplays under assumed names and for reduced wages. The less useful, such as Alvah Bessie, were simply out of luck. Having been brought West as a reward for his Party loyalties, Bessie was now exiled as punishment for them; it was poetic judgment à la Hollywood, and it secured him in his sense of righteousness. Herbert Biberman and a few other blacklisted moviemakers went to New Mexico and produced an agitprop epic called *Salt of the Earth.* The Hollywood Ten and their sympathizers pretended to believe that their dismissal from the film capital would result in a disastrous decline in the quality of American movies (not to mention the national plunge into fascism); it was a pardonable conceit, with even less substance than the industry's claim, invoked to repair Hollywood's damaged image, that Movies Are Better Than Ever. In fact, the absence of these writers mattered as little to the quality of America's movies as their presence, and when, at last, Dalton Trumbo was permitted to sign his own name again, it was attached to such extravaganzas as *Spartacus* and *Ben Hur* and *The Sandpiper.* The eulogy on these men, who were never able to forgive Hollywood for what it had allowed them to become, was written by Murray Kempton:

> Their story is a failure of promise: first, of the promise in themselves, and last, of the promise of the Hollywood which was so kind to them until they became an embarrassment and then turned them out. The promise at the beginnings of most of them appears now to have been largely smoke and thunder; the promise which vanished at their end appears to have been tinsel, as Hollywood is tinsel. They were entombed, most of them, not for being true to themselves, but for sitting up too long with their own press releases.

The Hollywood hearings brought forward no heroes. The writers, puffed up with a sense of martyrdom, made a burlesque of a Jeffersonian cadre. The producers, exemplified by Warner, were like those shrewd, fawning peddlers who appeared in silent films in the days when racial stereotypes were still thought fit for public comedy. As for the Committee itself, its premise in this investigation, that movies were being subverted by a Red underground in league with New Deal bureaucrats, was asinine; its methods were gross and its intentions despicable. The philosophy that flowered under the klieg lights of 1947 would be an inspiration for much of the Committee's later work: a philosophy that held not only that Communism was a subversive doctrine, not only that Communists in sensitive positions were threats to the nation, but that the presence in this land of every individual Communist and fellow traveler and former Communist who would not purge himself was intolerable; that the just fate of every such creature was to be exposed in his community, routed from his job, and driven into exile.

8

1948: Vintage Year

NINETEEN FORTY-EIGHT stands as the most celebrated year of the Committee on Un-American Activities, a year of threat and counterthreat to which the Committee responded with enormous gusto, grasping and sometimes throttling its opportunities. It was the year of the end of democracy in Czechoslovakia and a Soviet blockade in Berlin; of domestic spy scares, security checks, deportations and harassment of Communists; of the dismal fling of the Progressive Party. It was an election year, filled with decisions that would define the limits of the cold war in Europe and the extent of our reaction to it at home. These were matters of great promise to the Committee and in pursuing that promise it showed itself at its best and at its vicious worst. It held hearings out of which, for the first time in its ten years of existence, a law would actually emerge. In its mistrust of civilian scientists and intellectuals at large, it did what it could to destroy the reputation of a government official of unimpeachable loyalty. It brought into the open smoldering antagonisms toward the Democratic Administration and forced a test of the legislature's power to probe the activities of the executive branch. It tended the spy fears of the day, producing a record number of sensational headlines as its contribution to the Republican Presidential campaign. And with its presentation of the Hiss-Chambers drama, it touched a generation of liberals to their very souls.

On February 5 a subcommittee under Richard Nixon resumed hearings into "proposed legislation to curb or control
the Communist Party of the United States." The members of
the subcommittee were Vail, Peterson, McDowell, and F.
Edward Hébert of Louisiana, the last named replacing the
invisible Bonner, who had decided to give his energies to the
House Merchant Marine Committee. Two bills were up for
study: one, the effort of Representative Gordon L. McDonough,
would have outlawed the Communist Party; the other, from
Representative Mundt, called for the Party and its front groups
to be registered with the government. The Mundt bill was the
serious one. Chastened by the 1947 hearings and J. Edgar
Hoover's cautions regarding a total ban, the Committee majority from the outset favored the idea of registration which,
so it was claimed, would subject the subversives to exposure
rather than drive them underground.

Most of the witnesses during the seven days of hearings in
February agreed that registration was the preferable approach.
The veterans' groups and the Daughters of the American Revolution were still plumping for an outright ban, and they found
allies in James Burnham and Raymond Moley. But the witnesses from bar associations, law schools, and the ranks of
anti-Communist New Dealers like Morris Ernst, Louis Waldman, Donald Richberg and Adolf Berle (who would have a
busy time with the Committee this year) leaned toward registration. The C.P. itself and the American Civil Liberties Union[1]

---

[1] Representing the A.C.L.U. before the Committee, Arthur Garfield Hays
submitted the following measure for consideration by Congress:

A BILL to provide means to eliminate the Communist nuisance.
Whereas this was a happy land with no troubles until hordes of Commu-
nists overran us, causing high prices, strikes, conspiracies and treason; and
Whereas Communists have, since the beginning of our history, caused all
the hell-raising in the United States; and
Whereas experience during the late war proved conclusively that the
F.B.I., the police, the military and all of our courts and laws are incapable
of doing their jobs of apprehending traitors; and
Whereas treason is hard to prove under the Constitution of the United
States; and
Whereas Communists advocate deceit, confusion, and are traitors; and
Whereas one of our chief difficulties is that we cannot distinguish Commu-
nists from anyone else; and
Whereas there is a pressing need for some means of easy distinction; and

opposed any more laws on the subject, while Attorney General Clark, cool toward the whole matter, granted under the questioning of Nixon that the Mundt approach seemed better to him than the McDonough approach. Ferenc Nagy, in exile from Hungary, and George M. Dimitrov, in exile from Bulgaria, were called forward to speak of the villainies which the Communists had perpetrated upon their lands, and seventy-five-year-old Admiral W. H. Standley (ret.), former ambassador to the U.S.S.R. as well as former Chief of Naval Operations, was allowed to ramble a bit on how the Communists were infiltrating our schools and inducing workers to ask for higher pay, but the general tone of the hearings, particularly when Nixon was doing the questioning, was workmanlike, several cuts above what the Committee's recent performances had given reason to expect. (Where they might have strayed without Nixon was demonstrated on February 11, when the young man slipped on an icy street and fractured his elbows. The hearings scheduled for that day thus fell into the slack hands of McDowell, which allowed Rankin, who had been kept more or less in order on his previous visits to the hearing room, to take over for an entire morning. In a surrealistic interrogation of Adolf Berle, Rankin spoke feelingly of how the white folks of Mississippi were being slandered and harassed by officials in the Justice Department who kept accusing them of unkindnesses toward their Negro neighbors.)

Out of these hearings, in April, came the Mundt-Nixon bill to "protect the United States against un-American and subversive activities." It required the registration of the Communist

---

Whereas we have all sorts of investigations, committees, commissions, but no machines to read a man's mind: Therefore be it

Enacted by the Senate and House of Representatives of the United States of America in Congress assembled:

1. That all suspected Communists or people we don't like be submitted to a mental test.

2. That we appropriate $10 billion to set up a commission to invent a mental reading machine which when applied will say "Communist" when the individual is not a loyal citizen.

3. Until such machine is fully developed, all Communists must wear boots, red shirts, fur caps (both male and female), and grow beards (both male and female).

4. This law shall be self-enacting and shall take effect immediately.

Representatives McDowell and Hébert declared themselves not amused.

Party and its front organizations; the attorney general was given the responsibility of naming the subject groups, and they were allowed an appeal and a court review. As the bill made it a crime to attempt to establish a totalitarian dictatorship under foreign domination and, further, declared that the Communist Party was trying to do exactly this, there were grounds for the belief that the C.P. would in effect be outlawed, since any Communist who registered might thereupon be jailed for his part in the ubiquitous conspiracy. The confusion on this point was dramatized in a nationally broadcast debate between the leading contenders for the Republican Presidential nomination, Governor Thomas E. Dewey of New York and Harold E. Stassen of Minnesota, as the bill was being argued over in the House. Both gentlemen appeared to favor it: Stassen favored it because it would outlaw the Communist Party; Dewey favored it because it would not.

The House debate was held soon after the issuance of another Committee report which showed, with quotations from Karl Marx, William Z. Foster and numerous Communists in between, that their Party advocated the overthrow of this republic. Nixon, handling the bill calmly through three days of acrimonious exchanges, took the position that it would outlaw solely subversive activities, whereas its opponents, notably Celler, Javits, and Holifield, insisted that it was clearly aimed at doing by indirection what could not be done directly under the Constitution—wiping out the Communist Party. As Javits interpreted the bill, if the Communists didn't register, they would be subject to prosecution for defying the law, and if they did register, they would be admitting their guilt as conspirators, by the law's definition. "If perchance it should become law," prophesied Holifield, "—and in these days of hysteria anything is possible—the Supreme Court will kill it as dead as the Alien and Sedition Laws of 1798." Nixon, for his part, kept to the substance of the case, but some of his allies let loose: "The world is dividing into two camps," announced Michigan's Dondero: "freedom versus Communism, Christian civilization versus paganism, righteousness and justice versus force and violence." To which South Carolina's Bryson called amen: "It is already later than we think. The security of this nation demands that all Communists within our borders be rendered politically and economically impotent." Mundt invoked the name of J. Edgar Hoover. Marcantonio matched him with cries of fascism. In a year when the nation was busily looking for ways to deport, dismiss, blacklist, and jail its Communists, the Mundt-Nixon bill swept through the House by a vote of 319 to 58.

Senate hearings were held at the end of May—a formality because there was small chance so late in the Congressional session of passing a highly controversial measure for which the Truman Administration had no enthusiasm. The bill was opposed by the entire left—from Americans for Democratic Action to the C.I.O., then engaged in exiling its own Communists, to the Socialist Party and, of course, the Communists— but it was the Progressive Party that made the cause its own. The Wallace campaign rested on the faith that the new party— whose sponsors suspected that they might be called upon to register as a Communist front—was the people's bulwark against plutocratic truculence abroad and totalitarian repression at home. Causes were required from which vast quantities of smoke could be stirred to conceal the fact that the fires within were very tiny indeed. So Mr. Wallace testified against the legislation, and June 1 found thousands of marchers in Washington picketing the White House, cheering Marcantonio's invective and Paul Robeson's baritone, and stalking Congressmen's offices in the interests of defeating a bill that had no chance of passing for that session. It was, spokesmen for the Progressives agreed, a splended success, one of a series of splendid successes that kept many of them in a constant state of self-delusion until November.[2]

---

[2] The near unanimous verdict after election day was that the Communists had suffered a defeat of monumental proportions, and had given a conclusive demonstration of their political incapacity. But the Committee on Un-American Activities made as much of the Wallace campaign as did the Wallaceites themselves. In a pamphlet, *Communism and Education*, published early in December 1948, as part of the series, *100 Things You Should Know About Communism*, the Committee declared: "Communism gained new recruits through the Wallace campaign, made new contacts and tapped fresh money. The largest vote cast for Communism in this country was registered in 1948 behind Wallace's name."

Chairman Thomas played no great part in his Committee's formulation of a Communist-registration bill. Legislative activity had never been of compelling interest to him, and, moreover, he was ill during the early part of the year. He was still at Walter Reed Hospital on March 1, recuperating from an attack of gastrointestinal hemorrhages, when he issued from his bedside a preliminary report to the full Committee from a subcommittee consisting of himself, Vail, and the docile Wood, on the subject of Dr. Edward U. Condon, director of the National Bureau of Standards. The technique of releasing a so-called preliminary report as a means of publicly indicting individuals and organizations without going through the rigors of formal hearings had been brought to an art by Dies and Matthews. Now Thomas employed it, against the advice even of Stripling, to call Condon "one of the weakest links in our atomic security."

If the charge had had any substance, it would have been serious. Condon, one of a handful of American physicists who had made a contribution to basic atomic energy theory, had been closely involved with the development of the A-bomb since 1939. He was only forty-six when the Committee delivered its broadside, but he had behind him a decade of work in which he had earned the trust of his employers in industry, the gratitude of government officials, and the esteem of his fellow scientists. The subcommitte report was akin to those exposés that appear each season, as books and magazine articles, where the writer's conclusions so far exceed his evidence that his sincerity is called into doubt; somebody has evidently assigned him the job and he, as a professional, has done what he could with what he has, allowing irrelevancies to creep in where useful and attempting to work up some semblance of indignation along the way. The report took care to mention that Condon's wife was of Czechoslovak descent and that he had been recommended to head the Bureau of Standards in 1945 by none other than Henry Wallace, who was Secretary of Commerce that year and whom the report identified flatly as the Communists' candidate for vice president. It placed a sinister interpretation on Condon's "associations" with East European officials, whom he could hardly have helped associating with while carrying out his own official obligations, as well as with unnamed Americans "who are members of the Communist Party." It managed to garble his membership in the American-Soviet Science Society, set up in the postwar glow as an aid in facilitating an exchange of material with the secretive Russians, to make it appear that the attorney general had put the organization on his subversive list. It was an associated group, the National Council of American-Soviet Friendship, that had made the attorney general's list, and that not until December 1947. By the time the report was issued, the scientists' group had drifted away from the National Council. "The members would be shocked beyond measure if they could read the full report in this case," said Rankin when inserting the document into the Record. How Rankin could have come to such a conclusion is a mystery since neither he nor any other member of the Committee had ever seen anything fuller or more shocking than what had been given to the press. Such is the power of reiteration, however, that a month after the report came out, Representative Vail demanded of the House: "The question is, can we entrust the very security of our nation in the hands of an individual who apparently sees nothing wrong in associating with card-holding members of the Communist Party, with associating with persons who are known to be agents of the Soviet Union and who affiliates with an organization which is in the control of Communists."

This was not the first assault by Thomas on Condon. During 1947 the Congressman had leaked three page-one articles, sprinkled with misstatements of fact, to the Washington *Times-Herald*, then owned by the McCormick interests, and had referred to the scientist unfavorably in two magazine articles. The reason for the barrage was not obscure. In attacking the probity, not to say the loyalty of Dr. Condon, whose repeated requests for an opportunity to reply went unhonored, Thomas was attempting to cast doubt on all of the scientists who had pressed, successfully, to have the Atomic Energy Commission placed under civilian control. His report concluded with the broad and unsubstantiated warning that "the situation as regards Dr. Condon is not an isolated one . . . There are other government officials in strategic positions who are playing Stalin's game . . ."

Edward Condon had been a scientific advisor to the Special Senate Committee on Atomic Energy, which reported out the McMahon bill that so angered the military community and its champions in Congress. He was known to be a liberal, and not of a noticeably anti-Communist stripe; in addition to his affiliation with the Soviet-American Friendship front, he had allowed his name to be used as a sponsor of a meeting of the Southern Conference for Human Welfare and was a friend of Harvard astronomer Harlow Shapley, the Progressive Party's leading recruit from the scientific community. Condon, like many scientists, had been irked during the war by what seemed to him extreme security restrictions on atomic research; he wrote Dr. Oppenheimer in 1943 that he found them "depressing," and he was on record as favoring a freer flow of technical information between East and West. He was not nearly as antagonistic to Russia as Thomas believed that every American scientist ought to be. Indeed, he had had the temerity in March 1946 to say that America ought to welcome Russian scientists to its laboratories, and to add, "I only mention Russia because she is right now the target of attack by those irresponsibles who think she would be a suitable adversary in the next world war." These were the opinions that invited Thomas's attention in the year in which the terms of all five members of the A.E.C. were due to expire.

Condon was not left to fight off Thomas on his own. In addition to the support of the usual array of groups opposed to anything the Committee did, he was backed by scientists throughout the country, by the Commerce Department's loyalty board, which hastened to issue him a clearance, by most newspapers and columnists, and by a number of Congressmen, notably Holifield of California. Less than a week after the release of the Condon report, the Committee came before the House with a request for an unprecedented $200,-000, twice the sum it had received the year before, to carry on its work for the balance of the year. There was no question about the House's acquiescence—the vote was 337 to 37, with Javits of New York the sole Republican in the minority—but even a few of its supporters expressed concern over the fact that in spite of repeated requests, before and after the issuance of the report, and repeated promises by Committee members ("If he's been put upon," said McDowell, "I'd rather the Committee took a shellacking than to have the public continue uncertain"), Condon had not been granted an opportunity to testify in his own behalf.

The chief defender of Condon, as it turned out, was the Truman Administration. A few days after the release of the report, the scientist was moved to the background as stage center was taken up by confrontations between Thomas and Truman, Republicans and Democrats, the Congress and the executive. A Presidential election was coming on, and the air was thick with alleged spy plots and charges of disloyalty among federal employees. Not for two decades had the Republicans been so confident. Never had the ordinarily peppy Mr. Truman been peppier. It was not in his temper to avoid a good scrap, or even to avoid reaching out for one, and in March 1948 the Thomas Committee positively forced itself upon him.

Mention was made in the Condon report of a letter sent by an unnamed former security officer in the Manhattan Project to an unnamed Congressman, who turned out to be Thomas himself. It was written in 1946, during the debate over whether control of the nation's developing atomic energy program should remain with the military or be put into civilian hands, a question to which Condon and Thomas were giving contrary answers. "May I suggest," wrote the security officer, "that you demand Dr. Condon's record of the F.B.I. It would be enlightening."

In September 1947, after Thomas had already begun his attacks on Condon, a Committee investigator was permitted by the Department of Commerce to look at the scientist's file. Included therein he found a letter from J. Edgar Hoover to Secretary of Commerce W. Averell Harriman, written in the course of a loyalty check which the department had authorized. The Committee investigator started to copy the letter, but was asked to desist before he could complete the job. The portion which he had managed to copy—with the exception of one sentence—was included in the Committee's report; it concerned mainly the association of the Condons with several individuals connected with the Polish embassy in Washington, including one man who was described by the F.B.I. as an "alleged Soviet espionage agent." The Hoover letter also noted that Condon "has been in contact as late as 1947 with an individual alleged, by a self-confessed Soviet espionage agent, to have engaged in espionage activities with the Russians in Washington, D.C., from 1941 to 1944." The self-confessed agent, it would later become known, was none other than the famous Elizabeth Bentley, and the alleged spy was Nathan Gregory Silvermaster, a government economist whom Miss Bentley had named as heading a Soviet spy group in Washington during the war. The sentence left out of the Committee report—inadvertently, according to Thomas—followed the reference to Silvermaster, and stated: "There is no evidence to show that contacts between this individual and Dr. Condon were related to this individual's espionage activities."[3]

Thomas demanded the original F.B.I. letter. Mr. Truman, who had ordered both the Commerce Department and the F.B.I. to send their copies to the White House, where they were locked away, directed the department and all departments to refer to him all requests for information relating to their loyalty programs. Thomas, still in hospital, promised that he would force the release of the letter before he was through. McDowell announced he was assigning all the Committee's investigators to the case. Nixon attacked the Commerce Department's loyalty procedures and demanded the letter. Vail told the House that Condon had associated with thirty or more persons "directly or indirectly" engaged in espionage for the U.S.S.R. Thomas, with the blessing of the House Republican leadership, offered

[3] This inadvertence was revealed by the Washington *Post*, to which the omitted sentence had apparently been leaked by the Commerce Department. The Administration made use of the *Post* in much the way the Committee made use of the *Times-Herald*.

a resolution which would order the Secretary of Commerce to surrender the report: "If President Truman, Secretary Harriman or anyone else thinks he can get away with withholding vital information, he is very much mistaken." Republican National Chairman J. Carroll Reece, in recognition of the fact that elections were only six months away, notified 20,000 G.O.P. officials that "It is time for a showdown between those who believe in the maintenance of our representative republic and exponents of the New Deal philosophy that the people are 'too damn dumb' to understand what their government does . . ." He mentioned impeachment.

At the end of April, the House by a vote of 300 to 29 took the extraordinary step of ordering the Secretary of Commerce "forthwith" to surrender the F.B.I. letter. The issue was presented to the House as one of Congressional prerogative—"whether Congress in the due performance of its functions of legislation can require the executive branch to submit to duly authorized committees of Congress information that is necessary to properly and fully perform the duties assigned to the Congress and its committees." Even Sam Rayburn, minority leader in the House and most loyal of Democrats, voted for it, remarking, "I'm going to be swept along with the crowd today, I guess." As the Senate had not concurred in the resolution, it carried no force of law and within an hour and a half of the vote, Truman reminded his press conference of President Jackson's response on a similar occasion—"The Chief Justice has made his decision; now let him enforce it." Enforce its resolution the House could not, and in mid-May it passed a bill designed to compel executive departments, though not the President's office itself, to produce information demanded by Congress. The vote this time, 219 to 142, was divided by party, and as the Senate showed no inclination to become bogged down so late in its session in a fight over a measure that would certainly be vetoed and might prove unconstitutional, the bill was allowed to wither.

Precedent, extending back to George Washington, was with Mr. Truman on this matter; at least six previous Presidents had rejected Congressional demands for information and escaped intact. Yet the Committee kept up a drumfire of criticism. Thomas blustered about the prerogatives of the House; Nixon explained coolly that he was thinking of Condon's best interests; and Vail conducted a set of secret hearings at which employees of the Bureau of Standards were asked whether Condon had ever pressured them to join the American-Soviet Science Society. Of the several issues raised by the Condon case, none was of larger consequence in 1948 than the fate of the loyalty program itself. The Truman program, distasteful as it was to many of its supporters, had been set up in part to keep federal employees from becoming casualties of snipers in Congress. At stake in the President's refusal to release material from Condon's file was the integrity of his program, which was being run with some degree of decency, and with it the livelihoods and reputations of thousands of persons, such as Condon, who were free of any taint of disloyalty. If their records were to be given over to men with the casual interest in fairness which Thomas had shown throughout his decade with the Committee or to men like Nixon who would walk where ambition led or to the unthinking Vails and McDowells and even the Rankins in Congress or to committee staff members with pals on the Hearst and McCormick newspapers, then no employee who had ever had a kind thought for the U.S.S.R. could sleep easy. A loyalty file, rich in allegations, hints, rumors, conjecture, was as tempting to such men as a key to the local arsenal would be to delinquent teenagers, and as risky for anybody in the neighborhood.

If the Condon affair needed any further resolution, it came in July when the Atomic Energy Commission, having gone over the scientist's complete file, including F.B.I. reports of his associations, announced that "The Commission considers that his continued clearance is in the best interests of the atomic energy program." In October, Nixon proposed what had been proposed by many before him—that Congressional committees should give accused persons an opportunity to testify in their own behalf before being publicly excoriated. No semblance of an apology was forthcoming from the Committee, not with elections approaching. The following December, however, the elections over, the case long out of the headlines, Condon no longer in particular need of apologies, Richard Nixon allowed in a radio interview that the Committee's handling of the Condon case had been "unfair." Condon, he said, "should have been heard by the Committee before any statement about him was made public." A few days later Mundt, Senator Mundt now, said he "concurred" with Nixon. And in the following year even Stripling, who had by then left the Committee, disclosed that he had objected to the release of the "weakest link" report on the grounds that Condon had not been heard, but that Thomas's impatience had prevailed. By restraining their criticism through the rousing summer and fall of 1948 and then voicing it as an aside in the Christmas season as the Committee was passing into the hands of the Democrats, Nixon and Mundt showed a nice feeling for the less demanding styles of political honesty.

In 1951, with the security packs in full cry, Condon's trustworthiness was again attacked by Vail, and when in August of that year he resigned as director of the Bureau of Standards, Vail and Harold H. Velde, the latter coming into eminence on the Un-American Activities Committee, announced that it was a resignation "under fire." At length, in September 1952, Condon was summoned before the Committee, mainly in order that he might be publicly questioned about the left-wing friendships he had maintained at the University of California Radiation Laboratory at Berkeley from September 1943 to February 1945. His critics were irked that he had lately invited several former colleagues who had belonged to a C.P. group at Berkeley and took the Fifth Amendment before the Committee in 1949 to stay with him while in Washington. He had known them as young men in California and refused to disown them even after their Committee appearances. He had gone so far in defense of one physicist suspected of Communist allegiance as to chide J. Robert Oppenheimer for his reported testimony regarding the man in executive session before the Committee. Although it was once again made evident that Condon's political sympathies had drawn him into the company of Communists and

Sovietphiles over the years, that he was reluctant to think ill of old friends, and that he had a constitutional antipathy to security arrangements, no one suggested any wrongdoing or even an identifiable indiscretion on his part; his worst known offense seemed to be imprudence. The purpose of putting the Committee's spotlight upon him again in 1952, when he was no longer in government employ, may be gathered from the summation of Representative Velde:

> I was an F.B.I. agent out there working at Berkeley, California, during that time. But it does appear to me, Dr. Condon, that while we do not want to cause you to be thought guilty by association with a lot of these Communists and espionage agents and so forth, it is a little peculiar that you seem to have hung around them like flies hanging around a pot of honey, and, in view of the fact that you did have at that time a very confidential assignment, I would say I am just a little bit impressed. I wonder if you could explain that for me—the fact that you had so many acquaintances, with the known Communists and espionage agents and so forth.

The unspoken assumptions and heavy innuendoes of this statement reflect the spirit of this hearing and, to an unhappy degree, of the year 1952. The Committee's annual report for that year took one final swipe at Condon, declaring him to be unqualified for any security position owing to his "propensity for associating with persons disloyal or of questionable loyalty and his contempt for necessary security arrangements." A few days later Condon was installed, amid enthusiastic applause, as president of the American Association for the Advancement of Science.[4]

Loyalty and the want of it were minor but insistent themes in the Presidential campaign of 1948. Committees in both houses of Congress issued denunciations of executive department laxity in ferreting out Reds and prosecuting spies, and

---

[4] Dr. Condon's security troubles were not yet over. In 1954, the Navy gave him a security clearance only to suspend it almost at once, causing him to resign from his position as head of research at the Corning Glass works. By October 1966, however, Condon, now a professor of physics at the University of Colorado, was considered sufficiently secure by the Air Force to be made head of its inquiry into the flying saucer phenomenon.

even Thomas Dewey, not the most demagogic of politicians, chided the Truman Administration for "Communist-coddling." Thomas, encouraged by the G.O.P. National Committee to hold open hearings during the pre-election months, sprang into action, and his Committee's contribution to the 1948 campaign, a substantial contribution, took up prime newspaper space throughout the month of September.

Having managed to obtain reports of security investigations from Manhattan Project days, the Committee focused anew on Thomas's favorite target, the scientists who had worked on developing the atom bomb. A subcommittee, under Mc-Dowell, was named to hold closed hearings into Manhattan Project espionage, and several times a week from September 2 on, reporters were informed of the witnesses summoned, the information elicited, and the great progress being made. Thomas announced that "a very important espionage case" was being studied, a case involving "one of the most important Soviet agents." It ranked, he said, as "the gravest matter" in the Committee's history. He planned to question a Russian schoolteacher who jumped out of the window of the Soviet consulate in New York to avoid being sent home, on the chance that she knew something about the grave matter. The Committee promised to reveal "a shocking chapter in Communist espionage in the atomic field." Nixon charged that Truman was preventing J. Edgar Hoover from testifying because he was "afraid of the political consequences." When one of the nominally secret witnesses took the Fifth Amendment Mc-Dowell called it "a typically Communist position," and he said that the evidence justified the indictment of three persons for wartime atomic espionage. Open hearings were ruled out because of the vital secrets that might be endangered, but a report was promised which would "shock the public" by showing that Presidents Roosevelt and Truman and Attorney General Clark had had the facts regarding a spy ring that obtained A-bomb secrets and had done nothing about them.

Truman, engaged in his remarkable one-man Presidential campaign, was not backward about meeting these attacks. He took the occasion of the opening of a meeting in Constitution

1948: Vintage Year   241

Hall of the American Association for the Advancement of
Science to shake Dr. Condon's hand and give him a broad
grin. He warned, as the scientists themselves were warning
with a certain amount of hyperbole, that scientific work "may
be made impossible by the creation of an atmosphere in which
no man feels safe against the public airing of unfounded
rumors, gossip and vilification." While in Oakland, California,
on one of his whistle-stop trips, he remarked in the presence
of those who could be counted on to print it, that the House
Committee was "more un-American than the activities it is
investigating." And he predicted that J. Parnell Thomas would
not be sitting in the House for very much longer.

Finally, on September 28, the Committee issued its report,
which it likened to the 1946 report of the Royal Commission
that investigated the Canadian atom spy ring. The Committee
report was far too partisan a document to bear comparison
with the scrupulously prepared and dispassionate paper of the
Royal Commission, but the stories it told did indeed indicate
that the Russians had been trying to get atomic information
during the war, and in all likelihood had picked up some.

Three separate incidents were related:

In 1943 Steve Nelson, chairman of the C.P.'s western Pennsylvania district was visited late at night by a "Scientist X"
who worked at the University of California's Radiation Laboratories. (The scientist's name was withheld because he denied
everything in executive session; calling him "Scientist X" was
a favor to newspaper headline writers.) Soon after, Nelson
met a Russian official and handed him an envelope. Later,
another Russian official gave Nelson some money. (The Yugo-
slav-born Nelson, whose name had been dramatically Ameri-
canized from Stefab Mesarosh, refused to tell anything to the
Committee, which he described as "a gathering of political
pyromaniacs.")

In 1944 a Manhattan Project scientist had dinner with two
Russian officials at Bernstein's Fish Grotto in San Francisco
and they discussed some phases of atomic research. Whether
the Russians were told anything they shouldn't have been told

remained unsettled. The scientist involved conceded he may have been indiscreet, but not disloyal.

Also in 1944 a young physicist, who had been working with the Manhattan Project before he was called into the army on the recommendation of security officers who wanted him out of the way, asked another scientist whether he would like to meet one Arthur Adams, a veteran Soviet agent. The purpose of the meeting was to establish a new source of scientific information now that the first fellow was being removed from A-bomb work. The second scientist met briefly with Adams but said he got cold feet and never passed any information. The first scientist took the Fifth Amendment. Adams was not available for questioning, having fled the country when things got hot.

The Committee acknowledged that all of its information, evidently obtained from a source in army security, had been known to the government for several years, and it charged the Truman Administration with a "completely inexcusable" lack of action in these cases. The Justice Department issued a strong countercharge—that the Committee was indulging in "political activity in the field of espionage" in an election year. To the Committee's statement that "doubtless the Department of Justice has conclusive evidence" on which to base a prosecution, the department replied that "there is absolutely no competent proof here . . . of the actual or attempted communication, delivery or transmittal of information relating to the national defense to a foreign government or to one of its representatives," as required by the Espionage Act.

McDowell thereupon offered some estimates as to how many pieces of atomic information had actually been obtained by the Russians, and called for the impeachment of Attorney General Clark. When Mundt suggested early in October that the Committee cease its activities until after the election, Thomas dismissed the thought, promising to go right on exposing Communist infiltration, intrigue, and espionage wherever he found it. "As far as I am concerned," he said without a smile, "the election has nothing to do with it, nor has the election ever had anything to do with our investigations."

The report on atomic espionage presented all of the evidence at hand; the hearings had added nothing of substance to the information already known to the F.B.I. If Thomas had been in possession of additional evidence to bolster his case against the Justice Department, it would have been strikingly out of character for him to withhold it. As for the accusation that the attorney general himself was holding back evidence, that was at best speculative. The most that could fairly be said of the behavior of the Democratic Administration was that during the war, when relations with the U.S.S.R. were a matter of delicate concern, it was satisfied to stop seepages of information to our ally of the time by quiet means rather than complicate our diplomacy with spectacular arrests and trials. Whether Attorney General Clark had enough evidence to make a viable case against the accused scientists is moot—prosecutors do differ on how much evidence makes a case; but the highly inconclusive Committee report did not of itself support the charges of a "completely inexcusable" lack of action. It remained for the wartime head of the Manhattan Project, General Leslie Groves—no particular friend of the civilian scientists and certainly no enemy of the Committee—to remind everyone that "security was of course a part of the work on the atomic bomb. But at the time (the early 1940s) our major objective was to get the bomb so we could end the war and save American lives."

Leaving aside the timing of the A-bomb hearings—September of an election year—and Thomas's oft-proclaimed dissatisfaction with the atomic scientists' attitude toward military control, there remains the question of whether the revelation in 1948 of events that had taken place, under the eye of the F.B.I., in 1942–1944 was desirable. Insofar as it added to public sophistication about U.S.-Soviet relations even in the comradely war years, it no doubt had a certain value. But in order to turn the information into a political weapon, the Committee needed to make it appear that it had uncovered a nest of traitors who had done incalculable harm to America's security. On the evidence offered, it seemed that a few scientists had indeed allowed themselves to be led up the path by the Russians, but there was no evidence to support the deductions of Thomas and McDowell that any of them had actually passed along anything of any great utility. Still, the Committee had never before gotten quite so close to honest-to-goodness espionage, and it would prove loath to relinquish these cases.

We must now go back a few weeks, to July of 1948 and the beginnings of the Un-American Activities Committee's great case. Nearly twenty years have passed since Whittaker Chambers and Alger Hiss faced one another in a jammed hearing room and, like Bolingbroke and Norfolk before King Richard, hurled their accusations, denials, challenges. Their stories have been told in many books and innumerable articles, and the courts have made their judgment. Yet the drama has not staled, and the meaning of their experience is still good for an argument wherever middle-aged liberals gather.

It began with Elizabeth Bentley. Although she did not quite live up to the expectations aroused by the Beautiful Blonde Spy Queen title with which she was adorned by the New York *World Telegram* before her public appearance, her story of being a courier during World War II between Washington officials and Soviet intelligence operatives in New York was exciting enough on its own account. The "nutmeg Mata Hari," as A. J. Liebling dubbed her, had told her story to the F.B.I. in 1945. In 1948 she told it to the federal grand jury in New York which that July indicted twelve leaders of the Communist Party for violation of the 1940 Smith Act and before its term expired would indict Alger Hiss for perjury. On July 30 she told part of it in public to a subcommittee of the Senate Investigating Committee under Senator Ferguson, implicating a Commerce Department official named William Remington. The Remington-Bentley case made a companion theme to the Hiss-Chambers case. Remington, an unsinister young man who had been attracted to Communism in his teens and had the further misfortune to marry into a Communist family, admitted knowing Miss Bentley as a reporter of some sort but denied everything else. As soon as it become evident that Senator Ferguson was content to concentrate on the Remington case, as a means of pressuring the Administration to "tighten" its loyalty review procedures, Miss Bentley was summoned before the Un-American Activities Committee and encouraged, despite previous cautions regarding her testimony from the Department of Justice, to tell her entire story in public.

That Elizabeth Bentley was associated with a Communist underground in the early nineteen-forties is certain. Much less certain from her testimony was the extent of the involvement of the officials she named. Partly this was due to the nature of the operation. She knew most of her sources only through a contact and depended largely on hearsay for her opinions as to who was a thoroughgoing C.P. member, who a fellow traveler, who a hanger-on. She was not clear in many instances whether an official knew that he was involved with the Russians or believed that he was merely doing a good turn for the American Party. Her judgment of the quality and importance of the information that passed through her hands was extremely faulty.

Her testimony was further obscured by the mist in which she had lived out her strange adventure, a romantic mist composed of a plain girl's dreams of love, a lonely girl's desire for friendship, a naïve girl's idealism: "Employers, I had discovered, often fought bitterly against unionization because it meant they had to pay more wages." In her experience with Communism, she found everything she wanted most, a cause, a community, and then a lover: "Nothing mattered any more—I had found the man I loved." She was, for a few years, the heroine of all the bad novels she had ever read. The lover, a Soviet agent named Jacob Golos, she invested with the aura that certain types of teenagers save for uncles and professors of English. The political conspiracy in which he involved her became far grander in her imagination than there is any reason to believe it actually was; an official needed only to be spoken of favorably by one of the conspirators for him to become part of the conspiracy. Then in 1944 Golos died. "Goodbye, *golubchik*," she said. "You have left me a legacy and I will not fail you." But there was no legacy, except the discovery that all the Communists who did not love her fell short of the perfection of the one who had: "The international Communist movement, I realized, was in the hands of the wrong people."

Miss Bentley was received by the Committee with the warmth that it customarily accorded to friendly witnesses,[5] and she was allowed to tell her story without being pressed for any evidence aside from her recollections. Even Rankin, however, was taken aback by her reference to Lauchlin Currie, who had been a White House assistant under F.D.R. for six years. She charged that Currie, with whom she had never had any contact, had been a source of information as well as "a friend at court," because she had heard his name bandied about by a man she knew to be a Communist. Rankin, annoyed that the Committee was leaving the Remington case to the Senate, took objection to smearing "this Scotchman in the White House" by remote control. Miss Bentley implicated one other important official whom she had never met—Harry Dexter White, Assistant Secretary of the Treasury under Henry Morgenthau, who had helped design the Bretton Woods Monetary Plan, the Morgenthau Plan for Germany, and the World Bank. White, she said, used his influence to place C.P. members and fellow travelers in strategic positions in government.

Miss Bentley named a score of lesser known persons as members of two rings for which she acted as a courier during the war, and whatever doubts an observer might have been left with regarding specific incidents or the value of the information that had been collected and passed along to the Russians, he could hardly help concluding that U.S. security precautions regarding Communists during the war years were less than stringent. The central figure in the major Washington cell was Nathan Gregory Silvermaster, an economist who had worked in various government agencies for a period of twelve years, from August 1935 to November 1947. His record was thick with evidence of Communist sympathies and activities—a Civil Service Commission report in 1942 came to the conclusion that "Nathan Gregory Silvermaster is now and has for years been

---

[5] "Here," said Representative McDowell, "is an American citizen who delved into this business and now has the courage to walk through the valley of the shadow of publicity."

a member and a leader of the Communist Party and very probably a secret agent of the O.G.P.U.."—yet he was able not only to hold onto his jobs but to use his house as a photographic lab and transfer point for documents. Even granting, as the liberal press did not neglect to point out, that the Russians were our allies during this period and the C.P., U.S.A., was a patriotic institution, it is difficult to conceive how Silvermaster and some of the other men named by Miss Bentley could have hung on as long as they did without the services of some good angel or an extraordinary lack of interest on the part of our security services. The Committee would naturally be inclined to put the more sinister interpretation on the facts, and the facts seemed to bear out some of their suspicions. As a result of the investigations set off by Miss Bentley's charges, eleven State Department employees were abruptly dismissed from their jobs.

In search of corroboration for Miss Bentley's recollections, portions of which suffered from lack of outside support, Stripling turned to Whittaker Chambers. The name of this senior editor at *Time* magazine had been whispered to him during the spring Condon hearings by a New York newspaperman who had learned that Chambers was to be heard by a grand jury in New York. Committee investigators questioned Chambers and discovered that he had been a Communist and a courier more than a decade before, had told his story to various authorities beginning in 1939, but knew nothing about Condon. Now, in August, Stripling, looking to Chambers to help substantiate Miss Bentley's recollections, issued a subpoena, naturally notifying the Hearst papers of the fact before notifying Chambers himself.

Chambers opened his testimony with a statement composed in the portentous style that would mark all of his writings thereafter, with none of the glibness or plays on words for which his magazine was known. His opening speech was skillfully put together for dramatic impact, beginning with the revelation that he had reported what he knew—though without providing any supporting evidence and leaving ambiguous the possibilities of espionage—to authorities in Washington two days after the Hitler-Stalin pact, and ending with a call to still-hidden ex-Communists and to Communists whose better instincts had not been altogether corroded to join him in the good struggle for which he was courageously sacrificing himself. ". . . it is better to die on the losing side," he quoted himself as saying on his departure from the Communist camp, "than to live under Communism." The substance of his testimony was that he was attached during the mid-thirties to an underground apparatus in Washington, from which two members of Elizabeth Bentley's band had apparently been recruited. He named as his Communist associates of the time eight former officials whose objective, he said, was not espionage but infiltration of the government.[6]

The period he evoked, 1934–1935, was the dawning of the New Deal when young men from good Eastern colleges were drawn to Washington by a combination of job prospects and social revolution. Business opportunities were at a low level but federal jobs were opening up at a furious pace; the capital's bureaucracy increased by 50 per cent between 1933 and 1938. The new recruits knew nothing of the tawdrier side of the Communist Party finaglings of which Chambers had had a full measure since his involvement in 1925 and throughout the Third Period, the years of the C.P.'s toughest, most uncompromising position. Whereas the poet-rebel Chambers came to the Party in despair over post–World War I civilization, from family tragedy and rootlessness and a literary man's pursuit of life's drama, the young lawyers and economists came out of Harvard and the middle classes with great expectations both for their cause and for themselves. Where he was rhetorically fatalistic, they were inexpressibly hopeful. Whereas Chambers's future, in the underground or as a C.P. functionary, was as murky as his past and as depressing, their futures were bright under an Administration which needed them and, for a time, seemed to be allowing them their heads. At once successful bureaucrats and revolutionaries of high promise, they could

---

[6] They were John Abt, Henry Collins, Alger Hiss, Donald Hiss, Charles Kramer, Victor Perlo, Lee Pressman, Nathan Witt. The organizer of the group and its head until his death in 1935 was Harold Ware, son of the C.P.'s Mother Bloor. Only the Hiss brothers denied Chambers's story under oath.

look forward to splendid careers as the advance cadre of a new America. Chambers, beset always by self-doubt and fear, had nothing in common with these smart young men, keen lawyers, assistants to Supreme Court justices, officials not yet turned thirty but full of credentials, coming men who knew so well how to make their way in the world which turned its back to him. Yet for a few years they were bound together in a conspiracy, sophomoric but with a terribly serious side, that would prove more treacherous to the conspirators than to the nation.

Most of the men named by Chambers and Miss Bentley—none of them, with the exception of the unfortunate Remington, in government any longer—were lavish with indignation at the charges but sparing of details about their pasts. Summoned before the Committee, they took refuge in the self-incrimination clause of the Fifth Amendment. Nathan Gregory Silvermaster, the central figure in Miss Bentley's tale, called her "a neurotic liar" but refused to say whether he ever knew the lady. He protested against "this diabolical conspiracy" but refused to say whether he was a Communist. Henry Collins, a government employee for fifteen years, then director of the American-Russian Institute, belabored the poll tax and the Committee, made known that his forebears had come to these shores in 1640 and that he had fought in the Battle of the Bulge, denied that he had violated U.S. law or knew "a man named Chambers," but would not say whether he was a Communist—or, for that matter, a member of the American Legion. Abraham George Silverman, named by Miss Bentley as the contact with Harry Dexter White, said he was deeply shocked and took the Fifth Amendment. A typical statement came from Victor Perlo, an economist named by both Miss Bentley and Chambers as a leader of a Communist group, who had gotten into the Treasury Department through the good offices of Harry White and in 1948 was working at Wallace headquarters: "It is becoming increasingly clear that despite headline spy sensations, the people resent the failure of the special session of Congress to act on the urgent problems facing the country. The people will echo Mr. Wallace's call for more red meat and less red herrings." Perlo had prepared for the record a denial of all the charges, but modified it after Nixon warned him that he might be leaving himself open to a perjury indictment.

Lee Pressman, lately separated from the powerful post of general counsel of the C.I.O. because of his commitment to the Progressive Party, attacked the hearings as an effort to take people's minds off real issues, to smear the memory of F.D.R., and to discredit Henry Wallace. For the time being, Pressman would answer no questions regarding Chambers's recollection that around 1934–1935 he was a leader of a small Communist cadre in Washington that included Alger Hiss. Two friends and associates of Pressman, John Abt and Nathan Witt, whose flagrant Communist predilections as secretary of the N.L.R.B. had resulted in his removal from that post in 1941, appeared before the Committee with him. Both had been named by Chambers; both, like Pressman, were represented by an attorney who registered in their names objections to the inquiry on the grounds that it was outside the scope of Congress and that the Committee was unlawfully constituted owing to the presence thereon of John Rankin; both replied with the Fifth Amendment to all questions relating to their beliefs and associations. When McDowell sought to have them cited for contempt, they responded, "He regards as traitors those who supported Franklin Delano Roosevelt in his magnificent policy of complete unity with our wartime allies."

This set of hearings marked the first mass use before the Committee of the Fifth Amendment. Other witnesses, notably Browder and Foster in 1939, had refused to answer certain questions lest they incriminate themselves, but now the constitutional clause was being used by persons who had already testified before a grand jury and were charged with no indictable offense. There was, after all, nothing illegal about being a Communist in 1936, or even in 1944, and the three-year statute of limitations on the disclosure of confidential information had run out. In its report at the end of August, the Committee would vent its frustration by calling for laws to cope with "the new Communist tactic of evading detection and impeding the processes of legislative investigation through an unwarranted and unjustifiable misuse of the protections which the

Fifth Amendment to the Constitution rightfully provides for those unjustly accused or those decent, patriotic Americans who may at times be required to defend themselves in a court of law."

Nevertheless, the Committee did not at this point quarrel with the right to the Fifth of their presumably indecent, unpatriotic witnesses. Although Thomas was characteristically ungracious about allowing witnesses to consult with their attorneys,[7] there was satisfaction for him in hearing former New Dealers and present eminences of the Progressive Party discredit themselves in public; not only might their performances prove helpful to the Republican cause in November, but they could be taken as an affirmation of everything that he and Martin Dies had been saying for ten years about Communism and the New Deal, particularly as witnesses threw the New Deal mantle over them with such flourishes: "Because I have never attempted to conceal my strong advocacy of the rights of all New Deal principles," complained the deeply implicated Silvermaster, "I have been constantly harassed by groundless accusations of disloyalty." It would be some time before the Committee came to terms with the Fifth Amendment, but it learned quickly the publicity value of having an unfriendly witness refuse to answer a long string of Stripling's questions about his past associations. There was but a single conclusion that one could sensibly draw from the contagious reluctance to discuss the past; as Nixon spelled it out for a witness—"It is pretty clear, I think, that you are not using the defense of the Fifth Amendment because you are innocent."

Of the smaller group of men who, without availing themselves of their constitutional prerogatives, denied the Bentley-Chambers charges, three were of greatest consequence: Lauchlin Currie, the Harvard economist who served as administrative assistant to F.D.R. from 1939 to 1945 and whose name had

---

[7] During the Hiss hearings, Thomas and Stripling attempted to coerce a lawyer for one of the witnesses to give testimony regarding his advice to his client. When the lawyer refused to be sworn, Thomas lit into him. "The rights you have are the rights given you by this Committee. We will determine what rights you have and what rights you have not got before this Committee."

been dropped into a public hearing by Elizabeth Bentley; Harry Dexter White, international monetary expert and influential Assistant Secretary of the Treasury under Henry Morgenthau and first executive director of the International Monetary Fund, also mentioned by Miss Bentley and characterized by Whittaker Chambers as "a fellow traveler so far within the fold that his not being a Communist would be a mistake on both sides"; and Alger Hiss.

There was never any serious suggestion that Currie, who came to the hearing room accompanied by Dean Acheson, had been a full-fledged member of a conspiratorial group. As for Miss Bentley's description of him as "a friend at court," he had indeed exerted himself on one occasion to save Silvermaster from losing his job in government for sound reasons of security. Currie maintained that he had no inkling that his friend Silvermaster was a Communist, but "this Scotchman in the White House" evidently did have an affinity for left-wing circles in Washington, including, it would be shown in 1951, members of the Institute of Pacific Relations. He seemed to suffer from a sneaking respect for the Communists around him, an emotion that the Communists managed to make use of in his case as in others.

Harry Dexter White, who later would be named by Whittaker Chambers as one of those who had actually passed him confidential information, asked on his appearance before the Committee that he be permitted periodic rests, in deference to a heart condition. Thomas, with his ineffable bad taste, stopped the proceedings at one point to read out the request, adding, "For a person who had a severe heart condition, you certainly play a lot of sports." A few days later White died—according to that part of the nation which took the Wallace campaign seriously, martyred by the Committee. "Harry D. White," said Wallace himself, "my good friend and close associate on many New Deal committees, died Monday—a victim of the Un-American Activities Committee."

White, who had had a major hand in the Morgenthau Plan to reduce postwar Germany to a pastoral condition, made an intelligent and articulate witness, exasperating to Chairman

Thomas and very satisfying to the audience which, unabashedly partisan, chuckled at his ripostes and applauded his opening statement of his "creed," in which he declared himself in favor of freedom and opposed to discrimination. White had, through accident or design or possibly a beneficent indifference, forwarded the governmental careers of several of the named Communists; he interceded to help the suspect Silvermaster keep his job at the Board of Economic Warfare and took that old-line Communist with him to the Bretton Woods world monetary conference. The extent of his commitment was never made clear.[8] Chambers described him as an exceedingly nervous agent whom George Silverman was responsible for keeping in "a buoyant and cooperative frame of mind," and Miss Bentley recalled that Silvermaster had assured White that the information he provided was destined exclusively for the C.P., U.S.A., not for the Russians. Testifying a week after Silvermaster took refuge in the Fifth Amendment, White stated his conviction that his old friend was innocent and he was applauded by the audience for his fidelity. The death of Harry Dexter White, which may have been precipitated by his Committee appearance left his case unsettled, and it is only decent to reserve judgment on the charges that Whittaker Chambers made public afterward. But to remember him as a martyr is to invest that highly intelligent man with rather too much innocence.

The cases of Currie, White, and the two dozen other persons named as Communists and abettors of Communists—both those who denied the charges and those who refused to reply to them —soon passed from the attention of the Committee and the nation as all focused upon Alger Hiss.

Hiss stood out sharply from the other members of the Washington Communist group whom Chambers named in his introductory statement to the Committee—rather like a Man of

[8] "It is impossible not to fear," wrote Rebecca West, "that Harry Dexter White, this gifted and playful man, began by putting a finger in every pie, but ended in giving his whole body over to the rack. The printed record suggests that he served a cause that was not his by helping to build up within the closed system of the civil service another closed system, and that barbaric in character."

Distinction on a stroll through the C.C.N.Y. campus. Pressman, Abt, Witt, and Hiss, recently out of law school, had been Young Turks together in the legal department of the Agricultural Adjustment Administration during the earliest days of the New Deal, but in February 1935 their group lost out to more conservative forces. They went their separate ways, with Hiss embarking in 1936 on the most sedate way of all, a career in the State Department which would include an organizing role in the Dumbarton Oaks Conference, the Yalta Conference, and the meeting in San Francisco where the U.N. Charter was adopted. In 1947 he accepted the presidency of the Carnegie Endowment for International Peace.

Chambers said that he met Hiss in 1934, about the time that the young lawyer left the A.A.A. to go to work for the Nye Committee—which was investigating the munitions industry with the kind of go-get-'em spirit that most liberals would not find objectionable until it was exercised by the Un-American Activities Committee. Officiating at the introductions, said Chambers, was Harold Ware, son of the C.P.'s revered Mother Bloor and shepherd of young Communists in the capital, and J. Peters, the shadowy figure credited with being the mastermind behind Communist underground activities in this country. (Some weeks later Peters, a man of many pseudonyms whom the government was trying to deport, would appear before the Committee and good-humoredly decline to answer all significant questions.)

Unlike his alleged fellow Communists, Hiss lost no time in issuing a denial of Chambers's charges and asking the Committee for an opportunity to deny them under oath. This he was accorded on August 5, the day that President Truman, irritated by the recalcitrance of the Republican Congress, first termed the investigation a "red herring." All the revelations of Chambers and Miss Bentley, said Truman, were known to the F.B.I. and all had been studied by a grand jury and found insufficient for an indictment—and, anyway, why didn't Congress, which he had called into special session with the challenge to enact the 1948 Republican Party platform, get cracking on a program to control inflation? Hiss made an impressive witness, tall and lean, of forthright demeanor, excellent diction, and agreeable comportment. (Chambers was short and round and had a tendency to mumble and slouch.) So impressive were his seemingly unequivocal denials of Chambers's story that Rankin stepped down to shake his hand. In executive session afterward, the Committee members looked at one another in silent dismay, and Hébert suggested that the case be turned over to the Justice Department: "Let's wash our hands of the whole mess." The Committee had never pretended to be an impartial court; it had, as usual, identified itself with the prosecution. "Certainly," commented Mundt during Chambers's first appearance, before Hiss had been heard, "there is no hope for world peace under the leadership of men like Alger Hiss." Elizabeth Bentley and Whittaker Chambers had become the Committee's own, and if they were proved false, the Committee would have to bear the shame. "We've been had!" lamented one of the Republicans. "We're ruined!" For a few days afterward, the Committee diverted the press with the promise of "key witnesses," efforts to partake of the publicity generated by a couple of defecting Russian schoolteachers, and announcements that uranium had been shipped to the U.S.S.R. during the war.

Only Nixon, with the support of Stripling,[9] favored pursuing the case. Nixon had already shown himself to be by far the most competent member of the Committee. He studied up on the subject at hand, paid attention to testimony, and alone of the nine Congressmen was able to lead a witness, without badgering, along an orderly line of questioning. Chambers, soon to become the youthful representative's good friend and uncritical fan, attributed Nixon's insistence on continuing with the hearings to his possession of "one of those direct minds with an inner ear for the ring of truth." But in fact what Nixon showed when reacting to Hiss's testimony, which bowled over his colleagues, was an ear for the ring of equivocation. Asked by Stripling

[9] There is a slight difference of emphasis in the recollections of Nixon and Stripling as to which of them played the more forward role at this crucial hour. Nixon writes: "I was the only member of the Committee who expressed a contrary view, and Bob Stripling backed me up strongly and effectively." Stripling writes: "But, as I pointed out, with the aid of Rep. Nixon, a *prima facie* perjury was somewhere involved."

whether he had ever seen Whittaker Chambers, Hiss had replied: "The name means absolutely nothing to me . . ." While
under oath, he had avoided a categorical statement that he did
not know his accuser.

Two days after Hiss's appearance, Nixon, accompanied by
Hébert and McDowell, questioned Chambers secretly in a
courtroom of New York's federal courthouse on Foley Square.
Nixon realized that to prove that Hiss had been or still was a
Communist might be impossible, but to prove that he and
Chambers had known one another need not be unduly difficult
if Chambers could supply details of Hiss's private life in the
years 1934 to 1938. This Chambers seemed able to do in ample
measure. He told of the Hiss family's nicknames, their eating
and drinking habits, their furniture; he recalled that Hiss was
an amateur ornithologist who had once seen a rare prothono-
tary warbler; he said that Hiss had turned over a 1929 Ford
roadster to a C.P. member. He also mentioned what he had
oddly failed to mention at his first appearance, that Hiss knew
him not as Whittaker Chambers, but as "Carl."

Nine days later, during which period Nixon paid three visits
to Chambers at his farm in Westminster, Maryland, and became thoroughly convinced of his truthfulness, Alger Hiss was
called to an executive session in Washington. The aplomb of
his previous appearance had worn off; when Hébert charged
him with hedging, he expressed his indignation at the idea that
the testimony of a creature such as Chambers, "a confessed
former Communist and traitor to his country," should be
weighed equally by the Committee with the testimony of a
person such as himself. It was at this meeting that Hiss, though
wary now and reluctant to say too much, unknowingly confirmed many of the details of his life which Chambers had
provided. Midway through the session, Hiss, with a bit of
rigmarole, gave the Committee a name, George Crosley, which
he explained belonged to a magazine writer, a free-lance free-
loader who had hung about him during his Nye Committee
days. The name, he emphasized, had not been brought to mind
by the photographs he had seen of Chambers, but by a newspaper report to the effect that Chambers had displayed con-

siderable knowledge of the Hiss household. The Committee interpreted this to mean that Hiss now realized he could no longer get away with a flat denial.

At the conclusion of this session, on August 16, it was agreed that a confrontation between Chambers and Hiss would be arranged for August 25. But late on the night of the sixteenth, Nixon, persuaded that Hiss was lying, changed plans. Chambers and Hiss were suddenly summoned to meet in New York the very next evening. Nixon would subsequently deny charges that the change of plans was an effort to divert attention from the death of Harry Dexter White on August 16. As he explained it, the date was moved up in order to deprive Hiss of "nine more days to make his story fit the facts."

The executive session in Room 1400 of the Hotel Commodore did not take long. Hiss started it off with several complaints— the suddenness of the summons, the death of Harry White, a Committee leak to the *Herald Tribune* of his disinclination to take a lie detector test. Chambers was brought into the room. After a certain amount of stage business in which Hiss inspected his teeth, made a show of listening to his voice, and did some paltry cross-examining, the climax was reached. Hiss said: "I am perfectly prepared to identify this man as George Crosley." The session ended with Hiss advancing upon Chambers with clenched fists and challenging him to make his charges outside of the Committee hearing room: "I challenge you to do it, and I hope you will do it damned quickly." It is difficult to read the transcript of this encounter and not conclude, with Whittaker Chambers, that "Alger Hiss was acting from start to finish."

By the time of the public confrontation on August 25, the nation's excitement had been whipped up by various means. There were Nixon's briefings to the press about the "George Crosley" development: "He [Hiss] went to New York with him [Chambers], stayed in a house with him, loaned him money and a car, and he didn't know he was a Communist." There were the refusals to testify of most of the men named by Chambers—with the notable exception of Donald Hiss, Alger's brother, who denied knowing Chambers under any name whatever, thereby giving Chambers the lie but also depriving his brother of a possible corroborating witness for the George Crosley story. There were newspaper reports that Mrs. Hiss and others were being questioned in private and that detective work was being done on the Ford roadster. There were Truman's continued attacks on the Committee. And there was a long and angry letter to the Committee from Hiss insisting that they get down to the question of whether he had ever been a Communist, and pay attention to Chambers's spotty past as contrasted to his own shining record: "I too have had a not insignificant role in the magnificent achievements of our nation in recent times." He referred to all the important people, senators and cabinet members and federal judges and Eleanor Roosevelt, who knew and respected him. It was, as Nixon commented, a display of "innocence by association."

The August 25 hearing, the most dramatic as well as the most crowded public event in the Committee's history, lasted for nine hours; Hiss testified for six hours, Chambers for three. Nixon, Stripling, and the others pressed Hiss hard, particularly on details relating to his disposal of the already famous Ford roadster, which investigators had traced to a man who refused to state under oath whether he was a member of the Communist Party. Hiss was extravagantly careful. He prefaced nearly two hundred answers with "to the best of my recollection," and insisted that the Committee ask Chambers, whose story was notably more direct and more plausible than his own, whether he had ever been in a mental institution. Chambers replied that he had not, "period," and played his own part for all it was worth. Asked what motives he might have for seeking to ruin Hiss, he answered: "We were close friends. But we got caught in the tragedy of history. Mr. Hiss represents the concealed enemy we are all fighting. I am testifying against him with remorse and pity. But in this moment of historic jeopardy at which this nation now stands, so help me God, I could not do otherwise."

It was to be expected that the Committee report issued two weeks after the confrontation would describe Chambers's testimony as "forthright and emphatic" while that of Hiss was "vague and evasive." But even the hopes that liberals invested in Alger Hiss were severely strained that day. Before this performance, *The Nation* wrote of the Chambers-Bentley charges, "Any neurotic exhibitionist who can claim to have been a Communist is now assured of absolution, soul-satisfying publicity, and probably more material rewards in the shape of payment for exclusive newspaper stories, lecture contracts and good jobs." But a *Nation* reporter, commenting on the August 25 meeting, had to grant that the Committee's relentless questioning of Hiss as to dates and details had "elicited answers characterized by such persistent qualifications and evasions that an objective observer might have concluded that Hiss's claim of innocence had been compromised." A few days later, Chambers accepted Hiss's challenge and stated on *Meet The Press,* where he received a rough going over from reporters for the Washington *Post* and the Chicago *Sun,* that Alger Hiss was a Communist and "may be one now." Three weeks passed before Hiss responded, and even the Washington *Post* was led to comment that "Mr. Hiss has created a situation in which he is obliged to put up or shut up. Mr. Hiss has left himself no alternative." At the end of September, Hiss sued Chambers for libel.

Alger Hiss had no alternative from the first. In his shrewd article on the case, in *Commentary,* Leslie Fiedler explained Hiss's lies by grouping him with Remington and the Rosenbergs as examples of "the Popular Front mind at bay, incapable of honesty, even when there is no hope in anything else." But there is a simpler explanation. For known Sovietphiles like Lee Pressman and Henry Collins, taking the Fifth Amendment could do only marginal damage to their already dubious reputations. For persons out of public life, taking it would in all likelihood mean a passing personal injury. But the reputation of the president of the Carnegie Endowment for International Peace had to be unshadowed. Chambers, fascinated with conspiracy in all its forms, would take Hiss's denials as evidence that the man was still a member of the Communist apparatus which, in Chambers's imagination, was omnipresent, like SMERSH or THRUSH. In 1952 Chambers would ask whether there were "people who still believe that in 1948 Alger Hiss, impenitent and defiant to this hour, was still not an active Communist, working as such in close touch with some of the highest power centers in the country? Are there people who still do not see that in removing his power for evil in 1948, the secret apparatus that I had failed to smash singlehanded in 1938 was at least damaged?" But no evidence was ever adduced that Hiss had not simply drifted away from the Party in 1939 or 1940 as many young Communists did; Miss Bentley, so generous with names of wartime Washington officials, never volunteered that of Alger Hiss. In 1948 Hiss was defending a career, much too brilliant a career to survive the kind of smudge that lesser men may accept as part of life's game.

But circumstances demanded the pretense, for him as for Chambers, that there was a greater cause at stake in his fight for self-preservation. Hiss seized on the fact that Thomas, Mundt, and others on the Committee were itching to use his case as proof that the New Deal and the United Nations were tainted with subversion, and presented himself as a victim of a reactionary plot "to discredit recent great achievements of this country in which I was privileged to participate." Even after his case was decided, after he had served his time in prison, he concluded his singularly unpersuasive account of the entire affair with these words: "But nothing can take away the satisfaction of having had a part in government programs in which I strongly believed. I feel deep satisfaction that I took part in the creative efforts of the New Deal and in the formation of the United Nations. The democratic ideals which motivated me in government service continue to shape my outlook on life."

To the end, and beyond, Hiss made that plea to the liberal community, and a part of it, only too conscious of what the Committee was up to and unwilling to admit what could scarcely be denied, were caught in the snare; they made the cause of Alger Hiss their own. Their hearts went out to the personable young man who had stood at F.D.R.'s side at Yalta. They were eager to take Harry Truman's mindless sneers of "red herring" as something more substantial than the instinctive reaction of a highly political man in a difficult political situation—the Soviets acting up in Berlin, the Republicans in full cry after "Communists in government." These liberals would not concede that the Administration had done, for all practical purposes, nothing about Whittaker Chambers's story of a Washington Communist cell when he brought it to the State Department's security officer, Adolf A. Berle, a few days after the signing of the Nazi-Soviet pact. They would not, could not concede that many New Dealers, including F.D.R. himself, had been slow in taking the Communists as seriously as they deserved to be taken. Those who in 1948 associated themselves with the sad cause of Alger Hiss made an error for which the liberal cause would pay in the next half dozen years.

The maneuvers and polemics of both sides during the hearings, the Hiss trials, and afterward were generally exaggerated and at times ludicrous. Whereas Hiss claimed that he was the victim of a public hysteria whipped up by haters of Franklin Roosevelt, Chambers presented himself as the last hope of the West as it succumbed to atheistic Communism. Not only was the whole power complex of an infiltrated government and press bearing down on his head, but a conspiracy of immeasurable proportions was out to destroy him. However, as he made clear periodically, he had chosen to destroy himself for the sake of this lost and ungrateful civilization. The pudgy figure in a dark and unpressed suit wanted everyone to understand that he harbored the conscience of Raskolnikov and the mission of Jesus Christ. In the second Hiss trial, the defense would ring in a couple of psychoanalysts to explain, with appropriate phrases from their canon, that Chambers was a great liar. A better case can be made that Chambers was a truthful man, who on certain subjects could not quite separate the real from the fantastic.

For years Hiss had been the public man and Chambers the creature of the underground. Now it was Hiss who sought to conceal his past, while Chambers indulged in self-exposure worthy of Rousseau. Chambers thought of himself as a key symbol in the "crisis of the West"; he savored the allegory of himself—as time closed in on him, so history closed in on the rest of us. Despite the political notoriety he achieved, he was from first to last a literary man. He saw politics not as a battle of ideas or even of human beings, but of immense forces played out on a grand stage. What drew him to Communism in the twenties was not Marx, but Hauptmann, Ibsen, Gorky, not the plight of the working stiff but the blazing dream of revolution in which a rotten West would be annihilated. What sustained him during his years in the Party and in the underground were the heroic commitments, the sacrifices, the exhilaration of conspiracy. (On the evidence of his autobiography, *Witness,* the Communists' efforts at intrigue owed about as much to Harpo Marx as to Karl, but intrigue it undoubtedly was.) And when he fled the Party in 1938, in revulsion at the cruelty and hypocrisy of the Stalinists and their apologists in this country, he took with him two cherished possessions: a sense of ubiquitous peril and a vision of the Apocalypse. He also took God, with whom he had recently become reacquainted.

He was exasperated by those who followed the Hiss case as a kind of tennis match between two pros. For him it was the Force of History, represented by Alger Hiss in alliance with the greatest powers in the land, against one lone figure, Whittaker Chambers, who was sacrificing a fine career, a good name, and the family peace that he had belatedly found in a hopeless effort to show a blind, corrupt, ungrateful, irreligious nation how deep its infection went. He could write: "I am a man who reluctantly, grudgingly, step by step, is destroying himself that this country and the faith by which it lives may continue to exist." Chambers suffered during the Hiss case, and he wallowed in his sufferings; they were proof of what he most fervently needed to believe—that the West had been betrayed and was doomed and that he, atoning, was the unhonored messiah to the age. ". . . the world's instinctive feeling was against the little fat man who had stood up to testify for it, unasked. The world's instinctive sympathy was for the engaging man who meant to destroy it, was for Alger Hiss."

Chambers's literary bent became plain in his posthumous book, *Cold Friday,* a sandwich board proclaiming the end of the world. It reported that the critical hour for the West, after which there was no turning back, came when men transferred their faith from God to the machine. But this new faith was unsatisfying; who, after all, would give up his life for a gasoline engine? A vacuum had been created in men's souls, and into it surged the revolutionary forces of the century, proclaiming a godless faith for which men *would* be willing to die. The flabby, materialistic West could not withstand such a movement, and so for fifty years we have been afflicted by various forms of this dynamic revolutionary atheism—Russian Communism, Italian fascism, British Socialism, the American New Deal. All, in Chambers's system, had sprung from the same impulse, and were propelled toward the same authoritarian goal. The fitting end of the West would be its demolition by a product of its own technology, the hydrogen bomb. What decisively separated Whittaker Chambers from the temper of the democratic West was his belief that we urgently needed a faith for which men were willing to die, a "rallying idea . . . capable of being grasped and so overmastering millions of men . . ." He rejoiced in the robes of martyrdom. If the Hiss forces had any case at all, it was that Chambers would have been willing to destroy even an innocent Alger Hiss if, in his fiery reasoning, it served some greater purpose.

Whittaker Chambers was not, of course, the first hot American nor the last, although he gave signs of believing he was the only authentic specimen around at the time. Before we were a nation, the churches of New England were fortresses where preachers of Enthusiasm tried to stave off preachers of the Enlightenment. The Enthusiasts lost, and they have lost many other engagements during these two hundred years, but their spirit has never been entirely subdued. Its reappearance is generally accompanied by repression, brutality, and howlings in the night. It is also accompanied, often as not, by religious banners. Chambers was a peaceable, reflective, solitary man, afflicted by nightmares, some of which were real and some of which were real mainly to him. His life was dominated by a steaming imagination, which found its ultimate, incredibly satisfying, outlet in the Hiss case. Here was sufficient drama for the greediest taste, and the libel suit, which seemed at first to be an anti-climax, brought the action to new peaks of excitement.

During the pre-trial examination in November, Hiss's attorney made a routine request of Chambers to produce any letters or communications that he might have from Alger Hiss. Up until this hour, Chambers had made no public charge of espionage against anyone. Now, faced with the prospect of losing the libel suit, he went to New York and recovered from an unused dumbwaiter shaft in a Brooklyn apartment house a large envelope which he had entrusted to his wife's nephew ten years before, when he broke from the Communist apparatus. In it were sixty-five typed pages, copies or summaries of State Department documents; three memoranda in the handwriting of Alger Hiss; a long memo in the handwriting of Harry Dexter White; two strips of developed microfilm; and three cylinders of undeveloped microfilm. With the exception of the microfilm which the ever suspicious Chambers secreted in a hollowed-out pumpkin on his Maryland farm, the material was turned over to the Department of Justice. Upon learning that some new and important evidence had appeared, Nixon and Stripling, mistrustful of the attorney general and reluctant to relinquish so promising a case, paid a hurried visit to Chambers. He confirmed that he had indeed produced one "bombshell" and gave them to understand that he had another in safekeeping against the danger that the Administration might attempt to suppress the evidence in its possession. A press service dispatch published that morning provided substance for his fear: "The Justice Department's investigation of the Hiss-Chambers affair is about to die for lack of evidence, it was disclosed today. Unless something new turned up soon, officials said, there would be little use going to a grand jury with the information obtained so far." Nixon, about to embark on a vacation cruise in the Canal Zone, signed a subpoena *duces tecum* on Chambers for any and all documents he still had in his possession relating to his charges before the Committee. A few days later, with a blast of publicity, the existence of the microfilm, which had been retrieved by Committee investigators from its pumpkin, was made public. Stripling was photographed scrutinizing the film. Mundt told reporters that it contained "definite proof of one of the most extensive espionage rings in the history of the United States." Nixon was photographed hastening back from the Caribbean, and on his arrival in Washington voiced his concern over an "apparent lack of interest by the Department of Justice in getting to the crux of this case. It seems to be trying frantically to find a method which will place the blame for possession of these documents on Mr. Chambers."

An Administration which had repeatedly committed itself to a "red herring" interpretation of the Hiss case was fair game for such suspicions; it did have an interest in discrediting Whittaker Chambers. But the Committee's refusal through the month of December to let loose the evidence and forgo the spotlight it had enjoyed in August, owed something to politics as well. A triumph now would counteract the disheartening effects on the lame-duck Committee of Harry Truman's upset victory in November. Nixon's own stake in the case was tremendous; his career no less than Alger Hiss's hinged on the outcome. So the nation looked on while a committee of Congress disputed jurisdiction of a criminal case with the Justice Department.

With a federal grand jury reconvened, there was never any question about where jurisdiction belonged, but the Committee was able to exert great pressure on the attorney general's office in a variety of ways: by reporting that in the judgment of former high State Department officials Chambers's documents could have enabled the Russians to break the department's code; by calling Henry Julian Wadleigh, a former State Department employee implicated by Chambers;[1] by competing with the grand jury for witnesses; and by releasing the documents themselves piecemeal. At length, after much table-thumping and shouting and mutual recriminations, Nixon agreed to an accommodation whereby the Committee would retain possession of the microfilm but would make it available to the grand jury when it was wanted. On December 15, the

[1] Wadleigh, who took the Fifth Amendment, later confessed his part in the espionage operation, and Hiss attempted to shift onto him the guilt of purloining the compromising documents.

last day of the grand jury's life, Alger Hiss was indicted on two counts of perjury. The statute of limitations on espionage committed in 1937 and 1938 had long since run out, and the most that Hiss could be charged with was that he had lied when he said he never turned over State Department documents to Chambers and when he said he never saw Chambers after January 1, 1937. "Despite criticism from all sources from the President down," declared a victorious Nixon, "the indictment establishes beyond doubt the justification for committees of Congress investigating in this field."

Alger Hiss was convicted of perjury and given a five-year sentence at his second trial in 1950. It was the year of the outbreak of the Korean War and the onset of McCarthyism. McCarthy and his disciples relied heavily on the Hiss case to justify their ravages. They believed or pretended to believe that the Communist rings exposed by Chambers and Miss Bentley were but two of many such rings and that others, yet undiscovered, were continuing to eat away at the Republic's vitals. Partly because of Chambers's pleasure in fantasizing, partly because of Miss Bentley's eagerness to oblige, partly because of Alger Hiss's insistence on sticking to his story even after forty-four months in prison, much about the case remains dim. The Bentley and Chambers testimony taken together tended to show not that there was a widespread network of subversives in Washington during the thirties and forties, but that the Communists, at the height of their prestige, had succeeded in planting a handful of their own in government.[2]

[2] In his study, *The Communist Controversy in Washington*, Earl Latham writes: "Of the Communist problem in the prewar years in the federal government, the evidence supports certain summary statements. First, there does not seem to have been a planned and premeditated 'infiltration' of the federal agencies, certainly not at the start. Second, once the entry into the federal service by members of the Communist Party took place in the quick expansion of staff that began in 1933, some members of the Party formed in such groups. Third, most of the membership of the Party was pretty well scattered in ones and twos here and there, and the total—Chambers guessed about seventy-five—was not large. There were a half million federal workers in Washington alone. Fourth, there were small concentrations of members of the Party in the Department of Agriculture, certain congressional committees, and the National Labor Relations Board. Fifth, the aim of these groups seems to have been the promotion of left tendencies in the development of the public policies of the respective agencies. Sixth, the Party groups were not primarily organized for espionage. Seventh, in the three areas discussed—Department of Agriculture, congressional

Chambers maintained that Hiss was to the end a member of the Communist conspiracy, but there was no evidence that he did the Party's work after 1938—although Adolf Berle, who did not take a particularly serious view of Chambers's disclosures in 1939, recalled that toward the end of the war Hiss, then executive assistant to Assistant Secretary of State Dean Acheson (who could not believe that the Hiss boys could be *Communists*), showed a disposition to conciliate the Russians. The fact that Hiss did not come forward to confess the adventures of his youth may be marked up as readily to simple careerism as to continuing subversive intentions. It is a footnote to the affair that by becoming a liberal rallying point, Hiss proved of service to the McCarthyites. His case, in the headlines for so long, made it easy for them to exaggerate the dimensions of the internal Communist menace and to whip up a storm which did not last long but left ruins in its wake.

The last flurry of the Committee's 1948 existence was set off by the fatal fall from the sixteenth floor of a midtown New York office building on December 20 of Laurence Duggan, president of the Institute of International Education. Five hours after the body was found, Mundt, with the concurrence of Nixon, notified reporters that Duggan's name had been mentioned about two weeks earlier in a closed session of the Committee. Isaac Don Levine, the right-wing writer and editor who had taken Whittaker Chambers to see Adolf Berle in 1939, told the Congressmen that Chambers had at that time mentioned Duggan, then a State Department official, as one member of a six-man Communist apparatus which had been passing documents. Asked when he would release the other five names, Mundt quipped, "We'll name them as they jump out of windows." Apparently alerted by the Committee, the F.B.I. had questioned Duggan ten days before his death.

Duggan's superiors in the State Department, where he had

---

committees, and the National Labor Relations Board—the promotion of left tendencies was not allowed to prevail: there was a 'blow-up' in Agriculture, Senator La Follette brought the practice of hiring downtown personnel under restraint, and the bid for control of the N.L.R.B. was lost."

been a respected Latin American expert, came swiftly to his defense, and Chambers corrected Levine's recollection by explaining that he had mentioned Duggan's name only as someone he believed to be cooperating with the Communists; Chambers had had no direct contact with Duggan and had received no documents from him.[3] As protests built up after the posthumous attack, Nixon realized that he and Mundt had gone too far, carried away perhaps by their success with Alger Hiss, whose career resembled Duggan's. Hébert called the disclosure "a blunder, a breach of confidence and a violation of agreed upon precedure." Even Rankin considered it "atrocious." Mundt's defense was unspirited; his action, he explained, was meant as an aid to the New York City police, and a majority of the Committee in Washington at the moment—namely Nixon and himself—had approved it. The quicker-witted Nixon, however, saw the storm warnings and recognized that the moment had come to throw the cargo overboard; he told a television audience that as far as he was concerned Duggan was clear of charges of espionage. The protests continued, with Attorney General Clark, who was privy to the F.B.I. report on Duggan, declaring him to have been "a loyal employee of the United States government," and Mundt too decided that Duggan was "cleared," that the case was a "closed book." He and Nixon granted with the approach of Christmas Day that their hasty disclosure warranted "some honest criticism." They regretted the "misunderstandings" and "misinterpretations" which had accrued. Isaac Don Levine was not so easily put off. When Sumner Welles came to Duggan's defense, Levine countered, "Let Sumner Welles explain away Mr. Alger Hiss and how documents and microfilm were filched from the State Department when for all practical purposes Sumner Welles was Secretary of State." In this use of the Hiss case to bolster lightly

---

[3] Whereas Chambers remembered Laurence Duggan as someone whom he had been told would be "very sympathetic" to the Communist cause, Hede Massing, former wife of Gerhart Eisler and confessed espionage agent, went further; she said that Duggan agreed to give periodic verbal reports to a contact. She met Duggan through his close friend, Noel Field, another State Department official, who wound up in a Hungarian prison after a mysterious defection to the East. Whatever Duggan's role in the conspiracy, Levine's charges exceeded the existing evidence.

substantiated charges against a dead man, Levine displayed a mentality that would become quite popular in America in the near future.

The Committee arrived at the end of its great year balanced somewhat uncertainly between its dramatic victory in the Hiss case and the equally dramatic, if indecisive victory of its archenemy Harry Truman in the November elections. One hundred and one new Democrats were to take their places in the House in January, and according to one report, none of them had shown an interest in a seat on the Un-American Activities Committee. Harry Truman called it a dead agency, and the Committee's enemies were again dreaming of abolition. In deference to the changed circumstances, Mundt and Nixon, fresh from defaming the memory of Laurence Duggan, put forward a nine-point code, steeped in virtue and designed to make formal the rights of witnesses to counsel and other amenities, such as not having their names bandied about in public. And lest anyone had forgotten Alger Hiss, on December 30, the Committee issued its final report on the case, largely given over to details of Chambers's techniques as a courier.

Hopes for abolition of the Committee were, as always, unrealistic; the group had plenty of support around the country (where six "little" un-American Activities committees were at work in state legislatures), and not much outspoken opposition in the House. Whatever its fate in the Democratic eighty-first Congress, however, the Committee's composition would be radically changed. Mundt, who had flowered in collaboration with Richard Nixon, had been elected to the Senate. McDowell and Vail were among the less significant casualties of the Democratic sweep. Chairman Thomas had been elected for his seventh consecutive term from his safe district in New Jersey, but he had allowed his public activities to lapse shortly after being charged by the Justice Department with payroll padding, and his mission would never be resumed. Two days after the election, he came before a grand jury where, to the delight of many who had followed his career, he availed himself of the Fifth Amendment. Within the week he was indicted on charges of conspiracy to defraud the government. When these charges were first made during the election campaign, the florid, bristling sufferer from stomach ulcers called them a "dying gasp of reprisal . . . against one who has stood up against the enemies of this country and did not cower before them." But it was his career that died. While fighting subversives from January 1940 to January 1945, he billed the U.S. Treasury for salary payments to persons who did not in fact work in his office, and he pocketed the money. He was convicted, sent to the Federal Correctional Institution at Danbury, Connecticut (where he encountered Ring Lardner, Jr.), and was paroled after about nine months. Early in 1954 he attempted to return to Congress, presenting himself as "a fighter of the McCarthy type," but the Republican leadership, for whom one McCarthy at a time was proving sufficient, turned a deaf ear. A few years later he died. The poetry of the end of J. Parnell Thomas requires no gloss. It is enough to note that his talents as a public official flourished on the Un-American Activities Committee. His major appearances on the floor of Congress were in such causes as the impeachment of Frances Perkins for her failure to deport alien radicals and the denial of the benefits of the Wagner Act to unions with alien officers. Neither his record nor his personality were of a sort to awaken wide sympathy, and it was left to Martin Dies to remind us that Congressmen had been taking kickbacks since Congress began: "I hold no brief for Parnell's conduct, but what of the high crimes Administration favorites have committed with impunity?" It was a defense worthy of J. Parnell Thomas himself.

Another veteran of the Dies Committee was preparing his farewells at the end of 1948. Robert Stripling, having apprenticed at the feet of Martin Dies and come into his own at the right hand of J. Parnell Thomas, was now looking toward a career in the oil industry. He was a cold and tough investigator; the Communists were his quarry and everything else was irrelevant. Stripling was a professional, a status that he shared with Nixon; he organized his investigations for maximum impact and conducted them with a sense of order that the messianic Matthews had never been able to master. As a technician, Stripling made a significant impression on the operations of the Committee in his own time and for the future as well.

Of the Republicans, then, only Richard Nixon remained. He was, Dies wrote, "the only Congressman ever to profit by anti-Communist activity," adding sourly, "and he profited only because he backed away from it." Nixon's career was famously expedited by the Hiss case—he was Bolingbroke to Richard II, his bucket dancing in the air as Hiss's sunk down and down —but the qualities he showed on the Committee would have carried him forward in any event. He was smart, energetic, and a very fast learner of what he needed to know. He could be dogged yet agile; he had a nice instinct for when to bet high and when to cut his losses. The Committee had helped to make him, but he, more than any other member, had been responsible for giving the Committee its great year. As that year drew to a close, no one could doubt that Richard Nixon's future was exceedingly bright. As for the Committee itself, however, it would not again attain the resplendency of 1948.

9

★ ★ ★ ★ ★

1949-1950: In Contempt

A<small>T</small> the start of the eighty-first Congress the functioning of the Committee was delayed briefly as the Democratic leadership pondered means of taming it—since, despite the President's deepest desires, they lacked the votes for abolition. The taming process amounted to replacing Rankin and Hébert, both of whom had supported the States' Rights candidate in November, with Truman Democrats. "The word seems to have come down from Moscow to keep me off the Committee on Un-American Activities," commented Rankin when the Administration's intentions became known, and he who had led the way into the Promised Land was abruptly ejected. Renovating their rules to fit the occasion, the leaders of the House decided that no chairman of another committee could sit on the Un-American Activities Committee, thereby getting rid of Rankin, who supervised Veterans' Affairs; they decided further that every Democrat on the Committee must be a lawyer, thereby eliminating Hébert, a newspaperman. Named to join John Wood, chairman again, were Burr P. Harrison of Virginia, John McSweeney of Ohio, Morgan M. Moulder of Missouri, and the influential Francis E. Walter of Pennsylvania, who had been critical of some aspects of Committee behavior in the past. The Republicans, allowed only four members, courteously retained Thomas whose payroll padding case was in the courts,[1] and added Francis H. Case of South Dakota and

[1] After Thomas, convicted, resigned from Congress in January 1950, he was replaced by Bernard W. Kearney of New York, who had refused a seat on the Committee as long as Thomas remained.

Harold H. Velde, a newcomer from Illinois who had been an F.B.I. agent during the war. Richard Nixon made up the Republican complement. Frank Tavenner took over Stripling's post of chief of staff, and Louis Russell, another former F.B.I. man, became chief investigator. The Committee was granted $200,000 without debate.

It soon became evident that the changes were more than nominal. Newsreel and TV cameras were barred from the hearing room and Chairman Wood actually turned down an interview for the movies, an unheard of self-denial in Thomas's time. Wood confused the Committee's friends and foes by being a gentlemanly hunter of Communists; he was a conservative but he was not a red neck; and he was by no means a showy or particularly forceful personality. With Francis Walter instead of Rankin now lighting his way, the chairman went along at a less jarring gait than in his previous term. During the first months of the eighty-first Congress, despite persistent goading from the minority to show more zeal, there were no public hearings and no leaks from executive sessions. When in March Judith Coplon, an employee at the Department of Justice, was arrested as a Soviet spy, Nixon demanded an investigation. "This case," he announced, "shows why the department may be unfit and unqualified to carry out the responsibility of protecting the national security against Communist infiltration." But except for a short and profitless inquiry into a couple whose names had come up in the Coplon case—he an employee of the federal government, she of the U.N.—no investigation ensued. The Committee issued its reports (on atomic espionage, the Communist-run Paris Peace Conference, the need for new laws against Communists), held its closed-door meetings, and caused discontent within its own ranks. By the end of May stories began to reach the newspapers of dissatisfaction among both Republican and Democratic members. "I am disgusted," declared an unnamed Democrat, who could only have been Harrison or McSweeney. "It is hardly worth while to serve on a group that is doing so little. Some of us are getting tired of the policy of almost complete inactivity and keeping what little work we do completely secret.

It's time we began to fulfill our function of exposing Communists and un-American activities." *The New York Times* responded with an editorial commending the Committee for being vulnerable to this type of criticism. Over the next few months, the pressure to cast off the unaccustomed restraints would have some effect; for a moment that June it seemed that college textbooks might be investigated, but the impulse was quelled by a surge of protests.[2] At the end of the year such staunch opponents of the Committee as Representatives Holifield and Helen Gahagan Douglas were able to praise it for having "acted with more restraint and regard for civil liberties than ever before." The Committee, they agreed, in a nice phrase, had done "a fine job of what it had to do."

The greater part of the Committee's time in 1949 was taken up by a reprise, with embellishments, of the wartime atomic espionage cases which it had made public the year before. The F.B.I.'s evidence, though not conclusive, most seriously involved two young scientists who had been associated with the Manhattan Project. Clarence F. Hiskey, who had worked on the A-bomb at the University of Chicago, was suspected of passing information to the mysterious Soviet agent Arthur Adams. Scientist X, finally identified in October as Dr. Joseph W. Weinberg, a thirty-two-year-old assistant professor of physics at the University of Minnesota who had been with the University of California's radiation laboratory during the war, was alleged to have passed information to Steve Nelson for transmission to the Russians.

Hiskey was named a pre-war C.P. member by Paul Crouch, a long-time Party functionary lately turned informer. On his reappearance before the Committee in May, the analytic

---

[2] The textbook incident, which provided the Republicans with a unique opportunity to complain that the Committee was overly active, began with a petition from the Sons of the American Revolution for an investigation of the Communist infiltration of college texts. With the passive acquiescence of Chairman Wood, investigators mailed out letters to a random sampling of schools asking for a list of their textbooks. This caused such an outcry from the recipient educators that Wood was compelled to send another letter explaining that he had no intention of interfering with academic freedom. Whereupon the Republicans placed the entire blame for the abortive adventure on the Democrats.

chemist, then teaching at Brooklyn's Polytechnic Institute, denied any disloyal activities but again pleaded the Fifth Amendment, as he had the previous year, to all questions pertaining to the Communist Party, Arthur Adams, and other matters of particular interest. Weinberg, on the other hand, answered all the questions and denied all the charges. He described the accusations as a case of "mistaken identity" and was annoyed at the "Scientist X" designation that had been pinned on him. The Committee, in possession of the report of an F.B.I. agent who had audited from a nearby rooftop a meeting at Weinberg's home in August 1943, attended by Steve Nelson and four scientists with reputations as Communists, doubted Weinberg's testimony. In October it publicly accused him of lying under oath in denying that he had been a C.P. member and knew Steve Nelson or Nelson's secretary Bernadette Doyle.[3] By this time the scientists named as Weinberg's fellow cell members at the Berkeley campus of the University of California, when the Manhattan Project was under way, had pleaded the Fifth Amendment in both executive and open sessions to questions regarding their C.P. affiliations. And in a most acrimonious hearing, Steve Nelson took the Fifth on all questions having to do with his wartime activities in California.

The Committee's fascination with atom-bomb conspiracies during this period was grounded in fact, in politics, and in the general unease over the new weapon and the consequences of its development by the Soviet Union. The testimony which it heard, though vague in many particulars, was clear on one point—the Russians were most interested in the activities at the nation's radiation laboratories in the early nineteen-forties and had done what they could to tap friendly sources among the atomic scientists. In 1949 the U.S.S.R. exploded its first atomic bomb; in 1950, after sensational spy revelations in Canada and Great Britain, the Rosenbergs were arrested in this country. Together with such disquieting developments went the continuing mistrust in Congress, exemplified by the lamented Thomas, of civilian control of atomic energy—al-

[3] Weinberg was subsequently indicted for perjury, tried, and acquitted.

though all the hard cases of espionage uncovered took place while the army had custody of atom-bomb research. It was the old mistrust of the "practical" man for the brain-worker, adapted to new circumstances. As the House Committee's espionage hearings were under way in the Senate David Lilienthal, head of the Atomic Energy Commission, was being forced to defend himself against Senator Hickenlooper's discreditable charges of "incredible mismanagement."

Thwarted by the Fifth Amendment, the Committee employed against the former Berkeley scientists its most effective weapon—exposure. It was especially effective in this instance because all of the men occupied posts at major universities. One after another they came before the Committee, took the Fifth, and resigned from their jobs. (One, lately an associate professor of physics at Fisk University, was traced by a reporter to Oklahoma City where he was working as a utility company laborer at $1.20 an hour; when the reporter attempted to question him, he climbed to the top of a 110-foot water tower and refused to come down.) With the exception of Hiskey and Weinberg, the named scientists were charged only with having been Communists together during the war. For this youthful villainy, they could now be made to pay.

The justification for exposing the identities of the Berkeley scientists was that they had refused to cooperate in an investigation of substance. But the Committee, reacting to the frustration of being balked and succumbing to an underlying anti-intellectual animus, inflicted a similar penalty where it had no justification. Frank Oppenheimer testified before the Un-American Activities Committee a day after his famous brother Robert appeared at the Joint Committee on Atomic Energy in defense of David Lilienthal. Questioned first in closed session, then, suddenly and for no stated reason, in public, the younger Oppenheimer, who had resigned from the University of Minnesota's physics department before coming to Washington, conceded that he had belonged to the Communist Party from 1937 to 1941, while he was a college student, before the start of the Manhattan Project in 1942. He said that he had never turned over any information to any unauthorized persons, that he had no knowledge of anyone else doing so, and that he would have reported it had he had such knowledge. Although he conceded having met the Communist scientists at Berkeley, he was never accused of having been a member of their group or having done anything untoward during his time with the government. Where Oppenheimer balked was at questions about persons he had known during his Communist phase, in particular those who had been present at meetings with Steve Nelson: "Questions about political affiliations or sympathies or actions . . . seem to me not matters which I can talk about here, because the people whom I have known throughout my life have been decent and well-meaning people. I know of no instance where they have taught, discussed or said anything which was inimical to the purposes of the Constitution or the laws of the United States." His wife, who had been a C.P. member along with him, took an identical position. By shunning the Fifth Amendment, yet declining to answer certain questions, the Oppenheimers opened themselves to a charge of contempt. But Chairman Wood resisted bringing such a charge, explaining, "I don't know that that would do any good. I am not in favor of contempt action except in cases where a witness withholds information that is vital to Committee investigation." Why this sensible principle was not carried over to the practice of putting such witnesses on public display, Wood did not explain.

A similar instance of gratuitous publicizing came at the end of 1950 when David Hawkins, a professor of philosophy at the University of Colorado who had worked at Los Alamos as an aide to J. Robert Oppenheimer, told in executive session of his C.P. membership in the San Francisco area from 1938 to 1943. Hawkins and his wife, like the Oppenheimers, disclaimed all knowledge of espionage activities and refused to name persons they met when they were in their twenties and Communists—despite frivolous assurances from Representative Harrison that "we are not going to do anything to those people. We are not going to injure their reputations." The Hawkins's testimony, which provided some familiar reasons—such as depression and fascism—as to why students were still attracted to Communism in 1938, was promptly made public, but the subdued character of the Committee was evidenced by the fact that again Wood refrained from pressing for contempt citations. Still, given the craving, never satisfied, to turn up espionage plots, given the assumption held by several members that every Communist group was *per se* subversive and every member a likely spy, given their inability to view former Communists as individuals, and given the Committee's manner of operating, these hearings could hardly avoid injuring reputations. Nor, despite the improved procedures and the restraining influence of Wood and Walter, did all the Congressmen go out of their way to do so, particularly when the reputations in question were those of scientists or former Administration officials.

In June 1949 the Committee was reported by the Associated Press as ready "to break their first big case of industrial espionage." As it turned out, this was a case that had been broken before it had fairly been put together. Three witnesses who had worked in a Buffalo aircraft plant during the war told of how they had been solicited by one Andrei Schevchenko, a Soviet purchasing agent, to supply him with information about jet aircraft: "I am a Russian, that is true, and you are an American, but we can't let nationalities interfere with progress. Scientists must be international." The three had at once notified the F.B.I. and for three years they received $200 a week apiece for supplying Schevchenko with inconsequential and misleading data. What injected this routine incident with a certain promise for the Republicans on the Committee was the charge by one of the witnesses that former Secretary of State James F. Byrnes was responsible for letting Schevchenko get away after his efforts at espionage had been fully established. Questioned on this point, the witness explained that he had heard an F.B.I. agent complain that "Mr. Byrnes of the State Department says we can't touch him." The witness had taken as literal truth the grumble of a policeman prevented from hauling in a culprit for reasons of higher policy. The policy reasons were easy enough to grasp. It seemed more sensible during the war to keep the Russians happy with a flow of innocuous information rather than arrest one of their minor officials and bring on an intra-alliance fuss.

This case expired quickly for want of substance, but a few months later Velde, who had worked on the Scientist X affair as an F.B.I. agent during the war and was now building a reputation of sorts on the Committee, took the occasion of the Soviet announcement that they had an atom bomb to charge that the Russians had "undoubtedly gained three to five years in producing the atomic bomb" because of a soft official attitude. He declared that "there is a complete and indictable case against so-called Scientist X . . .", and that "Soviet espionage agents are still highly active in the continental United States." He called on the nation to "throw out of office those incompetents who regard their political lives as more important than our national security." Velde, along with Nixon and Case, was more than ready in December for the liveliest episode of the Committee's year, touched off by the accusations of G. Racey Jordan.

Jordan, who had been a lend-lease inspector at the Great Falls, Montana airport, a stopping-off place for planes en route to the U.S.S.R., came into prominence as a guest star on a Fulton Lewis, Jr., radio broadcast. The former Air Force major told a provocative tale of goings-on at Great Falls in 1943 and 1944—a tale in which he had tried without success to interest *Life* magazine before coming to Lewis, who until his death in 1966 was the nation's most popular radio voice of the lumpen right. Jordan maintained that several shipments of uranium and heavy water and many suitcases—some of which he had broken into, to find State Department documents with such labels as MANHATTAN ENGINEERING DISTRICT and URANIUM 92—had made their way to Russia via the Montana base. He said that in the spring of 1944 he had received instructions by telephone from the late Harry Hopkins to expedite a certain shipment and not report anything about it to his superiors. In a folder marked OAK RIDGE, he said he found a memo from Hopkins, then lend-lease administrator, to Soviet Deputy Premier Mikoyan, which read "Had a hell of a time getting these away from Groves." The Washington *Times-*

Herald printed the Lewis broadcast verbatim under the eight-column headline: HOPKINS ACCUSED OF GIVING REDS A-SECRETS.

The Joint Atomic Energy Committee as well as the Un-American Activities Committee quickly expressed interest in the story and three days after his broadcast Jordan came before the four Democratic members of the latter group, the Republicans all being out of town. Embellishing the tale outside the hearing room, Fulton Lewis told reporters that Henry Wallace had overruled General Groves in order to get the uranium shipments to Russia. Testifying two days later, Groves conceded that he had approved two relatively small shipments to the Russians in an effort to discover their sources of uranium and to avoid tipping them off to the uses to which we were putting the material; the Committee had been informed of these shipments some months before. Groves doubted that any heavy water, which he compared in value to diamonds, was shipped, and he denied ever being pressured to help out the Russians. He had never met or talked to Harry Hopkins or to anyone working for him and had had almost nothing to do with Wallace, about whose security rating he seemed to have some doubts. Walter commented afterward that in his opinion it was "highly improbable that many of the things Mr. Jordon said occurred did occur." Harrison called Jordan's account "inherently incredible."

Major Jordan would doubtless have gone into obscurity at this point had not Nixon, Case, and Velde entered a "protest in the strongest terms" at what they termed a "whitewash" accomplished in their absence. So in January the Committee took up Jordan's reminiscences again, focusing now on the only large shipment of uranium to Russia made during the war, one thousands pounds from a Canadian firm. Nixon did his best to pin responsibility on U.S. lend-lease officials, but could unearth no evidence of finagling by Hopkins or anybody else. The New York broker for the shipment, a sound business-man, stated: "No pressure from any source was used, or indeed necessary, to induce my company to fill these routine orders from the Russian Government out of readily obtainable supplies, in strict compliance with all applicable regulations, at a time when we were rushing all available supplies to our then ally." Henry Wallace came before the Committee to answer what he felt had been a slur by General Groves, and in a testy session, which Velde tried to steer onto the subject of the former Vice President's trips to China and the U.S.S.R., Wallace pointed out that his wartime Board of Economic Warfare had had no effective supervision over lend-lease.

Some weeks later a Committee staff member presented the results of his investigation of the Jordan charges. It appeared that in 1944 the Russians had shipped an astounding 1,700,000 pounds of documents via Great Falls and Jordan had complained about the quantity of stuff going through in the diplomatic pouch—but had made none of the more colorful charges he was to make under the auspices of Fulton Lewis. No White House stationery of the kind Jordan described as bearing Hopkins's signature was discovered. On a return visit to the Committee Jordan did his best to make his previous testimony conform to that of General Groves and the Committee's investigator, and added a new recollection—that among the documents he had seen bound for the U.S.S.R. were some folders marked FROM HISS and FROM SAYRE—the latter being special assistant to the Secretary of State in 1943 and Alger Hiss's superior.

The sensational elements of Jordan's story—those which suggested a conspiracy by New Deal officials to send atomic materials and secrets to Russia and had therefore aroused the interest of Nixon, Velde, and Case—were not substantiated by anything other than a diary that Jordan claimed he had kept during 1944. The diary was not subjected to scrutiny. Still, despite the understandable inclination of the liberal press to dismiss him as a fraud through and through, his experience did afford a glimpse of the sensitive and restless U.S.–Soviet lend-lease relations during the war. The Russians were continually pressing lend-lease officials for more and more supplies of all sorts, including uranium after they began their atomic researches in 1942. Many of the supplies, like the uranium, had no bearing on the war then in progress on the Eastern front, but our officials were loath to stir up a fuss which might have resulted in more complications than it was worth. The Russians were demanding and touchy; the Americans solicitous to the point of permitting them to send a mountain of intelligence matter—the bulk of it readily available material such as technical manuals and road maps—through the diplomatic pouch. A noteworthy, if unsinister, chapter in the history of the war, with a bearing on postwar relations as well. But espionage, not history, was the Committee's concern, and when despite the best efforts of the Republicans, the charges against Hopkins and Wallace fizzled, it turned to other things.

A second major area of Committee scrutiny in the eighty-first Congress, after atomic espionage, was the presence of Communists in the District of Columbia, in western Pennsylvania and Cincinnati, and in Hawaii. The District of Columbia hearings had to do with the membership of the Washington Bookshop and other front organizations and a predominantly Negro laborers' union. The Pennsylvania and Ohio hearings relied, heavily, on the lengthy testimony of Matthew Cvetic, who had worked for the F.B.I. in an undercover capacity through the nineteen-forties; the hearings touched a variety of organizations, such as the American Slav Congress, the Civil Rights Congress, and the Progressive Party, but focused particularly on Pittsburgh Local 601 of the United Electrical Workers, long known as a Communist-controlled union and expelled by the C.I.O. on that account in November 1949.[4] And the hearings in Honolulu, the Committee's first hearings outside the continental United States, had to do almost entirely with Harry Bridges's Longshoremen's Union, which was on strike in Hawaii during 1949.[5]

Although these hearings provided interesting details on the

---

[4] For a sense of the impact of Cvetic's testimony on the lives of some of the people he named, see Frank J. Donner's *The Un-Americans*, pp. 142–146. It was Cvetic, incidentally, who was the inspiration for that memorable film, *I Was a Communist for the F.B.I.*

[5] The Committee's investigation was used in the campaign to block Hawaiian statehood, but three of the five Committee members who went to Honolulu voted for statehood in 1950, and Representative Walter told a Senate Committee that they had found only a modest amount of Communist activity.

techniques of Communists for securing and utilizing power in
labor unions and other groups, they revealed nothing that had
not been known to the F.B.I. and, indeed, to many less professional observers of the embattled left-wing unions. Nonetheless, they are of significance in the Committee's history on several accounts. They were a means, in the case of the Electrical
Workers, of stirring up opinion against old-line Communist
leaders during their battle for survival against the C.I.O.'s
newly formed International Electrical Workers Union under
James B. Carey. Such intervention would prove effective in
other union fights too. The hearings were good for extensive
newspaper coverage in the areas concerned, and in coming
years the Committee would leave Washington with greater frequency. And they brought nearer to perfection a format that
would serve in many future investigations—a willing witness,
either F.B.I. informer or disenchanted Communist, followed
by unwilling witnesses who took the Fifth Amendment. "I don't
think a Committee like this or any subcommittee has a right
to go into any question of my beliefs, my associations or anything else," protested Julius Emspak, general secretary of the
U.E., presaging innumerable protests to come. Along with
some of the atomic scientists, these witnesses goaded the Committee to issue its critical challenge to the relevance of the Fifth
Amendment in such cases.

During the questioning of the reluctant scientists, Committee
members, particularly Nixon and Walter, had shown growing
exasperation at the uses to which the self-incrimination clause
was being put. There was little browbeating but, in repeated
colloquies, the Congressmen disputed with the witnesses and
their attorneys over their employment of the Fifth. Nixon told
one of the scientists that he didn't "see how the witness could
plead self-incrimination on whether or not another person was
a member of the Communist Party." But the witness refused
to answer twenty-seven questions anyway. When a lobbyist
for two left-wing labor unions took the Fifth, Representative
Harrison demanded of the chairman, "When are we going to
start citing someone for contempt?" Now and then a member
succumbed to snideness. When Clarence Hiskey, who pleaded

the Fifth Amendment in preference to discussing his relations with Arthur Adams, told the Committee that he believed in the federal Constitution, Velde responded: "I know you especially believe in the Fifth Amendment to the Constitution."

Finally, the Committee resolved to bring the issue to its first test and, on two days of August 1950, the House of Representatives was called upon to approve the contempt citations of fifty-six persons.[6] The question before the House, as Representative Walter presented it, was not complicated: "Has a committee of the Congress the right and authority to issue a subpoena requiring and compelling the attendance of a witness at a hearing of a committee and to require and compel that witness to answer such questions as within the judgment of the committee are pertinent and relevant to the matter under investigation? That is the sole issue."

And so it seemed to the House. Only Marcantonio argued that the Fifth Amendment had been appropriately taken, a defensible position which he could not help leaving for a fling into demagogy. "What are you really afraid of?" he asked his colleagues, and then told them: "You fear the people and their will for peace and freedom." Marcantonio was alone that day. Even Celler, a consistent opponent of the Committee, held that the claim of immunity had no merit in cases where the witnesses were attempting to protect others and not themselves. But constitutional questions were not uppermost in his mind. He felt that the dignity of a committee of Congress, however undignified its own behavior, was at stake. Referring to Emspak, the first person up for citing, Celler said, "The witness was brash, impertinent and utterly contemptuous of Congress. I cannot allow any witness to offer affront and insult to a Congressional committee as did the witness against whom the contempt citation is brought." Emspak was cited by a vote of 373 to Marcantonio, and the other citations followed in rapid course. The following day, as the balance of the fifty-six cases came up, Representative Cox made a victory speech: "I saw them run

[6] Of these, thirty-nine had taken the Fifth Amendment in Hawaii, five were officials of the United Electrical Workers, four were scientists, and the others, including Steve Nelson, were assorted Party members and sympathizers.

yesterday, people who have been the recipients of favors of the group that the Committee on Un-American Activities are now pursuing, who have received their financial assistance and their political support. I saw them turn and like frightened children run away."

The bounty of contempt cases presented to the courts by Congress in 1950 contained an assortment of constitutional questions, the most important of which were the following: Was the plea of possible self-incrimination available to witnesses testifying before legislative committees? What type of questions did the plea protect the witness from answering? What constituted a claim of the privilege? What constituted a waiver of the privilege? Was the Committee obliged to inform the witness that his answer was unsatisfactory? "It must come from the Supreme Court," Velde told the House, "whether we can force witnesses to answer questions that will help us in our investigative work. I think it must be decided once and for all."

Velde's question and each of the others were answered by the courts to the benefit of the defendants, all but three of whom were judged not guilty—the remaining three finally winning their cases in the Supreme Court, the Warren court, in 1955. Most of the defendants relied successfully on a 1950 ruling by the Supreme Court that it was a violation of the self-incrimination clause to compel a witness to testify before a grand jury on his knowledge of Communist Party operations after he had pleaded the Fifth Amendment. Justice Black wrote: "Whether such admissions by themselves would support a conviction under a criminal statute is immaterial. Answers to the questions asked by the grand jury would have furnished a link in the chain of evidence . . ."

Further, the courts allowed the defendants considerable leeway in their manner of stating that they were pleading the Fifth Amendment; declared that questions aimed at establishing a relationship between a witness and persons who had testified against him or who were themselves accused of subversion were incriminating—and that a witness was within his rights in refusing to acknowledge that he knew certain persons; stated, in the case of Steve Nelson, that the admission of Communist Party membership did not in itself constitute a waiver of the Fifth Amendment privilege; and informed the Committee that it had the responsibility of pressing the interrogation if it didn't like a witness's answers, and of specifically warning a witness, when his position was unacceptable, that he might be cited for contempt.

The meaning of these decisions, in Carl Beck's summary, was to broaden the applicability of the Fifth Amendment plea to any question that tended to incriminate, whether or not it, of itself, was incriminatory, and to narrow the possibility that a witness would lose his rights by default, entrapment, or confusion. The era of the Fifth Amendment was thus launched, but the Court's decisions placed no substantial limitations on the Committee's actions; it soon became apparent that the self-incrimination plea, albeit constitutional, would subject the pleader to public skepticism regarding his innocence. As Beck observes: " 'I refuse to answer on the ground that it might tend to incriminate me' has been legally sanctioned, reinforced, but socially devalued . . ." Henceforth, in the court of public opinion, resort to the Fifth Amendment would carry its own penalties.

Besides its planned hearings, the Committee made a number of sorties in 1950 prompted by events which seemed to one or another member to warrant its attentions, thereby giving the year's record a somewhat helter-skelter appearance.

In May came the return of William Remington, the young Commerce Department official named by Elizabeth Bentley as a source of information during the war. Like Alger Hiss, Remington had dared his accuser to repeat her accusations in unprivileged surroundings. Like Whittaker Chambers, Miss Bentley had responded on *Meet the Press*. Like Hiss, Remington had brought suit for libel—and here, for a time, the resemblance seemed to end. Remington was cleared by a Commerce Department loyalty board in February 1949. In 1950 the National Broadcasting Company and the program's sponsor, General Foods, agreed to settle his suit out of court. The settlement was not at all to the liking of Miss Bentley or her attorney,

Godfrey P. Schmidt. In preparation for the suit, Schmidt had sent an investigator to Tennessee to look into Remington's associations from September 1936 to May 1937, when at the age of eighteen he had worked as a messenger for the T.V.A.; Schmidt had been "pleased" with the results. Similarly affronted by the settlement of the suit and its implication that Remington had been untruthfully accused, the Committee took testimony in executive session from the sources unearthed by Schmidt, and followed this up with a staff investigation of its own. Two of Remington's T.V.A. acquaintances, both admitted former Communists, identified him as a Party member in Tennessee; a third took the Fifth Amendment.

At his public appearance before the Committee—on the day that President Truman released the loyalty files of eighty-one State Department employees under heavy fire by Senator McCarthy—Remington granted that he had been active in union affairs during his months in Knoxville, where he had worked in an interim between his freshman and sophomore terms at Dartmouth; that he might have associated and even roomed with Communists at that time; and that they might have taken him to be one of their own. (Speaking of that period, he referred to himself as "the kid.") But he denied Party membership emphatically: "It is impossible for me ever to have been a Communist." Again he gave his version of his relationship with Elizabeth Bentley in Washington; he believed she wrote for the newspapers and he passed on no confidential information. On the following day Miss Bentley appeared and repeated her story of receiving from Remington War Production Board statistics on airplanes as well as a formula for making synthetic rubber out of garbage, which, she pointed out, Remington thought was destined merely for the American Communist Party, not the Kremlin. Now the Remington case resumed a course parallel to the Hiss case. Remington was called before a grand jury and a few weeks later was indicted for perjury for falsely denying his C.P. membership. He was tried and convicted twice, the first conviction being set aside by the Court of Appeals, and he was sent to prison where he was killed by another inmate. The Committee took full credit for reviving the Remington case and for sending that feckless young man to jail.

In August another figure from the memorable year of 1948 was summoned to Washington. The Progressive Party was falling into disarray as a result of its leadership's Communist line on the Korean War. Henry Wallace himself, belatedly discovering who was running his people's army, quit, and conspicuous among the other departures was that of Lee Pressman. "It is obvious," commented Vito Marcantonio, New York State Chairman of the American Labor Party, with the charity that true believers reserve for apostates, "that Mr. Pressman is disappointed in the amount of fees he expected to get from the Progressive movement when he left the C.I.O."

On the day before Pressman honored his summons to the Committee, New York *Herald Tribune* reporter Bert Andrews, Representative Nixon's particular friend, wrote a somewhat sensational story about the secrets that Committee members hoped to draw out of their old acquaintance, and counsel Tavenner started the hearings with the warning that he would "not be satisfied with a mere perfunctory repudiation of the Communist Party." He wanted names. But Pressman was not in a giving spirit. He conceded what he had refused to concede two years before—that he had been a member of a Communist group in Washington in 1934 and 1935—but he pointed out a number of discrepancies in Whittaker Chambers's recollections. On the single question of surpassing interest to the Committee and the nation, he replied "I have no knowledge regarding the political beliefs or affiliations of Alger Hiss"; he said that Hiss had not been a member of the Washington group during his participation, yet he managed by the fastidious phrasing of his answers to leave the impression that he knew more about Hiss than he was prepared to tell.[7] When it came to other names, he was like the girl who will not jump into bed without twenty-five minutes of urging by her suitor lest she be thought of light virtue. Pressman explained to Chairman Wood how offensive

[7] In 1952 Nathaniel Weyl told the Senate Subcommittee on Internal Security that he had been a member of the famous Communist Party cell in Washington in 1934 along with Pressman and the others, and that Alger Hiss was one of their number.

it was to him to name names and then, in a strange scene, implored the chairman to demand that he do so. Wood, as was his custom, refused to demand anything of anybody, but Nixon finally said that he was insisting on an answer and Pressman thereupon let it be known that Witt, Abt, and Kramer were Communists with him in the thirties. All three, on being recalled by the Committee, again took the Fifth Amendment, as did Abraham George Silverman; Witt, still at it, volunteered a statement about "atomic bomb diplomacy," "frightening power of monopolies," "red-baiting," and "heightened attacks on the Negro people." With his appearance in August 1950, Lee Pressman departed public life. His epitaph was delivered by Richard Nixon, who, with his sharp nose for such witnesses, concluded that Pressman was not "coming clean." Pressman was tough and smart to the end and would doubtless have made an exemplary commissar. But history had not gone his way, the expectations to which his ability entitled him had collapsed, and he made his exit, still a young man, detested by anti-Communists from Nixon to the A.F. of L., and despised by his former comrades as only one's former comrades can despise one.

A few weeks later, the Committee heard in executive session Max Lowenthal, an attorney with a long record of government service, whose main offense was that he had written a book, soon to be published, that was highly critical of the Federal Bureau of Investigation. His summons by the Committee was a frank effort to discredit the book by discrediting its author; the questioning, aimed at stigmatizing him as a devotee of left-wing causes and persons, was as unfriendly as it was insubstantial. The Lowenthal hearings were made public in November, two days before the publication of his book. There is nothing to add to Professor Carr's summation of this incident: "That the Committee had any legitimate basis for questioning Lowenthal even in executive session is doubtful, in view of the questions actually put to him; that it had any justification for making public his testimony, beyond a desire to tar him as a person who had been investigated by the Un-American Activities Committee, is in no way apparent."

Carr also criticizes the appendix to the Remington, Pressman, Lowenthal hearings, composed of the names of selected persons referred to in the course of testimony, accompanied by selected associations, all presented as being information from the Committee's files regarding their "Communist record and activities." However obnoxious these associations, such as the National Lawyers Guild and the Anti-Fascist Refugee Committee, seemed to the Committee staff, to cite them as parts of an individual's "Communist record" was a leap, with malice aforethought, into hyperbole.

The possible consequences of this sort of uninhibited listing were illuminated a week after the Lowenthal hearing, when Hazel Scott, the Negro pianist (then married to Representative Adam Clayton Powell), came voluntarily before the Committee to protest that she had been smeared in *Red Channels,* a publication devoted to blacklisting people in show business, which was then being studied with utmost piety by radio and television executives. In a forceful statement against the newly prosperous blacklisters, Miss Scott contended that most of the affiliations credited to her by *Red Channels* were inaccurate. Her statement was received apathetically by the members present, except for Harrison, whom it aroused to a curious defense. He pointed out that *Red Channels* merely reprinted material from official publications, like those of the Un-American Activities Committee; hence, was it not unjust to blame entrepreneurs for simply giving wider distribution to reports from such reputable auspices? Miss Scott's suggestion that the publishers of *Red Channels* might check their facts before distributing to employers accusations against their employees made no impression on Harrison; the Committee had no quarrel with the logic that led from irresponsible listings to unconscionable pressures.

Among the other celebrities who came before the Committee during the eighty-first Congress were Edward G. Robinson and Jackie Robinson, the former to reply in executive session to an attack on him by *Red Channels* for his association with front groups over the years, the latter to point out, with other prominent Negroes in open session, that Paul Robeson's statement that American Negroes would not fight in a war against the U.S.S.R. "sounds very silly to me." Jackie Robinson's statement was forthright and sensible—"The fact," he observed, "that it is a Communist who denounces injustice in the courts, police brutality and lynching when it happens doesn't change the truth of his charges"—yet there was something troubling about citizens feeling compelled to come before an investigatory body to declare their allegiance to the flag. It was particularly troubling that persons whose livelihood was imperiled, as Hazel Scott's was, could find no better forum from which to reply. The choice before those attacked was not inviting. Once the charges had been circulated in public, it was impossible to ignore them and damnably hard to answer them with dignity.

The Committee's triumphant hour of the 1949–1950 Congressional session came not from any of these asides but, at last, from the passage of a law. In the spring of 1950 the Congressmen returned to the Mundt-Nixon bill of 1948. Eleven days of hearings were given over mainly to opponents of the measure, comprising the entire American left: liberals and socialists, Communists, Communist sympathizers and haters of Communists, each of them being asked at the outset whether he was at present or had at any time been a member of the Communist Party. With variations of style and emphasis, the witnesses opposed the idea of registering Communists and their hangers-on as discouraging to political freedom, but their words fell on ears filled with other noises.

In the year of the Korean War and the perjury conviction of Alger Hiss, the Congressional mood for anti-Communist legislation found expression in Senator McCarran's Internal Security Act, which incorporated the registration provisions first proposed in 1948. Both "Communist-action" and "Communist-front" organizations would have to register with the attorney general. In recognition of the fact that the Voorhis act of 1940, also aimed at getting the C.P. to register, had not managed to do so, the 1950 measure required further that officers of a subversive organization must register if the organization itself did not. In a bow to the Constitution, the new bill stated that be-

longing to such an organization was not of itself a crime, and
that registration was not to be used as evidence against an
individual in any prosecution. Did this mean that a registrant
could be certain that he would not be ensnared by the Smith
Act? No one could provide that assurance.

Mr. Truman tried to ward off the McCarran bill by sending
a special message to Congress on August 8, 1950 (the day that
Henry Wallace bade farewell to the Progressive Party), asking
only that existing sabotage and espionage laws be strengthened.
The burden of his message was given over to the warning that
the pending legislation was "so broad and vague in its terms
as to endanger the freedoms of speech, press and assembly
protected by the First Amendment. Some of the proposed
measures would, in effect, impose severe penalties for normal
political activities on the part of certain groups, including Communists and Communist Party-line followers. This kind of
legislation is unnecessary, ineffective and dangerous." He was
ignored. Three weeks later, the bill was passed in House and
Senate by crushing votes[8] and a strongly worded veto was
overridden easily in both Houses.

For the next decade and a half, the registration requirement,
like a lighted fire cracker in a Three Stooges' routine, would be
tossed about among the Communist Party, the executive
branch, and the courts without, however, going off. The jug-
gling started in April 1953 when the five-man Subversive
Activities Control Board, appointed by the President and con-

---

[8] The debate in the House, efficiently and fairly managed by Nixon, was
enhanced by contributions from every member of the Committee and John
Rankin, who after reading off a list of names that included the Rosenbergs,
Harry Gold, David Greenglass, and Morton Sobell, called the attention of the
House to the fact that "There is not a single Christian or a single white gentile
among those Communists which I have just named . . ." McSweeney, after
confessing that "I cannot understand a Communist," delivered himself of the
following poem:

> If you don't like your Uncle Sammy
> Then go back to your home o'er the sea;
> To the land from which you came—whatever be its name
> But don't be ungrateful to me.

> If you don't like the stars and Old Glory,
> If you don't like the red, white and blue,
> Then don't act like the cur in the story:
> Don't bite the hand that is feeding you.

firmed by the Senate, concluded that the Communist Party was a Communist-action organization and hence had to register with the attorney general. The Party, whose spokesmen had said flatly from the beginning that they had no intention of registering, appealed; the Court of Appeals upheld the statute; the Supreme Court returned the case to the board so that it might study challenges raised against the credibility of three of the attorney general's witnesses; the board reaffirmed its decision; the Court of Appeals sent the case back again so that the defendants might be given an opportunity to examine F.B.I. reports, in accord with a rule laid down by the Supreme Court in the 1957 Jencks case; the board again declared that the Communist Party must register; the Court of Appeals affirmed this ruling; and the Supreme Court agreed to review the case.

In June 1961, by a vote of five to four, the Supreme Court upheld the constitutionality of the registration requirement; in October the board's order became final; in December the Communist Party was indicted for its failure to register; it was found guilty in district court and was fined $120,000. In December 1963, a three-judge panel of the Court of Appeals for the District of Columbia reversed the conviction on the grounds that the government had not proved there was anyone alive willing to run the risk of incriminating himself by registering as an officer or member of a party that had been labeled "a criminal conspiracy," and in June 1964, the Supreme Court declined to review this decision. The Justice Department tried again, this time producing two F.B.I. informants who had been Party members and said that they would be happy to register the Party and submit a list of its members to the attorney general. On their testimony the Party was convicted in 1965. In March 1967, this conviction, too, was overthrown by the Court of Appeals, which pointed out that by subjecting the Communist Party "to the combined sanction of compelled disclosure and criminal punishment," the McCarran Act was "hopelessly at odds" with the constitutional privilege against self-incrimination. At this the Justice Department gave up. "The case is dead," said a spokesman.

Meanwhile, in May 1962, the attorney general had brought

action against ten C.P. members under the provision of the law that required individual members to register if the organization failed to do so, as was patently the situation. In November 1965, a unanimous Supreme Court ruled that the Justice Department could not require registration of individual members because even though they could not be prosecuted for their admission of membership, it might yet be used as evidence or as an investigatory lead that would subject them to prosecution under other federal laws "in an area permeated with criminal statutes." Thus, during more than a decade and a half of litigation, not one person, not one group ever registered under the 1950 law.

The Committee performed rites of resuscitation over the corpse of the Subversive Activities Control Board in August 1967. Mourners came forward to support a bill introduced by Committee Chairman Edwin E. Willis and others which would have the board determine who the Communists are and then have the attorney general enter their names in a public register. This would relieve Communists of the duty of incriminating themselves and, more to the point, give the vestigial S.A.C.B. something to do. (Shortly before these hearings, President Johnson demonstrated his opinion of the S.A.C.B. by appointing to it, as a $26,000-a-year wedding gift, the new husband of a former White House secretary.) In December 1967 a makeshift bill of this sort found its way through the ninetieth Congress, but its fate in the courts remains problematical.

The Internal Security Act remains to this day the outstanding legislative accomplishment of Richard Nixon, Karl Mundt, and the House Committee on Un-American Activities. Deformed, unfinished, sent before its time into this breathing world scarce half made up, its cruel fate, unlike that of King Richard, was to survive. Dragged along through the courts into a time when the internal Communist menace can barely be taken seriously even by Congressmen, its main accomplishment has been to confirm the solid virtues of judicial delay. This law designed to expose Communists has exposed itself and its makers, slight men who built careers upon the distracted times.

In June 1949, two days after the Committee had taken its pleasure of Frank Oppenheimer, Harry Truman held a lengthy press conference in which he suggested that the spy hunts and loyalty oaths then becoming popular were symptoms of the sort of hysteria that had come upon the nation after World War I, and that they would in time subside. But Truman was not destined to look upon that happy hour from the White House. In the early nineteen-fifties the nation's puzzlement and anxiety over the peculiar turns of the postwar world would find channels of expression in suspicion and vengeance. Soon Truman's own Secretary of the Navy would be plumping for preventive war. Senator McCarthy gave instruction by example on how the frustrations aroused by tension in Berlin, war in Korea, and a great Communist victory in China might be relieved if the guilt were only laid on Professor Owen Lattimore and pinkoes in the State Department. The arrest and trial of the Rosenbergs gave substance to the general unease and afforded the satisfaction of having flesh-and-blood people to punish for the disturbing realization that our enemies too possessed an atom bomb.

The Un-American Activities Committee would be nudged into the shadows as Senator McCarthy bestrode the land, but it contributed during this period to the public cultivation of a taste for quick, easy vengeance. Its repeated exhumation and glamorization of rather pallid espionage cases, its insistence on ever harsher laws, its continuing assaults on individuals—these showed the way. In December 1950, the Senate, envious of this pioneering role, created the Internal Security Subcommittee of the Senate Judiciary Committee, which, guided by Senators McCarran, Eastland, and Ferguson, would keep things churning during 1951 and 1952 with an investigation designed to bill the State Department and the Institute of Pacific Relations with the loss of China.

As long as the Truman Administration held office, a liberal White House facing a conservative Congress, the politics of Communist-hounding had irresistible allure. When the first Hiss jury was dismissed, Nixon and Velde immediately charged the judge with bias and threatened to call before the Committee the witnesses he had barred at the trial. In one of the more amusing public utterances of a career that has not been marked by wit, young Mr. Nixon said: "A handful of Administration apologists, who find themselves unable to defend Judge Kaufman's conduct in the Hiss case on the facts, are attempting to turn the case into a political issue which it is not."

The Congressional elections of 1950 went badly for Truman and very well for the Un-American Activities Committee. In the California senatorial race, Richard Nixon, campaigning almost entirely on the Communist issue and with more vigor than scruples, defeated Helen Gahagan Douglas, who had been one of the Committee's most persistent critics in the House. The *most* persistent critic, Vito Marcantonio, was beaten by an alliance of Democrats and Republicans in the East Harlem district which he had represented for eight terms. The Democrats lost twenty-eight seats in the House and five in the Senate, including that of the Majority Leader Scott Lucas. They retained a narrow numerical lead in both houses, but for practical purposes a coalition of conservatives would control the eighty-second Congress. The lesson that the victors took from the election was expressed by Republican National Chairman Leonard Hall, who attributed his party's gains to "resentment against the Administration's coddling of Communists at home and appeasement of Russia and Communist China abroad." This partisan sermon would be preached and acted upon most diligently until, in 1954, the trap that had been set for White House Democrats was found to be a hazard to White House Republicans as well.

10

★ ★ ★ ★ ★

1951-1952: Many Are Called

With Marcantonio gone, the only chiding that the Committee had to endure as it received $200,000 in the eighty-second Congress came from well-wishers. "Many people believe that there was a little slowdown in the Committee last year," noted the Republican Minority Leader Joe Martin, and Rankin did one of his turns: "While our boys are being killed or freezing to death in Korea, these Reds ought not to be permitted to undermine their country." Representative Walter found himself in the unusual position of defending the Committee against Representative Brown of Ohio for not publishing the testimony of an F.B.I. informer who had turned out to be an ex-convict and a mental case as well as a liar. It was Clare Hoffman of Michigan who brought his colleagues back to solid ground. "I do not know what the discussion is all about," he remarked, "but from past experience, I realize the Committee is going to get all the money it asks for and when it asks for it." The demands for increased activity would not go unheard. The message of the off-year election, the spurrings of Republican members[1] who knew themselves to be in the ascendance, the exhilarating examples of loyalty investigations in the Senate and around the country, the national suspicions, fears and cravings to strike back raised to a new pitch by the war in

[1] Joining Velde and Kearney were Donald L. Jackson of California, who replaced Senator Richard Nixon, and Charles E. Potter of Michigan, a severely disabled veteran himself soon destined for the Senate. Three Democrats—Wood, Walter, and Moulder—remained and their company was filled out by Clyde Doyle of California and James B. Frazier, Jr., of Tennessee.

Korea—these elements taken together would produce a most active two years. In 1951 and 1952 the Committee would hold more than a hundred days of public hearings at which more than three hundred persons would testify.

Again Hollywood called. Nowhere could the Committee find targets who were so celebrated and so vulnerable; publicity had created them, publicity could, and in a number of cases would, destroy them. In February Jackson and Potter gave out that they were dissatisfied with the "implied clearance" that had been issued to Edward G. Robinson after his voluntary appearance and soon the press was carrying the names of the well-known actors and lesser known, yet glamour-tinged writers and directors who had been subpoenaed. The lengthy list was made up of one-time C.P. members who had been scheduled for questioning before the abrupt cessation of the 1947 hearings, of Party-cause contributors whose names had been contributed by Paul Crouch and of others who were mentioned after the curtain went up.

One group of actors and writers, heirs to the spirit, the politics, and the attorneys of the Hollywood Ten, took the Fifth Amendment on the grounds that they would run the danger of self-incrimination if they answered any questions regarding their association with any organizations or persons who had been linked with subversive intentions. Had they been called in 1947, they would doubtless have taken the First Amendment and ended up in jail. Now there was no question of jail. The Committee was being roundly chastized for its wholesale contempt citations, and although Velde would have liked to go on with this losing game, the Democrats did no more now than dispute in an academic way a particular interpretation of the self-incrimination clause and point out to a witness the unfortunate impression he was leaving. As Wood put it to one man, "If you say [the question of whether you are a member of the Communist Party] would incriminate you, it leaves one conclusion in my mind and in the mind of every other fair-minded person within sound of your voice. Now, if in fact you are not a member of it, then your statement that it would tend to incriminate you isn't a true statement." The chairman raised this

argument repeatedly, to no avail, and his colleagues were sometimes moved to more forceful language. Moulder, far from the
most zealous inquisitor, told a writers' agent who had been one
of the prime movers within the Communist clique, ". . . your
refusal to testify so consistently leaves a strong impression that
you are still an ardent follower of the Communist Party and its
purpose." Moulder had no legal right to this impression, but
in the instance common sense could admit no other. Despite
frequent displays of skepticism, the Committee carried out its
interrogations without the emotion that had sputtered around
J. Parnell Thomas. Jackson, Potter, and Velde tended to be
argumentative and Doyle was long-winded, but Wood, bol-
stered by Walter, managed most of the time to keep things in
a reasonably low key; the resistant witnesses were by and large
not overly provocative.

At the other end of the witness range were those—notably
the writers Richard Collins and Martin Berkeley and the actor
Sterling Hayden—who had left the Party and now testified
fully and willingly about their former activities and associates.
Names were the food of the second Hollywood investigation—
not quite the delectable names of 1947 like Gary Cooper and
the mother of Ginger Rogers—but many more of them, writers,
directors, character actors, and here and there a star. The
hunger for names was a practical matter; if counsel Tavenner
had not been able to press witnesses for names and more names,
his interrogation would have amounted to very little. Despite
an occasional outburst by Velde about the Communist propaganda that was slithering through the movies, this proved to
be as profitless a line in 1951 as in 1947 and, deprived of the
target of the screen itself, the investigators naturally took aim
at individuals. On hand to whet the inquisitorial appetite was
Representative Jackson who was given to observations like
". . . it seems to me that the time has come to be an American
or not an American." When the writer-producer Carl Foreman
expressed a reluctance to name-drop, Jackson delivered a talk
about the casualties in Korea and concluded, ". . . the ultimate
test of the credibility of a witness before the Committee, as
far as I am concerned, is the extent to which he is willing to

cooperate with the Committee in giving full details as to not only the place of activities, but also the names of those who participated with him in the activities of the Communist Party . . ."

The heads of the motion picture industry took the Congressmen's concentration on names rather than on films as a sign of grace, and bowed joyfully to it. Their behavior in 1951 made 1947 seem an age of heroes. Having been assured that the Committee did not intend this time round to impose on the industry's higher movers, the Association of Motion Picture Producers publicly disassociated themselves from the witnesses, promised to invoke the 1947 Waldorf "interdict" against employees who took the Fifth Amendment, hailed the Committee for its endeavors, and spurred it on to root out Communists in government, in schools, on newspapers, in radio and television and in defense plants—anywhere, in fact, particularly if it wasn't Hollywood.

The main support that the first, hard-line takers of the Fifth Amendment received was from the Hollywood branch of the Council of the Arts, Sciences and Professions, a tainted relic of the Progressive Party. The unions washed their hands and turned away. As the Screen Actors Guild, Ronald Reagan presiding, informed Gale Sondergaard, wife of the Hollywood Ten's Herbert Biberman, on the day she took the Fifth, the Guild would fight against any secret blacklist, but "On the other hand, if any actor by his own actions outside of union activities has so offended public opinion that he has made himself unsaleable at the box office, the Guild cannot and would not want to force any employers to hire him." Not long after, Actors Equity made it clear that politically undesirable members would have to look elsewhere for solace: "This Council believes that all participants in the international Communist Party conspiracy against our nation should be exposed for what they are—enemies of our country and our form of government."

Hollywood was in a shaky position in the early nineteen-fifties. The moguls had felt the impact of television but had not yet regrouped their forces and accommodated themselves to the new prince of entertainment. Neighborhood movie theaters were shutting down by the dozens, and the government had recently forced the studios to divest themselves of theater chains in deference to the anti-trust laws. Under such blows of circumstance, the frail spirits of moviedom could hardly be expected to rise to the defense of Communists. The producers, the guilds, the craft unions formed themselves into the Motion Picture Industry Council, under the guidance of the anti-Communist A. F. of L. leader Roy N. Brewer, whose solitary purpose was to give the Un-American Activities Committee a franchise to investigate to its heart's content. In a statement to the Committee which was distributed by newsreel to the country's 18,000 movie houses, the Council declared:

> This country is engaged in a war with Communism. Eighty-seven thousand American casualties leave little room for witnesses to stand on the First and Fifth Amendments; and for those who do we have no sympathy . . . In time of crisis, we believe that the demands of American patriotism make necessary that witnesses respond to the call of their country, as represented by your Committee, and give you all the information necessary to the success of your objective.

The Hollywood Ten had all been members of the Communist Party. Now the Committee moved in on ex-Communists and on fellow travelers, and these found themselves in a difficult position. If they took the Fifth Amendment, their Hollywood careers would, for the foreseeable future, be ended. But to testify about their friends was for some a repugnant as well as an uncertain means of salvation. The first witness to struggle with the dilemma was Larry Parks, a young actor whose major film accomplishment had been his imitation of Al Jolson's mannerisms as he mouthed the words to *Mammy* in *The Jolson Story*. In his appearance, on the day that Alger Hiss went to jail, Parks became the first Hollywood personality to admit to having been a Communist; he had belonged to a small cell during the war. But he pleaded with the Committee not to make him name names. In his case, as in others to follow, Wood and Walter showed an inclination to defer to the witness' obvious sincerity. Why, Walter asked the unmoved Tavenner, was it essential to force Parks to give names "when we already know them"? The Committee never made up its collective mind on this subject; Parks was let off on condition that he testify fully in executive session. This he did, and the next day Velde, carried away with gratitude, extolled him on the floor of the House for being not only "a loyal and true American" but "a great actor." Encomiums notwithstanding, Parks was left with his career in limbo, the film he was scheduled to do for Columbia studios having been canceled when he received his subpoena.

Larry Parks's experience was not reassuring to the witnesses who followed. Whatever Chairman Wood's inclinations, he was in no political position to make deals with former Communists as to what they might testify about and what they could keep back; at the first hint of such leniency, Jackson and Velde would have gone to the nation with cries of Communist-coddling. Witnesses who belonged neither among the hard-core resisters ("If I have to choose between crawling in the mud with Larry Parks or going to jail like my courageous friends of the Hollywood Ten," announced the writer Paul Jarrico, "I shall certainly choose the latter") nor among the informers (screenwriter Martin Berkeley gave the Committee a hundred names) did not have many paths open to them. One was that taken by the director Edward Dmytryk, lately of the Hollywood Ten, who had been making $2,500 a week before the 1947 investigation and had not been employed since his release from prison. Dmytryk had been a C.P. member for only a few months during the U.S.-Soviet wartime alliance and, with his friend Adrian Scott, had left the Party around the time of the humbling of Albert Maltz. When Scott and Dmytryk were called before the Committee in 1947, their attorney, Bartley Crum, advised them to testify, but he had been beaten back by the hard-nose faction led by Lawson, who wanted a united front and a rousing issue. Sympathy for deserving causes such as the condition of the Negro rather than political discernment had brought Dmytryk into the ambiance of the Party. He was exploited more painfully than most fringe members, at last finding himself jailed and blacklisted for a faith that was barely his. In his 1951 appearance he gave only a few names of persons he had known as Communists, all of whom were known to the Committee too, but having gone through the forms, he was left to resume his career.

A year later this incident was repeated. Now it was Elia Kazan, famed director of stage and screen, who changed his mind. In executive session Kazan admitted to having been a Party member for less than two years in the nineteen-thirties when he was connected with the Group Theatre in New York, but refused to talk about his fellow members. Some weeks later, having experienced a dramatic change of heart, he informed the Committee: "I have come to the conclusion that I did wrong to withhold these names before, because secrecy serves the Communists and is exactly what they want. The American people need the facts and all the facts about all aspects of Communism in order to deal with it wisely and effectively. It is my obligation as a citizen to tell everything that I know." He did not, in fact, know a great deal; he produced a handful of stale names such as those of Clifford Odets, who was long out of the Party, Morris Carnovsky, who had already taken the Fifth Amendment, and J. Edward Bromberg, who had committed suicide after his reluctant appearance before the Committee some months earlier. The new Kazan also published an advertisement which told of his being inveigled into the Party during the depression, emphasized his hatred of Communists and urged all liberals to "speak out." Kazan's rhetoric outstripped the substance of his part, and some critics—particularly those on the left who could credit only uncooperative witnesses with principles—connected his self-imposed mission with the requirements of his career, an idea that may have been suggested by the conclusion of his public statement: "The main pictures I have made and the plays I have chosen to direct represent my convictions. I expect to continue to make the same kind of pictures and to direct the same kind of plays." Had he not testified, his expectations as regards pictures would surely have been disappointed.

The Committee had its most fun with big-name personalities who had never been Party members but had given of their money and their fame over the years to many causes sponsored by Communists. They were peculiarly vulnerable; they could not resist the Committee without ruining their careers but they could not cooperate without making themselves out to have been perfect fools. The most famous of them chose the latter course. Like José Ferrer, who in order to win an Academy Award for his portrayal of Cyrano de Bergerac despite opposition from the Motion Picture Alliance for the Preservation of American Ideals, had had to take out paid advertisements assuring Hollywood that he was no Communist. Ferrer, whose attorney for his appearance was Abe Fortas, tried to oblige the Committee in every way. He asked that Congress or the Justice Department set up a warning service to keep people like him out of trouble and assured the members that notwithstanding any petitions he may have lent his name to in the past, he was now opposed to the Committee's abolition. "When did you change your mind on that score?" asked Representative Kearney. "Well," Ferrer replied, "today, among other things." But even this did not save him from the reprimand of Velde for not voting in national elections.

John Garfield, too, did his best to make himself appear a simpleton, marvelously naïve about politics, who had helped support a variety of Communist fronts despite his firm hatred of Communism. Yet his performance was not quite silly enough to allay all suspicions. Tavenner wondered about him siding with China in its war against Japan, and when Garfield mentioned that he had once been given an unfavorable review by the *Daily Worker*, Velde, the former F.B.I. agent, quickly asked where he had gotten hold of a copy of that newspaper. Edward G. Robinson, whose estimable career had ground to a near halt since his credit in *Red Channels*, came once again before the Committee humble past the point of embarrassment: ". . . I feel that this is the only tribunal where an American citizen can come and ask for relief from smears, false accusations and innuendoes." He now realized that he had been imposed on by the Communists, and he was glad the Committee had exposed them and he wanted nothing more than for Representative Jackson to say publicly that he (Jackson) believed that he (Robinson) was not a member of the Communist Party.

It was difficult for persons whose professional lives were at stake to come out from their Committee encounters with much style. Among the witnesses who granted that they had been Communists but were so no longer and would be willing to discuss their own adventures without, however, answering questions about anybody else, the most eloquent statement came from Lillian Hellman. In a letter preceding her appearance, she wrote that she had been warned by her attorney, Joseph Rauh, that if she answered questions about herself she would have to answer questions about others or risk being held in contempt. She offered to waive the Fifth Amendment if the Committee would refrain from asking her about other people:

> I am not willing, now or in the future, to bring bad trouble to people who, in my past associations with them, were completely innocent of any talk or any action that was disloyal or subversive. I do not like subversion or disloyalty in any form and if I had ever seen any I would have considered it my duty to have reported it to the proper authorities. But to hurt innocent people whom I knew many years ago in order to save myself is, to me, inhuman and indecent and dishonorable. I cannot and will not cut my conscience to fit this year's fashions, even though I long ago came to the conclusion that I was not a political person and could have no comfortable place in any political group.

Chairman Wood had no choice but to reply that "the Committee cannot permit witnesses to set forth the terms under which they will testify." Had Miss Hellman and others who adopted her position—such as the talented writer, director and former Communist Robert Rossen—taken their chances instead of taking the Fifth, they might have been agreeably surprised. Despite the insistence of Jackson and Velde on names, Walter, as acting chairman, had on occasion allowed an earnest witness to speak of his past without repeating yet once again for Counsel Tavenner names which the Committee had in its possession many times over. With the contempt citations of 1949–1950 being shot down by the courts, Wood and Walter were not eager to trouble the Congress again so soon, and although they were not at all consistent about it, they more than once expressed their doubts as to the value of pressing a witness for redundant information.

It seemed for a time that the issue might come to a head in the case of a prominent Hollywood writer and producer named Sidney Buchman, who admitted that he had been in the Communist Party from 1938 to 1945, but refused to answer questions about persons who "never, to my knowledge, planned or committed or suggested an illegal act." Buchman did not take the Fifth, and at Tavenner's urging, Walter directed him to answer the questions. He still declined, his foresighted attorney taking pains to point out to Walter that a quorum of the Committee was not present, as Jackson had left the hearing room. Buchman was again subpoenaed, but now instead of appearing, he sought delays on suspect grounds of ill health while he brought a fruitless action in district court to test the validity of the subpoena. Buchman was cited for contempt —for refusing to obey a summons of the Committee. In contempt he indubitably was, and the House approved the citation by a vote of 316-0. He was found guilty and given a one-year suspended sentence and a fine of $150. The Committee had gotten its man, but the really interesting question, on the naming of names, remained unsettled.

Some of the testimony in the 1951–52 motion picture hearings was enlightening as regards the sociology of Hollywood. The Communist Party used its friends among the actors and writers mainly as big names for and big contributors to its innumerable causes. (The actors and writers, for their part, seemed to be attracted to the Party mainly out of a desire to *do* something—although one of them, an actor from New York noted for his tough-guy roles, recalled that he had been lured into a Marxist study group with the promise, "Get to know this stuff, and you will make out more with the dames.") A writer named George Beck told of being at a party for the *New Masses* with his agent, an important figure among the Hollywood Communists. When the time came round for fund raising the agent said, "Beck offers fifty. Is anybody going to match it?" It was matched whereupon the agent, without consulting the writer, called out, "Now Beck tops that with a hundred." And when that sum was met, he yelled, "Beck offers one hundred and fifty." Beck concluded the tale: "That is the contribution I made to the *New Masses*." Another client charged that after he left the Party, the same agent sabotaged his career by turning down assignments for him.

Budd Schulberg, who had belonged to the Party in the late thirties, provided a good case history of the clumsiness of commissars in dealing with independently inclined writers. When, while still a Party member, Schulberg was working on *What Makes Sammy Run?* John Howard Lawson insisted on seeing the manuscript. The young man refused to show it and was passed upward to the C.P.'s cultural chieftain V. J. Jerome[2] who harangued him about his incorrect attitude. When the book was published in the spring of 1941, a *Daily Worker* critic, insufficiently briefed by his superiors, wrote ". . . I've a feeling that all critics, no matter their carping standards, will have to admit they've found the Hollywood novel in *What Makes Sammy Run?*" Two and a half weeks later the critic, better instructed now, took back everything: "The first error I made was in calling the book the Hollywood novel."

The friendly witnesses were nearly unanimous regarding the inability of the Communists to influence the course of American films. The co-authors of *Song of Russia*,[3] that tribute to Soviet heroism, good works, and clean living, had been compelled to remove from their script words like "community" and to cloud the fact that much of the action took place on a collective farm. Nor were they permitted to have the Russian

[2] Jerome was the perfect Stalinist critic. When Hollywood finally got around to producing films about Negroes, such as *Home of the Brave, Pinky, Lost Boundaries,* and *Intruder in the Dust,* Jerome dismissed them not because of any aesthetic deficiencies but because they were designed "to strengthen the basic strategy of the white ruling class which seeks to conceal the imperialist source of Negro oppression and to blunt any kind of struggle against capitalism and war."

[3] The collaborators on this film, Richard Collins and Paul Jarrico, had been among the most active of Hollywood's Communists. In 1951 they broke up when Collins testified fully before the Committee and Jarrico took the Fifth Amendment. It was but one of many friendships that were shattered in the course of these hearings.

girl teach the American musician—born in Iowa—how to drive a tractor. An illuminating anecdote on the Communists' illusions regarding their influence on the minds of men had to do with the character actor who rushed into a friend's house one day yelling, "By golly, I got away with it!" What had he gotten away with? "Well, I was shooting this picture, and I had to wait for the elevator, so I pressed the button and there is a pause and the director said, 'Whistle something and fill in.' So I whistled four bars of *The Internationale!*" With such evidence, only the F.B.I.-trained Velde could continue to suspect that the Party had been cunningly sneaking propaganda into the movies. In its annual report for 1952 the Committee, while commending itself for blocking off Hollywood as a source of C.P. funds, backed away from its earlier charges that the movies had been corrupted, stating only: "Had these Communist efforts gone unexposed, it is almost inevitable that the content of motion pictures would have been influenced and slanted and become a medium for Communist propaganda." The investigation that had been billed as the cure for an epidemic now turned out to be an exercise in prophylaxis.

The 1951–52 assault on Hollywood quickly took its place among the most successful engagements in the history of the Committee. The idea that it was interested in persecuting anyone, declared Doyle early in the proceedings, was "damnably false," but there was nothing much else for it to be interested in. No espionage, no promise of legislation, no exposure of propaganda, and not much information except in the way of marginal sociology. It was a punitive expedition pure and simple, a purging of the undesirables. "If we could eliminate from the entertainment world people who decline to answer if they are members of the Communist Party, it would make me very happy," said Chairman Wood, and no spokesman from the cowering film industry—executive, guild leader, or union official—could bring himself to suggest that this was an odd undertaking for a committee of Congress. When in its annual report for 1951 the Committee criticized the studios for not getting rid of their Communists fast enough, the Motion Picture Industry Council's defense was that Hollywood had pioneered in firing Communists as far back as 1947 and was restrained now only by court rulings that unpopular political opinions were not sufficient grounds for breaking contracts. A few weeks later the studio executives and Eric Johnston made peace with the American Legion by agreeing to investigate more than two hundred employees listed in the Legion's bad books. The accused individuals were asked to refute, in writing, allegations concerning their loyalty. Other studios, meanwhile, were hiring their own "investigators," whose main job was to keep right-wing pressure groups pacified.

Bright names went, some temporarily, some forever, into eclipse; old friendships were demolished; men who had left the Communists in disgust learned that democracy can produce despotisms too. If the hearings revealed something about Communism in Hollywood, they revealed more about Hollywood itself, a soft place where giving in and selling out were so much a part of things that any effort to stand fast against the odds of the early nineteen-fifties was unthinkable. "The air has been cleared," said a studio executive in the fall of 1951, like a householder assuring the burglars that they have gotten everything of value and ought to try next door now. But it would be years before producers dared openly to defy the blacklist, before Hollywood's air would begin to be cleared of the eructations of this time.

The times, the propitious times, determined the extent and direction of the Committee's enterprise through the eighty-second Congress. So propitious were the times that the Committee's oldest, most reliable acreage, the loyalty of government officials, had attracted the attentions of others. Originally staked out by Martin Dies himself, it had now fallen to Senator McCarthy, making a name for himself with his onslaughts on the State Department, and by Senator Pat McCarran of Nevada, whose Subcommittee on Internal Security was engaged in reasonably informative, seemingly endless hearings designed to show how a group of Communist sympathizers in policy positions had betrayed Chiang Kai-shek. Succumbing to the building pressures, in April 1951 the President stiffened the test of loyalty for federal employees. Under his first executive order, a man could be fired if "reasonable grounds existed for belief that the person involved is disloyal to the government of the United States." Now all that was required was "reasonable doubt as to the loyalty of the person involved." Hundreds of cases were reopened.

Through the insistence of Velde, the Committee called into public hearing Oliver Edmund Clubb, a suspended State Department official soon to resign under the cloud of having sold out China to Owen Lattimore and the Institute of Pacific Relations. Clubb, a China specialist, had been named by Whittaker Chambers as having paid a visit to the offices of the *New Masses* in 1932. He had indeed done so, on a brief trip to New York, carrying a letter of introduction from a left-wing American journalist in China named Agnes Smedley. He described Chambers in his diary as "a shifty-eyed unkempt creature . . ." The Committee could not believe that a young Foreign Service officer could be interested, in 1932, in meeting and talking to intellectuals on the far left without some conspiratorial intent. Upon learning that Clubb had studied the Chinese revolutionaries in the early thirties, counsel Tavenner, an interrogator not ordinarily given to archness, asked, "As a result of your definitive study, did you arrive at the conclusion Chinese Communists were all agrarians?" The name of the deceased Miss Smedley came up again in the testimony of Major General Charles Willoughby, who had served as General MacArthur's intelligence chief. In his rambling testimony, Willoughby connected her with a Russian spy ring in the Far East before and during World War II. The general, who had already been heard by Senator McCarran's group and was being lionized by Washington votaries of General MacArthur (recently and abruptly relieved of his duties by the President), entertained the Congressmen with a statement on the "sinister background of world conspiracy," which took the Committee somewhat afield from its customary areas of concern.

Though the fall of China was a most promising subject now

that American troops were confronting Chinese troops in Korea, the Committee could not compete with McCarran and McCarthy, and except for a chance excursion such as those with General Willoughby and the unlucky Clubb, it tended domestic soil. As the Hollywood hearings demonstrated, even those who a few years before had protested against Communist-hunting expeditions now granted that the pursuit of Communists, wherever they might be found, was a natural right of Congress. In fact, it seemed to be a right of whoever cared to pursue them. From around the country came inspiriting reports of Communists being exposed, suspended, fired, evicted, tried, deported, boycotted, blacklisted, and physically set upon. The public temper invited, and the Committee joined in the sport.

When in June 1951, the Supreme Court affirmed the conviction of eleven Communist Party leaders on charges of advocating the overthrow of the government, Walter expressed the thought that the Committee might be "decisioned" out of a job. But in fact the decision had the opposite effect; it strengthened the use of the Fifth Amendment and, in a perverse way, made the Committee's work easier than ever. It did not really matter in most of the hearings of these years that most witnesses took the Fifth, for no information was being sought. The typical hearing opened with an F.B.I. informer or disaffected Communist who delivered himself of several score names of Party members he had encountered. The overriding purpose of the hearing was to spread on the public record names already known to official agencies. When those named appeared and took the Fifth Amendment, it was as satisfactory as a confession.

Although several witnesses comported themselves indecorously, the Wood Committee brought only two more contempt citations—which were approved by the Congress without a negative vote. One was against a Detroit Negro, Arthur McPhaul, who refused to give over the records of the Civil Rights Congress; the other against one Saul Grossman for failing to produce the records of the Michigan Committee for the Protection of the Foreign Born, as well as for refusing to answer questions relating to the records. In these citations, the Committee relied for precedent on the recently decided case of Rogers *v.* U.S. where the Supreme Court had ruled that since Mrs. Rogers had voluntarily testified that she was treasurer of the Denver Communist Party, she would not be further incriminated by handing over the Party's records. Both men were found guilty—Grossman on the single count of refusing to answer the question of whether or not he would produce the records and not on the production of the records themselves. On appeal, Grossman's conviction was reversed because he had not been specifically directed to answer the question for which he was held in contempt. (Called before the Committee again in 1956, he surrendered the records under protest.) McPhaul's conviction—he was sentenced to nine months and a fine of $500—was upheld by a five-to-four decision of the Supreme Court. The dissenters—Black, Douglas, Brennan, and Warren—maintained that although Congress did have the right to obtain the records in question, the Committee had not proved that McPhaul in fact had custody of them; hence, by holding him in contempt without demanding such proof, the courts had denied him the presumption of innocence to which every accused is entitled. But the rule of the majority was that the Fifth Amendment did not protect a witness from the requirement that he supply records kept in a representative rather than a personal capacity even though their production might tend to incriminate him. By 1960, when this case was decided, a five-to-four split was a common outcome in Supreme Court cases involving the Un-American Activities Committee.

Like super-heroes of the comic strips, members of the Committee swooped down on Los Angeles, Boston, Philadelphia, Chicago, and Detroit, confounded resident malefactors and flew off again. The ostensible purpose of most of the 1951–52 hearings was to look into Communist activities in important defense industries, a purpose general enough to take the Committee wherever it wanted to go and spacious enough to encompass anybody who lived in a city that could boast of some factories. The Los Angeles hearings, however, did not have even this excuse. In the course of the Hollywood investigation, mention had been made of Communist cells of doctors and lawyers in California. Former Communists were called and gave modest amounts of information along with a sizable list of names, most of which were connected with two organizations that had been in the fore of opposition to the Committee for years—the National Lawyers Guild and the Council of the Arts, Sciences and Professions. Both bore all the earmarks of Communist influence.

More than two dozen of the named lawyers came before the Committee on September 30 and October 1, 1952, and most of them behaved according to form. They were exceedingly talkative, highly argumentative, abusive of the witnesses who had named them, and disdainful of the Committee; formally counseled by Robert Kenny and his associates, they took the Fifth Amendment and other amendments with patriotic embellishments. Among those summoned were Ben Margolis and Charles J. Katz, advisors to the Hollywood Ten, who had developed the strategy of the First Amendment. They had been mentioned repeatedly in the testimony of former Communists as the Party's prime movers in Los Angeles, recruiters of bright young lawyers and proselytizers of not-so-bright actors. Margolis made a particularly trying witness. Hardly had he taken his place than he was delivering speeches—"I was born in New York City on April 23, 1910, and almost from the first day that I can remember I have hated tyranny and that is why I feel the way I do about this Committee . . . I have nothing but contempt for this Committee, and I will show it as long as I am up here." He was faithful to his word, unable even to resist arguing with Representative Jackson over which of them was more patriotic. Katz, an older man, was more subdued. He cautioned the Committee not to draw unwonted inferences from witnesses taking the Fifth Amendment "at a time such as this, in circumstances such as these"; he reminded the Congressmen that "it is the law that when one invokes the privilege of the Fifth Amendment, he admits no guilt, that the privilege exists for the innocent . . ." In coming months and years, the generous helpings of the Fifth Amendment being taken at Congressional hearings would come in for a great deal of analysis, cooler and more sophisticated analysis than that offered either by the witnesses who pleaded self-incrimination or by the Congressmen who received the plea with ill grace.

The most serious charge raised against the Committee's round-up of the Communist lawyers of Los Angeles was that it constituted an effort to discourage attorneys from taking on unpopular causes. Whether this was in fact in back of one or more of the Congressmen's minds, the effect could hardly be otherwise in a period when a public stand against the trial of the C.P. leaders or against the operations of the Committee was taken as evidence of Communist affinity. In a sense, the lawyers who had striven with some success to turn every good cause into a Communist cause were only getting their deserts when their own cause, however good, came to seem tainted. But such a set of hearings, when Communist lawyers were being threatened with disbarment and non-Communist lawyers were uneasy about taking on the defense of Party members, could only add to that political prudence which sapped the nation of its dissenting spirit in the early nineteen-fifties.

A few of the Committee's friendly witnesses became celebrities as a result of their appearances.[4] Twenty-nine-year-old Mrs. Mary Markward, who had served the F.B.I. from within the Communist Party of Washington, D.C., and Maryland for six years, received long applause from spectators after she

[4] The Committee took brief looks into Communist activities among veterans, peace groups, and farm organizations during this period, and in February 1952, it introduced the nation to Harvey M. Matusow, a twenty-six-year-old former C.P. member and professed authority on Communist youth groups, who put more than a hundred names into the record, including the members of the folk-singing group, The Weavers, who thereupon had their current engagement cut short owing to public protest. Matusow told of five-year-olds being taught such rhymes as:

> Jack Sprat could eat no fat.
> His wife could eat no lean.
> Because their Congress had done them in
> And picked their pockets clean.

After three busy years as friendly witness for the Senate Internal Security Subcommittee, the Permanent Investigating Subcommittee, the Subversive Activities Control Board, and the Justice Department and a campaigner for the Republicans in 1952, Matusow repented of being an ex-Communist, became an ex-ex-Communist, and zestfully took to exposing himself and those who had egged him on. He wrote a book, *False Witness,* and went to jail for perjury.

read out a batch of names already known to the Justice Department. The more interesting part of her testimony had to do with the Party's difficulties in getting reliable workers, a situation that made it easy for her, given her special incentive, to advance rapidly to the post of district treasurer. Tavenner, as always, was content to settle for names, but some of the Congressmen could not resist troubling the rather simple young woman with weightier matters. "Am I to understand," asked Doyle, who hated to let a witness go without some thoughtful exchange, ". . . that the Communist Party of the United States was definitely backing the projection of Soviet Communism in the nations of Europe right after the war . . . ?" More than thirty persons named by Mrs. Markward—left-wing union officers, ladies involved in the synthetic peace movement which the Communists had put together to oppose the U.S. role in Korea, Progressive Party boosters—took the Fifth Amendment.

Boston was covered by Herbert Philbrick, an advertising man who had cast off his Communist disguise in 1949 as a surprise witness at the trial of the C.P. leaders in New York. He had served the F.B.I. for nine years (a career that would soon become the basis, in a way, of a TV series) and he was able to provide the Committee with some fifty names, the most prominent being that of Dirk Jung Struik, professor of mathematics at the Massachusetts Institute of Technology. Professor Struik's political sympathies were well known: he was executive director of the Massachusetts Council of American-Soviet Friendship, a member of the Progressive Party, and a lecturer at Communist schools. Off the stand he called Philbrick a liar and explained that though he was a Marxist he had never joined the Party. On the stand he courteously pleaded the Fifth Amendment to a hundred questions. A few weeks later Struik was indicted, under the Massachusetts Smith Act, for conspiring to overthrow the government of the United States and the Commonwealth of Massachusetts. The indictment was dismissed in 1956 when the Supreme Court handed down its ruling against state sedition laws; Struik was censured by the

M.I.T. faculty for his want of candor but was retained in his teaching post.

Many of the names delivered by Philbrick belonged to organizers for the Electrical Workers (U.E.), which had been thrown out of the C.I.O. and was now fighting to keep its members from deserting for James Carey's International Union of Electrical Workers (I.U.E.–C.I.O.). The U.E., which had recently affiliated with the comradely Farm Equipment Workers Union, was the main subject of the Committee's 1952 hearings in Chicago and Philadelphia too. In Chicago pickets singing *Solidarity Forever* rushed into the Federal Building and pounded so loudly on the door of the hearing room that they drowned out the testimony. U.E. leaders charged that the Committee had come to Chicago to break its 26,000-man strike against International Harvester, a charge hotly denied by Chairman Wood. But three important union negotiators were compelled to appear before the Committee. They asked to be excused because they were busy with the strike and excused they were—but not before they took the Fifth Amendment.

In these hearings, the Committee relied, not on F.B.I. informants, but on union men who had broken with the Party. They drew a convincing picture of the way in which a disciplined cadre of Communists could control a large union and turn it to parochial uses. Policies and candidates determined on beforehand at meetings of the cadre, sometimes supervised by a C.P. functionary who did not even belong to the union, became the union's policies and the union's officers. Party membership became a requirement for the ambitious organizer, and he had to be prepared to oppose the Marshall Plan in the name of his local's electricians if the ruling came down. The issue of whether to strike or not to strike was tied in with the world strategy of the U.S.S.R. The hearing also recalled, however, the remarkable part that rank-and-file Communists of the thirties had played in building America's labor movement, the firings, jailings, beatings they had endured in the union's cause. They were a tough bunch, but not nearly as tough as the manipulators in New York, and many of them found themselves trapped by their own early commitment. There was nothing particularly lovable about the men who took the Fifth Amendment, but it was saddening all the same to be shown how unsightly were the ashes from the fires of the thirties.

The most noteworthy of the Committee's field trips was the one it made to Detroit, that "arsenal of democracy," as Wood identified it, in February and March of 1952. Announcements of this journey were issued by Michigan's Representative Potter, who was looking toward a Senate seat that fall. With this in mind and impressed with the impact of television coverage, as lately demonstrated by Senator Kefauver's crime investigations, Speaker Rayburn barred TV cameras from all committee hearing rooms. The Republicans cried foul, but the order stood. The Detroit hearings focused on Local 600, the United Auto Workers' largest local, representing more than 50,000 Ford Workers. Despite the victory of the Reuther forces in the U.A.W., Local 600 had never been entirely cleansed of Communists, and witness after witness took the Fifth Amendment, several of them most truculently. Potter played a prominent part in the questioning; when a particularly antagonistic Negro organizer got onto the subject of the hanging and bombing of Negroes in the South, Potter came back with the number of American casualties in Korea.

In airing the Communist records of Local 600's organizers and officers, the Committee provided Walter Reuther with an opportunity for a housecleaning. After the hearings, the U.A.W. took over the local, citing as cause the "overwhelming evidence" of Communist manipulation. Under the provision of the union constitution barring Communists, several lesser officials long known to be C.P. members were ousted, and the non-Communist position within the union was strengthened. It was easy to make an argument for the desirability of removing from union leadership persons who had demonstrated their subservience to the Communist Party; their tendency to turn the union into an ideological instrument had been amply documented. But there were other repercussions of the Detroit hearings that were harder to justify. Witnesses were fired from their jobs and hustled out of factories by fellow employees; a violinist was suspended by the Detroit Federation of Musicians; a student was expelled by Wayne University; two men were ordered evicted from a Detroit public housing project. Here, in this spontaneous collaboration of individuals and organizations of all sorts, lay the Committee's future. It could expose a man and leave his punishment to others. Those few years that comprise the McCarthy era were marked by a readiness to punish as well as by a propensity to accuse. The Committee, which had no direct means of getting at witnesses who took the Fifth, could now let them go, in confidence that some at least would be made to suffer for their sins. The Reds could not be hung, but with luck they might be fired by their bosses, abused by their neighbors, and harassed by local officials.

To a period steaming with suspicions, accusations, and investigations, the Committee contributed a report entitled *The Shameful Years*—a review of Soviet espionage from 1919 onward—which gained considerable popularity. Wood and his colleagues asked Congress for a law that would provide capital punishment or a life sentence for peacetime espionage. They asked for the admission of wiretap evidence in espionage cases, stricter passport requirements, and the revocation of military commissions held by persons who took the Fifth Amendment. They reached out repeatedly after newsworthy tidbits, which yielded no broth but kept the pot boiling. When, at the end of September, General Walter Bedell Smith, director of the Central Intelligence Agency, remarked while testifying in a $2 million libel suit brought by Senator McCarthy against Senator Benton, that "I believe there are Communists in my organization," he was hastily summoned by the Committee to explain himself. It turned out that there wasn't anything to explain; obviously if the general had known of any Communists in the C.I.A. he would have fired them. He had meant merely that, like all officials in highly sensitive agencies, he had to operate on the assumption that Communists had infiltrated his staff. General Smith used his appearance to give a strong commendation to Harry Truman for his support of the nation's security arms.

Chairman Wood, having decided to retire from Congress, was left with time on his hands during the fall of 1952, and while most committees remained idle after the summer adjournment, he busied himself with investigations, none of which was designed to benefit Adlai Stevenson's Presidential campaign. Stevenson was running against a powerful tide that reached from coast to coast. On the day in October that the Committee spent questioning doctors in Los Angeles, three New York City professors were suspended for declining to say whether they were Communists, and General Eisenhower, campaigning in Wisconsin, called for the reelection of Senator McCarthy in a speech from which a defense of General George C. Marshall against McCarthy's slurs had been cut out. Richard Nixon, who owed his nomination for the vice presidency at the age of thirty-nine to the Hiss case, made loyalty the principal weapon of his campaign, going so far as to argue that Stevenson was not fit to be President because he had submitted a deposition on behalf of Alger Hiss in his first trial for perjury.

In later years, when his behavior in the campaigns of 1950 and 1952 would come to seem somewhat careless, Nixon would appear before the nation a changed man, like the newly crowned Henry V matured past the riots of youth, putting Falstaff on notice, "Presume not that I am the thing I was." In later years, too, this period to which McCarthy lent his name would be remembered by some as a time of black repression, when the police state was upon us. That, of course, is a trick of memory. Even during his few years of cruelly used power, McCarthy was never free of attack. Richard Rovere reminds us that on most college campuses it was safer to be anti-McCarthy than pro-McCarthy. Yet many people were hurt; many more were frightened; caution was in the air. Liberals were stalled and on the defensive. Like the whiskey in *The Iceman Cometh*, liberalism had lost its kick and a kind of numbness had set in. The ideological certainties of the thirties had been cut away; the Stalinists, who with all their crudities and connivings had lent spirit to innumerable good causes, were consigned to limbo. Political innovation in America had entered a deep freeze that would last out the decade.

The Committee's work in 1952 ended with the Eisenhower landslide. The Republicans won a narrow majority in the House and for the first time in its history (and, as of this writing, the last), the Committee would be run by Republicans during a Republican Administration. This situation created a tension between the Easterners in the White House and the Midwesterners in Congress, between Establishment etiquette and Populist passions that would explode in the Army-Mc-Carthy hearings of 1954. As 1952 came to a close, however, Harold Velde, chairman designate of the Committee on Un-American Activities, liberated from the bonds imposed by Wood and Walter, saw only opportunities ahead.

11

★ ★ ★ ★ ★

1953-1954: The Velde Capers

HAROLD H. VELDE'S main claim to election to Congress at the age of thirty-eight was that he had been an F.B.I. agent. "Get the Reds out of Washington and Washington out of the Red" was the slogan with which he captured the 1948 Republican primary. His credentials were appropriate to the season, and during his four terms in the House, Velde would find frequent occasion to recall them to his colleagues, to Committee witnesses, and to newspaper reporters. His record as a Congressman, as might have been foreseen, had more of an investigative than a legislative cast. Velde in no way resembled the gorgeous Everett McKinley Dirksen, whom he had replaced in the House. He had no stage presence at all, mellifluity was not one of his gifts, and his essays at lawmaking reached a high point with a bill that would have required the Librarian of Congress to list the books in the Library's collection that might be regarded as subversive. He also proposed instituting a loyalty oath as a requirement for participating in national elections. He voted with the Taft wing of his party—against foreign aid, for 90 per cent farm parity, for an end to rent control. In his opposition to public housing he was more Taft-wing than Taft himself.

For some observers chairman-presumptive Velde evoked the shade of Martin Dies, who had just been returned to Congress in the flesh with, he claimed, "about a hundred thousand names of persons engaged in subversive activities," and was more than agreeable to taking a place on the Committee he had sired.

[321]

Velde was agreeable, too, but the unforgiving Democratic leadership would have none of it. "I'm not especially wedded to this Committee," announced Representative Walter in a refreshing comment on a fellow Democrat, "but if it were necessary for no other reason than to keep from giving Dies a seat, I would remain a member. I don't think he has any constructive contribution to make to the Committee's work." Martin Dies did not get his seat.[1]

Under the chairmanship of the peaceable Wood, Velde and Jackson had acted as constant goads; they wanted more investigations and tougher investigations. Now the Committee was theirs; their Republican colleagues, with the sometime exception of Kearney, were of a like mind with them on most matters, a markedly conservative mind, and the Democrats, out of party loyalty and milder temperaments, took on a restraining role. They were not very effective. In the eighty-third Congress the Committee established a remarkable record of 178 days of taking testimony from more than 650 witnesses, most of whom answered questions with the Fifth Amendment.

The record was set with the help of subcommittees which Velde deployed through the country like a feudal monarch giving work to lesser lords. The spring weeks of 1954, when the Army-McCarthy hearings were occupying the capital's press corps and when Congressmen were beginning to look toward their constituencies with anticipation, proved an especially busy time. In Albany, a subcommittee led by Kearney, the upstate New Yorker, was exposing yet other officials of the United Electrical Workers as well as several state employees who resigned from their jobs rather than answer questions; a subcommittee led by the Californian Jackson was in San Diego exposing a mixed bag of Communists; a subcommittee in Detroit and environs led by Michigan's Kit Clardy was exposing, with the aid of an F.B.I. informant identified only as Witness X, college-educated "colonizers" from New York who had taken unskilled jobs in the auto industry—at the behest,

---

[1] The only change in the Democratic complement, which was reduced from five to four by the election, was the departure of Chairman Wood. To the three holdover Republicans were added Kit Clardy of Michigan and Gordon H. Scherer of Ohio.

one might reasonably infer, of C.P. headquarters; a subcommittee led by Velde of Illinois was exposing more left-wing union organizers in Chicago. There were also visits to Seattle where a woman, a Communist of some twenty years' standing who had been convicted and sent to the penitentiary for violation of the Smith Act, gave the names of hundreds of her former comrades from various walks of life; to San Francisco where I.L.W.U. officials were exposed; as well as to Philadelphia, Baltimore, and Dayton, Ohio, where, in September of the election year, Representative Scherer got his chance to be a subcommittee chairman in the vicinity of his constituency.[2]

The Hollywood and New York entertainment worlds were invaded yet again—with TV cameras in use now—as Velde, like a frugal housewife, squeezed out a last few names to fatten the industry blacklist. (By now the A. F. of L.'s American Federation of TV and Radio Artists had voted to expel or otherwise discipline any member who declined to answer questions about his Communist connections, past or present.) The main novelty in the Los Angeles hearings was that the undercover F.B.I. agent turned out to be a sixty-eight-year-old grandmother, who delivered herself of 120 names, mostly obscure. Another F.B.I. source reported that Communists were upset by radio soap operas because they didn't show woman's role in the revolutionary struggle, and Party theoreticians objected to stars lending their prestige to the capitalist system by reading commercials. In New York City, Artie Shaw wept with remorse over having been duped by the Communists; Lionel Stander whipped up a furious storm in the course of taking the Fifth Amendment; Jerome Robbins named a few Broadway names; and Robert Rossen repented of his 1951 refusal to speak, because he had decided that in the ongoing world crisis no one "can ever indulge himself in the luxury of individual morality" against the needs of national security. Rossen testified that he had been a Communist from 1937 to 1947 and had contributed about $40,000 to Party causes; he gave fifty-seven

---

[2] It was in these Ohio hearings that for the only time in the Committee's history, a former Congressman, Hugh DeLacy of Washington, took the Fifth Amendment.

names, most all of them well worn by now from Committee handling.

But to review all the campaigns of these two years is to court redundancy. They were neither more nor less justified than similar explorations under Wood—though they were run a shade, sometimes several shades, less pleasantly in accord with the chairman's inclinations. Clardy, a right-wing lawyer from Lansing, whom an excitable writer for *The Nation* dubbed a "junior McCarthy," took the honors for choler, with Scherer a hard breath behind. (During the Michigan visit, the two worked in tandem. Scherer charged a witness with perjury and, when the man tried to reply, Clardy shut him up.) The main purpose of the hearings—more often than not their only purpose —was to publicize the names of persons identified as having Communist affiliations and sympathies, past or present, and so submit them to the passions of the hour.[3] These years of the zealot gave a brutal twist to a precept of Epicurus, that least zealous of philosophers, who advised, "Let nothing be done in your life which will cause you fear if it becomes known to your neighbor."

What distinguished the Committee under the chairmanship of Velde was not so much the quantity of its investigations or their quality, as the direction they took. Never had the country experienced such an epidemic of investigations as it did in 1953 and 1954. With Senator Jenner directing the Internal Security Subcommittee and Senator McCarthy banging away at the State Department until the Voice of America cried uncle, then entering into his fatal battle with the army, investigations came to be the main business of a Congress that had no taste for innovative legislation—unless it was on the order of the Communist Control Act which was aimed at strengthening the security legislation of 1950 and applying it to "Communist-infiltrated organizations," but had the effect only of further muddying already muddy waters. The Administration, inclined

---

[3] Walter Reuther greeted the Committee with a sensible statement that urged witnesses to avoid taking the Fifth Amendment if possible, but emphasized that the United Auto Workers would resist the discharge or disciplining of any member on the sole ground that he had claimed the privilege against self-incrimination.

toward a generalized passivity on domestic affairs and having taken office with the promise of patching up Democratic security loopholes, could not actively discourage the new investigations, yet could not wholeheartedly encourage them either since no one could tell where they might lead. Four months after taking office, President Eisenhower mollified Congressmen by shifting the Truman test of suitability for federal employment from the question of loyalty to the broader one of security. Henceforth, the question would be "whether the employment and retention in employment of any civilian officer or employee . . . is clearly consistent with the interests of the national security." As 1953 began, there seemed to be no off-limits signs for the hunters of Communists, and the Velde Committee soon found itself entangled in two of the most sensitive areas of our national life—education and religion.

America's schools and colleges offered the investigators an inviting prospect on several counts. There were undoubtedly Communists, former and current, to be found there, men and women who had received their own schooling in the thirties and had imbibed the popular ideals of the period. Educated beyond the ability of the society to use or reward them, many entered the middle class at its bottom rungs, taking teaching jobs which offered low pay and uncertain status; they made up a classic body of disaffected intellectuals. Most had broken with Communism or drifted away years before, but some were still caught up in the dream. The Party offered them what the society withheld, a sense of mission and of consequence, and as long as that was true, nothing that had happened in Russia since their early commitment could shake their faith. They had paraded their beliefs in the thirties and forties, working for a multitude of Party-approved causes (most of which happened to be quite deserving in their own right), and now, in the fifties of the cold war, their livelihoods were at the mercy of whatever winds shook their local school boards or college administrations.

For mentalities like those of Velde, Jackson, Scherer, and Clardy, the groves of Academe were choked with the weeds of subversion. J. Edgar Hoover spoke for them when, in a talk on the spirit of free inquiry, he said, "Some professors have aided the Communist cause by tearing down respect for agencies of government, belittling tradition and moral custom and by creating doubts in the validity of the American way of life." Through its entire career, the Committee on Un-American Activities had had to put up with attacks from university professors, singly and in concert. Most of the scientists named in the Committee's investigation of wartime atomic espionage were holding down good posts at prominent universities when they were called to testify. It was intolerable to Velde to think that there should be a privileged sanctuary for the opponents of his Americanism, and for weeks before he assumed the chairmanship of the Committee he was promising to rout out Communists from the educational scene. The fact that Senator McCarran had set himself a similar task in the eighty-second Congress and that Senator Jenner intended to carry on the work in the eighty-third was no deterrent; it was the time of the investigator in the land and there were enough schools to go around.

Velde's announced intentions naturally aroused educators. In a talk to the annual convention of the American Association of School Administrators in February 1953, Mrs. Agnes Meyer, wife of the owner of the Washington *Post* and a diligent worker for better education, delivered an all-out denunciation of Jenner, McCarthy, and Velde, and in particular questioned the I.Q. of the last named. Velde responded as members of his Committee had responded to criticism for years, by associating Mrs. Meyer with "pinks and others following the Communist Party line" and by releasing her dossier, in which she was credited with writing a letter in 1947 to a pro-Russian magazine in praise of the Russians and being lauded for it by *Pravda*. This turned out to be a clerical error; the letter had in fact been written by a Mrs. Mayer, not Meyer, and she lived in Port Clements, B.C., not Washington, D.C. On having this pointed out to him, Velde fired a staff member whom he said was to blame.

This beginning did nothing to reassure educators about what

lay before them, and liberal journals made much of the incident. (Representative Franklin D. Roosevelt, Jr., went through the motions of offering a resolution to remove Velde from his chairmanship, whereupon the House yawned and by a vote of 315 to 2 gave the Committee $300,000.) But the question of whether members of the Communist Party had a place on any American faculty was one over which civil libertarians differed. Whereas Albert Einstein urged intellectuals not to testify, Norman Thomas, who bore the scars of attacks from both left and right, held simply that "The right of the Communist to teach should be denied because he has given away his freedom in the quest for truth." Thomas despised men like Jenner and Velde and was under no illusion regarding their intentions, but he defended their right to investigate Communists in positions of trust and sensitivity. In his view, teachers who had been Communists some time in their past deserved forgiveness—"But he who today persists in Communist allegiance is either too foolish or too disloyal to democratic ideals to be allowed to teach in our schools."

Many college administrators found themselves between two sets of pressures: one from faculty members who took the position that the only proper criteria for judging a teacher were his acts and intentions, not his ideology or associations; the other from trustees and state legislators who tended to be more concerned about the reputation of their institutions than the careers of an odd Communist or two. No working consensus was ever reached, but the administrators, while insisting on fair investigative procedures and extolling academic freedom, tended to side with the trustees. Whereas the American Association of University Professors adopted a resolution to the effect that membership in a legal organization was not in itself a disqualification for teaching and opposed the automatic dismissal of teachers who took the Fifth Amendment, the Association of American Universities resolved that present Communist Party membership "extinguishes the right to a university position." The latter group, which spoke for the heads of thirty-seven major institutions, maintained further that a teacher who took the

Fifth must bear the burden of proof of his fitness to continue teaching.

The conflict came to a head at Rutgers when two professors who had taken the Fifth Amendment before the Senate Internal Security Subcommittee were fired despite the backing of a faculty review committee. The president of the university, Webster Jones, argued that professional competence was irrelevant to this issue. He granted that the freedom of a witness to remain silent was his civil right, but emphasized that a university was a public trust, that "academic freedom entails the obligation to render an explanation as clearly and rationally as possible, whenever such an explanation is called for by duly constituted governmental bodies acting within the limits of their authority." He took as given the fact that C.P. membership was not compatible with freedom of inquiry. "It is no invasion of privacy but a necessary measure of protection of the freedom of all of us to seek to determine whether teachers and others in public positions of trust are committed to the discipline and program of the Communist Party."[4]

By this reasoning, the Communist teachers had no choice; they would be fired if they refused to speak and they would be fired if they spoke. Seen as conspirators, that was no more than they deserved, and to judge by the Party's own directives, one could only believe—as Norman Thomas and Sidney Hook believed—that Party members would hew to the Party line in whatever subject they happened to be teaching and so indoctrinate their students. But this belief involved a simplification both of what takes place in a college classroom and of what Party membership meant to the individual teachers. They made up a diverse bunch, intellectually and emotionally. There were few "conspirators" among them, and many good honest teachers. It was with this in mind that one group of educators, under Buell Gallagher, who had just been named head of the City College of New York, asked that the "kind and degree of involve-

---

[4] In 1956 Rutgers was one of six universities censured by the American Association of University Professors for, among other offenses, dismissing a faculty member who took the Fifth Amendment before a Congressional committee. The others were the University of California, Ohio State, Temple, Jefferson Medical College, and the University of Oklahoma.

ment" with the Communist Party be established before a man was dismissed.

Another notable dissent from the automatic dismissal rule came from a faculty group at Columbia University, led by Lionel Trilling. The Columbia professors criticized the school investigation as unnecessary because the number of teachers ever committed to Communism was negligible, and harmful because it was creating "an atmosphere of apprehension and distrust that is jeopardizing the cause of free inquiry and threatening the right to dissent." Regarding the Fifth Amendment, the Trilling group observed that its protection did not extend beyond the committee room and that its use entailed the drawing of inferences, bad or good, but that "it cannot be made a condition of membership in the teaching profession that a person surrender rights which are guaranteed by the law of the land." As for C.P. membership, the professors conceded that it "almost certainly implies a submission to an intellectual control which is entirely at variance with the principles of academic competence," yet concluded, with a bow to life instead of to logic (or to the president of their university, who took the opposite view), that "in the present state of affairs" wisdom suggested that there be no academic test of fitness other than an individual's demonstrated competence and personal integrity.[5]

For Chairman Velde the debate was academic. Turning about an article of faith frequently cited by civil libertarians, he said, "It's a lot better to wrongly accuse one person of being a Communist than to allow so many to get away with such Communist acts as those that have brought us to the brink of World War Three." The Administration, which was devoting 1953 to the placating of Senator McCarthy, looked on benevolently. As the House Committee's hearings approached, the recent president of Columbia University explained, in a manner

---

[5] In January 1967, a decade after the issue had gone the way of most issues, the Supreme Court came out on the side of the Trilling group. In voiding New York State's complex of loyalty laws for teachers, Justice Brennan, speaking for the five-man majority, declared invalid the provision that mere C.P. membership without "any showing of specific intent to further the unlawful aims of the Communist Party" is sufficient cause for dismissal.

that was becoming famous, that he would be the last one to curtail Congressional investigations but he was opposed to prejudging anyone's guilt, that he was all for academic integrity but "would have none of traitors." The Republican leadership, like a mother who doesn't mind what her children do as long as they don't maul one another while doing it, made a lazy effort to keep the Jenner group and the Velde group from colliding as they snatched at star witnesses. General Wilton B. Persons, the President's liaison with Congress, met with McCarthy, Jenner, Velde, and a man from the F.B.I. to work out some sort of combined program, and Velde explained that whereas Jenner would be searching for organized Communist activity and dealing with institutions, he would be concentrating on individual members of the Communist Party. This Velde saw as "coordination" rather than competition. As their investigations proceeded, however, all through 1953 and well into 1954, the main discernible differences were that the Jenner Committee was more efficiently run and got fuller newspaper coverage.[6]

Velde started off late in February with several witnesses of distinction who had belonged briefly to the Party during their student days at Harvard in the thirties. Robert Gorham Davis, professor of English at Smith, Daniel Boorstin, associate professor of history at the University of Chicago, and Granville Hicks, who had made no secret of his sympathies either during his Party days or after he broke away as a result of the Hitler-Stalin pact, were all treated courteously. The most insinuating question put to them was why they had not spoken out after their break, in the manner of Louis Budenz. Scherer, Clardy, and Jackson pressed them, somewhat defensively, for testimonials as to the fair treatment they were meeting at the Committee's hands. "Do you feel," Scherer asked Davis, "that

[6] Now and then Senator McCarthy took time out from his other work to interject himself into the area of education—by inveighing against the "smelly mess" at Harvard after that university declined to fire an ex-Communist teacher who pleaded the Fifth Amendment, or by threatening legislation to take away the tax exemption from foundations that gave money to any college with Fifth Amendment people on its faculty. "Touch their pocketbooks and they get religion," said Joe—but, for the most part, he left America's teachers to Jenner and Velde.

your experience today has interfered in any way with your academic freedom or the academic freedom of any professor at Smith College?" Walter, who was establishing himself as the Committee's voice of reason, held a calm conversation with Hicks, in the course of which he made the near-heretical statement, "I am sure that the Communist Party membership has been reduced considerably—certainly the eggheads have all gotten out of it . . . and I think the situation is exaggerated now." Clardy made up for this by notifying Hicks that Americans for Democratic Action was a Communist front. Both Boorstin, who believed that a Party member should not be permitted to teach in the public schools or in the social science departments of colleges, and Hicks, who thought it was better to let a stray Communist teach than strain the fabric of academic freedom, were allowed to have their reasonable says.

But the amiable tone did not last out even the second day of hearings. Soon witnesses, beginning with Wendell Furry, the Harvard physicist, and Barrows Dunham, the head of Temple's philosophy department, were taking the Fifth (Dunham refused to speak at all, beyond begrudgingly giving his name, address, and birthday), and Committee members were arguing with them about their rights to the self-incrimination clause and their views in general. When Furry said he didn't believe that the U.S.S.R. started the Korean War, Jackson countered: "Do you make a distinction in your mind as between one who seeks the overthrow of the government by force and violence in this country and one in the lines of North Korea who seeks the overthrow of the United States of America by force and violence in Korea?" (When, however, Tavenner got started on the remote case of Furry's wife's sister's husband, who had been involved in the 1946 Canadian spy trials, Kearney pulled him up short.) For months thereafter, subcommittees went about the country and exposed some teachers wherever they alighted. Like socialites who throw their little shooting parties when the society reporters are all occupied with more impressive events, the subcommittees lost out to the Jenner group in the competition for national publicity. But local newspapers did nicely by them, and though the game was small it was abundant. They were cheered on by J. Edgar Hoover himself who, delivering his periodic warning to the House Appropriations Committee that the Communist threat was bigger than ever, declared that "Every Communist uprooted from our educational system is one more assurance that it will not degenerate into a medium of propaganda for Marxism." Before the Jenner and Velde committees and the state and local groups they inspired to action were done with their season's shooting, hundreds of teachers, having taken the Fifth Amendent, would be removed from the nation's schools and colleges by resignation, dismissal, and suspension.

To those who interpreted this record as a diminution of academic freedom, the Committee majority usually explained that they were in no wise concerning themselves with what anyone taught; they were merely out to get Communists, in schools as elsewhere. But if some of the objections to the hearings were overwrought, the defense was rather too cool; it drew too nice a line between pursuing individual Communists and influencing entire faculties. Although the investigators stayed clear of matters of curricula and brought up the subject of classroom indoctrination only in a general way, their campaign could have but one effect. It was an incitement to the dimmest right-wingers around the country, whose hatred of Communism took in everything that went under the head of progressive education. Along with the more potent McCarthy and Jenner investigations, it acted as an inhibitor of classroom controversy. And it undoubtedly contributed to that much-lamented phenomenon of the fifties known to magazine readers as the Silent Generation.

The Committee's encounter with the churches began in an offhand manner on March 9, 1953, when Velde, being interviewed on the Mutual Network program, *Reporters' Roundup,* allowed as how it was "entirely possible" that he might get into the "church field." It was not an entirely original idea, the Committee, in a 1951 report, having "observed with dismay the inordinately large proportion of clerics among the persons who are aiding or supporting the Communist 'peace' campaign in this country," and Velde made it explicit that he was interested in individuals, not in the churches themselves. "We would not be investigating the churches any more than we are now engaged in investigating the colleges and universities." Not a day passed before other members of the Committee were disassociating themselves from the notion of such an investigation. Kearney was "absolutely opposed." Even Jackson said it was "unwarranted." Everybody wanted it understood that Velde was speaking strictly for himself, and the Republican House leadership lectured the chairman on the subject. In an unaccustomedly strong statement, President Eisenhower told his press conference that he could see no possible good being accomplished by questioning the loyalty of America's churches—which, to be just, Velde had certainly not done. Walter's demand for a Committee resolution forbidding the chairman to announce an investigation not approved by the full Committee was acceded to without dissent.

But the matter was not to be laid so easily to rest. The Committee's opponents—including quite a number not known for their piety who were nonetheless willing to become champions of religion if that was what was needed to knock Velde flat— did not have it all their own way. From evangelical enclaves within the Protestant fold support began to build up for an investigation. Fundamentalists had long fumed over the kind of Protestantism preached and practiced by the National Council of the Churches of Christ in the U.S.A., which represented the country's largest, wealthiest, most respectable Protestant communities. Flickering here were vestiges of the long fight between Enlightenment and Enthusiasm in America's churches, as well as the familiar political tensions between big cities and rural areas, between the outward-looking Eastern seaboard and the provincial Midwest. Soon the American Council of Christian Churches, fourteen Protestant denominations that had banded together in 1941 "to offset the modernist, socialist influence of the National Council of Churches," was circulating a petition among clergymen asking for an investigation. "The searchlight on religious leaders has long been needed," announced the Council's general secretary. Mail favoring an investigation began arriving at Committee offices.

This support for Velde had an immediate effect. On March 17 Representative Jackson ("I am a Congregationalist by birth and breeding. The little white church across the street from my birthplace in South Dakota holds a special place in my affections") delivered a long speech in the House, in which he took back his initial, "hasty" reaction to Velde's radio statements. Now, he declared, he was "happy and proud" to associate himself with them. And he singled out as his particular target the foremost critic of the Committee among high Protestant officials, G. Bromley Oxnam, Methodist Bishop of Washington and one of the presidents of the World Council of Churches. "Having served God on Sunday and the Communist front for the balance of the week over such a long period of time," said Jackson, "it is no wonder that the bishop sees an investigating committee in every vestry." Jackson received an ovation for his speech.

Now the fire that seemed to have expired at the lighting flared again, and it would stay alive for many months. Bishop Oxnam, in the center of the flame for most of that time, was no prayerful martyr; he gave as good as he got. After Velde counseled a group of churchmen in Chicago to ponder the new "sin" of subversion when they were inclined to criticize proposals to search for Communists among the clergy, Oxnam told a group in Philadelphia that "There are some who insist that the hallelujahs of religion shall always support the hurrahs of the state." He challenged the Congressmen "to name one clergyman who holds a position of large responsibility in any Protestant church who is a member of the Communist Party." The bishop himself had never been charged with being a Communist, but he was much inclined to the social gospel and from time to time, in response to an attack by him on its methods, the Committee would release from its files an item connecting him with some Communist front. The *ad hominem* method of replying to criticism, ever popular with the Committee, aroused Oxnam to demand a full and open hearing. This he received— but not before another drama concerning Communists among the clergy and starring J. B. Matthews had been performed on another stage of the Capitol.

Matthews had come into his own during the cold war. Among the "consultants on Communism" who had formed themselves into a profession of sorts, serving state legislators, American Legion posts, the public relations departments of large and nervous companies, and the banquet chairmen of patriotic organizations, J. B. Matthews occupied a position roughly equivalent to that occupied by Joe McCarthy among the nation's investigators. As part of his educational works, Matthews contributed articles on aspects of the internal Communist peril to the *American Mercury*—once the playground of H. L. Mencken, now a backyard lot where right-wingers threw empty bottles into the air so that they might watch them crash— and it was only natural that the subject of Communist clergymen having been raised by Velde and seconded by Jackson, Matthews would have something to say in behalf of their position. (The May issue of the magazine had carried his article on *Communism and the Colleges*.)

Reds and Our Churches was published in the July 1953 issue of the *Mercury* and was inserted into the Congressional Record by Representative Clardy, who commended it to all members. Designed as a defense of Velde against the burst of criticism that followed his mild remarks on radio, the article led off with this sentence: "The largest single group supporting the Communist apparatus in the United States today is composed of Protestant clergymen." Matthews went on to report that in the previous seventeen years the Communist Party had enlisted the support of at least 7,000 clergymen (compared to barely 3,000 college professors)—"Party-members, fellow travellers, espionage agents, Party-line adherents and unwitting dupes." The way Matthews had arrived at this imposing figure was by adding up the names of clergymen he had found signed to petitions, resolutions, advertisements, and whatever in support of causes favored and promoted by Communists—notably the Stockholm Peace Appeal during the Korean War and pleas for clemency for the Rosenbergs. The reference to espionage agents was hyperbole, and the article named no card-carrying cleric.

As Matthews's clippings and calculations demonstrated, Communist causes had over the years held a continuing attraction for a segment of the Protestant clergy, and if Matthews's interests had run along a different path, he might have begun a worthwhile discussion as to why this should have happened. Was it that in addition to being more open to pleas for peace and mercy than their brethren among the fundamentalists, who still preached the religion militant, or among the Catholic priesthood, which was by and large willing to leave social justice to another place, Protestant clergymen were suffering from some ambiguity of role? They and their congregations were very much in this world, but what in heaven's name was their job? Well, one job they might reasonably take as their own was to bring the teachings of Jesus to bear on war or on capital punishment or even on the inequities of capitalism, and though harboring no particular affection for Stalin, they might have been imprudent enough to lend their signatures to petitions framed precisely to catch men of excess good will and scant political sophistication. It was scarcely a sin, after all, to believe that the execution of the Rosenbergs was an act of cruelty. These were matters that might have borne speculation, but they were no part of J. B. Matthews's trade.

About a week before his article's appearance Matthews had been named executive director of Senator McCarthy's Permanent Subcommittee on Investigations. The Democrats on the committee—Senators McClellan, Symington, and Jackson—had been showing increasing pain over McCarthy's stunts during these high-flying days, and the Matthews article presented them with an opportunity for a burst of ground fire. They denounced it as "a shocking and unwarranted attack against the American clergy," and with the support of Senator Potter called for Matthews's removal. (Even old Senator Byrd criticized Matthews and worked behind the scenes for his dispatch, but Senators Dirksen and Mundt, the senior Republicans on McCarthy's committee, held their peace.) McCarthy resisted for a day, but gave in after Nixon had a private chat over lunch with Mundt, and President Eisenhower spoke up, delivering his first direct shot at McCarthy, who had been having a rollicking time lately creating havoc in United States libraries abroad with no visible sign of displeasure from the White House. Upon receipt of a telegram from the co-chairmen of the Commission on Religious Organizations of the National Council of Christians and Jews, which labeled Matthews's article "unjustifiable and deplorable," the President replied that he shared their convictions. It had all the earmarks of a preconceived maneuver, and McCarthy "very reluctantly" accepted Matthews's resignation.

The Democrats did not let the matter rest there; when the subcommittee voted a Republican four to a Democratic three to give Chairman McCarthy authority to hire and fire staff members, they walked out of the committee and stayed out for several months. "If they don't want to take part in uncovering the graft and corruption of the Truman-Acheson Administration," commented McCarthy, "they are, of course, entitled to refuse." The remaining Republicans, however, did not accede to McCarthy's wish to call Matthews before them to give his evidence; they suggested that he go to the House—and the Un-American Activities Committee agreed to hear him.

But that hearing would never be held. In April of the following year, after experiencing some investigational vicissitudes, the Committee reversed itself. For one thing, Matthews did not exude an odor of success after his removal from his briefly held job; in fact he did not smell at all good. For another, the prospect of reawakening the Communist clergy dispute had become less enticing than ever after Bishop Oxnam's appearance. The Oxnam hearing, which filled the Old House Caucus Room, began at 2:30 p.m. on July 21 and, with a break for dinner, ran until 12:30 that night. The bishop's title, his record, and his firm but unprovocative manner made him a very different sort of witness from those to whom the Congressmen had lately been subjected, and the encounter offered an unusually clear view of the nature of the Committee and its dominant members and staff.

Although material from the Committee's files had been used

against him by the fundamentalists, not even a former F.B.I. agent could call Oxnam a Communist and not even a Communist could call him a reliable fellow traveler. His associations with Communist fronts had been few and fleeting and his entire history, actions as well as words, left no doubt that he was opposed to the Party, to its ideology, and to its vassals in this country. He was not much of a theologian, but he was too smart a man of affairs to play the dupe for very long—he never signed the Stockholm Peace Appeal. The worst he had done was to allow the use of his name by a few organizations to whose activities he did not pay sufficient attention. He had also lent his efforts to a host of liberal causes, been against Franco, and, along with everybody from Mike Quill to Leverett Saltonstall, had belonged to the National Council of American-Soviet Friendship during the war. And, finally, he was a critic of the Committee on Un-American Activities. "It seems singularly peculiar," said Clardy before the hearing, "that every time he's taken a stand he's taken that stand against the Committee and not on our side." The case against him was scantily fleshed, but Clardy, Jackson, and the newly hired counsel, Robert L. Kunzig, tried to make a meal of the bare bones.

Kunzig conducted most of the questioning, and it is not easy to say how much of his performance should be laid to simple ineptitude, how much to a shrewd assessment of the need to jazz up an exceedingly weak set of charges. He made a hash of chronology, jumping about over the decades and landing as far back as 1923; glossed over all events of the previous thirty years, including the ups and downs of America's relations with Russia; and made absolutely no distinctions regarding the nature of involvement with a front. Even where Oxnam reasonably explained or flatly denied an alleged association with a given person or group, Kunzig proceeded to fill the record with previously taken testimony and citations relating to that person or group, thereby leaving the impression with the inattentive listener that he was saying something about the witness at hand.

Since Oxnam had been an active member of the American Civil Liberties Union since 1946, Kunzig quoted a Fish Committee report from 1931 that held that the A.C.L.U. (which divested itself of its Communists in 1940) was closely allied to the Communist Party. When Oxnam testified that he had accepted an invitation in 1943 to become chairman of the executive committee of the Massachusetts Council of American-Soviet Friendship from Dirk Struik—the M.I.T. mathematics professor who had recently taken the Fifth before the Committee—Walter remarked, with no justification, "The fact of the matter is, this professor was a Russian spy, was he not?" When Oxnam admitted that he had belonged to the Committee on Militarism in Education in 1935, when it was opposing compulsory R.O.T.C. in the colleges, Kunzig recalled that ten years before that the group had been given $10,000 by the Garland Fund, which was subsequently cited as Communist by the Dies Committee. Oxnam admitted being "editorial advisor" of a magazine called the *Protestant Digest* from 1940 to 1942, not giving much time to the job and quitting when informed by Roger Baldwin that Communists were running it. Whereupon Kunzig noted that the publication had made the attorney general's list in 1947, tagging on this interesting legal point—"I might add the lists are retroactive." Kunzig also quoted Louis Budenz as saying the *Protestant Digest* was anti-Catholic; when Oxnam sought to defend himself against the implication that *he* was anti-Catholic, Velde delivered the punch line, "I regret very much that you brought the subject of anti-Catholicism up at all."

Although certainly not disposed in Oxnam's favor, Velde made a polite chairman. He occasionally admonished the audience, which was distinctly pro-Oxnam, to restrain itself, but allowed the bishop to reply fully and more often than not quite effectively to Kunzig's questions and innuendoes. When Oxnam complained about the Committee's habit of releasing inaccurate information about his activities which had been clipped from the *Daily Worker,* Velde chided him kindly: "In response to a question a while ago you indicated that you didn't know about your being listed on letterheads of certain organizations until you learned through our files that you were listed. I feel that you, as a good American citizen, should appreciate the fact that our Committee made this knowledge about you available." There is no reason to assume he was joking; Velde rarely joked.

Walter's position through the long day was never quite certain. He agreed with Oxnam that raw information of the sort that had been distributed about him should be confined strictly to the Committee, not given out, but he was peeved at the bishop for joining with those who opposed the McCarran-Walter immigration law, a matter that Walter brought up abruptly and the relevance of which no one questioned. There was never any doubt about where Jackson and Clardy stood; they were undeviating anti-Oxnamites. After Oxnam told of breaking off relations with Harry F. Ward, his teacher years before at the Boston School of Theology, because of Ward's Communist sympathies, Jackson made much of a tribute that Oxnam had paid in 1939 to Ward's accomplishments, and Clardy wanted to know why Oxnam hadn't turned his old professor in to the F.B.I. The only outspoken friend Oxnam had on the Committee was Doyle, whom Velde did his best to quash. It was Doyle who objected to Kunzig's producing documents from the year 1923 without advance notice and to the counsel's practice of listing citations of organizations to which Oxnam denied belonging. And it was Doyle who, at the end of the session after midnight, moved "that the record show in these hearings that this Committee had no record of any Communist Party affiliation or membership by Bishop Oxnam." To the astonishment of Oxnam and everyone else, the motion was immediately seconded by Jackson. But the Congressman relented no further. He objected to a second motion by Doyle asking that a note to the effect that Oxnam had denied membership in an organization be affixed wherever Kunzig had inserted the citations for such an organization—and the motion was defeated.

A photograph taken afterwards showed a smiling Velde shaking Oxnam's hand—but had the bishop in fact been cleared? Not according to Walter, who, thinking perhaps of the hard words which his immigration law was still suffering from the liberal community, said: "I don't know why anyone would say he was cleared because no one ever charged him with anything. I think the hearing demonstrated very clearly that the Communists are using well known and highly placed persons as dupes and the bigger the name the better for their cause. I place Bishop Oxnam as being in this category." That the Communists had used the bishop's name was certain, but his record by no means bore out Walter's conclusion. What the hearing showed was how narrowly men like Jackson and Clardy construed anti-Communism—one had to turn in old friends to the F.B.I. and be a supporter of the Committee on Un-American Activities. It showed how little men like Velde and Kunzig cared for orderly investigation. And it showed how entrenched the Committee was in the mechanically vindictive method of establishing individual guilt pioneered by J. B. Matthews. Bishop Oxnam deserved a much more generous apology from the Committee than he could ever have hoped to receive.

But if, despite the Committee's best efforts, Bishop Oxnam could not be remade to fit the image of a model fellow traveler, there were a few such among the Protestant clergy. Like Harry Ward, their identities were no secret. Five of them had been named by J. B. Matthews in his famous article[7]—but only after years of having contributed their names to Communist causes of impressive diversity and number. As Reinhold Niebuhr wrote, they had long been "protected by anti-Stalinist 'liberals' in the church who foolishly thought that the 'prophetic' spirits in the church were bound to be accused of disloyalty and therefore that the charge of Communist sympathies was a validation of the 'prophetic spirit.'"

The most energetic of this small but busy group was Jack R. McMichael. In 1939, still a seminarian, the lanky and loquacious young man from Georgia had appeared before the Dies Committee in his capacity of chairman of the American Youth Congress. He was subsequently ordained, and since the

[7] The five clergymen described by Matthews as "top pro-Soviet propagandists" were: Harry F. Ward, professor emeritus of the Union Theological Seminary; Kenneth Ripley Forbes, executive secretary of the Episcopal League for Social Action; Jack R. McMichael, executive secretary of the Methodist Federation for Social Action; Willard Uphaus, coordinator of the American Peace Crusade; and Joseph F. Fletcher, professor of Christian Social Ethics at the Episcopal Theological School in Cambridge.

end of World War II had been executive secretary of the Methodist Federation for Social Action, a loosely affiliated church organization concerned entirely with the affairs of this world, which the Committee had attacked in a 1952 report and from which McMichael's political proclivities had caused Bishop Oxnam to resign. In June 1953, with the heat on, McMichael gave up his post and took a small congregation in northern California. In July, a few days after Bishop Oxnam's appearance, he was called to Washington and placed in the witness chair.

McMichael had been identified as a member of the Young Communist League and the Communist Party in closed hearings of the Committee by two professional ex-Communists whose fortune it was rarely to be subjected to cross-examination, Manning Johnson and Leonard Patterson, and by a husband-and-wife team of undercover F.B.I. informants. McMichael denied their charges; indeed, he denied even knowing any of them, and had a fine time turning his appearance into a vaudeville routine with overtones of a revivalist session. He talked on and on in a Georgia drawl, made long speeches and little jokes, referred with mock officiousness to a set of diaries he had brought with him, and carried off a performance that threw the Committee into a worse tizzy than usual, as he notified it that he had to answer to Almighty God and not to it or to the attorney general. McMichael prefaced his denial of Party membership with a reference to "my six-year-old girl and my eight and ten-year-old boys" who had heard the charge over the radio. He told Velde, ". . . we are fellow Methodists and we understand each other . . ." While denying membership in a list of organizations mentioned by one of the informants, McMichael observed, "He refers to the Federal Bureau of Investigation. I have never been a member of that." When counsel Kunzig, driven desperate, shouted at him, McMichael replied, "I used to sell boiled peanuts as a little boy. I can speak as loudly as you." His tactics were particularly effective against Clardy, who began to behave like a slugger being jabbed maddeningly by an opponent with much faster footwork. When Clardy pressed him for an answer to a question about his student activities, McMichael said, "Thirteen years ago, brother —whatever your name is—that's quite a long while." He talked tirelessly without rancor, and when Clardy, steaming, hollered at him, "Be still!" he replied amicably, "I am not moving very far." At length the unhumorous Velde, who had been pounding his gavel for silence with as much effect as if he were commanding the sun not to rise, caught the spirit of the occasion: "The chair," he announced to McMichael who had been calling for an opportunity to deliver another short speech, "will allow you two minutes to make any derogatory statements you may want concerning this Committee." The event ended in inconclusive exhaustion as Velde, relieved of getting rid of the young man, handed a transcript of the proceedings over to the Justice Department for a possible perjury indictment. But although the Committee's informants had excellent reason to assume that McMichael had been a Communist in the nineteen-thirties and early forties, assumptions were not the stuff of which successful indictments are made.[8]

After this ordeal, Velde called no more clergymen. The Committee had come up with only one minister—a Los Angeles Unitarian—whom it had dead to rights and who had already taken the Fifth in 1951. But the bulk of the testimony from informants concerned ministers who had worked for Communist-directed causes but could not be pinned down as Party members. So Velde did what the Committee had periodically been criticized for doing before and had periodically vowed not to do again—he made public accusations that had been elicited in closed session from the old ex-Communist Benjamin Gitlow and the young ex-F.B.I. man Herbert Philbrick against several clergymen, who immediately denied being Communists but were not invited to testify. Philbrick, who had recently con-

[8] McMichael was accompanied at his hearing by Frank J. Donner, an attorney just beginning his encounters with the Committee. In 1961 Donner published a book, described as "the first fully documented account of the notorious House Committee on Un-American Activities," in which he gave this summary of McMichael's appearance: "In the 1953 hearing of the Rev. Jack R. McMichael, the Committee left no stone unturned in its brutal drive to ruin him. It refused to permit him to explain his answers, put words in his mouth and used highly questionable evidence against him." None of this is entirely untrue, but like so many of the attacks on the Committee, it conveys neither the flavor of the hearing nor the character of the witness.

tributed to the *Christian Herald* an articled entitled *The Communists Are After Your Church,* had been induced to gives names of suspect ministers by Clardy and Kunzig against his own sounder instincts. "Mr. Philbrick," urged Kunzig, "seeing as we are here in executive session and this testimony being confidential, do you feel you could tell the Committee the names of these ministers in the Boston area whom you, as you said, have a pretty good idea were the ones that you feel were members of the Communist Party?" Philbrick allowed himself to be thus inveigled, and three months later his confidential testimony was made public. Embarrassed in October at being quoted as the author of charges which he could not prove in July (his testimony being of this sort, "He is one of the individuals who, I am sure of in my own mind, is operating under Communist Party discipline"), Philbrick criticized the Committee for releasing his testimony "prematurely," before "all facts had been assembled and the probe completed . . ."

Public indignation, however, was directed mainly at Gitlow. Whereas a majority of the Protestant ministers named had been named before by Matthews, Gitlow added in passing two rabbis who, he said, had "carried out the instructions of the Communist Party or collaborated with it" more than thirty years before. They were Stephen S. Wise and Judah L. Magnes, both deceased, both men of outstanding reputations. (Gitlow also put John Haynes Holmes of New York's Community Church in this company.) He could not have selected more eminent rabbis if he had tried, and whatever one thought of their political tendencies in 1920, labeling them Communist functionaries was too much. Although Gitlow's testimony was based entirely on his memory of Party life at a time when associating with Communists was a much different proposition than it was in 1953, there was no way to refute him except to recall the good works which the two had done. These were widely recalled, and the Committee came in for another lambasting from press and pulpit. Velde had attempted a cheap coup and had been caught at it.

The cries of the Committee's opponents that it was engaged in an attack on religious freedom and was violating the line between church and state were hardly justified by anything Velde or Jackson actually did. Still there was no question that their investigations had been fueled by the un-Christian feelings of the evangelical sects toward their upper-strata brethren. Fundamentalist enthusiasm, however, could not carry one very far in national politics, and for want of any real news, the investigation soon petered out. In January 1954 Velde held a makeup meeting with a small unrepresentative but respectable Protestant-Catholic-Jewish group, and in its annual report for 1953, the Committee observed in the section devoted to religion that "only a very small number of clergymen in the United States have been consistent fellow travelers with the Communist Party," and even offered some excuses for those who had been misguided. What had begun with a bang ended in a mumble.

Although the Committee was well financed during the eighty-third Congress, receiving $575,000, more than any House investigating committee had ever received, and although it did a prodigious amount of testimony taking, it operated always under the shadow of others. The pursuit of individual Communists in schools around the country was minor league sport compared to the exhibitions that Joe McCarthy was putting on at the expense of the State Department and the military. So it was only natural that when an opportunity seemed to present itself to play in the majors, Velde would rise to it eagerly. The apparent opportunity came in November 1953, when Attorney General Brownell reopened the case of Harry Dexter White. In a speech to the Executive Club of Chicago, Brownell charged that in January 1946, President Truman had nominated White, then Assistant Secretary of the Treasury, to be executive director for the United States in the International Monetary Fund, despite an F.B.I. report delivered a month before which had reviewed White's activities as a Soviet spy. Another F.B.I. report, said Brownell, was delivered to Pennsylvania Avenue before White's Senate confirmation in February. Truman replied to Brownell, in words he would have to take back, that he knew nothing about any F.B.I. report: "As soon as we found White was disloyal we fired him." White's resignation in April 1947, after the Justice Department had failed to get a grand jury indictment against him, was accepted by Truman with "sincere regret and considerable reluctance."

There was not much question that the attorney general had the facts of the case straight, but no one could miss the political instigation behind his charge, whose phrasing conjured up black doings at the White House: "Harry Dexter White was known to be a spy by the very people who appointed him to the most sensitive and important position he ever held in government service." The speech had been cleared with Sherman Adams, Eisenhower's chief of staff, with Press Secretary James Hagerty, and, in a vague way, with Eisenhower himself. Brownell's resort to F.B.I. files was a particularly sensitive point. If Congressional committees to which such material had been barred under Truman could now get hold of it or if the Republicans were planning to strew about selected items in preparation for the 1954 elections, the country was in for a bitter political harvest. Senator Jenner immediately announced that his committee planned to reopen the White case, and his first announced witness would be Truman's former military aide and crony, Major General Harry H. Vaughan, to whom the F.B.I. reports had assertedly been handed. Thereupon, the Un-American Activities Committee also subpoenaed Vaughan, and there was speculation that a joint meeting might be held.

Now Velde made a spectacular move, his try for the big leagues. Taking the position that his Committee had a parent's prerogative on anything having to do with Elizabeth Bentley and Harry Dexter White, irked by Jenner's effort to lay first hands on the child ("We should get in the act," Velde's man Kunzig told the other Committee members), the chairman, on his own authority, sent forth subpoenas to James F. Byrnes, governor of South Carolina, who was Secretary of State in 1946 and remembered the F.B.I. warnings about White; to Supreme Court Justice Tom Clark, who was attorney general in 1946; and to Harry S. Truman. Sending a subpoena to a former President was a novel idea, untested in law, but Velde's intent was clear as day. The first attacks came from the Democrats on his Committee. Walter, to whom Velde was careful to defer during hearings, called the enterprise, "the most incredible, insulting, un-American thing that I've encountered in my twenty-one years in Congress." He charged that, in a race for headlines with Jenner, Velde had violated the Committee rule—adopted after the chairman's off-the-cuff remarks about an investigation of the clergy the previous spring—that required approval of a Committee majority for any major investigation. Doyle, in California, wired his strenuous opposition. Kearney, the Committee's only Eastern Republican, added his displeasure.

That was but the beginning. Had Harold Velde been a more notable figure, what came upon him now might be compared to those late scenes in *Richard III* when the king's allies presumptive decline to do combat or go over to the enemy. Velde's subpoenas were politely rejected by all parties. President Eisenhower, defending his predecessor's patriotism, said that he (the President) would not have subpoenaed him (the former President). The House Republican leadership sent a forceful emissary to the Committee's Republicans to get them to leave the field to Jenner. Jenner shrugged off Velde's ambitior s for a joint hearing of Vaughan, giving the Congressman a front-row seat to the Senate hearing as ironic consolation. When Velde announced that he intended to question the foreman of the grand jury that had heard the evidence in the White case, the Justice Department stepped in and forbade the man from testifying, grand jury proceedings being secret. The chairman was left with no witnesses, no audience and few supporters. Newspapers that had backed Eisenhower in 1952 and were critical of Truman's handling of the White case were yet more critical of Velde's presumption. Brownell, following the President's lead, said that he had not meant to impugn Truman's loyalty, merely to suggest that "laxity" on matters of security had prevailed in the White case. And after being invited to appear before the House Committee, the attorney general chose to appear before the Senate Committee instead and did so, together with J. Edgar Hoover, before the biggest audience of the investigating season, not counting radio and television.[9] Richard, in his difficult hour, called for a horse; Harold Velde was left promising the readers of *U.S. News* that he would not give up the field.

The Harry Dexter White affair was a victory for the Republicans—but a dangerous one. Truman, in a television talk, reversed himself, conceding that he had discussed the White case with members of his Cabinet; White had been allowed to take a post with the International Monetary Fund, he explained, so that the F.B.I. might carry on its investigations with a view toward getting an indictment. But the next day J. Edgar Hoover told the Jenner Committee that the F.B.I. had not been a party to any such arrangement, that his opinion had not been solicited, and that had it been up to him, he would have had White fired. Brownell's original statement of the facts of the case had been substantially correct; Truman's had been untrue. But Velde's initiative showed how easily such public charges could get out of hand, or, more precisely, get into irresponsible hands. By the end of 1953, the Administration had plenty of reason to be cautious about encouraging aspiring McCarthys.[1]

The Truman subpoena was not the only source of discontent within the Committee as 1954 began. The Agnes Meyer gaffe, the arousal of the clergy, the discharge of numerous staff members whose places were taken by persons more compatible to the new chairman (Robert Kunzig quite upstaged his associate counsel, Frank Tavenner)—these rankled Democratic members and gave special pause to the independently inclined Kearney, who charged publicly that the staff was wasting money and "jockeying for advantage over one another, trying to get raises which are undeserved and engaging in backbiting." Staff dissension reached such a pass that Velde appointed a subcom-

[9] Sherman Adams tells us in his memoirs that Brownell hoped his accusation "would take away some of the glamour of the McCarthy stage play."

[1] Through the fall and winter of 1953 and into 1954, the Committee made halfhearted efforts to get the Civil Service Commission to release its records of an employee of the Mediation and Conciliation Service who had been cleared for his job four times despite a record of cooperating with Communists in an A.F. of L. union. But the Administration abided by Truman's 1948 directive denying such papers to Congressional committees.

mittee of himself, Walter, and Kearney to look into it. While they were looking, in January 1954, Velde generated an uproar by firing Louis J. Russell, an F.B.I. alumnus who had been named chief investigator by Chairman Wood in 1949. When Velde explained that Russell had acted in ways that had embarrassed the Committee, Walter—against whom Velde already held a grudge for backing Truman's story about why he hadn't fired Harry Dexter White—commented sarcastically that Russell "didn't call for an investigation of religion." In fact, said Walter, "Whatever constructive work has been done by the Committee was done by him." But though Kearney shared his feeling that Russell was being made the goat for Committee blunders, the chief investigator was past defense. He had showed the poor judgment to borrow $300 from Edward G. Robinson, a former witness; the loan may have been innocent on both sides, but Russell was cooked.[2] The issue, however, remained alive. In March, ex-General Kearney returned to the attack, declaring the staff situation to be "rotten" and "intolerable" and threatening to quit if it was not cleared up. He said that one of Velde's appointees, who was supposed to have been fired in January for inefficiency, was still at work, and he was particularly irritated at the news that Velde had taken a staff man back to Illinois to assist him in a primary fight. Velde's response was that Kearney had unfortunately "fallen for the sucker pitch" of "left-wing editorialists and extremists."

Although Velde won in the primary, his taste for adventure was quelled by the cuffings he had received in 1953. He was, politically speaking, a frivolous man, but he had never shown the joy in his work that Martin Dies exuded. The second half of his term as chairman, coinciding with Joe McCarthy's time of troubles, offered fewer incentives to his chastened spirits and he played it safe. More than eighty days of hearings were held in 1954, but they were of a routine sort, subcommittees settling in various cities, calling up resident Communists, asking the

---

[2] Courtney E. Owens, who had been with the Committee for six years, was named to succeed Russell.

customary questions, and getting the customary refusal to testify on grounds of the Fifth Amendment. When a number of
witnesses were cited for contempt, the courts, as if parties to
the teasing of Harold Velde, returned fewer indictments than
he sought and very few convictions indeed.

12

★ ★ ★ ★ ★

The Fifth Amendment

THE Committee, its spokesmen somewhat apologetic about troubling the House yet again, pressed twenty-nine contempt citations against witnesses who appeared before it in 1953 and 1954. The citations fell into two categories, the larger having to do with persons who had pleaded the Fifth Amendment on questions regarding residence, schooling, and employment, which Committee members felt could not possibly incriminate them. The others involved witnesses who challenged the pertinency of inquiries into their political activities and associations but did not stand on the Fifth Amendment.

The former batch of citations brought the Committee unmitigated disappointment. A Detroit grand jury refused even to indict six persons who had declined to answer questions during a disorderly set of hearings conducted by Clardy, whose technique of dealing with obstreperous witnesses was to match their abuse with his own. In other cities, where indictments were issued, district courts acquitted the defendants—including Barrows Dunham, the first to be cited. Where district courts convicted, a court of appeals reversed the conviction. And the four cases in which convictions were upheld at the appeals level—on the grounds that an answer to the question, "Where do you live?" would not have been incriminatory—were reversed by the Supreme Court. Even answers to such innocuous questions, held the Court, might be dangerous. All but one of the eighteen persons cited for misuse of the Fifth Amendment went free, and that one would certainly have gotten off too had he carried forward his appeal, as his offense was no different from the others.

The decisions in these contempt cases carried to its utmost limit the principle laid down by the court in 1950 when it ruled in favor of a man who had refused to tell a grand jury about his knowledge of the workings of the Communist Party. As we noted earlier, Justice Black stated on that occasion, "Whether such admissions by themselves would support a conviction under a criminal statute is immaterial." The crucial point was that the witness' answers to the grand jury questions "would have furnished a link in the chain of evidence needed in a prosecution . . . for violation of (or conspiracy to violate) the Smith Act." Now, in the mid-fifties, it was established that virtually any question, no matter how seemingly trivial or remote from criminal activities, fell under this cover.

Legally, then, the question was settled, but the repercussions of taking the Fifth Amendment were by no means exclusively legal,[1] and they led to an emotional debate among respectable persons as to what inferences one might reasonably draw when a witness would not say whether he or she was a Communist on the grounds that "no person . . . shall be compelled in any criminal case to be a witness against himself." Prominent liberals took the position that no inferences whatever should be drawn, since an individual might in his past have done something altogether innocent which could now get him into trouble with the law. The most important statement of this position, widely distributed by the Fund for the Republic and widely quoted by liberal press and jurists, was set down by Dean Erwin N. Griswold of the Harvard Law School. It was a large-hearted argument by a man who had allowed his distress at the way legislative inquiries were being conducted to fog his thinking. In order to defend the no-inference rule, Griswold offered the hypothetical case of a professor who joined the Communist Party in the nineteen-thirties or -forties, limited

[1] At the height of the "Fifth Amendment–Communist" vendetta, the New York State senate unanimously passed a bill authorizing employers to fire any employee who pleaded self-incrimination, and in Washington, D.C., a secondhand piano dealer who took the Fifth before the Committee was denied the renewal of his license to buy and sell secondhand merchandise.

his activities solely to study groups, and quit in disillusionment at the outbreak of the Korean War. On being haled before a Congressional committee some years later, Griswold went on, such a man would be justified in taking the Fifth Amendment on the grounds that "Persons have been prosecuted under the Smith Act for membership in the Communist Party plus something else." Even though our hypothetical professor had no inkling of what the "something else" might be, what other evidence might be adduced against him, he had a right to take the Fifth, and any inference that he was therefore guilty of anything would be unwarranted. Griswold also invented the case of a non-Communist who feared that if he testified, his innocent membership in front groups in the past might be construed as evidence of Communist affiliation and so land him in trouble.

Dean Griswold's examples and the even more fanciful hypothetical cases thought up by others of the no-inference persuasion were deficient in one major regard: they had little to do with the reality of Congressional investigations. Witnesses who in fact told the Committee about their past membership in the Communist Party or front groups, far from being charged with anything, were fulsomely thanked and commended for their patriotism. No study-group Communists were ever prosecuted; the big Communist trials involved long-time C.P. leaders and functionaries. As for men like Hiss and Remington, it was their perjury, not their Party activities, that sent them to prison. Moreover, as Sidney Hook showed in a devastating retort to Griswold, the no-inference principle ran squarely against common sense. One might cherish the Fifth Amendment, agree with the dean that it represented "one of the great landmarks in man's struggle to make himself civilized,"[2] and defend sturdily the right of every man to take it and the duty of every court to respect it, yet not be able to blink away the presump-

[2] Griswold's light argument fairly blew away in its own rhetoric: "I believe the Fifth Amendment is and has been through this period of crisis, an expression of the moral striving of the community . . . a reflection of our common conscience, a symbol of the America which stirs our hearts . . . very nearly a lone sure rock in a time of storm . . . a symbol of the ultimate moral sense of the community . . ."

tion that a man who chooses to be silent rather than to speak has something to hide; even Dr. Griswold's hypothetical professor, though guiltless of any crime, *had* been a member of the Communist Party. The question was, in Hook's words, "Not knowing whether a person is innocent or guilty, what can reasonably or naturally be inferred from a refusal to answer a pertinent question, put by someone authorized to ask the question, on the ground that a truthful answer would tend to be incriminating?"[3]

The liberal community had not always been enamored of witnesses who would not speak up. It showed small sympathy for the discomfiture of businessmen in the Congressional hearings of the nineteen-twenties and -thirties and did not strain to invent hypothetical circumstances to prove that Frank Costello was pure in spirit because he preferred not to answer Senator Kefauver's questions in 1951. In 1936, then Senator Hugo Black, in his much-quoted *Harper's* article on Congressional investigations, evidenced great annoyance with unresponsive witnesses; he started his article with Woodrow Wilson's line, "If there is nothing to conceal, then why conceal it?"[4] The change of heart was of course due to the change in feeling on the left toward Congressional investigations since the campaigns of Martin Dies. There was concern over the investigators' tendency to pry into witnesses' ideas as well as their activities; there was distaste for the constant efforts to get witnesses to inform on old friends; there was sympathy for those whose careers were jeopardized by a subpoena; and there was an unmistakable indulgence toward the Communist

[3] There was a period when witnesses, advised that an answer to *any* question regarding past activities might jeopardize their right to the Fifth Amendment on the question of Communist Party membership, simply took the Fifth down the line. In these instances, the Committee's counsel and members frequently asked about espionage activities of which there was no evidence as well as about far-fetched and inconsequential matters designed to show up the witness as uncooperative or build up his refusal-to-answer score for the benefit of the press or simply for the sake of amusement. In regard to the rote Fifth Amendment response to such questions, no inference was warranted except that the Committee was taking advantage of the witness' situation.

[4] Conservatives have not failed to remind liberals of their earlier tolerance for the browbeating of witnesses. John J. McCloy said in 1953: "If the liberals had been more expressive when the so-called Congressional investigations of the thirties were studiously violating personal rights and when business was the target, there would have been less likelihood of excesses in this day and age."

witnesses that neither racketeers nor businessmen aroused. However much one objected to the Committee's motives and methods, a study of the hearings over the years left little doubt that the overwhelming majority of witnesses called before it had been correctly marked down as members or former members of the Communist Party; in 1953, 280 persons were heard, there being sworn testimony of their Communist affiliation in each case, and in every case but one—the Rev. Jack McMichael —the witnesses either admitted membership or pleaded the Fifth Amendment.

It was easy to sympathize with those—by no means a majority—who would have agreed to tell about their pasts if only the Committee then refrained from pressing them for information about former associates. But even under the generous limits allowed by the courts, the protection of third parties was not a valid reason for taking the Fifth Amendment. One might find the Committee and all its works obnoxious, but that was not a valid reason either. Giving witnesses an extensive benefit of the doubt and assuming that their reliance on the Constitution was founded on some reason other than a disinclination to testify against themselves, they were committing perjury. Telford Taylor, after building up an historical case for the no-inference position, was constrained to point out that most witnesses had no "solid legal and practical necessity" for taking the privilege and were "playing into the hands of those extremists who are trying to make the Fifth Amendment synonymous with guilt and subversion." It required a thorough suspension of disbelief on the part of a spectator to hear a man take the Fifth and draw no inferences from it—other than to conclude, as some did, that the fellow was a martyr. In a cogent essay on the subject, C. Dickerman Williams wrote ". . . The self-incrimination privilege benefits society through the compulsion which it exerts on enforcement officers to prove their cases by external evidence rather than by confessions extracted from suspects. But it does not mean that a given individual found in a compromising situation shows his innocence by failing to make a full disclosure." His shaft was aimed at those who overlooked the positive duty of citizens to testify before legally constituted bodies and who refused to concede that witnesses who did speak out about their past Communist associations were by no means all vile informers and witch hunters. As a matter of fact, as Alan Westin emphasized, they were carrying out a responsibility to the democratic community which the silent witnesses had relinquished.

Taking the Fifth Amendment was an act not of heresy but merely of self-protection. Used promiscuously, in response to questions about one's birth or education, as Carl Beck wrote, it "makes a mockery of a constitutional privilege established for the protection of the individual from the arbitrary exercise of power. By subverting this privilege, these witnesses eroded its efficacy and thereby contributed to the rejection by the public of the worthwhileness of the self-incrimination plea." It is presumptuous to ask anyone to be a martyr—but then a man who hides should not expect to be presented with a martyr's crown. Yet, in reaction against McCarthy's yawps about "Fifth-Amendment Communists" and against the invidious notion that once a man took refuge in the Fifth he thereby lost all claim to the ordinary needs of life, such as a job, some well-meaning persons surrendered their wits altogether and took to defending a prudent reliance on the self-incrimination clause not only as a sign of innocence but of positive nobility. It was, and remains, an example of the befuddling sentimentality that is a bane of liberal opinion.

As for the investigators and prosecutors who found themselves frustrated by the courts' comprehensive definition of self-incrimination under the Fifth Amendment, they were, in a way, to blame for their own fix. They had for years been demanding ever more stringent laws against Communists; the existence of such laws now constituted the rationale for the taking of the Fifth. Casting about for a corrective, the investigators hit upon the idea of offering witnesses immunity from prosecution, which had been tried in other circumstances over the years. A grant of immunity, it was argued, would enable a court or committee to overleap the constitutional bar against compelling someone to testify against himself. Such a law, the product of Attorney General Brownell, with investigators in both Houses of Congress serving as godfathers, was passed in August 1954. The Compulsory Testimony Act provided that in any case involving a danger to the national security, a United States attorney might, with the approval of the attorney general, ask the court to instruct a witness that he would not be excused from giving evidence on the ground that it might incriminate him; once instructed, no such witness could thereafter be prosecuted on the matter in question and so he could not claim the Fifth Amendment. A Congressional committee could ask the district court to grant immunity if two-thirds of the committee approved. Critics of the immunity law pointed out that it might not protect a witness against prosecution in a state court and would certainly not protect him from such side effects as losing his job. Some accustomed defenders of the underdog opposed the bill for the unexpected reason that it would provide an escape hatch for the guilty. The new law was quickly tested and upheld by the Supreme Court. Justice Frankfurter, speaking for the majority, took pains to praise the virtues of the Fifth Amendment, even quoting Dean Griswold, but the immunity law was nevertheless constitutional, he explained, because "once the reason for the privilege ceases, the privilege ceases." Justice Douglas, in the minority with Justice Black, quoted Dean Griswold more extensively than Justice Frankfurter. Douglas argued, as he would on other occasions, that the framers of the clause against self-incrimination meant much more than their bare words conveyed. In his view, the clause was designed in part "to prevent any Congress, any court and any prosecutor from prying open the lips of an accused to make incriminating statements against his will."

Not long after the new law took effect, Representative Walter, its major advocate in the brief House debate, suggested that it be used against a man from Flint, Michigan, whom Clardy, acting chairman of the Detroit subcommittee, called "one of the most contemptuous witnesses that it has been my experience to hear." The witness countered, "You have been one of the most contemptuous persons I have ever faced," and Clardy directed Tavenner to take appropriate steps. But despite the fact that there was good reason to believe that the witness had been sent to Flint as an auto union "colonizer" by the Communist Party, the immunity law was not invoked. Commenting on the failure to compel witnesses to testify after being granted a weapon with which to do so, Carl Beck wrote:

> The fact that the Committee has not exercised this power would seem to indicate either that it realizes that its investigations are not of enough importance to warrant granting immunity or that full testimony by racalcitrant witnesses would point up the weaknesses of the Committee, and perhaps raise the legal question of the pertinency of certain information to the legislative purpose and function of a Congressional investigation.

For all the commotion of the hearings and the anger of the Congressmen at being defied and often scolded by witnesses, it had been apparent for some time that the Fifth Amendment was sufficient for the Committee's purposes. The main object of virtually every public appearance lay in the appearance itself. This observation played a part in two Supreme Court decisions which determined the fates of those witnesses who were cited for withholding their cooperation from the Velde Committee—and, later, the Walter Committee—on grounds other than the Fifth Amendment. These decisions still stand as the court's major statements on the scope of the Committee on Un-American Activities.

The first decision concerned John T. Watkins, a vice president of the Farm Equipment Workers Union, who admitted in the Chicago hearings in April 1954 that although he had never been a card-carrying Communist, he had cooperated with the Party "to such a degree" between 1942 and 1947 "that some members may honestly believe that I was a member of the Party." Having conceded so much, Watkins then delivered a principled statement, framed by his attorney Joseph Rauh, in which, in contrast to those who wrapped themselves in the spacious folds of the Fifth Amendment, he bared his breast and invited the Committee to do its worst:

I would like to get one thing perfectly clear, Mr. Chairman. I am not going to plead the Fifth Amendment, but I refuse to answer certain questions that I believe are outside the proper scope of your Committee's activities. I will answer any questions which this Committee puts to me about myself. I will also answer questions about those persons whom I knew to be members of the Communist Party and whom I believe still are. I will not, however, answer any questions with respect to others with whom I associated in the past. I do not believe that any law in this country requires me to testify about persons who may in the past have been Communist Party members or otherwise engaged in Communist Party activity, but who to my best knowledge and belief have long since removed themselves from the Communist movement. I do not believe that such questions are relevant to the work of this Committee—nor do I believe that this Committee has the right to undertake the public exposure of persons because of their past activities. I may be wrong and the Committee may have this power, but until and unless a court of law so holds and directs me to answer, I must firmly refuse to discuss the political activities of my past associates."

Having singled out the most sensitive aspect of the Committee's way of life, Watkins stuck to his resolve. As names were put to him by Kunzig, he replied regarding persons he believed still belonged to the Party and refused to talk about the others, despite directives from the chairman. He was cited for contempt, indicted, found guilty in district court, and given a twelve-month suspended sentence and a fine of $500. A divided Court of Appeals ruled against his contention that the Committee had exceeded its authority with him, holding that the questions put were pertinent and that the exposure of names was incidental to its legislative purpose. The case went to the Supreme Court, which in 1957 reversed this decision.

Opponents of the Committee rejoiced over the court's ruling.[5]

[5] The court handed down three other decisions along with that on Watkins that satisfied civil libertarians. In one five California Communists convicted under the Smith Act were freed and a new trial was ordered for nine others. In a second a professor at the University of New Hampshire was upheld in his refusal to tell the state attorney general about his lectures at the university or his efforts in behalf of the Progressive Party. In the third the court ruled unanimously that Dean Acheson had violated his own regulations in 1951

The Washington *Post* viewed the decision as "a landmark in the long struggle to keep Americans free from oppressive and arbitrary governmental power," and Alan Barth told readers of *The New Republic* that "civil liberties have come back into fashion." After reviewing what he took to be the rules newly laid down for Congressional investigating committees by the court, Barth concluded: "The Un-American Activities Committee, as presently conceived, cannot possibly operate under those strictures." The applauders were misled by a combination of their desires and the Chief Justice's prose. Writing for the majority, Warren declared that "there is no Congressional power to expose for the sake of exposure," that "no inquiry is an end in itself; it must be related to, and in furtherance of, a legitimate task of the Congress." He referred to the "confusing breadth" of the Committee's "excessively broad charter." He spoke of the First, Fourth, and Fifth Amendments and described the post–World War II investigations by Congress as involving "a broad-scale intrusion into the lives and affairs of private citizens." These were all points that the Committee's critics had been making for two decades, but though his remarks would sustain the critics for years to come, the Chief Justice was merely indulging himself. Hosannas were unwarranted.

The issue decided in the Watkins case was, in fact, a narrow one; it centered on the Committee's obligation to inform a witness as to why specific questions were pertinent. In this, said the majority, Justice Clark dissenting, the Committee had clearly failed. Its authorizing resolution, the remarks of the chairman and Committee members to Watkins, and the nature of the proceedings all suffered from the "vice of vagueness." The hearing presumably had to do with legislation to deny the services of the National Labor Relations Board to Communist-controlled unions, but of the thirty names put to Watkins, seven were not connected with any union—one person operated a beauty parlor and one was a watchmaker. When Watkins

---

when he dismissed John Stewart Service, a career Foreign Service officer who came under attack during the *Amerasia* affair, for his alleged sympathy to the Chinese Communists.

questioned their pertinency, Velde replied with a reference to the Committee's franchise to look into "subversion and subversive propaganda"—a "woefully inadequate" reply, according to the court. Watkins was acquitted, then, not because of any inherent defect in the Committee, but because his right to due process had been violated when he was not adequately informed as to why the questions put to him were pertinent. In a concurring opinion, Justice Frankfurter stated the crux of the matter without Warrenesque embellishment:

> Prosecuting for contempt of Congress presupposes an adequate opportunity for the defendant to have awareness of the pertinency of the information that he has denied to Congress . . . Accordingly the actual scope of the inquiry that the Committee was authorized to conduct and the relevance of the questions to that inquiry must be shown to have been luminous at the time when asked and not left, at best, in cloudiness.

Although Representative Jackson charged that the court had rendered his Committee and the Senate Subcommittee on Internal Security "innocuous as two kittens in a cageful of rabid dogs" and David Lawrence devoted a three-page editorial in *U. S. News* to the theme that "Treason has won its biggest victory," the Watkins decision was merely procedural. The Committee would thereafter take more care in setting forth the purposes of its hearings and the pertinency of its questions, but neither the acclamations of its enemies nor the forebodings of its friends were justified.

How little justified they were was made evident in 1959, when the court handed down its ruling in the case of Lloyd Barenblatt. Barenblatt, a young psychology instructor who had taught for a term at Vassar, came before the Committee in June 1954, during one of its hearings on "Communist Methods of Infiltration (Education)," after being named as a C.P. member during his student days at the University of Michigan. In a lengthy brief, which Velde would not permit him to read but did allow into the record, Barenblatt explained that he would refuse to answer questions about his association with the Communist Party or with the Michigan Council of the Arts, Sciences and Professions on the grounds that they intruded upon his personal life and the Committee did not have the authority to ask them. He took care to state, "I do not invoke the Fifth Amendment in declining to answer," and he did not raise the question of relevance, as Watkins had two months before. His conviction of contempt in district court was affirmed by the Court of Appeals and then reaffirmed in the light of the Watkins decision. In December 1958 the case came before the Supreme Court, where the fires of hope sparked in liberal hearts by the Watkins decision were ground out. The court's decision, written by Justice Harlan—joined by Frankfurter, Clark, Whittaker, and Stewart—examined one after another the main judicial arguments that had been leveled against the Committee and dismissed them all.

Was the authorizing resolution vague? Yes, but it had been defined by the "persuasive gloss of legislative history."

Was the Committee authorized to investigate Communists in education? A teacher had no immunity from being questioned merely because he was a teacher—"an educational institution is not a constitutional sanctuary."

Were the witnesses' rights to freedom of speech and association under the First Amendment abridged by the investigation? Perhaps, but these rights had to be balanced against the need of the government to preserve its existence.

Was the witness adequately apprised of the subject of the investigation and the pertinency of the questions? Incontestably.

Would the fact that the Committee had no motive other than to expose Barenblatt as a Communist invalidate his conviction? Although "there is no Congressional power to expose for the sake of exposure," the motives of the Committee were not sufficient to vitiate an investigation if a legislative purpose was being served, as was the case here.[6]

Justice Black—with the concurrence of Warren and Douglas and partial concurrence of Brennan—delivered a ringing dissent

[6] Beck notes that although the majority used the Committee's history to add precision to its vague mandate, it declined to use that same history as a guide to its motives.

that still lifts spirits wherever the Committee's opponents gather (sometimes lifting them so high that they overlook the fact that they lost the case). The authorizing resolution, argued Black, was too vague to support any conviction for a refusal to testify. He objected to the notion of a balancing test of national security against the rights guaranteed by the First Amendment. He charged—and here Brennan joined him— that it was clear as day that "exposure and punishment is the aim of this Committee and the reason for its existence." The record in the Barenblatt case showed that there was no purpose to the investigation except "exposure purely for the sake of exposure," and Barenblatt's rights were impaired by the Committee's ability to inflict "humiliation and public shame."

So were the liberal hopes raised by the Watkins decision cast down. Whatever the Commitee's intentions and whatever its effects, it was constitutional. The majority of the court showed itself as reluctant as ever to impose standards of conduct on an arm of the Congress, and it showed itself responsive to the exigencies, vital or merely fashionable, of national security. Still, it was a near thing for the Committee. The rebuff of the Watkins case, the close decision on Barenblatt, the powerful dissent, the criticism implicit in the Harlan ruling—these had a chastening effect, at least to the extent of bringing more order into its proceedings during the late fifties and into the present decade.

But we have run ahead of our story. It was inherent in the work of the Committee—partly because of its broad mandate, partly because of the type of Congressman attracted to a career of Communist-tracking, and partly because of the strategies and manners of many witnesses—that its tone and direction were determined largely by bad tempers. (What could be expected of Clardy or Scherer when a witness took to yelling at them, as one did in Seattle, that they were "phony Congressmen" who "ought to be investigated by psychiatrists"?) During the eighty-third Congress, the Committee formalized its rules of procedure with eight unexceptionable provisions designed to prevent unilateral decisions on the part of the chairman and rash actions on the part of the staff and to protect the reputations and rights of witnesses, particularly by inviting persons named as Communists to appear, yet the hollering and the mutual recriminations did not abate. As for the Committee's habit of exposing for no other purpose than exposing, it was clear by now that there was no alternative to this but to go out of business. At the end of its term, the Velde Committee issued a report on "Neo-Fascist and Hate Groups," but its trade was frankly in Communists and there was nothing to be done with Communists except to expose them.

And then, as always, there were political requirements and temptations. Led by the indefatigable Richard Nixon, the Republicans made Communists-in-government the great issue of the 1954 elections. Senator McCarthy having received his censure in the Senate, the Communist issue was in the hands of more respectable forces, civic-minded pyromaniacs. During his thirty-three-state campaign for Republican candidates, Nixon bore down hard on Truman for losing six hundred million people to the Communists in seven years. He made much of the fact that the Communist Party and Americans for Democratic Action agreed on the desirability of recognizing Red China and on the undesirability of the Eisenhower security program and of "the Committee which brought out the evidence which convicted Alger Hiss." Three weeks before the election the Civil Service Commission, egged on by Nixon, announced that 6,926 federal employees had been dismissed or had resigned under the new security program, leaving the impression that these were all subversives appointed by Truman; a year later it was disclosed that more than 40 per cent of them had been hired after the Republican Administration took office, and most of those dismissed had not been charged with disloyalty.

The Democrats recaptured control of both chambers that November, but their margins were slim—twenty-nine seats in the House, one in the Senate—and, for most purposes, the Republican-Southern coalition remained in effective charge. For the Committee, however, it meant a seemingly more consequential change. Clardy, the ill-tempered lawyer whose affectation it had been to address people as "Witness" rather than by name, had been defeated in Michigan and was replaced on the Committee by an affable Democrat from Louisiana, Edwin E. Willis. And, of course, Harold Velde had to give over his gavel of office to Francis E. Walter. Liberal hearts leaped when a day after the election the chairman presumptive proposed nothing less than the abolition of the Un-American Activities Committee and the transfer of its functions to a subcommittee of the House Judiciary Committee which, it was understood, he would head. But the House Minority Leader Joe Martin let it be known that he would oppose such a move and the scheme was prudently dropped. "I don't propose," said Walter, "to take any step that would lend color to the phony Communist issue raised so frequently by the Republicans in the last campaign. This is not a political issue."

As 1954 came to a close, the Committee's opponents, an optimistic lot, had new grounds for optimism. Whereas every previous chairman had been a Congressional nonentity until the Committee shed its lustre upon him, Walter, who had come to the House in the year of Franklin Roosevelt's first election, was a power in his own right—chairman of the House Democratic Patronage Committee and ranking Democrat on the Judiciary Committee. He had voted against making the Un-American Activities Committee permanent, and had been named to it by loyal Democrats in an effort to protect the Administration from excessive abuse. His behavior was not altogether predictable, but he did object to several of Velde's adventures, and he was not given to joining Clardy, Jackson, and Scherer in the harassment of witnesses. Liberals held his sponsorship of the restrictive McCarran-Walter immigration law against him (on a 1952 campaign stop in Walter's district, with the Congressman on the platform, Adlai Stevenson refrained from asking for his reelection), yet they might, in time, have warmed toward a man who said out loud that he did not like Martin Dies or Joe McCarthy; who opposed the setting up of a committee to investigate tax-exempt foundations; who rebuked Velde for reporting out the Communist Control Act without taking a word of testimony on the measure—"the most flagrant attempt to jam legislation down the throat of the Committee . . . that I have ever seen"; and who declared, in reference to Velde's hiring of a new investigator a day after he resigned from the Air Force because he had passed a secret document to the Committee, that "surreptitious methods of pilfering files will not be tolerated by the Committee."[7] Perhaps a new day, more or less, was dawning.

[7] The captain referred to did not stay long with the Committee. Hired in November 1954, he was retired in January 1955, and the following August was arrested for having filched the secret document. It was a report from the Air Force's Office of Special Investigations on Jay Lovestone, the A. F. of L.'s anti-Communist specialist, who had been expelled by the Communist Party in 1929. He was of interest to the Committee because he had been named in executive testimony in 1953 by a dismissed Labor Department official as the "kingpin" who placed Communists in government. The allegation was wild, but not too wild for Clardy to use as the basis of a charge as he was separated from national life that there was "a gigantic world-wide network of Communists, previously unidentified, even now in the State, Labor and other departments."

13

★ ★ ★ ★ ★

1955-1956: The Walter Committee

THE HEARINGS of the Committee for the years 1955 through 1960 reflect changes of consequence that took place in that half decade. In 1955 the loyalty-security mania had reached its crest and was already abating. The war in Korea was over; Stalin was dead; the Hiss and Remington and Rosenberg affairs were fading into history and so was the terrible McCarthy. The Republican in the White House was scarcely vulnerable to charges of being soft on Communism and the Democrats in Congress were not of a mind to press such charges. Just as the country, uplifted upon the rhetoric of John Foster Dulles, would be slow to recognize what was happening—at least until the 1956 events in Hungary scotched the brave talk of "liberation"—so the Committee, caught in its own music, seemed to be going about its business as usual . . . but in fact business was off. In the eighty-fourth Congress, the Committee's index tells us, there were 121 days of public hearings, a large number but well below Velde's record of 178 days. The backlog was being used up, and raw materials were not so abundant. The number of hearings in the following four years added together would not reach the 1955-1956 figure.

The annual report of the Committee for 1954 asked, as usual, for more severe punishments of Communists, including an amendment to the Smith Act to make proof of C.P. membership *prima facie* evidence that an individual was conspiring to teach and advocate the overthrow of the U.S. government; it also commended the Detroit school system for removing teachers who took the Fifth Amendment because "the delivery of a student into the tutelage of a member of the Communist Party has been responsible for the destruction of thousands of American homes." But otherwise the Committee's first weeks brought a strangely bright promise to its opponents. Chairman Walter again rebuffed an effort by Congressman Martin Dies, supported by Senator Joseph McCarthy, to come back to his old neighborhood.[1] Walter then announced that the Committee was overstaffed and overpaid, and soon counsel Kunzig and other Republican appointees "resigned." (Mrs. Harold Velde, the Committee's "official reporter," resigned along with them.) Walter asked Congress for $50,000 less for the year than the $275,000 that the group had gotten in 1954, a remarkable gesture on the part of a committee chairman. One of his economy measures was to do away with the leather-bound Committee identification cards ordered by Velde, the former F.B.I. man. Reports that the Congressmen had held a two-and-a-half-hour meeting devoted mainly to the subject of fair play for witnesses, like the promises that the Senate Investigations Subcommittee and the various loyalty boards were going to pay more attention to individual rights, were greeted by liberals with hopeful hearts. BACK TO THE AMERICAN WAY, called *The New York Times.*

The overture was unfamiliar. Not so the production. Walter never promised to leash up the Committee; what he promised was to "go after Communists as Communists," instead of as members of trades, professions, or avocations, and public hearings opened on the last day of February with a familiar bang. The third scheduled witness, John T. Gojack, vice president of the United Electrical, Radio and Machine Workers of America, that favorite Committee target, had barely taken his seat before he was denouncing the hearings as a "union busting venture." Gojack, a salty Midwestern organizer, was in fine fettle. He called the rival I.U.E.–C.I.O. "the only McCarthyite union in America," and wrote off the witnessess who

[1] McCarthy devoted part of a speech to Dies: "The leadership of the Democratic Party said, 'We won't put you on that Committee,' because they knew that Martin Dies wouldn't trifle with Communists. It was part of the continued effort to break Martin Dies."

had testified against him as two paid liars and one paid lunatic, but he declined to speak of the non-Communist affidavits he had signed and which were required of union officials by the Taft-Hartley Act. After lambasting the Committee for most of a morning, he complained to Representative Scherer, "You have been extremely provocative toward me. You have tried to provoke me into arguments here."

Gojack's only unorthodox act was to take the First Amendment rather than the Fifth when asked if he was a Communist at the moment in 1949 when the U.E. was expelled by the C.I.O., on the grounds that the Committee did not have the right to put such questions to him. He was cited for contempt without delay, but it would be more than eleven years before his case would be settled by the courts. His first conviction for contempt was thrown out by the Supreme Court in 1962 because his indictment had failed to specify the subject under inquiry by the Committee. A few months later he was reindicted for refusing to answer six questions, the first of which was, "Are you a member of the Communist Party?" He was found guilty and sentenced to three months' imprisonment and a fine of $200. The Court of Appeals upheld the conviction, but in June 1966 a unanimous Supreme Court voided it.

The American Civil Liberties Union, which filed a petition with the court in the case, hoped that the justices would take the opportunity to review the question of the Committee's constitutionality, and reverse its 1959 Barenblatt decision. The A.C.L.U. argued that since the world conditions which had led the court to choose national security over individual rights in 1959 had changed, the justification for invading the First Amendment rights of witnesses no longer existed. Justice Black agreed with the A.C.L.U., but the majority of the court, in a reprise of the Watkins decision, made their ruling on narrower grounds. The "question under inquiry," wrote Justice Fortas, was neither properly authorized nor specifically stated, and its purpose was not clearly understood even by members of the subcommittee, whose jurisdiction, moreover, had not been properly defined. Once again the high court cuffed the Committee but resisted knocking it flat.

A few weeks after the Gojack hearings there occurred a political sensation which, though not strictly Committee business, belongs in this history for what it tells about Francis Walter and his altered course in the last decade of his career from a responsible and generally respected legislator to a man obsessed.

The undisguised intent of the McCarran-Walter Immigration Law of 1952, based as it was on a system of national origins quotas for admitting immigrants, was to keep Eastern and Southern Europeans and Asians of all sorts out of the country. Thus, the law, passed over Mr. Truman's veto when security was the national bugbear, constituted a considerable political handicap in large cities filled with Italians, Poles and Slavs, whose kinsmen in the suffering Old World were being frankly discriminated against; and during the 1952 election both presidential candidates promised to do something about it. Mr. Eisenhower redeemed this promise with the Refugee Relief Act of 1953, which was supposed to admit more than 200,000 non-quota immigrants by the end of 1956. It was a grudging piece of legislation, bound in with requirements that each refugee prove that a job and home awaited him here, and capped with the provision that the good work be administered by the director of the State Department's Bureau of Security and Consular Affairs, a former F.B.I. man named R. W. Scott McLeod, whose first impulse upon seeing huddled masses was to search them. McLeod, in debt to Senator McCarthy for his job, participated in the demoralization of the State Department in the fifties. So restrictive was the legislation and so fastidious was the administrator that by the end of 1954 only a minute percentage of the designated number of refugees had been granted entry, and of these the overwhelming majority, fortunately for them, had relatives in this country.

Pressed by liberal and minority groups, as well as by G.O.P. politicos in the big cities, to show more enthusiasm for carrying out the Administration's own law, the State Department in January 1956 hired Edward Corsi to be special advisor to the Secretary of State on refugee and immigration matters. It was an appointment that pleased both those who were worried

about votes and those who were worried about people. Corsi
was a prominent New York Republican who had been Commissioner of Immigration under both Hoover and Roosevelt.
An immigrant himself, having been brought here at the age
of ten, he was full of ideas for letting non-Anglo-Saxons onto
these shores. The State Department, more enamored of Corsi's
image than of anything he might actually recommend, sent
him off on a trip to Europe (accompanied by a former Texas
ranger who filed confidential reports with McLeod) and trusted
he would enjoy himself and not prove troublesome. But they
reckoned neither on Corsi's humanitarian passions nor on the
paternal feelings of Francis Walter for his immigration bill.
Corsi had been publicly critical of the McCarran-Walter law
before coming to Washington and in Walter's view that was
sufficient cause not only to declare him unfit for his new post
but also to question his loyalty. Relying on the Committee's
files, Walter attacked Corsi for having belonged to a few
Communist-front organizations in the nineteen-thirties, affiliations which Corsi denied and which Walter did not attempt
to substantiate. Instead, in the middle of March, he sent a
confidential letter to Secretary of State Dulles which took Corsi
to task for "having expressed contumacious disdain and contempt" for the laws he was supposed to be administering and
again referred to "Mr. Corsi's association with highly objectionable groups and organizations branded as subversive by the
attorney general and his neglect to resign from such organizations after their true nature had become a matter of common
knowledge . . ." These charges were flimsy, but Dulles could
not lightly disregard a complaint from the chairman of the
House Judiciary Subcommittee on Immigration Laws. Corsi
had known Dulles and Attorney General Brownell, both New
York Republicans, for years, but, as he later complained, "after
Walter made his unfounded charges, nobody spoke out. Nobody was around. I've never felt so much a stranger."

In April, Corsi, who had recently rented a house in Arlington
for six months, was belatedly informed that his appointment
had been a temporary one; now that his ninety days were
almost up, he was presented with the opportunity of "making

a survey with reference to the possibilities of land settlement in Latin America and other areas." A variety of reasons were advanced for exiling Corsi to exotic places—the same Dulles who had welcomed him in January as "the best qualified" man in the country to break the immigration logjam now found him unqualified because he was not a good administrator—but the credit belonged entirely to Francis Walter. If J. Parnell Thomas or Harold Velde had done this kind of job on Corsi, there would have been no cause for surprise, but Walter's career had been of a distinctly different sort. Up until his sponsorship of the immigration bill, he been no darling of the right wing, but he had invested so much of himself in that bill and been so hurt and angered by the outcry against him within the party he had served for so many years that after 1952 anyone who criticized his law was marked in his mind as a probable subversive and could be fought on that premise. The conduct of the Un-American Activities Committee under his chairmanship becomes less mystifying if we allow that the same man who disdained Dies and McCarthy could for the last ten years of his life nourish and exercise a powerful grudge against the whole liberal community.

Despite the attentions of the Messrs. Scherer and Jackson,[2] the Committee's record in the eighty-fourth Congress was distinguished by unusual courtesy and coherence. The stuff of the proceedings, however, was much the same as it had been for the past few years. Like a TV format come to weary middle age, the operations settled into the established informant–Fifth Amendment pattern. A policewoman from Brook-

---

[2] Both Congressmen continued to be irritated by the use to which the Fifth Amendment was being put, and could be counted on to dispute a witness' right to the Fifth, to press subcommittee chairmen to demand answers to their questions, and to threaten contempt proceedings. During hearings in Los Angeles Jackson asked a former Communist whether she knew anyone named Francik Mizokljyk, "a Pole, I imagine." When the witness pleaded the Fifth, as she had been doing all along, Jackson announced that the name was totally fictitious; he had made it up to demonstrate that the self-incrimination clause was being used in response to questions that could not possibly incriminate anyone. He made his point, but only at the cost of revealing a frivolous attitude toward entrapping a witness before a Congressional committee. Scherer performed the same trick on a Newark paperhanger in September 1958; he used the name Joseph Stepovich, but refrained from identifying him as a Pole.

lyn gave several hundred names of Party members she had known in Flatbush in the nineteen-forties. The Committee to Secure Justice for the Rosenbergs, peace organizations in several cities, and a half dozen New York State summer camps were shown to be weighted with Communists. Two days were given over to "Attempts at Subversion and Espionage by Diplomatic Personnel"—which had to do with the peculiar activities of a man from the Soviet Embassy named Mikheev in openly approaching three government employees for information that was not classified. He was either an honest researcher or a delightfully inept spy. In either case, the Committee's script did not measure up to its title. And, in another hearing, former Representative Jerry J. O'Connell, a Montana Democrat who had been mentioned in friendly testimony as an accomplice of the Communists, conceded to the Committee that he had participated in quite an array of front organizations. In speaking of his own political philosophy, O'Connell, a hard-working fellow traveler, showed how much he owed to the pat phrases of the thirties: "I can be a non-Communist, and yet not anti-Communist, just like I can be a Democrat and yet not an anti-Republican."

Not all of the hearings were amiable. More than a thousand U.E. members demonstrated in front of the Newark hotel where Representatives Scherer and Doyle, described by the picketers as "a bunch of rats," were staying when they opened another investigation of Communist control of a big U.E. local. Events inside the hearing room, too, were stormy. The union organizers and business agents named as Communists by an unidentified F.B.I. source, as well as by former colleagues, were loud and insulting, given to expostulating on the subject of stool pigeons and union busters and fascists, but shy about their own activities. "Mr. Chairman, I say again that if you prefer to believe the word of stool pigeons and paid informers and other assorted finks, that is okay with me, except I will stand on the privilege of the Fifth Amendment." It was an ungallant display which left a clear impression that the stool pigeons, informers and finks were telling the truth about the U.E. officials. Three Newark teachers who took the Fifth were fired and turned to the courts for redress, and, as a result of the Committee's visit, the Newark City Council unanimously adopted a loyalty oath for all city employees.

Hearings in Los Angeles aimed at a rebellious Musicians Union local were timed to assist the national union beat down the rebels. Left-wing union officials were also called up in Seattle and Denver, and Communist influence in the Young Progressives of America, the Civil Rights Congress, and the Labor Youth League were aired in Milwaukee, where it was disclosed that two undercover F.B.I. informants had been conscientiously including one another in their reports to the home office. As the number of C.P. members declined, the proportions of delegates from the F.B.I. naturally increased, and in North Carolina, too, a pair of informants dutifully exposed one another for the Congressmen's benefit.

The Committee's files, which John Rankin had gone to such lengths to preserve from the Potomac River, were put to notable, if not novel, use during the eighty-fourth Congress. They were employed by Southerners against the civil-rights movement, which had gained great momentum with the Supreme Court school integration decision of 1954. In February 1956, States' Rights activists in Louisiana publicized the alleged Communist-front associations of Hulan Jack, Manhattan borough president and a Negro, when he visited New Orleans to participate in a Catholic interracial program. The information had been released by the Committee's staff director to Senator James O. Eastland of Mississippi, who courteously passed it on to his neighbors in Louisiana.

A few weeks later, as a prelude to a large civil rights march on Washington, Representative E. C. Gathings of Arkansas read into the Congressional Record the Committee's citations for leaders of the National Association for the Advancement of Colored People. Those listed included Roy Wilkins, A. Philip Randolph, Ralph Bunche, Robert Weaver, Morris Ernst, John Haynes Holmes—quite a distinguished roll. Each name was preceded by a disclaimer:

> The public record, files and publications of this Committee contain the following information concerning the subject individual.

This report should not be construed as representing the results of an investigation by or findings of this Committee. It should be noted that the individual is not necessarily a Communist, a Communist sympathizer or a fellow-traveller unless otherwise indicated.

Anyone who had followed the careers of most of the persons listed knew that although their battles in the Negro's cause brought them into alliance with Communists now and then, they were neither Party members nor facsimiles. By presenting the citations straight, without a critical gloss, and by notifying the Congress that 44.1 per cent of the N.A.A.C.P. leaders had been cited by the Un-American Activities Committee (a calculation that included Eric Johnston who had two "citations" to his name—both involving his position with the Motion Picture Producers Association at the time of the 1947 Hollywood hearings), Gathings sought to stigmatize the entire civil rights movement.[3] He was congratulated for his presentation by several Southern colleagues.

Succumbing again to the allure of show business, the staff of the Velde Committee had rounded up the names of another batch of Broadway people whom it was left to the Walter Committee to herd into the public corral. In July 1955 the news got out that about two dozen persons—most of them actors, with a scattering of other occupations—had been subpoenaed for August hearings at the U.S. Court House on Foley Square. Walter, who had begun his tenure as chairman with a vow not to investigate specific trades or professions, now promised to cover the "broad field" of entertainment in New York City. Pressed to explain the purpose of the investigation, he referred vaguely to Communist infiltration of the entertainment unions and to the filling of Communist coffers with Broadway salary checks, but neither line was pursued. Most of the witnesses were several steps below star rank and whatever their inclinations they could hardly have done much to keep the

[3] This was not the last time that Gathings would deliver this recital. After he read the citations into the Congressional Record again in 1963 during the debate on civil rights legislation, the Committee's staff director, Francis J. McNamara, told me, "We can't control what Congressmen do with the material."

Communist Party afloat. As for the unions, they had some time
since shaken off the remnants of Communist influence, and
a few days before the start of hearings, the American Federation of Television and Radio Artists authorized its local units
to take disciplinary measures against any member who failed
to answer questions before a Congressional committee. A recalcitrant performer might be fined, censured, suspended, or
expelled on the charge of conduct prejudicial to the welfare
of the union. A.F.T.R.A. had previously condemned the blacklisting organization which called itself AWARE for circulating
lists of entertainment figures named in reports of the Un-
American Activities Committee, but by this vote the union
put itself on the side of those who held that resort to the Fifth
Amendment was sufficient reason to deprive a man or woman
of even the most innocent livelihood.

But for the cloud of the blacklist, the subcommittee's few
August days in New York would have been merely frivolous.
The blacklisters, however, went all out to turn it into an occasion. Representatives Walter, Willis, and Scherer were welcomed to New York by a statement signed by such anti-
Communist warriors as George Sokolsky, Eugene Lyons, Victor
Lasky, Manning Johnson, and Vincent Hartnett, who was then
making a living as a compiler of dossiers on show business
personalities. He called himself a "talent consultant" and
charged $5 a head for short reports, $20 for long reports. On
the evening of the first day of hearings Walter was guest of
honor at a rally, put on by a group called Alliance, Inc., Archibald B. Roosevelt presiding. "Is Joe McCarthy out of business?"
asked Archibald Roosevelt, and the audience yelled back,
"No!" There Walter, not entirely comfortable in the McCarthy
mantle, said that he hoped theatrical employers would be
"traditionally American and withhold judgment until they
know what all the facts are." (The American Civil Liberties
Union made its own contribution to the art of the pro forma
statement when it called on the Committee to confine its
questioning "strictly to conspiratorial acts.")

In its four days at the courthouse, which were honored by
visits from Bernard Baruch and Hamilton Fish and during

which the hiring of Elizabeth Bentley as Committee consultant was announced, the Committee heard twenty-three witnesses, most of whom had previously been mentioned by Martin Berkeley, Elia Kazan, Lee J. Cobb, or Jerome Robbins or who were in AWARE's bad books. One young man, briefly exposed to the C.P.'s Broadway branch in the forties, cooperated with the Committee and was assured by Walter that in the cold war his contribution might be equal to that of a division of infantry. The other witnesses declined to answer the critical questions; eighteen of them took the Fifth Amendment; one took the First Amendment; three took no amendments. A few were obnoxious in the hard-line style; their main objection to the blacklist seemed to be that it was not directed aaginst people they didn't like, such as Kazan and Cobb. (Before the anti-Communists found it in their power to blacklist Communists, the Communists did what they could to keep anti-Communists from working. But they were not nearly so effective at it.) "Is this the Kazan that signed the contract for $500,000 on the day after he gave names to this Committee?" asked a producer who had been dropped by C.B.S. in 1951 upon being mentioned as a candidate for a Committee subpoena. "Would you sell your brothers for $500,000?" But for the most part the hearings were placid. The most serious offense revealed in the professional lives of the accused had to do with a skit presented at a New York State summer camp by Elliot Sullivan, an actor who had been featured in some eighty movies and seventy-five radio shows before being set down in the blacklister's bible, *Red Channels*. The skit had to do with two sneaky-looking fellows selling the Bill of Rights to each other; after the sales were completed, they both revealed themselves as F.B.I. agents and arrested one another. The Congressmen felt that this was a insult to the Bill of Rights since the sale price was only one dollar.

Sullivan, who two weeks earlier had taken the Fifth Amendment before the Committee, now stood on the First Amendment and was duly cited for contempt along with an actor named George Tyne, who questioned the pertinency of his alleged Communist connections to the Committee's work, and the folk singer Pete Seeger, bard of the Wallace movement and a popular figure in Communist-front festivities. Seeger put on a folksy manner in the witness chair, presenting himself as a "banjo-picker" who knew nothing of Communists, but just went around the world making the common people happy with his songs. But when the usual questions were put to him, he dropped the stage business and objected calmly and succinctly to the intrusion on his privacy: "I am not going to answer any questions as to my associations, my philosophical or religious beliefs, or how I voted in any elections or any of these private affairs. I think they are very improper questions for any American to be asked, especially under such compulsion as this."[4]

Tyne and Sullivan were acquitted of contempt in 1961, when the district court found their indictments "fatally defective" because the government had not submitted the Committee's resolution ordering the hearing. Seeger was sentenced to a year in prison—after a trial in which Chairman Walter was put on the stand—but in 1962 the Court of Appeals unanimously reversed the conviction on the grounds that *his* indictment was defective too, for much the same reason. Seeger's indictment had included the Committee's authorization to its clerk to undertake the entertainment investigation, but had omitted specific authorization for the subcommittee hearings. The judges, responding to the government's contention that this omisison was a "hypertechnical" point, took a high road:

> A defendant, faced with possible loss of liberty, should not at the commencement of the prosecution, be made to guess whether the inquiring body has power to exact his testimony . . . We are not inclined to dismiss lightly claims of constitutional stature because they are asserted by one who may appear to be unworthy of sympathy. Once we embark upon shortcuts by creating a category of the "obviously guilty" whose rights are denied, we run the risk that the circle of the unprotected will grow.

[4] Despite the surge of popularity of folk singing in the late nineteen-fifties and early sixties, the talented Seeger was not seen on network television between 1950 and 1967. In September 1967, the producers of the Smothers Brothers Comedy Hour and executives at C.B.S. judged that the weather had cleared sufficiently to hire him. So, finally, he appeared, but was not permitted to sing a song critical of President Johnson.

Nevertheless, for all the fine language, the Committee had unquestionably authorized the Seeger hearings, and the court's decision did indeed rest on a technicality that saved the judges from confronting Seeger's claim that his constitutional rights had been violated.

Although there was not much in the way of an immediate future for the subpoenaed entertainers in the movies, television, or radio, most of them would continue to find theater work. (Zero Mostel, the outstanding talent among those called up in August, could not make it in from California owing to professional commitments and so did not take his Fifth Amendment until October.) Broadway, relatively free of political censorship and dependent on a small, liberal, big-city clientele, was not susceptible to the pressures that could put a local movie house out of business or give a TV sponsor the shakes, and off-Broadway liked nothing better than to have its little-noticed productions picketed. Still, the employment opportunities of entertainers who had been marked down as Communists were diminished and there were protests, demonstrations, and exposés on the left against the existence of a show-business blacklist watched over by kindred spirits of Joe McCarthy. The Committee's majority, including the chairman, took these flurries personally and, in the spring of 1956, with the publication of a report on blacklisting by the Fund for the Republic, found a means of replying to them.

The Fund for the Republic, run by the erstwhile head of the University of Chicago, Robert M. Hutchins, had been set up by the Ford Foundation in 1951 to support activities "directed toward the elimination of restrictions on freedom of thought, inquiry and expression in the United States." Since 1953, when it was turned loose and became, in Hutchins's phrase, "a wholly disavowed subsidiary of the Ford Foundation," with fifteen million dollars to keep it going, it had directed its energies against everything that the Committee on Un-American Activities considered American. Its very first act was to give $25,000 to the American Bar Association for a study of Congressional investigating committees. It distributed works by critics of the investigations such as Telford Taylor, Alan Barth, and Dean

Griswold[5] and films of the impressive Ed Murrow–J. Robert Oppenheimer TV interview; it financed studies of the effects on individual rights of the federal security program; it gave $150,000 to the American Friends Service Committee for use in legal cases "to strengthen the right to freedom of conscience," $240,000 to the Southern Regional Council for "education in intergroup relations in twelve states," and $5,000 to a Quaker group in Pennsylvania for hiring a librarian who had invoked the Fifth Amendment. In 1955 it produced a *Bibliography of the Communist Program in the United States* which at once had to be revised because of charges from scholars of "inexcusable sloppiness," "distortion by omission," and a tendency to discriminate against sophisticated anti-Communist writers like Arthur Koestler, Dwight Macdonald, Max Eastman, and Bertram Wolfe, while including trivial material from the Party press. Hutchins, who had a reputation as a baiter of boobs to maintain, said in public, "I wouldn't hesitate to hire a Communist for a job he was qualified to do provided I was in a position to see that he did it"—and, indeed, the Fund had hired a newspaperman after he took the Fifth before a Senate committee.

This record was sufficient to bring down attacks from the American Legion, whose national commander charged that the Fund was trying to "persuade Americans that Communism is not and never has been a serious threat to the United States," from senators like John Bricker and representatives like B. Carroll Reece, and from Fulton Lewis, Jr., who called it "an extensive ideological political propaganda organization, promoting the doctrines of the Americans for Democratic Action and all points to the left of that, fighting the security programs by which the federal government tries to protect itself against every infiltration, fighting also the Congressional investigators who seek to expose Communists and the methods the Communists have used in the past to infiltrate our government up to the very highest level." In June of 1956 Francis Walter,

---

[5] The Fund made no pretense of objectivity in these matters. It put out 35,000 copies of the Griswold book, *The Fifth Amendment Today*, and only 1,000 copies of an effective rebuttal by C. Dickerman Williams.

who suspected the Fund's directors of lobbying for repeal of his immigration law, announced that he intended to investigate the body, with a view to answering the question, "Is this foundation, with its vast reservoir of funds and power a friend or foe in the nation's death struggle against the Communist conspiracy?" Two weeks later Walter said the investigation was being postponed, but in July it suddenly came to life again.

The largest grant allotted by the Fund in its first years was $300,000 for "an account of Communist influence in major segments of U. S. society," and one of the studies undertaken was of "Blacklisting in Private Industry." In context, "industry" meant the entertainment industry, and the end of June 1956 saw the publication of a two-volume *Report on Blacklisting* written by John Cogley, former executive editor of *Commonweal*. It charged that blacklisting had become an institution in movies, radio, and television, that hundreds of persons were being denied employment because of their Communist associations, and that industry leaders had given over responsibility for judging accused individuals to the very people who had promoted the blacklist in the first place. Executives in Hollywood deferred to the American Legion, while the producers, advertising agencies, and sponsors of radio and TV shows were guided by *Red Channels*—a list of alleged Communists in entertainment put out by three former F.B.I. operatives in 1950—and AWARE, formed in 1953 to "combat the Communist conspiracy in entertainment communications," whose main function was to issue bulletins on the backgrounds of performers. The Cogley report also told how several Communist-hunters, led by the columnist George Sokolsky and the former Hollywood A. F. of L. leader Roy Brewer, were engaged in a "rehabilitation" campaign for those unjustly accused or truly repentant—a mission which some of their allies frowned upon as soft on sinners. *Report on Blacklisting* was not a model of sound journalism. It made extensive use of anonymous informants—fearful members of a frightened industry;[6] printed

---

[6] Cogley later complained that those in the industry who had protested bitterly to him of blacklisting when assured of anonymity did not step forward to say a word in support of his report when it came under attack.

charges of vigilante activities without in all cases taking pains to check with the alleged vigilantes; and relied heavily on tales of individual injustice—mistaken identity and the like— instead of coming to grips with the central issue of whether it was justifiable to keep even a thrice-proven Communist out of a job that had nothing to do with the national security. Yet with these defects, this was by far the best report done up to that time on a subject that few knowing people in Hollywood or New York cared to talk about for publication. A blacklist there indubitably was, and industry leaders, true to their careers, had given it into the charge of zealots and con men; the masters of the mass media had entangled them-selves in loyalty oaths, security checks, and clearance procedures that were debasing to the accused and sources of temptation to their accusers.

Protests against Cogley's work were raised as soon as it was published. The Committee was on excellent terms with the American Legion and with AWARE, and Walter did not have to read the report to know that he disagreed with it on two counts. First, he denied there was any such thing as a blacklist and second, he wanted all Communists driven out of films, theater, radio, television, and, if feasible, out of the country. On July 10 he opened his "Investigation of So-Called 'Blacklisting' in Entertainment Industry—Report of the Fund for the Republic, Inc." The first witness was John Cogley, in 1953 a "personal assistant" to Robert Hutchins at the Fund for the Republic. He had been subpoenaed to appear instead of merely being invited, and from the outset it was evident that Walter had no great interest in the subject of blacklisting, but a driving desire to blacken Cogley's report and, through that, the Fund and all its works. The interrogation was conducted by Richard Arens, formerly with the Senate Internal Security Subcommittee, who had taken over as Committee staff director in May. Spurning the forms of objectivity, he attacked at once, beginning with a quotation from the conservative Catholic publication, *The Tablet*, to the effect that the liberal Catholic publication, *Commonweal*, was not Catholic at all. He brought two major charges against Cogley's report: first, that it had been assembled by persons of suspect background and second, that it did not give the Communist affiliations of the "sad cases" which it reported—"Did you at any place in your treatise list the Communist-front record of Larry Adler and of Paul Draper, which is as long as two arms?" In a sense, Cogley had brought this kind of attack on himself for basing his argument on cases of mistaken identity rather than granting at once that most of the blacklistees were or had been Communists (or had done their darndest to pass as such), and arguing against the black-list even in their desperate cases. As to the first charge, Arens was particularly unfortunate in the persons he picked out as Communist sympathizers. One was Dr. Maria Jahoda, a social scientist who had belonged to the Socialist Democratic Party in Austria before coming to this country in 1945 ("only in 1945," was the way Arens put it and he wanted to know whether Cogley had checked with the F.B.I. before hiring her); she had contributed an interesting paper on the diffi-culties encountered by *anti*-Communists in radio and television. Another was Paul Jacobs, who had belonged to the Young Communist League twenty years before and had taken part in the wars against Stalinists in labor unions and elsewhere ever since. And a third was Michael Harrington, a proudly confessed socialist. "You, of course, are aware of the fact," said Arens to Cogley, "that Lenin, the key philosopher of Communism, had said socialism is only one transition toward Communism." Doyle and Moulder showed some signs of sym-pathy for Cogley during his interrogation, but were even less effectual than usual.

The next day Arnold Forster, counsel of B'nai Brith's Anti-Defamation League and a major source of Cogley's informa-tion, told how he had prevailed upon influential right-wingers to help "rehabilitate" some unfortunates. Then came an honor guard of the country's preeminent blacklisters. James F. O'Neil of the American Legion said that blacklisting was reprehensible but that persons identified with the Communist apparatus should not be employed in the entertainment industry. Vincent W. Hartnett, the "talent consultant," and Paul R. Milton, a founder of AWARE, Inc., and Godfrey P. Schmidt, AWARE's president, and Roy M. Brewer, who had by now moved from union leader to industry executive, and Francis J. McNamara —formerly with the anti-Communist organ, *Counterattack,* at the time of his appearance director of the American Sovereignty Campaign of the Veterans of Foreign Wars, and today director of the Committee on Un-American Activities—agreed with O'Neil. McNamara said he liked to think of his work as similar to that of Dun & Bradstreet—handing out credit ratings on people—and nobody called Dun & Bradstreet a blacklisting outfit. These witnesses were treated with surpassing deference; they were permitted to say whatever they wished at their own length, and after listening to them Walter announced what he might have announced before the hearings began, that in his view "the Fund for the Republic report is a partisan, biased attack on all persons and organizations who are sincerely and patriotically concerned in ridding the movie industry and radio and television of Communists and Communist sympathizers."

Walter had promised that some of the allegedly blacklisted performers would be called to testify, and two—Gale Sondergaard and Jack Gilford—were subpoenaed. The careers of both had been buffeted by winds from the right, but instead of questioning them about their experiences, Arens put them, once again, through the Fifth Amendment ritual. He used them not for information about the blacklist but to drive home the point that those who complained of being blacklisted were in fact Communists. That, in the minds of Walter, Arens, Jackson, Scherer, and their friends among the veterans, was sufficient cause for denial of employment not only in entertainment but virtually anywhere—and it was the central point at issue in the Committee's sudden foray, a week after Cogley's appearance, into the Fund for the Republic's award of $5,000 to the Plymouth Monthly Meeting, whose library committee had hired a former Communist. "The Committee wishes to know," said Walter at the outset, "more about the factors which prompted the Fund for the Republic to consider the retention of a Communist a defense of 'democratic principles' worth $5,000 of its tax-exempt money."

This one-day hearing opened with the researcher who had looked into the case for the Fund. Arens directed his questions at showing that she had interviewed in the main persons favorable to the retention of Mrs. Mary Knowles, who had been having trouble finding a job since being named as a former Communist by Herbert Philbrick and taking the Fifth Amendment. The library committee of the Quaker Meeting hired her upon her assurance that she had not been a member of a subversive organization since 1947, and Arens brought forward four prominent residents who wanted Mrs. Knowles removed. The last witness, received more coolly than the four, was a member of the library committee who had voted to hire her. Such was the dissension among the Friends, whipped up by a band called Americans Alerted,[7] that the $5,000 gift was still being held in escrow, and several major benefactors of the library had withdrawn their support. Arens established the point that the Fund's award had fed controversy in Plymouth. But it was a small accomplishment for the director since the gift had been frankly designed to bolster resistance to the sentiment, assiduously promoted by his Committee, against giving aid, comfort, or sustenance to politically abhorrent persons.

Chairman Walter's justification for troubling himself over the case of a small-town librarian and a report on blacklisting was that the Fund for the Republic, being a tax-exempt operation, could not lightly spend its money on causes which he did not deem to be in the soundest interests of the United States. Although foundations were the province of another Congressional committee, the rationale was not absurd; liberal groups have often complained of the uses to which rightwingers like H. L. Hunt have put their tax-exempt money, the nub of the argument being that one man's education is another man's propaganda. But despite repeated requests for a full hearing from the Fund's prestigious directors—Paul G. Hoffman, John Lord O'Brien, Elmo Roper, and James D. Zellerbach

---

[7] Americans Alerted sent out flyers of this sort: "Did you also know that Mrs. Knowles is by no means the only Security Risk working or living in this immediate neighborhood? That Plymouth-Whitemarsh has been and still is being infiltrated?"

among others—and promises by Walter that there would be such a hearing for "this multi-million dollar propaganda machine which enjoys tax exemption," the Committee never picked up the challenge of an open confrontation. It chose instead the tactic of hit-and-run assault and verdict by press release.

A better ordered, more solidly fleshed set of hearings began in December 1955, when Herbert Fuchs, a former attorney for the National Labor Relations Board, told the Committee in public session what he had previously told it in executive session—that during most of his years with the government, from 1937 to 1948, he had been a participant in Communist cells made up of N.L.R.B. lawyers and other federal employees. Fuchs came to public attention in September 1955, midway between his executive testimony and his open hearing, when it was announced that he was being dropped from the law faculty of American University, in Washington, D. C., where he had been teaching since 1949. At his first meeting with the Committee in June, Fuchs refused to testify about others, whereupon the president of the university assured him of support. In July he changed his mind, named names, and was given a choice by the president of suspension or a leave of absence, both preliminary to the non-renewal of his contract. Representative Willis took note of the fact that American University was a Methodist institution in whose policies Bishop Oxnam had a substantial hand, and implied that the bishop was seeking to penalize Fuchs for cooperating with the Committee. The university, in an indefensible position, did not trouble to defend itself. When the ultimatum became known, Fuchs found himself championed by a peculiar alliance of Communist-hunters and civil libertarians, which included Representative Walter and Reinhold Niebuhr, Representative Scherer and the American Civil Liberties Union, the American Committee for Cultural Freedom and the *Saturday Evening Post*. Virtually the only groups that did not wear Fuchs's colors were those that had been loudest in their complaints over the firings of teachers who had refused to cooperate with Congressional committees.

During the hearings on federally employed Communists that followed Fuchs's testimony, the Emergency Civil Liberties Committee, several of whose more eminent supporters were themselves in process of taking the Fifth Amendment, sent a petition to the House of Representatives calling the investigation "illegal, invalid and contrary to the Committee's enabling resolution." The phrasing was standard but hardly compelling since the Committee, for a change, was actually looking into the activities of Communists in government agencies, a job that was historically within its compass if anything was.

Fuchs made a careful and believable witness. Among the former government employees he named were seventeen attorneys who, he said, had been in his Communist group at the N.L.R.B.—a fair number out of a legal review staff that rarely went above 115 and was sometimes as low as twenty-five. As the hearings proceeded, two of the persons named corroborated Fuchs's testimony and a third said he had socialized with the group but had never belonged to the Party; only one of the lawyers, a woman, denied the accusations. The others called up all took the Fifth Amendment.[8] Among these were two familiar faces, Edwin S. Smith, member of the N.L.R.B. until 1941, and Nathan Witt, the board's secretary for most of Smith's tenure and an intimate of Lee Pressman's before the Korean War came between them. By 1956 Edwin Smith, who had been indignant when charged with leftist leanings by Martin Dies, was a registered agent of the Soviet Union, in the trade of selling photographs of the U.S.S.R. and the People's Democracies to United States publications; he had already pleaded self-incrimination before a Senate committee.

The N.L.R.B. hearings followed accusations by Senator

[8] Most of those who pleaded the Fifth were associated with the National Lawyers Guild. Walter, who wanted to bar lawyers from representing witnesses before the Committee unless they swore they were neither Communists nor former Communists, had to endure hearing attorneys David Rein and Frank Donner take the Fifth and then having them reappear alongside clients in the hearing room. When some weeks later Leonard Boudin, an outstanding counsel for unfriendly witnesses, was called up and angrily denied ever having been a Party member, Walter's small supply of patience gave out and he demanded that the attorney be investigated for perjury—though there was no evidence against Boudin except his legal specialty. In 1960 Boudin was still representing witnesses and Walter was still calling him a Communist.

McCarthy that the agency was "literally honeycombed" with promoters of Communist movements; the board, now with a Republican majority, responded by putting three hundred more jobs into the "sensitive" category, which required F.B.I. clearance. Arens attempted in his questioning to draw a picture of Nathan Witt bringing his Communist protégés into the N.L.R.B. for the purpose of subverting the American labor movement. He demanded to know whether any "Communist organization masquarading as a labor union" was denied bargaining rights by the N.L.R.B. in the thirties, and had to be reminded that there was nothing in the Wagner Act damning Communist unions. The N.L.R.B. had previously been looked into by a special committee under Representative Howard Smith in 1940 and by a saner Senate committee in 1953, where evidence was adduced that Witt and Smith went out of their way to be of service to Lee Pressman and Harry Bridges. They were severely criticized by their N.L.R.B. colleagues and knowledgeable persons in the labor movement, and eventually removed. But the picture was not so simple as Arens would have liked.

As Fuchs did his best to explain, Communists in the thirties were heart and soul in favor of the Wagner Act and it required no dissimulation on their part to carry out its provisions with zeal: ". . . we told ourselves and were told that to be good Communists at the National Labor Relations Board the better job we did for the board and for the government, that was it." When asked whether decisions had been loaded in favor of Communist unions, Fuchs referred Arens to the records of twenty years past—a laborious pursuit which counsel did not undertake—and avowed, to Arens's incredulity, that the Communists in the N.L.R.B. were not faking their official duties. The point that Fuchs tried to get across was one the Committee always had difficulty in crediting: that in the nineteen-thirties, Alger Hiss notwithstanding, there was no question of divided loyalties for the majority of Communists in government. They were mainly talkers, not couriers, and they needed no directives from Moscow on how to conduct their professional duties. They were young, idealistic, ambitious, and they believed in the New Deal. Earl Latham points out what single-minded hunters of conspiracy invariably overlooked—"that there was a motion and life in the government service that was quite independent of any contrivance, responding to the restlessness of people interested in promotions, increases within grade, new opportunities, more challenging responsibilities, more interesting jobs; and responding also to the continuous creation of new agencies, and therefore of new chances of interesting and financially rewarding employment." Which is no more than to say what by the mid-fifties it was difficult to remember—that the Communists in government in the thirties were subject to all the minor vices common to ambitious young bureaucrats, and also partook of their virtues.

In the spring of 1956, the Committee turned to a subject close to the chairman's troubled heart. Complementing his anxiety over undesirable foreigners coming to this country was an annoyance that undesirable Americans should be able to leave it from time to time. He had been offended lately by a Court of Appeals decision that took from the State Department's Passport Office some of the arbitrary powers (such as denying passports without a hearing) it had exercised upon Americans wishing to travel abroad, and he had introduced a bill to restore to the Secretary of State power to prohibit passports to Communists and their sympathizers and to deny rejected applicants access to evidence against them that might compromise investigative sources. Meanwhile, he called upon Mr. Dulles simply to refuse passports to any persons against whom there was "adverse security information"—which would have meant defying the courts. Passport legislation was, strictly speaking, in the purview of the House Judiciary Committee, but Walter sought to aid his cause by producing before the Committee on Un-American Activities a number of persons who, he said, had participated in a "skillfully organized Communist passport conspiracy by which Party members and fellow travelers are enlisted to travel abroad in the service of Soviet propaganda and subversion." The reference was to voyagers who, defying government injunctions to shun Com-

munist lands, wound up at youth conferences and peace conferences in Warsaw and Peking, visited Prague and Moscow,
and took part in anti-American spectacles wherever they went.
One of them had, in the cause of peace and world amity,
delivered a broadcast from Peking in 1952 to the effect that
United States troops in Korea had packed three hundred
children into a building, set it afire, and then machine-gunned
the mothers who tried to rescue the children. Their host countries obliged them by stamping their visas on separate pieces
of paper rather than in their passports to make their return
to this country less troublesome.

The Committee had its facts in order, and most of the witnesses called up took the Fifth Amendment. One of the more
prominent, the Communist apologist and divine Willard Uphaus, who had lent his name to Communist charges that
America used germ warfare in Korea, was in an orotund mood.
He waved a Bible and reminded the Committee that "Jesus
stood before Pilate and He didn't answer a single question
when asked." To which Arens responded, "Well, He wasn't
asked whether He was hooked up with Communist conspiracy."
Where Uphaus took as his sermon Peace Through Brotherhood
("We are all human beings, sir," he observed when Walter
chided him for speaking of Republicans and Communists in
the same breath. "We are all children of God. They too are
beloved, just as well as other people."), Paul Robeson blew
the trumpets of proletarian war. His appearance was all hollering and thumping and gaveling and speechifying: ". . . I am
not being tried for whether I am a Communist, I am being
tried for fighting for the rights of my people who are still
second class citizens . . ." and ". . . in Russia [in 1934] I felt
for the first time like a full human being, and no colored
prejudice like in Mississippi and no colored prejudice like in
Washington . . ." On being asked whether he had made a
speech in Moscow praising Stalin, he threw back an indictment
that would be heard a decade later from James Baldwin and
LeRoi Jones and Black Nationalists: "You are responsible and
your forebears for sixty million to one hundred million black
people dying in the slave ships and on the plantations, and

don't you ask me about anybody, please." Robeson's great talent had raised him far above the run of American Communists, but his rhetoric did not rise with him, and one could sympathize with Walter when he muttered, "I have endured all of this that I can," and abruptly adjourned the hearing.

Robeson was threatened with contempt for his performance, but although he was inordinately contemptuous and although he was having passport troubles at the time, the Committee thought better than to give him yet another stage for his resonant defiance. Contempt citations were, however, brought against two other eminent witnesses who had been having difficulty prying their passports loose from the State Department: Otto Nathan, professor of economics at New York University and the executor of Albert Einstein's estate, and the playwright Arthur Miller. Neither could claim Robeson's degree of loyalty to the Kremlin, but both had been involved with the Party and its fronts and both, without taking advantage of the Fifth Amendment, refused to answer Arens's questions regarding their past associations. Their manners, however, were dissimilar, a reflection not only of their differing temperaments but the differing approaches of their attorneys. Nathan, accompanied by Leonard Boudin, whose own recent Committee appearance had been full of angry exchanges, assumed a righteous air. When asked whether he was a Party member, he referred Arens to a non-Communist affidavit he had signed in 1953 and when asked whether the affidavit was truthful, he took the question as an insult: "Mr. Chairman, I resent the implication that I have made a statement under oath which shouldn't be correct. I refuse to answer. I think there is a limit beyond which counsel may not be permitted to go." Nathan also refused, understandably, to hand over to the Committee the passport he had finally been granted by the State Department after a two-and-a-half-year delay. In declining to give answers to Arens, Nathan questioned the jurisdiction of the Committee and the purpose of the hearing and took the First, Fourth, and Ninth Amendments, but not the Fifth.

Whereas the Nathan hearing caused Arens to shout and

pound, Arthur Miller's appearance was notable for its air of sober amiability. Miller—accompanied by Joseph Rauh, who was identified with Americans for Democratic Action rather than with the National Lawyers Guild—readily conceded that he had run with the Communists during the nineteen-forties, though he didn't recall ever signing a C.P. application form. But he had learned his lesson: "I would not now support a cause or movement dominated by Communists." This declaration did not prevent the Committee's director from leading him through a review of his career[9] as a signer of statements put out by the Civil Rights Congress against anti-Communist legislation and the Un-American Activities Committee and in behalf of Gerhart Eisler and Howard Fast. Despite a certain fuzziness on a number of points, Miller made a credible witness. He was responsive, collected, and only moderately sententious. He was decently annoyed at the uses to which the Communists had put his play about witch hunting in Salem, *The Crucible* (Howard Fast interpreted it as a statement on the Rosenberg case), and graciously evasive about the rupture of his friendship with Elia Kazan since the latter's testimony. So reasonable was Miller in the witness chair that his prolonged attachment to and exploitation by Communists became difficult to understand. Where the playwright balked, toward the end of his appearance, was at the point where John Watkins—who had also enjoyed Rauh's counsel—had balked. Asked to give the names of C.P. members who had been at meetings he attended in 1947, he replied, in words similar to those Lillian Hellman wrote in 1952: "I could not use the name of another person and bring trouble on him. These were writers, poets, as far as I could see, and the life of a writer, despite what it sometimes seems, is pretty tough. I wouldn't make it any tougher for anybody. I ask you not to ask me that question."

[9] In his researches, Arens came across a one-act play that Miller wrote with Norman Rosten in 1938, on a Federal Writers project. Entitled *Listen, My Children*, it had to do with a Congressional investigating committee and opened upon the following scene: "In the center of the room, in a rocker, sits a man. He is securely tied to a chair, with a gag in his mouth and a bandage tied over his mouth. Water, coming from a pipe near ceiling, trickles on his head. Nearby is a charcoal stove holding branding irons. Two bloodhounds are tied in the corner of room."

The request went to no avail. Jackson and Scherer, the members most adamant about compelling witnesses to tell all, observed that if every witness were permitted to let his conscience be his guide as to which questions he would and would not answer, the Committee would be hard put to get any information from anybody. The only alternative they would grudgingly allow to full disclosure was the stigma of the Fifth Amendment.

Eight contempt citations were dispatched by the House on July 25, 1956, at the behest of the Committee on Un-American Activities—against Arthur Miller, Otto Nathan, Pete Seeger, Elliot Sullivan, George Tyne, and three witnesses who had withheld their cooperation at hearings in St. Louis in June —John W. Simpson, William E. Davis, and Anne Yasgur Kling. Only the citation against Miller was debated, a distinction he owed at least as much to his prominence as a writer as to the circumstances of his refusal to answer questions. Three New York Democrats took up his defense. Celler noted that he had been responsive and respectful and warned that citing so eminent a figure would do America no good abroad. Klein put into the record a study which Joseph Rauh had submitted to Chairman Walter of other witnesses who had refused to give names to a committee of Congress, yet escaped citation. And Multer asked Jackson: "Will the gentleman tell the House please what legislation has been interfered with because you do not know the names of certain persons associated with this man?" Jackson did not need to reply; Miller was cited by a vote of 373 to 9.

None of the July 1956 citations was upheld by the courts. The Seeger, Sullivan, and Tyne cases we have already reviewed. Of the St. Louis witnesses, Simpson and Davis—who had histories of affiliation with Communist-run unions—took the Fifth Amendment beginning with the question of where they were born and owed their acquittal to the courts' ruling that even such routine inquiries might somehow prove incriminating. Mrs. Kling, who had worked in C.P. offices in 1945–1946 and quit the Party in 1947, took her place beside John Watkins and Arthur Miller. "Mr. Tavenner," she said, "I will tell you anything that you want to know about myself and my activities, anything you want to know. I have nothing to conceal. I engaged in no criminal or illegal activity. But I am not a tattletale, and I don't want to snitch on anybody." Her lawyer relied on the Watkins case, which was then under consideration by the Supreme Court, and his client, who had testified politely and fully about her own activities, was acquitted in district court because she had not been informed by the Committee of the pertinence of the questions regarding individuals she had known. Nathan was acquitted for the same reason after the Watkins decision. Miller had to carry his case to the Court of Appeals,[1] which found in September 1958 that he had not been adequately apprised that he risked contempt if he refused to answer questions on grounds of conscience. Since Walter had agreed to defer pressing Miller for names until counsel Rauh submitted a brief, the witness "had a right to leave the hearing room thinking that the direction to answer was still suspended, if not abandoned." Thus the court managed, without becoming involved with substantive issues, to escape the embarrassment of sending an international celebrity to jail.

Walter brought 1956 to an end with hearings in a half dozen cities "to examine the widespread counterattacks which the Communists have launched in order to subvert the legislative and executive programs designed to thwart them." Specifically, the chairman was impatient with the continuing attacks on his immigration law. The leadership of both parties, not excepting the President, had gone on record during the 1956 campaign in favor of liberalizing the law, and Walter's purpose in the November and December hearings was to promote the belief that the liberalization campaign was Communist-direct-

---

[1] As Miller brought his appeal, the Committee released a reproduction of a card, dated 1943, in which "A. Miller," a "writer" of 18 Schermerhorn Street, Brooklyn—a former address of the playwright—applied for membership in the Communist Party. The card was not signed by Miller, who described it as "either a forgery or . . . done unknown to me." In the place set aside for the name of the person proposing the new member was the signature of "Sue Warren," a one-time acquaintance of Miller's, who had declined to answer any of the Committee's questions. Miller called the release of the ambiguous card "a transparent attempt to influence the course of my appeal," and so it was.

ed, aimed, in the words of his first witness, Archibald Roosevelt, at "bleeding-heart" Americans and "well-meaning people who have been brainwashed." Roosevelt said he didn't want the country turned into a "polyglot boardinghouse." The strategy of the hearings was transparent. In Washington, Youngstown, Chicago, Los Angeles, San Francisco, and Seattle, officials of the American Committee for the Protection of the Foreign Born, a Communist Party front of long standing, were called up and identified as Party members. One after another the witnesses, several of whom had been before the Committee on other occasions, took the Fifth Amendment. Walter sought by this display to show up the opposition to his law as merely Red. In this he was inadvertently allied to the Communist Party, which always enjoyed being accounted a leader of popular causes onto which it tagged as they went roaring past. As the A.C.L.U. of Northern California observed, "We don't need public hearings to discover that a handful of Communists has seized upon our harsh and discriminatory immigration laws as a means of making political hay."

These hearings were the most disorderly of the year. Having exhausted his deferentiality on Archibald Roosevelt, Arens, who had helped draft the McCarran-Walter law, gave way to this kind of question: ". . . when our boys were fighting and dying with their hands tied behind their backs, being mowed down by the Communist traitors over there, being shot down by North Koreans, which side were you on?" The more truculent witnesses met him on his own level. The secretary treasurer of the International Longshoremen's and Warehousemen's Union, who chose not to deny that he had written Communist tracts under another name, notified Arens, "You are a little two-bit publicity hound," and was shortly thereafter removed from the hearing room. When Arens called on a witness who had just been identified as a Party member by a former F.B.I. operative, to "look him in the face so that there will be no faceless informers here . . ." the gentleman replied, "You wouldn't care for me to puke over the table by looking him in the face." The unfriendly witnesses had harsh remarks for seeming comrades who had been serving the Party in behalf of the F.B.I., setting them down as paid informers and unworthy of belief—but not a single accused Communist took the opportunity to deny the allegation under oath. Several of the lawyers, too, were argumentative. In Los Angeles, A. L. Wirin and John W. Porter, accompanying Mrs. Rose Chernin Kusnitz, executive secretary of the Los Angeles Committee for the Protection of the Foreign Born (who had been convicted under the Smith Act and would, in a few months, be freed by the Supreme Court), kept inserting themselves into the questioning despite repeated warnings to be quiet. Arens, who enjoyed noting that some of the lawyers attending on witnesses had themselves been identified as Communists, took to asking Porter's clients whether they knew a Communist by the name of John W. Porter. He ragged the attorney further by calling him "Comrade Porter." Scherer, suffering from the barbs of Wirin, charged that Mrs. Kusnitz was lying when she said she had personally prepared a carefully phrased document stating her reasons for not testifying. Wirin seemed determined to force the Committee's hand, or at least drive Scherer to distraction, and the Congressman's comment gave him an opportunity to protest: "Do I have to sit and hear someone call my client a liar in this hearing? This is a disgrace." Scherer and Velde insisted that Wirin be ordered out of the room; Doyle, the acting chairman, acceded. No sooner was Wirin led away by a marshal, than co-counsel Porter withdrew because his client was no longer adequately represented, whereupon the questioning had to be put over to the next day. Ever afterward the Committee's opponents used this event and the ouster of attorney Daniel G. Marshall after a similar run-in with the sensitive Scherer as case studies in undue process.[2] Arens's aspersions and incitements during the Los Angeles hearings prompted the board of governors of the California State Bar to censure the Committee for its "grossly offensive" treatment of lawyers.

[2] Other evictions came early in the Los Angeles hearings, when a retired brigadier general noted for his activities as vegetarian and prohibitionist was led from the Federal building after attempting to denounce the Committee and Doyle. A few minutes later, a lawyer was ordered out because he guffawed at the chairman's observation that the hearings were aimed at helping Congress to legislate efficiently.

In this series of hearings, Francis Walter had his most direct confrontation with his enemies and the enemies of his law, the people who had been calling him a bigot up and down the land. After the November 1956 elections, Walter said that only one consideration was preventing him from giving up the chairmanship—his resignation would be interpreted as a victory "by my enemies." The campaign against the McCarran-Walter law was, in his mind, directed against him personally and as an embodiment of the national security; it impugned his integrity and threatened the republic. Moreover, it stood for all of the other movements that had been gaining force during his first term as Committee chairman, toward easing security restrictions in this country and reducing cold war tensions abroad. His immigration bill was a product of the cold war, and every sign of warmer relations with Russia brought nearer an immigration thaw as well. The Committee's reports and declarations during this period had one overriding message: "the menace of Communism remains unabated." In the spring of 1956 after Khrushchev's attack on Stalin, Walter brought together thirtynine persons whom he described as "authorities" on Communism—a group tilted heavily to the right by such publicists as James Burnham, Clarence Manion, William Randolph Hearst, Jr., Whittaker Chambers, Louis Budenz, Francis McNamara, and the national commander of the American Legion—and they came through with a report entitled *The Great Pretense*. The fruit of their thought was distilled in Walter's preface: ". . . antiStalinism is but a political artifice, fraudulent and more dangerous than any other produced by the Kremlin thus far." J. Edgar Hoover contributed a summation.

For the men who had obliged Walter by proclaiming this news, as for the Un-American Activities Committee itself, there could be no change in U.S.–Soviet affairs, barring defeat for one party and victory for the other. Their careers were built on the immutable menace of Communism. The anti-Communism which, for most of them, had begun in honest disillusion and justified outrage had hardened into unquestioning faith; having given themselves to one truth, they could tolerate no other, and now nothing that happened in the real world could shake their belief in the less complicated world whose gates they guarded. As for Francis Walter, concern for national security, pride of authorship, and personal sensibilities merged into a force that would compel him to stand until the end of his life like the pathetic king of legend against the inexorable tides.

14

★ ★ ★ ★ ★

1957-1960: Operation Abolition

THE rioting that took place in San Francisco's City Hall in May 1960 as a result of a visit by three members of the Committee on Un-American Activities has properly been celebrated as marking a critical stage in the Committee's history. It was startling in its violence, but the powder for the explosion had been scattered over many months. In the closing years of the decade,[1] as the nation tired of security checks, loyalty oaths, and unending investigations, and as relations between Russia and America warmed somewhat, the Committee gave itself to incantations directed at resuscitating the drooping spirits of vigilanteism. The voice was usually the voice of Chairman Walter, but the hands were the hands of Arens and Scherer and J. Edgar Hoover, of Legionnaires and blacklisters, informers and defectors, of aging ex-Communists trapped by the experience of the thirties and young careerists loath to give up the power of the fifties. Committee hearings were less frequent but the number of reports and "consultations," with consultants chosen for dependability, rose; month after month the

---

1 Walter remained chairman throughout these years, and there were only minor changes in the Committee membership. Robert J. McIntosh, a freshman Republican from Michigan, took the place of Velde, who did not run for reelection in 1956, and when McIntosh was defeated in the Democratic sweep of 1958, he was replaced by another Michigan Republican, August E. Johansen. In January 1958, Frazier went off to the Ways and Means Committee and was replaced by William M. Tuck, a former governor of Virginia. General Kearney did not run in 1958; his Committee seat went to another upstate New Yorker, William E. Miller. In the fall of 1960, Frank S. Tavenner, Jr., took over as staff director from Arens, who went to his rewards as a commissioner in the Court of Claims, and Alfred M. Nittle became Committee counsel.

Committee turned out old warnings in old packages. Walter and Arens showed more respect for the cause of Marxism-Leninism than the globe's bewildered Communists, as powerful nationalist impulses broke out in Eastern Europe, as the dispute between Russia and China flared, as Communist unity strained and shattered with the shattering of Stalinism. The world looked on in amazement—but the Committee's message was that nothing had changed, nothing could change except for the worse, Communism was Communism, revolution was perpetual. To prove which they quoted Marx, Lenin, and Hoover. They were the last, truest believers.

When the minuscule C.P. U.S.A. fragmented itself to near invisibility after the Soviets crushed the Hungarian rebellion in 1956, the Committee warned that numbers did not count, the Party was a greater menace than ever since it had now gone underground. Like so many Romeos coming upon the corpse of their beloved, the Congressmen cried to the heavens, "The Communist Party of the United States is not out of business; it is not dead; it is not even dormant." Once the Committee had worried that the Party was attracting more and more adherents. Now it worried over the decline in membership. Representative Tuck warned, "A conspiratorial force may actually weaken itself when it increases in size." After Nikita Khrushchev shook the underpinnings of the Communist world with his speech on the crimes of Stalin, the Committee warned that it was but part of a sinister hoax to get us to drop our guard. As modest talks began with the new Soviet rulers, the Committee warned that negotiation with the U.S.S.R. was sheer folly, that all trade was at our peril, that Soviet visitors to this country would only reinforce their preconceived notions of capitalism. In celebration of Khrushchev's trip to America in September 1959, the Committee put out a series of reports on *The Crimes of Khrushchev*. When Sputnik was launched, the Committee attributed the accomplishment to the theft by Communist conspirators of America's scientific secrets, and warned that espionage was still rife. When our U-2 plane was shot down over the Soviet Union, Walter cautioned the world not to be distracted by a mischance of U.S. espionage from the subject of Communist subversion. In the spring of 1959, as a U.S. exhibition was opening in Moscow, the Committee created a minor furor over the fact that works of left-wing artists were included, and had Ben Shahn and Philip Evergood in to take the Fifth Amendment to prove it. By suggesting that peaceful coexistence between the United States and the U.S.S.R. was a real possibility, witness Joseph Starobin, former foreign editor of the *Daily Worker* who had dropped out of the Party in 1953, set himself against both his late comrades and his present inquisitors. In a foreword to a Committee report on the history of Communist machinations issued in 1958, when talk of a summit conference and an agreement on nuclear testing were in the air, Walter lamented over "the sorry spectacle of otherwise intelligent American leaders willing to negotiate with Communism's masters at international conference tables as if there were a real foundation of sincerity and good faith."

In all of this, one could hardly miss the flowering of an obsession. Where sane men the world over breathed a bit more easily at every reduction in the long, dangerous international tension, Walter saw only new threats. To his fear of undesirable foreigners polluting these shores was added a fear of undesirable Americans catching or spreading infection abroad. He discerned a menace of vast proportions in the propaganda —incredible stuff—which Communist countries shipped to this country and even in the languishing foreign-language sheets that elderly men still managed to put out in New York and Chicago, and under his direction the Committee became a counter-propaganda agency. He was a Platonist in the sense that Russia's rulers were Platonists, seeing a danger to the state wherever one's citizens encountered unorthodox ideas. The Russians sealed their borders to protect their Marxist "science" from reality, yet Walter paid their discredited ideology the tribute of fear. His whole effort in these years when men began to reach out toward one another, tentatively, suspiciously, but hopefully withal, was toward closing up, clamping down, as if only so could he still his inner trembling.

These were desperate years for Francis Walter. In succumbing to zenophobic passions and committing himself utterly to

the ways of the Committee he had once criticized, he had forfeited his hope of succeeding Sam Rayburn as Speaker of the
House. He remained loyal to his party and retained influence
in the House, but he had become set in the dated style of
suspicion and repression just at a time when fresh fashions were
stirring the land. Not all the letters of support from American
Legion posts or testimonial dinners by the right-wing guard
could save him; he was embattled by reality and there were
moments in these indescribably frustrating years when he
could barely make out friend from foe. In June 1958 the Supreme Court, that unmistakable foe, ruled that the State Department had no authority to deny passports to applicants
because of their "beliefs and associations." The five-to-four
decision was handed down on June 17 to take effect on July
11. Since the government did not intend to ask for a rehearing,
the State Department instructed the director of the Passport
Office, Miss Frances G. Knight, to start issuing the passports
that had been held up. She began to do so on June 24, delivering passports to several dozen known and suspected Communists, including such old Committee antagonists as Paul
Robeson and Harry Bridges. Walter was well aware that Miss
Knight was no advocate of free travel for political undesirables
—she had cooperated with him in drawing up a bill to tighten
passport requirements and was in the bad book of liberals—
yet such was his grief and rage that he lashed out even at her,
charging in a letter to Secretary Dulles that while corrective
legislation was pending she was "going out of her way to issue
passports to these Communist agents . . ." But everyone knew
there was no hope for such legislation in that session of Congress; the lady had merely been doing what for her must have
been a distasteful job—only to have an ally compound her
distress. Such were the distractions of the time.

Of the reduced hearings between 1957 and 1960, some were
frivolous, in that mode of cruel frivolity which had become a
Committee specialty. In the spring of 1957 a subcommittee
under Moulder ("Now, of course, we are not worried about
communizing Beethoven and Bach, and we do not feel that

the performance of a concerto by a Communist is in itself subversive") visited New York City for the purpose of routing out some three dozen musicians associated with the Metropolitan Music School, the Symphony of the Air, and Local 802 of the Musicians Union who had been identified as Communists and duly took the Fifth Amendment. Arens, who often told witnesses he was not concerned with their beliefs, only with their actions, took full advantage of them. "What is your position on Communism?" he asked one musician. "Are you for it or against it?" The best known of the witnesses was Earl Robinson (whom Arens called "Mr. Robeson"), composer of *Ballad for Americans, Lonesome Road, The House I Live In,* and other synthetic and edifying folk songs. "I hope my music will always be used in the fight against fascism," declared Robinson to the delight of Arens who was trying to prove that the Party could employ friendly musicians for political purposes. Arens exhibited a notice printed in the *Daily Worker* in 1938 that a lecturer at the music school had spoken on "the bourgeois music culture in the period of monopoly capitalism," while another man, a guitar instructor, was responsible for a people's song called "Gol-dern Red."[2]

Having done what they could to damage the livelihoods of these detested persons, the Congressmen went back to Washington. But they returned to New York a year later to call up a dozen show business people—a conductor, a publicist, a director, as well as a few actors—who had somehow been missed on previous visits. Joseph Papp, a stage manager for C.B.S. and the guiding force behind the New York Shakespeare Festival which was putting on free plays in Central Park, was the biggest name the Committee could find this time around—and he indicated that he had left the Party several years before. The

[2] I went up to my boss one day to ask him for a raise.
   He wept and said he didn't have the dough.
Well I knew for all his crying that the plutocrat was lying,
   And *that's* just what I told the so and so.
   And what d'ya think he said?
   "Why you're nothing but a gol-dern Red (straight from
      Russia)
   You're nothing but a gol-dern Red.
Yes: and if the truth be told, you're receiving Moscow gold.
   Yes, you're nothing but a gol-dern Red. . . ."

show business mine was about worked out. Even Hollywood was recovering from the blackest days of the blacklist, and the Committee had to be satisfied with getting one man fired by N.B.C. and another canceled from the Ed Sullivan show. (Five distinguished trustees of the Stratford, Connecticut, American Shakespeare Festival, bankers all, resigned to protest the retaining of a stage manager who took the Fifth.)

The July 1959 hearing on the American National Exhibition in Moscow which, according to Walter, included the works of twenty-two artists with "significant" records of affiliation with Communist fronts and causes, was taken up mainly by one Wheeler Williams, president of the American Artists Professional League and the sculptor responsible for the statue of Senator Robert A. Taft at the Taft Memorial in Washington. The judges for the exhibition, he complained, had slighted traditional artists in favor of social protest paintings and "meaningless doodles," which failed to give a true image of America, as they contained "next to nothing to show the wondrous natural beauty with which God has endowed our beloved land, to portray its glorious history, its heroes or its valiant people of varied races, and nothing to picture the wondrous architecture of our cities or charm and beauty of our villages and towns." If there remained any question of the kind of art Mr. Wheeler liked, he resolved it by telling how impressed he was with the paintings of tractor drivers and milkmaids that the Soviets had sent to tour America.[3]

There were other hearings, not so ludicrous as the flight into art, but still gratuitous, as Walter and Arens, like marginal oil operators setting up their derricks adjacent to a rich strike, tried to draw off some of the publicity of sensational incidents as it gushed forth. Thus, the Committee owed its first big newspaper story of 1957 to the extravagant Boris Morros, Russian-born Hollywood composer and double agent whose testimony

[3] Asked to comment on this controversy, President Eisenhower said: "Now I think I might have something to say, if we have another exhibition anywhere, to the responsible officials of the methods they produce, or get the juries, and possibly there ought to be one or two people like that, like most of us here say, we are not too certain exactly what art is but we know what we like and what America likes—whatever America likes is after all some of the things that ought to be shown."

before a grand jury had lately resulted in several indictments of Americans on charges of spying for the U.S.S.R. and the flight to Czechoslovakia of Mr. and Mrs. Alfred Stern, he a millionaire investment broker, she the daughter of the late William E. Dodd, former U.S. ambassador to Germany. (". . . we are visiting this peace-loving country," Stern told reporters, "and enjoying an interesting and restful trip.") The Senate Internal Security Subcommittee had set a hearing for Morros, but Walter got to him first, took testimony in executive session, and had the triumph of being the one to bring Mrs. Stern's name into the story. Morros's tale of his twelve years as a counterspy made exciting copy, but he did not require the services of the Un-American Activities Committee to tell it. He told it over and over, with flourishes, in press conferences, on TV shows, in articles, and finally in a book. The Committee merely provided him with one more stage, and his appearance gave Walter a chance to announce, "The facts now in the possession of the Committee indicate that a number of American citizens have been and may still be involved in Soviet espionage." The facts he referred to have yet to be produced. In October he called a number of former federal employees who had known or worked with one of the implicated persons during their time with such government agencies as the O.P.A. and the B.E.W. All had already been questioned by the F.B.I.; all declined to testify regarding their own Communist affiliations. The Committee had no evidence against any of them and expected no cooperation, but went through the motions of a hearing which it then published under the title *Investigation of Soviet Espionage.*

Walter and Jackson charged onto page one again in February 1960, after the Pentagon repudiated an Air Force training manual briefly in use at the Lackland Air Force Base in Texas which instructed student reservists that Communists had infiltrated United States churches and that thirty of the ninety-five persons who had worked on a Revised Standard Version of the Bible for the National Council of the Churches of Christ were affiliated with subversive organizations. It was the Bishop Oxnam affair all over again. Right-wing fundamentalists, impassioned as ever against the liberal disposition and ecumenical inclinations of the National Council, had managed to plant the charges, taken mainly from the writings of J. B. Matthews and the Un-American Activities Committee's files, in the manual. One evangelist tract listed in the appendix was entitled, *The National Council of Churches Indicts Itself on Fifty Counts of Treason to God and Country.* Hardly had the recently appointed Secretary of the Air Force Dudley C. Sharp withdrawn the manual,[4] with the apologies of the Secretary of Defense, than he found himself summoned before Walter's Committee in closed session. Whereas other Congressmen were threatening to investigate the inclusion of the charges, Walter intended to investigate their withdrawal. The poor Secretary, under simultaneous attack from the right and the center, made himself as agreeable as he could, giving "this fine Committee" to understand that he had no quarrel with its work, but merely did not feel it was appropriate for the Air Force to get involved in the issue of whether there were Communists among the clergy. Pressed hard by Arens and eight of the Committee's members to say that he did not mean to repudiate the material in its files, he conceded, "I would say that I certainly agree with the assumption that the Communist Party would obviously in its activities attempt to infiltrate the churches . . ." On the basis of such observations, Walter told reporters afterward that Sharp had said "admittedly everything in the manual was true." Before leaving the witness chair, the Secretary had to endure a threat by Jackson that "some sort of hell [the word was changed to 'ruckus' in the record of the hearing] will break loose on the floor of the House" if the author of the tract were punished. When a group of Protestant ministers asked Walter for an apology, he invited them to testify about the material that the Committee had collected over the years. They wisely declined to be diverted from the issue, as they saw it,

---

[4] The Air Force was suffering a certain embarrassment over its instructional materials at this time. Other manuals had recently been found which taught the airmen how to wash the dogs and polish the shoes of officers, how to encourage drinking in open messes run for profit, and how to use dining utensils: "The fork is used to lift, turn or move large or small pieces of food in a sanitary and practical manner."

of the propriety of the Air Force "indoctrinating reservists on religious questions." For weeks after, Fulton Lewis, Jr., devoted a portion of his daily broadcast to attacks on the liberal clergy, and Jackson capped the incident by accusing the National Council of promoting obscene books by Communist sympathizers.

In August of 1960, Walter partook of yet another juicy news story when Speaker McCormack invited him to inquire into the case of Bernon F. Mitchell and William H. Martin, young bachelor friends who had suddenly left their jobs as cryptographers at the National Security Agency and gone off, presumably behind the Iron Curtain. McCormack expressed dissatisfaction with the Pentagon's assurances that the men had no information which could be "prejudicial to the security of United States communications," and it may have crossed his mind that a bit of publicity about a security slip under a Republican Administration could do no harm to the fortunes that November of John F. Kennedy. Unable to get other committee chairmen to take an interest in the event, he turned to the one committee where he could count on action. Walter immediately introduced a resolution in the House calling for a complete study of the personnel practices of all U.S. Intelligence agencies. It was too late in the session for anything to come of this, but the Russians kept his cause alive by putting on a news conference in Moscow at which Martin and Mitchell announced they had defected out of a fear that U.S. intelligence methods, particularly reconnaissance flights like that of the ill-fated U-2, would lead to war. Now the case could not be ignored. President Eisenhower told a news conference that he saw a need for a review of hiring procedures in sensitive agencies, and the House Armed Services Committee appointed a three-man subcommittee to study the matter—an effort to take the play away from the Un-American Activities Committee. When Walter asked the President to order various government agencies to make available to him the names of persons who had regained federal employment after being dropped as security risks—long a sore point with the Committee—the President replied as his predecessors had replied in similar instances, negatively, citing the separation of powers.

Both House committees held closed hearings into the case. Walter issued periodic charges, the testimony of N.S.A. officials to the contrary notwithstanding, that at least one of the defectors was a homosexual. The Defense Department refused to let him have the personnel files on the two, but he was given a defector named Artamonov, a former Soviet naval captain, whom he put on the stand in public hearing, to tell about Soviet intelligence machinations. Despite Walter's efforts, the Mitchell-Martin case made little impact; the main lesson to be drawn from it was simply that security cannot be foolproof, or defector-proof. Neither of the men was listed in the Committee's files, and although N.S.A. dutifully went through the motions of tightening its personnel procedures, nothing less than constant surveillance could have prevented their astonishing flight. What was significant about the response to the affair was that with elections only a few weeks away Democrats showed so little desire to make political capital of it. Walter's passions came out of pathology, not politics, but his colleagues seemed to recognize that the time of the security champion had waned. There was no disposition to reopen old wounds or to take fresh vengeance for them. They had had enough of charges of "softness" and so, it appeared, had the country. Reflecting on what Nixon would have made of an N.S.A. defection in 1952, one could only admire the Democratic leadership and give thanks for the altered temper of the country.[5]

Public hearings in the eighty-fifth and eighty-sixth Congresses, generally well covered in local papers, took subcommittees to thirteen cities, as well as to Puerto Rico, where

[5] Walter pursued the case into 1961, with unexpected results. The agency's head of personnel and its security chief were both compelled to resign: the former because he had once claimed on an employment application that he had been awarded a law degree by Harvard, when in fact he had spent only a year in Cambridge and had gotten his degree from a less prestigious establishment, and then compounded this offense by substituting a correct form for the boastful one; the latter because he had accepted an undisclosed favor from some party that did business with the government. The case also resulted in a tightening up of N.S.A. regulations, several other dismissals, and, as we shall note a few pages hence, a new piece of security legislation.

twelve witnesses were cited for contempt only to have their indictments dismissed in 1962, when a district court upheld their contention that in authorizing the Un-American Activities Committee to conduct hearings within the continental United States, the Congress had not meant to include Puerto Rico. The informant–Fifth Amendment pattern was followed in the majority of the hearings—John Lautner and Armando Penha being the most productive informants of the period. The emphasis was on the ritual exposure of Communists, numbers of whom had been exposed before, but some light was thrown on Party activities in these difficult years. It was shown that the Jefferson School of Social Science in New York, which had dissolved itself in 1955 shortly after being adjudged a Communist front by the Subversive Activities Control Board, had set up shop again at a different address as the Faculty of Social Science. This prompted Walter to introduce another of his security bills—this one to insure that an S.A.C.B. order against an organization would apply to any successor organization. Chicago hearings into the left-wing United Packinghouse Workers indicated that several union leaders had resigned their C.P. memberships not out of disillusionment with the Party but merely to abide by the technical provisions of the Taft-Hartley Act. Officers and members of the American Communications Association—which had been expelled by the C.I.O. in 1950 and was being investigated by the Senate Internal Security Subcommittee when the Un-American Activities Committee set sights on it—were shown to be working around installations that would be regarded as sensitive in case of emergency, and seamen with records of Communist activity were shown to be sailing American merchant ships. Hearings in Gary, Indiana, disclosed that college graduates from New York had concealed their educational attainments to take jobs in heavy industry, presumably at the behest of Communist headquarters.

These hearings were not as difficult to justify under the Committee's mandate as the others held between 1957 and 1960, which had no discernible purpose other than to publicize the names of alleged Communists and cause them as much trouble as possible with their neighbors and employers. But even here the information obtained was not compelling. By now, the Committee was like a tiresome uncle who insists on telling his old ghost stories in broad daylight to nephews with other things on their minds. All of the reluctant witnesses were known to the F.B.I., and none had ever been charged with any act of disloyalty to this country. The Faculty of Social Science made no effort at camouflage. The A.C.A. members had worked at their jobs for many years, and although there was no way of refuting the *possibility* that in case of war with Russia a pro-Communist teletype operator *might* blow up an R.C.A. installation or take home Defense Department messages, the Committee's conclusion that "Communists' penetration of sensitive communications facilities constitutes a direct danger to American security" was a highly colored summary of what the hearings had actually disclosed. As for the Communist "colonizers" in the steel industry, only a determined demonologist could find much menace in their conspiratorial pretensions; even John Lautner, usually amenable to the Committee's needs, made the point that the purpose of the "colonizers" was to reestablish a Communist foothold in heavy industry—a difficult enough task—not to blow up any steel plants. But the investigators were nothing if not determined to find concealed perils. Upon locating an identified Communist in New Haven who held an executive post with the Children's Services of Connecticut, Willis and Kearney took care to point out, "In this capacity she made the decisions as to what home should receive the children and what was the best plan for the child."

The careful statement of legislative purpose with which the chairman began each inquiry and the explanations of pertinence which Arens delivered to balky witnesses became part of the ceremony after the Watkins decision, but the hearings themselves bore little resemblance to those of committees that seriously weighed pending bills. At most, as in the passport-security hearings of 1959, which were aimed at discrediting the Supreme Court's 1958 passport ruling, an official in favor of security legislation would be invited to testify; the only opponents of such legislation called as witnesses were persons like Harry Bridges[6] or the general manager of the *Daily Worker*, who were asked not about their opinions of the bills but about their Communist associations, and were held up as frightful examples when they took the Fifth Amendment. There was never much pretense of considering more than one side of the case regarding a proposed law. Walter opened the passport hearings with a reference to the Supreme Court decision, and at once passed judgment on what had yet to be considered: "Today, now the bars are down. Communist agents, propagandists and Communist sympathizers have a blanket invitation to come and go as they will . . . this situation is of direct benefit to the international Communist movement, and of direct detriment to security interests of our nation."

Walter promised after the Watkins decision that Congress would "pass the type of legislation that even the Supreme Court will understand." But although he and Scherer proposed numerous measures designed to redo what the Supreme Court was in process of undoing in the whole field of security, it was a rare piece of legislation that was put in their charge. Scherer vented his annoyance that they were not even entrusted with his own bill that authorized the federal government to take measures to guard defense facilities against individuals believed disposed to acts of subversion. In its first twenty years of life, the Un-American Activities Committee produced one law—the Internal Security Act of 1950. As though exhausted by that uncertain accomplishment, in the ensuing ten years it held not a single hearing on a specific piece of legislation. (The Committee's champions sometimes take credit for the Communist Control Act of 1954, that mysterious measure which announced that the Communist Party "should" be outlawed, then did not quite outlaw it, but in fact the major provisions of the bill originated in the Senate and Velde reported it out over the vigorous objections of Walter, Doyle, and Frazier without troubling to hold any hearings.) In 1954 and again in

[6] Shipping out of West Coast ports had gone smoothly during the Korean War despite Bridges's adherence to the Communist line. Yet in 1959, as one of the few left-wing union leaders of the thirties still alive and kicking, he was exhibited as a prime threat by the Committee because he said he would advocate a boycott if Chiang Kai-shek tried to retake the Chinese mainland.

1962, the Committee reported two amendments of no great consequence to its Internal Security Act—the first calling for the listing of all printing equipment in the possession of Communist-action and Communist-front organizations, the other relieving the Defense Department of the requirement that it publish a list of strategic defense facilities from which Communist Party members were barred. (By requiring such a listing in the first place, the Internal Security Act had inadvertently abetted enemy spies.) In 1963 the Committee completed its record of legislative accomplishment when it produced another amendment to the Internal Security Act, giving the Secretary of Defense power to dismiss summarily any employee of the National Security Agency, "an example, just one more example," commented the *National Review* with no humorous intent, "of the continuing legislative usefulness of the House Committee on Un-American Activities . . ." This bill, which owed its life to the Mitchell-Martin defection, was signed into law in 1964, and is now being reviewed by the Supreme Court.

Straining to provide the exhibitions in various cities with some legislative aura, Walter pressed into service one Irving Fishman, a New York Customs official. Jurisdiction over ". . . the diffusion within the United States of subversive and un-American propaganda . . ." was explicit in the Committee's mandate, and Fishman leavened the parades of local left-wingers with data on the number of pieces of Soviet propaganda entering the country through New York or New Orleans or Boston. What Mr. Fishman had to say could have made a thin pamphlet, but between June 1956 and May 1960 he was called on to perform a dozen times—in Washington, Philadelphia, San Francisco, New Orleans, Buffalo, Boston, Atlanta, and Newark. The highlight of his appearance usually came when he reached into the mail sack he carried with him and produced a genuine piece of Communist propaganda.

The Committee's legislative record, or want of record, was used gleefully by critics to demonstrate that despite its large annual allocation and staff ($654,000 and fifty-six members in the eighty-sixth Congress), the Committee on Un-American Activities produced remarkably few laws, and this became a tender point during Walter's chairmanship. Whereas neither Thomas nor Velde had had any great legislative aspirations, Walter considered himself a lawmaker, and not a season passed without a stream of proposals issuing from his office. At the outset of the eighty-sixth Congress, he made known that he wanted jurisdiction over immigration and passport legislation. As chairman of the Judiciary Committee's subcommittee on immigration, he had to work under Emanuel Celler, the committee's liberal chairman, and the change would have relieved him of that frustrating connection. It would also have given him the power base to which he felt entitled after a quarter century in the House and would have given his Committee a true legislative function at last. But Speaker Rayburn, at the first news conference of the eighty-sixth Congress, said, "We're not going to do that," and that was that. So Walter, who had once been among the inner group of policymakers in the House, now had to content himself with calling for the passage of bills that were not in his committee's jurisdiction. His annual favorite became the Omnibus Security Bill, a hodgepodge of measures designed to reverse numerous Supreme Court decisions, prohibit Communist lawyers from practicing before executive departments and Congressional committees, tighten passport controls and regulations regarding aliens, and so forth. Some of these measures were adopted as parts of other laws handled by other committees, whereupon the Un-American Activities Committee and its defenders could claim them as the Committee's accomplishments. Indeed, hardly a piece of repressive legislation went through that, by this easy criterion, the Committee might not claim as its own, yet of the 12,000 bills filed in the House of Representatives in the eighty-sixth Congress, only eleven were referred to the Un-American Activities Committee—and not one of these was passed. Insofar as the Committee deserved credit for various executive orders on security and laws such as those which broadened the scope of the Foreign Agents Registration Act, the Espionage Act, and the Smith Act, it was in the role of publicist, not legislator.

In its single-minded drive after names, the Committee swept by certain observations of witnesses that might have given it profitable pause. Howard Fast, having at last broken with the Party upon discovering that Jews had been among those slaughtered by Stalin, was questioned in closed session and commented afterward that the Committee, with its implacable demands for names, had made it virtually impossible for a man to leave the Party and retain any dignity. Dignity was not the word that sprang to mind regarding Fast, but his point was well taken. The self-righteousness of the Committee's members and staff obstructed it in the performance of its avowed informational function. Faced with an ex-Communist, Arens required repentance, abasement, and conversion. His questions were designed to be asked, not answered. He demanded of a witness in Buffalo: "Are you now thoroughly disgusted with the fact that you have been associated with the Communist ideology, which is atheistic, which is the very antithesis of Christian morality as we know it in this country?" The less polemical, less ambitious Tavenner was better at drawing out information. In several sets of hearings, he encouraged men who had quit the Party after the Soviet intervention in Hungary to tell of their feelings and experiences despite the fact that they took the Fifth on naming former friends. Granted this much permissiveness, the witnesses spoke intelligently and with evident honesty about the crises of conscience that had been stirred in Party ranks by the events of 1956, and one of them observed, much as Howard Fast had, that the Committee's habit of asking every dissenter to become an informer was hindering open debate within the Party. (The Committee was inconsistent about pressing for contempt citations against witnesses who were willing to testify about themselves but balked at naming others without relying on the Fifth Amendment; their fates seemed to hang on the composition and temper of the day's subcommittee, and on whether Arens or Tavenner was handling the interrogation. At times Tavenner was truly startling. When a Los Angeles witness took the Fifth, the counsel said: "It is quite apparent, Mr. Chairman, there is no use asking him questions if he refuses to answer regarding his membership." Had this principle been strictly followed, the Committee could have conserved a great deal of energy.)

In another area, too, the Congressmen and counsel Arens, like tourists who have eyes for nothing but what is in their guide books, went hastily by a sight that deserved pondering. In March 1959 and again in May witnesses who had been publicly identified as Communists while they were in fact working within the Party for the F.B.I. told of the harrassment they had suffered from anti-Communist neighbors and fellow workers. A packinghouse worker in Chicago said that ". . . my family and myself have been discriminated very badly and hurt, cut up to pieces because people pointed and thrown bricks and slapped me in the face and done everything imaginable because the neighborhood I lived in, there are no Communists and they can't stand a Communist." The Congressmen were sympathetic but did not pursue the matter. The experiences of the F.B.I. informants merely confirmed the charges delivered from the Supreme Court bench, the floor of Congress, and lesser platforms that in its accustomed role of exposing Communists, the Un-American Activities Committee was in fact inciting to punishment. Subcommittee members had no sympathy to spare for what happened to non-F.B.I. witnesses after they left the hearing room and allowed no testimony on that subject. "The hearings are public," said Moulder blandly to a witness who feared for his job if his place of work were made known, "and what may result from your testimony in the form of publicity can't be controlled by this Committee." But the attentive listener could find echoes in informants' ordeals of the ordeals of hundreds of other people who were guilty of no known crime.

By Walter's time, the F.B.I. informant had become a major actor in the Committee's ceremonies. These men and women were not proper F.B.I. agents, but Communist Party members, nominal or disillusioned, who for reasons of patriotism or more obscure motives reported regularly on their activities and the people they met. While the Committee's research staff occupied itself with clipping names and associations from the *National Guardian* and feeding them into its endlessly growing files, it was the informants who supplied most of the matter required for hearings. As the Communist Party fell apart, they were permitted to break cover and testify. By and large, they had little news to impart once they had delivered up their lists of names, but they could be counted on to reply affirmatively when Arens or one of the Congressmen asked whether in their opinion the Communist Party was more of a menace now than ever before.

In its public pronouncements on the subject, the Committee always indicated that its cooperation with the F.B.I. consisted mainly of giving the Bureau access to its remarkable files. But it became evident during the chairmanship of former F.B.I. operative Velde that the relationship was not so one-sided. The Committee could usually boast of having one or more former F.B.I. men on its staff—as indeed could many of the vigilante operations that flourished in the nineteen-fifties. Friendly cooperation outside of channels presented no particular problem given an understanding between the F.B.I.'s director and the Committee's chairman or staff director, and it was clear that, through unofficial means, the Committee was getting at least as much help from the F.B.I. as it was giving. The cooperation reached a dramatic peak in 1959. Previously the Committee had used informants who had already broken with the Party, but in Pittsburgh in March and in Chicago in May and again in Washington in June 1960 the Congressmen had the satisfaction of unveiling F.B.I. agents who had been C.P. members in good standing "up to the present minute." What they had to say was of marginal interest—the Communists, reported the Chicago man, were "nothing but a bunch of rattle snakes"—but their debut under Committee sponsorship made for good newspaper copy. It was a performance that would have been impossible without the cooperation, or at least acquiescence, of J. Edgar Hoover.

Early in the life of the Un-American Activities Committee, Hoover had had reason to be annoyed at some of Martin Dies's adventures, but under Walter's chairmanship a close and mutually rewarding relationship bloomed between Committee and Bureau. The F.B.I. used the Committee to turn what Chairman Dies had early called "the light of pitiless publicity" on persons against whom it could take no other action—and in so doing reaped a fair amount of publicity for itself. The Committee used the prestige of the F.B.I. and its enduring director to bolster its own apocalyptic philosophy. When Hoover announced in 1958 that the Communist Party was "well on its way to achieving its current objective, which is to make you believe that it is shattered, ineffective and dying," the Committee hastened to incorporate his remarks in its record. "When it has fully achieved this first objective," the director of the F.B.I. went on, in words that have remained comfortably the same over the decades, like the old slippers that go with mindless evenings at home, "it will then proceed inflexibly toward its final goal." The two groups were under attack from much the same quarters and their spokesmen came quickly and warmly to one another's defense when a slur was cast. "Where in God's name would our nation be," asked Doyle of a disrespectful New York musician, "if the F.B.I. wasn't able to get patriotic American citizens to go into these organizations in which Communists, crooks, cheats and traitors infiltrate?" Not receiving a satisfactory response, he added, "You ought to be ashamed of yourself for attacking the F.B.I." At times the Congressmen's adoration verged on the blasphemous. "If you cannot trust the F.B.I.," Willis once asked, "whom are you going to trust?" Hoover reciprocated this worshipful regard by writing a letter to Walter when the Committee came under attack from the Emergency Civil Liberties Committee, to say that "real Americans" wouldn't be fooled by the campaign. The Committee and the Bureau behaved during these years like a pair of mischievously indiscreet lovers. They were not officially affianced and so had to maintain a certain distance in public, yet so fond were the glances they exchanged, so endearing the sentiments, that observers could hardly help speculating over what they did together when the lights were out.

The worshipful feelings that Walter, Arens, and Scherer held for the F.B.I. impelled them into one of the great Committee follies of the period. In May 1958 Cyrus S. Eaton of Cleveland, known as a bearer of odd opinions for a man who had made several fortunes in coal, iron, and steel (he wanted closer relations with the U.S.S.R. and recognition of Communist China), was interviewed on a television series designed by the Fund for the Republic. The seventy-four-old Eaton had recently taken to sponsoring an annual international meeting of scientists at his birthplace in Pugwash, Nova Scotia, and he used the TV interview to voice his disdain for the "scores of agencies" engaged "in investigating, in snooping, in informing, in creeping up on people." He said that they made "no contribution to the upbuilding of this country and its respect abroad," and added that there were no Communists to speak of in the United States, "except in the mind of those on the payroll of the F.B.I." Eaton spoiled his performance by announcing that "Hitler in his prime, through the Gestapo, never had any such spy organization as we have in this country today"—still it was certainly one of the more refreshing shows of the TV season. No one could recall that the F.B.I. had ever been criticized on a national network before, and assuredly not by a chairman of the board of the Chesapeake and Ohio Railroad.

For the right wing, it was heresy. Three days after the broadcast, a thousand New Yorkers gathered at Hunter College, under the auspices of AWARE and eighteen other anti-Communist organizations to listen to Roy Cohn, William Buckley, and Gordon Scherer—in the city with a subcommittee investigating entertainers—defend the Un-American Activities Committee, the Internal Security Subcommittee, and the F.B.I. Eaton, declared Scherer, had "made a tremendous contribution to the Soviet cause." Walter demanded equal time from the American Broadcasting Company and sent forth Arens to uphold the honor of the Federal Bureau of Investigation. While doing so, Arens made public the fact that Walter had signed a subpoena for the millionaire to come before the Committee and explain himself. Upon this incitement, the Committee's critics entered the fray. The A.C.L.U. called the subpoena action a "clear-cut demonstration of the Committee's power to coerce American citizens and penalize them for expressing their opinions on controversial issues." *The New York Times,* which a few months before had complimented the eighty-fifth Congress on the "total absence of irresponsible and merely punitive Congressional investigatory action," now denounced the Committee for "a preposterous and dangerous arrogation of unconstitutional power." Senators Humphrey and Douglas issued a gentle rebuke to the Committee on the floor of the Senate—Douglas called the action "perhaps impetuous" and "ill-considered." The subpoena was never served. After an angry confrontation in Scherer's office which ended with Walter walking out—"My stomach could not take it"—and Eaton charging he had been bullied and pushed around, the chairman blew a faltering retreat: "It is believed that no useful purpose can be served by permitting Mr. Eaton to repeat the groundless accusations that Iron Curtain countries have used for propaganda purposes." Insofar as there is a last word in this sort of argument, Eaton seems to have had it. A few weeks after the aborted meeting a Cleveland engineering magazine carried an article by the industrialist which observed that some members of the Committee were "not noted for their intellectual depth or high ethical standards."

The Eaton incident passed, but the sentiments that the eccentric industrialist expressed with such gusto were shared by members of the Establishment. Cold-war security innovations were being rejected wholesale by the Warren court,[7] and aggrieved feelings on the Committee, where each new decision was received like a death in the family, were worsened by the justices' treatment of the twenty-eight contempt citations that issued from the hearings of 1957–1960. (The Committee had by now laid permanent claim to the cup for contempt citations, having in its two decades instituted more of them than all the other committees of the Congress put together.)

The results of the earliest tests were not displeasing to the Congressmen, and left them unprepared for the rain of blows that followed. The first cases involved two witnesses who had the bad luck to be called up in July 1958, midway between the Watkins decision and the Barenblatt decision. The hearings,

---

[7] In 1956 the court curbed state sedition laws and put restraints on federal security risk dismissals. In 1957 it limited the application of the Smith Act. In 1958 it ruled that the Secretary of State did not have the power to deny passports on the grounds of an applicant's beliefs or associations. In 1959 it voided the use of secret informers in the industrial security program.

held in Atlanta, concerned Communist activity in the South. Willis, as acting chairman, and counsel Arens took pains to spell out the authority of the Atlanta subcommittee and the legislative purpose of the hearing: the possible amending of the Communist Control Act and the Foreign Agents Registration Act. (These ceremonious speeches constituted the sole changes in the Committee's manners as a result of the Watkins decision over which liberals had prematurely rejoiced.) The reluctant witnesses, both identified as Party members, were Carl Braden, field secretary of the Southern Conference Educational Fund, which, according to Arens, was "for all practical purpose" a successor organization to the Southern Conference for Human Welfare, and Frank Wilkinson of the Emergency Civil Liberties Committee, which had been set up with the clear purpose of combating the Un-American Activities Committee. Both men refused their cooperation: Braden charged that the Committee was in Atlanta to discredit integrationists and Wilkinson gave only his name, adding, "As a matter of conscience and personal responsibility, I refuse to answer any questions of this Committee." Neither took the Fifth Amendment. Having sought sanctuary among the dicta of Watkins, they were undone by the thrust of Barenblatt. The high court decided their cases in February 1961. Speaking for the same five justices who had formed the majority in the Barenblatt case, Justice Stewart observed that it was not the intention of Congress to immunize from interrogation by the Committee all those who were opposed to its existence. To the minority's plausible charge that Braden and Wilkinson had been called as witnesses *because* they opposed the Committee (Wilkinson was not subpoenaed until he arrived in Atlanta to stir up protests against the hearings, and Braden had been instrumental in drawing up a letter from two hundred Southern Negroes asking that the Committee stay out of the South), Stewart countered that it was not the function of the court to speculate on the motives of Congressmen.[8]

8 In his dissent, Justice Black deserted the judicial Muse for the Muse of the horror tale. The result of the Wilkinson decision, he wrote, was that "from now on anyone who takes a public position contrary to that being urged by

The Braden-Wilkinson decision remains the Committee's last major victory in the Supreme Court. In June 1961 the Court overturned the conviction of Bernhard Deutch, a young nuclear physicist and a recipient of one of the batch of contempt citations issued in 1954. Deutch had admitted to being a Party member between the ages of eighteen and twenty-one, but refused to answer any questions about individuals he had known in those years. The five-to-four decision, written by Potter Stewart, held that the government had not proved that the questions asked of Deutch, a student at Cornell at the time, were pertinent to the Committee's topic of inquiry, which was ostensibly Communist Party activities within the Albany area, with special reference to unions. In joining with Warren, Douglas, Black, and Brennan, whose aversion to the Committee had been repeatedly demonstrated, Stewart shifted the court's balance. In 1962 the same five-man majority rejected a group of six contempt-of-Congress convictions, two of which—Norton Anthony Russell and John Gojack—derived from the Un-American Activities Committee, because their indictments had not identified the specific subject under inquiry at the time of the defendants' alleged default. (Clark and Harlan dissented, while the ailing Frankfurter and the recently arrived White did not participate.) Moreover, in overturning convictions in a pair of cases—Frank Grumman and Bernard Silber—that arose out of the Committee's 1957 investigation into the communications industry, the court decided that it itself might take note of a faulty indictment even though the defendant made no mention of it in his appeal, thereby casting a shadow of uncertainty over nearly every contempt case then pending.

A still more ominous decision was handed down in 1963, in the case of Edward Yellin, who had refused to answer questions

the House Un-American Activities Committee should realize that he runs the risk of being subpoenaed to appear at a hearing in some far-off place, of being questioned with regard to every minute detail of his past life, of being asked to report all the gossip he may have heard about any of his friends and acquaintances, of being accused by the Committee of membership in the Communist Party, of being held up to the public as a subversive and a traitor, of being jailed for contempt if he refuses to cooperate with the Committee in its probe of his mind and associations, and of being branded by his neighbors, employer and erstwhile friends as a menace to society *regardless of the outcome of that hearing.*"

on grounds of the First Amendment in the 1958 hearings in Gary, Indiana. Here the court ruled for the defendant on the ingenious grounds that the Committee had failed to comply with its own Rule IV-A, which called for an executive hearing if, among other reasons, the majority of a subcommittee believed that a public hearing might unjustly injure a witness's reputation. Arens had turned down a request by Yellin's attorney for an executive hearing without giving the subcommittee an opportunity to consider the question. It would be an easy matter for the Committee thereafter to arrange its rules without disturbing in the slightest its accustomed methods of operation. The omen lay in the fact that this decision was the first on a Committee contempt case written since Felix Frankfurter had been replaced on the high bench by Arthur Goldberg. Now, even with Stewart joining Clark, Harlan, and White in dissent, the five-to-four majority which had given the Committee victory in the Barenblatt case and the Braden-Wilkinson case had conclusively swung the other way.

The cannon of the Supreme Court and Cyrus Eaton's six-shooter were not the only armament leveled against the temples of security in the late fifties, and the Un-American Activities Committee made a prime target. Anti-Committee protests there had always been, outside the hearing room and inside, from Communists, friends of Communists, and authentic civil libertarians, but now there were more protests and more vigorous ones. Some witnesses, particularly the hard-line C.P. members, raised cain as a matter of tactics. Some were incited by the snideness of Arens or the bullying of Scherer. Since no court ever held a witness in contempt of committee because he had behaved contemptuously, the only option available to the Congressmen when their patience was tried was to order troublesome persons from their sight, a penalty that was generally accepted like a medal.

The unfriendly witnesses followed as strict a pattern as the investigators, and charges of racism became popular accompaniments to the Fifth Amendment as the civil rights movement built up national momentum. In 1960 Paul Robeson, Jr., the Negro C.P. pillar Benjamin Davis, and Jesse Gray, the Harlem agitator, told off a subcommittee that was in New York to ask questions about the Vienna Youth Festival, where middle-aged officials of the Party from middle Europe had put their young American comrades through the usual anti-American exercises. In September 1958 a Negro witness in Los Angeles demanded of the Committee why it wasn't investigating the efforts being made in Little Rock, Arkansas, to nullify the Supreme Court's ruling on school integration, and across the country in Newark that month another Negro witness, on being asked where he was born, replied, "Mr. Arens, I was born in the state where yesterday the Reverend Martin Luther King was arrested by the courthouse at Montgomery, Alabama." The Newark hearings, the rowdiest of the 1958 season, had to be recessed on opening day owing to the noise. The following day a U.S. marshal took matters into his own hands and ejected the aforementioned Negro because the man called him Wyatt Earp. When the witness's lawyer objected, the marshal, incensed by suggestions from the audience that he belonged in Little Rock, warned, "I will throw you out too." Willis, chairman of the Newark subcommittee, afterward commended the peace officer for his "astute law enforcement and decorous conduct." As for demonstrations outside the building, such as those that greeted the 1959 subcommittee in San Juan, the unvarying response of the Congressmen was to credit them to the Emergency Civil Liberties Committee, formed in 1951 as a kind of benevolent and protective association for Communists in trouble, and they took to summoning activist opponents, like Frank Wilkinson and Carl Braden, who had tainted political records. In Chicago in 1959, two leaders of the Chicago Committee to Defend Democratic Rights, which had been organized to demonstrate against the investigation of the meat packers, were subpoenaed and charged with C.P. affiliations. By their behavior in the Committee room, such witnesses did nothing to refute the Committee charge that Communists were behind the opposition.

Rousing though a number of the hearings were between

1957 and 1960, they only served as curtain raisers to the great anti-Committee outburst of the period, the May 1960 demonstrations in San Francisco. California first worked its appeal on the Committee in Martin Dies's time, and it never flagged. No year passed between 1951 and 1960 that did not find a subcommittee in Los Angeles or San Francisco calling forth alleged Communists in entertainment, in education, in the professions, or merely at large. These visits were generally met by an angry opposition that featured but was by no means limited to familiar Communist apologists, and four days of hearings in San Francisco in June 1957, which opened a day after the Watkins decision had been delivered, did a great deal to broaden the base of protest. As a grim overture to these hearings, whose subject was the "extent, character and objectives of Communist Party activities within the professions," a young cancer researcher named William K. Sherwood committed suicide. He left a note expressing his anxiety over the publicity that was about to rain upon him: "My life and my livelihood are now threatened by the House Committee . . . I will be in two days assassinated by publicity . . . I would love to spend the next few years in laboratories but I would hate to spend them in jail." To settle the blame for a man's suicide on any exterior cause is a dubious enterprise, but the Committee's critics seized the opportunity. They exploited a statement that the biochemist had prepared—"The Committee's trail is strewn with blasted lives and the wreckage of youthful careers"—and a charge which his widow attempted without success to have put in the record: "You have helped to kill my husband and make my four children fatherless . . ." Whatever the justice of this accusation, it could not fail to impress upon the public what the Chief Justice had had in mind when in his opinion in the Watkins case he chastened the Committee for exposing for the sake of exposure. The suicide also drew attention to the fact that the San Francisco subcommittee, headed by Walter, was allowing the hearings to be televised in defiance of the no-TV rule laid down by Speaker Rayburn before the 1952 Detroit hearings and again when the Democrats recaptured Congress in 1955. (The televising of hearings in New

Orleans and in Baltimore earlier in the year had escaped notice.) Although Rayburn told reporters that his ban still held—"There will not be any more committee or subcommittee hearings in Washington or anywhere else televised or broadcast by radio. Period."—Walter permitted the TV cameras to continue operating, and it required a private meeting of the two men, who had once been close but had drifted apart as Walter went the way of the subversive hunter, to get the matter settled; there would be no television, period.

None of the people called to testify in June 1957—teachers, lawyers, doctors, actors, an architect, a radio broadcaster—were charged with having done anything remotely subversive, and if not for the suicide and the ensuing dispute over TV coverage, these hearings would not have been long remembered. But many Californians had not yet been able to forget them when the Committee, with great fanfare, again turned its attentions westward in 1959. Its actions in that year and the next seemed designed to test whether the temper of the country had really changed since Harold Velde roamed, and the answer was soon forthcoming. Early in June, Walter announced that 110 California teachers, seventy in Los Angeles and forty in the San Francisco area, had been subpoenaed for hearings later that month. They were a vulnerable group, for under a 1950 state law a loyalty oath was a prerequisite for obtaining teaching credentials. The Committee denied leaking their names, but a good number found their way into northern California newspapers. Protests followed; a spokesman for the northern California branch of the American Civil Liberties Union called the procedure "needless, sadistic harassment that cannot possibly be helpful for legislative purposes."

The harassment had only begun. Earlier in the year a Los Angeles subcommittee under Walter had taken two days of testimony in executive session from persons whom unidentified informants had named as having attended C.P. meetings. All took the Fifth, and the Committee released the transcripts a few weeks later without giving the source of its information or holding the anticipated public hearings. It was a case of run and hit. Now, in June, hearings of the subpoenaed teachers were postponed to September because, according to Walter, the ramifications of the situation were "so extensive and malignant" that further investigation was required. His action gave observers grounds for suspecting that there were too few ramifications rather than too many—indeed, that there was hardly any situation at all. The California Teachers Association, complaining that the leaking of names and the delay had put the subpoenaed teachers in the position of standing accused for an entire summer with no opportunity to reply, made the mistake of suggesting that the Committee pass along its information to local school boards, which could then hear the accused teachers in private. To everyone's amazement and his own evident relief, Walter accepted that proposal. He agreed to give the names to local boards so that they might interrogate the teachers and send the transcripts to the Committee. When the A.C.L.U. sought to enjoin the Committee from passing on its files—which, once again, were compilations of uninvestigated charges from unidentified sources—the material was hastily delivered to state authorities. The state's attorney general promised that he would keep the names secret, whereupon investigator William A. Wheeler, the Committee's California specialist, sent the names directly to county officials.

As a result of these maneuverings, several teachers lost their jobs. The price of this accomplishment to the Committee was high, however. It had taken the role of an adjunct police agency, supplying raw data to authorities with the power to punish. The role was not entirely untried, but it had not in recent years been played so nakedly. Unable to conceive that the California performance could find offense in the eyes of any but traitors and their dupes, the members of the Committee searched for Communist and fellow-traveling instigators of the ensuing protests. But if the protests—from newspapers, unions, and Episcopal, Methodist, and Quaker groups, among others—did not represent quite the groundswell of indignation that publicists on the left liked to pretend, they were not so mysteriously motivated that one had to go rooting about for Communists. How large a part this opposition played in turning back the Committee is a matter for speculation, but certainly the retreat heartened opponents for the battle soon to come.

Appropriately, it was a representative from California, James Roosevelt, who in these years raised aloft the standard in Congress against the Un-American Activities Committee. The flag had little starch to it. While individual Congressmen were willing to criticize the Committee for its random adventures, such as that involving the Air Force manual, even the most liberal of them had no spirit for an open confrontation. Through the nineteen-fifties, the Committee's annual appropriation rose steadily and passed the House with no semblance of debate. When it was given $305,000 in 1958, objection was uttered by a single legislator, Roy W. Wier, a Minnesota Democrat. (New York's Adam Clayton Powell said afterward that he was against the appropriation too because the Committee had not investigated the Ku Klux Klan.) A year later, with the appropriation up to $327,000, Wier was joined by Roosevelt, after the latter's proposal to turn the Committee's functions over to the Judiciary Committee had been allowed to perish in the Rules Committee. This proposal was unanimously rejected by the House Republican Conference, which took the unusual step of singling it out for rebuke, and Speaker Rayburn, concerned as ever for the Democratic Party's image, would not permit it to come to the floor; nevertheless, it was well publicized and had the effect of stirring up fresh waves of discontent with the Committee's practices. In April 1959 Harry Truman provided the discontented with a valuable quotation when he called the Committee the "most un-American thing in the country today." A week later, at the prodding of his friend and fellow Missourian Morgan Moulder, Truman added that he had had in mind the excesses of Martin Dies and Harold Velde, but the Committee's critics, who were in no mood for nice distinctions between one chairman and another, continued to make capital of the original, unqualified remark.

On April 25, 1960, Roosevelt rose again in the House to ask flatly that the Committee be abolished. His speech, "The Dragon Slayers," based mainly on the 1959–1960 record, was a good-humored, reasoned argument against the Committee's justification for existing. Referring to its constant warnings of possible espionage by Communists wherever unearthed, he granted that left-wing meat workers might conceivably poison the nation's meat supply, but made it plain that he was not considering becoming a vegetarian on that account. He said that he could see no end to the Committee's anxieties "except to say that such heretics cannot be permitted gainful employment, and then I suppose we should put them to death to avoid watching them starve." Roosevelt pointed out that whatever one thought of the Air Force training manual's remarks about the clergy, they were no business of the Un-American Activities Committee; Air Force manuals fell within the jurisdiction of the House Armed Services Committee. He noted that the $327,000 allocated to the Committee on Un-American Activities in 1960 was substantially more than the sums given most House committees, including such consequential bodies as the Ways and Means Committee and the Judiciary Committee, which actually handled legislation. The Un-American Activities Committee, in Roosevelt's summation, was expensive, useless, redundant, "sanctimoniously cruel," "an agency for the destruction of human dignity and Constitutional rights." Scherer's response ten days later was to say that such criticism was just the sort of thing that came from Communists.

The greater part of Roosevelt's speech in April 1960 was given over to the previous year's subpoenaing of teachers, and that clumsy affair was still green when, a few weeks later, Willis, Scherer, and Johansen presented themselves in San Francisco with the intention of questioning several dozen witnesses about "current operations" of the Communist Party of northern California. These were not, it turned out, the promised, delayed, suspended hearings of the California teachers; only six teachers took the Fifth Amendment on this visit. Most of the three days in San Francisco's City Hall were divided between two informants—Karl Prussion, who had left the Communist Party nine months earlier after more than twenty years in it on behalf of the F.B.I., and Barbara Hartle, a redeemed Communist who had made her peace with the Committee in 1956—and a handful of local C.P. lights. (Irving Fishman, the customs

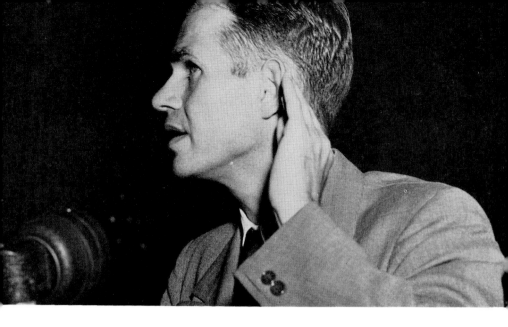

Alger Hiss claimed that the newspaper photograph above, published before his public confrontation with Whittaker Chambers, below, was what gave Chambers the idea of telling the Committee that the Hiss he knew years before was deaf in one ear. In the scene below, Hiss is third from left at the second table, for some reason smiling.

Posed around Robert
Stripling as if they were
studying the microfilm
found in Whittaker
Chambers's pumpkin were
(left to right) Committee
investigators Louis Russell,
William Wheeler, Robert
Gaston, Donald Appell,
C. E. McKillips.

The appearance of the
microfilm caused Richard
Nixon to interrupt a
Caribbean cruise and, with
the assistance of the Coast
Guard, hasten photogeni-
cally back to Washington.

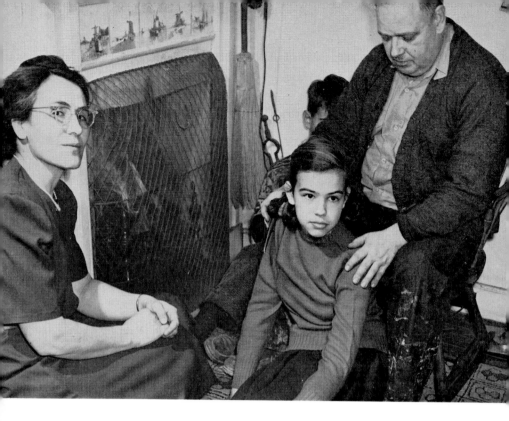

In the aftermath of their remarkable case, Chambers sought out the quiet of his Maryland farm and Hiss was taken to the penitentiary.

Did Chairman Velde's smiling handshake at the conclusion of Bishop G. Bromley Oxnam's ten hours of testimony mean that all was forgiven? Not exactly.

The gentleman pointing something out to Representative Francis Walter was Matthew Cvetic, one of the early Committee informants.

During the periodically renewed hearings on show business during the nineteen-fifties, (clockwise) the actor John Garfield apologized for his past enthusiasms; the choreographer Jerome Robbins gave the names of a few Communist associates; the bandleader Artie Shaw wept; and the playwright Arthur Miller announced that he was planning to marry Marilyn Monroe.

When fire hoses did not extinguish the anti-Committee demonstration in the San Francisco City Hall, the police took to dragging demonstrators down the marble staircase.

Flowers, applause, and a cute baby greeted Mrs. Dagmar Wilson, a leader of Women Strike for Peace, as she approached the Committee's witness chair.

Robert Shelton, the Ku Klux Klan head, shown here getting decked out for a rally and cross-burning in South Carolina, was more sedately received when his turn to testify arrived.

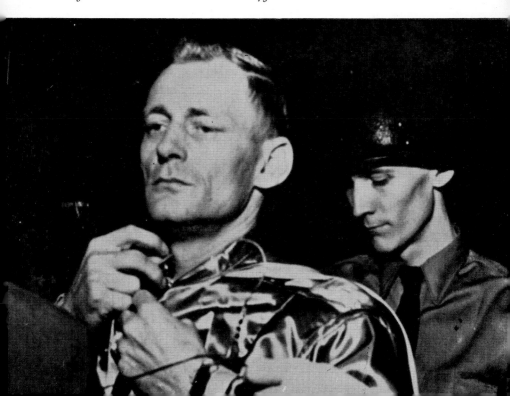

The high point of the hearings of opponents of the war in Vietnam came as attorney Arthur Kinoy was vigorously assisted from the room. A few days later, Representative Joe Pool, who had ordered Kinoy out, got a rousing reception from the Veterans of Foreign Wars.

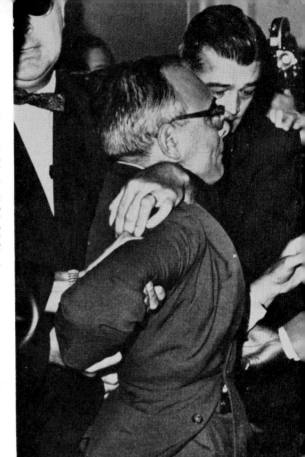

official whose appearance at Committee functions had become a custom, was also on hand, with his mail sack.)

The informants were superlatively obliging. In addition to supplying names, Prussion told the Congressmen that 10,000 Communists were enough to carry out an insurrection and Mrs. Hartle, who had been convicted under the Smith Act, replied in the affirmative when Arens asked, "You have found your way back to God and patriotism, is that correct?" Peaceful coexistence with the Soviets, she reported, was a snare and a delusion. The professional Communists, too, outdid themselves. They were extraordinarily obstreperous. They played to the TV cameras—in use again despite the events of 1957—and presented themselves alternately as champions of democracy and martyrs to the inquisition. They baited Congressmen and counsel with relish; one man addressed his long speech on the reasons why he was taking the Fifth Amendment to "Honorable beaters of children and sadists . . ." Another told Arens that he sounded "halfway like a nut." (Arens was in form, too. Questioning a witness who had visited the Far East some years before, he asked: "While you were there, did you make inquiries respecting the emasculation, the crucifixion of the Christian missionaries who had been teaching in Red China?") During a recess on the first day several witnesses, accompanied by a few members of the audience, made use of an available microphone to attack the Committee and sing *The Star Spangled Banner*. The Congressmen let this act, recorded by the TV cameras, proceed for a while, then called the riot squad to lead the singing group away. The master of ceremonies, Archie Brown, a Communist longshoreman, was removed twice that Thursday and so was not available when he was called to the witness chair. On Friday he was summoned again, but this time he couldn't make it because of the commotion taking place just beyond the doors of the hearing room. He finally did appear on Saturday, attempted to make a motion to "disqualify the Committee," and was ejected for the third time, thereby setting a record that still stands.

The great events of the May hearing occurred outside the hearing room. The days leading up to the Committee's visit were full of warnings. Students from the Berkeley campus of the University of California and San Francisco State College joined in demonstrations against the long-delayed execution of Caryl Chessman; hundreds of residents of the Bay Area attended a lively meeting of the Berkeley board of education at which two probationary teachers who had been subpoenaed the year before were given a hearing; student newspapers ran attacks on the Committee by faculty members and other groups that recalled the events of 1959; the one University of California student who had been subpoenaed—because he was a delegate to the 1959 national C.P. convention—did some agitating around campus; anti-Committee groups of various political shadings welcomed the investigators to San Francisco with protest meetings and statements. Emotions were building up, and as the Congressmen set to work on May 12, one thousand people, mostly students, demonstrated against them in Union Square, while several hundred others marched around City Hall and lined up before the doors of the hearing room.

On the second day of the hearings, Friday, the number of demonstrators had grown substantially. A fair degree of order was maintained outside City Hall, where loudspeakers were set up to relay the hearings. Inside the building, however, some two hundred students seeking admission to the hearing room grew incensed upon observing that most of the seats were set aside for friends of the Committee. Investigator Wheeler had issued passes, he explained on opening day, "to keep the Communists from stacking the meeting. We wanted some decent people in here." Wheeler feared that if spectators were admitted first-come-first-served, the hearings would get out of hand; the students were prepared to guffaw at appropriate moments and the hostile witnesses were prepared to play up to them. But by packing the hearing room, he provided the protestors with a real cause and an effective rallying cry. On the first day, before breaking into *The Star Spangled Banner*, the subpoenaed witnesses, led by Archie Brown, kept yelling for the Committee to "Open the doors! Open the doors!" On Friday morning the students gathered peacefully, but became restive as the hours passed and only a handful of their number were admitted. They were noisy enough to disturb a judge attempting to carry on his duties in another room of the building. The precise cause of the event that has entered the annals of the Un-American Activities Committee as "the Communist-led riots" remains shadowed in controversy. The police, backed by the Committee and J. Edgar Hoover, maintained afterward that a student leaped the barricade, assaulted a policeman with his own billy, and led a surge of students toward the hearing room. But the young man charged with this aggression was found not guilty. The students and their defenders maintain that at 1:15 p.m., with no particular warning and for no particular cause, the police turned high-pressure fire hoses on them. For the next half hour, they were washed out of the rotunda of the building and dragged bumping down City Hall's marble stairs, with an occasional assist from a policeman's club. "People should be able to differ without being disagreeable," commented Mr. Willis. Upwards of five dozen demonstrators, two of whom were alleged to be Communists, were hauled off to jail, the charges against all but one—the young man accused of jumping the policeman—being dismissed by a sensible judge two weeks later.

Giving way to their uncontrollable tic, the Congressmen on the scene at once blamed what Willis called "probably the worst incident in the history of the Committee" on the Communists. Scherer told the House that the riots were "clearly planned at the highest Communist levels" and J. Edgar Hoover accommodated the Committee with a report entitled *Communist Target—Youth; Communist Infiltration and Agitation Tactics,* which used self-congratulatory statements of Communist leaders to prove that "such a Communist coup has not occurred in the San Francisco area for twenty-five years." The Committee's most elaborate exposition of its view of the affair was presented in the form of a forty-five-minute movie, put together by a commercial firm in Washington out of subpoenaed TV newsreel films, and narrated by Fulton Lewis III. A tricky piece of work, replete with distortions and irrelevancies, gossip and surmise, it became a *cause célèbre* in itself, exciting protests and counterprotests wherever it was shown.

Events were presented out of sequence in order to strengthen the connection between Communists and students; a shot of Harry Bridges, who had nothing to do with the demonstrations, was inserted for flavor; as the film showed students being thumped down the stairs, Fulton Lewis III spoke feelingly of the trials of the police. (An amended version had to be produced to repair the more blatant distortions in the original.) *Operation Abolition*—the film's title was taken from a 1957 report on the Emergency Civil Liberties Committee—became an official document of the Committee and hundreds of prints were soon circulated to private groups and TV stations around the country, and seen by millions of people, to the profit of the Washington company. An excellent antidote, *Operation Correction*, produced by the Civil Liberties Union of northern California, used the same film strips with a different narration to expose the misleading techniques of the Committee's hired hands, but it never managed to catch up with the original. Nor did *Autopsy on Operation Abolition*, a pro-con documentary put out by the Catechetical Guild of St. Paul, a large publisher of Catholic educational aids.

Since the days of the Paris Commune, Marxists have taken to themselves credit for events in which they played but a passing part, and they have been supported in their pretensions by their heartiest foes. Something of what the Committee's spokesmen saw in the San Francisco disturbances, as set forth by Scherer in an astonishing harangue at the conclusion of the hearings, was visible even to objective eyes. Communists and their sympathizers in campus groups and the Emergency Civil Liberties Committee (Frank Wilkinson was on hand and so won a featured role in *Operation Abolition*) were prominent in the efforts to build up resentment against the Committee before its visit. At the hearings, the subpoenaed Communists did their utmost to incite a riot. And there was no doubt that the Party was delighted with the results. But that was all that Scherer, Hoover, and the others saw, all that they had ever seen in protests against the Committee; this time the explanation was not necessary, it was not sufficient. By calling the 5,000 students who demonstrated outside City Hall on the last day of hearings "victims of this despicable propaganda plot," Scherer displayed his own incapacity to sense the impulses at work among the young people at Berkeley and elsewhere around the country. The Committee's subpoenas and cancellations and the final growling withdrawal in California in 1959 had prepared the ground for the May 1960 demonstrations; Wilkinson and his cohorts had tended it, as did many non-Communists and anti-Communists; and the police had assisted in their inimitable way. But a demonstration of such proportions and such vehemence required something more than this. For the students, the upsurge in San Francisco proclaimed the end of a decade of cold-war hibernation; college campuses were becoming centers of national discontent over larger issues than the Un-American Activities Committee.

"Looking at the riots and chaos Communists have created in other countries, many Americans point to the strength of our nation and say, 'It can't happen here,'" wrote J. Edgar Hoover. "The Communist success in San Francisco in May, 1960, proves it can happen here." But the policeman Hoover had no inkling of what was really happening. In 1960 students had already been moved to action by the civil rights struggle; in a few years they would be holding teach-ins on Vietnam. Their protests would take diverse and sometimes puzzling forms—Caesar is supposed to have remarked on first hearing Brutus speak in public, "I know not what this young man intends, but whatever he intends, he intends vehemently"—but no Party line could accommodate them. Though the radicals of the thirties might march along with the radicals of the sixties when conditions seemed suitable, their dreams were not the same. The new activists spared no particular affection for the Soviet paradise; nor were their emotions locked up with the Moscow trials or the war in Spain. Their discontent was formless and pervasive. They saw after eight years of Dwight Eisenhower what the young have often seen, their destinies in the hands of old, cautious, unimaginative, unfeeling men, and they needed to break out. The campus at Berkeley became a testing place of this remarkably non-ideological, even anti-ideological movement, and the arrival of the Un-American Activities Committee, which had been engaged in the harassment of teachers, students, and political non-conformists for twenty years, was galvanic. "Nobody incited us, nobody misguided us," declared fifty-eight of the arrested students after the charges against them were dismissed. "We were led by our own convictions, and we still stand firmly by them."

To those who converged on City Hall, the Committee, represented by men made nervous and angry by any show of unorthodox opinion, stood as a symbol and tool of the Establishment, a deadening hand extended from Washington to quash the impulses of dissent wherever they might spring up. How could these young men and women, in their teens and early twenties, be expected to know that the Committee itself had been doing battle with the Establishment since its earliest days and that never had it been farther from the center of America's political life than in the year of the election of John F. Kennedy?

15

★ ★ ★ ★ ★

1961-1966: The Lean Years

IN 1961 and 1962, Francis Walter served the new Administration as a Congressional lieutenant. His long tenure and forceful personality, his strong position among the Democratic representatives, his reputation as a conservative, albeit aberrated, and a party regular, albeit temperamental, combined to make him a valuable contact for the White House in a Congress that was not enthusiastic over New Frontiers. But while he was concluding his career amid the expressed esteem of those who needed his services (at a dinner in his honor in 1961 Speaker Rayburn, letting bygones be gone, praised Walter for having "dug out more dens of disloyalty than any man who has ever lived in the United States"), his Committee, already a shadow, was fading, fading.[1] There were but forty-four days of published hearings in the two years of the eighty-seventh Congress, several closed to the public, few newsworthy.

Most of the organizations selected for the Committee's table made meager fare. They had a handful of members, little money, short lives, and no influence. There was the Fund for Social Analysis, set up early in 1958 as, frankly, "an informal organization of individuals interested in aiding Marxist research," whose function was to give modest grants-in-aid "for studies of problems posed by Marxist theory and its applica-

---

[1] Joining Walter on the Committee in the eighty-seventh Congress were four Democrats—Moulder, Doyle, Willis, and Tuck—and four Republicans—Scherer, Johansen, Donald G. Bruce, a freshman from Indiana, and Henry C. Schadeberg, a freshman from Wisconsin. Tavenner was director, Alfred M. Nittle, counsel, and John C. Walsh, co-counsel.

tion." The Fund's bent was evident from the names of grantors and grantees—Barrows Dunham, Russell Nixon, Herbert Aptheker—and though these scholars were not above making a bit of propaganda for their side, their pursuits were harmless as well as predictable. There was the National Assembly for Democratic Rights, organized at a Giant Freedom Rally in September 1961 as a response to the June decision of the Supreme Court upholding (temporarily) the McCarran Act. It was the creature of groups threatened by the law with forced registration. With W. E. B. Du Bois, John Abt, Rockwell Kent, Willard Uphaus, Carl Marzani, and Benjamin Davis among its sponsors and well-wishers, the exposure of this group as being "under concealed control of the Communist Party" was an exercise in the self-evident. There were the Medical Aid to Cuba Committee and Friends of British Guiana run, respectively, by admirers of Fidel Castro and Cheddi Jagan. To judge by the Committee's information, these groups had done nothing more than they were avowedly in existence to do: send medical supplies to Cuba and a printing press to the People's Progressive Party of then British Guiana. This set of hearings, which opened two weeks after the October 1962 Cuban missile crisis, was not the first or the last demonstration of Committee interest in Castro's supporters in this country. The Fair Play for Cuba Committee, the major pro-Castro group, had already been claimed by the Senate Internal Security Subcommittee, but on a trip to the West in April, Doyle and Tavenner had studied "Communist and Trotskyist Activity Within the Greater Los Angeles Chapter of the Fair Play for Cuba Committee" and found "a significant increase in the power and influence" of southern California's Trotskyists. (The Los Angeles visit was the first to that part of the country by a subcommittee since the demonstrations in San Francisco. Hundreds of pickets were at hand on opening day, but their interest fell off when it became apparent that whatever was being done was being done in closed session, with a minimum of publicity.)

A few certifiable C.P. functionaries who had quit or been ousted for "revisionism" or "ultra-leftist dogmatism" or other sins during the Party's late ideological turmoils were summoned but refused redemption at the Committee's hands. The Committee thereupon concluded, on the basis of a presentation by Francis McNamara, its staff authority, that the Communist Party was not a democratic institution. There were also hearings on the communications union, on Soviet propaganda outlets, on the World Youth Festival in Helsinki, on the oppressive conditions in Russia and China, and on Communist activities in Cleveland, in the course of which, once again, a man identified as a Party member by an F.B.I. informant turned out to be an F.B.I. informant himself. Taken in all, the Committee's record for the greater part of 1961 and 1962 was like summer television, heavily dependent on cheap packages and reruns.

The feature event of the eighty-seventh Congress came in December 1962 when a subcommittee under Doyle held hearings in Washington on Women Strike for Peace. As emperors once claimed descent from the heavens, so activist groups of every sort attribute their existence to a spontaneous urge of that contemporary divinity, the Ordinary American. In the case of W.S.P., it was the Ordinary American Housewife, and there was more substance to the claim than usual. The perils of radioactive fallout, particularly to young children, had been dramatically publicized during the last years of the Eisenhower Administration, and even the least political mother reading her copy of *Redbook* or watching television must have felt uncomfortable at the insistent connecting of her baby's bones to nuclear tests. The more political took quickly to the suggestion in September 1961 of a Washington, D.C., illustrator of children's books, Mrs. Dagmar Wilson, that women get together and work for a test ban, an avowed Kennedy goal that was meeting resistance in Congress, the Pentagon, and the Atomic Energy Commission, as well as in the Kremlin, which had a few weeks before broken a two-year moratorium and ordered a resumption of testing. The issue in the fall and winter of 1961–1962 was whether the United States would resume its own tests, and the major efforts of the rapidly and loosely organized W.S.P. were directed at discouraging such a response. In November 1961 tens of thousands of women in dozens of cities demonstrated for a test ban. In January 1962 some 1,700 women converged on Washington to picket the White House and buttonhole Congressmen. In February there was picketing at the United Nations. In April, shortly before the President ordered a new round of U.S. tests, fifty-one of the women made a well-publicized flight to Geneva to lend encouragement to the disarmament negotiators.

The Committee, which had preached in years of reports, consultations, and friendly testimony that anything less than a call for holy war against the Soviets was suspect, could only take a sour view of the ladies' activities, and the December hearings were arranged by the staff to make the best connection they could between Communists and the peace movement. The hearings were designed to show, as an obliging writer in the *National Review* commented afterward, that the women's activities "are—if not controlled by the Communists—at least of immense help to the Communist peace offensive." The staff began its demonstration, rather oddly, with a young New Yorker who, under F.B.I. instructions, had accepted $3,000 from a pair of Russian U.N. employees to finance his campaign for a seat in the state assembly. He was in no way connected with Women Strike for Peace or any other peace group. But Counsel Nittle managed to extract from his testimony the nugget that the Russians wanted him to emphasize in his campaign speeches such subjects as peace, disarmament, nuclear testing, and trade with the Communist bloc. As the hearings progressed, Nittle called a few leaders of peace groups other than W.S.P. who had substantial records as Communists or fellow travelers. Their relationship to W.S.P. was remote but sufficient for the Committee's purpose; despite the assurance of Chairman Doyle, aged seventy-five and vaguer than ever, that being for peace did not automatically make one a Communist, the hearings were arranged to cast the darkest shadow possible on the entire peace movement.

Among those attracted to Women Strike for Peace were numbers of veterans of leftist battles of the thirties and forties, some of them Party members. The nuclear test ban was much more than a Communist cause, but it was a cause in which apologists for the U.S.S.R. had an interest, particularly in the months when President Kennedy was pondering the resumption of U.S. tests. Having been through many previous wars, the old-timers moved into the organizational jobs that most of the W.S.P. supporters, young mothers and busy ones, were content to leave to others. The older women were experienced, they were enthusiastic, and they had no infants at home in need of diapering. It was a handful of such peace workers from the New York area on whom the Committee turned a jaundiced eye in December.

The witnesses and the scores of women, a few with babies, most with hats, who made up the greater part of the audience found more fun in the hearings than their interrogators. They rose and sat as one, laughed and applauded on cue. "This movement was inspired and motivated by mothers' love for their children," said the first woman to take the Fifth Amendment, an elderly resident of Scarsdale who, according to Nittle, had been a C.P. member when she taught in the New York public schools a decade or more before. "When they were putting their breakfast on the table they saw not only Wheaties and milk, but they also saw strontium 90 and iodine 131." Applause. (On the first day, too, a man who had worked for the F.B.I. for eleven months before quitting and writing a harsh article about J. Edgar Hoover was ejected when he yelled out an unfavorable opinion of the proceedings.)

On the second day there were bouquets for each witness. "It is nice to get the flowers while you can smell them, isn't it?" observed Doyle, who would be dead in three months. Nittle, attempting to demonstrate, with the help of a chart of organization, that the W.S.P. women were being manipulated by a clique of New York Reds, got into some baffling exchanges with witnesses who insisted that their operations were highly flexible, that jobs went to whoever would do them and the movement ran, somewhat haphazardly, by itself. "This appears to be a most elusive organization . . ." said Nittle as desperation set in. There was a touch of feigned ingenuousness in the testimony, but had Nittle ever watched the workings of his local P.T.A., he would have found it easier to believe or, at any rate, understand the ladies. Matters soon got quite beyond Doyle, who kept insisting that the last thing he intended was to discredit the peace movement; on the second day he had to apologize for having said on the first day, "So far as we know, she is a Communist now because there is no evidence that she is not. If she is not, here is an opportunity for her to clear it up."

Most of the witnesses took the Fifth Amendment, but three —a woman charged with being a member of the American Student Union and the Young Communist League at Vassar in the thirties, who burst into tears on leaving the stand; another, who testified that she had not been a C.P. member for at least five years; and a man who had been adjudged a Communist by the Subversive Activities Control Board in 1956— refused to discuss their past activities or present associations on grounds of the First Amendment. Reeling before adverse court decisions, the Committee made no effort to press contempt charges against any of them. Yet another witness put on display was Elizabeth Moos, mother-in-law of the unfortunate William Remington and a vintage worker in Communist causes; she had nothing special to do with Women Strike for Peace, having given her energies mainly to the Stockholm Peace Appeal and similar causes instigated from abroad. That the Committee summoned her at all was evidence of its intentions toward the W.S.P.

The final witness was Mrs. Dagmar Wilson, the Washington lady generally credited with having gotten the idea for Women Strike for Peace. Nittle made it explicit that he had no evidence of Communist sympathies on Mrs. Wilson's part, and embarked again on a line of questioning designed to show that W.S.P.'s Communists or former Communists were running things, perhaps under supervision of the Kremlin. Mrs. Wilson, affecting a certain giddiness, answered most of Nittle's questions, thereby adding to his confusion. The only question of consequence that Nittle put to her, the question that the Committee had been working up to for three days, was this: "I would like to ask whether you would knowingly permit or encourage a Communist Party member to occupy a leadership position in

Women Strike for Peace." Mrs. Wilson replied: "Well, my dear sir, I have absolutely no way of controlling, do not desire to control, who wishes to join in the demonstrations and the efforts that the women strikers have made for peace. In fact I would also like to go even further. I would like to say that unless everybody in the whole world joins us in this fight, then God help us." When Nittle pressed her on whether she planned to take any action to prevent Communists from assuming places of leadership or to eliminate those who had already attained such places, she answered, "Certainly not."

This answer, though understandable in the circumstances and refreshing after a decade in which it was rarely allowed in public that Communists were also human beings, was nonetheless glib. The precedent for these hearings was a 1960 investigation, by the Senate Internal Security Subcommittee under Thomas J. Dodd, of the National Committee for a Sane Nuclear Policy. As a result of Senator Dodd's initiative and amid heartfelt anguish, reluctant expulsions, and sad resignations, the leaders of SANE decided that they could not in the future abide the presence of Communists. In part, this was a merely prudential move; at stake was the future of a growing and effective organization whose goals would be jeopardized by any suspicion of Communist direction. But in the light of the entire history of American Communism, it was also sound policy on a higher level; as the SANE statement noted, members of the Communist Party are "not free . . . to apply to the misconduct of the Soviet or Chinese government the same standards by which they challenge others."

For Mrs. Wilson to take a similar stand publicly at the instance of the Un-American Activities Committee was unthinkable; it would have been interpreted as an admission of guilt and a note of retreat. Moreover, since W.S.P. was not so tightly controlled as SANE, even had she been so inclined, she would have had no ready way to remove the Communists, no charters to revoke or staff to be fired. W.S.P. was given mainly to the spectacular gesture—picketing the White House, a flight to Geneva. By the time of the hearings, the women had already experienced their greatest moments; the enthusiasm that had been so quickly generated would quickly wane. (The hearings before the Committee may actually have stimulated W.S.P. for a time. Upon leaving the Caucus Room, seventy women walked twenty blocks to the White House, bearing signs on the order of END THE ARMS RACE, NOT THE HUMAN RACE and PEACE IS AMERICAN.) The Senate's ratification of the test-ban treaty in September 1962 was a victory that would turn W.S.P., briefly a notable phenomenon, into just another peace group of mostly well-meaning women. As for the Communists among them, the worst they could do within such an organization was to add their inimitable anti-American touches to the signs they had printed up.

There was something excessive in handing out bouquets to witnesses who preferred not to incriminate themselves, and Mrs. Wilson's explanation of her position regarding Communists was not a model of clear thinking—"The solid support of the women for those who took the Fifth is an indication that we are simply not concerned with personal points of view" —but the ladies of W.S.P., like more objective observers, could not fail to discern the Committee's purpose in bringing on these hearings and they were in no mood to capitulate. It was an obvious and awkward attack on the supporters of a nuclear test ban and it left the well-meaning Doyle and the ill-prepared Nittle floundering in confusion, bathed in ridicule. It would be some time before the Committee again engaged itself with peace organizations, and then it would choose its subjects with more care.

On May 31, 1963, Francis Walter, ill since the beginning of the year, died of leukemia. He had brought to the chairmanship of the Committee a greater distinction, competence, and sense of legislative purpose than it had ever known. But like the respectable burgher turned loose in a brothel, he gave way to his surroundings and exhibited the more perverse side of his nature. It was as though he caught infection from the shades of men he knew to be inferior to him: Martin Dies, J. Parnell Thomas, Harold Velde. Many of the symptoms he despised in them reappeared during his chairmanship: malice, vindictiveness, irresponsibility, inanity—all flourished in the Committee hothouse, fertilized and tended by Arens and his staff. Whatever its psychological cost, sublimation is often a virtue in politics; in giving Walter an opportunity to act out, the Committee distorted a notable career. At the end, after serving in the House for more than fifteen terms, he was anathema on the left yet, except for certain ceremonial occasions, no hero of the right. In 1962 the Conservative Society of America gave his Committee its highest rating of all standing committees of Congress, but gave him a rating of zero on his voting record. "That means," explained Edith Kermit Roosevelt in her newsletter of the distant right, "Rep. Walter is listed by the hard-core conservative group as voting liberal-socialist 100 percent of the time." The Democratic leadership valued him, yet was periodically exasperated by his more manic moods. So complicated a figure was he that on his passing, the liberal Washington *Post* found for him respectful words which it had had no occasion to print while he lived. The Committee, like a bartender whose grief over a customer's passing depends on how much he drank, wrote in its memorial tribute, ". . . his many contributions in the field of national security will be an everlasting monument to his memory and will serve as a living inspiration to all those who serve after him." But it was those heady liquors of international security that betrayed the man.

The torch was handed on to Edwin E. Willis of Louisiana, who, his party's leaders could feel confident, would not use it to burn down the House, Willis, aged fifty-nine, had been in Congress for fourteen years without starting any fires. There were several other changes on the Committee in 1963. Scherer, the alleged Birchite, and Moulder, the putative liberal, retired, and Doyle, who had never wearied of his role of kindly Uncle Clyde though he wearied everyone else, died,[2] and was

---

[2] These departures left three Democratic vacancies, which were filled by Joe R. Pool of Texas, Richard H. Ichord of Missouri, and George F. Senner, Jr., of Arizona. The single Republican vacancy was taken by John M. Ashbrook of Ohio. Some months before these changes there was a major staff change: Francis J. McNamara became Committee director, with Tavenner staying on as general counsel and Nittle as counsel.

commemorated by the Committee in lines which he had himself composed:

> Four things you must do
> If you would make your record true;
> To think without confusion clearly,
> To love your fellow men sincerely,
> To act from honest motives purely,
> To trust in God in Heaven securely.

Under Willis, but through no fault of that gentleman, unenterprising though he was, the Committee now settled into the role of the aging rake, living in comfort, tended still by loyal retainers, rocking in his chair and musing idly upon the high times of a lusty youth. Then, without notice, roaring up from the rocking chair, pulling on his trousers, and tearing into town where, likely as not, a bunch of streetcorner troublemakers would be waiting for him, winking and elbowing one another at the sport in store. The question one now began to ask as the Committee charged forth on its infrequent adventures was not, as in the old days, what it was going to inflict on others, but what unpleasantness the others had planned for the Congressmen this time.

On September 12 and 13, 1963, for example, the Committee's Washington hearings of a group of young leftists who had paid a summer visit to Cuba erupted into the noisiest, most violent scenes since San Francisco. After repeatedly, and to no avail, warning his audience to desist from hurrahing every time a witness delivered himself of a rouser against the "racists that are sitting up here in front of me right now," Willis told the police, "Okay, throw them out," and with kicks, screams, and yells of "Fascist!" and "Police brutality!" and "It's like Nazi Germany!" thrown out they were.

The pandemonium in September was part of a series of hearings that occupied the Committee for much of 1963 and into 1964. (The 1964 hearings were quiet, except when a member of the American Nazi Party dashed down the aisle, vaulted a railing, and, hollering, "Down with Castro!", tried to slug a witness.) The Congressmen were bothered by the fact that known and suspected Communists seemed to be going to Cuba at their pleasure despite a State Department ban on such trips. The offenders were in the main members of the Progressive Labor Movement, the creation of two upstate New York men who had been expelled from the Communist Party in 1961 for their Chinese-Albanian tendencies. The P.L.M. youths led sizable groups of students, not all Communists, on visits to Cuba in the summers of 1963 and 1964—expenses paid by the Cuban government, with spending money thrown in. There they were feted by the Cuban Institute for Friendship Among the Peoples, and played ping-pong and baseball with their host Fidel. The P.L.M. leaders missed no opportunity to speak ill of the leaders and institutions of their own country, and they returned home with tales of the glories being wrought in the people's democracy to the south. (One young man, who went along in behalf of the F.B.I. brought home other tales; he became a friendly witness before the Committee.)

The Committee went after these pilgrims on two grounds: first, that they had violated the State Department regulation forbidding travel to Cuba, a charge being studied by a grand jury as well; and second, that they had acted as propagandists for a foreign regime while abroad and after their return. Although counsel Nittle tried to make something of a detective story out of the mechanics by which the group leaders had purchased their tickets and traveled to Cuba via Paris and Prague, the witnesses were anything but secretive about their journeys. They took the Fifth Amendment in response to questions about their fellows ("Certainly to know the names of individuals can be in no way of help to the Congress in framing legislation," said one. "It may be of help in framing individuals but not to frame legislation"), but they were voluble regarding the trip itself, the virtues of Castroism, the defects of the United States, their distaste for the Committee, and their faith in Marxism. The hearings thus became a series of high-school cafeteria debates, with victory on points going easily to the witnesses. For one thing, there was substantial doubt whether the State Department could in fact enforce the ban it had promulgated. Moreover, the witnesses were more practiced debaters, quicker-witted for the most part than any of the Congressmen who took them on and much sharper than counsel Nittle, who was subject to fits of confusion. The outburst on the second day was brought on as much by the incapacity of Chairman Willis to handle the argument of his witness, Phillip Abbott Luce, a young employee of the Emergency Civil Liberties Committee who had acted as press relations man for the touring students, as by the readiness of the P.L.M. partisans to demonstrate:

CHAIRMAN: Did you have knowledge of the State Department rulings that this trip or any other trip without validation of passport constituted a violation of the law and regulation I just quoted a while ago, whether you agreed with them or not? Did you have knowledge of that ruling by the State Department?

LUCE: I would be very lax in my homework if I did not, sir; but again, it is no law. It is Public Notice 179.

CHAIRMAN: You disagree with the ruling of the State Department?

LUCE: I not only disagree with it; it is absolutely and totally unconstitutional.

CHAIRMAN: Are you an attorney?

LUCE: I am not an attorney, but obviously I have as much knowledge of this as you since you cannot find what the law is.

CHAIRMAN: I quoted it to you.

LUCE: You did not quote it to me. You quoted a public notice. Public notices do not have the effect of law. And don't come on to me about that 1185 (b), because that is the Walter-McCarran Act . . .

. . . . . .

CHAIRMAN: And you don't agree with the law?

LUCE: It is not a law. It is a public notice. I do not agree with the public notice because I consider it unconstitutional. I would also like to say this to you, sir . . .

CHAIRMAN: Now we are getting down to it. In other words you take the position that this law and this regulation are unconstitutional?

LUCE: Sir, it is not a law. It is a public notice. Even if there was a law, however, even if there was a law, which there is not, I believe along with Thoreau, Emerson and other people throughout American history that certain rules and regulations must be broken. Now, we did not break a law. We broke a public notice. I want to make that very clear.

CHAIRMAN: But if in your opinion there was a law, you would say . . .

LUCE: I would consider it my duty to break that law as much as the Negro voters in the state of Louisiana and Danville, Virginia, Mr. Tuck, consider the breaking of the state laws when they try to vote.

(*Demonstration in hearing room.*)

CHAIRMAN: Get them out.

LUCE: "Get them out." Throwing them out for clapping. This may be something you can get away with in Louisiana or Virginia, but I can't understand it here.

The general quality of the debates may be appreciated in an exchange from the 1964 hearings, between Representative Senner of Arizona, not the blackest reactionary on the Committee, and a twenty-four-year-old P.L.M. enthusiast named Yvonne Marie Bond:

MISS BOND: This country has monopolies rather than the free enterprise that it is so highly touted to be. I pondered on the solution for these problems for a long time and I was cynical because I thought it had to do with the nature of man that things should always be thus. Then I discovered socialism and found that things don't always have to be.

SENNER: When you use the word "socialism," are you talking about communism? Are you not talking about communism when you say socialism? There is a difference, and you know it.

MISS BOND: Socialism is that stage of economic development before communism.

.　.　.　.　.

MISS BOND: I found out about socialism and the fact that man is able to change his environment and his economic and social structure. I started reading about countries which were socialist, such as Cuba, the Soviet Union and China and other socialist countries. Cuba especially impressed me because it was such a small place and because they seemed to have made such rapid development in alleviating malnutrition and poverty in such a short time. In recalling all the poor people and the

Negro people and the highly taxed workers and even middle-class people . . .

SENNER: Miss Bond, I think this eighty-eighth Congress has done more for education, civil rights and everything else to move this country in the direction of equal opportunities for all. If you will study history correctly, you will find that more millionaires have been made since World War II in this country than ever before in its history.

MISS BOND: While others remain poor. That is just a cure for the symptoms, not the disease.

SENNER: I want to ask you this question: What would happen to you if you would oppose Fidel Castro in the manner that you are opposing the United States government now? What would happen to you?

MISS BOND: That is a silly question because I would not oppose Fidel Castro simply to oppose him. It is not a matter of opposition for opposition's sake; it pertains to reality, to concrete things.

The troopers of the Progressive Labor Movement would, willy nilly, be lumped in with the new left, that catch-all for youthful discontents in the nineteen-sixties, but except in their willingness to flaunt their Marxist faith before the Congressmen, they were barely distinguishable from the old left. It was Cuba now instead of the U.S.S.R. that captured them, and Castro instead of Stalin, but their slogans, their pretensions, their simplifications were the stuff on which the radicals of the thirties had built their towers too. They could in one breath damn Representatives Willis and Tuck for coming from districts where Negroes were deprived of the vote, and acclaim the absence of elections in Cuba: "The Cuban people don't want an election. They honestly do not care to have an election at the national level at this time." Their debut under the Committee's auspices was sufficient to put off even so tried a friend of the left, old and new, as the journalist I. F. Stone who withdrew as moderator of a Town Hall panel discussion on travel to Cuba after the September 1963 hearings with the observation that the students' views "seem to me a mixture of naïveté, Negro nationalist distortions (understandable enough in the light of the Negro's anguish, but still distortions), and out-of-this-world leftism." The Town Hall meeting, presided over by the dependable Corliss Lamont, began with a search by a P.L.M. security band of suspicious-looking characters as they entered and by the forcible ejection of anti-Castroites. It ended on a heavy note of irony when the young radicals requested a police guard to lead them safely to the subway past a mean-looking crowd.

The Committee did not accomplish its announced purposes with these hearings. The students had the better of the legal argument over the State Department[3] ban as well as of the larger controversy over the freedom of Americans to travel wheresoever they would. "Why shouldn't they go?" Robert Kennedy is reported to have said of the first group when he was attorney general. "If I were twenty-one years old, that's what I would like to do this summer." The proposition, suggested by more than one Congressman, that the youths be compelled to register as foreign agents because of their affinity for Castro was silly and invidious. In putting the tiny P.L.M. group on public display, the Committee was in fact aiming beyond the issue of travel in Cuba. These students had all been active in more important protest movements on which the Committee, weighted with conservative Republicans and Democrats from the South, cast a baleful eye; they could be found in all the demonstrations for Negro rights and against the war in Vietnam, shouting the most fiery slogans, waving the wildest banners. "Mr. Maher," asked Representative Senner of a rich young man from Texas who had made the Cuba trip in 1964, "have you contributed any money to any groups to carry on street riots after the passage of the Civil Rights Act of 1964?" The Committee was assiduous in its search for discreditable people who could be blamed for disagreeable occurrences and was expert at finding them. "In any corner of the civilized world," observed Carlyle, "a tub can be inverted and an articulate speaking biped mount thereon." In a demon-

---

[3] In 1967 the Supreme Court upheld the action of a district court in dismissing the indictments against fifty-eight travelers to Cuba. The statute under which the government had attempted to prosecute them, the court observed, was inapplicable since the youths held valid passports at the time of their unauthorized journey.

stration of tens of thousands a couple of dozen P.L.M. extroverts never had any trouble attracting attention. What they lacked in good sense, they made up in audacity, and their exploits in the coming months and years would continue to be grist for the Committee's ever grinding mills.

On the first day of the turbulent September 1963 hearings five leaders of the Cuban pilgrimage were summoned to an executive session of the Committee and were asked to testify behind closed doors since, as Chairman Willis explained, a grand jury was inquiring into "matters relating to the subject of this hearing." The witnesses were not impressed, suspecting perhaps that Willis was losing heart for what promised to be a public ordeal, and the five insisted on their right to be exposed for exposure's sake. Willis conceded, and all lent their voices to the ensuing commotion.

In December 1964 a similar incident occurred, with different results. The Committee's preference for public hearings through the years was famous, in some circles notorious. Where closed hearings were allowed, it usually indicated that the Committee had not yet accumulated sufficient evidence to proceed openly or that public proceedings threatened to result in unfavorable public relations. There is dispute over which reason prevailed in December when a subcommittee under Joe Pool of Texas started an inquiry into the visit to this country in 1963 of Kaoru Yasui, dean of the law school at Hoesi University in Japan, a visit that had reportedly caused controversy between permissive and restrictive elements within the State Department. Yasui, director in his country of the Council Against Atomic and Hydrogen Bombs and a recipient of the Lenin Peace Prize, had come to the United States for a lecture tour arranged by the left-wing *National Guardian* and sponsored by prominent members of the peace movement. The Committee's staff, ever alert to such activity by such individuals under such auspices, sought information from the State Department on the events leading up to the visit, and then summoned for executive questioning three persons who had interceded in Yasui's behalf: Russell Nixon, general manager of the

National Guardian; and Dagmar Wilson and Donna Allen, leaders of Women Strike for Peace. Nixon, formerly Washington representative for the United Electrical Workers, presented no unusual problems. He had been identified as a Communist before the Committee on several occasions and had taken the Fifth in 1956. But the memory of the 1962 run-in with Women Strike for Peace was still fresh, and the Congressmen, who had nothing on the ladies, could not have wished for a repeat performance.

As a reminder of the earlier festivities, the witnesses received twenty large vases of flowers from W.S.P. chapters around the country at their appearance in Washington on December 7, 1964. There they, together with Nixon, refused to testify in secret. They pointed out that their formal representation to the State Department was part of the public record, and they saw no advantage to giving testimony in private which the Committee might later release, when and as it saw fit. Their testimony, they maintained, would neither endanger the national security nor defame innocent persons—the two official reasons for conducting hearings *in camera*. But Representative Pool, trying out for the role of Committee bully boy vacated by Clardy and Scherer, was not about to give the ladies another chance to make their interrogators look silly. He refused to open up the hearings, as was his prerogative under the Committee's rules, and the three witnesses were cited for contempt.

Since the House was not in session, Speaker McCormack transmitted the contempt citation to the U.S. attorney for the District of Columbia, upon being advised by the House parliamentarian that such a transmittal was mandatory. The three were indicted, tried, convicted, and given a suspended sentence of four to twelve months and fined $100 apiece. In August 1966 the Court of Appeals overturned their convictions. Once again, the judiciary based its ruling not on a substantive issue—the defendants claimed that a closed session would have violated their freedom of speech by depriving them of an opportunity publicly to deny any involvement in subversive activities—but on a close technical point. In a two-to-one decision, the court held that Speaker McCormack had erred in assuming he had no choice but to pass along the case to the U.S. attorney. In the absence of the Congress, according to the court, the speaker was required to subject the contempt citation to his independent scrutiny. The decision, which kept intact the Committee's five-year losing record in the courts, presaged nothing; had the House been in session, the citations would without doubt have been overwhelmingly approved. Yet the incident held significance for the future; once again the Committee had demonstrated a fascination with the peace movement and once again it had found a means of publicizing the part being played in it by people with records like Russell Nixon's.

Occupying most of the Committee's attentions in 1964 were three sets of hearings of passing note. Between February and May seven days were given to a batch of bills providing for the creation of a Freedom Commission and a Freedom Academy. These institutions, the idea for which had aroused enthusiasm on the political right for several years,[4] were hailed by its champions as the free world's reply to the Lenin School in Moscow. The Freedom Academy would, in the words of a chief sponsor, A. Sydney Herlong, Jr., of Florida,

> prepare not only government foreign affairs personnel, but also private citizens and foreign students, to understand Communist political warfare and subversion and to give them the capacity to organize all of the methods and means which free men can properly employ to defeat Communist subversion and political warfare, while seeking to build and preserve independent countries.

The Committee's hearings consisted almost entirely of testimony from ardent supporters: conservative Congressmen, a former Chief of Naval Operations, American Legion officials, professors from Catholic universities who had served the Committee as consultants, Herbert Philbrick, representatives of Radio Free Europe and the National Captive Nations Com-

---

[4] A bill authorizing a Freedom Academy passed the Senate by a voice vote in 1960, but met the resistance in the House of Francis Walter, who reportedly opposed the Academy out of fear that it would be infiltrated by Communists.

mittee, and similarly disposed experts. Only two witnesses—W. Averell Harriman, speaking for the Department of State, and Adolf A. Berle—restrained their rapture. The State Department preferred to set up a National Academy of Foreign Affairs, exclusively for government officials. Berle was in favor of a Freedom Academy with apologetically rendered reservations: "Let me say something here that I hope will not shock the Committee unduly. If a country, of its own accord and minding its own business, decides to build a situation not based on private property and not unfriendly to the United States, I do not think the United States would have any real right to object, nor perhaps should it object." In the circumstances, this diffident support for the self-determination of nations came as something radical. The other witnesses did not trouble Chairman Willis with reservations.

It was not often that the Committee devoted itself to a real bill, but the hearings, which continued into 1965, were so arranged that they became not so much legislative occasions as opportunities for the Committee's friends and clients to parade their patriotism, lament the national deficiency of anti-Communist zeal, and advance the view—so often advanced in the Committee's publications—that Communist successes in various parts of the world were all of a piece and were due to treachery on the part of the Reds and ineffectuality or worse on our part. They wanted stronger anti-Communist medicine than the State Department was willing to concoct, and they saw the proposed Freedom Academy as a combination training camp for commandos and Jesuit retreat where men would be presented with the Truth so that they might then go and set others free. The Committee recommended passage of a Freedom Academy bill in 1966, and little has been heard of it since.

In the continuing pursuit of Communists during the spring and early summer of 1964, subcommittees settled upon Buffalo and Minneapolis. The Buffalo event, picketed by a couple of hundred students, had its moments. The first unfriendly witness, an instructor at the State University, started off with a request to tape record his interrogation and when this was denied, carried out an inspection of the witness table to make sure it was not bugged. Another witness, who had taken the Fifth during the Committee's 1957 visit to the city, was joined in dissent by his wife, seated in the rear of the courtroom:

WOLKENSTEIN: Let me have my say. What is this? The United States or is this the Hitler Germany regime?

POOL: The witness will be seated. You are going to be held in contempt.

MRS. WOLKENSTEIN: Don't tell him that. You insulted our whole family.

POOL: Remove that lady.

WOLKENSTEIN: You will not remove that lady.

MRS. WOLKENSTEIN: I will not leave.

WOLKENSTEIN: You leave her alone.

MRS. WOLKENSTEIN: I will slap you if you touch me; that's my husband.

The lady was removed, swinging at the marshals as she went.

Despite such interruptions, the Buffalo and Minneapolis hearings proceeded in their ordered course. The F.B.I. informants gave names. The persons named took the Fifth. (Except for a man in Minneapolis, a lawyer, who willingly told the Committee that he had not been a member of the Communist Party since September 1950, but refused to answer questions about the years before that on the novel grounds that the Committee's resolution was limited to appraising the workings of the Internal Security Act and the Subversive Activities Control Act, both passed in September 1950; he did not invoke the self-incrimination clause, and the Committee did not press contempt charges.[5]) In both cities the chairman opened and closed the proceedings with a few remarks on the importance of his visit. In Minneapolis Willis took as his theme a statement by

[5] In 1966 the Supreme Court threw out the contempt conviction of a New Hampshire man, a former Communist, who had refused to answer questions put by his state's attorney general concerning his Party activities before the year 1957, when the New Hampshire Subversion Act became effective. Upholding his claim to the First Amendment, Justice Douglas wrote that "the staleness of both the basis for the investigation and its subject matter makes indefensible such exposure of one's associations and political past—exposure which is objectionable and damaging in the extreme to one whose associations and political views do not command majority approval."

Gus Hall, secretary general of the C.P., U.S.A.: "For the good of Minnesota, I would pledge that we do everything we can to build the Communist movement within the state." Willis went on from there:

Has the Communist Party lived up to the pledge made to the Communists of this district by Gus Hall? Is it pouring more money into this area, more literature, more speakers? Just what are the commissars of the Communist Party doing to build the Communist movement in this state? What have they done in the past? How have they done it or tried to do it? Who are their agents? What are they now doing to subvert the democratic process in this district? These are some, though by no means all, of the questions to which the Committee hopes to obtain answers.

But the Congressmen knew the answers they would get before they started. They were like celebrants at a ritual who have long lost the meaning of their ceremonies and go faithfully, dumbly through the forms. Fourteen witnesses identified as Communists were called in Buffalo and eleven in Minneapolis. Of these, several had been named in previous proceedings or had made no great secret of their affiliation. Others had broken with the Party during one of its recurrent traumas. The Committee found grave menace in the remaining handful of Party stalwarts and a few neo-Trotskyites.

Had the Congressmen actually listened to the tales of their informants—simple folk who strove to be obliging in generalities about ever-growing menaces but seemed to stay close to the facts regarding particulars—they might have been comforted. For what the informants had encountered during their years in the service of the F.B.I. (a Buffalo man reported to the F.B.I. on his Party activities from 1942 until 1962, probably a record) bore little resemblance to the apparatus of conspiracy that one encountered in the Committee's reports. What they found were a few aging men, stranded by events and seeking to return to the wide road they believed they once traveled. The Party was in sorry shape, low on members and on cash, torn by the dissension endemic to movements that have lost their base in reality. Its fading leaders reached out desperately for recruits and found themselves harboring spies; they tried to play the old game, to take over an N.A.A.C.P. chapter, a local P.T.A., a labor union, and were rebuffed or ignored. They found comfort in Marxist study groups where, with a few fellow addicts, they could smoke the pipes of revolutions past and dream on miracles to come. Only the peace movement and the civil rights movement were spacious enough to let them in and allow them the illusion that they were still at the hot center of American radicalism. This illusion the Un-American Activities Committee reinforced, like a physician who shares his patient's taste for opium. The Congressmen saw the Party not as the ailing thing it had become but as the mighty adversary it never quite was. In continuing to stage such public exhibitions around the country, the Committee's staff and membership were only responding to the ache of their own infatuation.

The next set of big-city hearings took place in Chicago, amid clamorous protests, at the end of May 1965.[6] Hundreds of youthful pickets walked, yelled, and sang in front of the old U.S. Court of Appeals building on Lake Shore Drive, while the F.B.I. took moving pictures from a strategic window, and dozens of demonstrators were arrested for lying under paddy wagons and crashing through barricades. The more significant protest, however, occurred within the hearing chamber, and it came not from the few teenagers who had to be carted away for joining in a chorus of *My Country 'Tis of Thee*, but from three subpoenaed adults who walked out on the Committee after objecting to its inimitable ways. Chairman Willis was unmoved by their objections and a district court judge in Chicago dismissed their petition for an injunction a day before the hearings were due to open, but the issues raised by the three may yet be put to a proper test.

To begin with, on May 13, twelve days before the start of the hearings, the names of most of the persons subpoenaed were

[6] Lyndon Johnson's resounding victory over Barry Goldwater in 1964 had its repercussions on the makeup of the Committee. The Democrats gained an extra place, which was filled by a young Atlanta moderate, Charles L. Weltner. Among the Republicans, only Ashbrook of Ohio survived into the eighty-ninth Congress, and he was joined on the Committee by John H. Buchanan, Jr., of Alabama and Del Clawson of California. On the death of Frank S. Tavenner, Jr., in 1964, William Hitz was named general counsel.

published in a Chicago newspaper. The leaking of names, contrary to the Committee's own Rule XVI,[7] was not unusual. Where it happened, Chairman Willis expressed mystification: "Now how those things leak out, I don't know." He insisted that the rule had never been violated, which caused some laughter in the hearing room in Chicago. In Minneapolis he promised to fire any staff member whom reporters identified as having given out names, and implied that enemies of the Committee were doing the leaking "in order to make us the scapegoat." In Chicago he put the blame on Richard Criley, an alleged Communist and head of the Chicago Committee to Defend the Bill of Rights. Criley, noting that the subpoenas had been entrusted for delivery to the police department's "Red Squad" and that the names were first printed in the Chicago *American,* a Hearst paper, said he was not at all mystified.

The most prominent of the published names was that of Dr. Jeremiah Stamler, director of the Division of Adult Health and Aging and the Heart Disease Control Program of the Chicago Board of Health, associate professor at Northwestern University Medical School, member of professional societies, recipient of research grants, winner of awards. Two days after his name had been publicized, Dr. Stamler signed an oath drawn up by the president of the Board of Health, to the effect that he had neither engaged in subversive activities nor consorted with subversive groups or persons during his association with the Board of Health. This declaration which, as Willis took care to point out, did not mention the word Communist, saved his job for a time, but the Congressmen were not to be put off so lightly. It was on behalf of Dr. Stamler and of an assistant of his, a research nutritionist named Yolanda F. Hall, that a wide-ranging challenge was brought against the Committee.

The first request by the attorneys for Stamler and Mrs. Hall was that all testimony relating to them be taken in executive session and that they themselves be questioned in private rather

[7] "No member of the Committee or staff shall make public the name of any witness subpoenaed before the Committee or subcommittee prior to the date of his appearance."

than in open hearing, in accord with House Rule XI, 26(m).[8] Chairman Willis turned down both requests, arguing that the witnesses who were likely to give defamatory evidence—two F.B.I. informants—had already been heard in executive session, and everyone mentioned by them as a member of the Communist Party had been sent a letter with the offer of an opportunity to appear voluntarily in a closed hearing. In this way, said the chairman, the Committee had complied with its rule, and he added that his invitations had all gone unacknowledged. He did not add that any witness who had accepted his offer would in all likelihood have been summoned to return in public anyway. (In June, a woman who had been ill during the Committee's visit to Chicago was heard in executive session in Washington. She declared she was not a Communist, that she believed Communists to be "a deceitful and disruptive force" and that "for a considerable period I have had no association or activity that could remotely be deemed Communist." But she pleaded the Fifth Amendment on questions relating to her past activities, and after a half hour Chairman Willis opened the hearings to the public. All of her testimony, public and executive, was included in the transcript of the Chicago hearings.) If a witness volunteered testimony in private, it could be released at the discretion of the Committee, and in no case would he be given an opportunity to cross-examine his accusers.

Ordinarily, demands to be allowed to cross-examine have been uttered in the secure knowledge that they would not be granted; whatever one's feelings about the police informer as a species, a reading of the record over the years gives little reason to doubt that the informers' charges before the Committee have, with some regrettable exceptions, been substantially accurate. But the evidence brought against Dr. Stamler and Mrs. Hall was not of the usual sort. It was irregular even by the Committee's standards, and the cross-examination requested by their attorney might have been enlightening.

Two informants gave testimony in Chicago, Negroes who

[8] Rule 26(m) provides "if the Committee determines that evidence or testimony at an investigative hearing may tend to defame, degrade or incriminate any person it shall—(1) receive such evidence or testimony in executive session . . ."

had served the F.B.I. as C.P. members during the nineteen-fifties and up until 1963, and counsel Nittle's questioning played hard on Communist participation in civil rights and peace organizations. Each identified several persons as Communists, their lists duplicating one another as there were evidently no longer enough prominent Party members extant in Chicago to keep two informants occupied without some overlap. But in their presentations, which took up the first day and a half of the Chicago meeting, neither informant mentioned the name of either Jeremiah Stamler or Yolanda Hall.

On the afternoon of the second day, after the informants had been excused, Nittle was questioning a man with a record of C.P. activity going back to the nineteen-thirties; in 1950 he was state education director of the Communist Party of Illinois. This witness had taken the Fifth Amendment more than forty times, when Nittle put this question: "While you were an instructor at the Chicago Workers School, did you also know Yolanda Hall?" Mrs. Hall's attorney objected strenuously to having his client's name slipped into the hearing in such a manner; the witness continued to take the Fifth Amendment; and Nittle proceeded with his line of questioning: "Did you then know Yolanda Hall to be a member of the Communist Party?" As a matter of fact, everyone knew that Mrs. Hall once belonged to the Party. In July 1949, testifying in behalf of the C.P. leaders being tried under the Smith Act, she had admitted as much. In 1949, too, she had taught political economy at the South Side branch of the Party's Chicago Workers School. That was the freshest evidence that was produced regarding Mrs. Hall, and opponents of the Committee charged that her subpoenaing was stimulated by property owners in her Chicago neighborhood who were incensed by her efforts in behalf of open housing for Negroes. By injecting her name into the hearings in the form of questions about events of fifteen years before which he knew would not be answered, Nittle lent credence to this charge.

Whereas the evidence against Mrs. Hall was stale, evidence against her superior, Dr. Stamler, was missing altogether. His name was not mentioned in testimony until the last day of hearings when Nittle made up for the oversight, again with questions to witnesses who, it was clear, had determined to give no answers to anything: "The Committee's investigation discloses that the person who served as the Illinois youth co-ordinator of the American Youth Crusade was Dr. Jeremiah Stamler. Do you know Dr. Stamler?" None of Nittle's questions had a more definite base: "The Committee is also informed . . ." "The Committee also possesses information, which it believes reliable . . ." Soon Nittle was saying: "Exhibits previously intro-duced indicate that you were a leader of the Communist-organized and -controlled American Peace Crusade at the same time Dr. Jeremiah Stamler was the coordinator of its youth branch in this state"—although in fact no exhibits were intro-duced that even mentioned Dr. Stamler. To another witness who had been taking the Fifth by rote, Nittle said: ". . . the Committee is in possession of information which it believes to be completely reliable, that in the years 1956 and 1957 you attended meetings of the Communist Party at the residence of Dr. Jeremiah Stamler. Is this true?" A moment later, he asked whether Dr. Stamler's wife, who had never been referred to up until that moment, had not acted as chairman of the alleged C.P. meetings.

The Committee had been pained over the years at the charge that "faceles informers" were used against its witnesses, and in fact there had been little basis to it since the time of Harold Velde. The informants' faces were not always of the highest type, but it was usually known whence the accusations came. In Dr. Stamler's case, however, they could be traced no further than the Committee counsel himself, who claimed no firsthand acquaintance with his subject. In an effort to give a semblance of substance to the wispy charges against Stamler, Nittle called back to the stand one of the informants and asked him a few questions about a meeting held in his home in 1959 and at-tended by Claude Lightfoot, a prominent C.P. official:

NITTLE: Was Dr. Stamler's name mentioned in the course of that meeting?
ARMSTRONG: (the F.B.I. informant): Yes.
JENNER (Stamler's attorney): Mr. Chairman, does the . . .

ARMSTRONG: I want to say here that Dr. Stamler's name was mentioned, but I myself did not even know Dr. Stamler at that time. But he was mentioned.

NITTLE: Now will you tell the Committee please . . .

ARMSTRONG: He was discussed, not mentioned.

. . . . .

NITTLE: Now will you tell us what was said by Claude Lightfoot, if anything?

ARMSTRONG: Well, in discussing Dr. Stamler, he just said that we have a noted heart specialist, a very renowned heart specialist.

JENNER: Mr. Chairman, you as a noted law teacher—I object on the ground that this is obvious hearsay.

CHAIRMAN: Your client will have an opportunity to face what you have been referring to as accuser and confront him and under oath to deny all this. Proceed.

JENNER: I request that opportunity.

CHAIRMAN: Proceed.

NITTLE: Will you proceed, Mr. Armstrong, to relate that.

ARMSTRONG: Well, he said that there was a noted heart specialist by the name of Jeremiah Stamler and he was a loyal Party member doing good work among the professional people. He did not discuss in detail and that is about the gist of it. Dr. Stamler. If you want to know more in other ways, maybe I can tell you.

NITTLE: That is all, Mr. Chairman.

That, indeed, was all. Nittle's questions to unresponsive witnesses were phrased to invite the inference that there was weighty support behind them: "The Committee is informed that at the time you were contacted by Dr. Stamler, you were advised by him that you were one of several persons chosen to give up their identity and to move to new areas to carry on in case Communist Party leaders were put away. Did he tell you that?" But the nature of the support was never disclosed. When asking the House for contempt citations against Stamler and Mrs. Hall in October 1966, Willis and Ichord quoted executive testimony by Staff Director McNamara to the effect that both subjects had been engaged in C.P. activities in recent years. The only source of information credited by McNamara was a newsletter put out by an arm of the radical right called the American Security Council. The Committee's staff director has always exercised considerable autonomy, and such was the Congressmen's faith in McNamara that it never occurred to them to check his evidence before making his charges public.

Stamler and Mrs. Hall were represented at the hearings by Albert E. Jenner, Jr., of the Chicago law firm of Raymond, Mayer, Jenner, and Block. Former president of the Illinois State Bar Association, senior counsel for the Warren Commission, member of the Federal Loyalty Review Board in the early nineteen-fifties, and a Republican, Jenner was not the prototypical counsel for witnesses before the Committee, and Chairman Willis allowed him extraordinary latitude, which he used to the full[9] in stating his objections. Jenner demanded an investigation of who had leaked the names of the subpoenaed witnesses. He objected to the Committee's refusal to hear his clients and all testimony regarding them in executive session and to allow him to examine all evidence and cross-examine the informants. He objected to the manner in which unattributed charges were placed in the record and asked permission to examine counsel Nittle. His protests that the investigation had no legislative purpose and was in violation of his clients' rights to due process had been made by many attorneys at many other hearings, but the events in Chicago gave them special force.

Jenner, a trial lawyer for many years, argued:

It is clear from what had occurred in these hearings on May 25 and 26 and to this point today—one, that public hearings are not needed and were not needed, because you have already heard Lola Belle Holmes and Lucius Armstrong [the F.B.I. informants] and others apparently in executive session and the repetition in these public hearings has served, as it could only serve, particularly under the type of examination of the distinguished counsel

9 Jenner did not appear until the final day of the Chicago hearings. On the first two days he was represented by an associate, Thomas P. Sullivan, who had the misfortune to be faced not with Willis, out ill, but with Joe Pool. When Sullivan attempted to object to the first injection of Yolanda Hall's name by counsel Nittle, Pool interrupted him continuously and had the marshals push him back into his chair.

for the Committee, to injure persons whom they charged and counsel has charged without being under oath to be or to have been members of the Communist Party; and, two, the questioning of my clients will be of a defamatory and prejudicial nature and be harmful to their good reputations, which they cherish.

He emphasized that Dr. Stamler and Mrs. Hall were not invoking the privilege against self-incrimination—"They have committed no crime and have been loyal to our country"—but were refusing to testify on other constitutional grounds. A few minutes later, by Jenner's direction, both witnesses walked out of the hearing room. (A third witness, Milton Cohen, also walked out defiantly, to the cheers of the spectators, and joined Mrs. Hall and Stamler in their suit. Unlike them, he had been identified as a C.P. member by the two informants. Although the ten other subpoenaed witnesses and their attorneys registered protests in much the same language as Jenner, they covered themselves by taking the Fifth Amendment, which had the effect of making their other arguments academic.)

In April 1966 the Stamler-Hall-Cohen suit against the members of the Committee was dismissed in district court on the grounds that the plaintiffs had no standing to sue. In November the Court of Appeals returned the case to the lower court for a hearing on the constitutional issues raised. In a two-to-one decision the judges maintained that although the constitutionality of the Committee had been sustained in the Barenblatt decision, the allegations in the present case—that the Committee was bent on exposing witnesses to public scorn, obloquy, harassment, and intimidation with no legislative purpose, but to deter them and others in the exercise of their rights under the First Amendment—warranted a hearing. (As of this writing, their case has not yet been reconsidered by the lower court.)

A few weeks before the Court of Appeals' decision, the Committee brought to the House its contempt citations against Yolanda Hall, Jeremiah Stamler, and Milton Cohen. Debate was hot. Pressed hard by Fraser of Minnesota for a reason why the request for an executive hearing was not granted, the unadept Ichord found himself arguing in *favor* of executive hearings: ". . . the hearings are in progress and you have all of these pickets outside and beatniks walking around and people trying to create disorder and you have a ruckus and disorder." Pressed by Yates of Illinois for the reason why Yolanda Hall had been called to testify, Willis replied: "Mr. Speaker, if I could answer that question in open forum, I should be glad to do so but some of these days I shall be happy to tell the gentleman from Illinois the reason therefore." Asked by Yates for the origin of the derogatory information about Stamler and Mrs. Hall that director McNamara had passed on to the Committee, Ichord conceded that he was in the dark. He did not know whether the information was true or not: ". . . this was a summary of what was in the files, of what the investigators and the F.B.I. had reported to the House Committee on Un-American Activities." Pressed by Hays of Ohio on whether friendly witnesses were paid by the Committee, Willis said that he was "getting sick and tired of all these dog-goned intimations about dishonesty." Hays had discovered that the Committee was paying some of its friendly witnesses when, as a member of the House Administration Committee, he was asked to approve their contracts. On raising the issue in the House he was met with indignation from members of the Committee: "My goodness," said Willis, "that has never been indulged in." Before the day was done, the indignation had turned to a reluctant admission that Hays was correct; some witnesses had been paid . . . but *honi soit.*

The members of the Committee could bear up under the slings of debate because they knew that they would be vindicated on the final vote. A motion to recommit to a select committee the first contempt resolution debated, the one against Milton Cohen, lost by 90 votes to 181. That was the best the opposition could manage. In fact, it established a new record. The citation against Jeremiah Stamler was put through by a vote of 174 to 37.[1]

The resolutions passed in October marked the second time in 1966 that the House was asked to vote on contempt citations

---

[1] In July 1967 the three were indicted by a federal grand jury in Chicago on the contempt-of-Congress charges, whereupon Dr. Stamler and his assistant were placed on "inactive status" by the Chicago Board of Health.

issuing from the Committee on Un-American Activities. On February 2 Willis asked for proceedings against seven officials of various Ku Klux Klan groups who had refused, during public hearings in Washington in October 1965, to turn over their records to the Committee. All took the Fifth Amendment, but Willis argued that, by the Supreme Court's 1960 decision in the McPhaul case, the plea of self-incrimination did not protect a witness against a request for documents held in an official capacity.[2] Objections to the citations on constitutional grounds as well as on grounds of simple distaste for the Committee were voiced by Representatives Ryan, Burton, Edwards, and others whose antipathy to the Ku Klux Klan was more pronounced than that of most of the Committee's members, but the contempt resolutions were voted rapidly one after the other. In October 1966 Robert M. Shelton, Imperial Wizard of the United Klans of America, received a maximum sentence of one year in prison and a $1,000 fine in district court. Three other Klansmen subsequently pleaded guilty, and their cases, along with the remaining three, who have pleaded not guilty, await the disposition of Shelton's appeal.

The proposal in 1965 for an investigation of the Klan originated with Charles L. Weltner, a natty young representative from Georgia, who owed his victory in the Democratic primary to Atlanta's many registered Negroes and its higher-income whites. During his first term in the House, 1963–1964, Weltner became the lone Congressman from the states of the Old Confederacy to vote for final passage of the Civil Rights Act of 1964. (At the end of his second term, in 1966, he withdrew from his campaign for reelection rather than run on the same ticket with Lester Maddox, the segregationist gubernatorial candidate.) Weltner sought and obtained a place on the Un-American Activities Committee in 1965 with the purpose of starting up an investigation of the Klan, which had resumed its abominable ways in resistance to the civil rights movement. On February 1 the young man from Georgia attacked the

---

[2] Arthur McPhaul, refusing to submit the records of the Civil Rights Congress in 1952, said: "I wonder if the Kluxers of Georgia have ever been asked to produce their records."

"invisible empire" on the floor of the House: "I believe I speak for the vast majority of Southerners in calling for action. For in doing nothing, we will inaugurate a second century for the Ku Klux Klan."

The novelty of having a Southerner and a member of the Un-American Activities Committee ask for such an investigation stirred considerable comment. The Committee had won the hearts of Klansmen at birth. A K.K.K. pamphlet of 1942 stated: "The vicious fight on the Klan sprang from the same source which has fought the Dies Committee from the day of its inception." An Imperial Wizard once paid Martin Dies the compliment of acknowledging that his program "so closely parallels the program of the Klan that there is no distinguishable difference between them." In those early years critics like Samuel Dickstein protested that the Committee was not doing enough to harass un-Americans on the right, and in truth there was small enthusiasm among its members for such adventures then or later. Francis Walter, forgetting the origins of his Committee, took the position that its investigative mandate covered Communists exclusively. As for the Committee staff, it was composed of professional Communist-hunters, set in their ways and not readily diverted; the K.K.K., after all, had never been put on anyone's subversive list. By 1965 the Committee's critics, though admiring of Weltner's initiative, took the position that the Committee should not be investigating anything, right or left, not even the universally despised Ku Klux Klan. They wanted federal legislation against the Klan, but they wanted it to originate in the Judiciary Committee.

Skepticism abounded in the Capitol that the K.K.K. investigation would get beyond what Chairman Willis called a "look-see," a "peek." (Also being peeked at were the Minutemen, the Black Muslims, and the American Nazi Party.) But on the evening of March 25, 1965, a Detroit woman, Mrs. Viola Gregg Liuzzo, who had been shuttling Negro civil rights workers back to Selma, Alabama, after the march to Montgomery, was shot and killed in her car. Four Klansmen—one of them later identified as an F.B.I. informant—were arrested, and before anyone had been brought to trial, President Johnson made a dramatic appearance on television, accompanied by Attorney General Katzenbach and J. Edgar Hoover himself. The President blamed the Klan for the murder—one of a series of murders of civil rights workers in the South that were resulting in the indictments but not the convictions of K.K.K. members—and suggested that Congress might wish to conduct an investigation.

The commission could have gone to the Judiciary Committee, but the Un-American Activities Committee won out because of its unrivaled immunity to charges of bias in behalf of Negro rights. In April the House voted the Committee an additional $50,000 for the investigation, over the objections of forty-three members, mostly liberals joined for the moment with a couple of arch-segregationists. (Where Ryan of New York feared that the investigation would be "the opening wedge of a witchhunt into civil-rights organizations," Walker of Mississippi wanted it to be extended to S.N.C.C., C.O.R.E., and S.C.L.C.) Of the six Negroes in the House, four voted against the appropriation and two did not vote. Civil rights leaders, wary of where the Committee might turn next, were unanimously opposed; they asked that the K.K.K. be studied by a special commission appointed for the purpose.

The Ku Klux Klan became the main business of the Committee in the latter half of 1965 and into 1966. A subcommittee of four Southerners—Willis, Pool, Weltner, and Buchanan—and one Northerner, Ashbrook of Ohio—the only Congressman from his state to vote against the 1964 Civil Rights Act—opened hearings in Washington on October 19; before they came to an end the following February, they had consumed thirty-seven days. The opening weeks ran simultaneously with the trial in Hayneville, Alabama, of Klansman Collie Leroy Wilkins for the murder of Mrs. Liuzzo. While an all-white jury in Hayneville was engaged in acquitting Wilkins, the Washington hearings were disappointing both those who had predicted a whitewash and those who had been hoping for a spectacle.

Robert M. Shelton, the ravaged-looking Imperial Wizard, had been expected to answer questions, but at the last minute he announced that he was taking the Fifth Amendment lest otherwise he forfeit his dignity as a free American and be eternally damned: "I am a God-fearing man." (For a Kluxer to take the Fifth like an ordinary Commie was poetry; for him to take the Fourteenth, as Shelton and his brothers in the faith repeatedly did, was epic.) Counseled by a soft-voiced, permanently apologetic attorney from Raleigh, North Carolina, the eminent Klansmen called on in the first days of the hearings all resorted to their rights under the Constitution. They racked up quite a record of Fifths, but it was not like the Chicago hearings of the previous spring. The Klansmen uttered their respectful declinations in quiet voices; there were no disturbances in the House Caucus Room, and the dozen or more uniformed police and plainclothesmen had nothing to do. After the first crowded day, the number of spectators fell off sharply.

Set beside the Klan's reputation and the grim event that had led to these hearings, the charges put in the record by the Committee's staff were trivial—yet the show had its moments. For those who had always known that the Klan was composed of clowns and clods, it was satisfying to learn that they thought of themselves as kligrapps (secretaries), klokards (lecturers), and kludds (chaplains). Donald T. Appell, the staff member in charge of the investigation, produced evidence that Wizard Shelton had been channeling his blood brothers' contributions into a Tuscaloosa account belonging to an invention of his called the Alabama Rescue Service and then taking the money out to buy himself a Cadillac and lesser staples at his nearby Piggly-Wiggly supermarket. He was alleged to have shaken down an engineering firm in trouble with the state, and had evidently been kicked out of the Alabama Knights of the K.K.K. for withholding dues from the reigning Wizard. The Grand Dragons of Virginia and North Carolina (where Klan checks were made out to one's local "improvement association" or "sportsmen's club"—"Your donation will be used to help make our community a better place to live") were impecunious drifters before their elevation in Shelton's Klandom, whereupon overnight they became affluent models for poor white lads all over the South. Dragon Jones of North Carolina even made a profit on the sale of sheets; the material cost him about $3.20

and the finished article, with peaked hat, went for $15. It was also disclosed that a lot of crosses had been burned and that the White Knights of the Ku Klux Klan of Mississippi had passed around a memorandum on permissible techniques of good-humored harassment; these included the use of itching powder, tear gas, snakes and lizards and mad dogs.

The hearings were broken off in November after the attorney general took exception to the Committee's calling two Klansmen indicted and freed in the murder of Lemuel Penn, a Negro reserve officer who was shot and killed in 1964 as he was driving home to Washington, D.C. from a training base in the South. The case, explained the attorney general, was before the Supreme Court. When the inquiry resumed in the new year, it turned from the account books toward more colorful matters. A Georgia Kluxer conceded that he was financing a movement against kosher food. A Grand Empress of the Klan, a lady in Cincinnati who had allegedly worked up schemes for killing the President, the Vice President, Martin Luther King, and others, was put on the stand. A former Klansman told of taking part in nightrider bombings of the homes of Negroes in McComb, Mississippi. A Louisiana man admitted that he had helped out in a flogging.

The hearings throughout were conducted in much the same manner as the hearings into Communist activities. The main differences were in the subdued responses of the witnesses who, off the stand, blamed not the Committee but Lyndon Johnson and Martin Luther King for their discomfiture. The Committee staff was able to produce some evidence of wrongdoing, mostly petty finaglings, rarely available in the case of Communists. Although there was no question that a majority of the Committee would have embarked on an investigation of the civil rights movement with pleasure, the fear of some liberals that the K.K.K. hearings would be turned into such a party was misconceived. It did justice neither to the political sense of the Congressmen nor to their personal attitudes. Far from wishing to defend the Ku Klux Klan, the Southerners were out to show that the Klansmen were crooks and freaks (Buchanan, in a burst of wit, called Shelton the Imperial Lizard) and had nothing in common with decent citizens of the South, like the members of White Citizens Councils who sit on juries.

The impact of these drawn-out hearings on the fortunes of the Klan is difficult to estimate. They may, oddly, have been a heavier blow than any a more respectable body could have delivered. The Committee's habit of asking questions that it knew would not be answered, its interest in matters that belonged to night court, its reliance on publicity to do the job of punishment, its infatuation with Fifth Amendment records—these might well have worked on the level where the K.K.K. operates most successfully. The North Carolina used-car dealer who startled the Committee while in the witness chair by resigning as treasurer of his Klavern (the White County Improvement Association) and turning over a batch of canceled checks, explained that he was disillusioned by the Klan leaders' refusal to testify. "Anyone who takes the Fifth Amendment," he told reporters, "either has something to hide or is a Communist." Men who could abide a little crowding of a pushy Negro might yet be offended by the idea of a Grand Dragon gouging lesser knights on the price of a sheet, or using the 50-cents-a-month Imperial Tax to buy molasses not for the gas tanks of civil rights workers but for his own table. What the Rev. Roy Woodle, former Grand Kludd of North Carolina, didn't like about his chiefs was that they wore diamond rings, traveled first class, and employed shills at rallies. He was annoyed that they weren't working harder to preserve segregation in the South.

The President had asked for laws against the Klan, which gave the Committee an opportunity to display its legislative incompetence. To produce a workable federal law that could cover what the bill put forward by Chairman Willis called "the reprehensible, terroristic activities of the Klan movement" required a certain finesse. Whatever qualities the Willis bill had, finesse was lacking; it was written in the go-get-'em style that typified the Committee's work. It provided severe penalties, up to life imprisonment, for any agent of a "clandestine organization" who would commit or "conspire to commit" a crime of violence. In hearings held in July 1966, a spokesman for the American Civil Liberties Union observed that the bill's definition of a "clandestine organization" was broad enough to cover college fraternities. Attorney General Katzenbach told the Committee he was concerned over the section of the bill that made it a crime to "willfully teach, advise or advocate" the use of violence, since the Supreme Court had questioned the Smith Act's prohibitions against teaching and advocating the overthrow of the government. The attorney general was also doubtful about a provision of the Willis bill, devised by Representative Weltner, that would have authorized the Justice Department to seek injunctions against acts of violence in the planning stage. Katzenbach, like officials of the civil rights organizations, preferred to rely on Title V of the Civil Rights Bill of 1966, which broadened federal criminal laws against harming or intimidating persons exercising their legal rights.

The majority of the Un-American Activities Committee did not support the Administration's civil-rights program (only two of the Committee's nine members, Weltner and Senner, voted for the ill-fated 1966 bill) and if one were of a suspicious mind, one might suspect that the crudely drawn Willis measure, which even Ichord found "unenforceable and unconstitutional," was designed with an eye less to confounding the Ku Klux Klan than to confusing the civil rights debate. In any case, the Committee approved its K.K.K. bill only at the close of the Congressional session, and it subsided without a murmur in the last days' business.

At about the same time that the K.K.K. bill was going under, another Committee product was actually passed by the House of Representatives. Conceived by Joe Pool, it made it a federal crime to give assistance to forces engaged in "undeclared war" with this country or to interfere with the movement of military personnel or supplies. That this hapless measure reached the floor of the House on October 12, 1966, was due to Representative Colmer of Mississippi, who exercised his privilege as a member of the Rules Committee to call up a resolution setting the terms of debate on the bill. That it passed, despite a notably inept presentation by Pool, Ashbrook, and Ichord, was due to the nearness of the November elections and the assurance that it would not get through the Senate where leaders of both parties had only scorn for it. As Representative Edwards, the Committee's foremost opponent and a candid man, observed during the debate in the House: "Indeed, I presume that this body has in mind a quick passage while holding its nose, secure in the knowledge that our indiscretion will be cured by quiet death in the other body; thus reemphasizing the wisdom of our founders in providing a bicameral Congress."

The Pool bill, one of several of a like nature put forward in 1966, came to the floor patched with amendments that could not cover its constitutional and logical holes. It was, as the attorney general explained in testimony before the Committee in August, flatly unnecessary. The Trading with the Enemy Act and other statutes made it unlawful to transfer funds to blocked countries, yet did not infringe on free speech or obstruct the work of the International Red Cross as the Pool measure would probably have done, and a variety of laws were already at hand to prosecute people for getting in the way of military traffic. Moreover, the offenses that had excited the Committee's legislative genius were hardly worthy of a second look. A handful of Vietcong rooters had raised a lot of hell and a little money ($1,500 evidently made its way to Czechoslovakia and from there, presumably, to the National Liberation Front) and collected some blood (which, so far as was known, never got close to Vietnam). Ramsey Clark, making his first appearance before the Committee as attorney general, offended the Congressmen by suggesting that pro-Vietcong elements in America did not constitute a threat to the land, that their noisy carryings-on near military bases amounted mainly to headline seeking:

> I would say that the people who stand in front of a troop train with the realization that they have no potential of stopping it, particularly when the train never slows down, continues ten miles an hour, and before it reaches them they scatter off the track, that is seeking publicity rather than an effort to stop a train that they know they cannot stop.

The Committee, which had recently decided that the American Nazi Party and the Minutemen and even the Black Muslims did not warrant their full attention, could not bring the same cool judgment to bear on the bearded youths and long-haired girls who waved the Vietcong flag in public.[3] The visceral revulsion of staff director McNamara and subcommittee chairman Pool and ranking Republican Ashbrook against these unkempt types combined with the opportunity to attack opponents of the war in Vietnam on their most bizarre flank, led to the Committee's hearings of August 1966. It was all of a piece with the carelessly drawn bill. The conduct of these hearings brought a new barrage of criticism upon the Committee and turned Joe Pool of Texas into something of a national figure.

The American Civil Liberties Union sought to block the August hearings and at the same time to start an action challenging the constitutionality of the Committee by going into district court for an injunction.[4] The A.C.L.U. argued that the Committee's mandate to investigate "propaganda" ran counter to the First Amendment. To everyone's surprise, a ten-day restraining order was granted, a day before the scheduled opening of the hearings, by U.S. District Judge Howard F. Corcoran, brother of the New Deal's Tommy Corcoran, who had been appointed to the bench by President Johnson in 1965. Never before had a committee of Congress suffered enjoinment, and Pool, with the approval of Speaker McCormack, announced

[3] Reporting to the House the decision not to pursue the American Nazi Party of George Lincoln Rockwell, Willis explained: "He wants to see front-page headlines about his organization. He would like to see his picture featured on nation-wide TV newscasts and spread over the pages of newspapers in all parts of the country. It would give him the publicity he not only wants, but desperately needs, at this point. I do not believe the Committee should accommodate him on this matter." Willis might have applied the same reasoning to the Progressive Labor Movement.

[4] The A.C.L.U.'s strategy of seeking injunctive relief followed from a 1965 Supreme Court decision extending relief to officers of the Southern Conference Educational Fund who had been harassed by Louisiana officials and threatened with criminal prosecution under the state's Subversive Activities and Communist Control Law. Concerned over the "chilling effect on free expression of prosecutions initiated and threatened in this case," the majority urged the lower courts to give the appellants declaratory relief that would enable them to test the provisions of the law, which was so vaguely worded as to be of doubtful constitutionality, before they were prosecuted under it.

that hearings would begin at 10 a.m. on August 16 as planned, injunction or no injunction. There were calls in the House for the impeachment of Judge Corcoran. A hastily summoned three-judge panel of the Court of Appeals dissolved the restraining order shortly before 10 a.m., and as the A.C.L.U. set forth on the long road of judicial review to attempt again to test the Committee's constitutionality, the hearings opened. Whatever the legal shortcomings of the brief-lived injunction, it was an omen which, had it been heeded, would have spared the Committee a disagreeable few days and considerable chagrin.

As the witnesses summoned for the Vietnam hearings[5] were of the same generation—mostly under thirty—and ideological bent—Progressive Labor—as those who had caused such a commotion at the 1963 Cuba-travel hearings, the Committee had every reason to look forward to a rousing time. An extraordinary force of federal marshals and Capitol police was laid on, and the officers were kept busy during the first four days of hearings carrying out witnesses and spectators, some fifty of whom were booked for disorderly conduct before things quieted down. But it was not the hissing, booing, cheering, hollering, screaming, kicking, and calls to "Get out of Vietnam!" that caused the Committee its greatest distress in August of 1966. All of this was, in a way, welcome, as showing up the bad manners of the Chinese-Albanian left. There were other developments, unforeseen, that were far from welcome.

The first witness was Phillip Abbott Luce, who had gone on the Cuba trip in the summer of 1963, had been a member of the Progressive Labor Movement for about six months of 1964, and had baited the Committee with particular skill on his last appearance. Luce, an articulate young man, began his 1963 testimony with an attack on a previous witness who had traveled to Cuba for the F.B.I., calling him "this creep, this fink." Now, in 1966, it was his turn to be called a fink and take

[5] The Committee preceded these hearings by subpoenaing membership lists of anti-war organizations from the University of California at Berkeley and the University of Michigan. Their compliance brought about a statement in July 1967 by the American Council on Education urging colleges and universities to resist all such future demands.

his seat amid a storm of catcalls. Having changed his mind about the P.L.M., he now regaled the Committee with its revolutionary program and the names of its leaders. Since the main objective of the P.L.M. was to draw attention to itself by staging picturesque incidents and since it had no life of any consequence outside of its rather frenetic public life, little that Luce said was news. Still, the Committee, which he had characterized in 1963 as "the scum of Congress," was appreciative, and his reformation was something to behold. Whereas in 1963 he had criticized Willis for ejecting demonstrators—"This may be something you can get away with in Louisiana or Virginia, but I can't understand it here"—in 1966 he criticized the demonstrators. Two months later, during the debate in the House over the contempt citations resulting from the Chicago hearings, Representative Hays named Luce as having received $1,000 from the Committee for services rendered. The contract had been quietly arranged by director McNamara. One of those unaware of it was general counsel William Hitz. After being fired by McNamara in October 1966, purportedly for not earning his $25,000 a year salary,[6] Hitz circulated to each member of the Committee a memorandum which disclosed that Luce had been offered the contract as a "consultant" more than a month before he testified.[7] Young Luce thereby became the first man in history to go from the employ of the Emergency Civil Liberties Committee to the employ of the Un-American Activities Committee. McNamara, Luce's patron and instigator of the Vietnam hearings, laid the failure to inform his colleagues of the contract to inadvertence.

The second day of those rowdy August hearings achieved a climax with the eviction from the Caucus Room of an attorney. Beginning with its efforts to obtain a restraining order, the American Civil Liberties Union had determined to make the Vietnam hearings an all-out test of the Committee's constitu-

[6] Chester D. Smith, a Defense Department intelligence specialist, was named in December to replace Hitz as general counsel.

[7] No one thought to remind Representative Ichord of his statement during the debate on the Stamler-Hall contempt citations: "There is nothing wrong with the Committee hiring a witness who might have testified before the Committee in regard to Communist activities at an earlier date, because that would be after the fact."

tionality, and an unusually forceful complement of lawyers, including the A.C.L.U.'s executive director, John de J. Pemberton, was present,[8] with an extensive list of objections to the proceedings. As Representative Pool had demonstrated during his few hours in the chair at the Chicago hearings, he had little patience for defense attorneys. "Mr. marshal, set this man down" was his natural response when a lawyer rose to make an objection. Pool, elected in 1963 to the Congressman-at-large seat once held by Martin Dies (after the leading candidate was opportunely indicted for income tax evasion), was distinguished in the House mainly for his shape; he stood about five foot six and weighed well over two hundred pounds. He was affable enough, but not versed in the parliamentary graces. Still, if he did not always grasp what the Eastern lawyers were complaining about, he knew they meant him no good. Unable to cope when they became argumentative, he tended to rely on a heavy gavel and on commands that they be quiet and sit down or else.

The incident that culminated in the ousting of counsel Arthur Kinoy, who had been on the defendants' side in the Chicago hearings too, began when a friendly witness, a writer for the *National Review*, mentioned the name of one of the subpoenaed witnesses. Kinoy objected, as attorneys had previously objected, to having his client named in open session and to being denied the right of cross-examination. Joined by his partner, William Kunstler, Kinoy persisted in his objections after they had been overruled. Voices became loud, and before Pool knew it, he was banging his gavel and ordering the lawyer taken away. The next day's papers showed the peppery little man, shorter even than Joe Pool and about a hundred pounds lighter, being hustled out of the hearing room by three or four marshals who seemed huge beside him. One had an armlock on his neck. By the time Pool, embattled by protesting lawyers and possibly troubled by second thoughts over the scene, agreed to allow Kinoy back into the hearing room, the

[8] Attorneys cooperating with the A.C.L.U. included William M. Kunstler, Arthur Kinoy, Jeremiah S. Gutman, Beverly Axelrod, and Frank J. Donner. In addition, Joseph Forer and Ira Gollobin were present and heard from.

lawyer had been taken off to the police station. (He was later convicted of disturbing the peace and is appealing.)

It was at this point that the hearings began to deteriorate into farce, with Joe Pool playing the fool of fate. First the lawyers, all of them, one after another, delivered formal statements of withdrawal, and two subpoenaed witnesses—the director of the new, small, and determinedly radical Free School of New York, where he taught "Marxism and American Decadence," and the founder of the U.S. Committee to Aid the National Liberation Front—simply walked out on the Congressmen.[9] The other witnesses, formally without attorneys now, were excused until next day, and the Committee turned with relief to an assistant district attorney from Alameda County, whose jurisdiction took in the campus at Berkeley. He told of the demonstrations around troop trains, military bases, and induction centers staged by a far-out, far-left group called the Vietnam Day Committee. (One of their pamphlets, *Brief Notes on the Ways and Means of "Beating" and Defeating the Draft*, advised: "Be an undesirable. Go for a couple of weeks without a shower. Really look dirty. Stink. Long hair helps. Go in barefoot with your sandals tied around your neck.") When a witness whose name was mentioned in the course of the friendly testimony rose to object, Pool had to be restrained by Ashbrook from ordering him thrown out of the room.

As the unfriendly witnesses reappeared, still without counsel, it became clear that the subcommittee was prepared to let them depart in peace. "I would suggest, Mr. Chairman, that you proceed as quickly as you can to conclude this part of the investigative hearing," advised Representative Ichord after the walkout of the lawyers. The Congressmen had already questioned two of the young leftists in the first days of the hearings and they had proved compulsively responsive about their opinions, joyfully abusive of the Committee, and exceedingly taxing.

[9] The A.C.L.U. brought a suit against the Committee in behalf of these two witnesses, Dr. Allen M. Krebs and Walter D. Teague, 3d. In September 1967, a three-member panel of federal judges ruled that they did not have jurisdiction to decide on the constitutionality of the Committee since it had been formed not by an act of Congress but by a resolution of the House of Representatives. The ruling is being appealed.

One managed to put the entire preamble of the constitution of the Progressive Labor Party into the record. When Pool asked the other whether he believed he "ought to help the Viet Cong, the North Vietnamese, so they can go back into battle and kill our boys," the witness retorted: "You are sending them there to die. And Johnson is sending them there to die, and they all, all this government and the big business are sending them there to die and bleed, and then you try to assume that I am against them."[1] As in the Cuba travel hearings, the new leftists enjoyed this sort of exchange more than the Congressmen, and Pool presently gave up the debate and contented himself with coaxing his witnesses to take the Fifth Amendment.

After the Kinoy arrest, the subpoenaed youths were offered an opportunity to have their testimony postponed for three months, a euphemistic way of getting rid of them, but most refused, preferring the opportunity to have a go at the Congressmen on the spot. The first of these, a student at Stanford, gave the Nazi salute as Pool was swearing him in. He responded willingly to questions about his part in collecting money for the North Vietnamese Red Cross, but refused to talk about those who had worked with him, spurning the repeated invitations of the Congressmen to avail himself of the Fifth Amendment: "I will not answer this question on the grounds that it nauseates me and I am liable to vomit all over this table." Three others did take the Fifth, among their numerous and vociferously presented objections to the Committee, but made no effort to conceal their sympathies, affiliations, or activities. They were voluble, sophomoric (while being sworn in, one

---

[1] Counsel Nittle, too, fell into exchanges with this young man from which he had trouble extricating himself.

GORDON: The blood of American G.I.s is on the hands of Johnson and on the hands of all those abetting and aiding him.

NITTLE: It isn't on the hands of President Johnson. The responsibility, you well know, rests in Peking and in Moscow.

GORDON: . . . Where is the Peking troops in South Vietnam? It is American troops that have gone in, forced to go there. Why are you covering this up?

NITTLE: Now will you tell us, please . . .

GORDON: You talk about blood, you talk about aid. What about if your aid in Vietnam is American bombs? They are killing our people there.

NITTLE: Will you tell us, please . . .

POOL: Let's have order.

held up a fist, with the middle finger erect, and a couple of them had to be dragged away from the witness chair), and splendidly vituperative. "I will proceed alone," said a West Coast organizer for the P.L.M., "to confront and take on this racist committee of cowardly, yellow-bellied reactionaries as representatives of the U.S. government, not of the people, that is conducting a genocidal war in Vietnam that is against the best interests of the American and Vietnamese people."

The last two witnesses uttered statements which were rare in the Committee's history—". . . yes, I am a Communist and I am proud to say that I am a member of the Progressive Labor Movement," and ". . . I am a P.L.P. member and proud to say that, proud to say I am a Marxist-Leninist, a revolutionary Communist." Most of this latter young man's testimony was given over to attacks on the Committee, the Johnson Administration, bosses, union stooges, racists, and other undesirables, and after he was carried off yelling, "The blood of the Vietnamese is on the American government!", the Committee had had enough. Chairman Pool concluded abruptly and lamely: "We have the information we set out to obtain. The need for enactment of the bill is clear. We see no need to continue the investigative phase of this hearing. All witnesses against whom subpoenas are still outstanding are hereby excused from their subpoenas." A young man in the uniform of the American Revolution, who had been waiting for three days to be called so that he could distribute parchment reprints of the Declaration of Independence, objected with such vehemence that he had to be hustled out of the room and off to the police station.

Joe Pool of Texas, modestly endowed in everything but flesh, desiring nothing more than the kind of satisfaction that had come so readily to other chairmen of other subcommittees, might be forgiven for wondering why this cross had been laid on him. Even Everett Dirksen commented after the hearings were cut short: "This spectacle can do the Congress no good." For years the Committee had trusted unwaveringly in the premise that the Communist Party was a secret conspiratorial organization whose members were dedicated to subverting the land and so had to be exposed. For years it had interpreted the

Fifth Amendment as a form of confession. For years witnesses whose livelihoods were in jeopardy had been baited for failing to speak up. Now none of this applied. Aesopianism was passé. The witnesses in August 1966 admitted they were Communists, advertised their anti-war protests, defied the Committee, and were not cited for contempt. The Committee was browbeaten in its very citadel.

Yet despite the embarrassment they suffered, the abuse they took, and the ineffectuality they displayed in dealing with this new species of radical, the members of the Committee could conclude the hearings with a certain satisfaction. It was not the familiar satisfaction of making middle-aged ex-C.P. members cower behind the Fifth Amendment; the students had too little to lose to let the Congressmen take their pleasure of them without screams and kicks. But the main purpose of the hearings had been noisily served. The nation had been shown that the peace movement was infested by a rude bunch of America-haters; to those who subscribed to the reasoning of the Committee, protests against the war in Vietnam could henceforth be written off.

As for the exuberant young members of the Progressive Labor Movement, for them the August appearance was like a second shot on the Ed Sullivan show. One must resort to show business for a comparable case of so much being made of so little. To accept the estimate of Phillip Abbott Luce, there are a thousand card-carrying P.L.M. members in the entire country, and their ideology owes at least as much to good old American exhibitionism as to the writings of Chairman Mao. In their disgust with their own country and disdain for liberals and everybody else over the age of thirty, they cannot acknowledge how much of the defiance they showed in the hearing room was subsidized by that part of square America which brought down McCarthy and is reflected in the Warren Court. Arrogant, short-tempered, long-winded, they were peculiarly effective against the Un-American Activities Committee; when Joe Pool was in the chair, the House Caucus Room was no place for philosophers or gentlemen.

These last vaudeville-like hearings of 1966 were great fun, but it was the kind of fun that leaves a bad aftertaste. What we were witnessing was a confrontation between the benighted and the loud-mouthed, a monster film in which the worst of the stand-patters met the worst of the dissenters, and each fed on the other. It was an indecent display, but fans of both sides claimed a victory. "Those of us who sat listening to the spirited answers of the subpoenaed witnesses," wrote a leader of Women Strike for Peace, "derived a vicarious satisfaction from the experience." She saw emerging from the brawl "the beginning of a new unity among peace, civil liberties and civil rights advocates" —a return to the united front. And a few days after it was all over the Veterans of Foreign Wars gave Representative Pool a gold medal, three cheers, a parade, a standing ovation, and a chorus of *For he's a jolly good fellow*. Pool was touched. He said: "The House Committee on Un-American Activities is now in its greatest hour."

16

★ ★ ★ ★ ★

1967 . . . : Un-American?

As the House Committee on Un-American Activities rounds out the third decade of its existence,[1] it appears to be succumbing to the allure of the two great protest movements of our time. The attraction, to be sure, is perverse—there is something about the spectacle of people picketing for peace in Vietnam or marching for votes for Negroes that sets teeth on edge around the Committee's offices—but its recent gestures are at one with the spirit that has brought the Committee the special place that it occupies in the Congress and in the country. Foreign perils and domestic turbulence have provided the stuff of its labors since Martin Dies set about exposing the Detroit sit-down strikes as part of a Moscow-directed insurrection, and now the clouds of war and civil discontent are full of promise. In truth, the Committee cannot prosper without threats abroad and fears at home; it owes its most resplendent hours to the postwar confrontation in Berlin, the Communist victory in China, espionage cases in New York and Washington, war in Korea—and lacking in such fertilizing events, the early nineteen-sixties brought a series of dry seasons. Hearings have been rowdy, inconsequential, humiliating. The Committee

---

[1] Edwin E. Willis of Louisiana remains chairman in the ninetieth Congress. The Democrats on the Committee are William M. Tuck of Virginia; Joe R. Pool of Texas; Richard H. Ichord of Missouri; and John C. Culver of Iowa—a newcomer who has dissented from all of the Committee's 1967 legislative proposals. The Republicans: John M. Ashbrook of Ohio; Del Clawson of California; Richard L. Roudebush of Indiana; and Albert W. Watson of South Carolina. Francis J. McNamara remains staff director; Chester D. Smith is general counsel; Alfred M. Nittle is counsel.

has suffered rebuff upon rebuff from the courts. It has encountered increasing opposition in Congress and out. Once its tales
of Soviet espionage made the front pages, but hearings in
April 1967 into even that colorful subject went unattended.
A parched decade.

But now it may be that those lowering clouds, seeded by
the frustrations of Vietnam and the fears in our simmering
cities, are about to open again. Did not the President use the
occasion of presenting the Medal of Honor to a marine's widow
to contrast her husband's sacrifice with the "hostile placards
and debating points" of the war's critics "thousands of miles
away from the battlefield on which he fell"? Has not the Secretary of State reported that "the Communist apparatus" is hard
at work on peace demonstrations? Has not our former ambassador in Saigon warned that "disunity in America prolongs
the war" in Vietnam? Has not our most celebrated general
concurred? And did not the House of Representatives pass a
bill, by a vote of 386 to 16, to make public mutilation of the
flag a federal crime? This is Committee weather. Representative Pool, whose conduct of the raucous 1966 hearings into the
Progressive Labor Movement was unedifying to the point of
burlesque, has become a prophet. "The voice of Congress this
year," a Northern liberal was quoted as saying in June 1967,
"is old Joe Pool."

The Committee's main contribution to the anti-dissent chorus
of 1967 came in the form of a report released on March 31, two
weeks before the Saturday set for major peace demonstrations
in New York and San Francisco. The report was a typical Committee document in its casual association between the evidence
adduced and the judgment rendered. It reviewed the busy part
that Communists—particularly students urged on by Bettina
Aptheker, daughter of Herbert—had played in the planning for
the event, and from this trampoline leaped to the assertion:
"Such success as the instigators and organizers of Vietnam
Week may have in staging anti-U.S. demonstrations April 8–
15, and in turning out large numbers of people for the New
York and San Francisco demonstrations may be attributed
primarily to the Communists." The motives behind the report

do not bear much scrutiny; it was gotten together and issued
to discredit the protests in advance and to discourage participation. (In a revealing foreword, Chairman Willis explains
that he is not opposed to "honest and responsible dissent from
American policy by patriotic Americans" which will add to the
public's "appreciation of the basic correctness of the policy
our Government is pursuing.") On the day the demonstrations
were held and scores of thousands marched on both coasts,
the President let it be known that the F.B.I. was keeping its
eye on anti-war activity, and Joe Pool demanded that Governor
Rockefeller call out troops and tanks to safeguard property.[2]

Civil rights presents trickier terrain. Chairman Willis cannot but be sensitive to the fact that today more than ever his
Committee is dominated by Southerners and conservative Republicans, with not a single Eastern or Western liberal among
them. Should he undertake a direct assault on a prominent
civil rights group, as his predecessors once assaulted the
N.A.A.C.P., he would be vulnerable on that account and would
have to be prepared for a powerful show of resistance. While
diehard Southerners may continue to use the Committee's files
to discredit Negro and white activists, it is not likely that Mr.
Watson of South Carolina will have his way, that the cautious
Willis will plunge directly into the whirlpool of civil rights. Yet
the attraction is surely there, has been there since Martin Dies
rebuked left-wingers for giving the poor Negro the idea that
he ought to have a measure of equality. "I deplore the fact,"
said Dies in 1942, "that throughout the South today subversive
elements are attempting to convince the Negro that he should
be placed on social equality with white people, that now is the
time for him to assert his rights."

Just as one may get at the Vietnam dissenters via the youths
who cause commotions at military bases, so one may find an
access route into the civil-rights movement. In October 1966
Chairman Willis announced that his Committee was under-

---

[2] Two former stalwarts of the Committee, ex-Representatives Donald C.
Bruce of Indianapolis and Fulton Lewis III, who helped put out *Operation
Abolition*, have produced a film about anti-war demonstrations, entitled *While
Brave Men Die*, which they are showing with reported success to the Daughters
of the American Revolution and similar audiences.

taking "a preliminary inquiry" to determine the extent to which "subversive elements" were involved in "organized rioting, burning, looting and other tragic acts of violence . . ." (This announcement came a few weeks after Joe Pool had placed in the Congressional Record an article by the ever reliable J. Edgar Hoover on the theme "Communist influence is being injected into civil disobedience.") By the mid-nineteen-sixties the remarkable surge of support for the Negro's claims had ebbed; the backlash was being felt. In the fall of 1966, Republicans used "law and order" as a dominant campaign theme, with evident effect. The perennial riots in Negro ghettoes, terrifying in themselves and in what they reveal of the rage that festers in our cities, were taken by a number of legislators as an invitation for a reprisal against the civil-rights movement. As the Un-American Activities Committee prepared its part in the counterattack, dozens of "anti-riot" bills were pending before the House Judiciary Committee.

When a group of civil-rights leaders expressed concern over the Committee's 1966 initiative and petitioned the House to block it, Willis declared: "We have no intention of investigating the civil-rights movement or the opinions or positions of any individual or organization on the civil-rights issue. Those things are none of our business . . . The Committee on Un-American Activities . . . has no jurisdiction in such matters and it has no intention of trying to inject itself into them." Roy Wilkins could not have said it more succinctly—but Willis could not let the subject go at that. He added: "If we should learn in the course of our investigation that a certain organization is actually controlled and dominated by the Communists carrying out the work of the Communist Party, we would not hesitate to investigate their operations." The preliminary inquiry was entrusted to Representative Tuck of Virginia, one of the members who had been urging an investigation of Communist infiltration of civil-rights groups, and the staff—which for practical purposes *is* the Committee—went scouting for what it manages to find wherever it looks.

So far a direct encounter between the Committee and the civil-rights movement remains only a promise. There is pressure for it, but there is strong pressure against it from powers in the House who have no taste for a repetition of the rowdy hearings of the recent past. Willis does not usually flout the wishes of his party's leadership, but the subject is alive and kicking for all it is worth. In the summer of 1967, a few days after the Newark, New Jersey, ghetto erupted, a bill making it a federal crime to cross state lines to incite a riot swept through the House of Representatives by a vote of 347 to 70. Edwin Willis served as floor manager. After the Detroit outbreak, the worst yet, he let it be known that the evidence of "subversive influence" gathered by Committee investigators "will justify public hearings." Hardly had the fires of Detroit burned themselves out when a Presidential commission and two Senate groups were inquiring into the subject of riots in the cities, but the Un-American Activities Committee was not to be denied. In August the gist of a "secret" staff study was leaked to newspapers; to no one's surprise, it drew attention to the role of militant Negro groups and Communists in whipping up hatred of authority among Negroes. The promised hearings opened in October 1967 and as this is written are ambling unprovocatively along under Governor Tuck, while the Senate Permanent Subcommittee on Investigations, covering much the same subject, is getting most of the newspaper space.

The Committee's present interests represent no break with tradition, and its knack for attaching itself to popular passions is again creating tactical difficulties for its opponents.[3] The young men who court notoriety by waving the Vietcong flag and burning the American flag are prime exhibits for Edwin Willis, who characterizes Vietnam dissenters as "Communists, fellow travelers and a motley collection of unkempt hippies and beatniks, cowardly draft card burners and treasonous flag burners and the ilk that will unite with them." And riots in the cities are invitations for repressive action to men who have

---

[3] In writing of the opponents of the Committee in this chapter, I mean those who sometimes act as defenders of individual Communists but are not the Party's collaborators or apologists—that is, persons more likely to contribute to the American Civil Liberties Union than to the Emergency Civil Liberties Committee and more responsive to the pronouncements of Americans for Democratic Action than to those of the National Lawyers Guild.

fought every effort to ease the conditions of ghetto life. (A day after it passed the anti-riot bill, the House turned down a measure to fight rats in the nation's slums. Only two members of the Committee, Willis and Culver, voted for this bill.) An understandably frightened public is understandably receptive to calls for tougher laws, more police, harsher penalties.

To add to the liberal burden, those, like the staff of the Committee, who set themselves the task of finding Communists and fellow travelers in the peace and civil-rights movements will find them without having to look very hard. When *The New Republic* ran an editorial mocking the Committee's report on Vietnam Week, Bettina Aptheker, that chip off old Herbert, chided the editors for not giving the Communists sufficient credit for their role in the April 15 marches. Moderate peace organizations like SANE gave them credit enough to abstain from official participation that day. Just what attitude to adopt toward self-advertising Communists, old style and new, Moscow-oriented and Peking-oriented, has been a cause of fresh soul-searching among liberal intellectuals in the nineteen-sixties. The old resentments have cooled, and most liberals seem ready to grant that it is silly in 1968 to go on rating ex-Communists by the day and month in 1939 or 1945 or 1956 that they quit the Party, rather like the French émigré nobles in Coblenz who divided the imagined spoils of the restoration according to the date that one fled France. Nor are liberals eager to abet the hunters of Reds by giving our Communist remnants more attention than their condition warrants. Yet the issues that seemed to have been battled out in the nineteen-thirties will not lie quiet in the post-Stalin era. Is it becoming for men who champion freedom in its full variety to make common cause, even in the noblest pursuits, with the champions of totalitarianism? Is it moral? Is it practical? Can such collaboration benefit the liberals' high purposes or will it in fact work against them?

Whereas the non-Communist left is divided over these questions, the Communists and the scourges of Communists are, as usual, allied. The Communists have often followed, with regard to their lay organizations, the model of gamblers who put hirelings without criminal records in nominal charge of their enterprises in Las Vegas; just as the syndicate makes sure to get its regular cut, so the Party has made sure to take a substantial share of credit for all benefits proceeding from the worthy groups. The investigators of the Committee on Un-American Activities, suspicious of all leftward-leaning organizations and all their works, have for thirty years delightedly given the Communists their claimed share of credit, and more. Issues of great moment—from the New Deal to industrial unionism to a nuclear-test ban—have enjoyed the Committee's attentions. In most cases there has been substance to the charges of Communist machinations just as there has been substance to the countercharges of red herring. Sorting out the charges and countercharges has fallen to mere liberals, who have sometimes pretended that the Communists were social democrats at heart and have sometimes responded to the Committee's incursions by looking the other way. But there have always been voices among them that were at once sophisticated about the Communists and unfearing of the Committee, and these have been heard to better effect in recent years.

Liberal opposition peaks regularly in odd-numbered years, when the new House of Representatives meets and goes through the formality of adopting the rules of the previous Congress, including all of its standing committees. This occasion brings forth editorials and petitions and calls for abolition from Congressmen like Edwards of California and Ryan of New York. But abolition has never been a realistic goal. As Representative Edwards sadly remarked in 1965, "A standing committee once established is immensely difficult to get rid of, even though its mandate is probably unconstitutional and its behavior embarrassing and belittling to the Congress."

The Committee's opponents in the House have therefore directed their attacks toward its appropriation, which must be approved annually. In the eighty-ninth Congress, it received $848,000, over and above its basic staff budget of about $162,000; this was the fourth highest appropriation among the twenty standing committees of the House, substantially more than the sums given to such productive arms of the Congress as the Committee on Interstate and Foreign Commerce, the Committee on Banking and Currency, or the Committee on the Judiciary. So it came as a notable victory for the opposition when in April 1967 the $400,000 requested by the Committee for its year's work was cut to $350,000 by the House Administration subcommittee entrusted with reviewing such appropriations. Then the opponents rounded up ninety-two votes for a motion which would have compelled the Committee to justify its budget at open hearings. There were 304 votes against this motion, but not since the Committee's establishment as a permanent body in 1945 had the liberals in Congress managed to rally such an expression of dissatisfaction with its behavior.

Yet even on this day of victory, only forty-three representatives voted against the actual appropriation, an improvement over 1961 when there were only six opposing votes, but far from the smell of success. The liberals owed their modest achievement of April 1967 to the display put on by the egregious Joe Pool at his Vietnam hearings of the previous summer and, barring some even more flagrant episode, there is no reason to suppose that they will do much better in the future. The Committee can continue to rely on a staunch body of supporters in the House as well as on the disinclination of Congressmen to register an unfriendly vote which will have to be explained to American Legion posts back home.

A more likely source of an effective blow to the Committee is the judiciary, which has already delivered it so many slaps for bad manners and has quite undone its preeminent legislative accomplishment, the Internal Security Act of 1950. The Committee's four doughty foes—Warren, Black, Douglas, and Brennan—remain on the bench, and they have been joined by two juniors from whom Willis, Pool, *et al.* have no reason to look for indulgence. The dossier of Thurgood Marshall has periodically been plucked from the Committee's files and waved about by arch-segregationists. And it was Abe Fortas who wrote in gloomy 1953 that "the [Congressional] hearing has become a weapon of persecution, a useful tool to the demagogue, a device for the glory of the prosecutor and of shame for the accused."

If the Stamler-Hall-Cohen case that originated in the Chicago hearings of 1965 or the Krebs-Teague case that came out of the 1966 Vietnam hearings should find its way up to the high tribunal while this six-justice group is intact, the Committee stands to receive a sharper rebuff than it received in the prematurely acclaimed 1957 Watkins decision. At any rate, such is the liberal hope. No court can do away with the Committee, but if the witnesses who walked out in Chicago and Washington are upheld in their major arguments against the Committee's status and procedures, unfriendly witnesses of the future will have been provided with a sturdy shield for defiance. They will not be able to prevent any Congressman from making any accusations he wishes, but they may be relieved of the obligation to participate in their own pillory.

The points scored annually by liberals in Congress against the Committee's existence are barely contestable—and for all practical purposes Committee members gave up contesting them some time ago, relying instead on evocations of the Communist menace and their own patriotism. The Committee's annual expenditure and the size of its staff, so much larger than most committees of the House, represent an exorbitant cost for so meager a legislative record.[4] Its files of names and affiliations, which Chairman Willis cites often as being of inestimable help to federal investigators of all sorts, arouse special disquiet among liberals; not only do they presume that they are listed therein, but they question the propriety of a committee of Congress keeping political dossiers on citizens. And, of course, liberals continue to be put off by the Committee's uncivil methods of carrying out its uncertain mandate. But valid as the reiterated criticisms are, they do not quite explain the vehemence with which liberals, along with virtually the entire intellectual community,[5] have rallied against the Committee.

[4] Responding in 1965 to criticisms that the normal Committee complement of between fifty and sixty staff members seemed excessive, Representative Ashbrook, the Committee's ranking Republican, explained: "Without sufficient staff we might well have a fishing expedition here and there and stray into paths which lead to irresponsibility."
[5] In 1961 a professor of classics at the University of Illinois named Revilo P. Oliver (destined to become an adornment of the Birch establishment) who

There are few causes in our history that have kept liberal passions at the boil for so long. "Frankly," Chairman Willis has said, "while I do not question their sincerity, I just do not understand these people."

They are not so difficult to understand. For thirty years the most cherished ideals of liberalism and many of its heroes have been among the Committee's main targets. Liberals have had their motives impugned and their patriotism questioned. They have seen associates and acquaintances harried by investigators and have read of the ordeals of witnesses with whom they could easily identify. Their responses to the recurrent assaults have not always been intelligent or entirely honest. There were periods, before the outbreak of World War II and in the early postwar years, when many liberals, bemused by the dream of the Popular Front or having tolerated it to their later chagrin, fought back by denying the undeniable and defending the indefensible. On finding themselves vulnerable to the Committee's charges, some have cried like hurt children at their tormentors, "You're one too!," accusing the Committee itself of being un-American. Such has been the liberal contribution to the debasement of political discourse.

Had Martin Dies and J. B. Matthews and their successors contented themselves with arguing that the Communist Party or the German-American Bund was un-American because it conducted its affairs by the grace of a foreign state, one would have been hard put to challenge them. But the Communists were never sufficiently satisfying game; Dies was out to get the New Deal, and as he and Thomas and Velde moved on to fellow travelers and others, the Committee's rationale became increasingly tenuous. Soon the Congressmen were taking logically impermissible shortcuts; it was no longer a man's loyalty to the U.S.S.R. that made him a likely subversive but his adherence to causes favored by those who were loyal to the

---

wished to show that not all intellectuals despise the Committee made public a statement in its defense signed by 139 college administrators and teachers from seventeen schools. To fill out his company, Professor Oliver had to mine institutions like Catawba College, the Chicago Lutheran Theological Seminary, and Roberts Wesleyan College, thereby confirming what had been apparent for years—that the country's intellectuals despise the Committee.

U.S.S.R. So the famous files were built up, wherein support of Loyalist Spain, antagonism to the Smith Act, and, of course, any expressed hope for the disappearance of the Committee all became black marks in one's dossier. It was guilt by extension. The Communist Party, that band of social climbers, always loved to brag of its roots in American radicalism. The claim was humorous coming from the Soviet fan club, but the causes to which the Communists gave their considerable energies, such as industrial unionism and Negro rights, did have authentic roots and, like an army company straying beyond reach of its supply station, the farther the Committee moved from paid functionaries of the Party, the weaker became its lines of support.

No critic of the Committee will take exception to these unoriginal observations, but they bear on the liberal side of the debate too. Just as there is nothing historically un-American about wanting to do away with A.T.&T. or the Catholic Church, so there is nothing un-American about union-busting or anti-Semitism or the Ku Klux Klan, and unless one is prepared to blank out large and significant patches of our history, there is nothing un-American about the Un-American Activities Committee. An organization, as J. B. Matthews taught, may be known by the company it attracts, and none of the men who have led the Committee in its endless campaigns represents anything unique in our national political life. The swaggering demagogy of Martin Dies was run-of-the-mill stuff back in Texas. The unstinting bigotry of John Rankin showed him to be the true representative of the voters in his home district, scarcely an alien or the son of an alien among them. And what is un-American about the brutality of J. Parnell Thomas, the cunning of Richard Nixon, the mindless opportunism of Harold Velde, the zenophobia of Francis Walter, the stupidity of Joe Pool? The fact that such are the men who have found a home with the Committee is revealing, but not on account of any want of "Americanism."

The Committee's Americanism runs deep. It can trace its ancestry to colonial times, when we hounded religious eccentrics, and to the Revolution, when we tyrannized Tories. The fear of Jacobinism that brought us the Alien and Sedition Laws in the eighteenth century was not unlike the fear of Bolshevism that brought us the Internal Security Act in the twentieth century. In World War I we imprisoned socialists, pacifists, and German sympathizers, and in World War II, with the Committee's blessing, we forced thousands of people to leave their homes and gather in camps because they were of Japanese descent. For three decades the Committee has labored in behalf of America's nativists, preserving the verities of the small town against adulteration by the big city, shoring up pietist truths against erosion by the social gospel, defending the flag from soilage by aliens, intellectuals, crackpots. It is precisely the Committee's Americanism that is so troubling, in its reminder that this is not the land exclusively of Lincoln and Jefferson.

In a time like the present, when our repressive instincts are under reasonable control, the Committee exists to keep us from smugness, from forgetting how suddenly an external or internal threat or imagined threat can bring a relapse into that delirium where common sense mingles with common superstition, intelligence rides with ignorance, and honest men find themselves in league with charlatans, self-aggrandizers, and maniacs. The Committee, like the distemper itself, has raged and subsided, has invigorated the political body and ravaged it, has compelled us to confront real weaknesses at the very moment that it was sapping our fundamental strengths. At times the fever has been efficacious, a stimulant to an apathetic constitution, but more often it has been all pains and rashes which left the body debilitated, even disfigured. Invariably the nation has recovered, but not without casualties. Lacking these casualties, the people whose reputations and livelihoods have been blithely hazarded, the Committee's career would lack meaning. They are its achievement. It has established a record not of laws but of Fifth Amendment pleas and contempt citations and disrupted lives. The proudest exhibit of the Committee's thirty years is its spacious files filled with the names, associations, activities, and public utterances of thousands of Americans.

From the start the Committee has been egged on by the

nation's entire lumpen right. Whatever foray it rode out upon, it wore, and still wears, the colors of Legionnaires, policemen, and ladies of the D.A.R., fundamentalist congregations in the South and Midwest and McCarthyite Catholics in Boston and New York and vigilantes everywhere. Trapped by a terrible nostalgia, these truculent cheerleaders of repression are fighting against the sense that their economic, social, and political positions have deteriorated, that control of their country's destiny, and their own, is slipping inexorably away. Their neighborhoods are changing; the country is changing. They are not, most of them, readers of poetry or, indeed, much else, but they might find words for their feelings in Yeats: "Things fall apart; the centre cannot hold; Mere anarchy is loosed upon the world." Alas, they can look for no Second Coming. Their passions cry for outlet, and since they cannot declare war on all America, or even concede that it is some genius of America itself that is doing them in, they set out after Reds, pinks, blacks, foreigners, beatniks—conspirators all. The Un-American Activities Committee is the engine of their vengeance, and for thirty years it has run on flesh and blood.

The endless harassment of individuals for disagreeable opinions and activities has created the greatest anxiety, revulsion, indignation, outrage among liberals. In protesting against the Committee's bloodlettings, liberals are only affirming their position in the war between the enthusiasts and the men of the Enlightenment which already raged when our country began. Between the Committee and the liberal spirit no reconciliation is possible, for the Committee embodies the drive to ban, censor, forbid, jail that has cursed the land for two hundred years. Whether or not the emotions stirred by the war in Vietnam and by the ghetto riots will reinvigorate the Committee, whether or not the Congress will limit its appropriation or the courts narrow its range, the division between freedom and security, between the pardoners and the punishers will not be healed. It is wider and deeper than the division between right and left in America, where the left has its doctrinaires and the right its libertarians. The awareness that even if the Committee were abolished tomorrow the gulf would remain, dangerous as ever, will deter no one from carrying a placard for abolition. Nor can it solace those who have been hurt during the years of rampage. But let us hope that the thought that the Committee on Un-American Activities can inflict on the nation only what the nation in its paranoiac seizures is willing to endure, may provide some small comfort for the unquiet shade of Sam Dickstein.

Appendix I

Chairmen of the House Committee
on Un-American Activities

1938–1944: Martin Dies, Jr. (D., TEXAS)
1945: Edward J. Hart (D., N.J.)
1945–1946: John S. Wood (D., GA.)
1947–1948: J. Parnell Thomas (R., N.J.)
1949–1952: John S. Wood (D., GA.)
1953–1954: Harold H. Velde (R., ILL.)
1955–1963: Francis E. Walter (D., PA.)
1963: Edwin E. Willis (D., LA.)

Appendix II

Hearings and Reports of the
House Committee on Un-American Activities

SPECIAL COMMITTEE: 1938–1944

Public Hearings

Vol. 1: Aug. 12, 13, 15–20, 22, 23, 1938; Washington, D.C.

Vol. 2: Sept. 15–17, 1938; New York. Sept. 28–30, Oct. 4–6, 1938; Washington, D.C. Oct. 11–13, 1938; Detroit. Oct. 17–22, 1938; Washington, D.C.

Vol. 3: Oct. 24–27, Nov. 4–6, 14–17, 19, 21, 1938; Washington, D.C.

Vol. 4: Nov. 19, 22, 23, 28, Dec. 1, 5–9, 14, 1938; Washington, D.C. (supplement) Dec. 15, 1938; Washington, D.C.

Vol. 5: May 18, 22–24, 31, June 1, 1939; Washington, D.C.

Vol. 6: Aug. 16–18, 21–24, 28, 29, 1939; Washington, D.C.

Vol. 7: Sept. 5–9, 11–13, 1939; Washington, D.C.

Vol. 8: Sept. 18–20, 22, 23, 25, 27, 1939; Washington, D.C.

Vol. 9: Sept. 28–30, Oct. 5–7, 9, 11, 13, 14, 1939; Washington, D.C.

Vol. 10: Oct. 16–21, 23–25, 28, 1939; Washington, D.C.

Vol. 11: Oct. 28, 30, 31, Nov. 1–3, 27, 29, 30, Dec. 1–3, 1939; Washington, D.C.

Vol. 12: Feb. 7, 8, 10, March 25, 28, 29, April 2–4, 1940; Washington, D.C.

Vol. 13: April 11, 12, 19, 23–25, May 6, 8, 9, 21, 1940; Washington, D.C.

Vol. 14. Aug. 29, 1940; Washington, D.C. Oct. 1, 2, 4, 1940; Newark. May 21, 22, 26, 27, 29, June 10, 12, Aug. 11, 1941; Washington, D.C.

Vol. 15: June 8–12, 15–18, 1943; Los Angeles. June 18, 1943; Parker, Arizona. July 1–3, 6, 7, 1943; Washington, D.C.
Vol. 16: Nov. 29, 30, Dec. 1, 6–9, 20, 1943; Washington, D.C.
Vol. 17: Sept. 27–29, Oct. 3–5, 1944; Washington, D.C.

Executive Hearings Made Public

Vol. 1: Sept. 20, Oct. 6, 9, 11, 12, 14, 1939; Washington, D.C. Nov. 9, 10, 1939; New Orleans. Nov. 17, 18, 1939; Chicago. Nov. 20, 1939; Detroit.
Vol. 2: March 9, 11, 1940; Miami Beach. March 21, June 3, 1940; Washington, D.C. July 8, 1940; New York. July 8–11, 1940; Austin. July 16, 17, 1940; Beaumont, Texas.
Vol. 3: July 17, 1940; Chattanooga. July 18, 1940; Houston. July 19, 22, Aug. 5, 1940; Beaumont, Texas. July 26, 1940; Washington, D.C. Aug. 6, 1940; Orange, Texas. Aug. 16, 17, 1940; Los Angeles. Aug. 19, 20, 1940; San Francisco.
Vol. 4: Oct. 2, 3, 1939; Chicago. Aug. 23, 24, 1940; Kansas City, Mo. Aug. 26, 27, 1940; New York. Oct. 1, 2, 1940; Newark. Oct. 17, Nov. 6, 8, 1940; Los Angeles.
Vol. 5: Nov. 2, 1940; St. Louis. Nov. 18, 1940; Chicago. Dec. 11, 20–22, 1940; March 4, Aug. 5, 7, 8, Dec. 18, 19, 1941; Washington, D.C.
Vol. 6: Oct. 30, 1941; Jan. 15, 16, 19–22, 26, March 26, April 17, 1942; Washington, D.C.
Vol. 7: March 23, 29–31, April 1, 2, 5–9, 16, 1943; Washington, D.C. April 19, 1943; New York.

Reports

House Report No. 2. Annual Report. Jan. 3, 1939.
House Report No. 1476. Annual Report. Jan. 3, 1940.
House Report No. 1. Annual Report. Jan. 3, 1941.
House Report No. 2277. Annual Report, Part 1. June 25, 1942. Part 2 (minority views on annual report). July 7, 1942.
House Report No. 2748. Annual Report. Jan. 2, 1943.
House Report No. 717. Japanese in the United States (including minority views on war relocation centers). Sept. 30, 1943.
House Report No. 1161. The Peace Now Movement. Feb. 17, 1944.
House Report No. 1311. C.I.O. Political Action Committee. March 29, 1944.

Report of a Special Subcommittee on the Tule Lake Riot. 1944.
Minority Views on Tule Lake Segregation Center. 1944.
Index to Hearings, Volumes 1–14, Reports, 1939–44; Appendixes I-V. 1942.

Appendixes

Appendix I. A compilation of original sources used as exhibits to show the nature and aims of the Communist Party, its connections with the U.S.S.R. and its advocacy of force and violence. 1940.

Appendix II. A preliminary digest and report on the un-American activities of various Nazi organizations and individuals in the United States, including diplomatic and consular agents of the German government. 1940.

Appendix III. Preliminary report on totalitarian propaganda in the United States. 1941.

Appendix IV. German-American Bund. 1941.

Appendix V. Transport Workers Union. 1941.

Appendix VI. Report on Japanese activities. 1942.

Appendix VII. Report on the Axis front movement in the United States—Nazi activities. 1943.

Appendix VIII. Report on the Axis front movement in the United States—Japanese activities. 1943.

STANDING COMMITTEE: 1945–1967

79th Congress

Hearings on Office of Price Administration. June 20, 21, 27, 1945.
Hearings on Communist Party. Sept. 26, 27, Oct. 17–19, 1945.
Hearings on Gerald L. K. Smith. Jan. 30, 1946.
Hearings on Joint Anti-Fascist Refugee Committee. April 4, 1946.
Hearings on Louis F. Budenz. Nov. 22, 1946.

House Report No. 1996. Sources of financial aid for subversive and un-American propaganda. May 10, 1946.
House Report No. 2233. Annual Report. June 7, 1946.
House Report No. 2742. Annual Report. Jan. 2, 1947.

80th Congress

Hearings on Gerhart Eisler. Feb. 6, 1947.

Hearings regarding Communism in labor unions in the United States. Feb. 27, July 23–25, 1947.

Hearings regarding Leon Josephson and Samuel Liptzen. March 5, 21, 1947.

Hearings on H.R. 1884 and H.R. 2122, bills to curb or outlaw the Communist Party of the United States. March 24–28, 1947.

Testimony of William C. Bullitt. March 24, 1947.

Testimony of J. Edgar Hoover. March 26, 1947.

Testimony of Eugene Dennis. April 9, 1947.

Testimony of Walter S. Steele. July 21, 1947.

Testimony of Victor Kravchenko. July 22, 1947.

Hearings regarding Hanns Eisler, Sept. 24–26, 1947.

Hearings regarding Communist infiltration of the motion-picture industry. Oct. 20–24, 27–30, 1947.

Hearings on H.R. 4422 and H.R. 4581, proposed legislation to curb or control the Communist Party of the United States. Feb. 5, 6, 9–11, 19, 20, 1948.

Hearings regarding Communist espionage in the United States Government (including interim report on hearings, Aug. 28, 1948). July 31, Aug. 3–5, 7, 9–13, 16–18, 20, 24–27, 30, Sept. 8, 9, 1948.

Excerpts from hearings regarding investigation of Communist activities in connection with the atom bomb. Sept. 9, 14, 16, 1948.

Hearings regarding Communist espionage in the United States Government, Part II. Dec. 7–10, 14, 1948.

House Report No. 209. Communist Party of the United States as an agent of a foreign power. April 1, 1947.

House Report No. 271. American Youth for Democracy. April 17, 1947.

House Report No. 592. Southern Conference for Human Welfare. June 16, 1947.

House Report No. 1115. Civil Rights Congress. Nov. 17, 1947.

Report on Dr. Edward U. Condon. March 18, 1948.

Report on proposed legislation to control subversive Communist activities in the United States. April 10, 1948.

House Report No. 1844. Protecting the United States against un-American and subversive activities. April 30, 1948.

House Report No. 1920. The Communist Party of the United States as an advocate of overthrow of government by force and violence. May 11, 1948.

Report on Soviet espionage activities in connection with the atom bomb. Sept. 28, 1948.

Second report, Soviet espionage within the United States Government. Dec. 31, 1948.

Annual Report. Dec. 31, 1948.

81st Congress

Documentary testimony of Gen. Izyador Modelski. March 31, April 1, 1949.

Hearings on Soviet espionage activities in connection with jet propulsion and aircraft. June 6, 1949.

Hearings regarding Steve Nelson. June 8, 1949.

Hearings regarding Toma Babin. May 27, July 6, 1949.

Testimony of Paul Crouch. May 6, 1949.

Testimony of Philip O. Keeney and Mary Jane Keeney and statement regarding their background. May 24, 25, June 9, 1949.

Hearings regarding Communist infiltration of radiation laboratory and atomic bomb project at the University of California, Berkeley, Calif. (vol. I). April 22, 26, May 25, June 10, 14, 1949.

Hearings regarding Clarence Hiskey (including testimony of Paul Crouch). May 24, 1949.

Hearings regarding Communist infiltration of minority groups (part I). July 13, 14, 18, 1949.

Hearings regarding Communist infiltration of minority groups (part II) (testimony of Manning Johnson). July 14, 1949.

Hearings regarding Communist infiltration of labor unions (part I). Aug. 9–11, 1949.

Hearings regarding Communism in the District of Columbia (part I). June 28, 29, July 6, 12, 28, 1949.

Hearings regarding Communist infiltration of radiation laboratory and atomic bomb project at the University of California, Berkeley, Calif. (vol. II) (identification of Scientist X). Aug. 26, 1949; July 1, Sept. 10, 1948; Aug. 14, Sept. 14, 27, 1949.

Hearings regarding Communist infiltration of labor unions (part II) (security measures relating to officials of the UERMWA-CIO). Dec. 5, 6, 1949.

Testimony of James Sterling Murray and Edward Tiers Manning (regarding Clarence Hiskey and Arthur Adams). Aug. 14, Oct. 5, 1949.

Hearings regarding shipment of atomic material to the Soviet Union during World War II. Dec. 5, 7, 1949; Jan. 23–26, March 2, 3, 7, 1950.

Exposé of the Communist Party of western Pennsylvania (part I) (based upon testimony of Matthew Cvetic, undercover agent). Feb. 21–23, March 13, 14, 24, 1950.

Hearings regarding Communist activities in the Territory of Hawaii (part I). April 10–12, 1950.

Hearings regarding Communist activities in the Territory of Hawaii (part II). April 13–15, 1950.

Hearings regarding Communism in the United States Government (part I). April 20, 21, 25, 29, May 4–6, 1950; July 30, Aug. 7, 1948; June 8, 1950.

Hearings regarding Communist activities in the Territory of Hawaii (part III). April 17–19, 1950.

Hearings on H.R. 3903 and H.R. 7595 (legislation to outlaw certain un-American and subversive activities). March 21–23, 28–30, April 4, May 2–4, 1950.

Exposé of the Communist Party of western Pennsylvania (part II) (based upon testimony of Matthew Cvetic). March 24, 25, 1950.

Testimony of Philip A. Bart (general manager of Freedom of the Press, publishers of the *Daily Worker*, organ of the Communist Party) and Marcel Scherer (coordinator, New York Labor Conference for Peace and formerly district representative of District 4, UERMWA-CIO). June 21, 1950.

Hearings regarding Communist activities in the Cincinnati, Ohio, area (part I). July 12–15, Aug. 8, 1950.

Hearings regarding Communist infiltration of minority groups (part III) (testimony of Josh White). Sept. 1, 1950.

Hearings regarding Communism in the United States Government (part II). Aug. 28, 31, Sept. 1, 15, 1950.

Exposé of the Communist Party of western Pennsylvania (based upon testimony of Matthew Cvetic and documents of C.P. of western Pennsylvania) (part III). June 22, Sept. 28, Oct. 13, 21, 1950.

Hearings regarding Communism in the District of Columbia (part II). Dec. 6, 11–13, 1950.

Testimony of Edward G. Robinson. Oct. 27, Dec. 21, 1950.

American aspects of the assassination of Leon Trotsky. July 26, Aug. 30, Oct. 18, 19, Dec. 4, 1950.

Hearings regarding Communist infiltration of radiation laboratory and atomic bomb project at the University of California, Berkeley, Calif. (vol. III). Dec. 20–22, 1950.

Hearings regarding Communist infiltration of labor unions (part III). Aug. 29, 30, 1950.

Hearings regarding Communist espionage. Nov. 8, Dec. 2, 1949; Feb. 27, March 1, 1950.

Testimony of Hazel Scott Powell. Sept. 22, 1950.

House Report No. 1954. Review of the Scientific and Cultural Conference for World Peace. April 26, 1950.

House Report No. 1951. American Slav Congress. April 26, 1950.

House Report No. 1952. Report on atomic espionage (Nelson-Weinberg and Hiskey-Adams cases). April 26, 1950.

House Report No. 1953. Congress of American Women. April 26, 1950.

House Report No. 1950. Annual Report for 1949. April 26, 1950.

House Report No. 2986. Hawaii Civil Liberties Committee—a Communist front. Aug. 24, 1950.

The Communist "peace petition" campaign (interim statement). July 13, 1950.

House Report No. 3123. National Lawyers Guild. Sept. 21, 1950.

Report on the *Honolulu Record*. Oct. 1, 1950.

House Report No. 3248. The National Committee to Defeat the Mundt Bill—a Communist Lobby. Jan. 2, 1951.

House Report No. 3249. Annual Report for 1950. Jan. 2, 1951.

82d Congress

Hearings regarding Communist activities in the Territory of Hawaii (part IV). July 6, 1951.

Communist infiltration of Hollywood motion-picture industry (part I). March 8, 21, April 10–13, 1951.

Communist infiltration of Hollywood motion-picture industry (part II). April 17, 23–25, May 16–18, 1951.

Communist infiltration of Hollywood motion-picture industry (part III). May 22–25, June 25, 26, 1951.

Hearings relating to Communist activities in the defense area of Baltimore (part I) (based on testimony of Mary Stalcup Markward). June 19–21, 26–28, July 11, 13, 1951.

Hearings relating to Communist activities in the defense area of Baltimore (part II) (Maryland Committee for Peace and Baltimore County Committee for Peace). June 28, July 10, 12, 1951.

Hearings relating to Communist activities in the defense area of Baltimore (part III). June 19, 20, 26–28, July 10, 12, 13, 1951.

Hearings on American aspects of the Richard Sorge spy case. Aug. 9, 22, 23, 1951.

Exposé of Communist activities in the state of Massachusetts (based on the testimony of Herbert A. Philbrick). July 23, 24, Oct. 10, 11, 1951.

Communist infiltration of Hollywood motion-picture industry (part IV). Sept. 17–19, 1951.

Communist infiltration of Hollywood motion-picture industry (part V). Sept. 20, 21, 24, 25, 1951.

Hearings regarding Communist activities among farm groups. Feb. 28, March 9, 1951.

Communist tactics among veterans' groups. July 13, 1951.

Testimony of Oliver Edmund Clubb. March 14, Aug. 20, 23, 1951.

Communist infiltration of Hollywood motion-picture industry (part VI). May 10, Sept. 10–12, 1951.

The role of the Communist press in the Communist conspiracy. Jan. 9, 10, 15–17, 1952.

Communist infiltration of Hollywood motion-picture industry (part VII). Jan. 24, 28, Feb. 5, March 20, April 10, 30, 1952.

Communist activities among professional groups in the Los Angeles area (part I). Jan. 21–26, April 9, 1952.

Communism in the Detroit area (part I). Feb. 25–29, 1952.

Communism in the Detroit area (part II). March 10–12, April 29, 30, 1952.

Communist activities among youth groups (based on testimony of Harvey M. Matusow) (part I). Feb. 6, 7, 1952.

Methods of Communist infiltration in the United States Government. May 6, June 10, 23, 1952.

Communist infiltration of Hollywood motion-picture industry (part VIII). May 19–21, 1952.

Communist activities among professional groups in the Los Angeles area (part II). May 22, July 8, 1952.

Testimony of Lynne L. Prout. Feb. 14, 1952.

Communist activities in the Chicago area (part I). Sept. 2, 3, 1952.
Communist activities in the Chicago area (part II). Sept. 4, 5, 1952.
Testimony of Dr. Edward U. Condon. Sept. 5, 1952.
Communist activities among professional groups in the Los Angeles area (part III). Sept. 30, Oct. 1, 2, 1952.
Communist activities among professional groups in the Los Angeles area (part IV). Oct. 3, 6, 7, 1952.
Communist infiltration of Hollywood motion-picture industry (part IX). Aug. 19, Sept. 29, 1952.
Testimony of Gen. Walter Bedell Smith. Oct. 13, 1952.
Communist activities in the Philadelphia area. Oct. 13–16, 1952.
Communist infiltration of Hollywood motion-picture industry (part X). Nov. 12, 13, 1952.

The March of Treason. Feb. 19, 1951.
House Report No. 378. The Communist "Peace" Offensive. April 25, 1951.
House Document No. 137. Guide to Subversive Organizations and Publications. May 14, 1951.
House Document No. 136. 100 Things You Should Know About Communism. May 14, 1951.
House Report No. 1229. The Shameful Years. Jan. 8, 1952.
House Report No. 2431. Annual Report for 1951. July 2, 1952.
House Report No. 1661. Review of the Methodist Federation for Social Action. March 27, 1952.
House Report No. 2516. Annual Report for 1952. Jan. 3, 1953.

83d Congress

Communist methods of infiltration (education). Feb. 25–27, 1953.
Communist methods of infiltration (education) (part II). March 12, 13, 17, 18, April 14, 16, 1953.
Investigation of Communist activities in the Los Angeles area (part I). March 23–25, 1953.
Investigation of Communist activities in the Los Angeles area (part II). March 26–28, 1953.
Investigation of Communist activities in the Los Angeles area (part III). March 30, 31, 1953.
Investigation of Communist activities in the Los Angeles area (part IV). April 7, 8, 1953.

Investigation of Communist activities in the Los Angeles area (part V). Dec. 2, 1952; Feb. 17, March 12, 27, April 7, 13, 1953.

Communist methods of infiltration (education) (part III). April 21, 22, 1953.

Communist methods of infiltration (education) (part IV). April 23, 27, 1953.

Investigation of Communist activities in the New York City area (part I). May 4, 1953.

Investigation of Communist activities in the New York City area (part II). May 5, 1953.

Investigation of Communist activities in the New York City area (part III). May 6, 1953.

Investigation of Communist activities in the New York City area (part IV). May 7, 1953.

Communist methods of infiltration (education) (part V). April 29, May 19, 26–28, 1953.

Communist methods of infiltration (government-labor) (part I). April 17, May 14, June 9, 1953.

Francisek Jarecki, flight to freedom. July 1, 1953.

Soviet schedule for war, 1955. May 13, 14, 1953.

Investigation of Communist activities in the Columbus, Ohio, area. June 17, 18, 1953.

Communist methods of infiltration (education) (part VI). June 22, 24, 29, July 1, 1953.

Testimony of Stephen H. Fritchman. Sept. 12, 1951.

Communist methods of infiltration (government-labor) (part II). July 20, 1953.

Investigation of Communist activities in the New York City area (part V). July 6, 1953.

Investigation of Communist activities in the New York City area (part VI). July 7, 1953.

Investigation of Communist activities in the New York City area (part VII) (based on the testimony of Manning Johnson). July 8, 1953.

Investigation of Communist activities in the New York City area (part VIII) (based on the testimony of Manning Johnson). July 13, 14, 1953.

Investigation of Communist activities in the Los Angeles area (part VI). March 21, 1951; June 2, 1953.

Investigation of Communist activities in the Albany, N.Y. area (part I). July 13, 14, 1953.

Investigation of Communist activities in the Albany, N.Y. area (part II). July 15, 16, 1953.

Investigation of Communist activities in the Los Angeles area (part VII). Sept. 4, 1953.

Testimony of Dr. Marek Stanislaw Korowicz. Sept. 24, 1953.

Hearings regarding Jack R. McMichael. July 30, 31, 1953.

Investigation of Communist activities in the Philadelphia area (part I). Nov. 16, 1953.

Investigation of Communist activities in the Philadelphia area (part II). Nov. 17, 18, 1953.

Communist methods of infiltration (government-labor) (part III) (based on testimony of James McNamara). Sept. 15, 1953.

Investigation of Communist activities in the San Francisco area (part I). Dec. 1, 1953.

Investigation of Communist activities in the San Francisco area (part II). Dec. 2, 1953.

Investigation of Communist activities in the San Francisco area (part III). Dec. 3, 1953.

Investigation of Communist activities in the San Francisco area (part IV). Dec. 4, 1953.

Investigation of Communist activities in the San Francisco area (part V). Dec. 5, 1953.

Investigation of Communist activities in the Los Angeles area (part VIII). Nov. 23, 1953.

Communist methods of infiltration (education) (part VII). May 15, 1953.

Testimony of Bishop G. Bromley Oxnam. July 21, 1953.

Communist methods of infiltration (entertainment) (part I). Jan. 13, 1954.

Investigation of Communist activities in the Philadelphia area (parts III, IV). Feb. 16, 17, 1954.

Communist methods of infiltration (education) (part VIII). April 21, June 8, 1953; April 12, 1954.

Investigation of Communist activities in the Baltimore area (parts I-III). May 18, March 25, 26, 1954.

Investigation of Communist activities in the Chicago area (parts I-III). March 15, 16, April 29, 1954.

Investigation of Communist activities in the Albany, N.Y. area (parts III–VI). April 7–9, 1954.

Communism in the District of Columbia-Maryland area (testimony of Mary Stalcup Markward). June 11, 1951.

Investigation of Communist activities in the State of California parts I-X). Feb. 1, 24, March 1, April 12, 19–22, 1954. Sept. 11, 1953.

Investigation of Communist activities in the state of Michigan (parts I-V) (Detroit). April 28–30, May 3–5, 7, 1954.

Investigation of Communist activities in the state of Michigan (parts VI, VII) (Lansing). May 10, 11, 1954; June 8, 1953.

Investigation of Communist activities in the state of Michigan (parts VIII-X) (Flint). April 30, May 12–14, 1954.

Communist methods of infiltration (education) (part IX). June 28, 29, 1954.

Communist activities among youth groups (based on testimony of Harvey M. Matusow) (part II). July 12, 1954.

Investigation of Communist influence in the field of publications (*March of Labor*). July 8, 15, 1954.

Hearings regarding Communism in the District of Columbia (part III). July 14, 15, 1954.

Investigation of Communist activities in the Pacific Northwest area (part I). Oct. 3, 1952; March 16, May 28, June 2, 9, 1954.

Investigation of Communist activities in the Pacific Northwest area (parts II, III) (Seattle-Hartle). June 14, 15, 18, 1954.

Investigation of Communist activities in the Pacific Northwest area (parts IV-VIII) (Seattle). June 14–19, 1954.

Investigation of Communist activities in the Pacific Northwest area (parts IX, X) (Portland). June 18, 19, 1954.

Investigation of Communist activities in the Pacific Northwest area (part XI) (Appendix). June 14–19, 1954.

Investigation of Communist activities in the Philadelphia area (part V). July 30, 1954.

Investigation of Communist activities in the Dayton, Ohio, area (parts I-III). Sept. 13–15, 1954.

Investigation of Communist activities in the state of California (part XI). Sept. 17, 1954.

Investigation of Communist activities in the Dayton, Ohio, area (part IV). Nov. 17–19, 1954.

Investigation of Communist activities in the state of Michigan (parts XI-XII). Nov. 17–19, 1954.

Communist methods of infiltration (entertainment) (part II). Dec. 14, 1954.

Communist methods of infiltration (government-labor) (part IV). Jan. 13, Dec. 15, 1954.

Investigation of Communist activities in the state of Florida (parts I, II). Nov. 29, 30, Dec. 1, 1954.

House Report No. 1694. Organized Communism in the United States. May 28, 1954.

House Report No. 1192. Annual Report for 1953. Feb. 8, 1954.

Colonization of America's Basic Industries by the Communist Party of the U.S.A. Sept. 3, 1954.

Preliminary Report on Neo-Fascist and Hate Groups. Dec. 17, 1954.

The American Negro in the Communist Party. Dec. 22, 1954.

Report on the *March of Labor*. Dec. 22, 1954.

House Report No. 57. Annual Report for 1954. Feb. 16, 1955.

84th Congress

Investigation of Communist activities, New York area (part I) (testimony of Jean Muir). June 15, 1953.

Investigation of Communist activities in the Fort Wayne, Ind. area. Feb. 28, March 1, April 25, 1955.

Investigation of Communist activities, New York area (part II) (youth organizations). March 16, 1955.

Investigation of Communist activities in the Seattle, Wash. area (parts I, II). March 17–19, June 1, 2, 1955.

Investigation of Communist activities in the Milwaukee, Wis. area (parts I, II). March 28–30, May 3, 1955.

Investigation of Communist activities, New York area (parts III, IV). May 3–6, 1955.

Investigation of Communist activities in the Newark, N.J., area parts I, II). May 16–19, July 13, 1955.

Investigation of Communist activities, New York area (part V) (summer camps). July 25, 28, 29, Aug. 1, 1955.

Investigation of Communist activities in the Ohio area (testimony of Keve Bray). July 13, 1955.

Investigation of Communist activities in the Los Angeles, Calif. area (parts I–IV). June 27–30, July 1, 2, 1955.

Investigation of Communist activities in the San Diego, Calif. area. July 5, 6, 1955.

Investigation of Communist activities (The Committee to Secure Justice in the Rosenberg Case and affiliates) (parts I, II). Aug. 2–5, 1955.

Investigation of Communist activities, New York area (parts VI–VIII) (entertainment). Aug. 15–18, Oct. 14, 1955.

Investigation of Communist activities in the Los Angeles, Calif. area (part V). Oct. 13, 1955. (*Note:* Part VI of the Los Angeles hearings, held April 18–21, 25–29, 1955, were executive and have not been released).

Investigation of Communist infiltration of government (parts I, II). Dec. 13–15, 1955.

Investigation of Communist infiltration of government (parts III–V). Feb. 14–16, 21, 23, 24, 28, 29, March 1, 1956.

Investigation of Communist activities in the North Carolina area. March 12–14, 1956.

Investigation of Communist activities in the Los Angeles, Calif. area (part VII). April 16, 1956.

Investigation of Communist activities in the Los Angeles, Calif. area (part VIII) (testimony of Nikolai Khokhlov—thought control in Soviet art and literature; discontent of the Soviet people with Communist leadership). April 17, 1956.

Investigation of Communist activities in the Los Angeles, Calif. area (parts IX, X). April 19–21, 1956.

Investigation of Communist activities in the Rocky Mountain area (parts I, II). May 15–18, 1956.

Investigation of the unauthorized use of U.S. passports (parts I–IV). May 23–25, June 12–14, 21, 1956.

Investigation of Communist propaganda in the United States (part I) (foreign propaganda—entry and dissemination). June 13, 1956.

Investigation of Communist activities in the St. Louis, Mo. area (parts I–IV). June 2, 4–6, 8, 1956.

Investigation of Communist propaganda among prisoners of war in Korea (Save Our Sons Committee). June 18, 19, 1956.

Investigation of Communist infiltration of government (part VI). June 20, 28, 1956.

Investigation of so-called blacklisting in entertainment industry (report of the Fund for the Republic, Inc.) (parts I–III). July 10–13, 17, 18, 1956.

Investigation of Communist propaganda in the United States (part II) (foreign propaganda—entry and dissemination in Philadelphia, Pa., area). July 17, 1956.

Investigation of the award by the Fund for the Republic, Inc. (Plymouth Meeting, Pa.). July 18, 1956.

International Communism (testimony of Ernst Tillich). Sept. 10, 11, 1956.

Investigation of Communist activities in the New Haven, Conn., area (parts I, II). Sept. 24–26, 1956.

Investigation of Communist activities in the Los Angeles, Calif., area (part XI). Dec. 16, 1953; June 6, July 5, 1956.

Hearings on attempts at subversion and espionage by diplomatic personnel. May 10, 11, 1956.

Investigation of Communist activities in the Youngstown and northern Ohio areas. Nov. 26, 27, 1956.

Investigation of Communist propaganda in the United States (part III) (foreign propaganda—entry and dissemination in the San Francisco, Calif., area). Dec. 10, 11, 1956.

Communist political subversion (part I). Nov. 12–14, 28, Dec. 11, 13, 14, 1956.

Communist political subversion (part II) (appendix). Nov. 12–14, 28, Dec. 2–8, 11, 13, 14, 1956.

House Report No. 1648. Annual Report for 1955. Jan. 17, 1956.

House Report No. 2189. The Great Pretense—a symposium on anti-Stalinism and the 20th Congress of the Soviet Communist Party. May 21, 1956.

House Document No. 206. Trial by Treason—The National Committee to Secure Justice for the Rosenbergs and Morton Sobell. July 17, 1957.

House Document No. 226. Guide to Subversive Organizations and Publications (revised). Aug. 5, 1957.

House Report No. 53. Annual Report for 1956. Feb. 11, 1957.

International Communism (part I—revolt in the Satellites) (consultation). Oct. 29, 30, Nov. 1, 17, 20, 1956.

85th Congress

International Communist propaganda activities. Jan. 30, 1957.

International Communism—Red China and the Far East (testimony of Chiu-Yuan Hu). Feb. 1, 1957.

Investigation of Communist propaganda in the United States (part IV) (foreign propaganda—entry and dissemination in the New Orleans, La., area). Feb. 14, 1957.

Investigation of Communist activities in the New Orleans, La., area. Feb. 15, 1957.

Investigation of Communist activities in the New Haven, Conn., area (part III). Feb. 26, 27, 1957.

Investigation of Communist Propaganda in the United States (part V) (New York City area). March 12, 13, 1957.

Investigation of Communist propaganda in the United States (part VI) (New York area). March 14, 15, 1957.

Investigation of Communist propaganda in the United States (part VII) (Chicago, Ill., area). March 26, 27, 1957.

Investigation of Communism in the Metropolitan Music School, Inc., and related fields (part I). April 9, 10, 1957.

Investigation of Communism in the Metropolitan Music School, Inc., and related fields (part II). Feb. 7, 8, April 11, 12, 1957.

Investigation of Communist activities in the Baltimore, Md., area (part I). May 7, 8, 1957.

Investigation of Communist activities in the Baltimore, Md., area (part II). May 9, 1957.

Hearings held in San Francisco, Calif. (part I). June 18, 19, 1957.

Hearings held in San Francisco, Calif. (part II). June 20, 21, 1957.

Investigation of the unauthorized use of U.S. passports (part V). July 26, 1957.

Investigation of Communist activities in the Newark, N.J., area (supplemental). July 24, 1957.

Investigation of Communist penetration of communications facilities (part I). July 17–19, Aug. 2, 9, 1957.

Investigation of Communist propaganda in the United States (part VIII) (Buffalo, N.Y., area). Oct. 1, 1957.

Investigation of Communist activities in the Buffalo, N.Y., area (part I). Oct. 2, 1957.

Investigation of Communist activities in the Buffalo, N.Y., area (part II). Oct. 3, 4, 1957.

Investigation of Communist penetration of communications facilities (part II). Oct. 9, 1957.

Investigation of Soviet espionage. Oct. 7–9, Nov. 20, 1957.

Investigation of Soviet espionage (part II). Feb. 28, 1956; Feb. 25, 1958.

Investigation of Communist infiltration and propaganda activities in basic industry (Gary, Ind., area). Feb. 10, 11, 1958.

Investigation of Communist activities in the New England area part I). March 18, 1958.

Investigation of Communist activities in the New England area (part II). March 19, 1958.

Investigation of Communist activities in the New England area (part III). March 14, 20, 21, 1958.

Investigation of Communist propaganda in the United States (part IX) (student groups, distributors, and propagandists). June 11, 12, 1958.

Communism in the New York area (entertainment). June 18, 19, 1958, May 8, 1958; April 1, 1957.

Communist infiltration and activities in the South. July 29–31, 1958.

Communist infiltration and activities in Newark, N.J. Sept. 3–5, 1958.

International Communism (part II—revolt in the Satellites) (Horvath, Kiss). March 20, 1957.

International Communism (Communist control of Estonia) (August Rei). March 10, 1957.

International Communism (The Communist mind) (Frederick Charles Schwarz). May 29, 1957.

International Communism (Communist penetration of Malaya and Singapore) (Kuo-Shuen Chang). May 29, 1957.

Who Are They? (part I—Khrushchev and Bulganin). July 12, 1957.

Who Are They? (part II—Mao Tse-tung and Chou En-lai). Aug. 23, 1957.

Who Are They? (part III—Zhukov and Konev). Aug. 30, 1957.

Who Are They? (part IV—Ulbricht and Kadar). Sept., 1957.

Who Are They? (part V—Tito and Gomulka). Oct. 11, 1957.

Who Are They? (part VI—Kim Il Sung and Ho Chi Minh). Oct. 25, 1957.

Who Are They? (part VII—Thorez and Togliatti). Nov. 22, 1957.

Who Are They? (part VIII—Lombardo Toledano and Prestes). Feb. 21, 1958.

Who Are They? (part IX—Hoxha and Gheorghiu-Dej). Aug. 5, 1958.

House Report No. 1182. Communist Political Subversion (the campaign to destroy the security programs of the U.S. Government). Aug. 16, 1957.

International Communism (the Communist trade offensive) (Marcus, Emmet, De Rochefort). June 26, 1957.

The Ideological Fallacies of Communism (Fineberg, Sheen, Polling). Sept. 4, 25, Oct. 18, 1957.

Operation Abolition. Nov. 8, 1957.

International Communism (the present posture of the free world) (Constantine Brown). Oct. 21, 1957.

International Communism (espionage) (excerpts of consultation with counterspy Boris Morros). Aug. 16, 1957.

International Communism (Communist designs on Indonesia and the Pacific frontier) (Gen. Charles A. Willoughby). Dec. 16, 1957.

House Report No. 1360. Annual Report for 1957. Feb. 19, 1958.

The Erica Wallach Story. March 21, 1958.

The Communist Program for World Conquest (Gen. Albert C. Wedemeyer). Jan. 21, 1958.

Communist Psychological Warfare (brainwashing) (Edward Hunter). March 13, 1958.

Chronicle of Treason (reprint of series of articles by Rep. Francis E. Walter, appearing in the *Philadelphia Inquirer,* Sept. 29–Oct. 3, 1957). March 3–9, 1958.

House Report No. 1724. Organized Communism in the United States (revised). May 14, 1958.

International Communism (Communist propaganda activities in Canada) (Milan Jakubec). April 3, 1958.

Communist Psychological Warfare (thought control) (Constantin W. Boldyreff). April 7, 1958.

International Communism (Communist encroachment in the Far East) (Maj. Gen. Claire Lee Chennault). April 23, 1958.

What Is Behind the Soviet Proposal for a Summit Conference? (Dallin, Bouscaren, Atkinson, McNamara). April 30, 1958.

The Ideology of Freedom Versus the Ideology of Communism (Dr. Charles W. Lowry). June 5, 1958.

Communist Strategy of Protracted Conflict. (Strausz-Hupé, Cottrell, Dougherty). May 20, 1958.

The Irrationality of Communism (Dr. Gerhart Niemeyer). Aug. 8, 1958.

International Communism in Yugoslavia (the myth of "Titoism") (Dr. Alex N. Dragnich). Sept. 15, 1958.

House Document No. 119. Patterns of Communist Espionage. April 20, 1959.

House Document No. 187. Annual Report for 1958. March 9, 1959.

86th Congress

The Kremlin's espionage and terror organizations (testimony of Petr S. Deriabin). Released, March 17, 1959.

Southern California district of the Communist Party—structure, objectives, leadership (part I). Sept. 2, 3, 1958.

Southern California district of the Communist Party—structure, objectives, leadership (part II). Sept. 4, 5, 1958.

Southern California district of the Communist Party—structure, objectives, leadership (part III). Feb. 24, 25, 1959.

Current strategy and tactics of Communists in the United States (greater Pittsburgh area) (part I). March 10, 1959.

Problems of Security in industrial establishments holding defense contracts (greater Pittsburgh area) (part II). March 11, 1959.

Problems arising in cases of denaturalization and deportation of Communists (greater Pittsburgh area) (part III). March 12, 1959.

Communist infiltration of vital industries and current Communist techniques in the Chicago, Ill., area. May 5–7, 1959.

Passport security (part I) (testimony of Harry R. Bridges). April 21, 1959.

Passport security (part II). April 22–24, June 5, 1959.

The American National Exhibition, Moscow, July 1959. July 1, 1959.

Communist training operations (part I). July 21–22, 1959.

Testimony of Clinton Edward Jencks. July 22, 1959.

Testimony of Arnold Johnson, Legislative Director of the Communist Party, U.S.A. Sept. 22, 1959.

Western section of the southern California district of the Communist Party (part I). Oct. 20, 1959.

Western section of the southern California district of the Communist Party (part II). Oct. 21, 1959.

Western section of the southern California district of the Communist Party (part III). Oct. 22, 1959.

Issues presented by Air Reserve Center Training Manual. Feb. 25, 1960.

Communist training operations (Communist activities and propaganda among youth groups) (part II). Feb. 2, 3, 1960.

Communist training operations (Communist activities and propaganda among youth groups) (part III). Feb. 4, 5, March 2, 1960.

Communist activities among Puerto Ricans in New York City and Puerto Rico (New York City) (part I). Nov. 16, 17, 1959.

Communist activities among Puerto Ricans in New York City and Puerto Rico (San Juan) (part II). Nov. 18–20, 1959.

Communist espionage in the United States (testimony of Frantisek Tisler). Released, May 10, 1960.

Testimony of Anthony Krchmarek and Charles Musil. May 26, 1960.

Communist activities among seamen and on waterfront facilities (part I). June 6–8, 23, 1960.

Communist penetration of radio facilities (CONELRAD–Communications) (part I). Aug. 23, 24, 1960.

Testimony of Capt. Nikolai Fedorovich Artamonov (former Soviet naval officer). Sept. 14, 1960.

Northern California district of the Communist Party—structure, objectives, leadership (part I). May 12, 1960.

Northern California district of the Communist Party—structure, objectives, leadership (part II). May 13, 1960.

Northern California district of the Communist Party—structure, objectives, leadership (part III). May 14, June 10, 1960.

Northern California district of the Communist Party—structure, objectives, leadership (part IV) (appendix). May 12–14, June 10, 1960.

House Report No. 41. Communist Legal Subversion (the role of the Communist lawyer). Feb. 23, 1959.

House Report No. 259. Report on the southern California district of the Communist Party—Structure, Objectives, Leadership, April 3, 1959.

Language as a Communist Weapon (Dr. Stefan T. Possony). March 2, 1959.

Communist Persecution of Churches in Red China and Northern Korea. March 26, 1959.

Control of the Arts in the Communist Empire (Ivan P. Bahriany). June 3, 1959.

Who Are They? (part X—Karl Marx). Aug. 28, 1959.

Communist Lobbying Activities in the Nation's Capital. Sept. 3, 1959.

The Communist Parcel Operation. Sept. 3, 1959.

Crimes of Khrushchev (part I). Sept. 4, 1959.

Crimes of Khrushchev (part II). Sept. 9–11, 1959.

Crimes of Khrushchev (part III). Sept. 10, 1959.

Crimes of Khrushchev (part IV). Sept. 21, 1959.

Crimes of Khrushchev (part V). Dec. 17, 1959.

Crimes of Khrushchev (part VI). Dec. 17, 1959.

Crimes of Khrushchev (part VII). Jan. 8, 1960.

House Document No. 336. Facts on Communism, Vol. I (The Communist Ideology). Feb. 9, 1960.

House Report No. 1251. Annual Report for 1959. Feb. 8, 1960.

Lest We Forget! A pictorial summary of Communism in action (Dr. Klaus Samuli Gunnar Romppanen). Jan. 13, 1960.

Communist Economic Warfare (Dr. Robert Loring Allen). April 6, 1960.

Communist Target—Youth: Communist infiltration and agitation tactics (J. Edgar Hoover). July, 1960.

Soviet "Justice": "showplace" prisoners versus real slave labor camps (Adam Joseph Galinski). April 4, 1960.

How the Chinese Reds Hoodwink Visiting Foreigners (Robert Loh). April 21, 1960.

House Report No. 2228. The Communist-Led Riots Against the House Committee on Un-American Activities in San Francisco, Calif., May 12–14, 1980. Oct. 7, 1960.

House Document No. 139. Facts on Communism, Vol. II (The Soviet Union, from Lenin to Khrushchev). April 13, 1961.

House Report No. 2237. Annual Report for 1960. Jan. 2, 1961.

87th Congress

Hearings related to H.R. 4700, to amend Section 11 of the Subversive Activities Control Act of 1950, as amended (The Fund for Social Analysis). May 31, June 7, Aug. 16, 1961.

Hearings relating to revision of H.R. 9120 and H.R. 5751, to amend the Subversive Activities Control Act of 1950. Sept. 13, 1961.

Manipulation of public opinion by organizations under concealed control of the Communist Party. (National Assembly for Democratic Rights and Citizens Committee for Constitutional Liberties) (parts I, II). Oct. 2, 3, 1961.

Communist penetration of radio facilities (CONELRAD—communications) (part II). Oct. 26, 27, Nov. 29, 1961.

Hearings on structure and organization of the Communist Party of the United States. Nov. 20–22, 1961.

Hearings relating to H.R. 9753, to amend section 3(7) and 5 (b) of the Internal Security Act of 1950, as amended, relating to employment of members of Communist organizations in certain defense facilities. Feb. 7, 1962.

Hearings relating to H.R. 10175, to accompany H.R. 11363, amending the Internal Security Act of 1950. March 15, 1962.

Testimony by and concerning Paul Corbin. Sept. 6, 13, Nov. 13, 27, 28, 1961; March 15, July 2, 1962.

Communist propaganda—and the truth about conditions in Soviet Russia (testimony of David P. Johnson). May 22, 1962.

"Intellectual freedom"—Red China style (testimony of Chi-chou Huang). May 24, 25, 1962.

Communist activities in the Cleveland, Ohio, area (parts I, II). June 4–7, 1962.

Communist outlets for the distribution of Soviet propaganda in the United States (parts I, II). May 9, 10, 17, July 11, 12, 1962.

Communist youth activities (Eighth World Youth Festival, Helsinki, Finland, 1962). April 25, 27, Oct. 4, 1962.

U.S. Communist Party assistance to foreign Communist governments (Medical Aid to Cuba Committee and Friends of British Guiana). Nov. 14, 15, 1961.

Communist activities in the peace movement (Women Strike for Peace and certain other groups). Dec. 11–13, 1962.

Rules of Procedure, Committee on Un-American Activities. Revised 1961.

House Report No. 25. U.S. Merchant Vessel and Waterfront Security Act of 1960. Feb. 23, 1961.

House Report No. 309. Amending the Subversive Activities Control Act of 1950 (parts I, II) (to accompany House Report No. 5751). April 26, Sept. 14, 1961.

House Report No. 309. Dissemination of Communist Propaganda in the United States (part II) (to accompany House Report No. 5751). Sept. 14, 1961.

Supplement to Cumulative Index to Publications of the Committee on Un-American Activities, 1950 through 1960. June, 1961.

House Report No. 1278. The Truth about the Film *Operation Abolition* (part I). Oct. 5, 1961.

House Report No. 1282. Manipulation of Public Opinion by Organizations Under Concealed Control of the Communist Party (National Assembly for Democratic Rights and Citizens Committee for Constitutional Liberties) (parts I, II). Nov. 30, 1961.

Guide to Subversive Organizations and Publications (and appendixes). Dec. 1, 1961.

House Report No. 1283. Communist Penetration of Radio Facilities (CONELRAD—communications). Dec. 5, 1961.

House Report No. 1278. The Truth about the Film *Operation Abolition* (part II). Dec. 27, 1961.

The New Role of National Legislative Bodies in the Communist Conspiracy. Dec. 30, 1961.

House Report No. 2559. Annual Report for 1961. Nov. 5, 1962.

House Report No. 1362. Publication in Federal Register of Lists of Defense Facilities. Feb. 19, 1962.

House Report No. 1665. Protection of Classified Information Released to U.S. Industry and Defense Contractors. June 28, 1962.

House Report No. 2120. Amending the Internal Security Act of 1950 to Provide for Maximum Personnel Security in the National Security Agency. Aug. 2, 1962.

Security Practices in the National Security Agency (defection of Bernon F. Mitchell and William H. Martin). Aug. 13, 1962.

The Communist Party's Cold War Against Congressional Investigation of Subversion. Oct. 10, 1962.

Communist and Trotskyist Activity Within the Greater Los Angeles Chapter of the Fair Play for Cuba Committee. Nov. 2, 1962.

House Report No. 176. Annual Report for 1962. Jan. 2, 1963.

88th Congress

U.S. Communist Party assistance to foreign Communist governments (testimony of Maud Russell). March 6, 1963.

"United front" technique of the southern California district of the Communist Party. April 24–27, 1962.

Violations of State Department travel regulations and pro-Castro propaganda activities in the United States (part I). May 6, 7, 23, 1963.

Violations of State Department travel regulations and pro-Castro propaganda activities in the United States (part II). July 1, 2, Aug. 5, 1963.

U.S. Communist Party assistance to foreign Communist parties (Veterans of the Abraham Lincoln Brigade). July 29, 1963.

Violations of State Department travel regulations and pro-Castro propaganda activities in the United States (part III). Sept. 12, 13, 1963.

Defection of a Russian seaman (testimony of Vladislaw Stepanovich Tarasov). Sept. 19, 1963.

Violations of State Department travel regulations and pro-Castro propaganda activities in the United States (part IV). Oct. 16, Nov. 18, 1963.

Hearings on bills providing for creation of a Freedom Commission and Freedom Academy (part I). Feb. 18, 19, 1964.

Hearings on bills providing for creation of a Freedom Commission and Freedom Academy (part II). Feb. 20, April 7, 8, May 19, 20, 1964.

Communist activities in the Buffalo, N.Y., area. April 29, 30, 1964.

Communist activities in the Minneapolis, Minn., area. June 24–26, 1964.

Testimony of the Rev. James H. Robinson. May 5, 1964.

Violations of State Department travel regulations and pro-Castro propaganda activities in the United States (part V). Sept. 3, 4, 28, 1964.

House Report No. 631. "United Front" Technique of the southern California district of the Communist Party. July 31, 1963.

House Report No. 108. Amending the Internal Security Act of 1950 to Provide for Maximum Personnel Security in the National Security Agency. March 13, 1963.

World Communist Movement: Selective Chronology, 1818–1957; Vol. II, 1946–1950.

House Report No. 1739. Annual Report for 1963. Aug. 10, 1964.

A Communist in a "Workers' Paradise" (John Santo's own story). March 1, 4, 5, 1963.

World Communist Movement: Selective Chronology, 1818–1957; Vol. III, 1951–1953.

House Report No. 971. Annual Report for 1964. Sept. 9, 1965.

89th Congress

Hearings on bills providing for creation of a Freedom Commission and Freedom Academy. March 31, April 1, 28, May 7, 14, 1965.

Communist activities in the Chicago, Illinois, area (parts I, II). May 25–27, June 22, 1965.

Testimony of Juanita Castro Ruz. June 11, 1965.

Testimony of Wladyslaw Tykocinski. April 6, 1966.

Hearings on bills to make punishable assistance to enemies of the U.S. in time of undeclared war (part I). Aug. 16–19, 1966.

Hearings on bills to make punishable assistance to enemies of the

U.S. in time of undeclared war (part II). Aug. 19, 22, 23, 1966.
Hearings on bills to curb terrorist organizations. July 20–22, 1966.
Activities of Ku Klux Klan organizations in the United States (part I). Oct. 19–22, 25, 1965.
Activities of Ku Klux Klan organizations in the United States (part II). Oct. 26–28, Nov. 1–4, 9, 1965.
Hearings regarding bills to curb terrorist organizations, July 20–22, 1966.

World Communist Movement: Selective Chronology, 1818–1957; Vol. IV, 1954–1955.
House Report No. 629. Freedom Commission and Freedom Academy. July 20, 1965.
Rules of Procedure, Revised. Sept. 14, 1965.
House Report No. 1928. Annual Report for 1965. Aug. 31, 1966.
House Report No. 1908. Obstruction of the Armed Forces. Aug. 29, 1966.
House Report No. 2335. Organizational Conspiracies Act of 1966. Oct. 21, 1966.
House Report No. 460. Annual Report for 1966. June 28, 1967.

90th Congress

Communist Origin and Manipulation of Vietnam Week (April 8–15, 1967). March 31, 1967.
House Report No. 326. Obstruction of the Armed Forces. May 31, 1967.
House Report No. 648. Organizational Conspiracies Act of 1967. Sept. 19, 1967.
House Report No. 733. Internal Security Act of 1950—Amendments. Oct. 4, 1967.

Notes

H refers to hearings before the Committee on Un-American Activities
R refers to reports of the Committee
C.R. refers to the Congressional Record

CHAPTER ONE

PAGE

4 ff. See Telford Taylor's *Grand Inquest* (New York, 1955) for a critical history of Congressional investigations, with particular reference to the Committee on Un-American Activities.

5　Frankfurter on investigations: *New Republic*, May 21, 1924, p. 329.

5　1919 investigation: U. S. Sen., 65th Cong., 3d sess. *Bolshevik Propaganda*—Hearings before a Subcommittee of the Judiciary. U. S. Sen., 66th Cong., 1st sess. *Brewing and Liquor Interests and German and Bolshevik Propaganda*—Report of the Subcommittee of the Judiciary.

6 ff. 1930 investigation: Debate—*C.R.*, May 22, 1930, pp. 9390 ff. Hearings—U. S. Cong., House, 71st Cong., 2d sess. Special Committee to Investigate Communism in the United States. Report—U. S. Cong., House, 71st Cong., 3d sess. Special Committee on Communist Activities in the United States—*Investigation of Communist Propaganda.*

7　(fn) Wilson on depression: *New Republic*, Jan. 14, 1931, p. 234.

7　Wilson on Fish: *New Republic*, Dec. 24, 1930, p. 58.

8　(fn) Foster on Comintern: Quoted in Howe and Coser: *The American Communist Party* (New York, 1962), p. 154.

10 ff. 1934 investigation: Debate—*C.R.*, March 20, 1934, pp. 4938 ff. Hearings—U. S. Cong., House, 73d Cong., 2d sess. Special Committee on Un-American Activities—*Investigation of Nazi Propaganda.* Report—U. S. Cong., House, 74th Cong., 1st sess. Special Committee on Un-American Activities—*Investigation of Nazi and Other Propaganda.* See also Howard M. Kline: *Some Practices of Congressional Investigating Committees,* p. 340 (Unpublished doctoral thesis, School of Citizenship and Public Affairs, Syracuse University, 1937).

11　Dickstein on camp: *N. Y. Times*, Aug. 24, 1934, p. 6.

12　Schlesinger on 1935: *The Politics of Upheaval* (Boston, 1939), p. 69.

12　Wilson on "informing function": *Congressional Government* (New York, 1900), p. 203.

13　Lippmann on "good precedents": *Forum*, Sept. 1930, p. 129.

13　Frankfurter on safeguards: *New Republic*, May 21, 1924, p. 329.

13 ff. Dickstein on Committee: *C.R.*, Jan. 21, 1937, p. 6106.

14 ff. Dickstein on Bundists: *C.R.*, April 27, 1938, p. 5881; *N. Y. Times*, May 23, 1938, p. 5.

18 ff. Dickstein–Cochran–Maverick debate: *C.R.*, Dec. 21, 1937, pp. 2031 ff.

20　Shannon on "foreign-born citizen": *Congressional Digest*, Nov. 1939, p. 282.

21 ff. Dies resolution debate: *C.R.*, May 26, 1938, pp. 7568 ff.

CHAPTER TWO

24 ff. See August Raymond Ogden's *The Dies Committee* (Washington, D. C., 1945) for a dispassionate survey of the Committee's activities from 1938 to 1944.

25 La Follette on Communists: *Collier's*, Feb. 8, 1947, p. 22.

25 ff. Thomas on Federal Theatre: *N. Y. Times*, July 27, 1938, p. 19.

26 Viereck subpoena: *N. Y. Times*, Aug. 4, 1938, p. 1.

26 Dies on radio: *N. Y. Times*, Aug. 10, 1938, p. 6.

26 ff. Dies before hearing: *H.*, Aug. 12, 1938, p. 2.

28 Metcalf hearing: *H.*, Aug. 12, 1938, pp. 3 ff.

28 Frey headlines: *N. Y. Times*, Aug. 14, 1938, p. 1.

28 ff. Historian on Frey hearings (Jerold S. Auerbach): *Journal of American History*, Dec. 1964, p. 435.

29 (fn) *New Republic* editorial: Nov. 13, 1939, p. 301.

29 Frey hearings: *H.*, Aug. 13, 15, 16, 1938, pp. 91 ff.

29 Sullivan report: *N. Y. Times*, Aug. 15, 1938, p. 1.

29 ff. Steele hearings: *H.*, Aug. 6, 17, 1938, pp. 277 ff.

30 ff. Poll: *N. Y. Daily News*, Oct. 31, 1938, p. 4.

31 Dobrzynski hearing: *H.*, Nov. 15, 1938, pp. 2207 ff.

32 Frey on industrial workers: Quoted in Howe and Coser: *American Communist Party*, p. 239.

32 T.W.U. witness: *H.*, Sept. 16, 1938, p. 1039.

32 *P. O. Quarterly*: April 1939, p. 235.

32 Thomas question: *P. O. Quarterly*, April 1939, p. 237.

33 Dies on Sullivan report: Ogden: *Dies Committee*, p. 58.

33 Frey on Brophy: *H.*, Aug. 16, 1938, p. 268.

34 Woll on Dewey: *H.*, Nov. 22, 1938, p. 2437.

34 J. Roosevelt church contributions: *H.*, Dec. 6, 1938, p. 2836.

35 Jemison hearing: *H.*, Nov. 22, 1938, p. 2435.

35 Ickes on Jemison: *The Secret Diary of Harold Ickes* (New York, 1954), Vol. 2, p. 506.

35 Dies on smears: *N. Y. Times*, Feb. 12, 1939, IV, p. 12.

35 ff. Dies autobiography: *Martin Dies Story* (New York, 1963), p. 67.

36 Howlers: See *N. Y. Times*, Nov. 6, 1938, IV, p. 10.

36 Starnes on Marlowe: *H.*, Dec. 6, 1938, p. 2857.

36 ff. For Matthews's apologia, see *Odyssey of a Fellow Traveller* (New York, 1938), published by John Cecil Rovere, head of the National Immigration Board, whose mission it was to keep refugees from Nazism out of this country because they were all Reds.

38 (fn) Madison Square Garden meeting: See Howe and Coser: *American Communist Party*, pp. 299 ff.

38 Matthews on big business: See J. B. Matthews and R. E. Shallcross: *Partners in Plunder* (New York, 1935).

40 Shirley Temple: *H.*, Aug. 22, 1938, p. 918.

40 (fn) Ickes and Perkins: *N. Y. Times*, Aug. 31, 1938, p. 1.

40 Kempton on fronts: *Part of Our Time* (New York, 1955), p. 154.

41 Consumers Research quotes: *Consumers Digest*, Feb. 1938. Quoted in George Seldes: *Witch Hunt* (New York, 1940), p. 136.

42 Matthews quotes: *Odyssey*, pp. 183, 267, 34.; *N. Y. Times*, Aug. 22, 1938, p. 2.; Kempton: *Part of Our Time*, p. 175.

43 Thomas on Federal Theatre: *N. Y. Times*, Aug. 10, 1938, p. 6.

43 (fn) Workers Alliance: *H.*, Sept. 15, 1938, p. 1007.

44 Federal Theatre hearings: *H.*, Aug. 19, 20, 22, 1938, pp. 775 ff.

44 Woodward–Flanagan hearings: *H.*, Dec. 5, 6, 1938, pp. 2729 ff. For Mrs. Flanagan's story of Federal Theatre, see *Arena* (New York, 1940).

PAGE

44   (fn) Woodward on "capitalistic press": *H.*, Dec. 5, 1938, p. 2807.
45   Rovere on Communist culture: Quoted in Kempton: *Part of Our Time,* p. 197.
45   Critic on Federal Theatre: *Commonweal,* July 14, 1939, p. 300.
45   (fn) Dirksen on Federal Theatre: *C.R.,* June 16, 1939, p. 7373.
46   Lavery on Federal Theatre: *Commonweal,* Aug. 4, 1939, p. 351.
47   Strecker case: 307 U.S. 22 (1940).
48   Bridges case: 326 U.S. 135 (1945).
48   Knowles hearings: *H.,* Oct. 24–26, 1938, pp. 1717 ff.
49   Minnesota hearings: *H.,* Oct. 17, 18, 1938, pp. 1359 ff.
49   Dies on "expedience": *N. Y. Times,* Oct. 18, 1939, p. 11.
49   Gadola–Barringer hearings: *H.,* Oct 21, 22, 1938, pp. 1674 ff.
50   Murphy defense: *N. Y. Times,* Oct 22, 1938, p. 1.
50   Dies on Murphy: *Martin Dies Story,* p. 124.
50 ff. F.D.R. on Murphy: *N. Y. Times,* Oct. 26, 1938, p. 1.
51   Dies pledge: *N. Y. Times,* p. 13.
52   Krock on election: *N. Y. Times,* Nov. 10, 1938, p. 15.
52   Dies on F.D.R.: *Martin Dies Story,* p. 138.
52   Ickes on Dies: *Secret Diary,* Vol. 2, p. 570.
52 ff. "Supreme Shouter": *N. Y. Times,* June 27, 1937, p. 20.
53   *Collier's:* Jan. 14, 1939, p. 50.
54   Ickes v. Dies: *Secret Diary,* Vol. 2, p. 504. *N. Y. Times,* Nov. 14, 1938, p. 12; Nov. 21, 1938, p. 1.
54   (fn) Ickes: *Autobiography of a Curmudgeon,* (New York, 1943), p. 298.
54   "Loaded Dies": *Secret Diary,* Vol. 2, p. 546; *N. Y. Times,* Jan. 17, 1939, p. 1.
55   First report: *R.,* Jan. 3, 1939.
55   Thomas on Perkins: *C.R.,* Jan. 24, 1939, pp. 702 ff.
55   Dies allocation: *C.R.,* Feb 3, 1939, p. 1128.
55   Ickes on Democrats: *Autobiography,* p. 573.
55   Rayburn on Dies: Quoted in *American,* May 1940, p. 22.
56 ff. *New Republic:* June 15, 1938, p. 144; Aug. 2, 1938, p. 50.
57   *Nation:* Aug. 27, 1938, p. 198.
57   Lawyers petition: *The Dies Committee—A Review of Its Proceedings.* Memo and Petition by Members of the American Bar to the Members of the House of Representatives, 1939.
57   Hook–Kirchwey: *Nation,* May 27, 1939, p. 603.
58   *New Republic:* June 15, 1938, p. 144.

CHAPTER THREE

59   Dies on fascists: N.B.C., Aug. 8, 1938; printed in *Vital Speeches,* Sept. 15, 1938, p. 731.
59 ff. Moseley case: *N. Y. Times,* May 19, 1939, p. 1.
60   For a round-up of the headlines, see *Nation,* June 3, 1939, p. 61.
61 ff. Moseley hearings: *H.,* May 22–24, 31, June 1, 1939, pp. 3285 ff.
61   Moseley call: *N. Y. Times,* May 21, 1939, p. 28.
62   Moseley speech: *H.,* May 31, 1939, p. 28.
63 ff. First Kuhn hearing: *H.,* Aug. 16, 1939, pp. 3705 ff.
64   Bundist testimony: *H.,* Aug. 18, 1939, pp. 3891 ff.
64   Second Kuhn hearing: *H.,* Oct. 19, 1939, pp. 6043 ff.
64   Ogden on pact: *Dies Committee,* p. 129.
64 ff. Browder on Nazi–Soviet agreement: Earl Browder: *Fighting for Peace* (New York, 1939); quoted in Howe and Coser: *Am. Communist Party,* p. 387.

65 ff. Browder hearing: *H.*, Sept. 5, 1939, pp. 4275 ff.
66   Hardman on C.P.: *New Republic*, Sept 17, 1930, pp. 122 ff.
67   Kazin on pact: *Starting Out in the Thirties* (Boston, 1965), p. 141.
67   Gitlow hearing: *H.*, Sept. 7–9, 1939, pp. 4529 ff.; Oct. 17, 1939, pp. 5981 ff.
67 ff. Krivitsky hearing: *H.*, Oct. 11, 1939, pp. 5719 ff.
68   Foster hearing: *H.*, Sept. 29, 1939, pp. 5323 ff.
69   Hicks resignation: *New Republic*, Oct. 4, 1939, p. 244.
69   Cameron on pact: *The Listener*, Oct. 21, 1965, p. 213.
70 ff. Ward hearing: *H.*, Oct 23, 1939, pp. 6213 ff.
70   Coffee on Ward: *C.R.*, Oct. 25, 1939, p. 879.
71   A.L.P.D. list: *N. Y. Times*, Oct 26, 1939, p. 1.
72   A.L.P.D. statement: *N. Y. Times*, Oct. 29, 1939, p. 27.
72   (fn) *Daily Worker*, Nov. 5, 1956; cited in Howe and Coser: *Am. Communist Party*, p. 496.
72   Baldwin on Communists: *New Republic*, March 18, 1940, p. 372.
72   (fn) A.L.P.D. Christmas card: *N. Y. Times*, Dec. 10, 1939, p. 1. For the debate in Congress on release of the A.L.P.D. list, see *C.R.*, Oct. 25, 1939, p. 485.
73   *Nation* on A.L.P.D.: Nov. 4, 1939, p. 485.
74   A.L.P.D. statement: *N. Y. Times*, Oct. 26, 1939, p. 14.
74   *New Republic* on Communists: Aug. 31, 1938, p. 90.
75   Dies v. Administration: "sordid procedure"—*N. Y. Times*, Oct. 28, 1939, p. 1; "grieved and pained"—*N. Y. Times*, Oct. 29, 1939, p. 22; 2,850 "known Communists"—*N. Y. Times*, Sept. 27, 1939, p. 1; F.D.R. on Dies —*N. Y. Times*, Sept. 30, 1939, p. 8; Thomas on Murphy—*N. Y. Times*, Oct. 23, 1939, p. 1; "most inappropriate"—*N. Y. Times*, Oct. 24, 1939, p. 12; Ickes on Murphy—*Secret Diary*, Vol. 3, p. 54.
76 ff. Curran hearings: *H.*, Oct. 28, 30, Nov. 2, 3, 1939, pp. 6457 ff.
77   Kempton on Curran: *Part of Our Time*, p. 86.
77 ff. Youth hearings: *H.*, Nov. 27, 29, 30, Dec. 1, 2, 1939, pp. 6829 ff.
78   Howe and Coser on A.Y.C.: *Am. Communist Party*, p. 359. A more favorable, more ingenuous picture of the A.Y.C. may be found in *American Youth Today* by Leslie A. Gould (New York, 1940), to which Mrs. Roosevelt contributed a strained foreword.
79   Mrs. Roosevelt on youths: *N. Y. Times*, Dec. 5, 1939, p. 8.
80 ff. Lash hearing, 1939: *H.*, Dec. 1, 1939, pp. 7062 ff.
80   *My Day* on Lash hearing: Quoted in *N. Y. Times*, Dec. 3, 1939, p. 34.
81 ff. A.S.U. meeting: *N. Y. Times*, Dec. 31, 1939, p. 11.
82   Lash hearing, 1942: *H.*, Jan. 21, 1942, pp. 2787 ff.
82   Dies and Lash on army: *N. Y. Times*, Jan. 24, 1942, p. 19.
82 ff. Dies on Lash: *U. S. News*, August 20, 1954, p. 56; Aug. 27, 1954, p. 95.
83   Dies on Trotsky and Rivera: *N. Y. Times*, Dec. 7, 1939, p. 22. On deportations: *N. Y. Times*, Dec. 25, 1939, p. 10.
83   Lovestone hearing: *H.*, Dec. 2, 1939, pp. 7096 ff.
84   Matthews on C.U.: *N. Y. Herald Tribune*, Dec. 11, 1939, p. 1.
84   Voorhis on Matthews: *N. Y. Times*, Dec. 12, 1939, p. 1.
85   *Business Week* on consumer movement: Dec. 10, 1939, p. 17.
85   For background on the C.U. report, see *C.R.*, Jan. 23, 1940, p. 601, and *N. Y. Times*, Dec. 12, 1939, p. 22.
85   (fn) Matthews on *Good Housekeeping: Partners in Plunder*, p. 50.
85 ff. Annual report, background: *Nation*, Jan. 13, 1940, pp. 36 ff.
86   Annual report: *R.*, Jan. 3, 1940.
86   (fn) Carey on U.E.: *C.R.*, Jan. 23, 1940, p. 583.
86   *N. Y. Times* editorial: Jan. 5, 1940, p. 18.
87 ff. House debate: *C.R.*, Jan. 23, 1940, pp. 572 ff.

PAGE

87 Gallup poll: *N. Y. Times,* Dec. 15, 1939, p. 21.
87 Dies speech: *N. Y. Times,* Jan. 7, 1940, p. 13.
88 Appropriation: *C.R.,* Jan. 25, 1940, p. 688.

CHAPTER FOUR

89 *Nation* on Christian Fronters: Jan. 27, 1940, pp. 89 ff.
89 ff. Pegler on Coughlin: *N. Y. World Telegram,* Jan. 23, 1940, p. 17.
90 Dies at rally: *Vital Speeches,* Dec. 15, 1939, pp. 152 ff. Delivered at "Mass Meeting for America" in Madison Square Garden, Nov. 29, 1939.
90 ff. Rules Committee: *N. Y. Times,* Jan. 23, 1940, p. 1.
91 *Nation* exposé: Jan. 27, 1940, p. 1.
91 Pelley booklet: *The Suppressed Speech of Maj. Gen. Moseley,* North Carolina, 1939.
92 Harold Weisberg: He has lately reappeared as the author of several books attacking the credibility of the Warren Report. See *Whitewash* (New York, 1965).
92 Pelley on "sucker": *N. Y. Sun,* Feb. 3, 1940, p. 17.
92 Stripling on forgery: *The Red Plot Against America* (Drexel Hill, Pa., 1949), p. 33.
92 ff. Hook on forgery: *N. Y. Times,* Feb. 1, 1940, p. 10; Feb. 4, 1940, p. 15; Feb. 7, 1940, p. 1. *C.R.,* Feb. 13, 1941, p. A637.
93 *Nation* on scoop: Feb. 10, 1940, p. 147; Feb. 17, 1940, p. 240.
93 (fn) Dies on conspiracy: *Martin Dies Story,* p. 115.
94 Stripling on Pelley: *Red Plot,* p. 34.
94 Pelley hearing: *H.,* Feb. 7, 1940, pp. 7201 ff.
94 Pelley on Dies: *N. Y. Sun,* Feb. 6, 1940, p. 3.
95 Dies on Communists: *N. Y. Times,* March 27, 1940, p. 13.
95 ff. Dies on C.P. raid: *U. S. News,* Aug. 20, 1954, p. 67.
96 C.P. raid decision: 33 F. Supp. 619.
96 Dies on decision: *N. Y. Times,* May 4, 1940, p. 6; April 6, 1940, p. 4.
96 ff. C.P. officials hearings: *H.,* March 25, 28, 29, April 3, 4, 1940, pp. 7335 ff.
97 Contempt cases: For a review of the Committee's contempt cases from these early ones up to the mid-1950's, see Carl Beck's *Contempt of Congress* (New Orleans, 1957).
98 Ogden on publicity: *Dies Committee,* p. 201.
98 ff. Celler on "dose of salts": *C.R.,* June 22, 1940, p. 9036.
99 (fn) Marcantonio on Smith Act: *C.R.,* June 22, 1940, p. 9034. See also Howe and Coser: *Am. Communist Party,* p. 418.
99 Abraham Lincoln Brigade hearings: *H.,* April 23, 24, May 8, 1940, pp. 7727 ff.
99 ff. Union hearings: *H.,* April 23, 24, May 8, 1940, pp. 7892 ff. Quill quotes —pp. 8093, 8106, 8111.
101 Leech hearing: *H.:.* July 16, 1940, pp. 927 ff.
102 Actors' testimony: See *Executive Hearings,* Aug. 16, 17, 20, 26, 27, 1940.
102 Rankin on actors: *C.R.,* March 6, 1946, p. A1150.
102 (fn) Havenner case: San Francisco *Chronicle,* Oct. 30, 1944, p. 7. For Havenner's recital of the facts, see *C.R.,* Jan. 11, 1945, p. 206.
102 ff. Dorothy Parker speech: *Directions,* April 1940, p. 4.
103 ff. Patman—Byoir hearings: *H.,* Aug. 29, 1940, pp. 8164 ff.; Aug. 11, 1941, pp. 8829 ff.
104 ff. Dies speech: *C.R.,* May 17, 1940, p. 6295.

105 ff. Quotes on saboteurs: Dies—*N. Y. Times*, Oct. 19, 1940, p. 4; chemist—*H.*, Oct. 1, 1940, pp. 8232 ff.; Starnes: *N. Y. Times*, Oct. 3, 1940, p. 1; Dies on lists—*N. Y. Times*, Oct. 22, 1940, p. 13; Hercules plant—*N. Y. Times*, Sept. 18, 1940, p. 25.

105 Willkie on Committee: *New Republic*, March 18, 1940, pp. 370 ff.

105 ff. Dies on Willkie and F.D.R.: *N. Y. Times*, Aug. 28, 1940, p. 21; on sabotage—*N. Y. Times*, Nov. 13, 1940, pp. 1, 4.

107 ff. Sumners on foreigners: *C.R.*, Nov. 25, 1940, p. 13738.

108 Voorhis on "totalitarian state of mind": *C.R.*, Nov. 25, 1940, p. 13736.

109 ff. White Book—including Zapp quotes: *Appendix II*, 1940.

109 *N. Y. Times* editorial: Nov. 23, 1940, p. 8.

110 Jackson charge: *N. Y. Times*, Nov. 24, 1940, p. 1.

110 Dickstein on Fassbender: *C.R.*, Jan. 21, 1941, p. 214.

110 ff. Dies on Jackson: *N. Y. Times*, Nov. 24, 1940, p. 32.

111 Dies on strikes: *N. Y. Times*, Nov. 27, 1940, p. 12.

111 ff. Dies—F.D.R. exchange: *N. Y. Times*, Nov. 26, 1940, p. 14. *C.R.*, Feb. 11, 1941, p. 895; Nov. 18, 1941, p. 9203. *Newsweek*, Dec. 9, 1940, p. 15. *U. S. News*, Aug. 20, 1954, p. 58. *Martin Dies Story*, p. 143.

113 Dies on million dollars: *N. Y. Times*, Nov. 30, 1940, p. 9. On "personal relief"—*N. Y. Times*, Dec. 3, 1940, p. 1.

113 Gallup poll: *N. Y. Times*, Dec. 4, 1940, p. 19.

113 ff. Dies—F.B.I. exchange: *New York Times*, Dec. 1, 1940, p. 47; Dec. 11, 1940, p. 17; Dec. 17, 1940, p. 1.

114 ff. Bund report: *Appendix IV*, 1941

115 Kunze hearing: *H.*, Oct. 1, 1940, pp. 8251 ff.

115 (fn) K.K.K. hearing: *H.*, Oct. 2, 1940, p. 8313.

115 Axis report: *Appendix III*, 1941.

115 ff. Annual report: *R.*, 1941.

117 Committee extension: *C.R.*, Feb. 11, 1941, pp. 886 ff.

CHAPTER FIVE

118 Ogden on Committee: *Dies Committee*, p. 249.

118 Filene and I.P.A.: Edward L. Bernays: *Biography of an Idea* (New York, 1965).

119 I.P.A. retort: *N. Y. Times*, Feb. 23, 1941, p. 116.

119 *Mr. Dies Goes to Town: Propaganda Analysis*, Jan. 14, 1940, pp. 43 ff.

120 ff. S.W.O.C.–Dies v. Murray: *C.R.*, March 24, 1941, pp. A1352 ff.; March 26, 1941, pp. A1423 ff. and 2574 ff.; March 31, 1941, pp. A1509 ff.

122 Dies on campaign: *Martin Dies Story*, pp. 78 ff.; *N. Y. Times*, July 11, 1941, p. 8.

123 A.P.M. Hearings: *H.*, May 21, 22, 1941, pp. 8391 ff.

124 Dies on Hitler and Stalin: *N. Y. Times*, June 24, 1941, p. 3; Oct. 20, 1941, p. 1.

125 O.P.A.—Dies v. Henderson: *C.R.*, Aug. 8, 1941, pp. 6926 ff.; *N. Y. Times*, Sept. 8, 1941, p. 1. *C.R.*, Nov. 28, 1941, pp. 9201 ff.

126 Brady on socialism: Quoted in *C.R.*, Nov. 25, 1941, pp. 9211 ff.

127 Dies–Watson: *C.R.*, Nov. 28, 1941, pp. 9201 ff. *N. Y. Times*, Nov. 27, 1941, p. 22.

127 F.C.C. on Dies: *Newsweek*, Jan. 5, 1942, p. 7; *C.R.*, Feb. 12, 1942, p. A505.

127 ff. Dies on Cowley: *C.R.*, Jan. 15, 1942, pp. 407 ff.

128 Dies on O.C.D.: *N. Y. Times*, Feb. 9, 1942, p. 9.

129 (fn) Dies on Japan: Quoted in *C.R.*, March 11, 1942, p. 2296.

129 Yellow paper: *Appendix VI*, 1942.

129 Voorhis on Yellow Paper: *C.R.*, Feb. 24, 1942, p. A726.
129 ff. Eliot–Dies–Marcantonio: *C.R.*, March 4, 1942, pp. 1921 ff.; March 6, 1942, pp. 2030 ff.; March 7, 1942, pp. 2055 ff. and A880 ff.
131 Debates on Committee: *C.R.*, March 11, 1942, pp. 2282 ff.; March 30, 1942, pp. 3216 ff.; Vote—April 28, 1942, p. 3754.
131 ff. Dies–Wallace: *N. Y. Times*, March 30, 1942, p. 1.
132 (fn) *New Republic:* April 6, 1942, p. 445.
132 Dies on defense agencies: *C.R.*, Jan. 15, 1942, p. 409.
132 ff. Cox on Parmalee: *C.R.*, March 30, 1942, p. 3204.
133 ff. Vaughn case: *C.R.*, March 30, 1942, pp. 3213 ff.; July 9, 1942, p. A2876. *N. Y. Times*, July 19, 1942, p. 24. *C.R.*, Feb. 18, 1943, p. 1110.
134 U.D.A. report: *R. #2277, Special Report on Subversive Activities Aimed at Destroying Our Representative Form of Government*, 1942.
134 ff. *New Republic* supplement: May 18, 1942.
135 Dies on subversives: *N. Y. Times*, June 24, 1941, p. 3; Oct. 20, 1941, p. 1.
136 Attorney General's report: U. S. Cong., House, 77th Cong., 2d sess. Document No. 833—*Report of the Federal Bureau of Investigation*, Sept. 3, 1943.
136 ff. Dies reply: *C.R.*, Sept. 24, 1942, pp. 7441 ff.
137 (fn) Cushman: *American Political Science Review*, Feb. 1943, p. 47.
137 Annual report: Part One, June 25, 1942. Part Two (dissent), July 7, 1942.
137 ff. Thomas on whitewash: *C.R.*, Jan. 8, 1943, p. 60.
138 Axis report: *Appendix VII*, 1943.
138 Ickes on Voorhis: *Secret Diary*, Vol. 3, p. 379.
138 *Nation* supplement: Oct. 3, 1942.
138 ff. Voorhis on rules: *C.R.*, Feb. 8, 1943, p. 724; Feb. 10, 1943, p. 807.
139 ff. Dies–Rogers: *C.R.*, Feb 1, 1943, pp. 474 ff.
140 Hendricks amendment: *C.R.*, Feb. 5, 1943, pp. 645 ff.
142 Treasury Dept. on Pickens: *N. Y. Times*, Feb. 7, 1943, p. 20.
142 ff. Pickens debates (including Hoffman quote): *C.R.*, Feb. 8, 1943, pp. 697 ff.; Feb. 9, 1943, pp. 732 ff.
144 ff. Kerr Committee: U. S. Cong., 78th Cong., 1st sess. Special Subcommittee of the Committee on Appropriations: *Hearings on the Fitness for Continuation in Federal Employment of G. B. Watson and W. E. Dodd, Employees of the F.C.C., and Robert Morss Lovett, an Employee of the Department of the Interior.*
145 Dies on Dodd: *Martin Dies Story*, p. 168.
146 ff. Lovett: See his autobiography, *All Our Years* (New York, 1948), written, incidentally, in the Ridgefield, Connecticut, home of Martha Dodd Stern.
147 Ickes on Lovett: *All Our Years*, pp. 346 and 291.
147 ff. Lovett quotes: *H.*, April 16, 1943, p. 3522. *All Our Years*, pp. 302 and 291.
148 ff. Watson–Dodd–Lovett debate: *C.R.*, May 18, 1943, pp. 4581 ff.
149 McKellar on "unjust provision": *C.R.*, May 26, 1943, p. 6407.
149 ff. Dirksen on bureaucracy: *C.R.*, May 17, 1943, p. 4552.
150 F.D.R. on "unwarranted encroachment": *N. Y. Times*, July 14, 1943, p. 1, and *C.R.*, Sept. 14, 1943, p. 7521.
150 Courtney–Hoffman: *C.R.*, Feb. 8, 1943, p. 698.
150 ff. Watson–Dodd–Lovett case: For a partisan, yet illuminating analysis of the constitutional issues, see "participant-observer" Frederick L. Schuman's article in *American Political Science Review*, Oct. 1943, pp. 819 ff.
151 ff. Court decisions: 66 F. Supp. 142 (1945). 328 U.S. 303 (1946).

PAGE

152 ff. Relocation: For a concise report on the relocation problem, see *Fortune,* April 1944, pp. 8 ff. It is more extensively treated in Morton Grodzins's *Americans Betrayed* (Chicago, 1949).

153   Denver *Post* report: June 4, 1943. Cited in Ogden: *Dies Committee,* p. 279, as "a positive misstatement."

153   Dewitt on "Japs": Quoted in *Fortune,* April 1944.

153   Rankin on "blood test": *C.R.,* June 28, 1943, p. 6684.

153   Thomas on food: Statement made May 19, 1943, cited in *H.,* July 6, 1943, p. 9650.

153 ff. Relocation hearings: Los Angeles–*H.,* June 8–12, 15, 16, 17, 1943, pp. 8833 ff.; Washington–July 1, 3, 6, 7, 1943, pp. 9391 ff.; Dillon Meyer–July 6, 1943, pp. 9599 ff.

156   Relocation reports: *R.,* Sept. 30, 1943. *Appendix VIII,* 1943.

156   Dies on race hatred: *N. Y. Times,* June 27, 1943, p. 13.

157 ff. Winchell–Dies: *C.R.,* March 27, 1944, pp. 3128 and A1523; March 9, 1944, pp. 2434 ff. *N. Y. Times,* March 27, 1944, p. 9.

159 ff. C.I.O.–P.A.C. report: *R.,* March 29, 1944.

159 ff. P.A.C. attacks: *C.R.,* March 9, 1944, p. 2434. *N. Y. Times,* July 29, 1944, p. 26; Aug. 3, 1944, p. 16; Oct. 4, 1944, p. 17; Oct. 30, 1944, p. 9.

161   Dies retirement: *N. Y. Times,* May 13, 1944, p. 1. *Martin Dies Story,* p. 82.

162   Thomas on exposure: *N. Y. Times,* May 14, 1944, p. 28.

162   Dies return: *N. Y. Times,* July 15, 1954, p. 10.

CHAPTER SIX

167 ff. The first six years of the Standing Committee's existence are the subject of Professor Robert K. Carr's estimable *The House Committee on Un-American Activities, 1945–1950* (Ithaca, N.Y., 1952).

168   Rankin motion: *C.R.,* Jan. 3, 1945, pp. 6 ff.

169   "Flat-footed": Stripling: *The Red Plot Against America,* p. 50.

169   Hoffman–Voorhis–Rankin: *C.R.,* Jan. 4, 1945, pp. 46 ff.

169 ff. Biddle on Hart: *N. Y. Times,* Jan. 14, 1945, p. 4.

170   Mundt survey: *N. Y. Times,* Jan. 23, 1945. *Life,* March 26, 1945, p. 30. *Liberty,* Sept. 22, 1945, pp. 11 ff. Brookings Institution–*Suggested Standards for Determining Un-American Activities,* Washington, D.C., 1945.

170   Rankin on $50,000: *C.R.,* March 7, 1945, p. 1856.

171   Rankin on O.P.A.: *C.R.,* Nov. 21, 1945, p. 10885.

171 ff. O.P.A. hearings: *H.,* June 20, 21, 27, 1945.

172   Rankin on Hollywood: *N. Y. Times,* July 1, 1945, p. 20.

172 ff. Hart resignation: *C.R.,* July 2, 1945, p. 7142. Mundt statement–*C.R.,* July 3, 1945, p. 7186.

173   Rankin on subversives: *C.R.,* July 9, 1945, p. 7377.

173   Rankin on Chaplin: *C.R.,* July 19, 1945, p. 7738.

173 ff. Rankin on Jews: *C.R.,* Feb. 19, 1946, p. A872; Feb. 27, 1946, p. 1727; July 18, 1945, p. 7739; Feb. 11, 1946, p. 1225; Oct. 24, 1945, p. 1032.

174   (fn) Pegler on Rankin: *C.R.,* April 30, 1945, p. A2369.

174 ff. Radio commentators: Adamson–*N. Y. Times,* Oct. 19, 1945, p. 21. Report–*R.,* June 7, 1946. Rankin–*C.R.,* Oct. 24, 1945, p. 1032. Wood bill–*N. Y. Times,* Nov. 22, 1945, p. 24. Spokesman–*Ibid.,* Nov. 7, 1945, p. 25. Advertisement–*Ibid.,* March 14, 1945, p. 18.

176   Duclos on Browder: *Daily Worker,* May 27, 1945, p. 1.

176   Browder hearings: *H.,* Sept. 26, 27, Oct. 17, 19, Nov. 8, 1945.

176   J.A.F.R.C. rally: *N. Y. Times,* Sept. 25, 1945, p. 1.

PAGE

177 Thomas on Laski: *C.R.*, March 28, 1946, p. 2746.
177 ff. J.A.F.R.C. charges: *N. Y. Times*, Jan. 2, 1946, p. 15. *C.R.*, March 28, 1946, p. 2745. (fn) Report: *R.*, June 7, 1946.
178 J.A.F.R.C. hearings: *H.*, April 4, 1946.
179 Contempt citations: J.A.F.R.C.–*C.R.*, March 28, 1946, pp. 2744 ff.; April 16, 1946, pp. 2761 ff. Lamont–*C.R.*, June 26, 1946, pp. 7589 ff. Morford–*C.R.*, Aug. 2, 1946, pp. 10748 ff. Marshall–*C.R.*, July 31, 1946, pp. 10592 ff. (fn) Marcantonio delay–*C.R.*, July 29, 1946, pp. 10406 ff. See Beck: *Contempt of Congress*, and Carr: *House Committee*, Chapter XI.
180 ff. Court decisions: Holtzoff–72 F. Supp. 58 (1947). Barsky *et al.*–167 F. 2d 241 (1948).
181 Fast on fascism: *N. Y. Times*, June 18, 1948, p. 10. (fn) See Lillian Hellman's introduction to Dashiell Hammett's *The Big Knockdown* (New York, 1960).
181 Beck summary: *Contempt*, p. 35.
181 ff. Smith hearing: *H.*, Jan. 30, 1946.
182 ff. Atom spies: Adamson–*N. Y. Times*, March 8, 1946, p. 3; March 27, 1946, p. 1. Rankin–*N. Y. Times*, June 27, 1946, p. 4. Rankin on McMahon bill–*C.R.*, July 19, 1946, p. 9448. Adamson on army–*N. Y. Times*, July 12, 1946, p. 5. Wood–*N. Y. Times*, Oct. 24, 1946, p. 6.
183 ff. Debate on Committee: *C.R.*, May 17, 1946, pp. 5209 ff.
184 ff. Budenz–Eisler: *N. Y. Times*, Oct. 14, 1946, p. 12; Oct. 16, 1946, p. 6. *N. Y. World Telegram*, Oct. 17, 1946, p. 1. *N. Y. Times*, Oct. 18, 1946, p. 1. Eisler on "provocation"–*N. Y. Times*, Dec. 23, 1946, p. 15.
185 Budenz hearings: *H.*, Nov. 22, 1946.
185 Eisler on C.P.: *N. Y. Times*, Dec. 12, 1946, p. 9.
185 ff. Eisler hearing: *H.*, Feb. 6, 1947.
186 Rankin on federal payroll: *N. Y. Times*, Dec. 26, 1946, p. 11.
187 Thomas on atom bomb: *N. Y. Times*, Nov. 27, 1946, p. 4.
187 Shapley hearing: *N. Y. Times*, Nov. 15, 1946, p. 14.
187 ff. Rankin–Adamson on investigations: *N. Y. Times*, Dec. 4, 1946, p. 44; Dec. 27, 1946, p. 1.
188 Adamson on democracy: See *C.R.*, Feb. 5, 1946, p. A508. Pearson–*C.R.*, Feb. 1, 1946, p. 1230.
188 Thomas–Adamson break: *N. Y. Times*, Dec. 28, 1946, p. 3; Jan. 1, 1947, p. 2.
188 ff. Annual report: *R.*, Jan. 2, 1947.
189 Kreml: Stripling, *Red Plot*, p. 57.

CHAPTER SEVEN

190 ff. G. Eisler hearing: *H.*, Feb. 6, 1947.
191 Contempt citation: *C.R.*, Feb. 18, 1947, pp. 1127 ff.
191 ff. Josephson hearing: *H.*, March 5, 1947.
192 Dennis hearings: *H.*, March 26, April 9, 1947.
192 Contempt citations: *C.R.*, April 22, 1947, pp. 3813 ff.
193 Dennis case: 171 F. 2d 986 (1948); 339 U.S. 162 (1950).
193 Josephson case: 165 F. 2d 82 (1947).
193 Eisler case: 338 U.S. 189 (1949).
194 Thomas on passports: *C.R.*, April 22, 1947, p. 3804.
195 Truman loyalty order: Executive Order #9835 (1947). 12 Fed. Reg. 1935.
196 ff. Anti-Communist hearings: *H.*, March 24–28, 1947. Bullitt–March 24; Green–March 25; Johnston–March 27; Hoover–March 25; Earle–

PAGE

March 28; V.F.W.—March 27; Tenney—March 26; (fn) McCarthy—March 28.

197 ff. Kravchenko hearing: *H.*, July 22, 1947.

198 Kravchenko-Gromyko: *N. Y. Times,* July 24, 1947, p. 4.

198 Steele hearing: *H.*, July 21, 1947.

198 Carr on Steele: *House Committee,* p. 53.

199 Allis–Chalmers hearing: *H.*, Feb. 27, 1947.

199 Union hearings: *H.*, July 23–25, 1947.

199 ff. Reports: Communist Party—*R.*, April 1, 1947. American Youth for Democracy—*R.*, April 17, 1947. Southern Conference—*R.*, June 16, 1947. Civil Rights Congress—*R.*, Sept. 2, 1947.

200 (fn) Civil Rights Congress: *America's Thought Police* (New York, 1947).

200 (fn) Thomas poem: *N. Y. Times,* June 13, 1947, p. 8.

201 Gellhorn on Southern Conference: *Harvard Law Review,* Oct. 1947, p. 1197. See also *American Scholar,* Spring 1948, pp. 139 ff.

202 Thomas—McDowell on fascism: *N. Y. Times,* June 13, 1947, p. 8. *C.R.*, June 13, 1947, p. A2831.

202 ff. L.A. hearings: *N.Y. Times,* May 15, 1947, p. 1; May 16, 1947, p. 1; May 17, 1947, p. 8. *C.R.*, June 6, 1947, p. A2687.

204 Thomas—Eisler exchange: *N. Y. Times,* May 13, 1947, p. 19.

204 ff. H. Eisler hearings: *H.*, Sept. 24–26, 1947. State Dept. official—Sept. 26, p. 156; Stripling quotes—*H.*, Sept. 24 and *N. Y. Times,* Sept. 27, 1947, p. 1. Eisler song—*H.*, Sept. 24, p. 156; (fn) Rankin—Sept. 24, p. 60; Welles—Sept. 24; Messersmith—Sept. 25.

207 ff. Hollywood hearings, first week: *H.*, Oct. 20–24, 1947. Warner—Oct. 20; attorney ejected—Oct. 20, p. 118; Disney—Oct. 24; Ryskind, Oct. 22. Trumbo on unfriendly witnesses—*The Time of the Toad* (Hollywood, Calif., 1949). Mrs. Rogers—Oct. 24; Cooper—Oct. 23; Montgomery, Murphy, Reagan—Oct. 23; Menjou, Oct. 21.

210 ff. Hollywood hearings, second week: *H.*, Oct. 27–30, 1947. Lavery—Oct. 29; Brecht—Oct. 30, and (fn) *Bertolt Brecht Before the Committee on Un-American Activities*—Folkway Records, FD 5531. Wilson on Communists—*New Republic,* Dec. 24, 1930, p. 158. Lawson—*H.*, Oct. 27; Kenny—Oct. 28; Maltz—Oct. 28; Trumbo—Oct. 28; Dmytryk—Oct. 29; Lardner—Oct. 30, and (fn) *Saturday Evening Post,* Oct. 14, 1961, p. 38.

213 ff. Maltz incident: *New Masses,* Feb. 12, 1946, p. 19, and Oct 12, 1946, pp. 24–25. See Daniel Aaron's *Writers on the Left* (New York, 1961), p. 386.

214 ff. Lawson–Maltz–Bessie quotes: *N. Y. Times,* Nov. 17, 1947, p. 14, and Nov. 3, 1947, p. 19. Alvah Bessie's *Inquisition in Eden* (New York, 1965), p. 99, and (fn) *The Un-Americans* (New York, 1957). *H.*, Oct. 27, 1947, p. 296.

215 ff. Hollywood Ten's films: For a content analysis, see Dorothy B. Jones's *Communism and the Movies: A Study of Film Content,* in John Cogley's *Report on Blacklisting* (New York, 1956), Vol. 1.

216 Agee on *Mission to Moscow: Nation,* May 22, 1943, p. 749.

216 October hearings: *H.* Oct. 20–24, 27–30, 1947. Rand—Oct. 20; Taylor—Oct. 22; M.G.M. script supervisor—Oct. 22.

216 McNutt–Johnston: *N. Y. Times,* Oct. 27, 1947, p. 26, and Oct. 26, 1947, p. 54.

217 (fn) Stripling–Johnston: *H.*, Oct. 27, 1947, pp. 314 ff.

217 Johnston to writers: Quoted in Gordon Kahn's *Hollywood on Trial* (New York, 1948), p. 5.

217 Warner on livelihoods: *H.*, Oct. 20, 1947, p. 53.

218 Waldorf decision: *N. Y. Times,* Nov. 26, 1947, p. 1.

218 Hearst editorial: Quoted in Kahn: *Hollywood on Trial,* p. 139.

PAGE

220 (fn) Warren: *N. Y. Times,* Dec. 7, 1947, p. 66.
220 Thomas quotes: *C.R.,* Nov. 20, 1947, p. A4211. *H.,* Oct. 29, 1947, p. 401.
221 Russell on Oppenheimer: *H.,* Oct. 30, 1947.
221 Stripling on "broken record": *Red Plot,* p. 75.
221 ff. Contempt citations: *C.R.,* Nov. 24, 1947, pp. 10769 ff.
222 Wallace on Ten: *N. Y. Times,* Jan. 29, 1947, pp. 10769 ff.
223 Contempt case: 176 F. 2d 49 (1949).
223 Trumbo on government regulation: *Time of the Toad,* p. 17.
224 Bessie career: See *Inquisition in Eden.*
224 Biberman career: See his *Salt of the Earth* (Boston, 1965).
224 Kempton on Ten: *Part of Our Time,* p. 182.

CHAPTER EIGHT

227 ff. Communist control hearings: *H.,* Feb. 5, 6, 9–11, 19, 20, 1948. Burnham –Feb. 19; Moley–Feb. 11; Ernst–Feb. 11; Waldman–Feb. 6; Richberg –Feb. 6; Berle–Feb. 11; Clark–Feb. 5; Nagy–Feb. 6; Dimitrov–Feb. 19; Standley–Feb. 9; (fn) Hays–Feb. 10, p. 208.
229 Communist control report: *R.,* May 11, 1948.
229 ff. House debate: *C.R.,* May 17–19, 1948. Javits–May 18, p. 5860; Holifield–p. 5873; Dondero–p. 6020; Bryson–p. 6022.
230 (fn) Communism report: *R.,* Dec. 4, 1948.
231 ff. Condon report: *Report to the Full Committee of the Special Subcommittee on National Security,* March 1, 1948. For a critical analysis of the report and of Thomas's campaign against Condon, see the pseudonymous Louis Welborn's *The Ordeal of Dr. Condon,* in *Harper's,* January 1950, pp. 46 ff. Also, Representative Holifield's presentations to the House–*C.R.,* July 22, 1947, pp. 9770 ff. and March 9, 1948, pp. 2435 ff.
232 Rankin–Vail on report: *C.R.,* March 2, 1948, p. A1306, and April 1, 1948, p. 4001.
232 ff. Thomas on Condon: Washington *Times-Herald,* March 23, 1947, p. 1; March 25, 1947, p. 1; July 17, 1947, p. 1. *American* magazine, June 1947, p. 16. *Liberty* magazine, June 26, 1947.
233 Condon on Russia: Quoted in *C.R.,* March 9, 1948, p. 2443.
234 McDowell on Condon: *N. Y. Times,* March 7, 1948, p. 1.
234 ff. Hoover letter: Condon report, *Report to the Full Committee . . . ,* p. 4. Washington *Post,* March 4, 1948, p. 1.
236 Thomas on Truman: *N. Y. Times,* April 8, 1948, p. 1.
236 Reece letter: *N. Y. Times,* May 2, 1948, p. 32.
236 House order: *C.R.,* April 22, 1948, pp. 4777 ff.
236 Truman reply: *N. Y. Times,* April 23, 1948, p. 1.
237 A.E.C. clearance: *N. Y. Times,* July 16, 1948, p. 1.
238 Nixon on Condon: *N. Y. Times,* Dec. 20, 1948.
238 Mundt on Condon: *N. Y. Times,* Dec. 23, 1948, p. 8.
238 Stripling on Condon: *Red Plot,* p. 86.
238 Vail attack: *C.R.,* April 23, 1951, pp. 4214 ff.
238 Velde on resignation: *N. Y. Times,* Aug. 11, 1951, p. 7.
238 ff. Condon hearing: *H.,* Sept. 5, 1952.
239 Condon in report: *R.,* Dec. 28, 1952, pp. 73 ff.
240 Atomic espionage hearings: *H.,* Sept. 9, 14, 16, 1948.
240 Committee members' quotes: Thomas–*N. Y. Times,* Sept. 14, 1948, p. 1, and Sept. 18, 1948, p. 1; Nixon–*N. Y. Times,* Sept. 25, 1948, p. 1; McDowell–*N. Y. Times,* Sept. 22, 1948, p. 8, and Sept. 26, p. 1.

241   Truman on investigation: *N. Y. Times*, Sept. 14, 1948, p. 1, and Sept. 23, p. 1.
241 ff. Atomic espionage report: *R.*, Sept. 28, 1948.
242 ff. Justice Dept. dispute: Justice Dept.—*N. Y. Times*, Sept. 30, 1948, p. 1; McDowell—*N. Y. Times*, Oct. 1, 1948, p. 1; Thomas—*N. Y. Times*, Oct. 5, 1948, p. 1; Groves—*N. Y. Times*, Sept. 11, 1948, p. 1.
244   Books by principals in the Hiss–Chambers case include: Whittaker Chambers's *Witness* (New York, 1952); Alger Hiss's *In the Court of Public Opinion* (New York, 1957); Elizabeth Bentley's *Out of Bondage* (New York, 1951); Richard Nixon's *Six Crises* (New York, 1962), pp. 1–71; Robert Stripling's *Red Plot*. Other books include Ralph de Toledano and Victor Lasky's *Seeds of Treason* (New York, 1950); Alistair Cook's *A Generation on Trial* (New York, 1952); Fred Cook's *The Unfinished Story of Alger Hiss* (New York, 1958); Lord Jowitt's *The Strange Case of Alger Hiss* (New York, 1953); Meyer A. Zeligs's *Friendship and Fratricide* (New York, 1967).
244   "Blonde Spy Queen": *N. Y. World Telegram*, July 21–23, 1948, p. 1.
245 ff. Bentley hearing. *H.*, July 31, 1948. Miss Bentley's quotes on Golos are taken from her book, *Out of Bondage*.
246   Bentley on Currie: *H.*, July 31, 1948, p. 553. Rankin on Currie–*H.*, p. 557.
246 ff. Civil Service on Silvermaster: *H.*, Aug. 3, 1948, p. 613.
247 ff. First Chambers hearing: *H.*, Aug. 3, 1948.
249 ff. Hearings of the accused: Silvermaster—*H.*, Aug. 4, 1948; Collins—Aug. 11; Silverman—Aug. 12; Perlo—Aug. 9; Pressman—Aug. 20; Witt—Aug. 20; Abt—Aug. 20.
250   Witt–Abt statement: *N. Y. Times*, Oct. 1, 1948, p. 12.
250 ff. Committee report: *R.*, Aug. 28, 1948.
251   (fn) Thomas to lawyer: *H.*, Sept. 8, 1948, p. 1310.
251   Silvermaster on disloyalty: *H.*, Aug. 4, 1948, p. 590.
251   Nixon on Fifth: *H.*, Aug. 12, 1948, p. 837.
252   Chambers on White: *H.*, Aug. 13, 1948, p. 906.
252   Currie hearing: *H.*, Aug. 13, 1948.
252 ff. White hearing: *H.*, Aug. 13, 1948; Thomas to White–p. 881.
252   Wallace on White: *N. Y. Times*, Aug. 18, 1948, p. 5.
253   White "Creed": *H.*, Aug. 13, 1948, p. 878.
253   Chambers on White: *Witness*, p. 29.
253   Bentley on White: *Bondage*, p. 164.
253   White on Silvermaster: *H.*, Aug. 13, 1948, p. 898.
253   (fn) Rebecca West on White: London *Sunday Times*, March 22, 1953, quoted in *C.R.*, May 26, 1953, p. A2963.
254   For the A.A.A. story, see Arthur M. Schlesinger, Jr.'s *The Coming of the New Deal* (Boston, 1958), pp. 77–80.
254   Chambers on Hiss: *Witness*, p. 338.
254   Peters hearing: *H.*, Aug. 30, 1948.
254   Truman on "red herring": *N. Y. Times*, Aug. 6, 1948, p. 1.
254 ff. First Hiss hearing: *H.*, Aug. 5, 1948.
255   Hébert suggestion: *Six Crises*, p. 10.
255   Mundt on Hiss: *H.*, Aug. 3, 1948, p. 579.
255   Republican's lament: *Six Crises*, p. 10.
255   (fn) Nixon–Stripling: *Six Crises*, p. 10, and *Red Plot*, p. 116.
255   Chambers on Nixon: *Witness*, p. 355.
256   Hiss on Chambers: *H.*, Aug. 5, 1948, p. 647.
256   Second Chambers hearing: *H.*, Aug. 7, 1948.
256 ff. Second Hiss hearing: *H.*, Aug. 16, 1948.
257   Nixon explanation: *Six Crises*, p. 30.

PAGE

257   First Hiss–Chambers confrontation: *H.*, Aug. 17, 1948. Hiss on Crosley
       –p. 975; Hiss challenge–p. 988.
257   Chambers on Hiss "acting": *Witness*, p. 605.
257   Nixon's briefings: *N. Y. Times*, Aug. 22, 1948, p. 13.
257 ff. Donald Hiss hearing: *H.*, Aug. 13, 1948.
258   Hiss letter: *N. Y. Times*, Aug. 25, 1948, p. 1.
258   Nixon comment: *Six Crises*, p. 43.
258 ff. Hiss–Chambers public confrontation: *H.*, Aug. 25, 1948.
258   Disposal of Ford: *H.*, Aug. 26, 1948.
258   Chambers's quotes: *H.*, Aug. 25, 1948, pp. 1176, 1191.
258 ff. Report on Hiss case: *R.*, Aug. 28, 1948.
259   *Nation* articles: Aug. 14, 1948, p. 173; Sept. 4, 1948, p. 251.
259   *Meet the Press* interview: *N. Y. Times*, Aug. 28, 1948, p. 251.
259   Washington *Post* editorial: Cited in *Six Crises*, p. 45.
259   Fiedler on case: *Commentary*, Aug. 1951, p. 110.
259 ff. Chambers on Hiss: *Witness*, p. 445.
260   Hiss defense: *In Court*, pp. 102, 419.
261   Psychiatrists: For an elaborate psychoanalytic exegesis on Chambers,
       see Zeligs: *Friendship and Fratricide*.
261 ff. Chambers on himself: *Witness*, pp. 715, 769; *Cold Friday* (New York,
       1964), pp. 67, 12.
264   Justice Dept.: *N. Y. Times*, Dec. 2, 1948, p. 3.
265   Mundt–Nixon on microfilm: *N. Y. Times*, Dec. 4, 1948, p. 1, and Dec.
       7, p. 1.
265   Officials on code: *H.*, Dec. 7, 1948.
265   Wadleigh hearing: *H.*, Dec. 9, 1948. For Wadleigh's story, see *N. Y.
       Post*, July 11–24, 1949.
266   Nixon on indictment: *N. Y. Times*, Dec. 16, 1948, p. 1.
266   (fn) Latham on thirties: *The Communist Controversy in Washington*
       (Cambridge, Mass., 1966), p. 149.
267   Berle on Hiss: *H.*, Aug. 30, 1948, p. 1296.
267 ff. Duggan case: Nixon–*N. Y. Times*, Dec. 1, 1948, p. 1. Mundt–*N. Y.
       Times*, Dec. 25, 1948, p. 1. (fn) Hede Massing: *This Deception* (New
       York, 1951). Criticisms and retractions: *N. Y. Times*, Dec. 3, 1948, p.
       1, and Dec. 25, p. 1. Levine on Welles: *N. Y. Times*, Dec. 23, 1948,
       p. 1.
269   Truman on "dead agency": *N. Y. Times*, Dec. 10, 1948, p. 1.
269   Mundt–Nixon code: *N. Y. Times*, Dec. 28, 1948, p. 1.
269   Hiss case report: *R.*, Dec. 31, 1948.
269 ff. Thomas jailed: *N. Y. Times*, Nov. 9, 1948, p. 1.
270   Thomas released: *N. Y. Times*, Feb. 8, 1954, p. 11.
270   Dies on Thomas: *Martin Dies Story*, p. 84.
271   Dies on Nixon: *Martin Dies Story*, p. 179.

CHAPTER NINE

272   Rankin on Moscow: *N. Y. Times*, Jan. 16, 1949, p. 1.
273   Nixon on Coplon: *N. Y. Times*, March 6, 1949, p. 2.
273   Short hearing: *H.*, May 24, 1949.
273   Democrat on "inactivity": *N. Y. Times*, May 29, 1949, p. 10.
274   Editorial: *N. Y. Times*, May 31, 1949, p. 22.
274   Holifield–Douglas: *N. Y. Times*, Dec. 26, 1949, p. 13.
274   Crouch hearing: *H.*, May 6, 1949.
274 ff. Hiskey hearing: *H.*, May 24, 1949.
275   Weinberg hearing: *H.*, April 21, 1949.
275   Accusation: *R.*, Sept. 29, 1949.

PAGE

275   Scientists hearings: *H.*, April 26, 1949; May 25, 1949; June 10, 1949; Sept. 27, 1949.

275   Nelson hearing: *H.*, June 8, 1949.

276 ff. Oppenheimers hearing: *H.*, June 14, 1949; Oppenheimer quote—p. 358.

277   Wood on contempt: *N. Y. Times*, June 15, 1949, p. 1.

277 ff. Hawkins hearing: *H.*, Dec. 20, 1950.

278   A.P. on "espionage": *N. Y. Times*, June 5, 1949, p. 3.

278   Espionage hearing: *H.*, June 6, 1949.

279   Velde on espionage: *N. Y. Times*, Sept. 26, 1949.

279   Jordan broadcast: Washington *Times-Herald*, Dec. 3, 1949, p. 1.

280   First Jordan hearing: *H.*, Dec. 5, 1949.

280   Lewis embellishment: *N. Y. Times*, Dec. 6, 1949, p. 1.

280   Groves hearing: *H.*, Dec. 7, 1949.

280   Walter–Harrison: *N. Y. Times*, Dec. 8, 1949, p. 1.

280   Republican protest: *N. Y. Times*, Dec. 9, 1949, p. 1.

280 ff. Second Jordan hearings: *H.*, Jan. 23, 24, 1949; broker quote—Jan. 24, p. 1039.

281   Wallace hearing: *H.*, Jan. 26, 1949.

281   Staff investigator hearing: *H.*, March 2, 1950.

281   Third Jordan hearing: *H.*, March 3, 1950.

282   D.C. hearings: *H.*, June 28, 29, July 6, 12, 28, 1949; Dec. 6, 11–13, 1950.

282   Pennsylvania–Ohio hearings: *H.*, Feb. 21–23, March 13, 14, 24, 25, June 22, July 12–15, Aug. 8, Sept. 28, Oct. 13, 21, 1950.

282   Honolulu hearings: *H.*, April 10–15, 17–19, 1950.

283   Emspak hearing: *H.*, Dec. 5, 1949; quote—p. 839.

283   Nixon on Fifth: *H.*, April 26, 1949, p. 302.

283   Harrison demand: *N. Y. Times*, July 13, 1949, p. 19.

284   Velde to Hiskey: *H.*, May 24, 1949, p. 397.

284 ff. Contempt citations: *C.R.*, Aug. 10, 1950, pp. 12234 ff., and Aug. 11, 1950, pp. 12284 ff.

285 ff. Constitutional questions: For this summary of the questions raised by the contempt cases, as for much else in this chapter, I am indebted to Professor Beck.

285 ff. Court decisions: Supreme Court on Fifth Amendment—340 U.S. 59 (1950); leeway for defendants—96 F. Supp. 491 (1951); incriminating relationship—349 U.S. 1950 (1955); Nelson case—103 F. Supp. 215 (1952); C.P. membership no waiver—349 U.S. 155 (1955); Committee's responsibility—349 U.S. 219 (1955).

286   Beck summary: *Contempt*, p. 86.

286 ff. Remington hearings: *H.*, April 20, 21, 29, May 4, 5, 1950; Remington quote—May 4, p. 1817; Bentley testimony—May 6.

288   Marcantonio on Pressman: *N. Y. Times*, Aug. 12, 1950, p. 30.

288   Andrews's story: N. Y. *Herald Tribune*, Aug. 7, 1950, p. 1.

288 ff. Pressman hearing: *H.*, Aug. 28, 1950; Pressman quote—p. 2845.

289   Witt–Abt–Kramer hearing: *H.*, Sept. 1, 1950.

289   Silverman hearing: *H.*, Aug. 31, 1950.

289   Nixon on Pressman: *N. Y. Times*, Aug. 29, 1950, p. 1.

289   Lowenthal hearing: *H.*, Sept. 15, 1950.

289   Lowenthal book: *The Federal Bureau of Investigation* (New York, 1950).

289   Carr quote: *House Committee*, p. 203.

290   Appendix to hearings: *Hearings Regarding Communism in U. S. Government*, Part II, pp. 2960–61.

290   Scott hearing: *H.*, Sept. 22, 1950.

290   E. G. Robinson hearings: *H.*, Oct. 27, Dec. 21, 1950.

290 ff. J. Robinson hearing: *H.*, July 18, 1949; quote—p. 479.

PAGE

291 Mundt–Nixon bill hearings: *H.*, March 21–24, 28–30, April 4, May 2–4, 1950.

292 Truman messages: *C.R.*, Aug. 8, 1950, pp. 12018 ff. Veto—*C.R.*, Sept. 22, 1950, pp. 15629 ff.

292 Internal Security Act: Public Law 31, 81st Cong., U.S. Code Title 50; Sections 781 and 811.

292 (fn) House debate: *C.R.*, Aug. 29, 1950; Rankin—p. 13725; McSweeney —p. 13733.

293 Jencks case: 77 S.C. 1007 (1957).

293 Constitutionality upheld: 81 S.C. 1357 (1961).

293 1963 reversal: 11 U.S. App. D.C. (1963).

293 1967 reversal: Citation not available at this writing.

294 1965 ruling: 86 S. Ct. 194 (1965).

294 1967 hearings: Transcript not available at this writing. See *R.*, Oct. 4, 1967, the Committee's report on H.R. 12601, the Willis bill, with a dissent by Culver. For House passage, see *C.R.*, Nov. 28, 1967.

295 Truman press conference: *N. Y. Times*, June 17, 1949, p. 1.

295 I.P.R. investigation: For an illuminating review of these hearings, which many on the left refused to take seriously, while some on the right made too much of them, see Latham: *Communist Controversy*, pp. 296 ff.

295 ff. Nixon on Hiss case: *N. Y. Times*, July 13, 1949, p. 19.

296 Hall on Communist-coddling: *N. Y. Times*, Nov. 19, 1950, p. 20.

CHAPTER TEN

297 Allocation: *C.R.*, Feb. 8, 1951, pp. 1151 ff.

298 Jackson–Potter on Robinson: *N. Y. Times*, Feb. 10, 1951, p. 6, and Feb. 23, 1951, p. 24.

298 ff. Hollywood hearings: *H.*, March 8, 21, April 10–13, 17, 23–25, May 10, 16–18, 22–25, June 25, 26, Sept. 10–12, 17–21, 24, 1951; Jan. 24, 28, Feb. 5, March 20, April 10, 30, May 19–21, Aug. 19, Sept. 29, Nov. 12, 13, 1952.

298 Wood on Fifth: *H.*, Sept. 21, 1951, p. 1703.

299 Moulder on Fifth: *H.*, April 24, 1951, p. 385.

299 Collins hearing: *H.*, April 11, 1951.

299 Berkeley hearing: *H.*, Sept. 19, 1951.

299 Hayden hearing: *H.*, April 10, 1951.

299 Jackson to witness: *H.*, Sept. 19, 1951, p. 1627.

299 ff. Jackson to Foreman: *H.*, Sept. 24, 1951, p. 1753.

300 Actors Guild to Sondergaard: *N. Y. Times*, March 21, 1951, p. 41.

300 Actors Equity on exposure: *N. Y. Times*, April 20, 1951, p. 25.

301 M.P.I.C. statement: *H.*, Sept. 17, 1951, p. 1416.

301 ff. Parks hearing: *H.*, March 21, 1951.

302 Velde on Parks: *C.R.*, March 22, 1951, p. 2890.

302 Jarrico on Parks: *N. Y. Times*, March 24, 1951, p. 9.

302 Dmytryk hearing: *H.*, April 23, 1951.

303 Kazan hearing: *H.*, April 10, 1952; quote—p. 2407.

303 Kazan advertisement: *N. Y. Times*, April 12, 1952, p. 7.

304 Ferrer hearing: *H.*, May 22, 1951.

304 Garfield hearing: *H.*, April 23, 1951.

304 ff. Robinson hearing: *H.*, April 30, 1952.

305 Hellman hearing: *H.*, May 21, 1951; letter—p. 3541; Wood to Hellman —p. 3546.

305 Rossen hearing: *H.*, June 25, 1951.

306 Buchman hearing: *H.*, Sept. 25, 1951.

538 NOTES

306   Buchman contempt citation: *C.R.*, Feb. 5, 1952, pp. 826 ff.
306   Actor on dames: *H.*, April 23, 1951, p. 4364.
306 ff. Beck's donation: *H.*, Sept. 25, 1951, p. 1817.
307   Client's complaint: *H.*, Sept. 19, 1951, p. 1525.
307   Schulberg hearing: *H.*, May 23, 1951.
307   (fn) Jerome: *N. Y. Times*, May 20, 1951, II, p. 5.
308   Actor on *Internationale*: *H.*, Sept. 19, 1951, p. 1602.
308   1952 report: *R.*, Jan. 3, 1953.
308   Doyle on persecution: *H.*, April 11, 1951, p. 215.
308   Wood on elimination: *N. Y. Times*, Sept. 22, 1951, p. 8.
308   1951 report: *R.*, Feb. 17, 1952.
309   Executive on cleared air: *N. Y. Times*, Sept. 30, 1951, II, p. 5. See Cogley's *Report on Blacklisting*.
310   1951 loyalty order: #10241 (1951) 16 Fed. Reg. 3690.
310   Clubb hearings: *H.*, March 14, Aug. 20, 23, 1951.
310   Willoughby hearings: *H.*, Aug. 9, 23, 1951.
311   Supreme Court on C.P. leaders: 341 U.S. 494 (1950).
311 ff. McPhaul, Grossman contempt citations: *C.R.*, June 20, 1952, pp. 8625 ff.
312   Rogers v. U.S.: 340 U.S. 367 (1951).
312   Grossman appeal: 229 F. 2d 775 (1956).
312   McPhaul appeal: 81 S. Ct. 138 (1960).
312 ff. Los Angeles hearings: *H.*, Jan. 21–26, April 9, May 22, July 8, Sept. 30, Oct. 1–3, 6, 7, 1952. Margolis–Sept. 30; Katz–Oct. 1.
314   (fn) Matusow: *H.*, Feb. 6, 7, 1952. *False Witness* (New York, 1955).
315   Doyle on C.P.: *H.*, July 11, 1951, p. 739.
315   Philbrick testimony: *H.*, July 25, 1951.
316   U.E. negotiators hearing: *H.*, Sept. 3, 1952.
317   Detroit hearings: *H.*, Feb. 25–29, March 10–12, April 29, 30, 1952.
318   *The Shameful Years: R.*, Jan. 8, 1952.
318 ff. Smith hearing: *H.*, Oct. 13, 1952.
319   Rovere on McCarthy era: *N. Y. Times Magazine*, April 30, 1967, pp. 23 ff.

CHAPTER ELEVEN

321   Dies on subversives: *N. Y. Times*, Nov. 25, 1952, p. 18.
322   Walter on Dies: *N. Y. Times*, Nov. 24, 1952, p. 12.
322 ff. Spring 1954 hearings: Kearney in Albany–*H.*, April 7–9; Jackson in San Diego–April 12, 19–22; Clardy in Detroit–April 28–30, May 3–5, 7, 10–14; Witness X–April 30; Velde in Chicago–March 15, 16, April 29.
323   Other hearings: *H.*, Seattle–June 14, 19, 1954; San Francisco–Dec. 1–5, 1953; Philadelphia–July 30, 1954; Baltimore–May 18, March 25, 26, 1954; Dayton–Sept. 13–15, 1954; (fn) DeLacy–Sept. 14, 1954.
323   Agents in L.A.: *H.*, March 28, 31, 1953.
323   Shaw hearing: *H.*, May 4, 1953.
323   Stander hearing: *H.*, May 6, 1953.
323   Robbins hearing: *H.*, May 5, 1953.
323 ff. Rossen hearing: *H.*, May 7, 1953.
324   *Nation* on Clardy: Feb. 13, 1953, p. 132.
324   Scherer–Clardy in Michigan: *H.*, April 30, 1954, p. 5207.
324   (fn) Reuther: Quoted in Taylor: *Grand Inquest*, p. 213.
325   Eisenhower executive order: #10450 (1953), 18 Fed. Reg. 2489.
326   Hoover on professors: *N. Y. Times*, Nov. 14, 1954, p. 75.

PAGE

326   Agnes Meyer talk: *N. Y. Times,* Feb. 18, 1953, p. 1.

326   Velde on Meyer: *N. Y. Times,* Feb. 18, 1953, p. 1.

327   Thomas on teachers: *N. Y. Times Sunday Magazine,* Feb. 8, 1953, p. 8.

327   A.A.U.P. resolution: *N. Y. Times,* March 29, 1953, p. 20.

327 ff.   A.A.U. resolution: *N. Y. Times,* March 31, 1953, p. 1.

328   Jones on Fifth: Quoted in *C.R.,* March 17, 1953, p. 2021.

328 ff.   Gallagher position: *N. Y. Times,* March 7, 1953, p. 10.

329   Trilling position: *N. Y. Times,* Nov. 8, 1953, p. 28, and Nov. 26, 1953, p. 30.

329   (fn) Supreme Court: 87 S. Ct. 675 (1967).

329   Velde on Communists: *N. Y. Times,* Feb. 9, 1953, p. 28.

329 ff.   Eisenhower on investigations: *N. Y. Times,* Feb. 26, 1953, p. 16, and Jan. 17, 1953, p. 6.

330   (fn) McCarthy: *N. Y. Times,* Jan. 6, 1954, p. 13.

330 ff.   Education hearings: Davis—*H.,* Feb. 25, 1953; Boorstin—Feb. 26, 1953; Hicks—Feb. 26, 1953. See also Hicks's *Part of the Truth* (New York, 1965), pp. 266–269. Furry—Feb. 26, 1953; Dunham—Feb. 27, 1953.

332   Hoover warning: *N. Y. Times,* April 5, 1953, p. 32.

332   Velde on churches: *N. Y. Times,* March 10, 1953, p. 1.

332   1951 report: *R.,* April 25, 1951.

333   Opposition to investigation: *N. Y. Times,* March 11, 1953, p. 12.

333   Eisenhower on churches: *N. Y. Times,* March 20, 1953, p. 1.

333 ff.   American Council on investigation: *N. Y. Times,* March 11, 1953, p. 12.

334   Jackson on investigation: *C.R.,* March 17, 1953, pp. 2017 ff.

334   Velde to churchmen: *N. Y. Times,* May 17, 1953, p. 32.

334   Oxnam retort: *N. Y. Times,* June 27, 1953, p. 18.

335   Matthews article: *American Mercury,* July 1953; reprinted in *C.R.,* June 27, 1953, pp. A3904 ff.

337   Eisenhower on article: *N. Y. Times,* July 10, 1953, p. 1.

337   McCarthy on Democrats: *N. Y. Times,* July 11, 1953, p. 1.

337 ff.   Oxnam hearing: *H.,* July 21, 1953. See also Oxnam's *I Protest* (New York, 1954).

338   Clardy on Oxnam: *N. Y. Times,* April 23, 1953, p. 17.

340 ff.   Walter on Oxnam: *N. Y. Times,* July 23, 1953, p. 7.

341   Matthews article: *American Mercury,* July 1953.

341   Niebuhr on "prophetic spirits": *Christian Century,* Aug. 19, 1953, p. 936.

341 ff.   McMichael hearings: *H.,* July 20, 21, 1953.

343   (fn) Donner: *The Un-Americans* (New York, 1961), p. 102.

343   L.A. Unitarian hearing: *H.,* Sept. 12, 1951.

343 ff.   Gitlow hearing: *H.,* July 7, 1953.

343 ff.   Philbrick testimony: *H.,* July 6, 1953.

344   Philbrick criticism: *N. Y. Times,* Oct. 2, 1953, p. 8.

345   1953 report: *R.,* Feb. 8, 1954.

345 ff.   Brownell on White: *N. Y. Times,* Nov. 7, 1953, p. 1.

346   Kunzig quote: *N. Y. Times,* Nov. 11, 1953, p. 1.

347   Walter on subpoena: *N. Y. Times,* Nov. 11, 1953, p. 1.

348   (fn) Adams: *First-Hand Report* (New York, 1961), p. 140.

348   Velde in *U. S. News:* Nov. 29, 1953, pp. 65 ff.

348   Truman talk: *N. Y. Times,* Nov. 17, 1953, p. 1.

348   Hoover testimony: *N. Y. Times,* Nov. 18, 1953, p. 1.

348   Kearney charge: *N. Y. Times,* March 23, 1954, p. 1.

349   Walter quotes: *N. Y. Times,* Jan. 17, 1954, p. 29, and Jan. 16, 1954, p. 7.

349   Kearney–Velde: *N. Y. Times,* March 23, 1954, p. 1, and March 26, 1954, p. 8.

CHAPTER TWELVE

351 ff. Once again I am indebted to Carl Beck's *Contempt of Congress* for the review of the Fifth Amendment cases.

351 ff. Contempt citations: *C.R.*, May 11, 1954, pp. 6375 ff.; July 23, 1954, pp. 11598 ff.; Jan. 5, 1955, pp. 11 ff.

351 ff. The following took the Fifth Amendment: Ole Fagerhaugh; Barrows Dunham; Bolza Baxter; George Tony Starkovich; Thomas G. Moore; John Rogers MacKenzie; Donald M. Wollam; Herbert Simpson; Mrs. Millie Markison; Benjamin F. Kocel; Paul Ross Baker; Curtis Davis; Evelyn Gladstone; Marvin Engel; Martin Trachtenberg; Carl Harvey Jackins.

The following took the First Amendment or objected to questions on grounds of pertinency, or both: Bernhard Deutch; John T. Watkins; Mrs. Goldie E. Watson; Lawrence Baker Arguimbau; Marcus Singer; Horace Chandler Davis; Lloyd Barenblatt; Lee Lorch, Robert M. Metcalf; Norton A. Russell.

The following purged themselves of contempt, and proceedings were dropped: Wilbur Lee Mahaney, Jr.; Francis X. T. Crowley; Richard E. Adams.

352 Court reversals: They were based on 341 U.S. 479 (1951). 1950 precedent: 340 U.S. 159 (1950).

352 ff. Griswold: *The Fifth Amendment Today* (Cambridge, Mass., 1955). For a more garbled essay taking Dean Griswold's position, see "Does Silence Mean Guilt?" by Laurent B. Frantz and Norman Redlich, *Nation*, June 6, 1953, pp. 471 ff.

353 ff. Hook: *Common Sense and the Fifth Amendment* (New York, 1957), p. 33.

354 Black on witnesses: *Harper's*, February 1936, p. 275.

354 (fn) McCloy on liberals: May 2, 1953 address, quoted in Taylor: *Grand Inquest*, p. 82.

355 Taylor: *Annals of the American Academy*, July 1955, pp. 114 ff.

355 Williams: *Fordham Law Review*, Vol. 24, 1955–56, p. 19.

356 Westin: *Commentary*, June 1953, pp. 537 ff.

356 Beck on Fifth: *Contempt*, p. 112.

356 ff. Immunity law: 64 Stat. 745.

357 Critics of law: See Leonard Boudin's *The Fifth Amendment, Freedom's Bastion*, *Nation*, Sept. 29, 1951, p. 258.

357 Frankfurter decision: 350 U.S. 422 (1955).

357 Walter suggestion: *H.*, Nov. 17, 1954, pp. 7116 ff.

358 Beck on immunity: *Contempt*, p. 121.

358 ff. Watkins hearing: *H.*, April 29, 1944.

359 Appeals Court: 233 F. 2d 681 (1956).

359 ff. Supreme Court: 354 U.S. 178 (1957).

359 (fn) Other decisions: 354 U.S. 298 (1957); 354 U.S. 234 (1957); 354 U.S. 363 (1957).

360 ff. Reactions to Watkins decision: Washington *Post*—June 19, 1957, p. 6; *New Republic*—July 1, 1957, pp. 9 ff.; Jackson—*C.R.*, June 27, 1957, p. 10534; Lawrence—*U. S. News,* June 28, 1957, pp. 152 ff.

361 ff. Barenblatt hearing: *H.*, June 28, 1954.

362 Appeals Court: 252 F. 2d 129 (1958).

362 ff. Supreme Court: 79 S. Ct. 1081 (1959).

363 Seattle hearing: *H.*, June 14, 1954.

364 Neo-fascist report: *R.*, Dec. 17, 1954.

365 ff. Walter quotes: on Communist issue—*N. Y. Times*, Nov. 17, 1954, p. 6; on Dies, McCarthy—*C.R.*, Aug. 4, 1954, pp. 13324 ff.; on Communist

Control Act—*C.R.*, Aug. 16, 1954, p. 14642; on employee—*N. Y. Times,*
Dec. 22, 1954, p. 15.
366   (fn) Clardy: *N. Y. Times,* Dec. 16, 1954, p. 20.

CHAPTER THIRTEEN

367   Number of hearings: See *Supplement to Cumulative Index to Publications
of the Committee on Un-American Activities, 1955–1960,* Washington,
D.C., June 1961.
367   Annual report: *R.,* Feb. 16, 1955.
368   (fn) McCarthy: *N. Y. Times,* Jan. 15, 1955, p. 7.
368   *Times* editorial: Jan. 23, 1955, p. 12.
368   Walter promise: *N. Y. Times,* Jan. 21, 1955, p. 7.
368 ff. Gojack hearings: *H.,* Feb. 28, March 1, 1955.
369   First Supreme Court decision: 369 U.S. 759 (1962).
369   Second Supreme Court decision: 86 S. Ct. 1689 (1966).
371 ff. Corsi case: Walter on Corsi—*N. Y. Times,* April 16, 1955, p. 1; Corsi on
charges—*N. Y. Times,* April 10, 1955, p. 1; State Dept. on Corsi—*N. Y.
Times,* April 9, 1955, p. 1.
372   (fn) Jackson: *H.,* June 28, 1955, p. 1535.
372   (fn) Scherer: *H.,* Sept. 3, 1958, p. 2787.
372 ff. Various hearings: Brooklyn policewoman—*H.,* May 3, 1955; peace
groups—Aug. 2–5, 1955; summer camps—July 25, 28, 29, Aug. 1, 1955;
diplomatic personnel—May 10, 11, 1956; O'Connell—June 1, 2, 1955
(quote) p. 594.
373 ff. Various hearings: Newark—*H.,* May 16–19, 1955; Los Angeles—April
16, 1956; Seattle—March 17–19, June 1, 2, 1955; Denver—April 15–18,
1956; Milwaukee—March 28–30, May 3, 1955; North Carolina—March
12–14, 1956.
374 ff. Gathings: *C.R.,* Feb. 23, 1956, p. 3215, and July 29, 1963, pp. 1359 ff.
375   Walter on entertainers: *N. Y. Times,* July 20, 1955, p. 1.
376   AWARE—A.F.T.R.A.: See John Henry Faulk's *Fear on Trial* (New
York, 1964); also Louis Nizer's *The Jury Returns* (New York, 1966),
Chapter 4.
376   A. Roosevelt on McCarthy: *N. Y. Times,* Aug. 16, 1955, p. 1.
376   A.C.L.U. on Committee: *N. Y. Times,* Aug. 15, 1955, p. 5.
376 ff. Entertainment hearings: *H.,* Aug. 15–18, 1955. Quote on Kazan—Aug.
18, p. 2440; Sullivan—Aug. 16 (also Aug. 1, 1955); Tyne—Aug. 15;
Seeger—Aug. 18 (quote) p. 2449.
378   Appeals Court on Seeger: 203 F. 2d 478 (1962).
379   Mostel hearing: *H.,* Oct. 14, 1955.
380   Communist bibliography: Arthur Sutherland and others: *Bibliography
of the Communist Program in the United States* (New York, 1955).
380   Criticisms of bibliography: See *N. Y. Times,* Oct. 29, 1955, p. 1.
380   Hutchins on Communist: *N. Y. Times,* Nov. 8, 1955, p. 34.
380   Legionnaire on Fund: *N. Y. Times,* June 11, 1956, p. 1.
380   Lewis on Fund: Quoted in *New Republic,* Sept. 26, 1955, p. 4.
381   Walter on Fund: *N. Y. Times,* June 11, 1956, p. 1.
381   Blacklisting report: Cogley: *Report on Blacklisting.*
381   (fn) Cogley: *N. Y. Times,* Aug. 15, 1956, p. 28.
382 ff. Blacklist hearings: *H.,* July 10–13, 17, 18, 1956. Cogley—July 10;
Forster—July 11; O'Neil—July 11; Hartnett—July 12; Milton—July 13;
Schmidt—July 13; Brewer—July 12; McNamara—July 13; Walter on
Fund—July 13; Sondergaard—July 13; Gilford—July 18.
385   Knowles hearing: *H.,* July 18, 1956. Walter quote—p. 5457.
385   (fn) Americans Alerted: Quoted in *New Republic,* Aug. 27, 1956, p. 13.

PAGE

386   Walter on tax exemption: *N. Y. Times*, Aug. 30, 1956, p. 12.
386 ff. N.L.R.B. hearings: *H.*, Dec. 13–15, 1955. Fuchs–Dec. 13.
386   *Saturday Evening Post* editorial: Dec. 10, 1955, p. 12.
387   E.C.L.C. petition: *N. Y. Times*, Feb. 15, 1956, p. 9.
387   Additional N.L.R.B. hearings: *H.*, Feb. 14–16, 21, 23, 24, 28, 29, March 1, June 20, 28, 1956. Smith–March 1; Witt–March 1; (fn) Rein–Feb. 21; (fn) Donner–June 28; (fn) Boudin–June 12; on lawyers, see *R.*, Feb. 23, 1959, and Walter's reiterated charge against Boudin–*H.*, Aug. 23, 1960, p. 1879.
387   McCarthy accusation: *N. Y. Times*, Nov. 16, 1955, p. 15.
389   Latham on employees: *Communist Controversy*, p. 129.
389   Walter on travel: *N. Y. Times*, May 23, 1956, p. 21.
389 ff. Passport hearings: *H.*, May 23–25, June 12–14, 1956. Uphaus–May 23 (quote), p. 4372; Robeson–June 12 (quotes), pp. 4499, 4506; Nathan– June 12 (quote), p. 4552; Miller–June 21 (quotes), pp. 14522, 14529. (fn) *Listen My Children–C.R.*, July 25, 1956, p. 14528.
393 ff. Contempt citations: *C.R.*, July 25, 1956, pp. 14491 ff. Simpson hearings –*H.*, June 4, 5, 1956; Davis hearing–*H.*, June 6, 1956; Kling hearing– *H.*, June 6, 1956 (quote), p. 4923. Multer to Jackson–*C.R.*, July 25, 1956, p. 14535.
394   Miller appeal: 259 F. 2d 187 (1958).
394   (fn) C.P. card: *H.*, July 26, 1951, pp. 1345 ff.; Miller quote–*N. Y. Times*, Aug. 25, 1957, p. 20.
394   Walter on "counterattacks": *N. Y. Times*, Nov. 12, 1956, p. 15.
395   Roosevelt hearing: *H.*, Nov. 12, 1956.
395 ff. Various hearings: Washington–*H.*, Nov. 12–14, 1956; Youngstown– Nov. 26, 28, 1956; Chicago–Dec. 3, 4, 1956; Los Angeles–Dec. 5–8, 1956; San Francisco–Dec. 11, 1956; Seattle–Dec. 13, 14, 1956.
395   A.C.L.U. on hearings: *N. Y. Times*, Dec. 10, 1956, p. 55.
395   Arens on Korea: *H.*, Dec. 5, 1956, p. 6712.
395   I.L.W.U. secretary-treasurer: *H.*, Dec. 11, 1956, p. 6681.
395   Party member on informer: *H.*, Dec. 3, 1956, p. 6491.
396   Wirin–Porter: *H.*, Dec. 7, 1956.
396   Marshall ouster: *H.*, Dec. 8, 1956.
396   (fn) Lawyer ouster–*H.*, Dec. 6, 1956.
396   California state bar: *N. Y. Times*, March 28, 1957, p. 24.
397   Walter on chairmanship: *N. Y. Times*, Nov. 21, 1956, p. 8.
397   Committee quote: *R.*, Jan. 17, 1956.
397   *The Great Pretense: R.*, May 21, 1956.

CHAPTER FOURTEEN

400   Committee on C.P.: *H.*, Sept. 5, 1958, p. 2902.
400   Tuck on C.P.: *H.*, Nov. 18, 1959, p. 1615.
400   *Crimes of Khrushchev: R.*, Jan. 8, 1960.
401   Shahn–Evergood hearings: *H.*, July 1, 1959.
401   Starobin hearing: *H.*, March 15, 1957.
401   1958 report: *R.*, May 20, 1958.
402   Supreme Court on State Dept.: 78 S. Ct. 1113 (1958).
402   Walter letter: *N. Y. Times*, June 23, 1958, p. 15.
402 ff. Musicians hearings: *H.*, Feb. 7, 8, April 9–12, 1957. Moulder quote– April 9, p. 612; Arens quote–April 10, p. 747; Earl Robinson–April 11 (quote), p. 72; (fn) *Gol-Dern Red–*April 9, p. 661.
403 ff. Show-business hearings: *H.*, May 8, June 18, 19, 1958.
404   American exhibition hearing: *H.*, July 1, 1959. Wheeler quote–p. 918.
404   (fn) Eisenhower comment: *N. Y. Times*, July 2, 1959, p. 3.

PAGE

404 ff. Morros story: *N. Y. Times*, Aug. 18, 1957, p. 1.
405　Stern on trip: *N. Y. Times*, Aug. 21, 1957, p. 1.
405　Morros book: *My Ten Years as a Counterspy*, with Charles Samuels (New York, 1959).
405　Walter on espionage: *N. Y. Times*, Aug. 22, 1957, p. 3.
405　Espionage hearings: *H.*, Oct. 7–9, 1957.
406　Sharp hearing: *H.*, Feb. 25, 1960. Sharp quote—p. 1301; Jackson to Sharp—p. 1316.
406　Walter on Sharp: *N. Y. Times*, Feb. 26, 1960, p. 6.
407　Jackson on N.C.C.C.: *C.R.*, April 20, 1960, pp. 8430 ff.
408　Artamonov hearing: *H.*, Sept. 14, 1960.
409　Faculty of Soc. Sci. hearing: *H.*, July 21, 22, 1959.
409　Chicago hearings: *H.*, May 6, 7, 1959.
409　A.C.A. hearings: *H.*, July 17–19, Aug. 2, 9, Oct. 9, 1957; Aug. 23, 24, 1960.
409　Seamen hearings: *H.*, July 7–8, 23, 1960.
409　Gary hearings: *H.*, Feb. 10, 11, 1958.
410　New Haven hearings: *H.*, Feb. 26, 27, 1957; quote—p. 179.
410 ff. Passport security hearings: *H.*, April 21–24, June 5, 1959.
411　Walter on Watkins decision: *N. Y. Times*, June 20, 1957, p. 12.
411　Scherer annoyance: *H.*, March 11, 1956, p. 408.
411　Communist Control Act: P.L. 83-637.
412　Printing equipment: P.L. 83-557.
412　Defense facilities: P.L. 87-474.
412　N.S.A.: P.L. 88-290.
412　*National Review:* Oct. 9, 1962, p. 255.
413　Omnibus Security Bill: See *Annual Report* for 1957, Feb. 19, 1958, p. 4.
413　Critics and defenders: See Frank Donner's *The Un-Americans* and William Buckley's *The Committee and Its Critics* (New York, 1962).
414　Fast on Committee: *N. Y. Times*, Feb. 22, 1957, p. 2.
414　Arens demand: *H.*, Oct. 2, 1957, p. 1651.
414　Tavenner technique: See *H.*, Oct. 22, 1959, p. 1229.
414　Witness's observation: *H.*, Sept. 3, 1958, p. 118.
414　Tavenner question: *H.*, Oct. 22, 1959, p. 1264.
415　March hearing (Pittsburgh): *H.*, March 10, 1959.
415　Chicago hearing: *H.*, May 7, 1959, p. 637. Packinghouse-worker quote —p. 637.
415　Moulder on publicity: *H.*, Oct. 22, 1959, p. 1256.
416　Pittsburgh and Chicago hearings: *H.*, Oct. 22, 1959, p. 1256.
416　Washington hearings: June 7, 1960.
417　Hoover on C.P.: *H.*, Sept. 5, 1958, p. 2903.
417　Doyle on Hoover: *H.*, April 9, 1957, p. 678.
417　Willis on Hoover: *H.*, May 9, 1957, p. 1069.
417　Hoover letter: *N. Y. Times*, Nov. 14, 1957, p. 39.
418　Eaton interview: *N. Y. Times*, May 5, 1958, p. 1.
418　Scherer on Eaton: *N. Y. Times*, May 8, 1958, p. 29.
418　Arens on subpoena: *N. Y. Times*, May 20, 1958, p. 40.
418　A.C.L.U.: *N. Y. Times*, May 21, 1958, p. 28.
418 ff. *Times* compliment: Sept. 1, 1957, IV, p. 8.
419　*Times* criticism: Sept. 24, 1958, p. 20.
419　Douglas–Humphrey: *C.R.*, May 29, 1958, p. 9830 ff.
419　Walter retreat: *N. Y. Times*, July 1, 1958, p. 36.
419　Eaton last word: *N. Y. Times*, July 11, 1958, p. 17.
419 ff. Braden–Wilkinson hearing: *H.*, July 30, 1958; Wilkinson quote—p. 2681.
420　Court decisions: Wilkinson—81 S. Ct. 567 (1961); Braden—81 S. Ct. 584 (1961).

PAGE

421 ff. Other decisions: Deutch—81 S. Ct. 1587 (1961); six contempt convictions—82 S. Ct. 1038 (1962); Silber—82 S. Ct. 1287 (1962); Grumman —81 S. Ct. 1560 (1962); Yellin—347 U.S. 109 (1963); Hartman (note) —82 S. Ct. 1574 (1962); Turoff (note)—291 F. 2d 864 (1961); Shelton (note)—327 F. 2d 601 (1963).

421 ff. Here, in summary, are the outcomes of the contempt cases that arose between 1957 and 1960. Frank Wilkinson and Carl Braden were convicted and sentenced to twelve months in jail for refusing to answer questions in the 1958 Atlanta hearings without taking the Fifth Amendment. Paul Rosenkrantz was given three months for doing the same thing in the 1958 Boston hearings. Donald C. Wheeldin got thirty days and a fine of $100 for failing to respond to a subpoena in Los Angeles in 1958. No true bill was delivered against Edwin A. Alexander, who testified extensively in Chicago in May 1959 about his disillusioning experiences with the Communist Party but refused to give names on grounds of conscience. The indictment against Sidney Herbert Ingerman, who took a similar position in Buffalo in 1957, was dismissed. The Supreme Court's 1962 decision in the case of Norton Anthony Russell that his indictment had been insufficient was applied to the benefit of Louis Earl Hartman, who had relied on the newly delivered Watkins decision in San Francisco in June 1957, and to Martin Popper, an attorney who had declined to talk about his alleged C.P. membership in the Washington passport hearings of April 1959. (Russell was reindicted and acquitted in March 1964 because it had not been shown that he was aware of the subject under inquiry at his hearing in 1955—another effort by the judiciary to tighten up Committee procedures.) The Supreme Court's decision regarding executive hearings, handed down in the case of Edward Yellin, an alleged "colonizer" who was uncooperative in Gary, Indiana, in February 1958, benefited three other witnesses cited in Gary—Robert Lehrer, Alfred James Samter, and Victor Malis. Also benefiting from the Yellin decision were Frank Grumman and Bernard Silber, in their retrial after their first conviction had been overturned for a faulty indictment, and Sidney Turoff, who had defied the Committee in Buffalo in October 1957. (Turoff's first conviction was reversed by the Court of Appeals, which found the admission in his trial of detailed testimony of his C.P. activities to be highly prejudicial.) The indictment against Harvey O'Connor, head of the Emergency Civil Liberties Committee, who threw his subpoena to the floor when it was served on him at a rally in Newark in September 1958, was dismissed following a ruling by the Court of Appeals in a related case that a subpoena must be authorized by the full committee and is invalid if authorized by the chairman alone. And, as already noted, twelve contempt citations growing out of the visit to San Juan were dismissed upon the district court's decision that the Committee had no jurisdiction beyond the limits of the continental United States.

423 Robeson–Davis–Gray hearings: H., Feb. 2–5, 1960.

423 Los Angeles Negro: H., Sept. 3, 1958.

423 Newark Negro: H., Sept. 4, 1958; quote—p. 2837.

423 Newark hearings: H., Sept. 3–5, 1958 (recess), p. 2902.

423 San Juan hearings: H., Nov. 18–20, 1959.

423 Chicago hearing: H., May 5, 1959.

424 San Francisco, 1957: H., June 18–21, 1957.

424 Suicide note: N. Y. Times, June 18, 1957, p. 23.

424 Widow's charge: N. Y. Times, June 19, 1957, p. 18.

425 Rayburn on TV: N. Y. Times, June 21, 1957, p. 12.

425 A.C.L.U.: San Francisco Chronicle, June 6, 1959, p. 1.

PAGE

425 Los Angeles hearings: *H.*, Feb. 24, 25, 1959.

426 Walter on postponement: S. F. *Chronicle*, June 12, 1959, p. 7.

427 Truman on Committee: *N. Y. Times*, April 30, 1959, p. 17.

427 ff. J. Roosevelt speech: *C.R.*, April 25, 1960, pp. 864 ff.

428 Scherer response: *C.R.*, May 5, 1960, p. 9649.

428 ff. San Francisco, 1960 hearings: *H.*, May 12–14, 1960. Prussion–May 13; Hartle–May 12 (quote), p. 1957; Fishman–May 12; "Honorable beaters. . . ."–May 13, p. 2065; "halfway like a nut"–May 13, p. 2013; Arens on emasculation–May 14, p. 2135; Brown appearance–May 14.

430 Wheeler on "decent people": S.F. *Chronicle*, May 13, 1960, p. 1.

431 *Communist-Led Riots:* R., Oct. 7, 1960.

431 Willis on disagreeable people and "worst incident": S.F. *Chronicle*, May 14, 1960, p. 1.

431 Scherer on riots: *C.R.*, June 2, 1960, pp. 11760 ff.

431 *Communist Target–Youth: R.*, July 1960.

431 Views of riots: For contrasting views, see Donner: *The Un-Americans*, pp. 190 ff. and Buckley: *The Committee*, pp. 176 ff.

432 *Operation Abolition: R.*, Nov. 8, 1957.

432 Scherer harangue: *H.*, May 14, 1960, pp. 2170 ff.

433 Hoover on riots: *Communist Target–Youth.*

434 Students' statement: *N. Y. Times*, June 2, 1960, p. 3.

CHAPTER FIFTEEN

435 Rayburn on Walter: *N. Y. Times*, June 26, 1961, p. 18.

435 ff. Fund for Social Analysis hearings: *H.*, May 31, June 7, Aug. 10, 1961.

436 National Assembly for Democratic Rights hearings: *H.*, Oct. 2, 3, 1961.

436 Cuba–British Guiana groups hearings: *H.*, Nov. 14, 15, 1962.

436 Fair Play for Cuba Committee: *R.*, Nov. 2, 1962. *H.*, Nov. 20–22, 1961.

437 Communications union hearings: *H.*, Oct. 26, 27, Nov. 29, 1961.

437 Soviet propaganda hearings: *H.*, May 9, 10, 17, July 11, 12, 1962.

437 Youth festival hearings: *H.*, April 25, 27, Oct. 4, 1962.

437 Russia–China hearings: *H.*, May 22, 24, 25, 1962.

437 Cleveland hearings: *H.*, June 4–7, 1962.

437 ff. W.S.P. hearings: *H.*, Dec. 11–13, 1962.

438 *National Review* on W.S.P.: Jan. 15, 1963, p. 24.

438 ff. W.S.P. hearings: New Yorker–*H.*, Dec. 11; Scarsdale lady–Dec. 11, p. 2074; Doyle on flowers–Dec. 12, p. 2126; Nittle on elusiveness–Dec. 12, p. 2139; Doyle apology–Dec. 12, p. 2126; Vassar lady–Dec. 12; former C.P. lady–Dec. 11; alleged Communist–Dec. 13; Mrs. Moos–Dec. 12; Dagmar Wilson–Dec. 13 (quote), p. 2200.

441 SANE statement: Quoted in *Nation*, March 11, 1961, p. 201. See Dodd's speech, *C.R.*, May 25, 1960, pp. 11632 ff.

442 Wilson on Fifth: *N. Y. Times*, Dec. 14, 1962, p. 1.

443 E. K. Roosevelt on Walker: *Between the Lines*, April 8, 1962.

443 Tribute to Walter: *R.*, Aug. 10, 1964, p. 157.

444 Tribute to Doyle: *R.*, Aug. 10, 1964, p. 158.

444 ff. Cuba hearings: *H.*, May 6, 7, 23, July 1, 2, Aug. 5, Sept. 12, 13, Oct. 16, Nov. 18, 1963; Sept. 3, 4, 28, 1964. Friendly witnesses–Sept. 12, 1963; witness on "framing"–Sept. 4, 1964, p. 2080; (fn) Supreme Court on travel–87 S. Ct. 574 (1967); Luce–Sept. 12, 1963, pp. 756–7; Bond –Sept. 3, 1964, pp. 2040–1.

445 For details of the Cuba trip, see Phillip Abbott Luce's *The New Left* (New York, 1960), pp. 61 ff. For an account of the formation and character of the P.L.M., see Jack Newfield's *A Prophetic Minority* (New York, 1966), pp. 149 ff. Also Luce, pp. 81 ff.

PAGE

448   Cuba elections quote: *H.*, Sept. 28, 1964, p. 2185.
448 ff. Stone on leftists: *N. Y. Times*, Sept. 14, 1963, p. 1.
449   Kennedy on Cuban travel: See Arthur Schlesinger, Jr.'s *A Thousand Days* (Cambridge, Mass., 1965), p. 700.
449   Senner question: *H.*, Sept. 4, 1964, p. 2150.
451   Nixon–Wilson–Allen case: 369 F. 2d 198 (1966).
452 ff. Freedom Academy hearings: *H.*, Feb. 18–20, April 7, 8, May 15, 20, 1964. Herlong–Feb. 20, p. 939; Harriman–Feb. 20; Berle–May 20 (quote), p. 1467; 1965 hearings–*H.*, March 31, April 1, 28, May 7, 14, 1965.
453 ff. Buffalo hearings: *H.*, April 29, 30, 1964. Minneapolis hearings: *H.*, June 24–26, 1964. Instructor–April 29; Wolkenstein–April 29, pp. 1608–9; Minneapolis lawyer–June 25, 1964; (fn) Court decision–86 S. Ct. 1148 (1966); Willis-Hall quotes–June 24, p. 1687.
456 ff. Chicago hearings: *H.*, May 25–27, 1965.
457   Names published: Chicago *American*, May 13, 1965, p. 1.
457   Willis on leaks: *H.*, May 25, 1965, p. 344.
457   Willis in Minneapolis: *H.*, June 25, 1964, p. 1834.
457   Willis–Criley exchange: Chicago *Daily News*, May 19, 1965, p. 1.
457   Stamler–Board of Health: *N. Y. Times*, June 3, 1965, p. 17.
458   Executive session made public: *H.*, June 22, 1965, pp. 557 ff.
459 ff. Chicago hearings: Nittle questions regarding Hall–*H.*, May 26, pp. 429, 436; Nittle questions regarding Stamler–May 27, pp. 508, 511, 524; Nittle–Armstrong exchange–May 27, p. 549.
461 ff. McNamara on source: *C.R.*, Oct. 18, 1965, pp. 26444, 26458.
462 ff. Jenner objections: *H.*, May 27, 1965, pp. 537 ff., 544, 547.
463   Appeals Court decision: 371 F. 2d 413 (1966).
463 ff. Contempt citations: *C.R.*, Oct. 18, 1966, pp. 26384 ff. Ichord on executive hearings–p. 26450; Willis on Hall–p. 26412; Ichord on information –p. 26458; Willis on paid witnesses–pp. 26459, 26393.
465   K.K.K. citations: *C.R.*, Feb. 2, 1966, pp. 1657 ff.
465   McPhaul case: 81 S. Ct. 138 (1966). (fn) McPhaul on Kluxers: *C.R.*, June 30, 1952, p. 8626.
465   Weltner on K.K.K.: *C.R.*, Feb. 1, 1965, p. 1592.
466   K.K.K. pamphlet: Quoted in *Nation*, Oct. 3, 1942, p. 309.
466 ff. Johnson on TV: *N. Y. Times*, March 27, 1965, p. 1.
467    $50,000 appropriation: *C.R.*, April 14, 1965, pp. 7740 ff.
467 ff. K.K.K. hearings: *H.*, Oct. 19–22, 25–29, Nov. 1–4, 1965. (Transcript of the 1966 hearings not available at this writing.) Shelton–Oct. 20; used-car dealer–Oct. 22 (quote) Washington *Post*, Oct. 23, 1965, p. 1; Woodle–Oct. 22.
470   Willis bill: (H.R. 15678) *C.R.*, June 14, 1966, pp. 12503 ff.
470 ff. Hearings on Willis bill: *H.*, July 20–22, 1966.
471   A.C.L.U. on Willis bill: *H.*, July 21, 1966.
471   Katzenbach on bill: *H.*, July 20, 1966.
471   Ichord on bill: *C.R.*, April 5, 1967, p. 3531. See also *R.*, Sept. 19, 1967, where Culver joins Ichord in opposition.
471   Pool bill: (H.R. 12047) *C.R.*, Oct. 12, 1966, pp. 2517 ff. Edwards on passage–p. 25183.
472   Hearings on Pool bill: *H.*, Aug. 19, 22, 23, 1966. Attorney General– Aug. 23, p. 1337. See also *R.*, May 31, 1967, which contains Culver's dissent.
473   (fn) Willis on Nazi Party: *N. Y. Times*, Feb. 10, 1966, p. 2.
473 ff. Vietnam hearings: *H.*, Aug. 16–19, 22, 23, 1966.
473   (fn) Court decision: 85 S. Ct. 1116 (1965).
474   (fn) American Council on Education: *N. Y. Times*, July 15, 1967, p. 27.

PAGE

474 ff. Luce testimony: *H.*, Aug. 16, 1966. Prior appearance—*H.*, Sept. 13, 1963. See *The New Left.*

475   Luce payment: *C.R.*, Oct. 20, 1966, p. A5454.

475   (fn) Ichord: *H.*, Aug. 18, 1966, p. 2649.

476 ff. Vietnam hearings: Kinoy ouster—*H.*, Aug. 17, pp. 1026–27; asst. D.A.— Aug. 17 (pamphlet quote) p. 1078; Ichord quote—Aug. 17, p. 1070; preamble to P.L.M. constitution—Aug. 17, p. 1023; witness to Pool— Aug. 16, p. 986; (fn) Nittle–Gordon exchange—Aug. 14, p. 984; Stanford student—Aug. 18, p. 1169; West Coast organizer—Aug. 19, p. 1203; "yes, I am a Communist"—Aug. 19, p. 1195; "I am a P.L.P. member"— Aug. 19, p. 1205; Pool conclusion—Aug. 19, p. 1212.

479   Dirksen on hearings: *N. Y. Times*, Aug. 21, 1966, p. 2.

481   W.S.P. leader: Donna Allen in *Liberation*, Oct. 1966, p. 7.

481   Pool to V.F.W.: *N. Y. Times*, Aug. 27, 1966, p. 15.

CHAPTER SIXTEEN

483   Espionage hearings: Transcript not available at this writing.

483   President's statement: *N. Y. Times*, May 3, 1967, p. 5.

483   Rusk statement: *N. Y. Times*, April 17, 1967, p. 9.

483   Lodge statement: *N. Y. Times*, April 27, 1967, p. 10.

483   Flag-burning bill: (H.R. 10480) *C.R.*, June 20, 1967, pp. H.7488 ff.

483   Liberal on Pool: *N. Y. Times*, June 19, 1967, p. 28.

483   Report on peace demonstrations: *R.*, March 31, 1967. Willis foreword— pp. 1–2.

484   Dies on social equality: Quoted in Gellerman's *Martin Dies* (New York, 1944), p. 245.

484 ff. Willis on "preliminary inquiry": See *C.R.*, Jan. 30, 1967, pp. 720 ff.

485   Hoover article: *C.R.*, Aug. 29, 1966, pp. 2007 ff.

485   Willis to civil rights leaders: *C.R.*, Jan. 30, 1967.

486   Anti-riot bill: (H.R. 421) *C.R.* July 19, 1967, pp. H.8924 ff. See *N. Y. Times*, July 27, 1967, p. 1, for Willis on riots.

486   "Secret" staff study: *N. Y. Times*, Aug. 3, 1967, p. 16.

486   Fall 1967 hearings: No transcript available at this writing.

486   Willis on dissenters: *C.R.*, May 8, 1967, p. A5178.

487 ff. *New Republic* editorial: April 29, 1967, pp. 3–4.

487   Bettina Aptheker: *New Republic*, June 10, 1967, pp. 34–35

488   Edwards on Committee: *C.R.*, Feb. 25, 1965, p. 3647.

489   Fortas on hearings: *Atlantic*, Aug. 1953, pp. 42 ff.

490   (fn) Ashbrook: *C.R.*, Feb. 25, 1965, p. 3658.

490   (fn) Oliver: *N. Y. Times*, Jan. 29, 1961, p. 43.

491   Willis on liberals: *C.R.*, Feb. 25, 1965, p. 3667.

Selected Bibliography

Association of the Bar of the City of New York. *The Federal Loyalty-Security Program*. New York, 1956.

Barth, Alan. *The Loyalty of Free Men*. New York, 1952.

———. *Government by Investigation*. New York, 1955.

Beck, Carl. *Contempt of Congress*. New Orleans, 1957.

Bentley, Elizabeth. *Out of Bondage*. New York, 1951.

Bessie, Alvah. *Inquisition in Eden*. New York, 1965.

Biddle, Francis. *The Fear of Freedom*. New York, 1951.

Buckley, William F., and the editors of the *National Review*.

———. *The Committee and Its Critics*. New York, 1962.

Carr, Robert K. *The House Committee on Un-American Activities, 1945–1950*. Ithaca, N.Y., 1952.

Chambers, Whittaker. *Witness*. New York, 1952.

———. *Cold Friday* (edited by Duncan Norton-Taylor). New York, 1964.

Cogley, John. *Report on Blacklisting* (two volumes). New York, 1956.

Dies, Martin. *The Trojan Horse in America*. New York, 1940.

———. *The Martin Dies Story*. New York, 1963.

Donner, Frank. *The Un-Americans*. New York, 1961.

Gellerman, William. *Martin Dies*. New York, 1944.

Griswold, Erwin N. *The Fifth Amendment Today*. Cambridge, Mass., 1955.

Hiss, Alger. *In the Court of Public Opinion*. New York, 1957.

Hook, Sidney. *Heresy, Yes–Conspiracy, No!* New York, 1953.

———. *Common Sense and the Fifth Amendment*. New York, 1957.

Howe, Irving and Lewis Coser. *The American Communist Party*. New York, 1962.

Kahn, Gordon. *Hollywood on Trial*. New York, 1948.

Kempton, Murray, *Part of Our Time*. New York, 1955.

Latham, Earl. *The Communist Controversy in Washington*. Cambridge, Mass., 1966.

Lovett, Robert Morss. *All Our Years.* New York, 1948.

Matthews, Joseph B. *Odyssey of a Fellow Traveler.* New York, 1938.

Nixon, Richard. *Six Crises.* New York, 1962.

Ogden, August Raymond. *The Dies Committee.* Washington, D.C., 1945.

Oxnam, G. Bromley. *I Protest.* New York, 1954.

Seldes, George. *Witch Hunt.* New York, 1940.

Stripling, Robert E. *The Red Plot Against America* (Edited by Bob Considine). Drexel Hill, Pa., 1949.

Taylor, Telford. *Grand Inquest.* New York, 1955.

Trumbo, Dalton. *The Time of the Toad.* Hollywood, Calif., 1949.

Warren, Frank A., III. *Liberals and Communism.* Bloomington, Ind., 1966.

Index

Abraham Lincoln Brigade, 99
Abt, John, 248 *n.*, 250, 254, 289, 436
academic freedom, 330–332
Acheson, Dean, 252, 267, 337, 359 *n.*
Actors Equity, 300
Adams, Arthur, 242, 274, 275, 284
Adams, Sherman, 346, 348 *n.*
Adamson, Ernie, 170–172, 174, 177, 182, 183, 187, 189
Addams, Jane, 38
Adler, Larry, 383
A. F. of L., 28, 32–34, 55, 76, 153, 187, 196, 289, 301, 323, 381
Agee, James, 216
Agricultural Adjustment Administration, 254
Agriculture, Department of, 84, 91
Alabama Knights of the K.K.K., 468
Alabama Rescue Service, 468
Alien and Sedition laws, 14, 229, 492–493
Allen, Donna, 451
Alliance, Inc., 376
Allis-Chambers Company, 199
Amalgamated Clothing Workers, 158
Amerasia affair, 360 *n.*
America First movement, 8
America First Party, 181
American Artists Professional League, 404
American Association for the Advancement of Science, 239–241
American Association of School Administrators, 326
American Association of University Professors, 327
American Bar Association, 380
American Bill of Rights, 74, 151, 377
American Civil Liberties Union, 8, 18, 30, 32, 43 *n.*, 72, 127, 155, 165, 227–228, 338, 369, 376, 386, 418, 425, 426, 470–471, 473–477, 486 *n.*
American Coalition Committee on National Security, 29–30
American Coalition of Patriotic, Civil and Fraternal Societies, 198
American Committee for Cultural Freedom, 386
American Committee for the Protection of the Foreign Born, 141, 395

American Committee to Save Refugees, 177
American Communications Association, 99, 409
American Council of Christian Churches, 333
American Federation of Television and Radio Artists, 323, 376
American Friends Service Committee, 380
American Gentile League, 17
American Labor Party, 100, 145–146, 160, 288
American League Against War and Fascism, 37, 39, 69–70, 141, 148
American League for Peace and Democracy, 19, 30, 37, 49, 54, 69–75, 77, 79, 85–87, 110–111, 126, 131, 133, 145, 148, 164
American Legion, 17–18, 25, 48, 49, 60, 90, 153, 154, 168, 223, 249, 309, 335, 380–383, 397, 399, 402, 452, 489, 493–494
American National Exhibition, 404
American Nationalists, Inc., 60
American Nazi Party, 444, 466, 473
American Patriots, Inc., 41
American Peace Crusade, 460
American Peace Mobilization, 123–124, 148
American People's Mobilization, 124, 148
American Revolution, 65, 479, 492
American-Russian Institute, 249
American Security Council, 461–462
American Shakespeare Festival, 404
American Slav Congress, 282
American-Soviet Science Society, 232
American Student Union, 75, 77, 81, 82, 86, 91, 145, 440
American University, 386
American Youth Congress, 75, 77–80, 82, 86, 123, 341
American Youth Crusade, 460
American Youth for Democracy, 199, 200
Americans for Democratic Action, 331, 364, 380, 392, 486 *n.*
Amtorg Trading Corporation, 6–8
Anderson, Clinton P., 144

[551]

Anderson, Paul Y., 57
Andrews, Bert, 288
anti-alien legislation, 98–99, 106–107, 244, 292, 315, 323, 352, 359 n., 367, 395, 413, 419 n., 429, 459, 471, 491–492
Anti-Defamation League, 383
Anti-Fascist Refugee Committee, 290
anti-Ku Klux Klan law, 17
anti-rat bill, 486–487
anti-riot bills, 485–487
anti-Semitism, 3–4, 10–12, 13–14, 34, 59–64, 90, 91, 94, 139, 167, 181, 215, 492
anti-war demonstrations, 483–487
Appell, Donald, 468
Aptheker, Bettina, 483, 487
Aptheker, Herbert, 436, 483, 487
Arens, Richard, 382–385, 388, 390, 391, 392 n., 395, 396, 399, 403, 404, 406, 410, 414–418, 420, 422, 423, 429, 443
Armstrong, Lucius, 460–462
Army-McCarthy hearings, 217 n., 320, 322
Ashbrook, John M., 433 n., 456 n., 467, 471, 473, 477, 482 n., 490 n.
Associated Farmers, 48
Associated Grocery Manufacturers of America, 84–85
Association of American Universities, 327
Association of Lithuanian Workers, 77–78
Atomic Energy Commission, 104 n., 232–233, 237, 276, 437
atomic espionage, 182–183, 187, 191–192, 239–269, 273–282, 295, 326, 333, 336, 367, 373
Austrian Social Democrats, 37–38
Austrian Socialists, 127
Autopsy on Operation Abolition, 432
AWARE, 376, 377, 381–383, 418
Axelrod, Beverly, 476 n.
Axis propaganda, 127

Bacall, Lauren, 220
Baldwin, James, 390
Baldwin, Roger, 26, 36, 72, 339
Bankhead, William B., 16, 55, 59
Banking and Currency Committee, 125, 489
Barbusse, Henry, 70
Barenblatt, Lloyd, 361–363, 369, 419, 420, 463
Barringer, John M., 49
Barsky, Edward W., 178, 180, 222, 223
Barth, Alan, 360, 379
Baruch, Bernard, 376
Beam, Harry P., 118
Beck, Carl, 181, 286, 356, 358, 362 n.
Beck, George, 306–307
Benson, Elmer A., 49, 70
Bentley, Elizabeth, 235, 244–255, 259, 260, 266, 286, 287, 346, 377

Bentley, Eric, 210 n.
Berger, Hans, 184
Berkeley, Martin, 299, 302, 377
Berle, Adolf, 227, 228, 261, 267, 453
Berlin, Richard, 85
Berlin blockade, 226
Bernays, Edward L., 118
Bessie, Alvah, 210 n., 212, 214, 215, 224
Biberman, Herbert, 210 n., 213, 222, 224, 300
Biddle, Francis, 130, 135–137, 151, 159, 166
Black, Hugo L., 151, 152, 193, 223, 285, 312, 352, 354, 357, 362, 363, 369, 420 n., 421, 489
Black Legion, 13–14
Black Muslims, 466, 473
Black Nationalists, 390
blacklisting, 381–386
Block, Louis, 71
B'nai Brith, 383
Board of Economic Welfare, 131–133, 140, 253, 281, 405
Bogart, Humphrey, 102, 220
Bogdanov, Peter A., 7
Bolshevik Revolution, 65, 146, 173
Bolshevism, 5–6, 492–493
Bond, Yvonne Marie, 447
Bonner, Herbert C., 170 n.
Boorstin, Daniel, 330, 331
Boudin, Leonard, 387 n., 391
Bowles, Chester, 172
Braden, Carl, 420–423
Brady, Robert A., 126, 127
Brecht, Bertolt, 210, 218 n.
Brennan, William J., Jr., 312, 329 n., 362, 363, 421, 489
Bretton Woods Monetary Plan, 246, 253
Brewer, Roy N., 301, 381, 384
Bricker, John, 380
Bridges, Harry, 29, 33, 46–48, 54, 55, 98, 99, 114, 121, 126, 128, 145, 282, 388, 402, 410–411, 432
Broadway theater, 375–379, 391–394
Bromberg, J. Edward, 303
Brophy, John, 33, 34
Broun, Heywood, 40, 41
Browder, Earl, 37, 39, 42, 45, 49, 54, 64–68, 70, 75, 89, 90, 111, 159, 163, 166, 175, 176, 250
Brown, Archie, 429, 430
Brown, Cecil, 174 n.
Bruce, Donald C., 435 n., 484 n.
Bryan, Helen R., 178, 179
Buchanan, John H., Jr., 456 n., 467, 469
Buchman, Sidney, 306
Buckley, William, 418
Budenz, Louis F., 184–185, 190, 191, 330, 397
Buffalo hearings, 453–456
Buford, 5
Bukharin, Nikolai, 191

Bullitt, William C., 196, 197
Bunche, Ralph, 374
Bund camps, 17, 18, 64
Bundists, 4, 17–19, 21, 28, 59, 63–64, 105, 106, 114–115, 117, 128–129, 491
Bureau of Standards, 231, 237, 238
Burnham, James, 227, 397
Byoir, Carl, 103–104
Byrnes, James F., 216, 278, 346

Cagney, James, 102
California Teachers Association, 426
Cameron, J. M., 69
Camp Fire Girls, 30
Campbell, James Erwin, 60
Canadian spy trials, 191, 241, 275, 331
Cantor, Eddie, 222 *n.*
capitalism, 83, 84, 111, 126, 144, 145, 147, 163, 208, 221–222
Caraway, Thad, 13
Carey, James B., 86 *n.*, 283, 316
Carnegie Endowment for International Peace, 254, 259
Carnegie Fund, 165
Carnovsky, Morris, 303
Carr, Robert A., 198, 289, 290
Case, Francis H., 272, 279–281
Casey, Joseph E., 66, 85, 87, 139 *n.*
Castro, Fidel, 436, 444, 445, 448, 449
Catechetical Guild of St. Paul, 432
Celler, Emanuel, 98–99, 174, 179, 182, 229, 284, 393, 413
Central Bank of the U.S.S.R., 115
Central Intelligence Agency, 318
Chamberlain, John, 38 *n.*
Chambers, Whittaker, 244, 247–269, 286, 288, 310, 397
Chaplin, Charles, 173, 199
Chapman, Oscar, 70
Chessman, Caryl, 430
Chevalier, Haakon, 221
Chiang Kai-shek, 174, 309, 411 *n.*
Chicago Committee to Defend Democratic Rights, 423
Chicago Committee to Defend the Bill of Rights, 457
Chicago hearings, 358, 409, 456–464, 476, 489–490
Chicago Workers School, 349
Children's Services of Connecticut, 410
Christian Front, 59, 89, 90, 92, 93, 163
church investigations, 332–345, 405–406
Churchill, Winston, 175
C.I.O., 15–16, 19, 28, 29, 31–33, 47, 49, 50, 52, 53, 55, 56, 71, 85, 86, 99, 107, 120–122, 130, 143, 158–161, 169, 183, 184 *n.*, 186–189, 199, 250, 282, 283, 288, 316, 368, 369
Citizenship Institute, 79
Civil Liberties Committee, 15–16, 25, 28, 29, 34
Civil Rights Act of 1964, 449, 467
Civil Rights Bill of 1966, 471

Civil Rights Congress, 72–73, 199–200, 214, 223, 282, 311, 374, 392, 465 *n.*
civil rights movement, 165, 374–375, 422–423, 448, 458–459, 466–467, 484, 487
Civil Service Commission, 125, 126, 246, 348 *n.*, 364
Clapp, Gordon, 104 *n.*
Clardy, Kit, 322, 324, 325, 330, 331, 335, 338, 340–344, 351, 357, 363, 365, 366 *n.*, 451
Clark, Dane, 216
Clark, Ramsey, 472
Clark, Thomas C., 180, 193, 228, 240, 242, 243, 268, 360, 362, 421, 422
Clawson, Del, 456 *n.*, 482 *n.*
Clubb, Oliver Edmund, 310, 311
Cobb, Lee J., 377
Coffee, John, 70, 73, 87, 116, 183
Cogley, John, 381–384
Cohen, Milton, 463, 464, 489–490
Cohn, Roy, 418
Cold Friday, 262
cold war, 64, 76–77, 189, 202, 213, 335, 419
Cole, Lester, 210 *n.*, 215
college investigations, 274, 315–316, 325–332
Collins, Henry, 248 *n.*, 249, 259
Collins, Richard, 299, 307 *n.*
Columbia University, 127, 329–330
Columbia University Club, 118–119
Comintern, 8 *n.*, 68, 190, 191
Commerce Department, 233, 235, 244, 286
Committee on Militarism in Education, 339
Commonweal, 381, 382
Communist Control Act, 324, 365–366, 411, 420
Communist espionage, 105, 182–183, 191–192, 197, 226, 235, 239–269, 273–282, 295, 326, 333, 336, 367, 373, 400–401, 404–405, 427–428, 482–483
Communist International, 6, 66, 185
Communist Party of the U.S., 66, 67, 69, 192, 245, 247, 253, 287, 400, 454–455
Communist Political Association, 176
Communist propaganda, 6, 22, 43–46, 104, 109, 127, 203, 210, 216–217, 221, 299, 308, 412, 437
Communist transmission belts, 65, 83
Compulsory Testimony Act, 357
Condon, Edward U., 231–235, 237–239, 241, 247
Condon report, 231–234
Congress Against War, 69–70
Congressional immunity, 104, 284
conscientious objectors, 146
Conservative Society of America, 443
Constitutional Educational League, 90
Consumers National Federation, 111

Consumers Research, 41, 83, 85
Consumers Union, 83–85, 127
contempt citations, 190–194, 211, 277–278, 283–286, 305–306, 311–312, 351–352, 375, 378, 391, 393–394, 408–409, 414, 419, 421–422, 451–452, 464–465, 475 n.
Cooper, Gary, 209, 299
Coplon, Judith, 273
Corcoran, Howard F., 473–474
Corcoran, Tommy, 473
C.O.R.E., 467
Corsi, Edward, 370–372
Coser, Lewis, 78
Costello, Frank, 354
Costello, John M., 152, 153, 155, 159
Coughlin, Father, 30, 42, 89, 91, 164, 181
Council Against Atomic and Hydrogen Bombs, 450
Council of the Arts, Sciences and Professions, 313
Counterattack, 384
Courtney, Wirt, 139 n.
Cowley, Malcolm, 127, 128, 204
Cox Committee, 144 n.
Criley, Richard, 457
Crop Insurance Program, 150
Crosley, George, 256–258
Crouch, Paul, 274, 298
Crum, Bartley, 211, 302
Cuba-travel hearings, 444–450, 474, 478
Cuban Institute for Friendship Among the Peoples, 445
Cuban missile crisis, 436
Culver, John C., 482 n., 487
Curran, Joseph, 75–77, 121, 123, 160
Currie, Lauchlin, 246, 251–253
Cvetic, Matthew, 282

Daily Worker, 6, 30, 38, 39, 66, 67, 96, 127, 134, 176, 184, 185, 201, 214, 304, 307, 339, 401, 403, 410–411
Daladier, Edouard, 67
Daughters of the American Revolution, 196, 227, 484 n., 493–494
Davenport, Russell, 204
Davies, Joseph E., 199
Davis, Benjamin, 423, 436
Davis, Robert Gorham, 330
Davis, William E., 393
Deatherage, George E., 60–62
defections, 268 n., 407–408, 412
Defense Department, 408, 410, 412
defense program, aliens in, 104–108, 111, 114
deficiency appropriation bill, 148–150
De Lacy, Hugh, 182, 323 n.
Demagogue Club, 52–53
Democratic Party, 29, 51–55, 101, 234, 296, 427
Dempsey, John J., 24, 51, 62, 65, 73, 85, 118
Dennis, Eugene, 192–193, 223

Department of Agriculture supply bill, 150
deportations, 207, 226
Detroit Federation of Musicians, 318
Detroit hearings, 317–318
Detroit riots, 486
Detroit sit-down strikes, 15–16, 21, 29, 49–51, 55, 161, 482
Deutch, Bernhard, 421
Dewey, John, 32, 34, 57
Dewey, Thomas E., 229, 240
DeWitt, John, 153
Dickstein, Samuel, 3–4, 9–24, 26, 28, 30, 110, 117, 466, 495
Dickstein Committee, 10, 30
Dickstein-McCormack hearings, 10–11, 103
Dies, Martin, 9, 13, 15, 16, 19–22, 24–30, 32–36, 41, 42, 45–65, 68, 70, 71, 73–75, 78, 80, 82–100, 102–105, 107–118, 120–136, 138–141, 143–145, 156–159, 161–166, 168–172, 180, 182, 186, 189, 200, 202, 231, 251, 270, 271, 309, 321, 322, 349, 354, 365, 372, 387, 416, 424, 427, 442, 466, 476, 482, 484, 491, 492
Dies Committee, 24–103, 118–120, 127, 130–131, 135, 137–143, 147, 152–166, 168–170, 175, 177, 179, 194, 198, 339, 341, 466
Dies resolution, 16, 19, 22–23
Dillinger, John, 56
Dimitrov, George M., 228
Dirksen, Everett M., 45 n., 141, 143, 149–150, 321, 336, 479
Disney, Walt, 208
Dmytryk, Edward, 212, 215, 218, 219, 222, 302
Dobrzynski, Zygmund, 31
Dodd, Thomas J., 441
Dodd, William E., Jr., 144, 145, 148, 150, 405
Dollfus regime, 37–38
Donner, Frank J., 82 n., 343 n., 387 n., 476 n.
Dos Passos, John, 38 n.
Douglas, Helen Gahagan, 179, 221, 274, 296
Douglas, Melvyn, 128, 222 n.
Douglas, Paul H., 32, 120
Douglas, William O., 193, 223, 312, 357, 362, 419, 421, 454 n., 489
Downey, Sheridan, 48
Doyle, Bernadette, 275
Doyle, Clyde, 297 n., 299, 308, 315, 340, 347, 373, 383, 396, 411, 417, 436–440, 442, 443
Draper, Paul, 383
Du Bois, W. E. B., 436
Duclos, Jacques, 176
Duggan, Laurence, 267–269
Dulles, John Foster, 367, 371, 372, 389, 402
Dumbarton Oaks Conference, 254
Dunham, Barrows, 331, 351, 436

Earle, George, 197
Early, Steve, 54
Earp, Wyatt, 423
Eastland, James O., 295, 374, 486
Eastman, Max, 380
Eaton, Cyrus S., 417–419, 422
Einstein, Albert, 327, 391
Eisenhower, Dwight D., 319, 320, 325, 333, 346, 347, 364, 370, 404 n., 407, 433, 437
Eisenhower, Milton, 155
Eisler, Gerhart, 184–185, 190–195, 204, 392
Eisler, Hanns, 204–207, 210 n., 223
Eliot, Thomas, 129, 130, 187
Eltenton, George C., 221
Emergency Civil Liberties Committee, 387, 417, 420, 423, 432, 446, 475, 486 n.
Emspak, Julius, 283, 284
Engels, Friedrich, 65, 185
Ernst, Morris, 227, 374
Esperanto Association of North America, 77–78
Espionage Act, 242, 413
Evergood, Philip, 401
Ezekiel, Mordecai, 71

Fabian Socialism, 209
Factory Acts, 7 n.
Faculty of Social Science, 409, 410
Fadiman, Clifton, 38 n.
Fahy, Jack, 144
Fair Employment Practices Commission, 179 n.
Fair Play for Cuba Committee, 436
Farm Equipment Workers Union, 316, 358
Farmer-Labor Party, 32, 49
Fascism, 6 n., 12, 15, 17, 19, 40, 56–57, 59, 62–63, 71, 79, 80, 86, 89, 90, 94, 103, 116, 117, 164, 202, 206–207, 230, 263, 403
Fast, Howard, 177, 181, 392, 414
F.B.I., 18, 47–48, 56, 103, 107, 110, 113–114, 132, 133, 158–159, 182, 184, 190, 234–239, 243, 244, 254, 267, 268, 273–275, 278, 279, 282, 283, 289, 293, 399, 405, 410, 415–418, 428,
Federal Communications Commission, 126–127, 140, 141, 144, 145, 151
Federal Council of Churches, 19
federal-employee investigations, 135–137, 140–152, 186–189, 237–244, 247, 287–288, 310, 386–389, 407–408
Federal Loyalty Review Board, 462
Federal Theatre and Writers Project, 25–26, 42–46, 55, 123
Federal Trade Commission, 85
Fellowship of Reconciliation, 38, 155
F.E.P.C. bill, 188
Ferrer, José, 304
Fiedler, Leslie, 259

Field, Marshall, 139, 198
Fifth Amendment, 238, 240, 249–251, 253, 259, 269, 274–277, 283–287, 289, 300, 301, 313, 323 n., 324 n., 351–366
fifth column, 106–107, 113, 122, 134
Filene, E. A., 118–119
First Amendment, 193, 210–211, 218 n., 220, 292, 298, 301, 313, 360, 362, 363, 377, 391, 421–422, 440, 454 n., 464, 473
Fischer, Ruth, 191
Fish, Hamilton, 6–10, 12–14, 18, 20, 30, 87, 116, 135, 143, 161, 176
Fish Committee, 9, 11–12, 24, 30, 34, 211, 338–339
Fishman, Irving, 412, 428–429
Flanagan, Hallie, 44, 46
Fly, James L., 127, 137
Flynn, Elizabeth Gurley, 175
Food, Tobacco and Agricultural Workers, 199
Forbes, Kenneth Ripley, 341 n.
Ford, Henry, 122
Ford Foundation, 379
Foreign Agents Registration Act, 128–129, 413, 420
Foreign Broadcast Information Service, 145
Foreman, Carl, 299
Forer, Joseph, 476 n.
Forster, Arnold, 383
Fortas, Abe, 304, 369, 489
Foster, William Z., 8, 68, 175, 176, 229, 250
Fourteenth Amendment, 468
Fourth Amendment, 96, 360, 391
Franco, Francisco, 99, 176, 177, 215, 338
Frankfurter, Felix, 5, 13, 151, 193, 357, 361, 362, 421, 422
Frazier, James B., Jr., 297 n., 399 n., 411
free speech, 175, 193, 222–223, 362, 451, 472
Freedom Academy, 452–453
Freedom Commission, 452
Frey, John P., 28–33, 50, 56, 107
Frey-Steele hearings, 29–30
Friends of New Germany, 11
Fuchs, Herbert, 386–388
Fund for Social Analysis, 435–436
Fund for the Republic, 352, 379–386, 417–418
Furry, Wendell, 331

Gadola, Paul V., 49, 50
Gailmore, William S., 174 n.
Gallagher, Buell, 328
Gallup Polls, 53–54, 87, 113, 220
Gardner, Ava, 220
Garfield, John, 199, 304
Garland, Judy, 220
Garland Fund, 339
Garner, John Nance, 16, 20, 54

Gathings, E. C., 374, 375
Gehrig, Lou, 130
Gellhorn, Walter, 201
General Motors, 28, 49–50
German-American Bund, 4, 17–19, 21, 28, 59, 63–64, 105, 106, 114–115, 117, 128–129, 491
German-American camps, 17, 18, 64
German Communist Party, 191, 205
German Library of Information, 109
German propaganda, 5, 104–105, 108, 109
German Railroad Office, 109
German-Soviet pact, 58, 65–67, 69, 71, 72, 76, 79, 81, 100, 112, 128, 133, 135, 160
German spies, 18, 28, 33, 103, 105, 117
German Tourist Bureau, 103
German Youth Movement, 17
Gilbert, Dudley Pierrepont, 60
Gilford, Jack, 384
Gitlow, Benjamin, 67, 68, 343, 344
Gojack, John T., 368–370, 421
Gold, Ben, 31, 121
Gold, Harry, 292 n.
Goldberg, Arthur, 422
Goldschmidt, Arthur, 144
Goldwater, Barry, 456 n.
Goldwyn, Sam, 218
Gollobin, Ira, 476 n.
Golos, Jacob, 245
Good Housekeeping, 84, 85
Gore, Albert, 144
Graham, Frank P., 202
Grand Dragons of Virginia and North Carolina, 468
Grapes of Wrath, 199
Gray, Jesse, 423
Great Atlantic and Pacific Tea Company, 103
Green, William, 196
Greenglass, David, 292 n
Griswold, Erwin N., 352–354, 357, 379–380
Gromyko, Andrei, 198
Grossman, Saul, 311–312
Groves, Leslie, 243, 279–281
Grumman, Frank, 421
Gutman, Jeremiah S., 476 n.

Hagerty, James, 346
Hall, Gus, 454–455
Hall, Leonard, 296
Hall, Yolanda F., 457–464, 489–490
Hammett, Dashiell, 181 n.
Hardman, J. B. D., 66
Harlan, John M., 362, 363, 421, 422
Harriman, W. Averell, 234, 236, 453
Harrington, Michael, 383
Harrison, Burr P., 272, 273, 277, 280, 283, 290
Harry Bridges Defense Committee, 126, 145
Hart, Edward J., 169, 171–173
Hart, Merwin K., 90

Hartle, Barbara, 428, 429
Hartnett, Vincent W., 376, 383
Harvard University, 330–331
Hatch Act, 159
Havenner, Franck, 102 n.
Hawkins, David, 277
Hayden, Sterling, 299
Hays, Arthur Garfield, 227 n.
Hayworth, Rita, 220
Healey, Arthur D., 24, 51, 62, 66
Healey's Irish Weekly, 10
Hearst, William Randolph, 127, 219
Hearst, William Randolph, Jr., 397
Hearst publications, 12, 60, 84, 85, 120, 128, 139, 153, 218, 237, 247
Hébert, F. Edward, 227, 255, 256, 268, 272
Hellman, Lillian, 181 n., 213, 305, 392
Henderson, Leon, 125, 126, 137
Hendricks, Joe, 140, 141, 143
Hepburn, Katharine, 220
Hercules powder-plant explosion, 105
Herlong, A. Sidney, Jr., 452
Hicks, Granville, 68, 69, 330, 331
Hill, Joe, 80
Hillman, Sidney, 56–57, 158–161
Hiskey, Clarence F., 274, 276, 283
Hiss, Alger, 165, 244, 248 n., 250, 252–269, 271, 281, 286–288, 291, 295, 301, 319, 353, 364, 367, 388
Hiss, Donald, 257
Hitler, Adolf, 10, 17, 26, 62–64, 66, 68, 71, 103, 104, 124, 139, 149, 157, 177, 206, 207, 418
Hitler-Stalin alliance, 58, 65–67, 69, 71, 72, 76, 79, 81, 100, 112, 128, 135, 160
Hitz, William, 456 n. 475
Hoffman, Clare, 142, 143, 150, 157, 163, 169, 297
Hoffman, Paul G., 385
Hollywood investigations, 29, 40 n., 86, 101–103, 172–174, 182, 187, 199, 202–203, 207–225, 298–309, 323, 404
Hollywood Ten, 210, 224, 298, 300–302, 313
Holmes, John Haynes, 344, 374
Holmes, Lola Belle, 462
Hook, Frank E., 91–93
Hook, Sidney, 57, 90, 328, 353, 354
Hoover, Herbert, 371
Hoover, J. Edgar, 47, 110, 113, 114, 183, 196, 199, 209, 227, 230, 240, 326, 332, 347, 348, 397, 399, 400, 416, 417, 431, 433, 439, 467, 485
Hopkins, Harry, 46, 54, 279–282
House Administration Subcommittees, 489
House Appropriations Committee, 148–149, 332
House Armed Services Committee, 407, 428
House Immigration Committee, 9

House Judiciary Committee, 108, 365, 389, 413, 428, 485
House Rules Committee, 6–8, 20, 87, 90–91, 121, 167, 168, 427, 471
House Ways and Means Committee, 428
Howe, Irving, 78
Huffman, Hazel, 123
Humphrey, Hubert H., 162, 419
Hungarian rebellion, 400
Hunt, H. L., 385
Hutchins, Robert M., 379, 380, 382

I Chose Freedom, 197
Ichord, Richard H., 443 *n.*, 461, 463, 464, 471, 477, 482 *n.*
Ickes, Harold L., 35, 40, 52–55, 65, 70, 75, 138, 144, 146–148, 151, 163, 170
impeachment, 46, 55, 94, 236, 242, 270, 474
Independent Citizens Committee of the Arts, Sciences and Professions, 102, 187
Institute for Propaganda Analysis, 118–120
Institute of Pacific Relations, 252, 295, 310
Internal Security Act, 291–294, 411–412, 454, 489, 492–493
International Electrical Workers Union, 283
International Labor Defense, 191, 199–200
International Longshoremen and Warehousemen's Union, 47, 282, 323, 395
International Monetary Fund, 252, 345, 348
International Red Cross, 472
International Seamen's Union, 76
International Student Service, 82
International Union of Electrical Workers, 316
International Workers Order, 95
Interstate and Foreign Commerce Committee, 488
Iron Curtain, 407, 419
I.W.W., 37

Jack, Hulan, 374
Jackson, Andrew, 52, 57, 236
Jackson, Donald L., 297 *n.*, 298, 299, 302, 304–306, 313, 322, 325, 330, 331, 333–336, 338, 340, 341, 345, 361, 365, 372, 384, 393, 405–407
Jackson, Gardner, 91, 92, 112, 166
Jackson, Robert H., 70, 108, 110, 111, 113, 194
Jacob, Hans, 174 *n.*
Jacobs, Paul, 383
Jagan, Cheddi, 436
Jahoda, Maria, 383
Japanese espionage, 128–131, 137, 153
Jarrico, Paul, 302, 307 *n.*
Javits, Jacob, 221, 222, 229, 234
Jefferson, Thomas, 52, 57, 493

Jefferson School of Social Science, 409
Jemison, Alice Lee, 35
Jencks case, 293
Jenner, Albert E., Jr., 324, 326, 327, 330, 346, 347, 460–463
Jenner Committee, 330–332, 348
Jerome, V. J., 205, 307
Johansen, August E., 399 *n.*, 428, 435 n.
John Reed Clubs, 36
Johnson, Lyndon B., 122, 166, 169, 184, 294, 457 *n.*, 466–467, 469, 473, 478
Johnson, Manning, 342, 376
Johnston, Eric, 196, 198, 217, 309, 375
Joint Anti-Fascist Refugee Committee, 176–178, 180, 190–191
Joint Atomic Energy Committee, 276, 280
Jones, LeRoi, 390
Jones, Webster, 328
Jordan, G. Racey, 279–281
Josephson, Barney, 201
Josephson, Leon, 192–193, 201
Josephson, Mrs. Leon, 201
Justice Department, 25, 54–55, 75, 87, 93, 108, 110, 111, 113–114, 128, 129, 135, 137, 145, 192, 194, 207, 228, 242, 245, 255, 264, 265, 269, 273, 293, 294, 304, 314–315

Kallett, Arthur, 84
Kamp, Joseph P., 90, 157
Katz, Charles J., 313
Katzenbach, Nicholas deB., 467, 471
Kaye, Danny, 22 *n.*
Kazan, Elia, 303, 377, 392
Kazin, Alfred, 67
Kearney, Bernard W., 272 *n.*, 304, 322, 331, 333, 347–349, 410
Keefe, Frank B., 144, 148
Kefauver, Estes, 317, 354
Kempton, Murray, 40, 77, 224
Kennedy, John F., 407, 434, 439
Kennedy, Robert, 449
Kenny, Robert, 210, 211, 313
Kent, Rockwell, 436
Kerr, John H., 144, 149
Kerr Committee, 144–149
Khrushchev, Nikita, 397, 400
King, Martin Luther, 423, 469
Kingdon, Frank, 135
Kinoy, Arthur, 476, 478
Kirchwey, Freda, 57, 90, 138, 204
Kling, Anne Yasgur, 393–394
Knight, Frances G., 402
Knights of Columbus, 170
Knights of the White Camelia, 60, 62
Knowles, Harper, 48
Knowles, Mrs. Mary, 385
Koestler, Arthur, 380
Korean War, 223, 266, 288, 291, 295, 297–299, 310–311, 315, 317, 331, 335, 352–353, 387, 390, 411 *n.*, 482
Kramer, Charles, 248 *n.*

Kravchenko, Victor A., 197, 198
Krebs, Allen M., 477 n., 490
Krivitsky, Walter, 67–68
Krock, Arthur, 52
Ku Klux Klan, 17, 115 n., 183, 427, 465–471, 492
Kuhn, Fritz, 15, 17, 28, 63–65, 89, 90, 115
Kunstler, William, 476
Kunze, Gerhard Wilhelm, 115
Kunzig, Robert L., 338–342, 344, 346, 348, 359
Kusnitz, Rose Chernin, 396
Kyffhauserbund, 129

Labor Department, 25, 29, 47, 55, 206
Labor Department supply bill, 150
labor strikes, 15–16, 21, 29, 47, 49–51, 55, 107–108, 111, 137, 161, 184, 187, 199, 316, 482
Labor's Non-Partisan League, 91
La Follette, Robert M., 15–16, 21, 25, 267 n.
La Follette Committee, 15–16, 25, 29, 34
La Guardia, Fiorello, 6
Lamont, Corliss, 179, 449
Landis, Gerald W., 170 n.
Landis, James M., 47, 48, 128
Lardner, Ring, Jr., 210 n., 212, 223, 270
Lash, Joseph P., 77, 80–83, 128
Laski, Harold, 176
Lasky, Victor, 376
Lasser, David, 141, 144
Latham, Earl, 266 n., 389
Lattimore, Owen, 295, 310
Lautner, John, 409, 410
Lavery, Emmet, 46, 210
law profession, 139, 290, 313–314, 387 n., 396, 486 n.
Lawrence, David, 361
Lawson, John Howard, 211, 212, 214, 215, 222, 302, 307
Lear, Edward, 22
League for Constitutional Government, 41–42
League of American Writers, 111, 147, 148, 177
League of Nations, 20
League of Women Shoppers, 84, 127
Lederer, Francis, 102
Leech, John L., 101, 102
Lenin, Nikolai, 65, 383, 400
Lenin Peace Prize, 450
Lenin School, 191, 452
Levine, Isaac Don, 267–269
Lewis, Fulton, Jr., 279–281, 380, 407
Lewis, Fulton, III, 431, 432, 484 n.
Lewis, John L., 31, 33, 56–57, 120, 160
liberals 53–54, 56, 62, 65–66, 71, 82, 86, 89, 90, 92, 98, 102, 117, 135, 138, 164, 165, 167, 233, 261
Library of Congress, 187, 188, 321
Liebling, A. J., 244

Lightfoot, Claude, 460–461
Lilienthal, David, 104 n., 276
Lincoln, Abraham, 57, 493
Lindbergh, Charles, 202
Lindeman, Eduard C., 120
Lippmann, Walter, 13
Liuzzo, Viola Gregg, 466–467
Long, Huey, 181
Lovestone, Jay, 83, 366 n.
Lovett, Robert Morss, 36, 144, 146–151, 164
Lowenthal, Max, 289, 290
Loy, Myrna, 220
loyalty oath, 152, 374–375, 425
Loyalist Spain, 145, 146, 491–492
Lucas, Scott, 296
Luce, Phillip Abbott, 446–447, 474–475, 480
Lusk, Clayton R., 5
Lusk Committee, 5
Lyons, Eugene, 376

MacArthur, Douglas, 310
McCarran, Pat, 295, 309–311, 326
McCarran Act, 291–294, 436
McCarran-Walter immigration law, 340, 365, 370, 371, 395, 397, 446
McCarthy, Joseph R., 5, 19, 158, 163 n., 186, 199 n., 266, 270, 287, 295, 309, 311, 318, 319, 324, 326, 330, 332, 335, 337, 345, 349, 356, 364–368, 370, 372, 376, 379, 387–388, 480
McCloy, John J., 354 n.
McCormack, John, 10–13, 15, 28, 98, 142, 157, 168, 407, 451–452, 473
McCormack Committee, 12, 18, 24–25, 28
McCormack-Dickstein hearings, 10–11, 103
Macdonald, Dwight, 380
McDonough, Gordon L., 227
McDonough bill, 227–228
MacIntosh, Robert J., 399 n.
MacLeish, Archibald, 127–128
McLeod, R. W. Scott, 370, 371
McMahon bill, 183, 233
McMichael, Jack R., 341–343, 355
McNamara, Francis J., 384, 397, 443 n., 437, 461, 462, 464, 473, 482 n.
McNutt, Paul V., 216
McPhaul, Arthur, 311, 312, 465
McSweeney, John, 272, 273
Madden, J. Warren, 151
Maddox, Lester, 465
Magnes, Judah L., 344
Maltz, Albert, 211–214, 221, 222, 302
Manhattan Project, 234, 240–241, 243, 275, 276
Manion, Clarence, 397
Mann, Thomas, 36
Marcantonio, Vito, 41, 43, 87, 99, 100, 117, 127, 130, 132, 142, 149, 160, 163, 178, 179, 182, 183, 184 n., 191, 195, 200, 221, 230, 284, 288, 296, 297

March, Fredric, 102, 199
Margolis, Ben, 313
Markward, Mary, 314–315
Marshall, Daniel G., 396
Marshall, George C., 179–181, 319
Marshall, Thurgood, 489
Marshall Plan, 316
Martin, Joe, Jr., 187, 297, 365
Martin, William H., 407–408, 412
Marx, Karl, 65, 111, 185, 205, 229, 262, 400
Marxism, 91, 101, 126, 163, 209, 216, 332, 435–436, 445, 456
Marxism-Leninism, 77, 400, 479
Marzani, Carl, 436
Mason, Noah M., 24, 32, 71, 73, 105, 123, 162
Massachusetts Council of American-Soviet Friendship, 315, 339
Massachusetts Institute of Technology, 315–316, 339
Mather, Kirtley, 119
Mattei, Albert C., 102 n.
Matthews, J. B., 24, 35–42, 56, 65, 67, 70, 74, 75, 77, 80, 81, 83–86, 91, 108, 111, 118–121, 125, 127, 146, 147, 159, 160, 162–164, 168, 187, 188, 231, 270, 335–337, 341, 344, 406, 491, 492
Maverick, Maury, 14, 19, 22
Mayne, David, 91–94
Mellon, Andrew W., 5
Mencken, H. L., 32, 335
Menjou, Adolphe, 203, 209
Mesarosh, Stefab, 241
Messersmith, George, 206
Metcalfe, John C., 28, 33
Methodist Federation for Social Action, 341–342
Metropolitan Music School, 402–403
Meyer, Agnes, 326, 348
Michigan Committee for the Protection of the Foreign Born, 311–312
Michigan Council of the Arts, Sciences and Professions, 361–362
Military Affairs Committee, 153
Miller, Arthur, 391–394
Miller, Clyde, 119
Miller, William E., 399 n.
Milton, Paul R., 383
Minneapolis hearings, 453–456
Minutemen, 466, 473
Mission to Moscow, 199, 207, 216
Mitchell, Bernon F., 407–408, 412
Mizokliyk, Francik, 372 n.
Moley, Raymond, 227
Molotov, Vyacheslav, 69, 198
Montgomery, Robert, 209
Moos, Elizabeth, 440
Morford, Richard, 179–181
Morgenthau, Henry, 246, 252
Morgenthau Plan, 246, 252
Morros, Boris, 404–405
Moseley, George Van Horn, 59–62
Mosier, Harold G., 24, 56

Mostel, Zero, 379
Motion Picture Alliance for the Preservation of Ideals, 208, 216, 304
motion-picture industry, 29, 40 n., 86, 101–103, 172–174, 182, 187, 199, 202–203, 207–225, 298–309, 323, 404
Motion Picture Industry Council, 301, 308–309
Motion Picture Producers Association, 196, 217, 300, 375
Moulder, Morgan M., 272, 383, 402, 415, 427, 435 n., 443
Mundt, Karl E., 135, 139 n., 152, 155, 170, 173, 176, 179, 183, 185, 192, 195, 197, 227, 230, 238, 242, 255, 260, 265, 267–269, 294, 336–337
Mundt bill, 227–228
Mundt–Nixon bill, 228–230, 291
Murdock, John R., 170 n.
Murphy, Frank, 48–51, 54, 55, 75, 193
Murphy, George, 209
Murray, Philip, 120, 121, 161
Murrow, Edward R., 379–380
Musicians Union, 374, 403
Mussolini, Benito, 104
Myer, Dillon S., 155, 156

N.A.A.C.P., 141, 374, 375, 455–456, 484
Nagy, Ferenc, 228
Nathan, Otto, 391, 393, 394
Nation, The, 30, 57, 73, 89–91, 93, 138, 204, 259, 324
National Academy of Foreign Affairs, 453
National Assembly for Democratic Rights, 436
National Association of Manufacturers, 85, 119, 120
National Captive Nations Committee, 452–453
National Citizens Political Action Committee, 159
National Conference of Christians and Jews, 215
National Council of American-Soviet Friendship, 176, 179, 232, 233
National Council of the Churches of Christ, 333, 405–406
National Federation for Constitutional Liberties, 136, 176, 179, 199–200
National Guard, 49–50
National Guardian, 415, 450–451
National Labor Relations Act, 107
National Labor Relations Board, 41, 55, 71, 105, 107, 150, 203, 250, 267 n., 360, 386–388
National Lawyers Guild, 139, 290, 313, 387 n. 392, 486 n.
National Liberation Front, 472
National Maritime Union, 75, 76, 105
National Republic, 29, 34
National Review, 412, 476

National Security Agency, 407, 408, 412
National Youth Administration, 78, 100, 150, 170
Native Sons of the Golden West, 154
Nazi Party, 94
Nazi propaganda, 5, 9–11, 104–105, 108, 109
Nazi-Soviet pact, 58, 65–67, 69, 71, 72, 76, 79, 81, 100, 112, 128, 135, 160
Nazi spies, 18, 28, 33, 103, 105, 117
Nazis and Nazism, 15, 18–19, 21, 22, 28, 33, 59, 79, 82, 90, 116, 138, 147
Negro suffrage, 191
Nelson, John E., 9
Nelson, Steve, 241, 274, 275, 277, 285
New Deal, 19, 22, 25–26, 28–29, 35, 42, 43, 48, 50–54, 61, 65, 70, 71, 92, 107, 122, 128, 134, 137–138, 142, 145, 159, 161, 163, 182, 187, 248, 251, 260, 388–389
New Frontiers, 435
New Masses, 69, 134, 141, 173, 213, 306, 307, 310
New Republic, The, 5, 29 n., 30, 56–58, 69, 70, 74, 127–128, 134, 139, 204, 360, 487
New York State American Labor Party, 160
New York State Economic Council, 90
Newark riots, 486
Niebuhr, Reinhold, 36, 40, 134, 341, 386
Nimmo, Ray E., 48
Ninth Amendment, 391
Nittle, Alfred M., 399 n., 438–442, 443 n., 445, 446, 459–462, 478 n., 482 n.
Nixon, Richard M., 186, 190–192, 196–199, 208, 222, 227–229, 235, 237, 238, 240, 250, 251, 255–258, 264, 271, 273, 279–281, 283, 288, 289, 292 n., 294–296, 297 n., 319, 336, 364, 408, 492
Nixon, Russell, 436, 450–452
Non-Sectarian Anti-Nazi League, 19
North Vietnamese Red Cross, 478
Novikov, Nikolai, 176
nuclear test ban, 437–439, 442, 448
nuclear tests, 437–438
Nudism in Modern Life, 131–133
Nye Committee, 254, 256

Oberwinder, Hellmut, 28
O'Brien, John Lord, 385
O'Connell, Jerry J., 373
O'Daniel, W. Lee, 122
Odets, Clifford, 203, 207, 213, 303
Odyssey of a Fellow Traveler, 24, 40
Office of Civilian Defense, 128
Office of Facts and Figures, 127–128
Office of Price Administration, 125, 126, 150, 171–172, 405
Office of War Information, 150

Ogden, August Raymond, 64, 98, 118
O.G.P.U., 67–68, 246–247
Oliver, Revilo P., 490 n.
Olson, Culbert, 48, 106
Omnibus Security Bill, 413
O'Neil, James F., 383, 384
Operation Abolition, 432, 484 n.
Operation Correction, 432
Oppenheimer, Frank, 276, 277, 295
Oppenheimer, J. Robert, 221, 233, 238, 276, 277, 379–380
Ornitz, Samuel, 213
O'Shea, Thomas Humphrey, 100
Owens, Courtney E., 349 n.
Oxford Peace Pledge, 81
Oxnam, G. Bromley, 334, 337–342, 404

Paine, Thomas, 57
Papp, Joseph, 403
Paris Peace Conference, 273
Parker, Dorothy, 102, 103
Parks, Larry, 301–302
Parmalee, Maurice, 132, 133, 140
passport frauds, 116, 191–193, 201
passport legislation, 318, 389–390, 402, 410, 413
Patman, Wright, 103, 104
Patterson, Ellis, 48, 182
Patterson, Leonard, 342
Paul Reveres, 34
peace demonstrations, 483–487
Pearl Harbor, 128–130, 152, 153, 155, 202
Pearson, Drew, 92, 170, 173, 188
Peck, Gregory, 220
Pegler, Westbrook, 89, 159, 174 n.
Pelley, William Dudley, 11–12, 62, 90–95, 181
Pemberton, John de J., 476
Penha, Armando, 409
Penn, Lemuel, 469
Perkins, Frances, 40, 46–48, 50, 54, 55, 94, 163, 166, 270
Perlo, Victor, 248 n., 249–250
Persons, Wilton B., 330
Peters, J., 254
Peterson, J. Hardin, 170 n., 190, 227
Philbrick, Herbert, 315, 343, 344, 385, 452
Pickens, William, 140–144
Pickens amendment, 142, 143
Political Action Committee (C.I.O.), 158–161, 169, 183, 184 n., 186
Pool, Joe, 450, 451, 454, 462 n., 467, 471, 473, 476–481, 483–485, 489, 492
Pool bill, 471–472
Popular Front, 37, 62, 65, 77, 89, 113, 176, 259, 491
Porter, John W., 396
Potter, Charles E., 297 n., 298, 299, 336
Powell, Adam Clayton, 290, 427
Powers, D. Lane, 144–146

Pressman, Lee, 121, 200, 248 *n.*, 250, 254, 259, 288–290, 387, 388
price-control legislation, 126–127
Progressive Citizens of America, 214, 220
Progressive Labor Movement, 445–450, 474–475, 479, 480, 483
Progressive Party, 213, 226, 230, 233, 250, 251, 282, 288, 292, 300, 315, 359 *n.*
Protestant Digest, 339
Prussion, Karl, 428, 429
Public Opinion Quarterly, 32
Public Works Administration, 52
Puerto Rico hearings, 408–409, 423

Quill, Michael J., 32, 99–101, 121, 123, 160, 338

Radio Free Europe. 452
Railroad Retirement Board, 140
Railway Audit and Inspection Company, 34
Rainer, Luise, 102
Rand, Ayn, 216
Randolph, A. Philip, 374
Rankin, John, 19, 80, 102, 117, 135, 143, 153, 158, 163, 167–172, 174–179, 182–191, 195–197, 202, 207, 215, 228, 232, 246, 250, 255, 268, 272, 273, 297, 374, 492
Rankin amendment, 168–169
Rankin Committee, 169–189
Rathborne, Mervyn, 99, 100
Rauh, Joseph, 305, 358, 392–394
Rayburn, Sam, 16, 55, 59, 167, 236, 317, 402, 413, 424, 425, 427, 435
Reagan, Ronald, 209, 300
Red Channels, 290, 304, 377, 381
Red Scare of 1919-1920, 5
Reece, J. Carroll, 236, 380
Reed, Susan, 201
Refugee Relief Act, 370
Reid, John G., 36
Rein, David, 387 *n.*
Relief Appropriation Act, 141
Remington, William, 244, 249, 259, 286–288, 290, 353, 367, 440
Report on Blacklisting, 381–382
Republican Party, 51–53, 164, 186–187, 189, 234, 236, 240, 254, 296
Reuther, Walter, 49, 199, 317, 324 *n.*
Reynolds Tobacco Company, 199
Ribbentrop, Joachim von, 69
Richberg, Donald, 227
riots, 6, 37–38, 187, 399, 430–434
Rivera, Diego, 83
Robbins, Jerome, 323, 377
Robeson, Paul, 80, 200, 230, 290, 390–391, 402
Robeson, Paul, Jr., 423
Robinson, Earl, 403
Robinson, Edward G., 199, 222 *n.*, 290, 298, 304–305, 349
Robinson, J. W., 170 *n.*

Robinson, Jackie, 290, 291
Rockefeller, Nelson, 484
Rockwell, George Lincoln, 473 *n.*
Rogers *v.* U.S., 312
Rogers, Ginger, 203, 208, 209, 299
Rogers, Lela, 203, 208
Rogers, Will, Jr., 140
Rolland, Romain, 70
Roosevelt, Archibald B., 376, 395
Roosevelt, Edith Kermit, 443
Roosevelt, Eleanor, 61, 65, 77–80, 82, 128, 159, 166, 170, 204–206, 258
Roosevelt, Franklin D., 9, 15–16, 21, 27, 42, 50, 52, 54, 55, 61, 67, 75, 79, 96, 105, 107, 108, 110–113, 122, 124, 142, 150, 157, 158, 160, 161, 166, 169, 175, 240, 246, 250, 251, 260, 261, 365, 371
Roosevelt, Franklin D., Jr., 327
Roosevelt, James, 34, 427, 428
Roper, Elmo, 385
Rosenberg trial, 275, 295, 333, 335, 336, 367, 373
Rossen, Robert, 305, 323
Rosten, Norman, 392 *n.*
Roudebush, Richard L. 482 *n.*
Rovere, Richard, 45, 319
Rural Electrification Administration, 170
Russell, Louis, 221, 273, 349
Russell, Norton Anthony, 421
Russian Revolution, 65, 146, 173
Rutgers University, 328
Rutledge, Wiley B., 193
Ryskind, Morrie, 208

sabotage, 6, 28, 83, 100, 104–108, 111, 114, 116, 130
Sacco-Vanzetti case, 164
Saltonstall, Leverett, 338
San Francisco subcommittee, 424
SANE, 441, 487
Schadeberg, Henry C., 435 *n.*
Schary, Dore, 218–219
Schenck, Nicholas, 218
Scherer, Gordon H., 322 *n.*, 323–325, 330, 363, 365, 369, 372, 373, 376, 384, 386, 393, 399, 411, 417–419, 422, 428, 431–433, 435 *n.*, 443, 451
Schevchenko, Andrei, 278
Schlesinger, Arthur, Jr., 12
Schlink, F. J., 85
Schmidt, Godfrey, P., 287, 383
school investigations, 119, 187, 228, 274, 315–316, 325–332, 372–373, 425–426
Schulberg, Budd, 307
Schuman, Frederick, L., 144
S.C.L.C., 467
Scott, Adrian, 213, 218, 219, 302
Scott, Hazel, 290, 291
Screen Actors Guild, 209, 300
Screen Writers Guild, 203, 208, 210, 213, 218, 223 *n.*
Secret Nazi police, 18

Seeger, Pete, 377–379, 393
Senate Internal Security Subcommittee, 295, 309, 324, 328, 382, 405, 409, 436, 441, 486
Senate Judiciary Committee, 295, 466, 467
Senner, George F., Jr., 433 n., 447–449, 471
Shahn, Ben, 401
Shameful Years, The, 318
Shapley, Harlow, 187, 233
Sharp, Dudley C., 406
Shaw, Artie, 323
Shaw, Irwin, 307
Shelton, Robert M., 465, 467–469
Sheppard, Morris, 122
Sherwood, William K., 424
Silber, Bernard, 421
Silver Shirts, 11–12, 73, 90, 91, 94
Silverman, Abraham George, 249, 253, 289
Silvermaster, Nathan Gregory, 235, 246–247, 249, 251–253
Simpson, John W., 393
Sinatra, Frank, 182, 199, 220
sit-down strikes, 15–16, 21, 29, 49–51, 55, 161, 482
Skouras, Spyros, 218
Smedley, Agnes, 310
Smith, Chester D., 475 n., 482 n.
Smith, Donald W., 55
Smith, Edwin S., 71, 387
Smith, Gerald L. K., 89, 164, 181–183
Smith, Howard, 107 n., 388
Smith, Walter Bedell, 318
Smith Act, 98–99, 107, 244, 292, 315, 323, 352, 359 n., 367, 395, 413, 419 n., 429, 459, 471, 491–492
Smith Committee, 144 n.
Smith-Connally bill, 158, 159
S.N.C.C., 467
Sobell, Morton, 292 n.
Social Justice, 30, 41–42
Social Security Act, 41
socialism, 36, 37, 41, 80–81, 126, 147, 209, 263, 447
Socialist Democratic Party, 383
Socialist Labor Party, 37
Socialist Party, 38, 40, 123
Sokolsky, George, 35, 85, 376, 381
Sondergaard, Gale, 300, 384
Sons and Daughters of the Golden West, 153
Sons of the American Revolution, 274 n.
Southern Conference Educational Fund, 420
Southern Conference for Human Welfare, 199–202, 233, 420
Soviet-German pact, 58, 65–67, 69, 71, 72, 76, 79, 81, 100, 112, 128, 135, 160
Soviet Secret Service, 201
Spanish Civil War, 99, 177–178, 215, 433

Spanish refugees, 176–179, 184
Stalin, Joseph, 54, 62, 65, 67, 69, 83, 112, 121, 173, 175, 197, 198, 207, 214, 233, 336, 367, 390, 400, 414, 448
Stalinism, 37, 38, 57, 66, 80, 82, 89, 400
Stamler, Jeremiah, 457–464, 489–490
Standard Brands, 171–172
Stander, Lionel, 323
Standley, W. H., 228
Starnes, Joe, 24, 32, 36, 45, 63–65, 77, 80, 87, 91, 94, 105, 123, 134, 159, 162
Starobin, Joseph, 401
Stassen, Harold E., 49, 229
State Department, 9, 105, 111, 186, 204–206, 247, 254, 264, 265, 267, 278, 279, 287, 295, 309, 402, 445, 446, 449–451, 453
Steadman, James H., 102 n.
Steel, Johannes, 174 n.
Steel Workers Organizing Committee, 120–121
Steele, Walter, 29, 34, 77, 198
Steele-Frey hearings, 29–30
Steinbeck, John, 213
Stepovich, Joseph, 372 n.
Stern, Alfred, 145, 405
Stern, Martha, 145
Stevenson, Adlai, 319, 365
Stewart, Donald Ogden, 102
Stewart, James, 220
Stewart, Potter, 362, 420–422
Stockholm Peace Appeal, 335, 338, 440
Stone, I. F., 448
Stripling, Robert E., 25, 92, 94, 153, 159, 188–192, 203, 205, 209, 212, 221, 231, 238, 247, 251, 255, 258, 264, 270–273
Struik, Dirk Jung, 315–316, 339
Student Congress Against War, 38
student demonstrations, 430–434, 453–454
Subversive Activities Control Act, 454
Subversive Activities Control Board, 292–294, 409, 440
Sudeten crisis, 18
sugar lobby, 21
Sullivan, Ed, 404, 480
Sullivan, Edward F., 29, 33, 34, 46
Sullivan, Elliot, 377, 378, 393
Sullivan, Thomas P., 462 n.
Sumners, Hatton W., 108, 183
Swing, Raymond Gram, 174 n., 204
Symphony of the Air, 403

Tablet, The, 382
Taft, Robert A., 209, 321, 404
Taft-Hartley Act, 368–369, 409
Tavenner, Frank, 273, 288, 299, 301, 304–306, 310, 315, 331, 348, 357, 393, 399 n., 414, 436, 443 n., 456 n.
Taylor, Robert, 203, 207, 216

Taylor, Telford, 355, 379
Teague, Walter D., III, 477 *n.*, 490
Teapot Dome scandal, 4
Temple, Shirley, 39–40
Tenney, Jack B., 199
Tenney Fact Finding Committee, 102, 172
textbook investigations, 104, 119, 274
Third International, 11–12
Third Reich, 109
Thomas, J. Parnell, 14, 22, 24–26, 32, 42–46, 55, 56, 65, 75, 82, 87, 94, 100, 131, 134, 137, 153, 156, 159, 162, 175, 177, 179, 182–190, 192, 194,–198, 200, 202, 203, 207–212, 214, 216–221, 231–238, 240–244, 251–253, 260, 269–273, 275, 299, 372, 413, 442, 491, 492
Thomas, Norman, 36, 327, 328
Thomas, R. J., 199
Thomas Committee, 30, 190–225, 234–239
Thompson, Dorothy, 204
Tone, Franchot, 120
Townsend, Francis, 181
Tracy, Spencer, 220
Trading with the Enemy Act, 472
Transocean News Service, 109–110
Transport Workers Union, 31, 32, 99–101, 105
Treasury Department, 249
Treasury–Post Office appropriation bill, 140–144
Trilling, Lionel, 329
Trojan Horse in America, The, 35, 108
Trotsky, Leon, 83, 173
Trotskyites, 37, 66, 436, 455
True, James, 34, 91
Trumbo, Dalton, 203, 208, 212, 222–24
Truman, Harry S., 186, 189, 195, 196, 207, 219, 234–236, 240–241, 254, 258, 260, 265, 266, 269, 287, 292, 295, 337, 345–349, 364, 370, 427
Truman Doctrine, 194
Truman Loyalty Order, 195, 219
Tuck, William M., 399 *n.*, 400, 447, 448, 482 *n.*, 485
Tyne, George, 377, 378, 393
T.V.A., 104, 134, 287

Ukranian Nationalist Federation, 34
Ulysses case, 132
Union for Democratic Action, 134–135
Unitarian Service Committee, 184
United American Spanish Aid Committee, 141, 177
United Auto Workers, 31, 107, 199, 317, 324 *n.*
United Electrical Radio and Machine Workers, 86 *n.*, 368
United Electrical Workers, 199, 282, 283, 284 *n.*, 316, 322, 373, 451
United Mine Workers Union, 33–34

United Nations, 165, 187–188, 198, 254, 260, 438
United Packinghouse Workers, 409
university investigations, 274, 315–316, 325–332
U.N.R.R.A., 177
Uphaus, Willard, 341 *n.*, 390, 436
U.S. Committee to Aid the National Liberation Front, 477

Vaughan, Harry H., 346, 347
Vaughn, David B., 133, 139
Velde, Harold H., 238, 239, 273, 279–281, 284, 295, 298, 299, 302, 304, 305, 308, 310, 320–327, 329, 330, 332–335, 339–350, 361, 365–368, 372, 396, 411, 413, 416, 425, 427, 442, 460, 491, 492
Velde, Mrs. Harold, 368
Velde Committee, 332, 358, 375
Veterans Affairs Committee, 169, 272
Veterans Against Discrimination, 188
Veterans of Foreign Wars, 197, 384, 481
Viereck, George Sylvester, 26, 103
Vietnam Day Committee, 477
Vietnam dissenters, 433, 483–484, 486, 487
Vietnam hearings, 473–481, 489–490
Vietnam War, 77, 472, 483, 494
Voice of America, 324
Voorhis, Jerry, 55–56, 62, 66, 71, 74, 85–87, 100, 105, 108, 113, 116, 123, 129, 131, 133, 135, 137, 138, 141, 156, 163, 169, 170, 186
Voorhis Act of 1940, 291
Vultee aircraft strike, 107–108

Wadleigh, Henry Julian, 265
wages and hours bill, 16, 20, 22, 171
Wagner Act, 41, 171, 270, 388
Waldman, Louis, 227
Waldorf interdict, 300
Waldron, Francis Xavier, 192
Wallace, Henry A., 131, 132, 137, 163, 166, 170, 200, 222, 230, 231, 249, 250, 252, 280–282, 288, 292
Walsh, J. Raymond, 174 *n.*
Walsh, John C., 435 *n.*
Walter, Francis E., 272, 273, 278, 280, 282 *n.*, 283, 284, 297, 299, 301, 305, 311, 320, 322, 331, 333, 339–341, 347, 349, 357, 365, 399–418, 424–426, 435, 442, 443 *n.*, 466, 492
Walter Committee, 358, 367–398
Walter-McCarran immigration law, 340, 365, 370, 371, 395, 397, 446
Walton, Sidney, 174 *n.*
Wanger, Walter, 218
war-agencies bill, 150
war hysteria, 67, 80, 100, 295
war industry, aliens in, 104–108, 111, 114
War Production Board, 140, 141
War Relief Control Board, 177, 178

War Relocation Authority, 152–156
Ward, Harry F., 36, 70–72, 147, 164, 200, 340, 341
Ware, Harold, 248 n., 254
Warner, Jack L., 207, 208, 217, 218, 224
Warren, Earl, 220 n., 360, 362, 421, 489
Warren, Lindsay C., 14–15, 21
Washington, George, 236
Washington Bookshop, 145, 282
Washington Committee for Democratic Action, 136
Washington Friends of Spanish Democracy, 125
Watkins, John F., 358–362, 392, 393, 420
Watson, Albert W., 482 n., 484
Watson, Goodwin, 126, 127, 141, 144, 145, 148, 150
Weaver, Robert, 374
Wechsler, James, 91
Weinberg, Joseph W., 274–276
Weisberg, Harold, 92
Welch, Joseph, 217 n.
Welles, Sumner, 204, 206, 268
Welsh, George A., 95, 96
Weltner, Charles L., 457 n., 465–467, 471
West, Rebecca, 253 n.
West Coast Japanese-Americans, 152–156
West Coast maritime strike, 47
Westin, Alan, 356
Weyl, Nathaniel, 288 n.
Whalen, Grover, 6, 8
Wheeler, William A., 426, 430
White, Harry Dexter, 246, 249, 252, 253, 257, 264, 345–349
White Book, 108–109
White Citizens Councils, 469–470
White County Improvement Association, 470
White Knights of the Ku Klux Klan, 469
Whitley, Rea, 56, 63, 65, 78, 80, 92, 94
Whittaker, Charles E., 362
Wier, Roy W., 427
Wilkins, Collie Leroy, 467
Wilkins, Roy, 374, 485
Wilkinson, Frank, 420–423, 432, 433
Wille und Macht children's camp, 11
Williams, Aubrey, 170
Williams, C. Dickerman, 355

Williams, Wheeler, 404
Willis, Edwin E., 294, 365, 376, 410, 417, 420, 423, 428, 431, 443, 444, 446, 448, 450, 454–458, 461, 462, 464–467, 470, 482 n., 484–487, 489–491
Willis bill, 470–471
Willkie, Wendell, 106, 124
Willoughby, Charles, 310, 311
Wilson, Dagmar, 437, 440–442, 451
Wilson, Edmund, 7, 38 n., 211
Wilson, Woodrow, 7 n., 12, 20, 107, 354
Winchell, Walter, 157–158, 170, 173, 174
wiretap evidence, 318
Wirin, A. L., 155, 396
Wise, Stephen S., 344
Witt, Nathan, 71, 250, 254, 289, 387, 388
Wolfe, Bertram, 380
Woll, Matthew, 34
Women Strike for Peace, 437–442, 451, 481
Wood, John S., 173, 174, 177, 178, 182, 183, 189, 190, 197, 272, 273, 277, 278, 288, 289, 299, 301, 302, 305, 316–320, 322, 324, 349
Wood, Sam, 208
Wood Committee, 311–312
Wood-Rankin Committee, 174–175
Woodle, Roy, 470
Woodward, Ellen S., 44
Workers Alliance, 13, 127, 141
World Bank, 246
World Council of Churches, 334
W.P.A., 25–26, 42–46, 55, 104, 123, 141

Yalta Conference, 175, 254, 260
Yasui, Kaoru, 450
Yeats, William Butler, 494
Yellin, Edward, 421–422
Yellow Paper, 129–131
Yellow Peril, 153
Yorkville Casino riot, 17–18
Young Communist League, 91, 96–97, 101, 342, 440
Young Progressives of America, 374

Zapp, Manfred, 109–110
Zellerbach, James D., 385